ACROSS

BEFORE

COLUMBUS ?

Evidence for Transoceanic Contact with the Americas prior to 1492

Edited by

Donald Y. Gilmore

Linda S. McElroy

New England Antiquities
Research Association
PUBLICATIONS, 94 CROSS POINT ROAD,
EDGECOMB. ME, 04556
PH/207-882-9425   FAX/207-882 8162-
e-MAIL/ KROSSPT@LINCOLN.MIDCOAST.COM

NEARA

The New England Antiquities Research Association
NEARA Publications 1998
Edgecomb, Maine

Across Before Columbus? is a publication of the New England Antiquities Research Association (NEARA), a non-profit organization chartered under the laws of the State of New Hampshire. NEARA was founded in 1964 to study the nature and functions of enigmatic stone structures found throughout the northeast, in their cultural context and as interpreted through relevant disciplines. Research on such lithic features as well as on broader questions relating to cultural diffusion is reported at semi-annual meetings and in the semi-annual *NEARA Journal*.

International Standard Book Number: 0-9663038-0-6

Library of Congress Catalog Card Number: 98-65323

Editing and layout: Linda S. McElroy and Donald Y. Gilmore
Cover design: Suzanne O. Carlson
Computer production: Linda S. McElroy, The ByteSmith

Printed in the United States of America by Mercantile Printing Company, Inc., Worcester, MA.

First Printing 1998

ACROSS BEFORE COLUMBUS?   CONTENTS

SECTION III LINGUISTICS, INSCRIPTIONS, AND GLYPHS — Continued

SECTION IV DIFFUSION AND VOYAGES

This volume brings to a wider audience most of the papers presented at the *America Before Columbus* (*ABC*) Conference, a Columbian quincentenary event sponsored by NEARA and held on the Brown University campus in Providence, Rhode Island, in June 1992. Many of these twenty-seven papers have been published elsewhere since the conference, either in the *NEARA Journal* or in other periodicals. For the present volume, most of the papers have been updated by their authors to include some new findings, and they are supplemented by an introductory essay as well as by commentaries on each of four sections. To encourage dialogue, the authors were also invited to respond to the commentaries if they wished and several have done so. The editors present concluding remarks.

Our revised title, *Across Before Columbus?*, reflects the major thrust of the book's content: evidence for transoceanic contact with the Americas across both oceans prior to 1492. And the question mark highlights the fact that this field of research and scholarly debate is very much a work in progress, with new evidence still to be found and only tentative conclusions possible at this time.

The papers, which cover a broad spectrum of investigation, have been gathered into four sections. These are not the same groupings of the conference itself, wherein papers were clustered for presentation by geographical areas. For this volume, however, groupings based on the papers' content seemed to provide a better way to focus reader attention on the parallels and contradictions inherent in the material itself, and to facilitate the commentators' critiques. The reader will find among the authors a mix of bold academic professionals and dedicated avocational researchers, neither group seemingly fettered by academic dogma or the fear of censure.

All papers do not adhere to the same scholarly standard—as one of our commentators points out; all authors are not academically credentialled for research. However, NEARA has long functioned as a forum in which serious scholars, without regard for credentialling, could present the results of their studies. Further, NEARA has consistently provided an opportunity for non-acrimonious debate and, at the least, for a courteous hearing, in the belief that many worthy ideas do arise from humble or unorthodox origins. In an era of rapid change, these functions have seemed appropriate, particularly for those who have not always found it easy even to gain a hearing for new ideas in an entrenched academic setting. The principle applied for inclusion of scholars at the original conference was primarily the relevance of their topic and evidence of serious research carried out over some period of time. As this volume purports to be the *Proceedings* of that conference, the only papers missing here are so either because of their authors' wishes or default.

The editors believe that *Across Before Columbus?* is a worthy sequel to *Man Across the Sea*, the 1971 volume of papers and commentary from a symposium held during the May 1968 meetings of the Society for American Archaeology in Santa Fe, New Mexico, and published by the University of Texas Press. Five of the researchers whose thought appears in the present volume (Carter, Jett, Kehoe, Kelley, and Sorenson) also participated in that conference nearly thirty years ago; some of their earlier research is included in *Man Across the Sea*. For readers interested in understanding more about the basis for the present papers, we suggest they read that important work; Roger Wescott's paper, *Types of Cultural Diffusion* (p. 255, this volume), provides background as well.

The ABC papers, like those from the Santa Fe symposium, reflect the multi-disciplinary approach necessary for research into post-glacial, but pre-Columbian, contacts across the oceans. The need to involve a number of disciplines was recognized by the editors of *Man Across the Sea* in their concluding remarks, where they stressed that, "The experts in each field must acquaint themselves with both the data and the most current thinking from the other disciplines. Cross-disciplinary evidence must be closely scrutinized and weighed with great caution. Particularly, we must guard against ideas becoming so imbedded that they are accepted as gospel without check or challenge." We would argue that there is need as well for cautious acceptance of a wider spectrum of methodologies in this kind of research than has generally been the custom in academic circles.

There is both challenge and dialogue in the content of the present volume. Do the findings suggest evidence for borrowing among cultures (diffusion), or for independent invention in the laboratory of the Americas, or even for some other as yet undefined combination? We urge the reader to consider the evidence without bias, keeping in mind that the search for truth is an ongoing process.

The Editors
January 1998

It was George F. Carter, Emeritus Professor of Geography at Texas A&M University, who encouraged NEARA to organize a conference during the Columbian quincentenary year on the subject of pre-Columbian diffusion to the Americas from across both oceans. NEARA is indebted to him for his guidance in the preparations for the ABC meeting which resulted, and for his contributions to the present volume. His introduction sets the scene for the papers that follow, and his research paper exemplifies the difficulties and anomalies as well as the excitement inherent in this body of scholarship.

NEARA and the ABC editors are also grateful to the many people who have made this volume possible, especially the twenty-six authors who have patiently collaborated in the editing of their work and the distinguished scholars who accepted our invitation to review this material and prepare commentary essays. NEARA also wishes to express its appreciation to the following participants in the ABC Conference whose contributions to the proceedings are not printed in this volume: Paul Bahn, Joseph Dishta, Evan Hadingham, Edmund Ladd, Murdena Marshall, Richard Nielsen, Jon Polansky, Parker Potter, and James Whittall, III.

To the NEARA volunteer teams who, in the first instance, contributed time, energy, and special talents to planning and conducting the ABC Conference; and, in the second, exhibited similar commitment to the production of this volume—those who patiently corresponded with sometimes inaccessible authors, who proofread the papers, designed and formatted the layout, selected and compiled the index entries, prepared the graphics, oversaw and standardized the computer production of final copy, and to the others who mobilized fund-raising and marketing efforts—to all these dedicated people go our sincere appreciation for their indispensable assistance. Particularly, we thank those NEARA members and friends whose contributions to the revolving fund have made it possible to finance, to publish, and to promote this publication. Finally, we wish to thank the fine professionals at Mercantile Printing Company who guided us through the final stages of the publication process.

INTRODUCTION

The Diffusion Controversy

GEORGE F. CARTER

Originality is certainly the rarest thing in this world,
and in the history of mankind original thoughts are appallingly sparse.
—Berthold Laufer, discussing Jade, 1912

In anthropology, the flow of ideas from one area to another is acknowledged as the master process. A. L. Kroeber (1948) once estimated from a study of California tribes that, at the most, only ten percent of any tribe's culture sets them apart from their neighbor. Kroeber finds that man is exceedingly good at borrowing ideas, and, as quoted above, Laufer is, if anything, even more emphatic on this. So far, there is little disagreement.

This happy agreement stops with a loud splash once a sea is met. The ocean suddenly becomes an impervious barrier to the flow of ideas. This is the so-called Monroe Doctrine of Anthropology. It may have arisen as a protest against the misguided notion that the Indians were unable to develop their civilizations all by themselves, and thus became a slur on the Indian race, assuming that there is such a thing as a uniform Indian race, something which I do not concede.

Nowhere is this more notable than in the treatment of the Mound-Builders. At first, all Mound-Builder achievements were attributed to mysterious people from overseas. No mere Indians could do this! The reaction was a forceful rejection of any suggestion that any of the Amerind cultures came from overseas contacts. Anyone suggesting anything to the contrary was attacked with ridicule and all kinds of specious reasoning and called a 'racist.' In so doing, the critics have become the racists, for, if the long runs of our studies are correct, then no civilization arose in isolation; and, if the American Indians accomplished this miracle, then they would have to be admitted as the master race. It is much more likely that the Mound-Builders were influenced by someone from somewhere. If this be the case, then they were just normal people, neither geniuses nor of weak natural ability.

The idea of the orderly development of all societies from savagery through a Neolithic/agricultural stage to civilization may be involved. Evolution was a powerful idea. Human development moving with regularity along a common path has had great appeal. Orderliness, regularity, societies following invariable laws of progress is an attractive notion. Some found this so attractive an idea that they felt there was no need for flows of ideas to account for similarities. For whatever reason or reasons, by the time of the founding of the Smithsonian Institution and the Bureau of American Indian Affairs, the denial of any overseas contacts was set in the concrete of dogma, and all contrary thought was summarily rejected.

If the demonstration of these laws of human cultural development is based upon the assumption that civilizations are totally independent of one another, then the several developments must be kept separate. No flows of ideas from one to the other can be allowed. However, the defense of this idea of separation of civilizations has gradually crumbled. In this century, all of the Old World civilizations have been found to be related: Egypt taking its beginning from Mesopotamia and all the developments in the West stemming from Near Eastern civilization—to Greece, to Rome, to England; India still poorly known but seemingly later, and China definitely late and showing clear evidence of influences from the south and west. An early and continuing interrelation of the civilizations of the Old World is now widely conceded.

At least in the New World, the growth of civilizations was totally separate from the Old World, or so the independent inventionists maintained. Even Peru and Mexico were once seen as independent developments, but that concept, too, has crumbled. The American civilizations are clearly interrelated and were so early on. The cultural evolutionists and independent inventionists were left with only two cases: the Old World cultural growth, and the New World. If this too collapses, then the whole structure comes tumbling down. One can sympathize.

Ideas that have persisted for over one hundred years and have filled shelves of books and reams of articles are not lightly tossed aside. Generations of students have earned PhDs and have gone on to teach what they learned as the basics of their field, namely, that New World growth was independent of the Old World. It has become a part of the cultural historian's fundamental beliefs, on a par with the law of gravity in physics. However, in all fields it is a regularity that anomalous data keep appearing that challenge long-held, basic beliefs, and, quite as one would expect, these anomalous facts are treated as errors made by maverick scholars, who are attacked with all the weapons at the disposal of scholars who cling to traditional explanations. When all else fails, ridicule and *ad hominem* attack, and at times guilt by association, are employed. Invoke Atlantis and Mu and insist that the work of scholars who present alternative views is more of the same (Williams 1991). It is shoddy work, but fashionable.

All recent attempts to call attention to evidence that suggests early contacts with peoples beyond the oceans have been greeted with animosity, although this is of course the opposite of how scholarship is supposed to operate. The question of contact or no contact should be viewed as open for inquiry. Is there good evidence that there actually were such exchanges? There has been a steady flow of scholars who tried to convince the anthropologists that there indeed was sound evidence for belief in the flow of ideas across the seas. Some of these pioneers, who have all too often been rejected with scorn, will be mentioned here.

Sir Grafton Elliot Smith (1915) is a classic case. He was a surgeon posted early to Egypt who was fascinated by the Egyptian culture. He is accused of seeing Egypt everywhere. Typically, this is exaggerated by his critics, and the massive data that he assembled and presented was ridiculed. Smith was aware of the influences that reached America from Southeast Asia, a theme that Heine-Geldern and Gordon Ekholm and others have developed in detail. I find that few of Smith's critics have read much if any of his work, usually none. It may stand as a good example of the role of 'education' in turning scholars completely off from reading interesting people.

At Berkeley in 1934, I was so indoctrinated in anthropology with anti-Smith doctrine that I read none of his work for fifty years. I backed into Elliot Smith when pursuing Amerind portrayals of the elephant, of which there is a startling supply. Here, I met a genial man of great breadth of knowledge, an excellent, witty writer. I doubt that any rational reader of Smith on the 'elephant in America' would doubt his finding that the Indians of Mexico were acquainted with the Asiatic Indian lore and adopted the role of this creature into American culture. That is but a single case. His work on Egyptian races and on mummies is classic. True, he tended to overemphasize Egypt's role in the origin of civilizations, and his conclusions need to be adjusted to contemporary evidence, but his contribution is a monumental mass of work worthy of study rather than cavalier rejection.

Smith stimulated much other work. Jackson's study of shells (1917) is a valuable collection of data, and it is there that one will find recognition of the significance of the cowry shell appearing in an Adena site. The cowry is not found in the Atlantic or in the Mediterranean, yet it was in the Adena culture and important in the Midewiwin society of the Algonkins along the Great Lakes. There is much more, but it tends to be lost in the fog of criticism of Smith and of all his school.

Picking other examples almost at random, there is the interesting work of Miguel Covarrubias, ethnologist, artist, and Olmec enthusiast (1954). His comparison of Asiatic and American Indian art is, or should be, convincing to anyone not mired in dogma. Parallel works by Ekholm (1950) and Heine-Geldern (1966) are more detailed and nail cultural items down to specific places and peoples in Southeast Asia and, at the same time, in Mexico. Shao's work (1983) follows along this line and focuses sharply on Shang and Chou influences in Mesoamerica. The northwest coast art, the familiar totem poles, are clearly Chou, if not earlier (Shang) art. The art field is specific as to time and people and even in part as to the route by which some of this came to America. It would be hard to find scholars with better credentials than Ekholm and Heine-Geldern.

This list could be pursued endlessly: Jett's classic study of the blowgun (1970) (Southeast Asia and tropical America); Tolstoy's study (1963) of bark paper-making (one area of Central America shows specific relationship to one island group in Asia); Randall Beirne's study (1971) shows that the ax types of America are dominantly from the Old World and that one ax type found in the Andes is known nowhere else except in Egypt. And we are back to Egyptians in America, and one must read Jairazbhoy and others to see that there is a huge complex of data all indicating that there was in some way massive Egyptian influence in America, either direct or indirect. Particularly notable are Jairazbhoy's illustrations of Egyptian gods and goddesses portrayed in Mayan manuscripts (1974). The portrayals of Nut, the Goddess of Night, and the goddess with a woman's bust but a scorpion's body are among the many striking items that Jairazbhoy points to. Even the association of the scorpion goddess is the same in Egypt and Honduras. She is always associated with the Milky Way.

Some of these studies, notably Jett and Beirne, are based on world-wide surveys and so test the notion that everyone just naturally does similar things. Such arguments overwork the principle of *elementen gedangken*, Bastion's notion of the uniformity of man leading to similar solutions over and over.

Many studies point directly to transoceanic influence on the Americas from the Formative Period right on to the Mediterranean rediscovery of America in 1492. The diseases said not to be here are now being found to have been present.[1] Tuberculosis is a classic case. The old claim that the required voyages could not be made are purely mythical and have long been laid to rest by Alice Kehoe (1971) and Thor Heyerdahl (1963), to mention just two—laid to rest if the critics have bothered to read the literature. Magnificent studies of the capability of the Polynesian craft have been demonstrated by actual voyages. The lowly log raft has been repeatedly sailed from Peru to Australia, and the Asiatic origin of this craft is obvious.

Belated attention has been focused on epigraphy in America. Belated, for the writing about inscriptions had lain unstudied for at least a century, though recorded, usually unwittingly. Barry Fell's work in this last quarter of a century has totally upset the picture (Fell 1982). The reaction to such findings as alphabetical writing all over the

Americas has been greeted with more heat than light. Fell's style of work often was not along the lines of the classic epigraphers and linguists, and this has become the focus of the attack. Within the epigraphic group, balanced, critical work has appeared, and the epigraphic base is steadily being firmed up.[2] Fell was seldom wrong on his identification of alphabets, and he usually found the appropriate language. The next step, getting the meaning, is more difficult. At times, it is obvious that Fell strained at meaning and pressed his material too far. Regrettable, but forgivable when his massive contribution is examined.

Everyone is a product of his time, and Kroeber is a good example. I have been criticized for venturing to point to some errors of judgment in Kroeber's work. He was indeed a great man in anthropology, and, since I was a student under him in the early 1930s, I can speak from first-hand knowledge of the man. This was a time of small departments, often a handful of notable men. At Berkeley, it was Kroeber, Lowie, Gifford, and Olsen. Only Ronald Olsen was open to the possibility of overseas contact with America. Lowie was impressed by the evidence that *patolli* (the Aztec game) was in some inexplicable way connected to *pachisi* (parchisi) in India. Kroeber denied any connection, largely because "it stood all alone," and thought this complex game was within the realm of possible re-invention. Kroeber was capable of citing case after case suggesting transoceanic diffusion and discarding each one with the statement that they would be good evidence except that "they stood alone."

One of my students took up the pachisi-patolli problem and, after consultations with the departments of psychology and of mathematics, calculated the odds against independent invention of such a complex game. He found that the odds were very high against any duplication—and he had omitted the equally complex set of beliefs associated with the game. His figure was something like one to the twenty-seventh power. If all of the religious meaning were factored in, the odds would go on out to astronomical figures. There is in anthropology another study of pachisi-patolli that minimizes everything and reaches the opposite conclusion. That researcher obviously failed to consult the psychologists and omitted reams of other data on the game.

Kroeber rejected the inscribed work on Easter Island as mere design. He reasoned that a people in the middle of nowhere could not have invented writing. It is obvious that, if they came from somewhere, they could have brought writing with them, as their own traditions say that they did. Today the material is deciphered. It is writing.

Kroeber cited data in one chapter that indicated the presence of a language in northern California with astonishing resemblance in details to Indo-European. He presented numerous traits shared by the Penutian languages of northern California and southern Oregon. For the Penutians, he lists the following: they say *kom* and *ko* when they mean 'come' and 'go.' He says this is "meaningless"

since it stands all alone. Later in the same chapter, he adds that the classificatory system is like Indo-European in the use of gender, the familiar masculine, feminine, and neuter. As he notes, this is rare in the world, being found principally around the Mediterranean. Some pages later we find: "Common to these two families (Penutian and Indo-European) are an apparatus of similar cases, including accusative, genitive, locative, ablative, instrumental, sometimes even a true nominative, plural by suffix, vowel changes in the verb according to tense and mode, a passive and several participles and modal forms expressed by suffixes, and pronouns either separate or expressed by endings fused with the tense-modal suffixes." To which he adds: ". . . of course, they appear there quite independently as regards their origin and history." Of course?

Even as a sophomore (1931) I could never accept this. Today, some professional linguists accept the Indo-European connection. Sadovsky (1984) links the languages through north Asia and sees in the Penutian languages evidence for repeated invasion of the Northwest of America (Oregon and northern California) by sea-borne incomers. The final finding is, I suspect, not yet in, but that there is a linguistic relationship is established. The case here is to illustrate that even the greatest minds are imprisoned in the dogma of their day.

As an aside, all are victims of patterns of thought. Nearly all discussion of transoceanic diffusion has centered on the Pacific. This is obvious and important, but it has deformed all studies to the detriment of transatlantic studies. Heine-Geldern, a truly impressive man and a sturdily independent thinker, has been trapped in the transpacific notion. So he goes to great lengths to bring influences to America via the Pacific even if the center of the data is in western Europe. The short, easy, direct route from western Europe is via the Atlantic. The La Tene culture of western Europe is much closer to America via the Atlantic than a route across much of Europe, all of Asia, and finally across the vast Pacific. Perhaps it did come to America via the Dongson culture of Southeast Asia, but the alternative is not even considered. The evidence for the transatlantic role is only slowly emerging.

I used Kroeber's great text for years to teach anthropology at Johns Hopkins University, for I felt that any geographer not soundly grounded in cultural studies would be a very weak geographer, and Kroeber's treatment of the subject was far and away the best available. That I disagreed with Kroeber on the question of transoceanic diffusion and on the antiquity of man in America was trivial when the whole of Kroeber's work is considered. I know of no one who is above criticism. In this case, I knew not only Kroeber's work but Kroeber as a person whom I greatly respected. Such ambivalent viewing of others, acknowledging their faults along with their strengths, is all too rare today.

I will use myself as an example of the emotions that one inherits and which thereafter influence all of one's thinking.

I graduated from the University of California with an AB degree in anthropology. I was totally convinced of the separateness of all American cultural growth, free of any contamination from the Old World, and I reacted angrily to any suggestions of overseas influences. I particularly abhorred G. Elliot Smith and all of his followers. And, of course, I did not read anything of theirs. However, my doctoral dissertation was in the world of cultural biology— maize, beans, and pumpkins in the American Southwest, all of which had spread from the early civilizations to the south. I became known for my work in tracing people by their domestic plants.

Presently, there landed on my desk a manuscript on the cytogenetics of cotton, and the data indicated that Old World cottons were spread from the Old World to the New World and hybridized here to produce a swarm of new hybrid cottons. Very few plants are capable of drifting great distances across the sea. Cotton demands the successful intervention of man to cross a sea.

This manuscript was from Stanley Stephens, a member of the Hutchinson, Silow and Stephens group. Cytogenetics is the examination under a microscope of chromosomes in the cells of plants. It is far from my area of knowledge, but the data and argument were impressive. I laid the manuscript down with shaking hands, for this called into question the whole matter of the inviolability of the American cultures. I set the manuscript aside for several days and then reread it. I still shook. Knowing that I was out of my depth, I sent it over to a geneticist to read, and he replied that the case was made and about as airtight as any scientific case gets. No scientist is willing to close any case entirely, for there must always be an opening for new data, new interpretations. While new developments in the cotton field continue, the central claim stands. Somebody brought Old World domesticated cotton to America and hybridized it with American wild cotton.

That passed the ball to me. Other plants were mentioned in passing: the sweet potato in Polynesia, and the *cucurbita maxima* on Hawaii. The cucurbitas are the American pumpkins and squashes, no candidates for natural transfer across wide seas. The cucurbita case had already been studied, and the plant was found to be *lagenaria*, the bottle gourd of African origin. I sighed with relief. I should have stopped, but I looked up the case of the sweet potato. There is a large and brisk literature about the plant. Its origin, its name, its place in myth, and evidence for its pre-1500 presence in Polynesia have been investigated, and some far-fetched hypotheses of natural spread have been dreamed up. The upshot is that the American sweet potato, complete with its name, was carried out into Polynesia where it is Carbon-14 dated to at least AD 800.

This work stimulated by Stephen's manuscript has led me far into the biological evidence for transoceanic carriage of plants, and ideas, and even chickens, across the world's oceans. (See separate paper in Section II.) Not

opinions, not authoritarian teaching, not peer pressure, but the hard evidence from biology, a field where independent invention does not apply, drove me from the security of standard cultural history into the wildly controversial position of the diffusionist. The list of transoceanic biological transfers is now lengthy and growing.

I relate all of this because it illustrates several things, especially the emotional upset that I felt when hit with seemingly solid evidence which called fundamental beliefs into question.

We are all emotionally attached to certain things. These are the mores of culture, beliefs held much more strongly than the folkways. Sixty years later I still remember the wrenching impact of the challenge to my firm beliefs. Only 'nuts' believed that anyone could have crossed the seas and disturbed the even, the natural, the inevitable flow of American cultural development. It is because of this personal experience that I can sympathize with those who resist the idea of transoceanic cultural impacts on the Americas. I once stood right there and felt as strongly as they do that the diffusionists were simply deluded fools, or at least deluded. It is these emotionally-held opinions that underlie much of our difficulty in getting a hearing. We are dealing not with scholarly, dispassionate criticism but with emotionally held opinions.

Some problems no longer exist. The voyage question has been answered. At some very early time, man became capable of crossing the seas. The most perplexing questions are those that depend on assumptions of the opposition. Where are the vast amounts of artifacts that contacts would supposedly bring, they ask? This one is best met by reviewing the problem of finding traces of such expeditions as that of de Soto. He toured the southeastern United States with a whole army, and of that passage virtually no trace can be found. Or the Norse case. There are inscriptions and artifacts in the New World and historic records in the Old World of the Norse discovering America. Much of this evidence indicates that these contacts were still under way at the time of Columbus' discoveries to the south (Hall 1982). Yet, consider the vast skepticism encountered in some quarters today even in the face of recent work that validates the long-rejected inscriptions (Hall, Nielsen, Chapman, and others).

Where are the burials and house remains? The portraits of eastern Indians indicate that they are European and not in the least Mongol—for instance, the portraits in Horan (1986), and the forensic reconstructions of Adena skulls (Webb and Baby 1957). The Adena skulls closely resemble those of the eastern Indians of the 19th century. Could it be that the innumerable Adena skeletons exhumed are actually of Europoids in America and blandly assumed to be 'mongoloids?' If this were so, the Adena houses and burials and a good deal more would be European evidence in America. If Webb and Baby are right, in dating the Adena to the time of the Old Copper Culture in America and the early Bronze Age in Europe, then things get even more interesting. Similar problems exist throughout the Americas, and the evidence has not even been considered dispassionately.

We need in-depth study of the data in both the Old World and the New at the appropriate areas and times. I am not aware of much effort by the critics, or for that matter by our side, spent to determine just what one should expect. Such studies are just beginning to appear. Perhaps the Old Copper Culture, the Adena, and the great stone works in New England are a unit and comparable to Old World cultural complexes. One can neither assert this nor deny it, for the requisite studies have not been made, though some good beginnings are under way. The evidence presented in architectural parallels is brushed aside. But is fitted megalithic stonework really repeatedly and independently invented? Or is it, as Heyerdahl insists, a world-wide phenomenon spread by sea? The same thing for the bronze clamps used to lock great stone blocks together. There are no developmental stages in America. When they appear at Tiahuanaco they are typical of a late stage (around 5th century BC) of a well-known sequence in the Old World, most especially in Greece (Ibarro Grasso 1982). There is a great need for such wide studies of traits, but what we have comes not from the critics but from interested non-professionals.

It was Henrietta Mertz, a lawyer, who first saw that the Bat Creek inscription was Hebrew. Cyrus Gordon supported her, and soon it was realized that the letters were Hebrew coin letters rather than normal Hebrew. It was an amateur who found the precise coin from which the letters were copied. It was an economist (McCulloch) who studied this material and had the wood from the find site carbon dated and the bracelets, so blandly assumed to be copper, analyzed and found to be brass. The whole complex dates to the earliest centuries of the present era. I have pointed out that the Green Corn ceremony, preserved into the present by the Yuchi, formerly residents in that area, is actually the Hebrew ceremony of Sukkoth. This I learned by reciting the details of the ceremony to the son of a Rabbi who burst out with: "That is Sukkoth!" And, as a final bit, Hebrew coins of that time have repeatedly been found in that same area. This then comprises the kind of complex of evidence that the critics often demand.

There are other such complexes. But this essay is not meant to be exhaustive, only illustrative of the problems that are addressed in the work which follows and for which this essay is intended to be an introduction. The gist of all this is that the diffusionists face an uphill battle. The resistance is emotional rather than scholarly.

In my view, the picture is complex, not simple. It is not one people at one time making contact with America. It was many contacts at varied times, now here, now there, and of differing intensity, from touch-and-go to trade, and even to settlement. Smith was right in seeing Egyptian influence in America. So was Leo Wiener (1920-22) in seeing

African contacts, though he overran his evidence woefully. Ekholm and Heine-Geldern and others were correct in seeing Asiatic influences. The Norse enthusiasts were, if possible, even more right than even they dreamed.

The claim of a very simple linguistic picture in the Americas is being challenged by competent linguists. Penutian is related to Nostratic in Asia. As yet unpublished, the Uto-Aztecan is influenced by Semitic, and this ties back into the appearance in the Southwest of very early Hebrew in the epigraphy. The epigraphy is both carbon-dated and identified, by the style of writing, as well before the time of Christ. It is difficult to separate this from the Hebrew writing, coins, ceremony, Carbon-14 dates, and brass bracelets, though just what the connection is and how and why is far from obvious. In one of his later papers, Fell presented evidence, more than he usually did in the form demanded by linguists, of Hamitic language influence along the Gulf Coast of America. The complexity of the contacts is far beyond any of our thinking today.

What then are we to do? In the face of attack by the independent inventionists we have only two paths. One is to continue to present sound evidence and count on the weight of the evidence finally to win out. The other path is to counter-attack the critics. There is no profit in battling with the emotionally committed. We must go on presenting sound evidence. We must continue to be critical of those presenting less than perfect cases even when we are sympathetic with their aim. Just as Kroeber is not above criticism, neither is Fell, as two classic cases. It is to the presentation of sound data that this volume is dedicated.

Hopefully, these studies will lead some scholars to examine dispassionately, unemotionally, the innumerable cases of parallels between Old World and New World cultures. We must respond to well-reasoned criticism, even though some of the demands are difficult to deal with. I have always liked the motto *Lux et Veritas*. Let there be light and the truth will prevail. Our aim must be to fan the flame of investigation so that the light will bring out the truth. The light will eventually prevail. It always does.

NOTES

1. On diseases, I cannot find a good general study of late enough date to cover the recent finds. Many of the diseases said not to be present were here, *e.g.*, tuberculosis. The whole syphilis case has changed. Syphilis was present world-wide in antiquity, and each area had its partial immunity. The local immunity was not transferable, and the New World strain raised havoc in Europe. Recent research has changed the whole picture of disease migration.
2. Kroeber is a most interesting scholar for his occasional lapses, which illustrate that he is only human. For instance, he ridicules the notion that writing of Easter Island and the Indus Valley could be connected, citing the great distance and the equally immense gap in time. Actually, there is writing later in time and in exactly the right places to link Easter Island and the Indus Valley.

REFERENCES

Beirne, Daniel Randall
1971 Cultural patterning as revealed by a study of pre-Columbian ax and adz hafting in the Old and New Worlds. In *Man Across the Sea: Problems of Pre-Columbian Contacts*. C. L. Riley *et al.*, eds. Austin: University of Texas Press.

Covarrubias, Miguel
1954 *The Eagle, the Jaguar, and the Serpent: Indian Art of the Americas*. New York: Knopf. Richly illustrated.

Ekholm, Gordon F.
1950 Is American Indian culture Asiatic? *Natural History* 59: 344-351, 382. I list only a single paper of many of these authors to serve as an introduction to their prolific work.

Fell, H. Barraclough
1982 *Bronze Age America*. Boston: Little, Brown. This is a useful introduction to Fell's work, but a major source of his writing is in *The Epigraphic Society Occasional Publications* (ESOP). There is now a critical literature that is balanced. See especially David H. Kelley's work and that of William R. McGlone and his associates, the latter a bit overly severe but valuable.

Hall, Robert A., Jr.
1982 *The Kensington Rune-Stone is Genuine*. Columbus SC: Hornbeam Press. There is a later expanded volume with supporting sections by other scholars. Lengthy articles by Richard Nielsen greatly expand the study of runes in America. The bulk of Nielsen's work is to be found in *ESOP*.

Heine-Geldern, Robert von
1966 The problem of transpacific influences in Mesoamerica. *Handbook of Middle American Indians*, Vol. 4, Archaeological Frontiers and External Connections. G. F. Ekholm and G. R. Willey, Eds. Austin: University of Texas Press. Heine-Geldern wrote much in German but also a considerable amount in English. For the little Roman head found in Mexico, dating to around the time of Christ, he suggests a transpacific contact rather than the much simpler transatlantic crossing. Here again, one sees a great mind imprisoned by 'accepted knowledge,' which seemed almost to require that transoceanic diffusion be transpacific rather than across the much closer and smaller Atlantic. Mediterranean influences almost certainly came transatlantic, and Asiatic, transpacific.

Heyerdahl, Thor
1963 Feasible ocean routes to and from the Americas in pre-Columbian times. *American Antiquity* 28:482-488.

Horan, J. D.
1986 *The McKenney-Hall Portrait Gallery of American Indians.* New York: Bramhall House. These are true-to-life portraits so realistic that individuals are easily recognized and are the type revealed by forensic reconstructions of Adena skulls.

Ibarra Grasso, Dick Edgar
1982 *América en la prehistoria mundial: difusión greco-fenicia*. [America in World Pre-history: Greco-Phoenician Diffusion]. Buenos Aires: Tipográphica Editora Argentina. Ibarra, here and in other works, places Tiahuanaco around 500 BC and as an eastern Mediterranean influenced site.

He cites portrayal of bronze swords, classic oil lamps, a rithon decorated in Tiahuanaco style, Greek-type bronze arthitectural clamps, etc.

Jackson, J. Wilfrid
1917 *Shells as Evidence of the Migrations of Early Cultures*. Publication 112, University of Manchester Press; and Longmans Green, London. This was preceded by numerous papers including the money-cowry. He was seemingly the first to see the importance of an Indian Ocean shell in the Adena culture.

Jairazbhoy, Rafique Ali
1974 Old World origins of American civilization, Vol. 1: *Ancient Egyptians and Chinese in America*. Totowa NJ: Rowman and Littlefield; and London: George Prior. One may quibble over details, but he is utterly convincing on the big picture.

Jett, Stephen C.
1970 The development and distribution of the blowgun. *Annals of the Association of American Geographers* 60(4):662-688. Jett's many papers include detailed studies, summary studies and theoretical works, all of great value.

Kehoe, Alice B.
1971 Small boats upon the North Atlantic. In *Man Across the Sea: Problems of Pre-Columbian Contacts*. C. L. Riley *et al.*, eds. Austin: University of Texas Press.

Kroeber, Alfred L.
1948 *Anthropology: Race, Language, Culture, Psychology, Prehistory*. New York: Harcourt, Brace. A completely revised edition of Kroeber's 1923 work, this is the best, simplest, most jargon-free text probably ever written for an introduction to anthropology.

Laufer, Berthold
1912 *Jade*. Dover Publications. [2nd edition published in 1946 by P. D. & Ione Perkins in cooperation with the Westwood Press and W. M. Hawley, South Pasadena CA.] On page 52 there is a brief but interesting discussion where he accepts mutual cultural exchanges between America and Asia.

Sadovsky, Otto J.
1984 The discovery of California: Breaking the silence of the Siberia-to-America migrator. In *The Californians* 2(6): 9-20. He finds relationships between Penutian and Siberian languages. The picture is very complex, but the inflow of Old World languages is certain.

Shao, Paul
1983 *The Origin of Ancient American Cultures*. Ames: Iowa State University Press

Smith, Grafton Elliot
1915 *The Migrations of Early Culture*. University of Manchester Publications No. 52. There is a long series of articles and books by Smith, and these are well summarized in the Sorenson and Raish bibliography. Of particular interest is: *Elephants and Ethnologists: Asiatic Origins of the Mayan Ruins*. 1924. London: Kegan, Paul, Trench, Trubner; and New York: Dutton.

Sorenson, John L. and Martin H. Raish
1990 *Pre-Columbian Contact with the Americas across the Oceans: An Annotated Bibliography*, 2 Vols. Provo UT: Research Press.

Stephens, Stanley G.
  1947 The cytogenetics of gossypium and the problem of the origin of New World cottons. *Advances in Genetics* 1:431-432. Stephens was a very careful scholar who tried hard in several papers to consider all the alternative possible explanations.

Tolstoy, Paul
  1964 Cultural parallels between Southeast Asia and Mesoamerica in the manufacture of bark cloth. In *Transactions of the New York Academy of Sciences,* 25:646-662. See also his 1974 Transoceanic diffusion and nuclear Mesoamerica in *Prehispanic America.* New York: St. Martin's. This is a classic case of sustained, detailed study of a single trait with remarkable results.

Webb, W. S. and R. S. Baby
  1957 *The Adena People,* No. 2. Ohio State University Press. See pp. 48-51. Not only are these obviously not Mongoloid but, equally obviously, are Europoid. A chart of Carbon-14 dates for Adena sites places the Adena in the Bronze Age. As often noted, there are similarities between the Old Copper Culture of the Michigan peninsula and the Adena culture.

Wiener, Leo
  1920-22 *Africa and the Discovery of America,* 3 Vols. Philadelphia: Innes and Sons. Reprinted 1971. New York: Kraus.

Williams, Stephen
  1991 *Fantastic Archaeology: The Wild Side of North American Prehistory.* Philadelphia: University of Pennsylvania Press. This illustrates the extremist in the anti-diffusionist camp. For a milder, but methodologically similar work, see *Lost Tribes and Sunken Continents,* Robert Wauchope, 1962. University of Chicago Press. Unfortunately, both stoop to guilt by association.

SECTION I

Artifacts, Sites, and Archaeoastronomy

TIWANAKAN 'JUBA TYPE' VESSEL
(N. Totten, Figure on page 32)

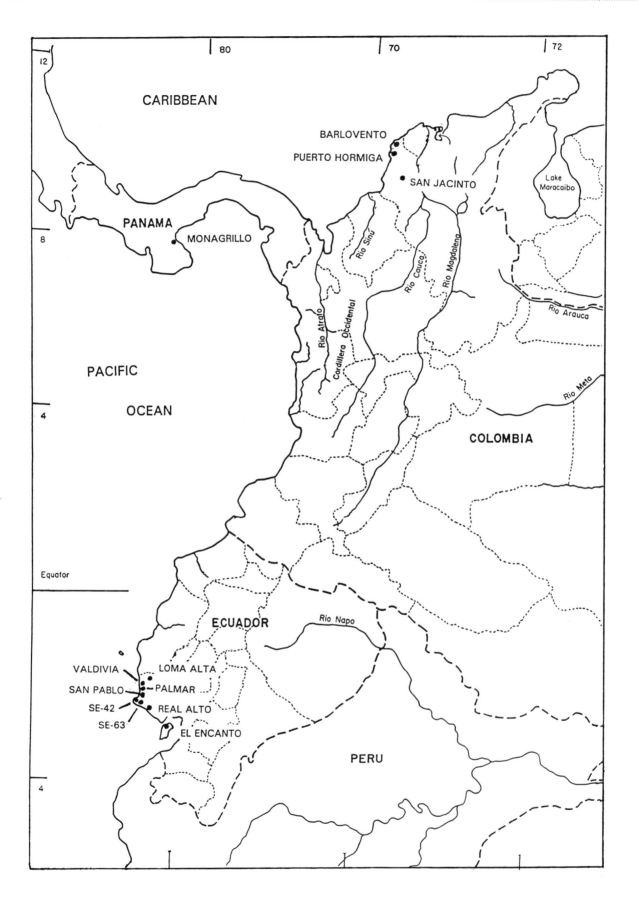

Figure 1 LOCATIONS OF VALDIVIA PERIOD **A** SITES MENTIONED IN THE TEXT

Jomon-Valdivia Similarities:
Convergence or Contàct?

BETTY J. MEGGERS

BACKGROUND

When Emilio Estrada invited Clifford Evans and me to work with him on the coast of Ecuador in 1954, we viewed it as an opportunity to make the contacts essential for exploring the eastern lowlands. As it turned out, we had the good fortune to participate in one of the most exciting events of New World prehistory: the definition of the Valdivia culture. Estrada (1956, 1958) recognized the pottery as early because of its similarities to ceramics of the Ancón and Guañape complexes of north coastal Peru, and his assessment was later confirmed by Carbon-14 dates. More detailed analysis of the Valdivia ceramics and comparison with the other complexes of similar age known at that time—Barlovento on the north coast of Colombia and Monagrillo on the Pacific coast of Panama—revealed only a few shared features (Evans, Meggers, and Estrada 1959).

Having been taught in graduate school that cultural development in the Americas was independent of that in the Old World, we did not think to look for more distant antecedents until Estrada pointed out some remarkable resemblances to Jomon pottery in Japan. He published the first detailed comparison in 1961. In 1963, we travelled from Tokyo to southern Kyushu, examining collections of sherds from Jomon sites. Comparing details of Jomon decoration with enlarged photographs of early Valdivia examples revealed an astonishing degree of similarity. Moreover, the contexts fulfilled the requirements that had been specified for distinguishing diffusion from independent invention: A complex of traits existed on each side of the ocean; the traits were free of functional constraints that might favor their independent duplication; the Early Middle Jomon assemblage was the product of some 6000 years of elaboration from simple beginnings, whereas the earliest Valdivia pottery had no local antecedents; the dates for Early Middle Jomon and early Valdivia were contemporary; and the Japan current provided a feasible route from west to east. In late 1965, we published a detailed description of the Valdivia ceramics and documented the Jomon similarities on twenty-six plates (Meggers, Evans, and Estrada 1965).

In January 1966, the hypothesis that pottery-making was introduced to the coast of Ecuador about 3000 BC by a group originating on the western island of Japan made newspaper headlines around the world. Ever since, the validity of the connection has been a focus of controversy. Many archaeologists have been favorably impressed (e.g.,

Ekholm 1964:496; Kidder II 1964:474; Matos Mendieta 1966; Jennings 1968:176; Schobinger 1969:264; Ford 1969; Reed 1971:108; Willey 1971:16), but others have been vehemently opposed (e.g., Lathrap 1973:1760-1763; Browman 1976:467; Paulsen 1977:653; Ravines 1982:67; Marcos 1988). There have been four principal foci of criticism: 1. the elements compared do not occur in early Valdivia; 2. they are dispersed in space and time in Ecuador and Japan; 3. the transpacific voyage could not have been made; 4. New World antecedents are more likely. I will attempt to demonstrate that these objections have no scientific validity (cf. Meggers 1987 for additional comments).

1. CHARACTERISTICS AND DATING OF EARLY VALDIVIA

The antiquity and characteristics of early Valdivia pottery are critical for tracing its origins and affiliations. Meggers, Evans, and Estrada (1965) presented a relative chronology divided into four periods—designated A, B, C, and D—based on quantitative analysis and seriation of pottery types from stratigraphic excavations. In 1966, Hill (1975) proposed a sequence of eight periods based on seriation of qualitative attributes. She considers her Period 1 antecedent to our Period A and lacking many of the features we used to compare early Valdivia with Early Middle Jomon ceramics, thus invalidating their affiliation (1975:25). Both the priority and the definition of Period 1 have been disputed by Norton on the basis of his excavations at Loma Alta (Figure 1), which produced decorated types and vessel shapes assigned by Hill to Period 2 in levels otherwise characteristic of Period 1. Norton interprets this as evidence that "the complete Valdivia 1 inventory was not present" at Punta Concepción, the site Hill used to define Valdivia 1 (1982:107).

The Carbon-14 dates from Loma Alta are relevant to evaluating the correctness of Hill's identification of Period 1 as pre-Valdivia A. The five dates she accepts for Valdivia 1 are 4495 ± 100 BP from Valdivia (G-31); 4460 ± 90 BP and 4450 ± 100 BP from SE-42 on the Santa Elena Peninsula; and 4370 ± 65 and 4330 ± 100 BP from Loma Alta (Table I). However, there are now at least thirty-two earlier dates from five sites that extend Valdivia A backward to 5620 ± 256 BP. Hill's dates for Valdivia 1 are thus not only more than a millennium more recent than most of those assigned to Valdivia A, but also later than many assigned to Valdivia 2.

Figure 2 EARLY MIDDLE JOMON POTTERY

a)	excised hour-glass motif	g - j)	sharp incising	o - q)	combing
b)	fingernail marking	k)	nicked rim	r)	interlocked lines
c, d)	rocker stamping	l)	zoned punctation	s - u)	broad incising
e, f)	multiple drag-and-jab	m, n)	finger grooving	v)	folded-over rim

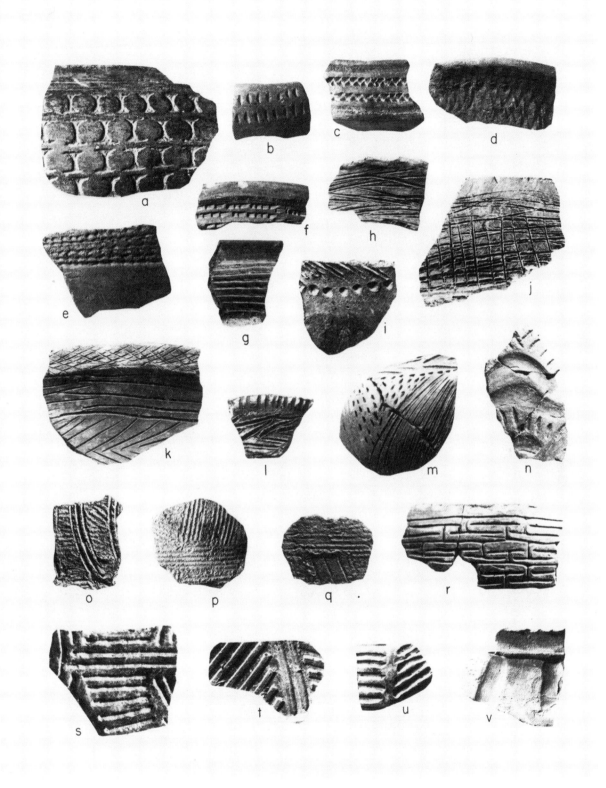

Figure 3 EARLY VALDIVIA POTTERY

a)	excised hour-glass motif	h - k)	sharp incising	o - q)	combing
b)	fingernail marking	l)	nicked rim	r)	interlocked lines
c, d)	rocker stamping	m)	zoned punctation	s - u)	broad incising
e - g)	multiple drag-and-jab	n)	finger grooving	v)	folded-over rim

Table I CARBON-14 DATES ASSIGNED TO VALDIVIA PERIOD **A**

DATE BP	LAB. NO.	SITE	PERIOD	INVESTIGATOR
4330 ± 100	HV-4673	Loma Alta	Valdivia 1	Hill
4360 ± 160	SFU-120	Loma Alta	Valdivia 2	Stahl
4370 ± 85	SI-1184	Valdivia	Valdivia B	Meggers *et al.*
4370 ± 65	SI-1055	Loma Alta	Valdivia 1	Hill
4375 ± 135	GX-7703	Loma Alta	Valdivia 2	Stahl
4390 ± 60	SI-84a	Valdivia	Valdivia A/B	Meggers *et al.*
4405 ± 90	SI-1311	El Encanto	Valdivia B	Stahl
4450 ± 90	SI-22	Valdivia	Valdivia A	Meggers *et al.*
4450 ± 200	W-631	Valdivia	Valdivia A	Meggers *et al.*
4450 ± 100	L-1042C	SE-42	Valdivia 1	Hill
4450 ± 120	SFU-105	Loma Alta	Valdivia 2	Stahl
4460 ± 90	I-7176	SE-42	Valdivia 1	Hill
4460 ± 130	SFU-122	Loma Alta	Valdivia 2	Stahl
4460 ± 100	ISGS-478A	Colimes	Valdivia 2	Stahl
4480 ± 140	M-1317	Valdivia	Valdivia A	Meggers *et al.*
4495 ± 100	HV-4840	Valdivia	Valdivia 1	Hill
4495 ± 160	GX-5266	Real Alto	Valdivia 2	Damp
4510 ± 95	HV-4674	Valdivia	San Pedro	Bischof
4510 ± 100	ISGS-478A	Colimes	Valdivia 2	Stahl
4525 ± 75	ISGS-477	Colimes	Valdivia 2	Stahl
4530 ± 55	SI-83	Valdivia	Valdivia A	Meggers *et al.*
4535 ± 55	HV-4639	Valdivia	San Pedro	Bischof
4540 ± 150	SI-84b	Valdivia	Valdivia A	Meggers *et al.*
4590 ± 120	ISGS-192	Loma Alta	Valdivia A	Norton
4620 ± 140	M-1322	Valdivia	Valdivia A	Meggers *et al.*
4630 ± 160	GX-7699	Loma Alta	Valdivia 2	Stahl
4675 ± 110	HV-4675	Valdivia	San Pedro	Bischof
4680 ± 75	ISGS-274	Valdivia	San Pedro	Bischof
4685 ± 95	I-7069	SE-63		Hill
4700 ± 75	ISGS-275	Valdivia	San Pedro	Bischof
4700 ± 100	L-1042D	SE-42	Valdivia 1?	Hill
4700 ± 270	GX-9460	Loma Alta	Valdivia 1	Stahl
4700 ± 300	ISGS-452	Real Alto	Valdivia 1	L & M
4750 ± 120	ISGS-146	Loma Alta	Valdivia A	Norton
4760 ± 80	H-4527/3810	Valdivia	San Pedro	Bischof
4760 ± 75	ISGS-468	Real Alto	Valdivia 1	L & M
4790 ± 160	SFU-110	Loma Alta	Valdivia 1	Stahl
4900 ± 170	GX-5268	Real Alto	Valdivia 1	Damp
4920 ± 120	I-7075	Loma Alta	Valdivia A	Norton
4920 ± 200	SFU-123	Loma Alta	Valdivia 1	Stahl
4960 ± 210	GX-9458	Loma Alta	Valdivia 1	Stahl
5000 ± 190	ISGS-142	Loma Alta	Valdivia A	Norton
5010 ± 120	I-7076	Loma Alta	Valdivia A	Norton
5050 ± 240	GX-9459	Loma Alta	Valdivia 1	Stahl
5150 ± 150	M-1320	Valdivia	Valdivia A	Meggers *et al.*
5240 ± 420	GX-9457	Loma Alta	Valdivia 1	Stahl
5275 ± 175	GX-7704	Loma Alta	Valdivia 1	Stahl
5495 ± 200	GX-5267	Real Alto	Valdivia 1	Marcos
5620 ± 256	ISGS-448	Real Alto	Valdivia 1	Marcos

Bischof 1980; Damp 1979; Hill 1975; Lathrap and Marcos 1975; Marcos 1988; Meggers *et al.*, 1965; Norton 1982; Stahl 1984

Hill does not consider factors other than chronology that might account for the absence of our early decorated types in her samples. The shallow and sparse refuse at the Punta Concepción site defining her Period **1** presents a marked contrast with the deep accumulations at Valdivia and Loma Alta. According to Hill (1975:2), "everyone who labored to find sherds . . . was conscious of how few sherds there were relative to the size of the site." This situation led Norton (1982:108) to propose that Punta Concepción represents "many relatively short visits by small groups . . . for the exclusive purpose of gathering shellfish." If so, the few vessels needed would not be expected to represent the full range of forms and decorations used at more permanent village sites of the same age.

I submit, therefore, that the incompatibility in dating and the atypical character of the site on which its definition is based make Hill's Valdivia 1 irrelevant for establishing either the content or the antiquity of the Valdivia ceramic tradition.

2. THE VALDIVIA-JOMON COMPARISON

The traits used to demonstrate the similarity between early Valdivia and Early Middle Jomon pottery have been criticized as temporally and spatially dispersed both in Ecuador and Japan. Muller (1971:70), for example, contends that "material from a very broad range in time and space from

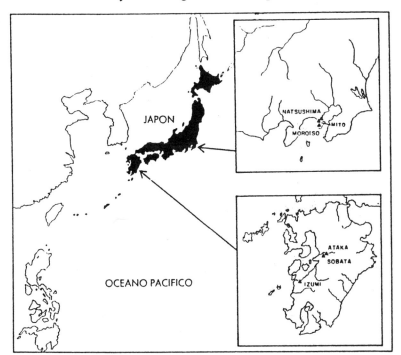

configuration of vessel forms and decorative practices that characterize the very beginning of Valdivia A."

These criticisms misinterpret the evidence provided in our monograph. Actually, sixteen of the decorative techniques diagnostic of Valdivia A have been identified in Jomon samples (Figures 2, 3). Twelve of these occur at the Sobata, Ataka, and Izumi sites (Figure 4), and most of the rest are present at other sites on Kyushu assigned to Early Jomon (Table II). All but one of the nine rim and base forms characteristic of Valdivia A also occur in the Middle Jomon samples from Kyushu, as does the only example of a possible tetrapod support (Meggers *et al.*:Figure 96). The existence of folded-over rims, both plain and finger-pressed, in Valdivia A, Izumi, and Sobata is particularly interesting since this treatment is typically late elsewhere in the New World (Figures 2v, 3v).

Furthermore, the Jomon and Valdivia traits are far more restricted in time and space than are those supporting Mesoamerican-Ecuadorian connections. For example, Lathrap *et al.* (1975:55) derive the "well known figurine tradition of West Mexico" from the figurines of the Chorrera tradition of coastal Ecuador, although more than a millennium separates the two occurrences (*op. cit.*: Figures 84, 85). Similarly, Collier (1982:9) asserts that "the significance of cultural similarities between early (Formative) Ecuador and the early cultures of the Pacific coasts of Guatemala and Mexico is beyond question," but he does not specify what the similarities are. Coe (1967:185)

Figure 4 LOCATIONS OF JAPANESE SITES
Ataka, Sobata and Izumi sites on Kyushu;
Jomon sites in the Tokyo Bay region

provides some examples: "a good case can be made for the introduction from Ecuador to Mesoamerica of metallurgy and such ceramic techniques as iridescent painting, rocker-stamping, and negative painting, and such traits as stirrup-spouts and the pottery mold. Coming in the other direction would be napkin-ring ear spools, chili-grater bowls, clay roller-stamps, the very odd three-pronged censers, and a host of other things." As Rivera (1982:401) has pointed out, however, "the origin of nearly all these traits has been somewhat vaguely situated in Mesoamerica as a consequence of the absence of sequences and well-defined local contexts."

By contrast, our study shows that two-thirds of the decorated techniques and eight of the nine rim and base treatments characteristic of Valdivia A on the coast of Ecuador occur at three western Kyushu sites that are contemporary with initial Valdivia (Figure 4).

Japan is compared with material from a very broad range in time in Ecuador." Feldman and Moseley (1983:155) acknowledge that "some of the decorative forms are indeed similar between Ecuador and Japan," but assert that "the occurrence of these traits is sporadic. They are scattered around the sequence, rather than clustered at the beginning." Lathrap (1967:97; 1973:1762) argues that "a careful study of the wealth of visual comparisons which the authors have made between Valdivia and various disparate Jomon complexes suggests that there is no single Jomon complex yet known that is particularly similar to the total

Table II VALDIVIA **A**

Decorative techniques at Jomon sites

TECHNIQUE	ATAKA	SOBATA	IZUMI	OTHER
Broad incising	X	X	X	X
Brushing		X		X
Combing	X	X	X	X
Corrugating				X
Excising	X		X	X
Fine hachure				X
Finger grooving	X	X	X	X
Fingernail marking	X	X	X	X
Folded-over rim		X	X	
Lobed rim	X		X	
Multiple drag-and-jab	X		X	X
Pseudo-corrugating				X
Red slipping	X			
Rocker stamping				X
Sharp incising	X	X	X	X
Shell stamping		X	X	X

3. OBSTACLES TO TRANSMISSION

Doubt has frequently been expressed concerning: a) the feasibility of a transoceanic voyage; b) the likelihood of any survivors; and c) the possibility that "a few exhausted fishermen" could have introduced new cultural traits (*e.g.*, Rowe 1966; Collier 1968:271; Davies 1979:71-2). The most extended critique is by McEwan and Dickson (1978), who estimate a minimum duration of five hundred and fifty-six days for such a crossing under ideal conditions and conclude "it is probably more likely that the drift voyage would have taken three times that long" (*op. cit.*: 366). They also consider that the weather "could have been extreme enough to prevent the survival of either the men or their craft" (*op. cit.*: 365).

a) Feasibility of the Voyage

The navigational skills of the early Jomon population are attested by archaeological evidence for their colonization of the Izo chain of small islands extending south from the Tokyo region for *ca.* 1000 km. This chain is divided into northern and southern segments by the fast-flowing Black Current, which is difficult to cross even today (Oda 1990:57). The more accessible northern islands were settled by the Earliest Jomon period, dating *ca.* 8000 BP. Multiple two-way crossings to the southern islands by 7000 BP are implied by the presence of obsidian from a source near Tokyo, as well as "considerable quantities of terminal Early-beginning Middle Jomon pottery clearly related to the Jomon pottery found on the main Japanese islands" (Oda 1990:60).

The ability of Jomon people to cross the swift Black Current repeatedly in both directions more than a millennium prior to the initial date for Valdivia pottery leaves no doubt that they could have survived a transpacific drift. The brevity and relative simplicity of the feat were demonstrated in 1980 by the successful voyage of the Yasei-go III, sponsored by the Ancient Pacific Cultures Research Project in Tokyo. This craft, a double canoe of the kind likely to have been in use by 5000 BP (Kadokawa 1979:2), was equipped with sails, a rudder, and a centerboard and was propelled solely by currents and winds. Departure from Shimoda, southwest of Tokyo, was at noon on May 8, 1980 (Fujimoto, pers. com.). Arrival at San Francisco was predicted for early July, but the Yasei-go III landed ahead of schedule on June 28 after travelling 9285 nautical miles in fifty-one days (Figure 5). The next stop was Acapulco, reached on August 11, after the craft weathered two hurricanes. The vessel resumed its voyage on September 27 and arrived in Guayaquil, Ecuador on October 12.

It is noteworthy that the greatest difficulties were encountered off the coast of Central America, which archaeologists tend to consider relatively smooth sailing. Adams (1967:534), for example, accepts the "evidence of far-flung contact via ocean routes" between Ecuador and Mesoamerica in part because "coastwise currents are favorable for such contact." Indeed, many of the most adamant opponents of trans-Pacific communication are willing to postulate repeated maritime voyages between Mesoamerica and Ecuador (*e.g.*, Coe 1960, 1967; Lathrap *et al.* 1975; Paulsen 1982). Feldman and Moseley (1983:146) suggest that seafaring contact "possibly even existed during the Pre-ceramic before 3500 BC."

Even opponents of transpacific influences credit the Valdivia population with the capacity to engage in deep-sea fishing. Lathrap (1975:22) states that "a small ocean catfish was by far the most common species represented" at Loma Alta, and that "the pattern of efficient marine fishing in Valdivia culture is also indicated by specialized fishing equipment." Feldman and Moseley (1983:147) agree that "the inference of early maritime navigation and contact receives support from animal remains in the Vegas and later Valdivia middens, where several types of deep-sea fish and shell fish have been found. The best explanation for their occurrence is that they were caught by people using watercraft capable of navigating on the open ocean."

b) Likelihood of Survivors

The ability of more recent Japanese sailors to survive long drifts has been documented for more than a century. Sittig (1896:530) reported the arrival of a junk on Oahu in December 1832, after a drift lasting eleven months, with nine living crew members. Another tabulation lists sixty cases between 1613 and 1876, thirty-three of which had one or more survivors. The longest drift was seventeen months. Of particular interest is a junk that deposited three crew members on the coast of Mexico in 1943 (Brooks 1876:53, 55). Although many drifts did not have survivors, enough did to indicate that this objection is not sustainable.

c) Introduction of New Cultural Traits

Whether "a few exhausted fishermen" could make an impact involves the questionable assumption that they would have arrived exhausted after a peaceful drift of several weeks. Even if they were exhausted, they certainly would have regained their normal state in a few days. Their capacity to introduce new ideas and skills is implied by the presence of Jomon-like pottery. This case is not unique. The existence of sherds, related to Initial and Early Jomon styles on Kyushu, not only on Okinawa but as far as South Korea, is attributable to a few individuals (Anderson 1987: 279). Interestingly, although Davies (1979:72) "persists in doubting that . . . [a] canoe could have reached Ecuador at all, much less changed the course of history," he argues in the case of the bottle gourd that "the act of one beachcomber who picked up a single specimen and cast it upon his rubbish heap would have suffficed for a debut to have been made in new surroundings" (*op. cit.*: 64). This kind of objection is impossible to prove or disprove in a particular case, but history is replete with successful introductions of a vast array of cultural traits by small groups. When, where, how, and if this happens varies, but whether it occurs is beyond dispute.

In short, the maritime skills of the Jomon and Valdivia populations, the rapidity of the voyage by the Yasei-go III, and the pervasive occurrence of cultural diffusion favor a trans-Pacific contact. The fact that modern Micronesians and Polynesians routinely make long journeys to distant islands in small craft is further evidence that we should not underrate the ability of earlier peoples to have survived similar long-distance excursions.

4. NEW WORLD ANTECEDENTS

Three principal alternative origins of Valdivia pottery have been proposed: a) derivation from the Puerto Hormiga complex on the Caribbean coast of Colombia; b) derivation from an inland antecedent; and c) derivation from an unknown New World ancestor.

a) Derivation from the Caribbean Coast of Colombia

Puerto Hormiga ceramics, known from a single site, share three of the distinctive early Valdivia decorative techniques: multiple drag-and-jab punctate, finger grooving, and broad-line incising (Reichel-Dolmatoff 1961, 1965). A motif characteristic of Valdivia Red Incised also occurs (Reichel-Dolmatoff 1965, Figure 3:5). Five Carbon-14 dates extend from 5040 ± 70 BP (SI-153) to 4515 ± 250 BP (I-1123).

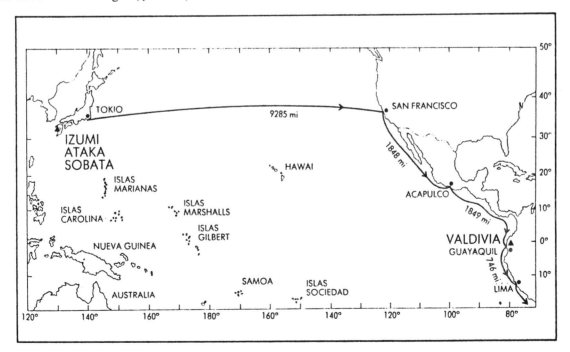

Figure 5 ROUTE OF THE YASEI-GO III AND DISTANCES IN NAUTICAL MILES
After stopping at Guayaquil, the voyage continued to Lima, Arica, and Valparaiso
where the vessel was donated to the Chilean Naval Museum.

Because a gap of several centuries separated our initial Valdivia date of 5150 ± 150 BP from the next earliest date, 4620 ± 140 BP (Table I), and because four of the Puerto Hormiga dates clustered between 5040 and 4875 BP, many archaeologists rejected the initial Valdivia date and assigned priority to Puerto Hormiga (*e.g.*, Lathrap 1967: 97; Coe 1967:185).   The relative simplicity of Puerto Hormiga ceramics also seemed to favor their greater antiquity. This interpretation is acceptable only when attention is restricted to locations within the western hemisphere. When the geographical context is expanded, the necessity of explaining the striking similarities between Valdivia **A** and the contemporary Early Middle Jomon ceramics becomes apparent (Meggers 1980).

b) Derivation from an Inland Ancestor

Norton (1982:109) has stated that "the accumulating evidence on the distribution and nature of the earliest Valdivia sites points increasingly to an inland origin of pottery in northwestern South America." McEwan and Dickson (1978:368) consider "the most compelling alternative explanation of the early Jomon-like ceramic complex at the Valdivia site is . . . an *in situ* cultural development whose antecedent forms inland in northwestern South America are only now being recognized and understood." Collier (1982:9) asserts that "the Tropical Forest connections are certainly strong and clear. We need only more adequate archaeological work east of the Andes to prove Valdivia origins beyond any question" (*cf.* Feldman and Moseley 1983:154).

These assertions are not supported by the archaeological evidence. Survey of the principal tributaries of the Amazon during the past fifteen years has defined dozens of ceramic complexes and produced several hundred Carbon-14 dates (Meggers *et al.* 1988). Neither the Carbon-14 dates nor the characteristics of the pottery support a tropical forest derivation for Valdivia. The Ananatuba Phase on Marajó Island (Meggers and Danon 1988) and the Barrancoid Tradition on the middle and lower Orinoco (Sanoja and Vargas 1983) are the earliest yet identified; both are distinct from Valdivia and at least two millennia more recent. The initial ceramics from eastern lowland Ecuador (Pastaza) and Peru (Waira-jirca) are also a millennium or more younger than Valdivia (Izumi and Sono 1963; Porras 1975).

Inland has also been used in the sense of *not on the shore*. Thus, although Loma Alta is only fifteen km. from the mouth of the Rio Valdivia, it has been described by Norton (1982:102) as an inland site. He concludes that "the discovery of inland early Valdivia sites weakens the transpacific hypothesis to the point where it becomes increasingly difficult to sustain" (1982:108). It is doubtful, however, that a location fifteen km. from the shore would have been considered *inland* by prehistoric people capable of making a thirty km. round-trip journey on foot during a single day. Nor does the occurrence of early Valdivia sites in the Guayas Basin rule out a transpacific introduction for the ceramic complex. Seaborne intrusions are

frequently postulated to account for traits observed hundreds of kms. from the coast (*e.g.*, Oberem 1982:344 and other papers given at this symposium).

c) Derivation from an Unknown New World Ancestor

Different objections have been expressed by Bischof and Viteri (1972). Based on excavation at the northeastern edge of Estrada's Cut **J**, Section **E**, at the Valdivia site, they concluded that "the fully ceramic Valdivia phase was preceded by the San Pedro phase, when well-made pottery was used in small quantities." Bischof's (1973:270) assertion that the discovery of the San Pedro complex discredits the hypothesis of Jomon antecedents for Valdivia has been taken up by others. Feldman and Moseley (1983:149) agree that "the presence of earlier pottery . . . seriously weakens Meggers' and Evans' argument that Valdivia pottery was derived from Japan," and Jett (1983:346) has withdrawn his previous support of a connection.

These judgments rest on two dubious assumptions: 1. that San Pedro pottery is distinct from and earlier than Valdivia; and 2. that the existence of an earlier ceramic tradition made coastal Ecuadorians immune to outside influence. The descriptions and illustrations of San Pedro pottery do not support Lathrap's contention that "the single vessel shape and decorative modes of this pottery . . . are outside the known range of Valdivia stylistic practices" (Lathrap *et al.* 1975:27). On the contrary, three sherds identified by Bischof as San Pedro among those illustrated by Meggers, Evans, and Estrada fall within the range of variation included in Valdivia Incised, and the single vessel shape is Valdivia form 18 (Meggers *et al.* 1965: Table A).

As for the temporal argument, the six dates assigned to the San Pedro complex by Bischof (1980:382) extend from 4760 ± 80 BP to 4510 ± 95 BP (Table I). The oldest is thus nearly a millennium more recent than the earliest Valdivia date, and the remainder overlap nine dates from early Valdivia contexts. These discrepancies in content and dating must be resolved before the priority and independence of the San Pedro complex can be accepted.

Nor is it clear why the existence of unrelated pottery would weaken the case for a Jomon-Valdivia connection. On the contrary, it could be argued that a group already making pottery would be receptive to new techniques of decoration.

CONCLUSION

I have attempted to show that the principal objections to a transpacific origin for Valdivia pottery incorporate misinterpretations of the evidence and incorrect logic. Although the opponents agree that all the initial ceramics discovered thus far are technologically advanced and that none is ancestral to Valdivia, they are unwilling to consider the possibility that New World antecedents may not exist. We cannot assume, however, that "the startling similarities . . . indicate the kinds of convergences that can occur when two unrelated ceramic traditions stress as their basic decorative concept the punching, pinching, dragging, brushing, combing, scraping, or otherwise mutilating of wet clay surfaces with a range of common household objects" (Lathrap 1967:97). First, we must establish that the traditions are not related.

I submit that existing archaeological evidence supports the conclusion that the Valdivia and Jomon ceramic traditions are related. I also submit that this relationship exemplifies the most important difference between our species and all others. We dominate this planet because we have substituted culturally determined behavior, which can be transmitted among unrelated individuals, for biologically determined behavior, which is transmitted from parent to offspring. The ability to adopt discoveries and inventions made in other times and places eliminates the need for each human individual or society to repeat complete developmental sequences, and diffusion is the mechanism by which the evolutionary potential of this capacity

is realized. The rapid technological elaboration and global dissemination of computers during the past decade exemplifies a process that has operated at an accelerating pace for millennia (Meggers 1985, ms).

If we accept this theoretical perspective, we are obliged to recognize that diffusion rather than independent invention is the prime mover of cultural change on a local as well as a global level (*cf.* Schneider 1977). Convergences may occur independently as a consequence of similar adaptive constraints, but there are no such constraints on the decorative techniques and motifs, rim treatments, and most other features of pottery. Indeed, it is the arbitrary nature of these elements that makes them the principal category of evidence used by archaeologists for tracing past cultural relationships. Accepting ceramic similarities as reliable indicators of communication *within* hemispheres requires acknowledging them to be equally reliable evidence of communication *across water*. The burden of proof to the contrary thus rests with the independent inventionists, not the diffusionists.

REFERENCES

Adams, Richard E. W.
  1967   Review of Ecuador by Betty J. Meggers. *American Anthropologist* 69:533-534.
Anderson, Atholl
  1987   Recent developments in Japanese prehistory: A review. *Antiquity.* 61:270-281.
Bischof, Henning
  1973   The origins of pottery in South America. Recent radiocarbon dates from southwest Ecuador. *Congresso Internazionale degli Americanisti.* Roma-Genova 1972, Atti 1:269-281.
  1980   San Pedro and Valdivia—Frühe Keramikkomplexe an der Kuste Sudwest-Ekuadors. *Beiträge zur Algemeinen und Vergleichenden Archaologie* 1:335-389. München: Deutches Archaologisches Institut.
Bischof, Henning and Julio Viteri Gamboa
  1972   Pre-Valdivia occupations on the southwest coast of Ecuador. *American Antiquity* 37:548-551.
Brooks, Charles W.
  1876   Report of Japanese vessels wrecked in the north Pacific Ocean from the earliest records to the present time. *Proceedings of the California Academy of Sciences*, 6:50-64. San Francisco.
Browman, David L.
  1976   Review of prehistory of North America by Jesse D. Jennings. *American Anthropologist* 78:467.
Coe, Michael D.
  1960   Archeological linkages with North and South America at La Victoria, Guatemala. *American Anthropologist* 62:363-393.
  1967   Directions of cultural diffusion: Review of Meggers 1966. *Science* 155:185-186.
Collier, Donald
  1968   Review of Ecuador by Betty J. Meggers. *American Antiquity* 33:269-271.

Collier, Donald
  1982   One hundred years of Ecuadorian archaeology. Pp. 5-33 in *Primer Simposio de Correlaciones Antropológicas Andino-Mesoamericano*, J. G. Marcos and P. Norton, eds. Guayaquil.
Damp, Jonathan E.
  1979   *Better Homes and Gardens: the Life and Death of the Early Valdivia Community*. PhD Dissertation. Alberta, Canada: University of Calgary.
Davies, Nigel
  1979   *Voyagers to the New World: Fact or Fantasy?* New York: William Morrow Co.
Ekholm, Gordon F.
  1964   Transpacific contacts. Pp. 489-510 in *Early Man in the New World*. J. D. Jennings and E. Norbeck, eds. Chicago: University of Chicago Press.
Estrada, Emilio
  1956   Valdivia, un sitio arqueológico formativo en la costa de la provincia del Guayas, Ecuador. *Publicación del Museo Victor Emilio Estrada*, No. 1. Guayaquil.
  1958   Las culturas pre-clásicas, formativas o arcaicas del Ecuador. *Publicación del Museo Victor Emilio Estrada*, No. 5. Guayaquil.
  1961   Nuevos elementos en la cultura Valdivia; sus posibles contactos transpacificos. *Publicación del Sub-Comite Ecuatoriano de Antropología*, Instituto Panamericano de Geografía e Historia, Guayaquil.
Evans, Clifford, Betty Meggers, and Emilio Estrada
  1959   Cultura Valdivia. *Publicación del Museo Victor Emilio Estrada*, No. 6. Guayaquil.
Feldman, Robert A. and Michael E. Moseley
  1983   The northern Andes. Pp. 138-177 in *Ancient South America*. J. D. Jennings, ed. San Francisco: W. H. Freeman and Co.

Ford, James A.
  1969 A comparison of formative cultures in the Americas: Diffusion or the psychic unity of man? *Smithsonian Contributions to Anthropology 11*. Washington DC.

Hill, Betsy
  1975 A new chronology of the Valdivia ceramic complex from the coastal zone of Guayas province, Ecuador. *Ñawpa Pacha* 10-11:1-32.

Izumi, Seiichi and Toshihiko Sono
  1963 *Andes 2: Excavations at Kotosh, Peru 1960*. Tokyo.

Jennings, Jesse D.
  1968 *Prehistory of North America*. New York: McGraw-Hill.

Jett, Stephen C.
  1983 Pre-Columbian transoceanic contacts. Pp. 337-393 in *Ancient South America*. J. D. Jennings, ed. San Francisco: W. H. Freeman Co.

Kadokawa, Haruki
  1979 *The Transpacific Experimental Sailing by "Yasei-go III."* Paper presented at ARGOS Conference, Lanham MD, September 13-14.

Kidder II, Alfred
  1964 South American high cultures. Pp. 451-486 in *Prehistoric Man in the New World*. J. D. Jennings and E. Norbeck, eds. Chicago: University of Chicago Press.

Lathrap, Donald
  1967 Review of Early Formative Period of coastal Ecuador by Meggers, Evans, and Estrada. *American Anthropologist* 69:96-98.
  1973 Summary of model building: How does one achieve a meaningful overview of a continent's prehistory? Review of 'An Introduction to American Archaeology, Vol. 2, South America' by Gordon R. Willey. *American Anthropologist* 75:1755-1767.

Lathrap, Donald W., Donald Collier, and H. Chandra
  1975 *Ancient Ecuador: Culture, Clay and Creativity 3000-300 B.C.* Chicago: Field Museum of Natural History.

Lathrap, Donald W. and Jorge G. Marcos
  1975 Informe preliminar sobre las excavaciones del sitio Real Alto por la Misión Antropológica de la Universidad de Illinois. *Revista de la Universidad Católica* 3:41-66. Quito.

Lathrap, Donald W., Jorge G. Marcos, and James A. Zeidler
  1977 Real Alto, an ancient ceremonial center. *Archaeology* 30:2-13.

Marcos, Jorge
  1988 Real Alto: la historia de un centro ceremonial Valdivia. *Bibl. Ecuatoriana de Arqueología 4*. Guayaquil: ESPOL.

Matos Mendieta, Ramiro
  1966 Un nuevo libro y una nueva teoría sobre arqueología Andina. *Boletin de la Sociedad Geográfica de Lima* 85:82-88.

McEwan, G. F. and D. B. Dickson
  1978 Valdivia, Jomon fishermen, and the nature of the North Pacific: Some nautical problems with Meggers, Evans, and Estrada's (1965) transoceanic contact thesis. *American Antiquity* 43:362-371.

Meggers, Betty J.
  1964 North and South American cultural connections and convergences. Pp. 511-526 in *Prehistoric Man in the New World*. J. D. Jennings, ed. Chicago: University of Chicago Press.

Meggers, Betty J.
  1967 Did Japanese fishermen bring the art of pottery making to Ecuador 5000 years ago? *The UNESCO Courier* 20(5):12-13.
  1971 Contacts from Asia. Pp. 239-259 in *The Quest for America*. Geoffrey Ashe and others, eds. London: Pall Mall Press.
  1980 Did Japanese fishermen really reach Ecuador 5,000 years ago? *Early Man 2* (4):15-19.
  1985 El significado de la difusión como factor de evolución. *Revista Chungará* 14:81-90.
  1987 El origin transpacífico de la cerámica Valdivia: una evaluación. *Boletin del Museo Chileno de Arte Precolombino* 2:9-31.
  m.s. Diffusion and the evolution of culture. *Proceedings of the Circum-Pacific Science Congress*. Seattle, August 1-6, 1989. In press.

Meggers, Betty J. and Jaques Danon
  1988 Identification and implications of a hiatus in the archeological sequence on Marajó Island, Brazil. *Journal of the Washington Academy of Sciences* 78:245-253.

Meggers, Betty J., Ondemar F. Dias, Enrico Th. Miller, and Celso Perota
  1988 Implications of archeological distributions in Amazonia. Pp. 275-294 in *Proceedings of a Workshop on Neotropical Distribution Patterns*. Rio de Janeiro: Academia Brasileira de Ciências.

Meggers, Betty J. and Clifford Evans
  1966a A transpacific contact in 3000 B.C. *Scientific American* 214:28-35.
  1966b Transpacific origin of Valdivia phase pottery on coastal Ecuador. *36o Congreso internacional de Americanistas, Actas y Memorias* 1:63-67. Sevilla.
  1983 Lowland South America and the Antilles. Pp. 287-335 in *Ancient South Americans*. J. D. Jennings, ed. San Francisco: W. H. Freeman and Co.

Meggers, Betty J., Clifford Evans, and Emilio Estrada
  1965 Early Formative Period of coastal Ecuador: the Valdivia and Machalilla phases. *Smithsonian Contributions to Anthropology 1*. Washington DC.

Muller, Jon
  1971 Style and culture contact. Pp. 66-78 in *Man Across the Sea*, C. L. Riley, J. C. Kelley, C. W. Pennington, and R. L. Rands, eds. Austin: University of Texas Press.

Norton, Presley
  1982 Preliminary observations on Loma Alta, an Early Valdivia midden in Guayas province, Ecuador. Pp. 101-119 in *Primer Simposio de Correlaciones Antropológicas Andino-Mesoamericano*. J. G. Marcos and P. Norton, eds. Guayaquil.

Oberem, Udo
  1982 Algunos hallazgos arqueológicos de la Sierra Ecuatoriana, indicios de posibles relaciones con Mesoamerica. Pp. 341-347 in *Primer Simposio de Correlaciones Antropológicas Andina-Mesoamericano*. Guayaquil.

Oda, Shizuo
  1990 A review of archaeological research in the Izu and Ogasawara islands. *Man and Culture in Oceania*, 6:53-79.

Paulsen, Allison C.
  1977 Differential survival of the Jomon-Valdivia hypothesis. *American Anthropologist* 79:652-653.

Paulsen, Allison C.
  1982   La secuencia de la cerámica de Guangala de la penin-
         sula de Santa Elena y sus implicaciones para un contacto
         prehistórico entre el Ecuador y América Central. Pp. 203-
         210 in *Primer Simposio de Correlaciones Antropológicas
         Andino-Mesoamericano.* Guayaquil.
Porras Garcés, Pedro I.
  1973   *El Encanto-La Puná; un Sitio Insular de la Fase Valdi-
         via Associado a un Conchero Aanular.* Quito.
  1975   El formativo en el Valle Amazónico del Ecuador: fase
         pastaza. *Revista de la Universidad Católica* 3:74-134. Quito.
Ravines, Rogger
  1982   *Panorama de la Arqueología Andina.* Lima: Instituto de
         Estudios Peruanos.
Reed, Erik K.
  1971   Commentary: Section 1. Pp. 106-111 in *Man Across the
         Sea.* C. L. Riley, J. C. Kelley, C. W. Pennington, and R. L.
         Rands, eds. Austin: University of Texas Press.
Reichel-Dolmatoff, Gerardo
  1961   Puerto Hormiga: un complejo prehistórico marginal de
         Colombia (nota preliminar). *Revista Colombiana de Antro-
         pología* 10:347-354.
  1965   *Excavaciones Arqueológicas en Puerto Hormiga
         (Departamento de Bolivar).* Bogotá: Ediciones de la Univer-
         sidad de los Andes.
Rivera Dorado, Miguel
  1982   Algunos rasgos Mesoamericanos en la costa de Esmer-
         aldas (Ecuador). Pp. 399-404 in *Primer Simposio de Corre-
         laciones Antropológicas Andino-Mesoamericano.* Guayaquil.
Rowe, John H.
  1966   Diffusionism and archaeology. *American Antiquity*
         31:334-337.

Sanoja, Mario
  1979   Las culturas formativas del oriente de Venezuela; la
         tradición Barrancas del Bajo Orinoco. *Biblioteca de la Aca-
         demía Nacional de la Historia, Série Estudios, Monografías
         y Ensayos* No. 6. Caracas.
Sanoja, Mario and Iraida Vargas
  1983   New light on the prehistory of eastern Venezuela. *Ad-
         vances in World Archaeology* 2:205-244. New York: Aca-
         demic Press.
Schneider, Harold K.
  1977   Prehistoric transpacific contact and the theory of culture
         change. *American Anthropologist* 79:9-25.
Schobinger, Juan
  1969   *Prehistoria de Suramérica.* Barcelona: Editorial Labor
         S. A.
Simoes, Mário F.
  1981   Coletores-pescadores ceramistas do litoral do Salgado
         (Pará): nota preliminar. *Boletim do Museu Paraense Emílio
         Goeldi, Antropologia* 78. Belém.
Sittig, Otto
  1896   Compulsory migrations in the Pacific Ocean. Pp. 519-
         535 in *Smithsonian Institution Annual Report.* to July 1895.
         Washington DC.
Willey, Gordon R.
  1971   *An Introduction to American Archaeology, Vol. 2:
         South America.* Englewood Cliffs: Prentice Hall.
Zevallos, Carlos, W. C. Galinat, D. W. Lathrap, E. R. Long, J.
  G. Marcos, and K. M. Klumpp
  1977   The San Pablo corn kernel and its friends. *Science*
         196:385-389.

King Juba Remembered:
a Working Hypothesis[1]

NORMAN TOTTEN

By the time we are finished, much of pre-Columbian history will have to be rewritten.
Alan Kolata—University of Chicago

Insight in archaeology is gained by the use of various forms of analogical argument
in conjunction with the evaluation of the physical evidence.
John Carlson—University of Maryland

I

This report of limited research into possible North African Berber influence in the Andes deals with one possible aspect of the origins of Tiwanakan and Moche civilizations. I have not visited Bolivia since 1975 and then only the site of Tiwanaku. My first-hand experience of Peru's pre-Columbian cultures is somewhat more extensive. Twice in the 1980s I led and lectured to groups there for Archaeological Tours of New York. I hope this paper provokes further testing, research, and reconsideration of Tiwanakan and Moche origins by others, not just simple or complex rehashes of currently accepted opinions.

'JUBA-TYPE' INSCRIBED POT

In 1978 I acquired an old pot from Bernheimer's Antiques, Cambridge MA. The piece had been in his private collection from before 1950. We both judged it genuine, with apparent script around its upper rim. Bernheimer said it could not be what it looked like, as no writing existed at Tiwanaku before Pizzaro.

Tiwanakan and Moche portrait vessels are smaller than human heads. This one is 14 cm. high, 11 cm. wide at top, 7 cm. wide at base, in monochrome black. Moustache, arrows, and inscription are incised. The pot is not as artistically refined as later painted Tiwanakan portrait vessels, nor as beautiful as the best stirrup-spouted Moche portrait vessels of about the same date.

Tiwanakan vessels in this category depict a man with a thin, black moustache and beard, wearing a turban with a decorated headband. Usually an arrow goes downward through each eye, then out below or at the bottom of the ears. The nose is aquiline, the jaws prognathous. Portrait pots in this category portrayed a single individual (or type): a culture-hero. For convenience in presenting my hypothesis, I will call such vessels the 'Juba type.'

II

Why Juba? Barry and Rene Fell stayed overnight in my home on their way from Harvard to retirement in San Diego in 1978. I showed Barry markings on the Juba pot, which occupied him during his flight. He deciphered them as corrupt Greek letters: "Jub Basileus, Jub Basileus," *i.e.*, King Juba, written twice.

IVB BA≤)ΛEV≳

FELL'S TRANSLITERATION OF THE JUBA 'INSCRIPTION'

Doubling designs on pottery was common practice in both Moche and Tiwanakan ceramic traditions, not a Berber transplant to America. The letters are degenerate compared with Greek writing in North Africa during Juba II's reign. Rulers' names and/or titles were frequently abbreviated on ancient Greek and Roman coinages.

WARREN COOK'S MACINTOSHIZATION OF INSCRIBED POT

III

The hand of Montesinos . . . about the use of paper and writing
. . . betray the credulous and uncritical mind
of the literary pirate.
Clements Markham

The question of whether or not there was anything resembling
hieroglyphics in pre-Incaic Peru is an important one, but one
which has never been solved.
Philip Means

No phonetic writing was in use in the Andes in 1532 when Pizzaro arrived. Both archaeology and the historic record attest to this. Whether one or more scripts had been employed centuries earlier is another matter. What is the documentary evidence for writing in the pre-Columbian Andes?

The only early extant chronicle to report that writing once existed in the Andes is Montesinos' *Memorias Antiguas Historiales del Peru* (first half of the 17th century). Montesinos borrowed without acknowledgement from earlier records now lost. Most likely he took the part dealt with here from Blas Valera's *Vocabulario Historico del Peru* (written before AD 1600).

According to Montesinos, the information was based on 16th-century interviews with Inka *amautas*, oral historian-astrologers using records kept on *quipus*. The amautas said that their Inka forebears once wrote on parchment called *quilca*, made from dried plantain leaves, and on stones. In evaluating this account, most objections that have been raised seem irrelevant and misleading. It does not matter what Montesinos thought about Ophir and Peru, or that he exaggerated numbers and dates, or even that he plagiarized Blas Valera. What matters is that we have an apparently valid record preserved indirectly from Inka oral historians that there had been writing in pre-Inka Peru (Markham's translation: 18, 53, 61, 62, 64).

Pedro de Cieza de Leon (1518-1560) was born and died in Spain. As a youth he went to South America, traveling from Panama and Colombia to Argentina. Cieza took part in various military expeditions and the founding of new Spanish cities. In 1547, Cieza journeyed on the main highway from Cuzco to La Paz. Along the way, he sought out the best local informants about Inka and pre-Inka civilization. Many remembered things before the Spanish arrived—tales, songs, traditions. Shortly after-

ward, Cieza wrote *Cronica General del Peru,* returning to Spain in 1550.

The Colla descended from a kingdom at the north end of Lake Titicaca, powerful before Inka conquest. They said that people who once lived on the largest island in Lake Titicaca had white skin and beards but were wiped out in later warfare. Cieza's *Del Senorio de los Incas* repeats the account of gentle white men who once lived on an island in Lake Titicaca. The color white had very deep symbolic significance in the pre-1500 Andes. Locals even referred to the conquering Spanish as *wiracochas*.

In chapter five, Cieza wrote that a greatly-venerated bearded white man called 'Ticiviracoca,' 'Tupaca,' or 'Arnauan,' obtained much power in the Titicaca area. Cieza heard stories about white megalith-builders who came by sea to the Peruvian coast, then moved inland to begin building Tiwanaku with iron tools.

One may question the historical accuracy of essentially oral traditions. It does not appear that Cieza significantly distorted the information he received. He even reported some variations in it, such as the name of Wiracocha. There are also related accounts by Montesinos, Betanzos, Salcamagua, and Molina.

The few surviving pre-1500 iron artifacts from South America are identified as made from meteorites. If iron tools were brought to Tiwanaku, there would have been no replenishment once they were used up. All of earth's free iron rusted hundreds of millions of years ago into oxides and requires smeltering ores to obtain it.

There is little doubt that Tiwanaku's monumental stone structures were built by exploiting local labor to support an elite ruling class. In our logic, this does not accord with Cieza's sanctified, peaceful Wiracocha. Andean logic did not require such an accord. The logic in ancient cultures was seldom Aristotelian.

IV

SECHÍN PRIEST
He wears a fez and *ogee* kilt. Note the solar arrows passing down through his eyes and face. He also holds a sacrificial mace-knife.

Arrows-through-the-eyes is an uncommon motif. The earliest example I know of is at the pre-Chavín site of Sechín (1300 BC). There, this symbol appears on bas-relief faces of priests holding instruments for human sacrifice. Arrows-through-the-eyes symbolism does appear elsewhere in the Americas, as shown below:

OLMEC
(Las Limas, Veracruz, Mexico.
Same date as Peru's Chavín)

ZAPOTEC
(Monte Albán, Mexico)

POST CLASSIC MAYA
(Madrid Codex)

Kilts worn by Sechín priests depict the earth mother's private parts, a symbol found later on Chavín and Tiwanakan pottery and in the southeast United States, where it is known as the *ogee*.

CHAVÍN CERAMIC BOTTLE
(500 BC) with engraved
ogee symbol from
North Coastal Peru.

The sharing of unusual motifs suggests the possibility of transmission from Peru's north coast to Tiwanaku, despite temporal differences between the civilizations. Arrows down from the forehead, through the eyes and out toward earlobes or below them visualize the concept that the first dynastic ruler descended from the sun, embodying divine intelligence, a common idea, an uncommon motif, employed also in ancient Costa Rica and Mexico.

DESIGNS ON TIWANAKAN POTTERY (Poznansky)

Top: Stylized raptorial bird-feline (condor-puma). Note the ogee where the three-feathered birdtail connects to the body. This is precisely what is worn by Sechín priests. From behind the ogee-kilt hangs the symbolic female birdtail.

Bottom: Detail of a beaker with solar eye symbols (circle-dot, pupil-iris), above which is a rectangular ogee.

V

Diodorus of Sicily, noted historian, wrote in 21 BC (*Historical Library*, book V, chapter 2), that Carthaginians had known about lands many days' sail west of North Africa. According to Diodorus, the islands had mountains and plains, navigable rivers, and lush vegetation. These references seemingly point to America. Caribbean islands fit the description; other islands in the Atlantic do not. Diodorus wrote, during the early part of Juba II's reign, that Carthaginians kept this knowledge secret in order to have a place of refuge, if needed.

CARTHAGINIAN-STYLE
GLASS BEAD

Similar information is conveyed in *On Marvelous Things Heard* (section 84), possibly written by a follower of Aristotle (d. 322 BC). It mentions a decree passed by the Carthaginian Senate regarding islands far out in the Atlantic:

"No one, under penalty of death, shall sail thither." It is well known that Carthaginians guarded in secret their ocean trade routes and marine technology. One Carthaginian is known to have sunk his warship to prevent its falling into enemy hands. Carthaginians guarded the Strait of Gibraltar to deny ships other than their own access between the Atlantic and Mediterranean.

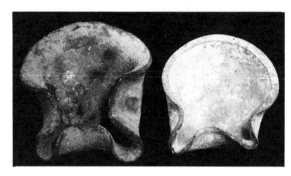

Top: CARTHAGINIAN SILVER COIN
This coin was minted in Sicily to pay troops (320-310 BC).
The obverse imitates a Greek Syracusan tetradrachm.
The reverse is totally Carthaginian with
bust of horse, date palm, Punic inscription.

Bottom: DOUBLE-SPOUTED SAUCER LAMP
Carthage, 4th century BC
ROMAN-PERIOD PUNIC LAMP
Malta, 1st century BC

Carthaginian and Roman coins and inscriptions have been found in scattered sites in the Americas. Maritime refugees from wars lost to Rome, especially the final one, fled to a refuge unknown to Rome—some to America? Refugees flee when they have the opportunity to escape destruction or enslavement.

VI

A Berber dynasty inherited Carthaginian territory and knowledge in North Africa's Maghreb. Pliny (*Natural History*, XVIII, 5) wrote: "Our Senate, after the fall of Carthage, gave its libraries to [North] African kings." Berber rulers of eastern Numidia ('nomad-land' between Mauretania and Carthaginian Zeugitana) began with Masinissa (202-148 BC), son of Gaya, king of the Massyles. Polybius (XXXVI, 16) called him "one of the best and most for-

tunate of men." Reared and educated in Carthage, he lived ninety-two years. His son Micipsa (148-118 BC) succeeded him.

MASINISSA'S TOMB, TUNISIA
(Photo: Warren Dexter)

COINS OF HIEMPSAL II, JUBA I, JUBA II

Micipsa's successors were Gulussa, Aherbal, Hiempsal II (left photo), then Juba I (60-46 BC, center photo). Cruel and arrogant, Juba was the preeminent Berber ruler during his own lifetime. He committed forced suicide when Julius Caesar defeated his ally Pompey, and Numidia became the Roman province of Africa Nova.

VII

Mauretania included Morocco and part of northwest Algeria. Augustus Caesar oversaw the future Juba II's (coin above right) education in Rome, and bestowed his throne. Juba II (25 BC-AD 23) was a gifted scholar, enamored of Hellenism. He married Cleopatra Selene (her name, not a title), daughter of Marc Antony and Egyptian queen Cleopatra VII. During Juba's forty-eight-year reign, Mauretania was a peaceful, prosperous nation. Historian and geographer as well as king, Juba II wrote about fifty scholarly works in Greek. Pliny in his *Geography* noted that he had requested information about the Canary islands from Juba II.

In AD 40, Roman emperor Caligula ordered the murder of Mauretanian king Ptolemy (AD 23-40), son of Juba and Cleopatra. Mauretania was split into two parts, both under direct Roman rule. Members of the Berber court knew that death or enslavement awaited them if caught.

There was no hope for escape to the east or north, where Rome reigned. The route south along Africa's west coast was unpromising: tropical diseases, poor harbors, unnavigable rivers, difficult seas, and hostile locals.

MOROCCAN BERBERS

Well-educated in things Egyptian, Greek, Roman, Carthaginian, Iberian, and Berber, privileged court refugees were neither nomadic tribesmen nor hill people engaged in petty clan warfare. This cultured elite inherited all the Mediterranean civilizations of their era. How many fled? Where did they go? We lack historical records.

BERBER WOMAN   MOCHE, PERU

VIII

Berber-type dress and physical features are depicted on some portrait vessels of AD 200-500. Ceramic pots shown at top of the next column depict Berber-like head gear and chin tattoos. Facial features (shape of eyes, nose, mouth) on the Moche pot at the left are indistinguishable from Berber.

Moche civilization arose in Peru's north coastal desert in river valleys where irrigation made it possible to supplement seafood with maize, beans, squash, and potatoes. Somewhat similar headdresses and chin tattooing, as shown at the right, were used by the Nazca culture along Peru's south coastal desert.

MOCHE   NAZCA

IX

In the 1960s, Bolivia's foremost archaeologist, Carlos Ponce Sangines, divided Tiwanakan culture into five periods (250 BC-AD 1200). These periods followed initial settlement of the site as a Chiripa-culture village (1000 - 250 BC). I suggest a reorganization of Sangines' phases to include a period of Berber influence, AD 100-200.

Revised dating, especially in the period of Tiwanaku's imperial collapse and abandonment of its central site are based on recent geological dating of severe droughts and the changing elevation of Lake Titicaca. Tiwanakan chronology will continue to be refined as excavation and dating methods proceed. The leading archaeological authority on Tiwanaku today is Alan Kolata.

TIWANAKU CULTURAL PHASES

ORIGINS	DATES
I Chiripa	1200-250 BC

Tiwanaku an Uru village. 'Yaya-Mama' style religious art lakeside, and 'Wankarani' herders (proto-Aymara) in the southern altiplano.

II Pukara	250 BC-AD 100

Tiwanaku dominated by culture from the opposite end of Lake Titicaca.

III Amalgamations	AD 100-200

Berber input, amalgamation, political independence. An edge over other settlements came partly from the charisma of added ideological and technological potential.

As Tiwanaku became a civilization, it developed massive architecture, intricate iconography, complex urban living for the elite, expansive statehood, and intensive raised-field agriculture. Commoners paid taxes in goods and labor.

CIVILIZATION	DATES

IV   AD 200-400

Tiwanaku dominates the south end of Lake Titicaca, develops an elite state religion, begins building a large city. **Monochrome black Juba portrait pots.**

V   AD 400-600

Early 'Classic' high civilization, artistic and technological zenith, early empire. **Polychrome Juba pots.**

VI   AD 600-800

Middle 'Classic' extends empire to southern Peru, northern Chile and Argentina. **Polychrome Juba pots.**

VII   AD 800-1100

Late 'Classic' urban renewal (800-900).   Sustained droughts after 1000 with a final prolonged drought 1050-1100. **Late Juba pots made in southern Peru.**

Tiwanaku had lunar and solar calendars, 50,000 people in the city, 125,000 in the altiplano, raised-field agriculture that produced 20 times more food than now, some paved roads, beautiful textiles, polychrome pottery, and refined ornaments.

STATUES AND HEADS
Large monolithic statues, heads of stone and pottery, reveal a variety of human types.

TIWANAKU'S SUN GATE
Its central figure is the Creator Wiracocha.

So far as I know, the objects Wiracocha holds have not been properly identified: a mace and bolas.   The inlaid winged ayar (in the next column) depicts these objects more realistically.   Many ayars flank Wiracocha in the Sun Gate image above.

About two hundred varieties of potatos were cultivated at different Andean altitudes.   When freeze-dried for indefinite preservation, they are called *chuñu*. Hardy (saline-tolerant, ultraviolet-radiation resistant) *quinoa*-type cereals also grew in the altiplano ('high plain'), 3850 m. above sea level.

Portrait pots that are not Juba types, appear to depict specific individuals.
(Author's photo of Tiwanakan portrait vessel in the British Museum. Not the Juba type, but very individual.)

X

Most Juba-type vessels depict ideograms, not inscriptions, on the headband and a few are plain. Thus far, the inscription is unique. The circle-dot, pupil-iris of the solar eye was used widely from ancient Egypt to China and in America with the meanings 'sun,' 'day,' 'light,' or 'time-period.'

The **S** abbreviated a connected double spiral of creation. The step-return symbolized cycles of birth-life-death-rebirth.

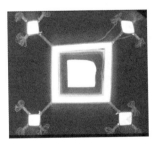

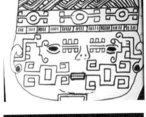

The five-part symbol found in cultures from Tiwanaku to Mexico had the same temporal meaning as a *quincunx*:

five ages of earth, the present sun-age at center with four previous sun-ages attached. I extrapolated this meaning from Mexican iconography, as it is found in the center of the 15th-century Aztec 'calendar' stone. The *ojo de dios* is another form of quincunx, with the present age (solar eye) central to four previous sun-ages.

TIWANAKU   COSTA RICA

TIWANAKU

Swastikas in ancient Eurasian and American cultures represented the creative motion of the sun and/or earth. Hopi include tribal migrations as part of this space-time symbol and celebrate a four-age universe rather than five.

XI

To propose a tentative sequence of headband designs in Juba vessels, I examined types 1 and 5 in my own collection, others by phototograph. Additional designs may exist. Portrait-pot fragments from archaeologically-excavated, dated strata need to be studied with this in mind to define typological sequences more precisely. Sangines offered to assist me in checking the archaeological evidence in Bolivia, but I have not had an opportunity to do so.

Painted Juba-type vessels belong to the Classic phases. During terminal phase, various localities produced pottery referred to as Coastal Tiwanaku, Tiawanacu-Wari, Atarco, and Epigonal. Portrait vessels ceased to be made at Tiwanaku itself, but the tradition, somewhat altered, continued in southern Peru.

Type 1. Transmission of a heavenly mandate through dynastic rulers had both visual and oracular dimensions. Similar ideas were expressed in different iconography in North Africa among Berber subjects of Juba II and his Egyptian wife Cleopatra Selene. The king in Egypt symbolized the sungod *Ra*. The queen's name indicates her as symbolic moon, an idea common in the ancient world, as female menstrual cycles approximate lunar cycles. *Selene* was the archaic Greek moon goddess, similar to Carthaginian *Tanit*.

Some ideas expressed in this paper are not now provable, but the vessel itself is fact. The pot seems to have united two originally-separate traditions: a) North African Berber face, moustache, headdress, primitively-written Greek inscription identifying King Juba; and b) Sechín-Chavín-Titicaca (also Costa Rica and Oaxaca) iconography to indicate divine solar origin and epiphany of the first dynastic ruler: sunlight rays iconed as arrows descending through the eyes to below the ears.

A variation of the solar arrow or spear fertilizing the feminine earth was painted in an Arizona *Bidahochi* (proto-Hopi) bowl and pecked in a New Mexico petroglyph. The petroglyph has been widely misunderstood.

XII

As traditions and iconography coalesced, degenerated writing forms were replaced by ideograms whose non-phonetic meaning continued to be understood for hundreds of years. Several generations must have passed between the first part-Berber rulers of Tiwanaku to the earliest-known Juba-type vessel. The inscription on the first Juba pot appears to have been phonetically meaningless to the potter, who probably copied it from an earlier prototype yet undiscovered.

The apparent immediate successor of the inscribed pot

is shown above, the inscription replaced with incised wavy vertical lines separated by diagonals and other forms. As phonetically illiterate potters dealt with traditional elements no longer understood, they and their patrons quite logically substituted ideographs for phonography. Transition from writing to geometrics is complete in this example, but its iconography is somewhat obscure.

XIII

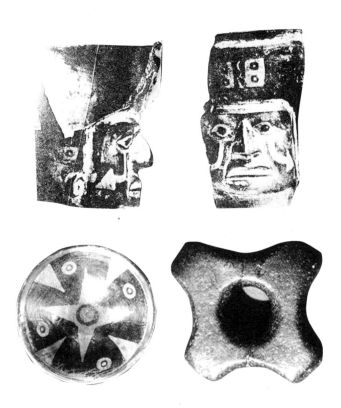

Type 2. Four suns around, or flanking, the Universal Present should belong to early phase V. The five-sun quincunx symbolized five ages (four past, and present), five directions (north, east, south, west, center). The sun's move-

ment across the sky divided each year by the winter solstice, spring equinox, summer solstice, and fall equinox. The Inka quincunx macehead dates about 1350-1400 AD.

INTIWATANA, MACHU PICCHU

Any vessel was viewed as receptive and holding life-needed fluid. The idea of suns tied to a common factor was expressed in the Inka *intiwatana* (**inti** meaning '= sun'; **watana** meaning 'hitching place'). Because the Inka so venerated intiwatanas, few escaped early Spanish destruction, but some can still be seen at Machu Picchu and Pisac.

XIV

Type 3. Suns in round or squared format tied to the present solar age belong logically to Middle Phase V. Costa

Rican pots with painted five-suns (shown below, left column) date 500-800 AD. Squaring the solar eye on Costa Rican and some Tiwanakan pots (shown below) may have originated in textile designs, as it is easier to weave squares than true circles.

XV

Type 4. Abstract animal motifs characterize Late Phase V. Self-assured faces of the first two periods gave way to faces with intense focus. The eyes are open wide in awe of seeing something 'other' during drug-induced states. This vessel flares slightly at top with no hint of turban, only a headband.

Similar designs were painted on Tiwanakan beakers and vessels with puma heads. Abstract motifs were incised on a small stone box probably used to hold hallucinogenic wilka powder. At Tiwanaku, powdered red wilka was sniffed like snuff; a *clyster* (enema syringe), was used to administer ayahuasca vine extract; and mescaline was imbibed in various ceremonies. Other hallucinogens, such as San Pedro cactus essence used on the Peruvian coast, may also have been available.

XVI

the cream-white color symbolized life, light, solar semen, foam of water, origins. For a fragile specific pottery type to endure so long indicates that the tradition it conveyed had great value.

XVII

Type 5. This vessel has an undecorated rim above the face. It is coastal Tiwanaku, southern Peru, Phases VI and VII, perhaps later. Exactly where this piece was made and found is unknown. Its ears are shaped and placed more as in life than on most previous Juba types. Symbolic sun-arrows have been replaced by geometrics high on each cheek, tattooed remnants of the arrow motif. The face is intense. Moustache and beard run together around an open mouth. Little arms are molded below the cheeks.

This final Tiwanakan Juba vessel ended the vessel type that evolved through 1000 years. Above and below the face,

CONCLUSIONS

There was no safe refuge for the Berber court in the Mediterranean, Europe, or Africa. Nor could they flee directly to East Asia. If they knew about lands far out in the Atlantic mentioned by Diodorus Siculus, they could have sailed west with prevailing winds and currents from the Canaries to America, the same route used in 1492 and by virtually all Spanish ships for the one hundred years following Columbus.

If 'Juba pots' have here been correctly interpreted, the elite refugees traversed Panama or traveled up Orinoco tributaries almost to coastal Ecuador, then continued south to Peru, where they found a climate much like the one they had left in northwest Africa.

I do not suggest that the Moche or Tiwanakan civilizations were created by Berbers. I propose that Mauretanian Berbers may have been a significant component, together with other components, in the creative mix of cultures giving rise to those civilizations.

When facts challenge theory, theory should be altered to accommodate facts. My case for Maghreb-to-Tiwanaku is underwhelming, but not invalid for this reason. It should be tested against existing evidence and new data as they come to light. Scholars should not expect wholesale transfers of Old World culture to America to prove limited connections; trips were few and far between.

If one just remains afloat and alive with the prevailing winds and currents from the Canaries, 3000 miles later he lands in the Caribbean or northern South America. During 3000 to 4000 years before 1492, many storm-tossed refugees perished at sea, and others disappeared like Roanoke and Columbus' first colony in Haiti. In some cases, however, there is reason to believe that explorers searching for natural resources, merchants, and well-educated refugees possessing some advantageous technologies may have significantly influenced indigenous cultures. After all, that was precisely what happened more massively following the 1492 voyage.

It does not matter whether Berbers came to America before Columbus or not, only whether that possibility is considered on the basis of facts and logic, within a valid framework of how creation occurs in humankind, and how civilizations have developed. Cases for other voyages and settlements have not been significantly addressed.

Hoffman has raised numerous points of critical concern about this paper. Several could be answered easily, but others would in total require at least a book-length essay to address with some adequacy. A minority of Berbers are negroid and dark-skinned, but most Berbers (without suntans) are as light-skinned as the general population of France. My article does not address race, but ethnicity and iconography.

Most dates used here are approximate. The early Juba pot has not yet been dated by laboratory techniques. As methods continue to be refined and new ones discovered, I have little doubt that it will be possible sometime in the future to augment the dating of excavated levels with even more accurate direct dating of pottery and many other artifacts.

My purpose was to set forth an intelligent hypothesis for testing, not a theory. One would expect prototypes to lose many non-indigenous features over a period of years. A non-indigenous part of the Juba-type vessel, maintained for as long as the type itself endured, was the distinctive moustache and beard.

The issue that Hoffman seemed to question most was the theoretical crossing by Old World refugees from the Caribbean to the Pacific. Panama's Darien and Colombia's Cordilleras are indeed rugged territories, once populated by often hostile groups.

If led by a guide and facing no hostiles, one can cross the Isthmus in the dry season by a combination of walking and dugouts in less than a week. The Orinoco route through Colombia would take longer. The earliest European explorers in the Darien observed that even traditional enemies had periodic truces for the exchange of goods, and gave special protection to traders. Darien Indians

living on the Caribbean coast told Balboa about the Pacific Ocean and guided him there so that he could discover it. Native Americans told him also about the Pearl Islands off Panama's Pacific Coast and of gold-rich lands farther south.

Ecuador's coastal Manteño were skilled navigators and renowned traders who ventured along the Pacific rim of South and Middle America in large balsa rafts equipped with sails and cabins. My Kuna manuscript has much more specific information about these topics. Although some research into this issue has been published (Jijón y Caamaño 1940; Lehmann 1947; Willey 1955; Evans and Meggers 1957; Coe 1960; West 1961; Edwards *et al.*), we still have much to learn about aboriginal sea navigation between the Americas.

POSTCRIPT

An example of how historians and anthropologists sometimes drag their feet in learning about or accepting findings made by scholars outside their fields is the invention of the compass. I continue to read references that say the compass was unknown outside China until far into the Middle Ages. The compass is useful to long-distance sailors in bad weather. In good weather navigators used the stars at night and sun by day to maintain their courses.

COMPASS DIAL BOWLS, LIRIA, SPAIN
ca. 100 BC – AD 100

Ceramic bowls and sherds excavated at Liria, Spain, in the general area of Valencia, were tentatively dated by archaeologists to 300 BC-AD 100. Drawings were published for the Museo Valenciana by Valls (1953) and Aparisi (1955). Fell (1976, 1979) deciphered them as Iberic and Iberian Greek inscriptions. His translations showed that the bowls served as compass dials in which magnetized needles and lodestones were floated on mercury.

OTHER LIRIA COMPASS DIAL BOWLS

Within the current Liria timeframe, there was considerable continuous trading by sea between southeast Iberia and northwest Africa's Maghreb. If a migration of elite Berber refugees to America occurred, they may have had such compasses with them.

Many of our ideas about past times were formulated more in ignorance than fact, then adopted with little serious further consideration. Human lives and scholarship require periodic renewals to survive the human tendency to dogmatize.

I do not expect this article or others in this volume to make a major dent any time soon in the current dogma that Native American cultures and civilizations developed in near-pristine isolation from the Old World (Asia, Europe, Africa). But who knows? The Juba-related Maghreb-to-Andes migration may some day become dogma. Then it will fall upon the adventurous to reconsider and challenge the new rut into which research bogs down before it moves ahead.

NOTE

1. Since this paper was presented at NEARA's *America Before Columbus* Conference held June 18 through 21, 1992, a number of books relevant to it have appeared. Note especially archaeologists Alan Kolata on Tiwanaku and Mike Moseley on coastal Peru. The author is indebted to the late Barry Fell, for deciphering the inscription, and the late Warren Cook, for leads on possible North African influence in South America. Also I wish to thank George Carter and Roslyn Strong (conference chairs), Warren Dexter, Don Gilmore, and Karla Urquidi of La Paz. Alan Kolata sent me relevant materials as I began to formulate this paper. Such assistance does not constitute agreement or disagreement with the paper's contents. I am also grateful to Curtiss Hoffman for an initial critique of this paper for its present publication.

Comalcalco: An Early Classic Maya Site

NEIL STEEDE

Comalcalco is a Maya city located in Mexico's Tabasco state, at the western edge of the Yucatan peninsula's base and near the southernmost curve of the Gulf of Mexico. When originally built, it was within a few miles of the coast, but the area's slow rise above sea level now places the ruins some twenty miles inland. In his day, Cortez could sail his ship directly up the Grijulva River to Comalcalco, which he did. The river subsequently silted up and stagnated; Comalcalco is built on what was the former delta, an area now called Rio Seco. The river, on a new course, empties some twenty miles further to the east. The area is still as swampy as it was in ancient times. Sited about two hundred and fifty miles west-northwest of Tikal, Comalcalco is the most western of all the great Maya cities which dot southern Mexico (Figure 1).

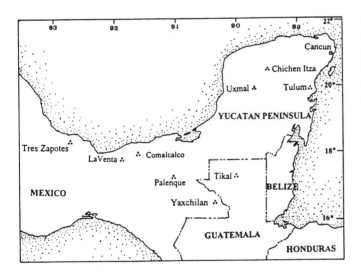

Figure 1   MAYA CITIES IN COMALCALCO AREA

Comalcalco is unique in many ways, but its most striking characteristic is that it appears to be constructed largely of fired brick. While the city is not the only one so built, brick structures from that time are extremely rare. Balancan and Tenosique both have brick structures. The only other known Maya cites of fired brick besides these are much smaller and are found in the immediate area of Comalcalco. They are believed to have been cultural satellites of Comalcalco, but possibly not dependent upon it.

Analysis of Comalcalco's special features raises many questions relating to possible pre-Columbian transoceanic contact. The brick itself is unusual enough, but there are many other aspects of the site which we find out of place in what is otherwise a supposedly totally Maya context.

DATING

Until recently, the dating of Comalcalco ruins has been guesswork at best. No laboratory testing had been done on any of the materials or artifacts. The only estimate of its age was based on two factors: a) architectural features, and b) the art style of the stucco bas-reliefs. Both were judged by analysts to be copies of the Classic Palenque style and, thus, Late Classic or even Post Classic (AD 800-1200) (Perez Campos and Silva 1992; Álvarez Aguilar et al. 1988; Andrews 1967; Peniche Rivero 1973). We totally disagree with this conclusion.

We believe that the style indicates a formative period rather than a decadent period (Steede n.d.a). Pottery types also seem to bear out this conclusion (Peniche Rivero 1973). Moreover, the hieroglyphics found at the site are simple in comparison with the baroque style displayed at Palenque. These factors have led us to conclude that Comalcalco probably dates from the 1st or 2nd century AD.

Since the 1992 presentation of this paper, Carbon-14 tests have been carried out on shell material in mortar from the ruins (Tomb of the Nine Lords of the Night) through Geochron Laboratories in Cambridge, Massachusetts, giving a date of 1620 ± 50 years BP (AECV #2022C). Those results demonstrate that much of the site was probably built starting toward the end of the 3rd century AD. At present, we have twenty-five more samples ready for testing when financing can be found. We have also received oral reports that forty-five samples of obsidian found in the ruins have been dated and that all are within the first two centuries AD. The obsidian samples are from the very earliest stages of brick construction. In the future, some may even give us BC dates.

ARCHITECTURE

The brick construction of the Comalcalco site is reminiscent of Mediterranean construction and particularly of Roman construction. To test this hypothesis, we prepared the two charts (Figures 2 and 3) which follow. While they display parallels with building techniques and styles found elsewhere, a strong argument could be made for contact with the Mediterranean or perhaps with India. Much more information is needed to confirm this hypothesis. Of interest

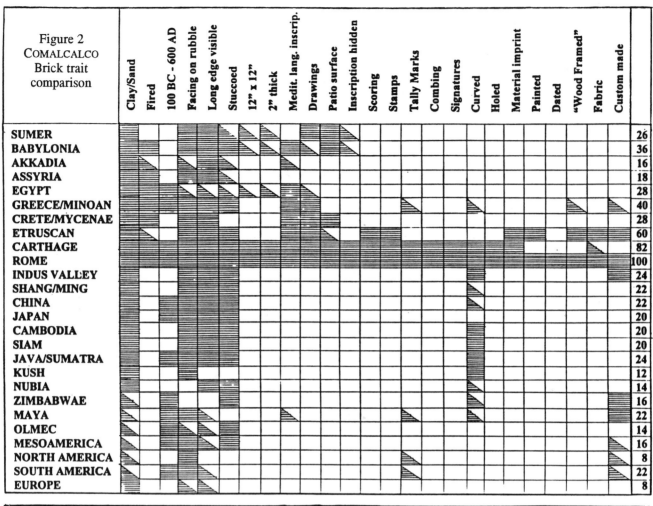

Figure 2
COMALCALCO
Brick trait
comparison

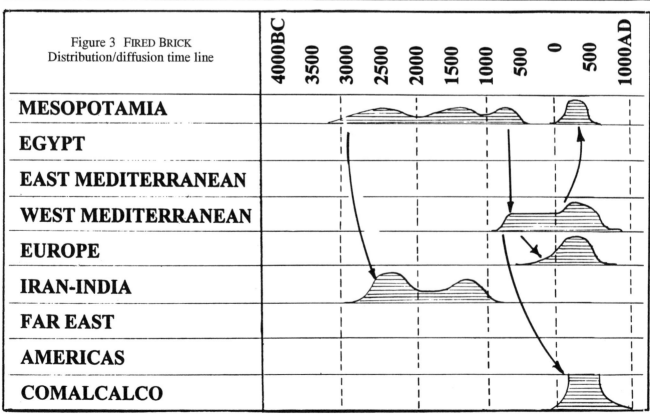

Figure 3 FIRED BRICK
Distribution/diffusion time line

is the fact that all of the stages of construction at Comalcalco with baked brick are identical. There do not seem to be intermediate and developing stages. The construction was always done exactly the same at each level at Comalcalco.

The mechanical construction of the site seems also to support the hypothesis. For example, all of the following features are found at Comalcalco: wing walls, buttresses, wall niches, cornice edging, corbel-arch vaulted rooms, and slightly curved corbelled arches. In addition, we found one case of a true bonding course, and while there is some evidence of footings, it is not yet conclusive. (These features are illustrated in Figures 4 through 7 below.) With some Carbon-14 dating complete, our assumption on dating is strengthened, suggesting that all of these items appeared together for the first time in Mesoamerica at Comalcalco. If confirmed, this finding would imply an amazing jump in construction technology. For, though we find these construction technologies in other parts of the world at earlier dates, we have thus far found no antecedents for them in Mesoamerica.

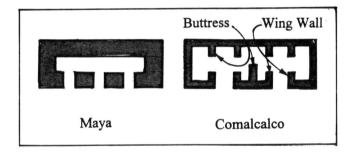

Figure 4 WING WALLS AND BUTTRESSES
These were widely used in Rome but are not found in
other Maya architecture.

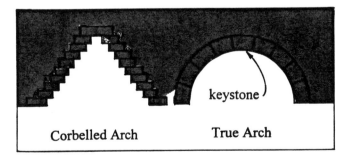

Figure 5 ARCH FORMS

Comalcalco's arches are corbelled and slightly curved, strengthening the arch, as in Roman corbelled arches. But the true arch, with keystone, is lacking or very rare in ancient Mesoamerica. Comalcalco's builders also placed empty pots in the fill over the arch to lighten the load, as done for a relatively short time in Rome; it was never done in other Maya construction.

At this point, the question obviously arises: if these construction technologies can be found in Comalcalco and if, in fact, they did come from the Mediterranean, why do we not find other construction technologies, such as true arches, with keystone (rare in this time in Mesoamerica) and true domes?

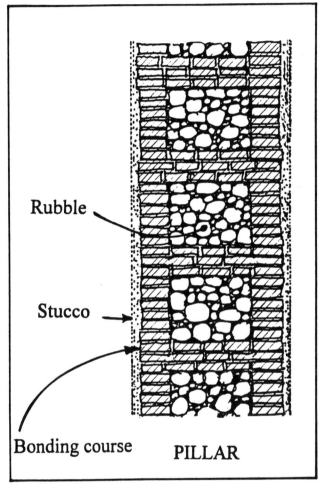

Figure 6 BONDING COURSES
These were found in Roman pillars and
at least one instance in Comalcalco.

Obviously, we don't know what the cultural intent, or thought, or mindset was at the time that Comalcalco was built. However, we can point to parallel cultures such as that of the early Brahmin in India which copied many Roman systems, but not all of them. In that case, we find the early Brahmin even using the Roman numeral system, as well as baked bricks. However, we find no domes in that time-frame in India, to our knowledge. Nor do we find any dress styles or hair styles as were used in Rome. Why did India choose to ignore these items? We may never have the answer to that, just as we may never have the answer to why the true arch or dome was not used in Comalcalco.

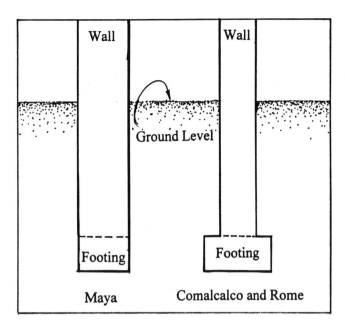

Figure 7 FOUNDATIONS
Extended footings allow thinner walls.

The mortar and stucco mixes in Comalcalco are comparable to 1st century mixes in the Mediterranean area (Littman 1957; Steede n.d.b). All mixes in Mesoamerica with which we have made comparison have less durability and strength than those found at Comalcalco. We are now trying to examine deeper levels at Comalcalco to see if we can find developmental stages for the mortar mixes found to date.

At the earliest brick stages, we have found no change in the mortar so far. The implication here is that a near-perfect mix appeared suddenly at Comalcalco, only to degenerate later into a less effective mix during the Classic Maya civilization (Littman 1957; Steede n.d.c).

As noted above, the cement mix found at Comalcalco is not found at other sites. We now know that Comalcalco dates earlier than these other sites. We do find, after the time of Comalcalco, that the Maya begin to raise buildings that are long-vaulted, corbel-arched buildings. This type of construction does not occur before this time (Coe 1987; Sanders 1968). It would seem therefore, that the cement mix was spontaneously found or possibly introduced at Comalcalco at a very early stage of the Maya civilization and then diffused into the surrounding areas in a less durable, weaker, or degenerated consistency.

BURIALS

The burials at Comalcalco are unique. The Tomb of the Nine Lords of the Night (the name found in glyphs on its inner wall) is very similar in construction to the Etruscan cube tomb. Although we have not found replicas anywhere else in Mesoamerica of Old World-style pot tombs, these, too, are found at Comalcalco.

We have identified a burial tomb from a later date which apparently was derived from them. This burial, later by several hundred years, was found in the area of Yaxchilan, some 200 miles southeast in Chiapas state, and can now be seen in the Museum of Art in New Orleans, Louisiana.

So, it can be demonstrated that Comalcalco tombs are very similar to constructions found in the Mediterranean. They are similar in their form and orientation, and identical in measurement. And yet, they have not been found at any other site, to date, in Mesoamerica. On the other hand, we do not find the example of the pot tombs, in which large urns were put over the bodies of the dead, diffusing from Comalcalco to other Mesoamerican sites. Why one diffused and the other didn't is not known to us at this time.

MEASUREMENTS

Evidence suggests that the entire Comalcalco site was laid out on the basis of the Roman measurement system. At least we can confirm that this site does not conform to the usual Maya system of measurement, featuring units of approximately eighteen inches, very similar to the Egyptian cubit. However, at Comalcalco, we seem to have the Roman system of feet and inches.

But, to simply measure out the site in Roman feet and inches does not prove that the Roman system was used. It is far too easy to fudge several inches here and there to prove a case. As an example, one may measure the length of a building and get a closed-feet measurement (that is, no extra inches), but one has to estimate the thickness of the now-eroded stucco and brick edges. This subjective estimating will always leave two or three inches of play. Thus, the case cannot be proven absolutely.

We have also measured the bricks themselves. The dimensions of the bricks prove to be much more revealing than those of the overall site. For, as most of the bricks are protected from erosion, they can be more precisely measured. We found that, on the basis of measuring one hundred and sixty individual bricks, 90 percent fell into an acceptable category of closed inches (within the tolerance of 1/32 of an inch). To carry this thought further, we wish for the reader to understand that bricks of at least ten different sizes were used in the construction of Comalcalco. All ten sizes would fit Roman inch measurements to within 1/32 of an inch. Molded bricks and cut bricks, whatever their size category might be, conformed to the closed-inch dimensions 95 percent of the time, while hand-molded bricks met this criterion only about 75 percent of the time.

But it is the consistency with which closed-inch sizing

was utilized for each size category that is the most remarkable. Now, we must compare these measurements with other known measuring systems to see whether similar percentages will be found. This would include measuring individual bricks of known Roman fabrication to see if the percentages show the same pattern. In most of the classical Roman construction, the pedlis brick was the most common. It was a standard 12 inches by 12 inches, by 1 or 2 inches thick. This standard had been set up by the Roman senate. Previously, inches were commonly used, but bricks could be 10 by 10, 10 by 8, 12 by 8, 12 by 10, etc., much as we find in Comalcalco.

We have recently found over sixty examples of bricks which have measuring marks on them. These marks seem to conform to Roman inches as well, spaced at one-half, one-quarter, and one-third of an inch (Figure 8). This finding certainly strengthens the hypothesis that the Roman measurement system was used at this site.

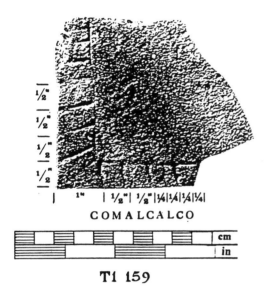

Figure 8 FRACTIONAL MARKS ON BRICKS

However, the argument is still not conclusive because there are other systems we have not yet tested which might also conform to these marks, Asian measuring systems, for example. Some have questioned why, or even if, the Romans used fractions of inches. Fractions such as one-half, one-quarter, and one-third inches, were constantly used in Rome, for example in sun-shadow, time-measurement systems (de Camp 1960).

INSCRIBED BRICKS

One of the most intriguing aspects of the Comalcalco bricks is that about three percent of them bear inscriptions. To the time of this writing, nearly 8000 of these inscribed bricks have been excavated. The inscriptions do

appear to have been done while the clay was soft, before firing. The inscriptions were never meant to be seen in the finished structure, as they were covered by mortar in the building process. This feature of brick manufacture has been observed in the Mediterranean area as well as in Asia. Although the act of inscribing is not in itself demonstrative of diffusion from the Old World to the New, it is the images we find inscribed on the bricks that do seem to suggest such diffusion.

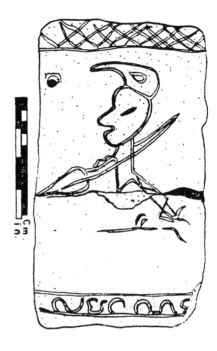

Figure 9 INSCRIBED BRICK
Figure, spear, and script

All the marks that appear to be texts are extremely short and, therefore, somewhat questionable. Barry Fell identified Roman, Greek, and Arabic scripts on these bricks, but it has since been fairly well demonstrated that many of his findings were mistaken (Fell 1989; Steede n.d.). While some

Figure 10 INSCRIBED BRICK
Head and possible lines of script

of the identifications may be accurate, most should be re-jected. At this time, several epigraphy experts are work-ing on the problem. But what is certain is that several of the bricks do have alphabetical marks on them which seem to be of Old World origin.

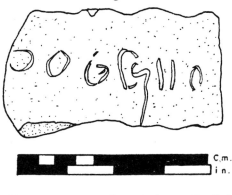

III   ·TI-2 I22   ·R 72

Figure 11 'Inscription' on Comalcalco Brick

The last 3200 of the inscribed bricks which we un-covered are being photographed at this time. We were fortunate in being allowed by both Tulane University and the Museum of Natural History in New York to photo-graph the more than four hundred inscribed Comalcalco bricks found in the 1920s by Blom and in the 1940s by Ekholm. We hope to find new clues among these items.

CONCLUSION

The features found at the Comalcalco site constitute some of the best evidence yet available in a cultural context for transoceanic contact. However, we recognize the need to move forward cautiously in our interpretation of this evi-dence. Even the best evidence can lose its effectiveness in support of the hypothesis if it is presented too hastily. We wish to avoid premature and possibly unjustified con-clusions. Hence, these observations are preliminary, and, as is so often the case in archaeology, the research needs further funding to continue the process of analysis. Never-theless, on the basis of our present knowledge of the site, we believe not only that Comalcalco is one of the most interesting and enlightening chapters of Mesoamerican history, but also that it could very well change Meso-american history as we now understand it.

NOTE

Permission has been given for the publication with this paper of some of our drawings of the inscriptions on several of the bricks, drawings which have been altered in certain insignificant re-spects. We regret that there have been earlier incidents in which other publications reprinted such drawings without authorization or appropriate credit; the related interpretation of the inscriptions served only to muddy the waters of investigation. We plan to publish photographs of the inscribed bricks, probably in late 1998, when our preliminary analysis has been completed.

REFERENCES

Álvarez Aguilar, Luis F., Maria G. Landa Landa, and José L. Romero Rivera
    1988   *Los Ladrillos de Comalcalco* (The Bricks of Comalcalco). Villahermosa: Government of Tabasco State, Instituto de Cultura de Tabasco.
Andrews, George F. *et al.*
    1967   *Comalcalco, Tabasco, Mexico: An Architectonic Survey of a Maya Ceremonial Center.* Eugene: University of Oregon.
Bell, Lewis K. *et al.*
    1990   *Full Measure.* Donald L. Cyr, ed. Santa Rosa: Stonehenge Viewpoint.
Blom, Frans
    1926   *Tribes and Temples: A Record of the Expedition to Middle America.* New Orleans: Tulane University.
Bodribb, Gerald
    1989   *Roman Brick and Tile.* Sutton Publishers.
Coe, Michael D.
    1987   *The Maya.* London & New York: Thames & Hudson, 4th edition.
de Camp, L. Sprague
    1960   *The Ancient Engineers.* New York: Ballantine.
Ekholm, G. F.
    1944   Unpublished field notes. New York: American Museum of Natural History.

Fell, Barry
    1989   *America B.C.* New York: Simon & Schuster, Pocket Books.
Littman, Edwin R.
    1957   Ancient Mesoamerican mortars, plasters and stuccos. *American Antiquity* 23:2,3.
Peniche Rivero, Piedad
    1973   *Comalcalco, Tabasco. Su cerámica, artefactos y enterramientos.* (Its ceramics, artifacts and burials). Thesis, Anthropology Department. Merida: University of Yucatan.
Pérez Campos, Elizabeth and Lorena M. Silva
    1992   *Comalcalco.* Archaeology Series. Cordoba, Mexico: Instituto Nacional de Antropologia e Historía.
Sanders, W. T. and B. J. Price
    1968   *Mesoamerica: The Evolution of a Civilization.* New York: Random House.
Steede, Neil
    1980s   Undated monographs. Independence MO: MLK Publications.
    a *The Dating of Comalcalco.*
    b *The Architecture of Comalcalco.*
    c *Fell's Studies on Comalcalco*

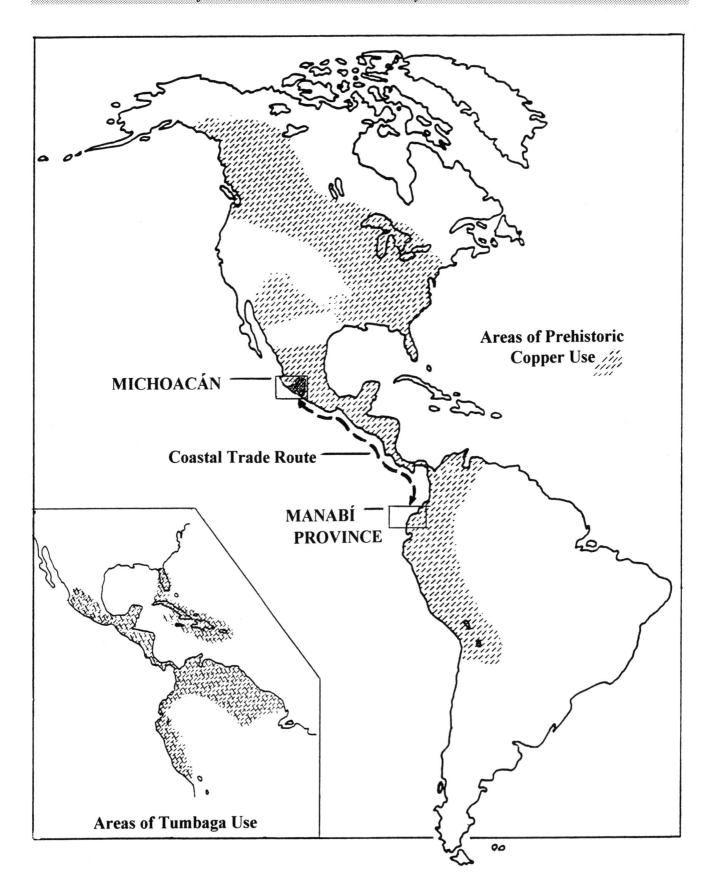

Figure 1 EARLY COASTAL TRADING IN THE AMERICAS

The Significance of Metallurgy
in the Purhépecha Religion

CELIA HEIL

INTRODUCTION

Metallurgy has been important in the culture of the Purhépecha[1] people of west Mexico's Michoacán area for many centuries. There is ample evidence that this technology may have been derived initially through trade with cultures further south in the Americas. Admittedly thinner evidence suggests that the metallurgy of Peru and Ecuador and its applications in Purhépecha culture may have been borrowed even earlier from cultures on the other side of the Pacific rim. As background, we should look first at what has been learned to date about pre-Columbian maritime capability on the west coast of the Americas as well as the early navigating capability of the people of Asia and the reach of their maritime efforts.

EARLY AMERICAN
MARITIME NETWORK

Early Spanish chronicles as well as more recent scholarly research leave little doubt that an active trading network existed along the Pacific coast of the Americas for well over a thousand years before the Spanish arrival. Important trading centers operated on the Manabí coast of Ecuador, run by the Manteño, at Chincha on the coast of Peru, and at Zacatula on the coast of Mexico (Hosler 1994:91; Jett 1983:362; Murra 1994:19-33). See Figure 1.

There is also documentation for the early appearance in Mexico of metal objects and metallurgical knowledge, apparently acquired through trade with South America. The commercial traffic from Chincha, including metallurgy and its applications, seems to have peaked about AD 1000, although, writes Dorothy Hosler, "Archaeologists recognize the existence of a maritime commerce along the coast since before AD 500" (Hosler 1994:91).

The research of Maria Rostworowsky records the presence, at the time of the conquest, of active coastal raft traffic off Peru/Ecuador, including northward shipment of Peruvian copper and lesser amounts of other raw materials. These rafts reportedly were capable of carrying up to 25 tons of cargo. Merchants from Panama and Ecuador also traded in large canoes along the coast, carrying, in addition to metals, significant quantities of textiles, seeds, cacao, highly-prized spondylous shells, furs, and feathers (Murra 1994; de la Cruz 1969:51).

Additional archaeological evidence shows a vast trade network in finished objects among the regions producing metal. In Chichen Itza, for instance, were found gold objects made in Colombia, Panama, Honduras, Guatemala, and southwest Mexico. Aztec merchants, the *Pochtecas*, carried their commerce to the areas of present-day Nicaragua, Guatemala, Panama, and Costa Rica. The Muisca, of the highlands of Colombia and traditionally called Chibcha, traded their salt cakes, textiles, and emeralds for raw cotton and gold (Acuesta and Rovira 1982:30-31).

ASIAN MARITIME CAPABILITY

Both China and Japan had commercial contacts south along the coast from Japan throughout the China Sea to Indonesia, as well as north to the cold and distant points of Siberia and Alaska (Thompson 1989; Jairazbhoy 1976). It is very likely that contacts with the Americas took place during this period.

At the beginning of the present millennium, China had the largest fleet in the world, with sixty-two warships carrying 28,000 sailors. By 1420, the Imperial Fleet of the Ming dynasty had two hundred and fifty high-sea galleons with seven sails, four hundred commercial galleons each capable of transporting one thousand metric tons of cargo, four hundred other warships with six hundred men each, and thirteen hundred and fifty smaller patrol ships based on their China Sea coastline (James and Thorpe 1994). Bernardino de Escalante, in what is considered the first western history of China, was also impressed by the vast navigation system, the quantity of ships, and the availability of wood and metal in China for shipbuilding (1577:55).

The Japanese were also excellent ship builders and navigators. They sailed along the coast of Southeast Asia and to the north along the Kuril and Aleutian island chains, and perhaps beyond, in search of mollusks and trade, under what was known as the 'Trade of the Red Seal Ships.' Their abilities to sail the oceans were later demonstrated when they established commerce with America shortly after the Spanish conquest, making the voyages across the Pacific Ocean without difficulty (Nuttall 1906). (See also Meggers in this volume for an even earlier probable Japanese drift voyage to the coast of Ecuador).

MICHOACÁN METALLURGY

Until recent years, it was thought that metallurgy had originated in the Near East, but new excavations in Southeast Asia reveal that bronze was being cast there in double molds before 3000-2300 BC, earlier than in India or China where it was previously held that bronze metalworking had begun (Solheim 1979:330-32).

In the New World, the so-called Old Copper Culture of eastern North America had been considered less significant than metalworking on the rest of the continent. In recent times however, radiocarbon dates of 3650 ± 600 BP and 5560 ± 600 BP, associated with metalworking, have been obtained in Wisconsin and its vicinity, and the artifacts are of surprising sophistication in style and execution for their age (Lópes-Valdés 1965:65). Some tribes made copper sheets by hammering raw ore and then polished them with abrasives found in native plants to give them a gold color (Acuesta and Rovira 1982:45).

South American metallurgical technology, as has been noted, seems to have moved northward with the coastal maritime trade, and this knowledge apparently included the skills of smelting, hot and cold hammering, and casting by both lost wax (*cire perdu*) and open molds (Acuesta and Rovira 1982:43; Hosler 1994:92). The Chavín of Peru appear to have been the innovators in metallurgy, probably before 500 BC, followed by artisans of Colombia and Ecuador. It could have been even earlier, however, as some samples have been dated to about 1500 BC in the high Andes, where hammering was the method, and there was particular interest in color (Hosler 1994:90).

While most research has suggested that metallurgy entered west Mexico from further south particularly in two specific periods, the 8th and 12th centuries AD, (Hosler 1985, 1988a, 1988b, 1994:93), more recent study by MIT's Hosler and Andrew MacFariane of the International University of Florida finds evidence that some artifacts from a much earlier period were manufactured with metal mined in west Mexico (Hosler and MacFariane 1996). This corroborates the archaeological studies of Adolphus Langenscheidt (1970), that mining and mineral exploitation in pre-Columbian Mexico was extensive and dates from 1200 BC. Further evidence was provided by the archaeological excavations in Amapa, Nayarit, in 1976, by archaeologist Rubén Cabrera Castro, establishing west Mexico as a center of creation and diffusion of metallurgy before AD 700 (Cabrera Castro 1976).

The Mexican anthropologist Nicolás León reported in 1889 that early Michoacán was a center of mineral wealth and that the Purhépecha people of Michoacán were skilled miners. A great number of shafts, galleries, mallets, anvils, and caves with metal remains had been found in the region. The walls of these mines show evidence of having been worked in primitive times with rude instruments (León, 1889).

Although metallurgy may have been introduced to Mesoamerica from South America, the technology could also have come from Southeast Asia. For instance, the pre-Columbian metalwork of Colombia is similar to metalwork of Southeast Asia's Dongson Culture, *ca.* 700 BC (Jett 1983; López-Valdés 1965:65; Solheim 1979:332). Heine-Geldern and the Swedish scholar Bernhard Karlgren called this culture 'Dongson' after Dong Son, a site in northern Vietnam south of Hanoi. The two scholars felt that the Dongson people introduced bronze and the geometric art decoration style into Southeast Asia (Solheim 1979:333).

Figure 2 PURIFYING METAL WITH BLOW-PIPES
Shown in the Florentine Codex

Moreover, it is also on the west coast of Mexico that we find many Asian cultural characteristics, in what today are the states of Chiapas, Oaxaca, Guerrero, Colima, Nayarit, and Michoacán. Among the most important of these possible borrowings from Asia is the pre-Columbian lacquer technology in Guerrero, Chiapas, and Michoacán, including the process of dry-lacquer. Possible Asian influence is also seen in early paper-making technology in the New World; we find that the Sumo people of Honduras, and those of Huaca Prieta, Peru, about 1500 years ago, were using tools very similar to or the same as those used in Asia (Heil 1995:37, 1996a; Jett 1983; Tolstoy 1991).

An important aspect of early metallurgy in Michoacán was the building of special storage houses for metal and metal objects. The objects were catalogued according to the quality and type of the metals, and whether they were used for religious offerings or as gifts of tribute (*La Relación* 1538-1541). One of the first steps in processing metals was to purify the metal through fire. The metal was placed inside a pit oven in the ground directly on the fire until it melted, thereby separating it from unwanted materials. The process was repeated as necessary until the metal achieved the desired purity. The Florentine Codex illustrates another type of clay oven and blow-pipes used to intensify the fire for metallurgy (Figure 2).

Throughout several centuries of metallurgical activity, and judging by the variety and abundance of certain objects found in Michoacán, the importance of the technology in their life is readily evident. Metal objects were part of their socio-political system, economy, language, technology, and, most importantly, their religion. It is known that the people of west Mexico considered metal to be sacred, and this is demonstrated in the technology as well as the use of most metal objects (Hosler 1994:91).

METAL OBJECTS IN
RITUAL AND CEREMONY

Metals used in the Michoacán culture were copper, gold, silver, and metal alloys (Hosler 1988a), from which were manufactured a variety of objects commonly used as offerings. The most reliable historic document of the Purhépecha, *La Relación de las ceremonias y ritos y población y gobierno de los indios de la Provincia de Mechuacan* (1538-1541),[2] mentions that the Purhépecha god, Kurikaueri, was adorned with gold loops. The document also says that the islanders of Xarákuaro, invited the nomadic Chichimecas to visit them. As a gesture of honor they cut their visitors' hair and gave each of them a gold tweezer to hang as a necklace (*La Relación* 1977:32). Metal objects worn as ornaments represented the social position, nobility ranking, and level of power of a person (Hosler 1994:88-89). The Purhépecha chief and the high priest wore metal ear pieces, bracelets, bells, and rings. The chief wore a gold necklace in the shape of a crescent moon inherited from his ancestors as a symbol of his rank (Figure 3).

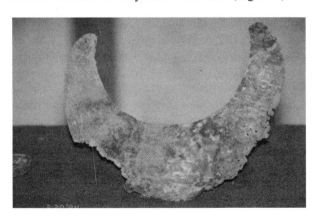

Figure 3 PRE-COLUMBIAN HAMMERED-GOLD JEWELRY
Crescent pendant

When a member of Michoacán nobility died, the body was cremated, and the ashes were buried with a metal mask and surrounded by gold, silver, and copper necklaces, bracelets, ear pieces, bells, open rings (Figure 4), and *hachuelas* or 'axe-monies.' The Purhépecha people believed that fire released the soul from the body. Slaves, relatives, and servants were selected to accompany their master to the underworld and were buried with him wearing metal offerings. Slaves, prisoners, and other humans offered in sacrifice to the gods wore silver objects if they were offered to the Moon goddess Xaratanga and gold if they were offered to Kurikaueri. Neither gold nor silver seems to have circulated as money. Instead, the Purhépecha and others along the west coast used copper hachuelas. With this as background, let's now examine some Purhépecha practices and uses of metal in more detail.

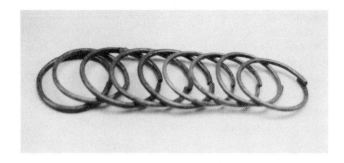

Figure 4 OPEN COPPER RINGS
(Approx. 1½ in. diameter)

BELLS

Bells appeared in Michoacán in the 10th century AD (Hosler 1988a) (Figure 5). Although various other metal objects and tools were forged, cast bells (using the lost wax method) make up 60 percent of metal objects fabricated (Hosler 1994:87). Some bells featured a loop at the top to hold or hang them; some were plain, and others had faces or animal figures. Their importance depended not only on the different shapes and sizes, but also on their color and sound (Hosler 1988a). Special care must have been taken in the combination of metals and percentage of tin and copper to produce alloys with the desired color and sound. In Asian manufacture, the proportions of metal in alloys were carefully measured to give the proper resonance in musical instruments, bells, and gongs.

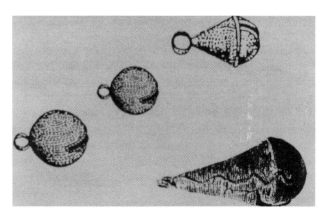

Figure 5 COPPER ALLOY CAST BELLS
Raised-wire design

The resonant qualities achieved in metal alloys, and the array of forms and sizes of the bells were of great importance in producing the desired variety of sounds. Sound was an essential aspect in shamanistic ceremonies and rites, a call to the spirits of deities to grant divine power to priests and the elite. The Purhépecha believed that the nobility obtained sacred power from their personal connection to the universe and their god Kurikaueri and that they were the intermediaries between the gods and the common people (Hosler 1996:96; Pollard 1993:133). Thus, the Purhépecha chief, like the Emperor of China, was an earthly form of their god and had direct connection with heaven (Pollard 1993:33). The color of the metal of ornaments worn by priests and nobility indicated the origin of power received from the deity, a belief also held in Peru. As with burial offerings, gold represented the sun and the god Kurikaueri, while silver signified the moon and the goddess Xaratanga (Hosler 1994:94).

Bells were used in various ceremonial ways, for instance, tied to ankles and wrists during rituals and religious dances. The priests and the elite had copper bells sewn on their garments for adornment, for religious significance, and for sound effects during rituals (Hosler 1994:87). The Dongson culture seems to have been the first to wear bells on their clothing as an adornment (López-Valdés 1965:73). The word to designate bell is the same in Nahuatl, Mixteca, and Purhépecha, an indication of an imported concept (Hosler 1994:96).

Metal bells had an important symbolism in the Buddhist religion. They were introduced to China with Buddhism in the year AD 65, and to Japan during the 6th century AD (Varley 1973). In Tibetan Buddhism the bell represents the spirit housing aspects of supreme wisdom. During rituals and prayers the bell is held in the practitioner's hand.

CRESCENT-SHAPED OBJECTS AND TWEEZERS

Next in importance seem to have been tweezers in all sizes, plain and elaborately decorated. These objects were usually in the form of a crescent moon or sea-shell, fan-like (Figure 6). They were carried by priests on official functions and seem to have been a sacred religious tool. The high priest carried specially-crafted large tweezers made of copper and tin alloys (Hosler 1994:88-89). Tweezers in that size would have been difficult to handle and could not have been functional as a depilatory instrument. Dorothy Hosler wrote in a 1985 study that " . . . the high proportion of tin in a composition of copper arsenic— between eight and twelve percent—found in the tweezers is far higher than necessary to ascribe to the mechanical function of the object. . . . [W]e must look to other functions of the tweezers—as a status symbol or display object." The special effort to achieve a specific color suggests that

Figure 6 COPPER TWEEZERS
(Approx. 4½ in.)

the tweezers had a ceremonial or religious significance.

HACHUELAS, PINS, AND RINGS

The *hachuela* is another object with the crescent or half-moon shape. Given the name of 'axe-monies,' they are found in beautifully-crafted metal pieces of the Moche culture in Peru.[3] Hachuelas have been found in abundance as burial offerings in tombs in Peru, Ecuador, and Mexico. In some tombs a copper bell or a hachuela is found placed in the mouth of the deceased. It was also an ancient Chinese custom to place a jade marble in the mouth of the dead. Copper was the metal most used by commoners (Grimberg 1990:7).

In addition to their function in ritual and as religious offerings, hachuelas were used to pay tribute and served as status symbols of wealth and nobility. Regarded as a primitive form of money, they were also sold in markets (Hosler 1988b). (Cacao beans were considered very valuable and were also used as money.) In Tibetan Buddhism the same curved form as the hachuela is an important symbol; it is probably a universal symbol, based on the crescent moon. The half-moon Buddhist ceremonial knife or chopper is used to symbolically sever attachments and ego from life, and it is a common object found in temples and in tombs (Museum of Fine Arts of Mongolia).

The Purhépecha also made needles and pins of diverse length and thickness. Some were plain and some decorated at one end with a bell or animal figure, and they were hammered or cast using the lost-wax method (Hosler 1988; Jairazbhoy 1976).

Metal open rings were another object produced in abundance in west Mexico. The open rings have been found in tombs arranged around the head, suggesting they may have been used to hold hair in place or simply for adornment (Hosler 1994:91). However, the rings were not actually holding hair. They were in clusters as were the axe-monies, in stacks by the body. The number and sizes of metal open rings and axe-monies found in burials appear to signify the status of the deceased (Hosler, Lechtman, and Holm 1990:20).

MIRRORS

Mirrors were shamanistic objects basic to both Asian and Mesoamerican cultures. It was believed in China that a mirror permitted the transition of the soul to other planes, to find the spirit of gods, and the souls of the ancestors (Barba de Piña Chan n.d:155). In China, mirrors were used during the Ch'i-chia culture, suggesting their use even before 2000 BC. Their significance was held to be representative of the universe and heavenly forces; they were worn for protection and as a status symbol, served as family heirlooms, and were given as funerary offerings (Loewe 1879).

Bronze mirrors of the Shang dynasty (1751-1112 BC), had a polished reflective face and were decorated on the reverse with symbols of heaven, the planets, calendric data, the I Ching, and other philosophic meaning based on the universe. Most bronze mirrors were round, representing universal space. By the Tang (618-906) and Song (906-1234) dynasties, bronze mirrors were not as abundant and had less Taoist symbols but more and more Buddhist elements (Barba de Piña Chan n.d:155-156, 158). By the 12th century, and during the Ming dynasty (1368-1644), China carried the Taoist concept of the circle as universal space.

In Japan, 'mirrors of the universe' seem to have had their beginning with the mirror given to the first emperor, symbolic of his nobility. In China and Japan, the reverse side of mirrors was inscribed with symbols of animals, and flowers, and with religious beliefs. Casting a mirror was compared to the creation of a new immortal soul, and polishing the mirror, to refining the soul. It became a tradition to carry a symbolically decorated bronze mirror as protection from evil spirits (Varley 1973).

In Michoacán, metal disks, called rodelas (Figure 7) were first manufactured by cold hammering. Like bells and mirrors of the universe, they were produced in large numbers, made of gold, silver, copper, and alloys. Decorated on the reverse side with symbols of nature and the universe, the Sun and the Moon, they were used in ceremonies and rituals. As in Asia, mirrors were considered precious by early Amerindian peoples, and several mirrors

similar to those made by Asians have been found in ancient burial sites on the coast of Panama and at other places in Central and South America.

Mirrors of the universe have been discovered in Peru, made of obsidian, and in Mesoamerica, made of stone. These were placed in shallow water facing the sun to produce a better reflection. Circular slate mirrors of the Early Classic period from Kaminaljuyu in Guatemala gave a reflection achieved by coating the surface with minute pyrite crystals. On the reverse were carved elaborate designs (Jairazbhoy 1976; Jett 1983). Mirrors coated with fine pyrite were also found in tombs on the highlands of Michoacán.

TOOLS

Although production of metal objects in Michoacán was primarily for ornamentation of the elite and for religious purposes, many utilitarian metal tools were also made, such as hatchets, hoes, and copper fishing hooks. While sharp points were devised for the coas (planting pole), no metal armament was made (Torres-Beltrán 1992:26). It is believed that Purhépecha metallurgists may have been the authors of the *Lienzo de Xukutákato*[4] (Figure 8) painted to commemorate the invention of metal agricultural tools: the *tarekua*, a planting stick used by Amerindians; the *angaru*, a type of axe with a curve similar to the machete (Figure 9); and the *teká'tzekua*, a hoe.

These metal agricultural tools were fabricated in Xiuquillan from copper and tin and were not found to have been made anywhere else outside of Michoacán. *Xiuquillan* means "the place where the plant kuriraxakua grows." In Purhépecha, *kuriraxakua* means 'fire-weed' (*La Relación*). It grows in salt water or among tequesquite, which is lava ash, probably containing burnable mineral elements from volcanic sources that helped make the strong fires required to work metals. This could explain the tree in the Lienzo that seems to be on fire. According to the anthropologist Nicolás León, the Lienzo was likely painted about the middle of the 10th century and altered in the 16th century by Spanish priests (León 1903a; *La Relación*).

COLOR

Golden-colored metal, other than gold itself, is referred to as *tumbaga*. A widely-used alloy in America, it was mainly a composition of gold and copper. The name is a word of Malayan origin that means 'copper.' The technology was also known in both India and China by the 3rd century BC. The most ancient objects of tumbaga come from Colombia where it seems to have its beginnings *ca.* AD 500 in the communities of Quimbaya, Tairona, and Muisca. Tumbaga was found in Peru, Mexico, and the Guayanas (see map). When tumbaga reaches its authentic proportion of 81 percent gold and 18.5 percent copper, it

Figure 7 PRE-COLUMBIAN COPPER RODELA
(Approx. 8 in. diameter)

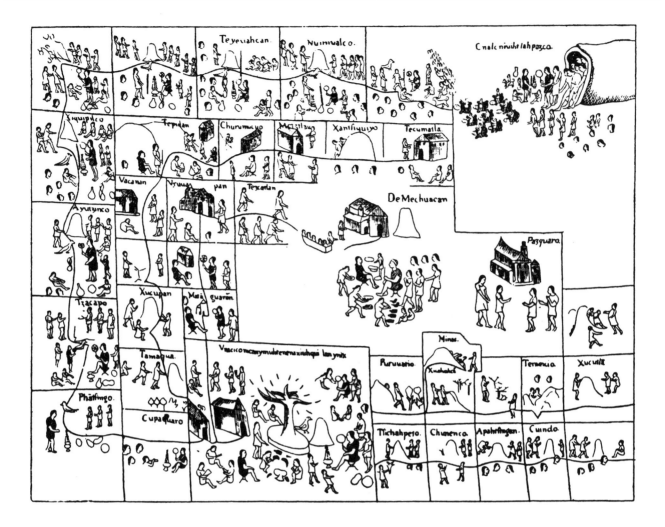

Figure 8 THE LIENZO DE XUKUTÁKATO (2.63 x 2.3 m.)

contains the best mechanical qualities, and its strength makes this material useful for manufacture of hatchets and other tools (Acuesta and Rovira 1982:21,43).

To make tumbaga from copper only, the object was immersed in an acid, a product obtained from various plants. The Purhépecha achieved a golden color by using copper with higher tin content for a look of pure gold (Hosler 1988b). It is possible that many of the metal objects of pre-Hispanic Michoacán thought to be gold were actually tumbaga. However, the copper and tin alloy which produces tumbaga was easily corroded, and is, therefore, prone to disappear.

Golden-hued copper hatchets were found in a tomb in Michoacán by the archaeologist Román Piña Chan, still preserving their golden color. He believed that they were either tumbaga or at one time were covered with a thin coat of gold. If these were utilitarian objects, there was no need to have them coated with gold; but if they were ceremonial objects, then there was no need for them to have been sharpened (Vargas 1990:77).

Behind the concept of tumbaga in Asia and India was the belief that under the right cosmological conditions a combination of non-gold metals could be turned into pure gold—alchemy.

FIRE

For centuries, Asian and Amerindian peoples sought to achieve harmony with the universe, and many symbols were created to represent this philosophy. For the Purhépecha, fire was sacred, and they regarded it to be a connecting force with the gods. This is evident in the importance they gave to maintaining a constant fire in the temples. *La Relación* mentions that bringing wood to the temples, for the fire to the gods, was a form of penitence, a gesture to gain their favors. The sacred fire was transported during migrations, and Zikuirancha, the Lord of Huayameo, said that during their journeys they always carried fire (La *Relacion*). In the Lienzo de Xukutákato is depicted a lantern in which they probably carried their sacred fire. This lantern, for a pre-Columbian America, is a very unusual item.

Figure 9 COPPER AXE OR *ANGARU*
(Approx. 14 in.)

A FINAL NOTE

Through knowledge of ancient objects, rituals, and beliefs, we may find understanding and the true meaning of Amerindian cultures and a final revelation of the trans-Pacific, pre-Columbian interchange with Asia. It is necessary to appreciate objects in their ceremonial and ritualistic context, whether that be Amerindians asking for rain or for a good harvest, or, through metal objects, establishing connection with the divine forces of the universe and the gods. These objects constitute a non-verbal world of signs and messages that hold abstract, religious, and spiritual concepts that need to be understood.

NOTES

1. *Purhépecha*—The people of Michoacán were called *Tarascos* by the Spaniards at the time of their invasion of Mexico, and that is how they are known today, but they prefer to be called by the name given to them by the people already living in the area, *Purhépecha*. According to Mary LeCron Foster (1993), *Purhépecha* means 'wanderers,' or 'those who are transplanted'; **p'ore** means 'to visit,' with the suffix **-pe** meaning 'interaction' or 'change'; **-cha** is the plural suffix. According to the historian Fray Bernardino de Sahagún, the name *Tarasco* is derived from the Purhépecha worship of the god or goddess Taras; adding the word **cue**, for 'temple,' it becomes *tarascue*, 'temple of Taras.' Other historians have translated tarasco as *tarháskua*, meaning 'son-in-law,' as the Purhépecha gave many of their women to the Spaniards.

2. *La Relación de las ceremonias y ritos y población y gobierno de los indios de la Provincia de Mechuacan* is an account of the history and customs of the Purhépecha. Written between 1538 and 1541, it has one hundred and forty-three pages and forty-four illustrations. In the introduction to the original, the authors explained that it was not their own work, that shortly after the conquest they wrote what was narrated to them by the elite elders of the council of Tzintzuntzan, the capital of the Province of Michoacán at the time of the conquest. It seems to be the work of the first friars to arrive in Michoacán, who are believed to be Friar Martín de Jesús de la Coruña and Friar Gerónimo de Alcalá. This is an assumption by some historians, since the authors never mentioned their names in the manuscript. The original work is in the Museum and Library of the Escorial in Madrid,

TIMELINE — MESOAMERICAN MINING AND METALLURGY

1250–400 BC   EARLY MINING IN MESOAMERICA

The Olmec were the first underground miners. They mined cinnabar, quicksilver, obsidian, crystalline quartz, and clays. Mining was continued by the Toltec and Maya. Evidence of pre-Columbian open-pit or underground mining methods is found at different locations of the Sierra Madre Occidental, south of San Luis Potosí, down to Guatemala and Honduras. Some of the most ancient pre-Hispanic mines were in Querétaro and Guerrero.

400–100 BC   THE MAYA ADDED THE MINING OF FLINT

100 BC–AD 700   LATE PRE-CLASSIC/EARLY CLASSIC

Miners perfected underground mining methods, and improved ore transportation, lighting, and hammering. There were prospectors, planners, administrators, and organizers within the consolidated mining industry. The main materials mined were obsidian, cinnabar, lead, tin, quicksilver, fine nephrite, jadeite; also, serpentine, chrysocolla, azurite, opals, copper, turquoise, and gold.

700–900   LATE CLASSIC

Metallurgy appeared on the west coast of Mexico. The Purhépecha of Michoacán and the Mixtec of Oaxaca became the foremost metal artisans in Mesoamerica at that time. The Mixtec (Oaxaca) fashioned delicate pieces in gold and silver. Centuries before the arrival of the Spaniards, the Mixtec smiths perfected the lost-wax technique. In Michoacán, copper was the base metal for alloys of gold, silver, tin, arsenic, zinc, and lead. Mesoamericans seemed to have knowledge of tumbaga and alchemy.

900–1200   EARLY POST-CLASSIC

The Toltec carried out intensive mining, mainly of obsidian.

1200–1500   LATE POST-CLASSIC

The Aztecs rose to prominence, but the most intensive and advanced pre-Columbian mining techniques were recorded in Michoacán and Oaxaca in copper, gold, and silver.

1492–1521   EUROPEAN INVASION OF MESOAMERICA

The first European miners arrived in the New World with Columbus' second voyage. Spain established in Seville the Casa de Contratación to control New World mineral exploitation and trade. At the time of the Spanish arrival, Mesoamericans were mining about thirty-five non-metallic minerals and approximately fourteen metallic materials.

(For additional information on metallurgy and mining, see *Minería Mexicana* 1984.)

Spain, and a copy of the original is in the Library of Congress in Washington DC, in the collection of papers of Peter Force.

3. *Axe-monies*—Jairazbhoy (1976) observes the following: "A recent study of the different types of axes analyzing their forms and world distribution concludes that the shaft-holed star mace may have diffused from Japan to Ecuador before AD 500, while the full-socketed axe could have come to Peru from South East Asia, and the grooved adz of Peru across the South Pacific from China."

4. *Lienzo de Xukutákato* (Linen of Jucutácato) describes a migration and metalworking. It is believed that it was painted about the middle of the 10th century to commemorate the invention of agricultural metal tools. Discovered only in the 19th century, it was found in the village of Jucutácato—thus its name. (By Spanish language standards, the name of the Lienzo is spelled as Jucutácato. The Purhépecha recently changed *c* to *k* and *j* to *x* in the spelling of their language.)

According to Nicolás Léon, who was the first to have it analyzed and copied, the Lienzo is painted with black vegetable ink on a crudely woven cotton cloth 2.63 by 2.3 m. It seems to have been altered in the 16th century by the Spaniards who added buildings and words in an attempt to explain it. The alterations were painted with a different type of ink and at a later date, although this information has been ignored by historians who give the Lienzo a post-Hispanic date (León 1903a).

The Lienzo consists of 33 squares, 30 of which are about the same size and contain drawings depicting the migration. Three larger drawings seem to represent more important events. The drawings depict human figures, a bird, a dog, turtles, and various domestic or religious utensils. Figures representing leaders wear red tunics which appear more oriental than Mesoamerican; the bird seems more like a dove than a Quetzal, hummingbird, or eagle, birds common in Mesoamerican codices. There is a lantern, a very unusual item even for a Mesoamerican post-Hispanic drawing. The leader figures hold the handle of a disk marked with eight divisions. There are mounds resembling *yacatas* or burial sites found in Michoacán. Yacatas have the same form and use as the stupa in the Buddhist religion.

REFERENCES

Acuesta, Domingo Mariano and Salvador Rovira Llorens
  1982 *Los Trabajos en Metal en la Area Andina.* Museo de América, Ministerio de Cultura, Dirección General de Bellas Artes, Archivos y Bibliotecas, Patronato Nacional de Museos, Madrid (1929).

Barba de Pina Chan, Beatríz
  n.d. *Interesantes parecidos entre algunas piezas de arte Chino y Maya, de los siglos IX al XII de nuestra era.* México: DEAS, Instituto Nacional de Antropología e Historia.

Cabrera Castro, Rubén
  1976 *Arqueología en el Bajo Balsas, Guerrero y Michoacán.* Mexico: Presa La Villita, Escuela Nacional de Antropología e Historia.

de Grimberg, Dora M. K.
  1990 *Los Senres del Metal: Minería y Metalurgía en Mesoamerica.* Mexico: Pangea Editores.

Escalante, Bernardino de
  1577 *Discurso de la navegación que los Portugueses hazen a los Reinos y Provincias del Oriente, y de la noticia que se tiene de las grandezas del Reino de la China.* Edición facsimilar comentada y publicada por Carlos Sanz, 1958, Sevilla, como Primera Historia de China.

Foster, Mary LeCron
  1993 Personal communication.

Heil, Celia
  1995 The pre-Columbian lacquer of west Mexico. Pp.32-39 in *NEARA Journal*, Vol. XXX, Nos. 1&2.
  1996a *El Maque Michoacano y las Lacas Asiáticos.* Morelia, Michoacán: V Congreso Mexicano de Historia de la Ciencia y la Tecnología.
  1996b *El Papel y el Papel Picado, Una Ciencia China o Amerindia?* Morelia, Michoacán: V Congreso Mexicano de Historia de la Ciencia y la Tecnología.

Hosler, Dorothy
  1985 *Pre-Columbian American Metallurgy.* 45th International Congress of Americanists.
  1988a Ancient west Mexican metallurgy: A technological chronology. *Journal of Field Archeology.* Boston: Boston University Quarterly, Vol. 15, No. 2.
  1988b *The Metallurgy of Ancient West Mexico.* Cambridge: MIT Press.
  1994 La metalúrgia en la antigha Mesoamérica: sonidos y colores. P.85 in *Semillas de la Industria.* Mario Humberto Ruz, ed. Centro de Investigaciones y Estudios Superiores en Antropología Social. México: Ediciones de la Casa Chata.

Hosler, Dorothy, Heather Lechtman, and Olaf Holm
  1990 Axe monies and their relatives (Ecuador/West Mexico). In *Studies of Pre-Columbian Art and Archeology*, No. 30. Washington: Dunbarton Oaks Research Library and Collection.

Hosler, Dorothy and Andrew MacFariane
  1996 Copper, sources, metal production, and metals trade in late post-Classic Mesoamerica. *Science* 273:1819-24.

Jairazbhoy, R. A.
  1976 *Asians in Pre-Columbian Mexico.* Enfield, England: Pika Printe Limited.

James, Peter and Nick Thorpe
  1994 *Ancient Inventions.* New York: Ballantine Books.

Jett, Stephen C.
  1983 Pre-Columbian transoceanic contacts. In *Ancient South Americans.* Jesse B. Jennings, ed. San Francisco: W. H. Freeman and Co.

Langenscheidt, Adolphus
  1970 *Minería Prehispánica de la Sierra de Querétaro.* Mexico: Secretaría del Patrimonio Nacional.

La Relación de las ceremonias y ritos y población y gobierno de los indios de la Provincia de Mechuacan: 1538-1541.
  Collection of papers of Peter Force. Washington: Library of Congress.
  1977 Facsimile reproduction of the above from manuscript c.IV.5.del Escorial, with transcription by José Tudela. Morelia: Editorial Basal.

León, Nicolás
  1889 Studies of the archaeology of Michoacán: The Lienzo of Jucutácato. In *Smithsonian Institution Annual Report.* Washington: Smithsonian Institution.

León, Nicolás
1903a *El Lienzo de Jucutácato*. Mexico: Imprenta del Museo Nacional.
1903b *Los Tarascos*. Mexico: Imprenta del Museo Nacional.

Loewe, Michael
1979 *Ways to Paradise*. London: Allen and Unwin.

López-Valdés, Pablo
1965 *Las Relaciones Prehispánicas Entre Asia y América*. GN 2, M6112, Tésis 91. México: Escuela Nacional de Antropologia e Historia, Universidad Autónoma de México.

Meggers, Betty
1971 Contacts from Asia. Pp. 239-259 in *The Quest for America*. Geoffrey Ashe, ed. London: Pall Mall.

Minería Mexicana
1984 Mexico: Edición publicada por la Comisión de Fomento Minero.

Murra, John V.
1994 Nos hazen mucha ventaja: The early European perception of Andean achievement. *Quincentenary Symposium, Seeds of Industry*. Washington: Smithsonian Institution.

Nuttall, Zelia
1906 The earliest historical relations between Mexico and Japan. *American Archaeology and Ethnology* 4(1):46-47. University of California.

Pollard, Helen Perlstein
1993 *Tariacuri's Legacy*. Oklahoma: Norman Publishing Division, University of Oklahoma Press.

Rostworowski, María
1970 Mercaderes del Valle de Chincha. *Revista Espanola de Antropología Americana*, Vol.5. Madrid.

Sahagún, Fray Bernardino de
1829 *Historia General de las Cosas de Nueva España* (General History of the Things of New Spain). *Ca.* 1558-1585, Fourth Edition. Mexico: Editorial Porrúa.
1957 *Sahagún y los Orfebres Precolombinos de México*. Mexico: Anales del Instituto Nacional de Antropología e Historia.

Solheim II, Wilhelm
1979 *New Light on a Forgotten Past*. Southeast Asia 2, Department of Anthropology, University of Hawaii.

Thompson, Gunnar
1989 *Nu Sun*. Fresno CA: Pioneer Publishing Co.

Torres-Beltrán, Ulises
1992 *La Identidad de los Tarascos*. XVI Coloquio de Antropología e Historia, Tradición e identidad en la cultura Mexicana. Zamora: El Colegio de Michoacán.

Vargas, Gustavo
1990 *Fusang, Chinos en América antes de Colón*. México: Editorial Trillas.

Varley, H. Paul
1973 *Japanese Culture*. Vermont and Tokyo: Charles E. Tuttle Co.

Yung Hua-king
1973 Fusang, in the book of Shi Zhou-ji. *Oriental Studies*, Vol. VIII, No. 1. México: El Colegio de México

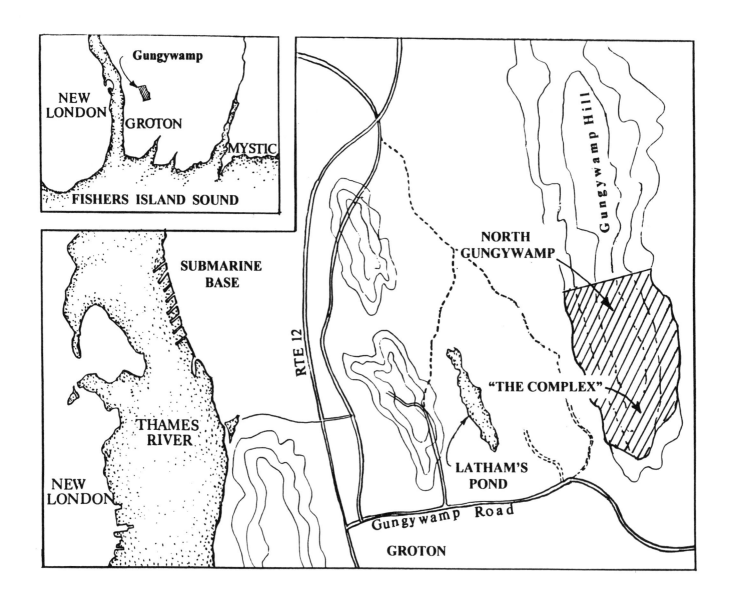

Figure 1 NORTH GROTON AREA AND GUNGYWAMP

The Gungywamp Enigma:
Serial Occupation of an Ancient New England Site

DAVID P. BARRON

ORIENTATION

The Gungywamp Complex is located on fifty-five acres of land belonging to the YMCA within the Gungywamp range of hills in North Groton, Connecticut, and about one mile east of the Thames River (Figure 1). The topography of the area includes many ledges, rock outcroppings, swamps, bogs, cliffs, and hills. It is densely wooded with second-growth trees and undergrowth. Contained within the complex is a vast array of lithic structures and features which have, until recently, defied explanation. Prior to our involvement, skeptics had dismissed the site as nothing more than a 'pre-industrial farmstead.' This characterization was made in spite of the fact that there is no tillable soil present, no discernible source of water, and no evidence of farm buildings beyond the ruined foundation of one old Colonial English half-house (*ca.* 1783).

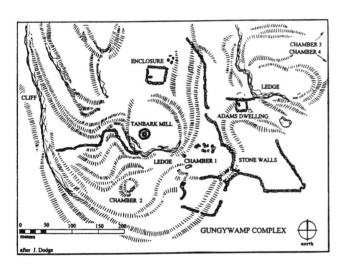

Figure 2 SOUTHERN GUNGYWAMP COMPLEX

Members of the Gungywamp Society field team have been conducting surveys and excavations within the complex and on neighboring land since 1979, finding over the years sufficient information to make a formal presentation to the Smithsonian Institution in Washington in May, 1994. The major goal of the presentation was to call attention to the site as a place of significant importance for academic and professional archaeologists to consider. We asked them to seriously evaluate the potentials of what we have found and cited our rationale which justifies future investigations. Apparently, our presentations were convincing enough for several gentlemen to approach us at the conclusion, indicating that "we'll have to go back to our offices and re-think American history."

AMERINDIAN FOCUS

Although we have found no Native American artifacts within the southern part of the Complex itself (Figure 2), an extension of the site about three-tenths mi. northward (the 'North Gungywamp') is replete with evidences of Amerind cultures (Figure 3). These finds include an entire northerly hillside filled with rock cairns, ruins of a 'meeting-house' shelter, quartz projectile points or fragments, and a fascinating site designated as Ledge Shelter II. The so-called meeting house structure ruin consists of a U-shaped earthen berm, covering an area of approximately 3 m. by 4 m. and about 20 cm. high; two hearths were found in the open end. Excavation of this feature produced a single Woodland era projectile point and some random turn-of-the-century items (old car spring, base of early light bulb, etc.).

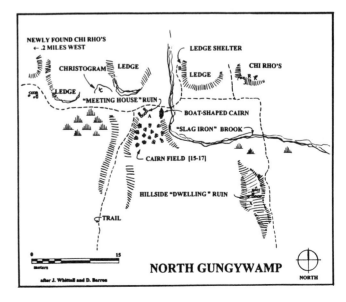

Figure 3 NORTH GUNGYWAMP

The nearby Ledge Shelter II site (at **B** on Figure 3) is a naturally-created, three-sided 'cave' approximately 3 m. wide by 2 m. deep by 2 m. high, located at the base of a rock outcropping about 11 m. high. This site required several years of excavation, analysis and curating. Notable among the artifacts retrieved were five different types of pottery, a most unusual tightly-grained hammerstone showing a man's profile, several dozen projectile points, scrapers, drills, and incised soapstone pipe fragments. Carbon-14 radiocarbon tests from charcoal in a hearth isolate the third horizon at around 770 BC (see Barron and Mason 1995). This date falls within the time frame of a Susquehanna-style broadpoint discovered less than one m. away within this same third horizon; this style of point was manufactured in the period 1500 to 500 BC. Connecticut State Archaeologist, Dr. Nicholas Bellantoni, has visited the site several times and has suggested that the lowest horizon might well be dated to 2000 BC or earlier.

EUROPEAN CONNECTION

Directly adjacent to the Native American materials, in the North Gungywamp, we have discovered several ancient, early Christian-style carvings. These include a crude 'Christogram' which was examined and identified by the late Dr. Barry Fell. He predicted that "whenever you find a Christogram like this you are bound to find some *chi rho*s." Indeed, just three years later, while completing an excavation on the ruins of a nearby stone chamber, we found several anciently-devised *chi rho* symbols and other less-easily identified carvings (Figure 4). These symbols were incised into the granite outcropping at chest-high level and hidden beneath heavy lichen and moss covering.

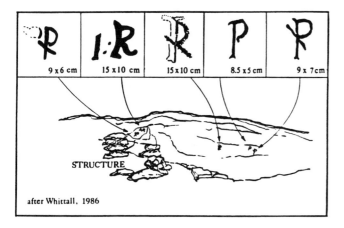

after Whittall, 1986

Figure 4 INSCRIPTIONS AT NORTH GUNGYWAMP

Together with Jim Whittall of the Early Sites Research Society, I undertook my third research trip to the British Isles in search of early Christian sites. Mr. Whittall discovered some excellent references and drawings of early

*chi rho*s, and we were able to identify those in the North Gungywamp as belonging to the transitional *chi rho* variety, which were in use in Europe somewhere between AD 500 and AD 700. This time-frame was to have greater significance within the complex itself. The carvings strongly suggested that some early Christian adventurers had been in the area long enough to expose some of the native populations to Christian symbols. As recently as the summer of 1996, three more *chi rho* symbols were discovered on the face of a rock ledge 200 m. west of the original carvings. These were of the same depth, erosion, size, and crude nature as the first-discovered symbols but lacked lichen covering due to direct sun exposure and rainfall.

COLONIAL INFLUENCES

At least two ruins which we have excavated are readily identified as being of Colonial derivation. One, the so-called Adams Dwelling (see Figure 2), surrendered hundreds of china fragments, iron pot portions, buttons, glassware, clay pipes, nails, spikes, fractured bricks, and animal bones. This site is datable to 1783, when Nathaniel Adams gave his "one room house" to his eldest daughter Hanna. The Adams family was a mercantile group in the present-day Groton-Ledyard area. At least two of the Adams clan were involved in the 1781 Battle of Fort Griswold in Groton. The analysis of artifacts showed no signs that the dwelling had burned down, nor had it simply rotted away. We opined that, when Hanna finally married, she and her husband dismantled the structure, taking all salvageable brick, window glass, iron work (fireplace crane and hooks), beams, and planks.

During the summer of 1995, we completed much of the stabilization and preliminary survey of a Colonial type ruin in the North Gungywamp (see **X** on Figure 3). Strangely enough, the only artifacts we found were a total of twelve hand-wrought nails and fragments on the easterly side of the site. This one-room dwelling was literally dug into a steep hillside and had its fireplace located in the northerly stone wall. The structure was positioned within eight m. of a boggy swamp. No well or outhouse remains were discovered. Further archaeological excavation is warranted at this site, including the clearing of surrounding undergrowth and investigation of the laid-stone flooring. For now, and until otherwise proven, we consider this ruin to be Colonial.

It should be noted here that, in the three hundred acres of YMCA land involved, only two ruins are clearly identifiable as being of Colonial origins. The Adams dwelling is located just within the major complex; the Hillside structure is isolated on a barren slope about one tenth mile north of the complex on private land. The lack of settlement remains from possible pre-Viking Christian explorers in the area (if, indeed, they were here at all) remains an enigma. It is possible, of course, that such a settlement may have been some distance away or beneath today's bogs and ponds. We have found evidence of these people in the form of markings on lithics and strongly suspect a cultural co-existence between them and native populations, but their actual habitats have so far avoided detection. The topography within the complex, including the North Gungywamp, is extremely rugged, making our task of discovery all the more difficult.

THE COMPLEX MYSTERIES

In leaving the North Gungywamp area and heading south along the eastern ravine trail, we begin to encounter a series of unusual lithic features, including one of three extant small stone bridges with single standing stones, two lines of standing stones, and numerous random, irregular stone walls. Seventeen overflights, undertaken some years ago, noted a pattern of stone wallings which looked akin to what a schizophrenic spider might have produced. We may have historic documentation of these stone walls in a letter from John Pynchon, November 30, 1654, to his mentor, John Winthrop the Younger:

> Sir, I have a report of a stone wall[ing] and strong fort within it, made all of stone, recently discovered at or neare Pequet. Here [Springfield MA] there are many strange reports [of this] and I would like to know the truth of it fro[m] yourself (D. P. B.'s brackets).

Within the complex itself are no fewer than four semi-subterranean dry-walled stone chambers (or ruins thereof). All of them have been excavated in recent years, by either Early Sites, Gungywamp, or a combined effort. No significant artifacts have been discovered which would help to date their construction. However, about twenty years ago, Carl Vogt and his brother Frederick came upon the hidden entrance to a small stone chamber in the Complex. Once they opened it, they discovered a small black pot on the dirt floor of the chamber. Years later, Carl recounted how they removed the pot, cleaned out the 'bird's nest' in it (possible cremational remains?), and took it to the anthropology department of a local college for assistance in dating. On returning for information several weeks later, they were confronted with a total denial of the pot's existence. No amount of prodding could resolve the loss of the pot. Both men felt the pot was made of bronze, but they were stymied at this point. Our subsequent attempts to trace down the missing artifact resulted in a frustrating blank.

One of the most significant aspects of our research into these chambers involved the archaeoastronomy associated with the larger, intact Chamber One. The so-called 'illuminaire shaft,' built into the rear upper wall, was discovered by accident. It permits a beam of light from the equinoctial sunset to penetrate into the dark confines on only two days of the year, illuminating the entrance to the hidden beehive chamber situated in the north wall of the structure. This beehive chamber had been sealed shut with rocks and was discovered only accidently by Early Sites excavators. The equinoctial sunset event, which we first observed several years ago, began a series of investigations and reports. Color, as well as black and white photos, taken six months apart clearly show the consistency with which this light beam was focused.

Vance Tiede, our astronomy researcher, has carried out many hours of personal observation on this illuminaire effect and has discovered several more significant solar and lunar alignments, many of which coincide with what are observed elsewhere as church holidays and Gaelic days. These findings strongly suggest that the chamber is a calendar site, as one might expect of a people moving toward dependence on cultivated food and the consequent need for calendrical precision. In eastern North America, one would expect this around AD 900.

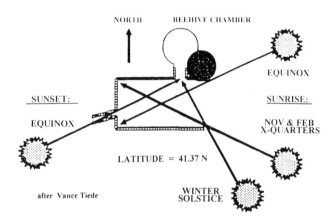

Figure 5 CHAMBER 1, SOUTH GUNGYWAMP

The so-called 'Tan Bark Mill,' consisting of two concentric circles of worn stone, and located near the edge of a rock ledge above the chambers, has given a Carbon-14 date of AD 455 ± 175 years (Geocron Lab No. GX15 986). This period overlaps our proposed 'window of inspection' time frame, AD 500 to AD 700. James Whittall has also discovered a similar crushing mill located on the Isle of Sark in the Channel Islands. That mill is dated somewhere within the same period. These mills were used to crush tree bark for tanning hides.

RESOLUTION

To date we have made no *absolute* claims of great antiquity for the Gungywamp Complex and continue to have good relationships with our State Archaeologist, Dr. Nicholas Bellantoni. We do submit that the data which we can present is sufficiently convincing to warrant serious consideration from the academic and professional communities.

Unresolved at this time is the location of the place where the ancient explorers may have lived during their stay. Except for the Amerindian items found in the North Gungywamp, the lack of in-ground artifacts within the Complex is a frustration. However, we do consider the carvings and architectural features to be reliable artifacts. So, too, are the Pynchon letter, the dating of the Isle of Sark grinding mill, and the archaeoastronomy within Chamber One.

This is no simplistic 'Occam's Razor' debate, nor is it a clearly defined theory which is substantiated by undeniable 'proof.' The site has gained a certain amount of notoriety and recognition. Film and TV crews which have documented much of our finds include Ted Timreck for NOVA, Italian Public TV, a German film company, a Tennessee video company, and numerous others. Laughingly, we comment to touring visitors that people in Rome, Berlin, London, and elsewhere know more about the Gungywamp than do residents of Groton, Connecticut.

If progress has been made through the activities of the Gungywamp Society, it would have to be recognized in the Society's vast reduction of vandalism, its role in public education, and the discovery of many more hidden features within the Complex.

In summary, there is a strong potential that dating the site between AD 500 and AD 700 presents a realistic window for future research.

REFERENCES

Barron, D. P. and Sharon Mason
  1995 *The Greater Gungywamp,* 3rd edition. Noank CT: The Gungywamp Society.
Bridenbaugh, Carl, ed.
  1984 *The Letters of John Pynchon*, Vol. 1. Boston: The Colonial Society of Massachusetts.
Caukins, Frances M.
  1852 *History of New London, Connecticut.* New London: New London Historical Society.
Coombs, Elizabeth
  n. d. Former stone ruins in Connecticut. *Early Sites Research Society Bulletin*, 7(2):19-20.
Dodge, John E.
  1965 *Gungywamp Site, Groton, Connecticut.* Storrs: Office of the State Archaeologist.
Kra, Renee, ed.
  1981 New England megaliths: Fact and fancy. *Bulletin of the Archaeological Society of Connecticut,* No. 44. Washington CT.
Trumbull, James Hammond
  1850 *The Public Records of the Colony of Connecticut Prior to the Union with New Haven Colony*, May 1665. Hartford: Brown & Parsons.
Whittall, James P.
  1976 Gungywamp Complex, Groton CT, Archaeological Report 1974. *Early Sites Research Society Bulletin,* 4(1):15-27.
  1986 Stone structures, North Gungywamp Complex. *Early Sites Research Society Bulletin,* 13(1):10-17.
  1991 Vernal equinox light channel, Chamber One, Gungywamp Complex, Groton CT. *Early Sites Research Society Bulletin* 18(1).
  1991 Radiocarbon dates associated with stonework in New England. *Early Sites Research Society Bulletin,* 18(1).
Whittall, James P. and David P. Barron
  1991 Double ring of stones, the Gungywamp Complex. *Early Sites Research Society Bulletin,* 18(1).

Earth, Stones, and Sky:
Universality and Continuity in American Cosmology[1]

JAMES W. MAVOR, JR. AND THE SPIRIT OF BYRON E. DIX

INTRODUCTION

Our use of the term 'American' is purposely vague because it can include those with long genealogical and cultural roots on the North American continent as well as immigrants arriving over hundreds and thousands of years. Americans before Columbus probably had as much knowledge as those of today, but it was more general and diverse. Today, we are specialists, and both we and the earlier Americans would have great difficulty in surviving in the other's environment. The Americans in our story are primarily in the earlier mode of living.

The sky is universal and holistic. Everyone watches the sky and sees mostly the same objects. The traditional stories comprise a universal language, and people everywhere and in all of time have responded with myths that are similar in character. George de Santillana and Martha von Dechend conclude that myth expresses the "variety and recurrence of the cosmos . . . . Myth has no historical basis, but history is driven by mythical forces" (de Santillana and Dechend 1969).

In ancient times, the people who lived all around the top of the world erected stone mounds, standing stones, stone chambers, and all manner of stone structures. They were also adapted to life at the edge of and on the sea. They lived under the blanket of the Aurora Borealis, a powerful natural environment that is very delicately balanced, and which we today call electrical fields. It is accepted that the early people all over North America came through the arctic, a place which surely affected their beliefs and practices. It may be that the arctic is the source of their emotional, physical, and spiritual strength in resisting changes to their ways through millenia. On the other hand, New England's native traditions and the excavation of burials suggest that the souls of men and women go to the Southwest (Simmons 1970). The two theories seem not to be mutually exclusive.

We focus on the universality of the sky because it may provide a way toward understanding the nature of the peoples we are studying. An observer of the sky at the same latitude anywhere around the globe can see the same seasonal sun paths and over the course of a year see all the same star patterns. Astronomy is known as the most holistic of sciences. We believe that a most important element in our understanding of past peoples is to recognize their awareness of the sky.

Structures created by Maritime Archaic peoples in the arctic are similar to structures found in New England and further south. These peoples used stone, earth, and wood to make dwellings with long passageways; standing stones were probably part of a system of markers for piloting and navigation. The accounts of earliest contact between Native Americans and Europeans confirm that the natives were accustomed to seagoing boats and prepared for deep-sea voyages.

The American skin boat has had at least 5000 years of development and was reportedly seen in Norway as early as AD 1300 (Johnstone 1980). Also, American Indians were reported to have reached the German and Irish coasts 2000 years ago (Cassidy 1968). Alice B. Kehoe suggests that the presence of woodworking tools and fishing gear in Archaic cultures of North America and ground slate knives and points in Scandinavia in the 3rd millenium BC could be explained by two-way voyages across the Atlantic made by cod fishermen in skin boats (Johnstone 1980). Tools found in Maritime Archaic cultures in Labrador and dated to 7500 years ago are similar to woodworking tools used in the 19th century AD by the Indians of northwestern United States to build seagoing vessels. Archaeologists Bruce Bourque, James Tuck, and William Fitzhugh believe that Atlantic Maritime Archaic people of 7500 to 4000 years ago were seafaring people who hunted cod and swordfish offshore in substantial boats (Timreck 1987). It was far easier to sail east than west in the north Atlantic, a fact which has been repeatedly demonstrated during several past centuries; the Norse voyages to Greenland and America were made against the prevailing currents and winds, by following the edges of the land masses.

We have chosen to discuss several stone structures in America dating from about 1300 to 100 years ago. They provide markers which lie along our path to understanding early Americans. We have described most of them in previous publications, but here we see them as part of a continuous, cultural process.

NEW ENGLAND'S STONE MOUNDS

Freetown is in a part of southeastern Massachusetts characterized by lakes, swamps, groups of stone mounds, and much Indian lore. We focus on one stone mound of a group of one hundred and five on the edge of a white cedar swamp that we studied in 1983, the last occasion on which we conducted an archaeological excavation (Mavor and Dix 1989). We had been attracted by similarly grouped stone mounds on Cape Cod where there are unique patterns of siting, typically on the flanks of kettle holes near the sea. As we talked to our friends among the people of this region, we got the impression that each mound and each individual stone has its own personal story and that only those intimately involved know the story.

There are many views of why mound groups were built: some undoubtedly resulted from farmers clearing fields; others could be so-called 'manure stones' for fertilizing, boundary markers, grave markers, memorials, vision quest sites, collapsed Indian shrines, astronomical sight-line markers, etc. They could have been, and some surely were, built by Native Americans as well as European and other colonists during several thousand years. It is certain that there are hundreds of thousands of man-made stone mounds in groups in New England. It is also certain that the origins of most of them are unknown to archaeologists because they have not studied them. Some people in the past have gone to considerable trouble to respect and protect them, for example, at the Watuppa Indian reservation in Freetown state forest.

We believe that the mound groups, each of which number from ten to two hundred mounds, represent markers for places of shamanic ritual, including the vision quest. They are located in places on the natural landscape that are particularly important in maintaining the balances of nature. They were the locations of important events, including astronomical sighting to mark important dates such as the solstices and equinoxes (Mavor and Dix 1989).

In the western part of the United States, in Canada, and northern Mexico, there are living and historical traditions among natives of the use of similar groups of stone mounds for shamanic ritual purposes. The stones were usually selected and piled in the hope that spiritual powers would be granted. Fasting and showing respect for the celestial bodies are also a part of the ritual, which is practiced among the Yurok of northern California and the Seri of northern Mexico. Since the Yurok are Ritwan speakers, distantly related to the Algonquians linguistically, there may be a widespread ritual which is connected by linguistic lines (Haviland and Power 1981). The Yurok and their culturally similar neighbors, the Wiyot, have a number of words expressing the sacred which correspond to the Algonquian. *Gudatrigakwitl* is the Wiyot, and *Wohpekumeu* or *Gard* the Yurok name for the creator known as *Kichtan* in Algonquian. *Woge* is the Yurok spirit within rocks. *Sa'atl* is the Yurok dwarf-like spirit of creeks and swamps and also means 'sanctity of place.' *Ki-we-sona* is a Yurok expression for the spiritual quality of things, comparable to the Algonquian *Manitou* (Kroeber 1976; Powers 1976).

In Canada, along the shores of Lake Superior, the practice of grouping stones into mounds for ritual purposes may go back to 3000 BC (Emerson 1960). In the East, local traditions of the stone mounds seem largely to have disappeared among Native Americans because of disease, enforced migration, and cultural change due to the pressures of foreign cultures. In eastern North America today, the descendants of Indian communities replaced many of the numerous local traditions and myths with a pan-Indian culture based in large part on universal aspects of Native American cultures throughout North America (Mavor and Dix 1989). At the same time, groups of Native Americans in different localities have different lifestyles. While they usually have in common that Life is Ceremonial and Sacred, the ceremonies may be different. gkisedtanamoogk, member of the Wampanoag Nation of Massachusetts, writes, "I believe in the Sacredness of the Sweat Lodge according to the Lakota (Sioux) Way; I believe in the Sacredness and the integrity of the Sundance. And I believe we are here to Support and Respect each other" (gkisedtanamoogk and Hancock 1993). When we discuss stone mounds and our findings with people in far-off places, they typically see their own heritage in them (Mavor and Dix 1989).

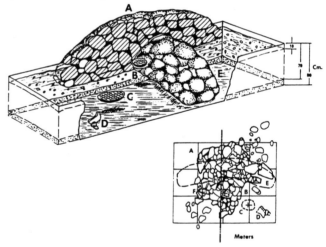

Figure 1 ISOMETRIC DRAWING OF FREETOWN MOUND

The Freetown mound which we chose to excavate was triangular in shape and oriented true north and south. Chief Little Horse of the Wallamonopaug Tribal Council participated in the excavation and performed a ceremony over the mound before we started work (Figure 1) (Mavor and Dix 1989). During disassembly of the mound **A** into its 992 component stones, we found a curved structure **E** at a depth of 0.8 m. that we interpreted as a prayer seat, or shrine, architecturally similar to many other structures found in New England and acknowledged as Indian shrines in the western part of the United States and around the world. At **B** we found a deposit of charcoal from which two samples were Carbon-14 dated to 790 ± 150 years (Geochron Lab No. GX9684) and 875 ± 160 years (Lab

No. GX9683) before AD 1950 (Mavor and Dix 1983; Hoffman 1988). There were two white quartz boulders in the mound, one on top center and the other shaped like an owl that felt waxy to the touch (Figure 2).

Figure 2 OWL-SHAPED QUARTZ BOULDER
From stone mound excavation

Feature **C** is a large deposit of red ochre, and feature **D** appears to be a manitou stone that was propped up before the mound was built over it. Charles Willoughby published a photograph, without comment, of a similar stone in an Archaic red paint cemetery (Willoughby 1935). We compare these two stones in Figures 3a and 3b. Manitou stones seem to represent the spiritual quality of things, places, and ideas. We have found variations in the shape of this type of artifact, usually like a human head and shoulders, all over the world, including Polynesia, Ascension Island, Japan, Siberia, and Australia.

A PREHISTORIC OBSERVATORY

In Upton, Massachusetts, we investigated an underground stone chamber which appears to have both Native American and European origins. It was brought to our attention by Malcolm Pearson, who at one time owned the property on which it is located (Lat. 42°, 11' N; Long. 71°, 35' W) (Figure 4). It is built into a hillside and is circular, with a corbelled dome and a long tortuous passage which is aligned to the summer solstice sunset. This passage was the impetus for a series of measurements which went on for years. The array of stone mounds and stone rows on Pratt Hill, one and a half km. to the northwest, led us to develop an elaborate astronomical scenario for the chamber as an observation place or shrine. It also led to a date of AD 720 ± 25 based on the change of setting position of several stars, due to precession. This date is contemporary with Fort Ancient and Late Hopewell

cultures in the midwest, and was a time of cultural unrest in the eastern woodlands.

Figure 3a FREETOWN MANITOU STONE
Found in mound excavation

Figure 3b STANDING STONE
Archaic Indian burial (Willoughby 1935)

The chamber is near John Eliot's praying village of Hassanamessett, the seat of the Nipmuck nation in the 17th century. It is also located near the source of all the major waterways of eastern Massachusetts, within the Blackstone drainage close to its watershed with the Assabet. The headwaters of the Quinebaug and Charles Rivers are within 5 km. of the site. These environmental characteristics alerted us to what we saw later as a pattern; Native American sacred places coincide with conjunctions of natural features, usually water, rugged topography, seismic activity, and subtler circumstances such as the presence of contact geology, where quartz and metals such as copper, lead, gold, and silver are found (Mavor and Dix 1989).

The Upton chamber structure is of particular interest because of the way in which the weight of the dome is transferred to the passageway. Usually this is done with a massive lintel stone, thick enough to take the bending load. Here, there is a gradual transition from the corbelled arch of the passage roof into the corbelled dome of the chamber, which does not require a lintel stone. There is a chamber with a corbelled dome in East Thompson, Connecticut, but to our knowledge, the Upton corbelled passage is unique in New England. The sophistication of the design and unquestionable, specific similarity to European chamber tombs incline us to the belief that it was the product of experienced and ancient builders (Mavor and Dix 1989). Not only is New Grange in Ireland built in this way but so are some early Christian monastic buildings in County Kerry. Chamber tombs on the Iberic peninsula are found with this same design as well. It may be important that Mayan arches and corbelling are significantly cruder than the Upton chamber. They seem not to have developed beyond a high, peaked arch with a short lintel, at least where soft limestone was the only rock available locally. On the other hand, aspects of the chamber and structures nearby have similarities to many Native American structures.

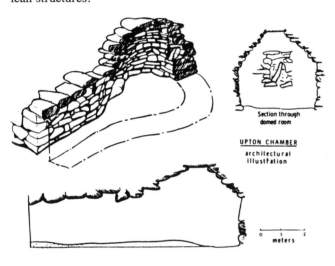

Figure 4 UPTON CHAMBER

Feature **J** on the Pratt Hill plan (Figure 5) is a stone mound that is directly in front of a narrow gap in a stone row. The gap is three feet wide, and the mound blocks the gap completely. To an observer looking from the chamber toward the hilltop, the stone row would be perceived as continuous, whereas it is not. This may be a distinctly American feature, and is found throughout the midwestern Mississippean, Adena, and Hopewellian structures.

Because of its unique structure and the astronomical date, we are open to the suggestion that the Upton chamber could have been built under the influence of Irish monks in the 8th century. If that were true, the monks or other Europeans who would have been here at that date and left remains of this prominence certainly would have had genial relations with the Native Americans and exchanged cultural traits both ways (Mavor and Dix 1989; Dix and Mavor 1980). The astronomical orientations would have been consistent with Irish participation. At least eight

oratories of early Christian Ireland are aligned to solar or stellar events (Mavor 1985). Also, navigation and astronomical knowledge always go hand in hand. St. Brendan set out "towards the summer solstice," on his voyage to the island of the paradise of saints in the 6th century AD. During the few centuries following, Irish monks sailed from Ireland to Iceland and the Faroes, voyages which were as difficult as the Norse voyages from Norway (Taylor 1971).

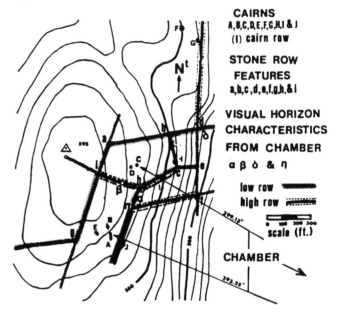

Figure 5 PRATT HILL PLAN

The northern end of the field of view from the chamber is marked by the summer solstice sunset at a conical mound **C**. The sun is shown setting over mound **C** in Figure 6. Also on Pratt Hill, there are examples of two types of stone row: high narrow rows which could serve as fences, and low wide rows which could not. Sometimes they intersect. With the help of Malcolm Pearson, we were able to locate precisely the stone mounds and rows on Pratt Hill with respect to the chamber. The hill is one and one-half km. away and in a heavily-wooded area. Malcolm provided a powerful strobe light which he set up at each structure in turn. We sighted the flash by looking through a transit telescope set up at the chamber; by communicating with walkie-talkies, we made repeated measurements to increase our accuracy. The results of these measurements show that the shapes of some stone mounds suggest effigies, and some have depressions, symmetrically located in the stone structures, which seem unlikely candidates for tree intrusion or falls. They can be interpreted as vision pits, such as were found in eastern Canada and called *puckasaw* pits by archaeologists J. Norman Emerson and William C. Noble (Emerson 1960; Noble 1968). The medicine men of the society would have gone to these pits to seek visions to solve the social problems of the day.

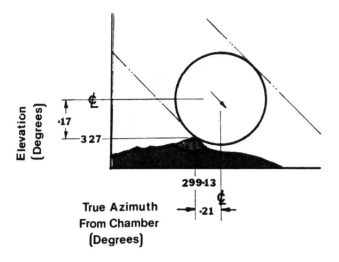

Figure 6 SUMMER SOLSTICE SUNSET
At the Upton mound

The horizon, as seen from within the chamber, is only six degrees wide. But an observer, in the darkened room, has enhanced vision of the horizon outside because his pupils dilate, enabling him to see subtle details and contrasts. The zig-zag passage to the chamber may have been designed in this way to limit the amount of light that enters the chamber. With this feature, the relatively faint, third magnitude stars in the field of view would be visible on the horizon and even brighter in ancient times with less air pollution. These stars, having a common date of setting at markers on Pratt Hill, are on the threshold of visibility at the horizon of three degrees elevation.

In New England, trees complicate astronomical interpretation of the landscape. We try to look at the landscape with the trees mentally stripped away. From reading the histories of New England, we found that when the first colonists arrived there were fewer, but larger, trees, mostly widely spaced with no brush, in contrast with today's dense forest of smaller trees. This more open forest resulted from periodic burning off of the underbrush in the spring and fall, which kept the landscape open and certainly made the astronomy much easier than it is today (Cronon 1983; Patterson 1988).

HELIACAL PHENOMENA

Since we had located a solstice marker that was visible from within the chamber, we looked for events that would have been suitably marked by the largest mounds, **A** and **B**. Together, these mounds have a total width of 30 m., with a gap between, as seen from the chamber. We picked the Pleiades as a likely candidate because they are, next to the sun and moon, the most interesting bodies in the sky, judging from historical records. If the mounds marked the setting of the Pleiades, the date would have been AD

720 ± 25. At that time, Electra, the first of the eight brighter Pleiads to set, and Alcyone, the brightest Pleiad, set precisely in the gap between mounds **A** and **B**, which taken together span just the width of the setting Pleiades cluster. These mounds also mark the momentary appearance and last setting of the cluster just after sunset (heliacal setting) in early April at the southern extremity of the field of view from within the chamber (Figure 7). An important historical record supports the observation of the heliacal behavior of the Pleiades in early New England. Giovanni da Verrazzano wrote to the king of France, in AD 1524, that the natives of southern New England sowed their seed at the time of the first rising of the Pleiades (Tarrow 1970; Mavor and Dix 1989).

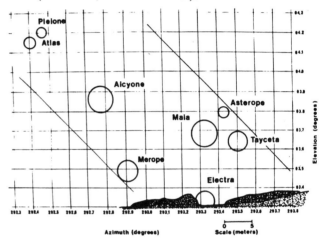

Figure 7 HELIACAL SETTING OF THE PLEIADES
At Upton mounds **A** and **B** in AD 710

For a long time, a cosmological riddle existed. Where did the celestial bodies go after they descended below the horizon, usually to return the next morning? While ancient people based many myths on the event because they did not know the answer, they certainly observed that the sun takes longer (about four minutes in our time) to return than the stars, and this fact has been an important basis of calendars throughout history. The resulting phenomenon, in which the stars appear momentarily on the horizon near sunrise and sunset, occurs as four events each and every year for each star. Thus, a star has four dates attached to it, so that if you know the map of the sky well, as the ancient people did, and you can count days, you have a calendar of as much complexity as you wish. Not only that, it is not necessary to have horizon markers on the land to construct this calendar, only an observation point marker. Some ancient people, probably for convenience and redundancy, did use horizon markers. Historically, the most commonly used of these four dates was the one when the sun and star were near the same horizon. This sunrise event, called heliacal rising, requires the star to appear momentarily just above the horizon before sunrise on the first day after the star has been invisible for months. The sunset event, heliacal setting, requires the star to appear momentarily just above the horizon after sunset on the last day before the star becomes invisible for months (Figure 7).

Heliacal phenomena have lost their significance in modern astronomical texts (Bruin 1979). However, they have a long history of calendrical use (Aveni 1972; Lockyer 1894; Bruin 1979). Analysis and prediction of heliacal events go back at least as early as 320 BC (Bruin and Vondjidis 1971). The observational problems of atmospheric variability and visual acuity remain. Ancient observers could probably do better than we can today because we are hampered by increased air pollution, less visual acuity, and less dedicated experience than those of ancient times.

Some of the medicine wheels of the Rocky Mountains are horizon markers for the heliacal rising of bright stars (Williamson 1984; Kehoe and Kehoe 1979; Eddy 1974; Robinson 1980, 1981). In the Southwest, pueblo peoples, who were settled in villages, used land markers, whereas the Navajo, who were more mobile, did not (Williamson 1984). The Navajo traditionally use the heliacal rising of the Pleiades (Delyehe) to mark the end of the planting season, and, in the fall and winter, the Pleiades provide them with a celestial clock (Williamson 1984). In Arizona, the Pima begin their calendar year with the June solstice, when the Saguaro fruit is gathered. Oral tradition preserves a complex astronomical event which is part of the ceremony, from which several metaphors of their language grew. At periods of from four to eight years, the Pleiades, the sun, the new moon, and Venus are seen together near the northeastern horizon in the morning of the June solstice (Hoskinson 1992).

The date of the heliacal rising of the Pleiades changes with the passing years and therefore signals different events in different epochs. It takes place today on June 25, just after the Pima Indians' summer solstice and harvest festival. In Verrazzano's time, AD 1525, the heliacal rising took place on June 10, at the end of the planting season. In AD 720, the proposed construction date of the Upton chamber, the Pleiades heliacal set, shown in Figure 7, occurred on April 8 and the heliacal rise, not visible from the chamber, on June 9.

These heliacal rise and set dates were determined by computer simulation by the author using the Redshift astronomy program (Maris 1994). The heliacal star and sun altitudes relative to the horizon, that are required for heliacal events and were observed by N. Lockyer, were used (Lockyer 1894). The Pleiades are represented by Alcyone, the brightest and central star. Accuracy of the heliacal dates is $\pm$ 2-3 days, depending upon visual acuity and atmospheric conditions.

The currently accepted date for introduction of maize agriculture in southern New England is about AD 900, and we know from Verrazzano that the heliacal rising of the Pleiades signalled sowing time in AD 1525. Evidently, the heliacal setting in 720 either would not have signalled corn planting or the climate then was warmer

than it was in 1525. Even though historical records support an intimate and continuing connection between astronomy and agriculture, astronomical records by paleolithic shamans probably had a strong and ancient role in culture independent of agriculture (Marshak, 1972).

A DRAGON'S LAIR

Calendar One, the first place we studied, is a high natural bowl in central Vermont open to the south. The drawing in Figure 8 shows a number of features: a stone chamber **A** in the center of the bowl, dug into a natural mound of rock; an all-weather spring **B**; standing stones **J** and **K**; stone mounds; and petroglyphs **L**. The hills surrounding the bowl have natural peaks and valleys which mark the dates of a solar calendar, as viewed from within the bowl. These natural features are reinforced by standing stones on the ridges. The landscape seems to cradle time; it appears to be a place of great natural power or sacred character that has been reinforced by stonework which led us there and allowed us to understand it.

This kind of place is found in the lands of all cultures. In China, they call it a dragon's lair, symbolized by a dragon and a tiger locked in sexual intercourse. The places in China are remarkably similar to Calendar One. They have a prime source of water and usually a twin-horned peak on one horizon, comparable to Calendar One's east ridge, and a single-horned peak on another, comparable to the west ridge, which, with a saddle between, form a natural bowl. Vincent Scully refers to them as natural megarons (Scully 1962).

In the center of the bowl, two standing stones are wedged deeply into the bedrock. We interpret this device as an arrangement for positioning an observer's feet accurately. The observer could witness the equinox and solstice sunrises and sunsets from here using the natural horizon contours and standing stones. Two yards from the site, we found a firepit which we dated by Carbon-14 sample (Geochron Lab. No. GX8629) to 580 $\pm$ 130 years before AD 1950. Not far to the east of the chamber, along the line to the equinox sunrise, there is a C-shaped stone mound and an extensive pavement made with stone fragments, which was excavated by James Whittall (Mavor and Dix 1989). This carbon date is contemporary with Middle Woodland settlements at Skitchewaug, just east of Calendar One on the Connecticut River, which show definite evidence of cultivation at this period (Petersen 1978).

We started excavating Calendar One in 1978 with a cautious dismantling of part of a stone mound; we got going in earnest in 1980 with the removal of many tons of dirt and some artifacts from the chamber during an excavation that went on for three years. The chamber is oriented toward the point of sunrise on the equinox at a steep elevation of 15 degrees, as shown in Figure 9. This puts the line to the sunrise perpendicular to the back, or west, wall of the

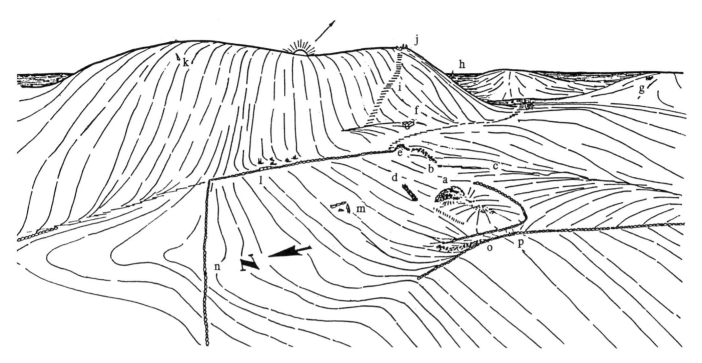

Figure 8 ISOMETRIC DRAWING OF CALENDAR ONE

chamber. The sun's rays must have passed through a gap in the roof of the chamber if they shone on the back wall, and if there was a roof. Perhaps a light box like that at New Grange and in ancient Mexican structures was utilized. The chamber is geometrically complex as shown in the drawing with oblique walls parallel to others (Figure 9).

The chamber was erected within a hole 1 m. deep quarried into bedrock by man using tailing removal tools of a type described by Fowler (1966). We found the typical three strata of soil. The bottom layer, a green material of clay-like consistency, was found within the chamber on bedrock. A consensus of geologists thought that this layer was the soil laid down just after the last glacial recession about 10,000 years ago. We don't claim that as the date of the structure, but stone artifacts were found within this green layer both inside the chamber and outside between the chamber walls and the quarried bedrock. They appeared to be magic stones placed as donations at the time of construction of the chamber. The green soil in the chamber was either placed by man to form a thin compacted floor or laid down by natural causes. In the central part of the chamber we found a tapered hole carved into the bedrock to a depth of 40 cm. The proximity of the chamber to the all-weather spring led us to consider that it might have been a sweat lodge (Mavor and Dix 1989).

During the excavation we became aware of the importance of bedrock to the people who lived there in ancient times. It seems to have been a special part of their world that required special respect. Whenever we encountered bedrock in our excavations, which was almost always, it showed signs of having been worked or of donations having been made on it. This impression is acquired

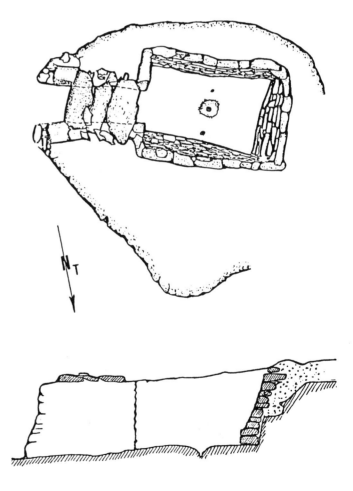

Figure 9 CALENDAR ONE STONE CHAMBER

readily in upland Vermont because the bedrock there is always near the surface.

NINETEENTH CENTURY RITUAL STONEWORK

We move on to the near-present and places where the traditions of ritual stonework continue. In Holliston, Massachusetts, there is a nearly-circular walled stone mound, on a golf course, which is 30 m. in diameter and 7 m. high containing about 5000 tons of quarried traprock (Figure 10). When we learned about this mound, we were astonished to hear that no investigation had ever been made of its origins. However, there are two prominent theories: one, that it was built by Indians; the other, that it was built by a farmer in the 1930s to make work during the depression. We attacked this problem in our customary manner. We became familiar with the landscape, we talked to local people, we examined the local cemeteries, and we read the local genealogy, history, and archaeology. In particular, we looked for evidence of astronomy.

Byron found a large perched boulder in a stone row not far from the mound. He sat on the boulder at the summer solstice and observed the setting sun rolling down the stepped edge of the mound. About a mile away there is a traprock quarry on a hilltop which fills with water in the spring. It overflows through a massive earthwork funnel to pour down the hillside and collect in a dammed-up pond. It then seeps underground to emerge around the great mound on the golf course. All about the quarry there are stone platforms, mounds, and stone rows that seemed related to the quarry. There was an underground chamber, apparently still in use.

We came across some reasonable answers to the enigma posed by the mound rather quickly, to our surprise, that is, in a couple of years. We believe that we know how the

mound was built, when it was built, and the names of some of the people involved. We have only a vague idea of why it was constructed. But most important of all, as it turned out, the investigation opened the door to 'invisible Indians,' descendants of Native Americans living among the general population, who prefer not to be recognized but who carry on many of the old traditions (Mavor and Dix 1989). Between the time of these discoveries about the mound and Byron's death, he and I visited many Indian cemeteries in New England with a view to learning more about who built the recent stone structures and why. Indian cemeteries in Massachusetts typically contain small unmarked stones and are near places having the stone mounds, stone rows, chambers, perched boulders, and the like which, in our view, characterize a Native American sacred area.

Our method was to observe the landscape ourselves, read the historical and archaeological record, and then draw our own conclusions without reference to the views of present-day Native Americans. We arrived at this procedure because we approached the subject like most western researchers, expecting patterns of consistency, and because we found differing and conflicting views among the Native Americans we met. This left us confused and uncertain but with the opinion that the ancient traditions had been lost. Later, through astronomy, becoming aware of 'invisible Indians,' and by consulting present-day Native Americans, we found that we were wrong about the traditions. They do exist, and they are inconsistent and conflicting because they are personal, local, and holistic and should be respected as such.

The great stone mound at Holliston was, in our view, built by Native Americans and Irish immigrant workers from the Miller Hill quarry about a mile away; we believe it was built as ritual landscape architecture in the mid-19th century. They used gin poles and power-driven machinery. This is such recent history that there may be living today persons who knew their ancestors who built the mound; I therefore feel it is not my place to publish any more on the subject unless the descendants request it.

We found a great many massive earthworks in the Nashoba area of Massachusetts, covering about 600 m. square (Mavor and Dix 1989). These works are accompanied by a group of stone mounds and serpentine stone banks. The entire complex reminds us of the large group of ancient, concentric, earthen banks at Poverty Point in Louisiana because of its geometry and setting at a river oxbow. Byron and I first learned of this spectacular site in 1984, when Byron detected it outlined by the contours of a USGS topographic map. Since then, we have mapped the stone and earthen works and inquired about the area's history. One representative of the owners, a large organization, confessed complete ignorance of the site, and others could find nothing of its history except evidence which showed that it was there fifty years ago. The earthworks could be a sand and gravel workings that used

Figure 10 GREAT STONE MOUND
Holliston, Massachusetts

modern earth-moving equipment, but it could also be a Native American sacred place, even inspired by Poverty Point, as suggested by comparisons of their plans (Mavor and Dix 1989). This type of problem plagues every investigation into recent sites which may be ceremonial. Not only can we expect technology to change the means of construction, but also the ceremonial and religious nature of the places.

These works may have been built between 1840 and 1870 by Native Americans working on the nearby railroad. There are many astronomical features. In Figure 11, Byron is shown sitting in an earthen bank enclosure watching the sunrise on the winter solstice over a conical earthen mound. Byron witnessed this event for three years, and, each time, he observed that someone had been there a day or two before and had built a tiny fire of twigs on top of the mound. There are other possible evidences of Native American donations in the general area: old bedsprings, whiskey bottles, rusted hardware, and milk buckets, left in special places to honor them. Near the mounds, a steel screen has been formed into a cage large enough to accommodate a sitting person. At each of the corners of its rectangular base, there is a tree about 15 years old growing up through the cage; plantings which are similar are customary in erecting Plains Indian prayer seats. There are other possible evidences of Native American involvement in this site in the form of donations.

Frank Speck wrote of caches of whiskey bottles which mark sacred places, and it has been customary among historic Indian tribes to avoid throwing things away, especially durable objects such as buckets, milk pails, bedsprings, bicycle parts, appliances, and other objects usually considered to be trash by the dominant cultures (Speck 1924, 1945). We have found a pattern throughout New England of caches of this sort of material associated with what we believe to be Indian ritual stonework and earthworks. While we cannot be sure in every case whether or not such caches are Indian donations, many are located deep in the forest far from any habitation where access could only be by foot, and they are accompanied by the familiar stone piles, rows, perched boulders, and changing natural landscape. This site is a long-term work in progress, which includes genealogical investigations of individuals connected with the site.

A large boulder at a busy intersection in Fitchburg, Massachusetts is in fragments held together by steel straps. Local people, who worked the quarry on the top of a hill overlooking the city, apparently felt that this rock, though broken apart, was so important that they gathered up its pieces, carried them down to the city, and assembled them into the shape of the original boulder. Named 'Rollstone,' the rock may have been removed from the quarry for preservation because it had been a rocking stone that was considered sacred by Native Americans (Mavor and Dix 1989). In a possibly similar case in Wrentham, a large Indian mortar was hauled to the center

of town from a site where it was associated with earthen mounds (Hoffman 1996).

Figure 11 WINTER SOLSTICE SUNSET AT NASHOBA
Byron observing over conical earthen mound

SKYWATCHING SHRINES

It seems fitting to complete this essay with a look at a different and comprehensive astronomical approach to what might have taken place at skywatching places in New England. We made a general study of both closed and open stone structures comparing those in New England, from the perspectives of architecture and natural setting, with Native American structures found throughout America. We inferred that the universality of the celestial objects would cause similar responses among geographically distant ancient people. Therefore, we reasoned, similar structures in similar settings might be expected to have similar functions. We noted that numerous stone enclosures on Cape Cod and in Foxboro and Wrentham, Massachusetts, as well as many in New Hampshire, Rhode Island, and Vermont bore a remarkable similarity to pueblo sun temples, from which astronomical observations are made (Mavor and Dix 1989).

There are specific similarities between New England structures and the sun shrines of the Tewa, Hopi, Zuni, and Anasazi in New Mexico. The sun shrines are still used there to tune the agriculturalists and hunters into the cycles of the sky (Mavor 1994). Archaeological surveys in New Mexico suggest that there may be hundreds of shrines associated with prehistoric pueblo ruins (Dougherty

1980). Our surveys of New England imply a similar density of shrines. New Mexico has 'world shrines,' which are larger than most shrines; they are located in places which have particularly spectacular distant mountain-peak and valley horizons all around, thus providing suitable markers from which to observe many celestial events and festival dates. Unlike New England landscapes, those in the west are not obscured by trees. In Arizona, the Pima, mentioned previously, draw shamanic power from the distant mountains surrounding their shrines. We can expect the same practice at the Anasazi shrines of New Mexico.

Figure 12 BOULDER RING IN MASSACHUSETTS
Possible skywatching shrine

Aside from these architectural comparisons, Byron and I were struggling with the concept of 'invisible Indians.' Repeatedly, we saw subtle evidence of recent ritual use of stone and earthen structures and, in the case of Holliston and Stow, Massachusetts, evidence that ritual stone mounds, rows, and earthworks were built during the 19th century. We inferred from this that there exists both a recent as well as present-day network of ritual activity that is not generally known and may have several explanations.

I have been studying New England coastal structures which may be sunshrines and considering the possibility that the astronomical observations that were made from them were more elaborate than heretofore believed. In fact, they may have been comparable to those in the west at which the sun, stars, moon, planets, supernovas, and eclipses were observed. I have postulated that coastal sites in New England, where views are unobstructed by the typical densely-wooded landscape, might not only offer an opportunity to broaden one's perspectives in experiencing these special places, but also offer a means to test the hypothesis that the New England sites were as expressive of a comprehensive cosmology as those in New Mexico and elsewhere.

We have discussed at least three ways to locate celestial events on the horizon which could be used for building calendars or myths. We can use fixed markers on the land as reference points for the positions of rising and setting of the sun, moon, stars, and planets. We can observe heliacal events referred to fixed markers on the horizon. We discussed heliacal events at the Upton stone chamber previously. We can observe the dates of stellar, heliacal events, and the positions of stars on the horizon referred to other stars, the constellations, and the sun (Figure 7).

We have chosen a site, in Falmouth, Massachusetts, which is representative of many in southeastern Massachusetts. It is located on a small, level, earthen platform near and projecting from the top of a hill elevated 30 m. above sea level. It overlooks the ocean where promontories and islands provide horizon markers that can be used for astronomical events. The observation place has a boulder circle (Lat. 41°, 32' N; Long. 70°, 39' W) about 2 m. in diameter built tangent to and integral with a stone row oriented to 42° true (Figure 12). Nearby, there are an embrasure (local diversion in stone row), a manitou stone in a row (Mavor and Dix 1989), a group of four stone mounds, and true west of the boulder ring a 60 cm. diameter stone circle that has been used as a hearth. There are at least four alignments to fixed markers on the land horizon. The equinox sunset is marked precisely by the small, center island of a vernal pool that seems to have been ritualized by stonework. I calculated that in AD 1150 ± 100, the rising of the bright southern star Fomalhaut occurred at a distant seacliff and that its setting occurred at a hilltop identified by a straight stone row pointing from the boulder ring. The rising of the bright northern star Vega occurred over a greater range of dates but included those above, again at the point where a straight stone row leading from the ring meets the horizon.

If we take a larger view of the eastern panorama from the stone ring, we notice a striking feature, symmetry of the whole horizon about the bluff at East Chop on Martha's Vineyard Island, where Fomalhaut rose in AD 1150. On the left, or north, a stone row extends from the shrine (by our definition we can properly call this stone ring a shrine regardless of when it was used or by whom) to a hilltop where Vega, the brightest star in the constellation Lyra, rose in AD 1150. The row extends past the shrine to the southwest to another hilltop where Fomalhaut, the brightest star in Pisces Australis, set. The East Chop bluff marks the exact mid-point of the angle between the two rows. To the north of East Chop, there is ocean, and to the south, there is land. The Cape Cod bluff marks the rise of Aldebaran, the brightest star in Taurus. If we follow the horizon from the point of Alcyone rise, the brightest Pleiad, south over the sea, from Aldebaran to Fomalhaut, we encounter the stars Rigel, Sirius, and Antares, respectively the brightest stars in Orion, Canis Major, and Scorpius. The entire eastern part of the horizon

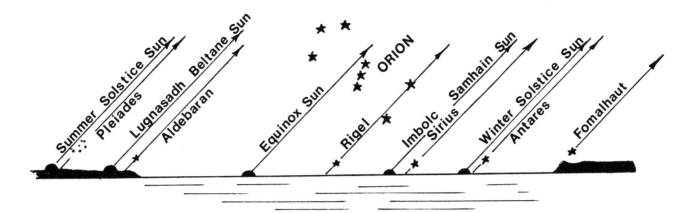

Figure 13 PARTIAL EASTERN HORIZON FROM MASSACHUSETTS BOULDER RING

Table I FOURTEEN CALENDRICAL RISE EVENTS (AD 1150)
All except Vega are shown in Figure 13.

EVENT	STELLAR FIRST RISING* or SUNRISE	TRUE AZIMUTH	MARKER
Vega rise	November 10	41°	stone row
Summer solstice sunrise	June 21	57	near sea cliff
Pleiades rise	June 6	62	near sea cliff
Beltane sunrise	May 6	67	near sea cliff
Lugnasadh sunrise	August 7	67	near sea cliff
Aldebaran rise	June 11	71	at sea cliff
Equinox sunrise	March 21, September 23	90	sea horizon
Rigel rise	July 9	103	sea horizon
Imbolc sunrise	February 4	112	sea horizon
Samhain sunrise	November 8	112	sea horizon
Sirius rise	July 31	111	sea horizon
Winter solstice sunrise	December 21	123	sea horizon
Antares rise	November 30	123	sea horizon
Fomalhaut rise	May 2	137.58	at sea cliff

* See earlier discussion in section titled HELIACAL PHENOMENA.

between northeast and southwest can be organized into a calendar using the heliacal rise dates of these six stars. They extend from early May to the end of July, and then again within November. The panorama lies between the two major hills of the horizon and is bisected between land and sea by the rising of Fomalhaut. Table I and Figure 13 summarize these and other relevant rise data for the sun and stars.

By way of comparison with other American archaeo-astronomical sites, some of the medicine wheels in the Rocky Mountains comprise calendars based on the dates of first rising before sunrise (heliacal) of the stars Fomal-haut, Sirius, Rigel, and Aldebaran, which are about thirty days apart. Some medicine wheels are dated to the same epoch as the Massachusetts site (Eddy 1974; Robinson 1980, 1981). But a calendar based on the dates of first or last rising or setting of stars does not require precise alignments to star positions. It requires only enough orientation for the stars to be identified as they rise or set and the ability to count days to the nearest solar event. These medicine wheel remains imply that more stellar alignments were probably used to complete a calendar of 12 or 13 months. The skywatching shamans tell us that sky-watching is an old religious response. It is not a by-product of culture but a basic maker of culture (Krupp 1983).

Applying these inferences to the southeastern Mass-achusetts site reveals that, indeed, Sirius, Rigel, and Aldebaran—which were chosen at the medicine wheels because they rise first heliacally about thirty days apart—appear on the horizon at positions which make them easily recognized by their place with respect to observed horizon markers on the land. I identified a total of twenty-one alignments on the landscape of the Massachusetts site: four are physically in place with a suggested date of AD 1150; seventeen are postulated as likely, but marked by the positions of other celestial bodies and events having cyclic behavior. In Table I, it can be seen that the Pleiades, Aldebaran, equinox sunrise, Rigel, Sirius, Antares, and Fomalhaut all have rising positions along the eastern sea and land horizon with six intervals between. In addition, the four places of rising on the horizon of four of these stars are paired with solar events: the Pleiades rise close to summer solstice rise; Aldebaran rises with Lugnasadh and Beltane sunrise; Sirius with Imbolc and Samhain sunrise; and Antares with winter solstice sunrise. I suggest the use of these elements of the eight-part solar calendar here because it is used by New England Wabanaki Indians; I also use the ancient Celtic names for four dates on the calendar to remind us of the universality of these events.

The case is not proven by these particular postulated alignments, nor is it intended to be. But they do suggest that we should look for more astronomical alignments in New England than just sunrises and sunsets. Twenty-one alignments from the observation point to a horizon marker on the land are not unusual for a Tewa or Hopi shrine in the Southwest. Traditions hold that many more were used in the past. Some involved more subtle astronomical events on the horizon or higher in the sky, and may have been observed using only star maps memorized by the skywatchers as a reference, with no markers on the land. Even those who have been studying ancient astronomy may have limited their understanding unnecessarily by concentrating on proven, intentional astronomical sightlines. Archaeologists who do not consider astronomical thought are likely to be omitting an important aspect of past cultures.

There is a fallacy in the view that if a 20th-century man can't understand these concepts, how could they have been understood 4000 years ago? However, Wood (1978) supplies a possible answer: "The complexity of modern scientific papers is in order to test hypotheses . . . . The techniques that were developed (by ancient man) for laying out and measuring geometrical shapes could have been very simple."

In New Mexico and Arizona, the sun priests, or observers, and the organizers of ritual dance are the sacred clowns; among the Rio Grande pueblos, they are members of the Koshare clan. So far as is known, social organization in New England's Woodland period, before contact with Europeans, was quite different from that in the Southwest. It had a looser clan structure than the sedentary southwestern cultures, and there were no hereditary positions. But, since the tradition of stone and earthen works, as well as observational astronomy, has been forgotten, or gone underground, and archaeology does not recognize it, the social structures connected with this tradition may have disappeared. There may remain one intercultural connection, however, the sacred clowns, who, oral tradition states, still exist and hold leadership positions in ceremonial matters among the Micmac of the northeastern United States and Canada. And there is an artifact that suggests a possible presence of the Koshare clan in Vermont.

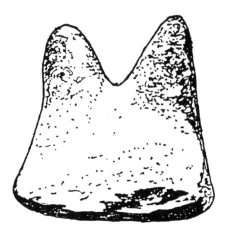

Figure 14a KOSHARE SYMBOL STONE
Found at prehistoric Tewa Pueblo (Barnett 1973)

Figure 14b STONE FOUND AT **J** OF CALENDAR ONE
Center stone of a group of fallen standing stones
(See Figure 8)

A worked piece of basalt was found in a pueblo ruin in the Chama valley of New Mexico. It was in the shape of a two-horned headdress, the symbol of the Koshare clan, and used at meetings of the fraternity (Barnett 1973) (Figure 14a). We mentioned standing stones in our earlier discussion of Calendar One; we once excavated a group of fallen standing stones at the southern end of the east ridge. One stone was 2 m. long and had originally been set upright in a notch in the bedrock. This point, called **J** in Figure 8, is the highest elevation at Calendar One, and also features a notched stone marking the equinox sunrise as viewed from the stone chamber in the bowl. It is clearly the most prominent place in Calendar One with a distant mountain view all around (Mavor and Dix 1989). At the center of the group of recumbent standing stones, we excavated a piece of stone, shown here in Figure 14b, which is identical in form to the Koshare symbol. This correspondence suggests a possible connection between the two cultures. It also implies that the group of recumbent standing stones may be a collapsed skywatching shrine (Figure 14c).

CONCLUSIONS

I have cited the astronomical traditions of the Native Americans of New Mexico because their traditions are well-known among non-Indians and are still practiced by the pueblo Indians. I have also cited the medicine wheels of the ancient Plains Indians because their natural environment provides the means for investigating similar skywatching structures in New England.

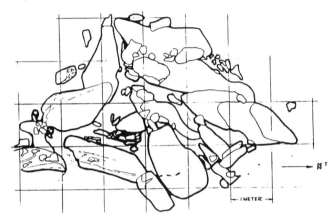

Figure 14c GROUP OF FALLEN STANDING STONES
East ridge, Calendar One
(Mavor and Dix 1989)

It would be unreasonable to expect that practices of a universal nature would exist all over North America except in New England where most knowledge of the shrines and detailed knowledge of the sky seem to have been lost. But ceremonies remain, and their framework implies a much greater reliance on the sky in the past than today.[2] Calendars were probably only stepping stones to the main reasons for watching the sky. They led to the seeking of visions and the creation of myths, which in turn helped to transform the awesome scale of the cosmos to the dimensions of everyday experience.

END NOTES

1. This chapter began with a lecture at the *America Before Columbus* Conference at Brown University in 1992. Byron Dix and I gave one of our customary joint illustrated 'happenings' which we hoped would produce more than twice the effect of one speaker; they were always spontaneous except for the choice of slides and the title. Byron died in April, 1993, and I was asked to produce an essay for the *NEARA Journal* based on our presentation. I concluded that a verbatim transcript would not convey its spirit. Instead, I summarized the main points of the lecture, retained 'we' in the present tense and added thoughts of mine that we might have had were we still working together. This paper is a revision of that essay, also authored by the spirit of Byron Dix and myself, that has been brought up-to-date with both corrections and additional material, carefully reviewed and, I hope, clarified.

2. The Wampanoag lunar calendar of thirteen moons is described by Bingham (1970). It is marked by events such as planting, growing of crops, harvesting, fishing, freezing and thawing. gkisedtanamoogk outlines a Wampanoag ceremonial calendar based on the sun and stars as well as the moon. Most of the ceremonies of the thirteen month calendar are for *Weachamin*, mother of all vegetation, who is helped by Grandmother Moon and Mother Earth. A four-day ceremony in the spring during planting time is followed by a ceremony for the grown plants. Later, a first-berry ceremony is celebrated at the summer solstice. The Green Corn ceremony occurs in September, and, also in September, the hunting ceremonies start. These involve the spirits of Bear, Deer, and Moose. At this time there is the harvest and the honoring of spiritual leaders and Creator. Many festivals occur around the time of the vernal equinox. These include the Feeding of Ancestors, Sap Flowing, Return of the Fish. The Moon ceremony begins at this time also and marks the awakening of Mother and the New Year.

There are many ceremonies, and ceremonies within ceremonies, at the winter solstice. One is the Sweat Lodge ceremony which begins with the first new moon after the group of stars known as Elders in the Sky is above us at sunset. There are ceremonies for the New Moon and Full Moon, and for the Star Nations or constellations.

There are four main directions and four phases of the seasons, marked by the sunset, sunrise, sun directly above and directly below, at the June and December solstices and spring and fall equinoxes. The circumstance of the sun being directly overhead, when mentioned in northern latitudes, must have been learned from people to the south, for the actual event occurs only in the tropics. There are several numbers that are important in the ceremonies. They include 3, 4, 7, 8, and 10. The Wabanaki recognize an eight-part calendar, which was also known in other parts of the world in ancient times, perhaps as much as thousands of years ago. The Wampanoag ceremonial calendar also includes many ceremonies for events and beings that non-Indians would consider non-religious, ceremonies for people and events of all kinds reflecting the sacredness of all things (gkisedtanamoogk 1993).

REFERENCES

Aveni, Anthony
   1972 Astronomical tables intended for use in astro-archaeological studies. *American Antiquity* 37(4).
Barnett, Franklin
   1973 *Dictionary of Prehistoric Indian Artfacts of the American Southwest*. Flagstaff: Northland.
Bingham, Amelia G.
   1970 *Mashpee, Land of the Wampanoag*. Mashpee: Mashpee Historical Commission.

Bruin, Frans
1979 The heliacal setting of the stars and planets. *Proceedings of the Koninkijke Nederlandse Akademia van Wetenschappen*. Amsterdam: North Holland.

Bruin, Frans and A. Vondjidis
1971 *The Books of Autolykos*. American University of Beirut.

Cassidy, Vincent H.
1968 *The Sea Around Them*, p. 78. Baton Rouge: The Louisiana State University.

Cronon, William
1983 *Changes in the Land*. New York: Hill and Wang.

de Santillana, George and Hertha von Dechend
1969 *Hamlet's Mill*. New York: MacMillan.

Dix, Byron E. and James W. Mavor, Jr.
1980 Possible astronomical alignments, date and origin of the Pearson stone chamber. *Early Sites Research Society Bulletin* 8(1):3-16.

Dougherty, Julia D.
1980 *An Archaeological Evaluation of Tsiping Ruin*. Albuquerque NM: USDA, Forest Service.

Eddy, John
1974 *Science* 184:1035.

Emerson, J. Norman
1960 The Puckasaw Pits and the religious alternative. *Ontario History* 52(1):71, 72.

Fowler, William S.
1966 The Horne Hill soapstone quarry. *Bulletin of Massachusetts Archaeological Society* 27(2):17.

gkisedtanamoogk and Frances Hancock
1993 *Anoqcou: Ceremony is Life Itself*. Portland ME: Astarte Shell.

Haviland, William A. and Marjory W. Power
1981 *The Original Vermonters*, p. 6. Hanover: University of Vermont.

Hoffman, Curtiss
1988 Radiocarbon dates for Massachusetts: An annotated list. *Bulletin of Massachusetts Archaeological Society* 49(1):31.
1996 Personal communication. September 21.

Hoskinson, Tom
1992 Saguaro wine, ground figures, and power mountains: Investigations at Sears Point, Arizona. In *Earth and Sky*. Ray Williamson and Claire Farrar, eds. Albuquerque: University of New Mexico.

Johnstone, Paul
1980 *The Sea-Craft of Prehistory*, pp. 40, 221. Cambridge: Harvard University Press.

Kehoe, Alice B. and Thomas F. Kehoe
1979 *Solstice Alignment Boulder Configuration in Saskatchewan*. Ottawa: National Museum of Canada.

Kroeber, A. L.
1976 *Handbook of the Indians of California*. New York: Dover.

Krupp, E. C.
1983 *Echoes of the Ancient Skies*. New York: Harper and Row.

Lockyer, N.
1894 *The Dawn of Astronomy*. London: Cassell.

Maris Multimedia
1994 *Redshift*. London: Multimedia Astronomy Computer Program.

Marshak, Alexander
1972 *The Roots of Civilization*, p. 12. New York: McGraw-Hill.

Mavor, James W., Jr.
1994 *New Mexican Sun Shrines Compared With Stone Structures of New England*. Meeting of Early Sites Research Society. Newburyport, Massachusetts, January.
1985 Astronomy and shamanism among the Culdee monks. *Early Sites Research Society Bulletin* 12(1).

Mavor, James W., Jr. and Byron E. Dix
1983 New England stone mounds as ritual architecture. *Early Sites Research Society Bulletin* 10(2):8.
1989 *Manitou*. Rochester VT: Inner Traditions International.

Noble, William C.
1968 Vision pits, cairns and petroglyphs at Rock Lake, Algonquian Park, Ontario. *Ontario Archaeology* 11:63.

Patterson, Willliam and Kenneth E. Sassaman
1988 Indian fires in the prehistory of New England. Pp. 107-136 in *Holocene Ecology in Northeastern North America*. New York: Plenum.

Petersen, James
1978 *Aboriginal Ceramics in the Connecticut River Valley*. Typescript on file, Department of Anthropology, University of Vermont, Burlington.

Powers, Stephen
1976 *Tribes of California*. Berkeley: University of California.

Robinson, Jack H.
1980 Fomalhaut and Cairn D at the Big Horn and Moose Mountain Medicine Wheels. *Archaeoastronomy* III(4):15.
1981 Astronomical alignments of the Fort Smith Medicine Wheel. *Archaeoastronomy* IV(3):14.

Scully, Vincent
1962 *The Earth, The Temple, and the Gods*. New Haven: Yale University.

Simmons, William S.
1970 *Cautantowit's House*. Providence: Brown University.

Speck, Frank G.
1924 Native tribes and dialects of Connecticut, a Mohegan diary. *American Bureau of Ethnology*, No. 43. Smithsonian Institution.
1945 The memorial brush heaps in Delaware and elsewhere. *Bulletin: Archaeological Society of Delaware* 4(17).

Tarrow, S.
1970 Translation of the Cellere Codex. In *The Voyages of Giovanni da Verrazzano*. L. C. Wroth, ed. New Haven: Yale University.

Taylor, E. G. R.
1971 *The Haven Finding Art*. New York: Elsevier.

Timreck, Ted
1987 *Secrets of the Lost Red Paint People*. Boston: NOVA TV Documentary.

Williamson, Ray A.
1984 *Living the Sky*, p. 165. Boston: Houghton and Mifflin.

Willoughby, Charles
1935 *Antiquities of the New England Indians*, p. 23. Cambridge: Harvard University.

Wood, John Edwin
1978 *Sun, Moon and Standing Stones*. Oxford: Oxford University.

An Ancient Solar Observatory
at Willow Creek, California

JOHN H. RUDOLPH

BACKGROUND

Credit for discovery of the summer solstice sunrise alignment effect at Willow Creek (CA-LAS 32) belongs to Professor Robert E. Connick and his wife, Dr. Frances Connick, of Berkeley CA, who presented a paper at the AURA International Congress on Rock Art at Darwin, Australia in 1988. We heard the presentation there, and we visited the site with Professor Connick on June 20, 21, and 22, 1989, to witness the solstice event. The Connicks had discovered this alignment in the 1960s but had not made their discovery public until the 1988 conference. They have produced two excellent papers on the site, one on the solar alignment event, *A Summer Solstice Petroglyph Site;* the other on the variety of petroglyphs in the area, *Varieties of Petroglyphs and Implications For Their Use and Chronology at Willow Creek Near Susanville* (CA-LAS 32).[1]

This paper has been prepared to record new information about the site subsequent to the Connicks' discovery, namely: the summer solstice sunset event; the autumnal equinox sunrise alignment; the autumnal equinox sunset event; the confirmation of the fifty-nine-day summer solstice prediction event; the sun light-shaft illuminating the top circle of the 'sun/moon gauge' (formerly called the 'tree glyph'); and the light finger moving into and across the 'super-pi' glyph.

INTRODUCTION
The Cosmos

Early man was imbedded in nature in a way that we are not. He observed the phenomena of the stars and the constellations, the sun, the moon, the planets, and special celestial events. These early people did not perceive the sky as we understand it. To them, the sky was an entity filled with powerful and threatening forces (Marshack 1972; Mayer 1975; Hudson 1984; and Brennan 1983).

Cultural Context

The seasons were of both pragmatic and mystical concern; they were observed; notations were made, and means were devised for prediction. It has been found that hunter-gatherers, in this case the early people of California, had the need and obtained the knowledge and sophistication to record, memorialize, and predict the celestial events that marked the seasons. Undoubtedly, ceremonies and celebrations were held on the occasions of seasonal importance. To the early people, the sky was a place populated with powerful beings who competed and struggled with each other. The outcome of these struggles could have dire or beneficial consequences for humankind. The native peoples could help stave off disaster and maintain the cosmic balance by performing certain ceremonies at the proper time of the year. It was crucial to them, apparently, to know when the solar year began (Hudson and Underhay 1978).

The Indian tribes found in this general area on the invasion of the white man in the 1850s were: the Northern Maidu (northeastern dialect); the Northern Paiute (Uto-Aztecan); the Atsugewi (Hokan family); the Shasta; the Wintu; the Yana; the Nomlaki; the Konkow and the Achomawi (Hokan family) (Heizer and Whipple 1951; Hudson 1984). (Refer to Figure 1, next page.)

Alfred Kroeber's 1925 work, *Handbook of the Indians of California*, discusses some of the methods Indians used to keep track of time and the seasons earlier in this century. For instance, we find:

> The Maidu calendar recognizes 12 lunations with more or less descriptive epithets. It opens in spring, appears to contain *no clear reference to the solstices*, and to possess no fixed points. There is no mention of a device for correction, and it may be presumed that the Maidu dispensed with any, leaving a lunation unnamed whenever their moons ran too far ahead of the year as determined by seasonal events. . . . On the whole, *a more distinctly unastronomical calendar than that of the Maidu can hardly be imagined.* . . . Four seasons were recognized by the Maidu . . . Spring: . . . flowers. Summer: . . . earth, dust, or dry. Autumn: . . . seeds, or acorn bread. Winter: . . . snow (Kroeber 1925:437, 439; JHR italics).

The Northern Paiute were part of the Uto-Aztecan family . . . the California Paiutes are better to be known as Shoshonean distributed from Oregon to Southern Mexico. The culture was generally poverty stricken (in California) due to the difficulty of keeping alive on the high plateau country. No references to calendar or seasons could be found regarding the Paiutes (Kroeber 1925).

William R. Palmer, University President and official of Cedar City, Utah, collected stories from the Paiutes. Many of these stories indicate a great knowledge of practical astronomy according to Nal Morris (Morris 1995).

In the 'Knowledge and Beliefs' section of his 1942 work on cultural elements, Ermine Voeglin recorded the contemporary observing habits of many tribes. The Atsugewi "Cut off knot each day to measure number of days which have elapsed, in order to know when to attend celebration" (Voeglin 1942:234/4423). As for the Western Atsugewi, they:

> Watch where sun rises for shortest day; know when shadow is at certain place sun is going to 'back up' and that it will snow. . . . Watch where light strikes on center post of living house or sweat house, but no marks on pole. . . . Mainly watch shadow from Soldier Mt. ("it goes to Jim Hunt's place") for solstices (Voeglin 1942:234/4436, 4450, 4451).

Among the Western Shasta:

> Every village had marks for observation. . . . Year begins in winter solstice, when for 2-3 days the sun rises and sets over the same marks (in the large assembly house) . . . there are flat rocks, set around base of center post; the shadow from post . . . is observed and note taken of where it falls on rocks at base of post . . . but for ordinary places, people watch where sun rises and sets between certain trees. (Informant now uses mark on board by his door . . .) Years counted from 1 winter solstice to next. Rising of Pleiades, morning star, especially observed (Voeglin 1942:234/4436, 4437, 4439a, 4450, 4451).

As for the Eastern Shasta, "Marks made on center pole of assembly house with chalk" (Voeglin 1942:234/4450). Among the Valley Maidu:

> Old woman . . . keeps 1 variety of seed after another in finely netted bag, and eats different sort each month. . . . variety of seeds she has in sack . . . often settles argument [among men about month] (Voeglin 1942:234/4443).

The Middle Wintu determined two solstices:

> Old men watch where sun rises over certain rocks or trees every morning throughout year; also observe where sun sets. . . . During solstices sun stays for 3 days, oscillating . . . on third morning it looks around and is ready to go N or S, depending on time of year (Voeglin 1942:234/4457, 4447).

The Southern Wintu, however, observe only the winter solstice because people ". . . want spring to come; don't bother about summer solstice" (Voeglin 1942:234/4447).

The above excerpts from Kroeber and Voeglin give the impression that the tribes of northeast California were rather unsophisticated about celestial events. But Hudson and Underhay (1978), Hudson (1984), and Mayer (1975,

1977) present convincing evidence that these and other California tribes, or their predecessors, were indeed very knowledgeable and sophisticated about astronomical observations. Hudson describes a complex philosophical and mythical framework involving celestial objects, people, and other beings, with rituals to maintain the cosmic balance involving the sun, the moon, certain stars, and constellations. Hudson cites evidence that eclipses could be predicted. An elite group developed to observe, record, interpret, and conduct ritual activities to assure proper interaction of the society and the gods (Hudson 1984). Mayer shows petroglyphs that match constellations and makes a convincing case for the acceptance of Miller's hypo-

Figure 1 TRIBAL TERRITORIES IN CALIFORNIA (Hudson 1984)

thesis that petroglyphs throughout the southwest recorded the supernova event of AD 1054 (Mayer 1977).

Other sites in the west demonstrate early man's need and capacity to measure, note, and record the various seasonal events. At Parawan Gap, Utah, Nal Morris has been investigating an elaborate and ingenious arrangement of cairns, light/shadow alignments, glyphs, and systems of counting to achieve precise determination of salient events of the year (Morris 1995). At Little Blue Table, Idaho, well-marked 'stations' where the horizon features were watched have been verified as sun-watching positions to determine the various seasonal points of importance.

It is clear that the people of these cultures "needed to

know not only where they were in place, but also in time" (Morris 1994). They had 'appointments' to keep with migrating game animals, ripening plants, roots, berries, seeds, and nuts as well as with other members of their tribe who spread out across the landscape for hundreds, perhaps thousands, of square miles of essentially trackless territory over the course of a year.

Cultural Conclusion

The various Indian tribes in the area of northern California (Atsugewi, Achomawi, Maidu, Wintu, Paiute and Shasta) (Figure 1) seem to have kept track of the seasons in various informal ways. In fact, the indigenous people living in the area in the 1800s, while noting the change of seasons, did not carry on the intense and meticulous observations indicated by the sophistication of the Willow Creek Observatory. It appears that the tribes present at the time of contact with the Europeans were late-comers to the area and that other people were the ones who used and embellished the Willow Creek site, possibly at a very early time. Alternatively, the tribes present in the 1800s could have been the direct descendants of the earlier people, but the traditions of acute astronomical observation could have degraded over time.

Throughout California, according to Hudson (1984), the hunter-gatherer tribes developed cultural, religious, mythic, and practical involvement in the celestial events with considerable sophistication.

It is worth noting that the most elaborate, carefully drawn and inscribed glyphs associated with alignments at Willow Creek seem to be the oldest. Later glyphs, although repeating many of the same symbols as those found in the earlier engravings, are less carefully done; they are not as deep and, in many cases, are merely marks scratched through the desert varnish. This suggests the possibility that the knowledge of and commitment to astronomical observation and recording was brought into the area from elsewhere and, over time, faded in practice and content.

At this point, there has been no attempt to date these glyphs with any of the scientific methods available. It is possible that the oldest of the carvings are very old. A site near Lakeview, Oregon, has revealed a portion of an escarpment of basalt covered with closely-packed glyphs, including a glyph of concentric circles. This panel of glyphs has been concealed by drifted soil, and the lower portion runs down *below* a layer of Mt. Mazama ash (now Crater Lake) indicating that this panel of glyphs, presumably covering the one hundred and twenty foot long cliff-face, was created prior to 4750 BC (Cannon and Ricks 1986). The connection to Willow Creek is tentative at this time.

Geographical Context

The Willow Creek site is situated in the northeast section of the state of California in the Great Basin area. A well-known petroglyph site, designated as CA-LAS 32,

it is north of Susanville CA, at 40.469° N, 120.44° W, about sixty miles east of Mt. Lassen volcano. The site is marked on USGS topographical maps as "petroglyphs."

Local Environment and Site

The country is high desert plateau with sage and rabbit bush mixed with sparse grass and occasional junipers and pines. The climate is dry, cold in winter, and hot in the summer. The desert floor is littered with basalt boulders and stones weathered out of the underlying lava floor. Honey Lake can be glimpsed to the south and is still a considerable body of water. It is much diminished from its size when the climate was wetter at the close of the last glaciation and when man perhaps first entered this area. Elevation is approximately 1300 m. (4275 feet).

The subject site is located on the eastern rim of Willow Creek Canyon in an outcropping of basalt that forms a ridge running generally northeast to southwest, rising about thirty feet above the surrounding plateau, and dropping about two hundred feet into the canyon on the west side. Two natural caves in the outcropping, one facing northeast and the other facing southwest, are the principal features of interest at the site. The main events observed are the summer solstice sunrise and sunset events, the autumnal equinox sunrise and sunset events, and the summer solstice predictor event.

Procedure

To record the petroglyphs accurately, I employed photography, video, and rubbing. For the latter, I used sheets of TYVEK, a DuPont product, taped to the rock face with the all-purpose 'duct-tape.' India ink was dabbed on a small bag of muslin filled with local grass, using a kitchen sponge as a reservoir. Too much ink smeared the surface of the TYVEK, but a partially dry muslin bag, rubbed vigorously across the surface, brought out the pattern of the rock carving with startling accuracy. Subtle details were revealed which were invisible to both eye and camera. This procedure protected the petroglyph from any abrasion, no ink soaked through the TYVEK onto the rock, and neither TYVEK nor ink touched the bottom of any glyph.

THE SUNRISE CHAMBER

North End Environs

The north end of the outcropping, which contains the 'Sunrise Chamber' (Figure 2), is heavily embellished with petroglyphs, all diagrammatic or geometric in nature. There are only two depictions of humans, and only one figure of an animal and one of a 'bird' can be found in the area. Directly above the entrance, and above the aperture that admits sunlight during the summer solstice, is a pecked vertical line painted with red ochre.

Figure 2 SUNRISE CHAMBER ENTRANCE

'Signboard'

There is a distinctive panel of glyphs above the entrance (Figures 3, 4). Some, like the deeply-pecked vertical line directly over the Sunrise Chamber light opening, are painted with red ochre. The crossed square on the left, according to Moran and Kelley (1969), is an ancient Chinese symbol for 'field,' 'world,' and by extension, 'the universe,' but in this context it may represent

Figure 3 SUNRISE CHAMBER 'SIGNBOARD'
Above entrance

the year with four seasons. There are two small circles adjacent to this glyph, connected with short lines, possibly symbolizing the sun and the moon. The next symbol to the right is not completely clear, but the photograph and the rubbing show a vertical line rising from a small circle with several horizontal branches. A long horizontal line caps the stem, curling into a small circle on the right and looping around and down on the left to return to the small circle at the base. Over this figure runs a horizontal serpentine.

Farther to the right, there appear to be two vertical red ochre lines followed by a very prominent pecked and red-painted oval pierced by a vertical line. This latter is similar

to the Chinese sign for ". . . middle or center, which the Chinese have used as the symbol for their country since 680 BC to this day" (Lindqvist 1989). Some similar glyphs are interpreted as atlatls, others are called 'phi' signs. This glyph is painted with red ochre, which seems to have protected the engraving from weathering, as the neighboring rock is now almost flush with the left side of the painted engraving; the weathering has made the rubbing indistinct even though the red ochre makes the figure very clear. The stem is shown by the rubbing to turn back on itself just as it does in a similar glyph at CA-INY 272 (Schmidt 1992). This panel of glyphs looks like a signboard announcing the importance and, possibly, the authorship of the earliest work at the site (Figures 3, 4). The ochre appears to be very old, but this should be verified by scientific analysis if possible. It is impossible to determine who carved the glyph or who applied the red ochre or when.

The Approach to the Sunrise Chamber

On the approach to the entrance, there are two boulders protruding from the ground with inscriptions that are not yet understood but are clearly not depictions of animals. Outside the entrance on the right is a large (four-ton) block of stone that has fallen over from its original position

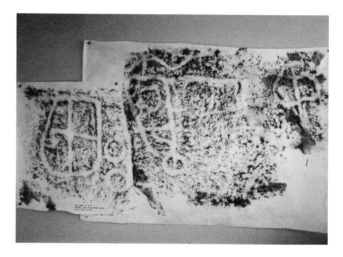

Figure 4 RUBBING OF THE 'SIGNBOARD'

(Figure 5). We determined by measurement that this stone was originally upright but separated from the larger block immediately to the south. Petroglyphs can be seen running down and underneath it where it would be impossible to peck them today. Those that can be seen on the under surface consist of zigzag lines and concentric circles. The rubbing reveals much that cannot be seen with eye or camera (Figure 6).

Adjacent to this stone is the larger block, mentioned above, still standing in place to the south. The top is deeply inscribed and heavily eroded, the glyphs being eroded down at the same rate as the surrounding surface. To the right of the chamber entrance and above the fallen stone, the rock face is covered with carefully designed and deeply inscribed

Figure 5 FORMER TOP OF FALLEN STONE
To the right of Sunrise Chamber entrance

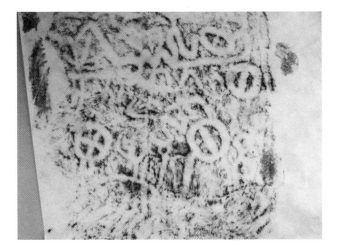

Figure 6 RUBBING OF STONE IN FIGURE 5

glyphs (Figure 7). The concentric circles on each of the rock's lower edge may be sun symbols. They may have come from the appearance of the sun with its aurora and halo rings. The circles are connected by a short line and seem to signify "here is the place that the sun turns the corner." Above are six connected circles that could represent a constellation, possibly the Pleiades. These symbols are drawn in the same way that both Chinese and Aztec constellations were drawn (Moran and Kelley 1969; Aveni 1980).

Above the entrance at the top of the basalt outcrop on an irregular, but generally horizontal surface, is a panel of glyphs having a serpentine figure with twelve turnings plus a smaller lobe (which may indicate an understanding that some years contain more than twelve full moons) connected to a circle with a dot in the center. There is a line through six of these loops. This may represent the cycles of the Lunar year as seen in similar glyphs at Newgrange (Brennan 1983). The other glyph in this panel is a circle connected to a wavy line from which lines extend to loops or circles. A small serpentine comes in from the right around the first-mentioned circle heading the lobed

serpentine (Figure 8).

To the west of the entrance is a large boulder with a sloping, slightly concave face directed easterly, covered with a complex of glyphs. Nearer the entrance on the south face of an angular boulder is a petroglyph which is completely invisible except when struck by a tangent beam of sunlight. Four circles set in a vertical row, connected by a line, are closely associated with another vertical line; that line has a circle at each end and a short crossbar at midpoint which has a 'lobe' at each end. These may be representations of constellations, Andromeda on the left, Cygnus on the right, both of which set in the northwest, the direction one looks when viewing this glyph (Figure 9).

Figure 7 INSCRIBED ROCK FACE
Outside Sunrise Chamber entrance

The carvings at this site appear to cover a broad range of time, as some are almost completely weathered away and cannot be seen unless the light strikes at a tangent to the rock face; others are very clear and seem to be almost new, being lightly pecked through the desert varnish. The latter are done more crudely but reflect many of the same motifs as the more ancient-appearing carvings.

Connick and Connick (ms) describe these variations and discuss the petroglyphs in their paper mentioned above. They classify them as "Great Basin Abstract: VULGARIS, being lightly pecked through the rock surface and hardly patinated; PROMINENT, being deeply carved and somewhat patinated; and CLASSIC, being deeply carved, carefully made and heavily patinated, weathered and eroded." While these classifications are helpful in cataloging the glyphs, they do not give us a clue as to what they mean or what purpose they served for the people who made and used them. It is my belief that the petroglyphs at this site are associated with the use of the site and, therefore, are astronomical in content and meaning. Some seem to be markers and gauges; some seem to be symbols of the sun, the moon, and constellations.

Figure 8   VERTICAL VIEW OF 12½-LOBED SERPENTINE

Several glyphs west of the main ridge of basalt had not been scrutinized by me prior to 1995. I believed that there were no figures of human beings (anthropomorphs) or animals (zoomorphs) except for the bird glyph in the sunrise chamber at the site. However, on a large pinnacle standing away from the main escarpment, there are several impressive glyphs. Two circles with crosses mark the top of this rock on a facet that faces northeast. A group of glyphs seen best from a small ledge to the south of the pinnacle consists of a three-ring concentric beside which, and touching, is the figure of a person with upraised arms. To the left of that is a sharply-carved five-fingered glyph

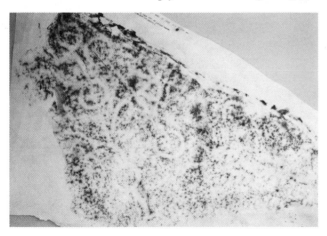

Figure 9   STONE TO WEST OF FALLEN STONE
Rubbing of south face

resembling a hand, but clearly not a hand. Nal Morris suggests that this design, found in many sites throughout the Great Basin, is a device to commemorate the five important sunrise or sunset positions on the horizon, namely, summer solstice, cross quarter, equinox, cross quarter, and winter solstice. The concentric circles are positioned so that when an observer stands on the ledge and looks up at the circles, then up past the pinnacle, he is looking in the direction of the north star around which all the other stars revolve in concentric circles. Alternatively, this glyph could represent the sun, as suggested for other glyphs at the site.

Figure 10   'CALENDAR' GRID AND 'ORION' FIGURE

Farther to the south, on the south face of a standing pinnacle, is a grid with twelve squares, one of which has a diagonal line through it. Can this represent the twelve ordinary full moons of the year, with the diagonal indicating that in some years there is a thirteenth? To the right of this grid is a pattern of tight fissures that have been pecked to show the figure's importance, possibly Orion Figure 10). The figure seems to stand on a narrow horizontal ledge. Orion sets in the west with his three-star belt in a horizontal position.

Still farther to the south, is a large, slightly concave rock surface of a slab that fell from the escarpment. On it are several glyphs, one showing three circles connected by a line, positioned so it matches the three stars of Orion's belt when it sets. Another possible representation of Orion's belt is carved in the vertical rock face to the left of the Sunrise Chamber entrance (Figure 11). The top circle is offset to the left just as it is on Orion's belt. Shadows cast from the left outline the circles and lines exactly during the summer solstice morning. When one stands at the entrance to the chamber and looks at this glyph, then raises his view to the sky, he is looking in the direction where stars of Orion's belt rise vertically exactly in the east.

Elements of the Sunrise Chamber

This cave is a narrow fissure opening to the northeast. It is about three feet wide at the entrance, narrowing to

Figure 11 GLYPH WHICH MAY REPRESENT ORION'S BELT

one foot wide farther in, and it extends back about twenty-one feet. The floor of the chamber slopes upward toward the rear (Figure 12). The roof is formed by very large slabs of stone covering most of the fissure except for the rearmost portion, which is open to the sky. There is a keystone-shaped boulder, almost concealing the entrance, wedged between the sides of the chamber. This stone has been carved, inscribed, and modified in shape. Halfway back in the chamber, the crevice narrows where another roughly triangular boulder is wedged between the walls,

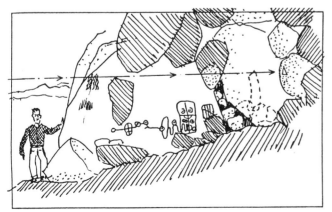

Figure 12 SECTION THROUGH SUNRISE CHAMBER
Path of summer solstice light forming a triangle

about six feet above the floor. This hanging stone seems to have been carved away on one side (Figure 13).

The rear of the chamber then becomes wider with side crevices providing somewhat more space. The rear wall consists of unmarked, rounded boulders, but the Connicks recall that when they first visited this site in the 1960s, there were several large stones in the rear of the room that have since been removed, presumably lifted out through the roof hole. One in particular is five feet long, slightly-bowed, triangular in section, and now rests above the chamber. The remains of a glyph on what was once the top of this stone suggest that it may have been the target stone for the summer solstice light triangle. There is a small boulder near the floor, wedged between the walls, with a seven-legged glyph on it (Figure 14).[2] The corners of the walls of the chamber have been rounded off, in contrast to the sharp corners of the naturally-split rock elsewhere in the basalt outcropping. Areas of the rock walls had been dressed prior to the carving of the elaborate glyphs on the walls of the chamber.

Figure 13 THE 'HANGING STONE'
Cut-away side forms the light triangle.

Petroglyphs Inside the Sunrise Chamber

Within the Sunrise Chamber are the boldest and, seemingly, the oldest of the rock carvings. The most prominent of the glyphs, 'the Grand Sunrise' glyph, on the east wall, is a long serpentine beginning at a small circle. It passes through an oval divided into six parts, rising and falling to connect a series of small circles and circles with central

Figure 14 RUBBING OF 'SUPER-PI' GLYPH

dots, finally entering the lower left quadrant of a large 'seasons diagram' glyph, where, after three loops or nodes, it crosses the vertical centerline of the 'seasons diagram' and loops back on itself (Figure 15).

This looping back is very similar to astronomical notations in the Boyne Valley of Ireland (Brennan 1979, 1983). I believe that this diagram shows the sun passing through the second quarter of the year and crossing the mid-line, after which it turns and begins to move back toward the south. The large, rounded quadrangle is divided vertically and horizontally and contains several circles with dots in the four quadrants. This glyph superficially resembles a large mask, but it may be a diagram of the year with its four seasons. Above this 'seasons diagram' is a complex figure looking somewhat like a bird rising from the carcass of another bird below (Figure 16). The eye of this bird, itself a circle and a dot, is illuminated during the summer solstice.

Figure 15 RUBBING OF THE 'GRAND SUNRISE GLYPH'

These glyphs are carved one to two inches wide and up to one inch deep into the basalt. Edges are very worn and eroded, and the patina appears the same inside the

glyph as on the mother rock. These inscriptions all give an impression of great antiquity.

The Summer Solstice Sunrise Event

On the morning of June 21, the interior of the chamber is quite dark prior to the actual sunrise. As one crouches in the cramped chamber watching the back wall of the cave, there is not much light until the edge of the sun peeps above the rim of the horizon, which is about twenty miles away and slightly elevated at 0.81 degrees. The azimuth at the instant of the sun's appearance is 58.4° E of N (Connick and Connick ms). At this instant, there appears on the back wall of the chamber a bright, crisp triangle of red light approximately six inches on a side with its point up (Figure 13). It is difficult to convey the drama of this event in words. The bottom of the triangle of light is shaped by the top of the 'keystone' at the entrance, which has been chipped and worked. The right side of the triangle is formed by the stone to the right of the entrance that has the two concentrics previously described in Figure 7. The left side of the triangle is shaped by the hanging stone halfway up the passage. It appears that this stone has been carved away on its west side to shape the light triangle.[3]

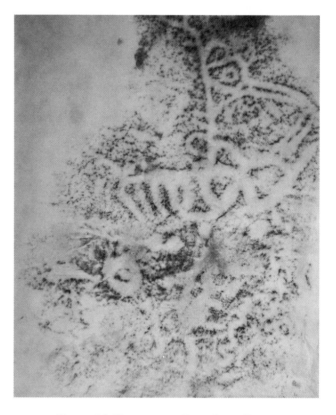

Figure 16 RUBBING OF BIRD-LIKE GLYPH

The combination of projected light and attendant shadows on the serpentine leading to the 'seasons diagram' illuminates the loops and circles of the serpentine in sequence, as seen in Figure 17, until this part of the glyph is

Figure 17 SUMMER SOLSTICE SHADOWS
'Grand Sunrise Glyph' serpentine

completely illuminated and a shadow cuts across the top of the serpentine, the whole sequence standing out in stark relief. Because the moving sunlight strikes obliquely across the stone face, the changes in the lighting are very rapid, and only minutes are required for this entire dramatic display. Finally, the line dividing the light and shadow bisects the 'seasons diagram' diagonally from upper left to lower right, cutting through the upper left sun symbol, through the intersection of the axes, and through the lower right sun symbol, touching the top of the larger circle in the same quadrant (Figure 18). This display seems to express the idea that half the year has passed. It also demonstrates knowledge that the summer solstice occurs off the true north-south and east-west axes.

Meanwhile, back at the chamber entrance, the finely cut glyph of six parallel lines on the east wall of rock on each side of a shallow vertical ridge has a light-shadow play moving across it, created by a notch cut in the overhanging lip above the glyph. As the sun moves high in the sky around midday, this shadow seems to mark the time of midday on the solstice. Exactly how this shadow-play works needs further study at the summer solstice.

West Wall Glyphs and Equinox Sunrise Event

On the west wall of the Sunrise Chamber is a complex panel that has some unusual characteristics. The rubbing reveals what photographs and close observation did not, that the tight serpentine seems to curl under itself in several places, which is most unusual for petroglyphs found in North America (Figure 19). This coiling gives the inscription a three-dimensional or visceral quality for which there is no obvious interpretation.

The stacked chevrons are another unusual feature of this same glyph that seem to have a definite purpose. At sunrise on the equinox, September 22, 1992, with the first beam of light of the rising sun, a vertical shadowline fell precisely along the points of the five stacked chevrons (center of Figure 19).

Figure 18 LIGHT/SHADOW LINE
On the 'Seasons Glyph'

THE SUNSET CHAMBER

Elements of the Sunset Chamber

This chamber is another natural cave formed by the splitting away from the main mass of basalt of a very large slab of rock that leans out toward the west, overlooking Willow Creek canyon. The split creates a passage about six feet wide, with a roof of large slabs of rock which span the space between the outer leaning wall and the mother rock on the east side of the chamber. The axis of this

Figure 19 WEST WALL RUBBING
Sunrise Chamber

cave is oriented generally east-west, and the floor of the chamber slopes downward as one enters (Figure 20).

On the right or south side, wrapped across the 'nose' of a rounded vertical edge of the rock, is a glyph consisting of concentric arcs. These lines form a series of six concentric half-circles which cross the 'nose' and form another series of five concentric half circles to the east of the 'nose.' The smallest inner circle on the left looks like an eye. There is no eye on the right. I call this the 'Sunset Mask.' Farther into the cave, five parallel, wavy, but essentially vertical, lines rise from a complex of inscriptions below to meet the roof slab above (Figure 21).[4] To the left of these lines is a short double serpentine.

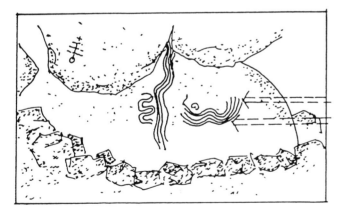

Figure 20 SECTION THROUGH SUNSET CHAMBER

Deeper into the cave is a glyph looking like a stylized tree, located far up underneath a large boulder which makes up part of the interlocked roof of the chamber (Figure 22). Because of its inaccessible location, we were barely able to make a rubbing. Like other glyphs at the site, this one has a stem that begins in a small circle, then rises vertically with seven cross-bars or branches. At the top is a circle with dot, offset to the left of the stem. This glyph appears to be a gauge of some sort, but, at our first

observations, no light seemed to strike it. However, on June 19, 1993, after the narrow crack above had been cleaned of debris, the sun was high enough in the sky to cast light on the upper offset circle.[5]

On a large boulder resting on the west wall deep within the chamber is a pecked series of horizontal lines. These are partially concealed by another boulder which must have fallen into its present position after the glyph was inscribed. The lines are very clear and distinct, but their purpose is not known at this time. They may be part of some unfinished work.

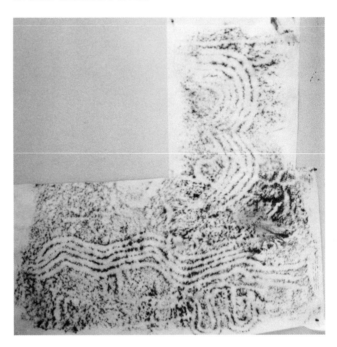

Figure 21 SOUTH WALL RUBBING
Sunset Chamber

Figure 22 EAST WALL SUN-MOON GAUGE
Sunset Chamber

The Summer Solstice Sunset Event

At sunset I observed a long shaft of light, six inches wide, coming to a point exactly like a pencil, which was shaped by the conjunction of the roof slab and the outer support rock at the mouth of the chamber (Figure 29). As the sun moved lower, this pointer traced around the outer ring of the right hand concentrics until it reached the top of the ring, level with the inner circle. It then pulled away to the right as the sun set (Figures 23 and 24).

Wondering whether there might be some alignments on the occasion of the equinoxes, we determined to return to the site on the occasion of the autumnal equinox.

Autumnal Equinox Sunset Event

On September 19, 1992, accompanied by Rollin Gillespie and Nal Morris, both accomplished archaeoastronomers, I visited the site again at the autumnal equinox. We were richly rewarded.

At sunset on the 22nd a shadow cast by a knob of rock to the right of the concentric double half-circle glyph formed what first looked like a human profile whose nose, acting as a pointer, moved up through the concentric rings, changing shape as it moved (Figures 25 and 26). When the point of the shadow reached the innermost ring, it then moved out along the top ends of the rings to the very top of the

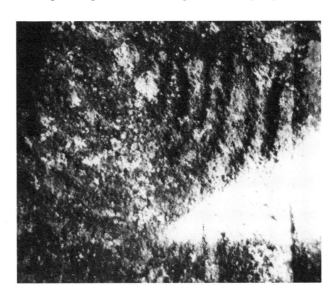

Figures 23 and 24 SEQUENCE OF LIGHT POINTER TRACING THE OUTER RING OF THE 'SUNSET MASK'
Sunset on the Summer Solstice

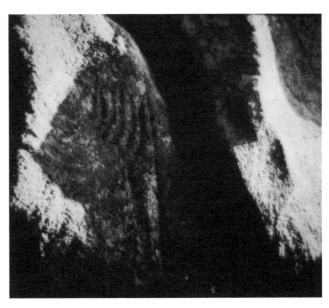

Figures 25 and 26 SHADOW SEQUENCE ON THE 'SUNSET MASK' AT SUNSET ON THE AUTUMNAL EQUINOX
Hand points to worked knob of rock which creates the shadow play across the glyph.

outermost ring where it held while the last limb of the sun sank below the horizon. This spot was identical to that touched by the light pointer at the summer solstice sunset.

I must say that this event moved us deeply. Had we just seen a silhouette of the ancient astronomer? Upon close examination of the knob of rock which cast the shadow, we could see that it had been worked to create the desired effect.

Predictions

The equinox sunset event inspired us to investigate the possibility of an alignment involving the glyph to the left of the five parallel lines, the three-lobed, double-lined serpentine (Figure 27). By stretching a string from the center lobe to the apparent intersection of the stones forming the solstice light pointer (Figure 29), we determined that the 279.5° azimuth and the 9.40° elevation predicted April 23, 1992 at 17:53 and August 17, 1992 at 17:59 standard time for an alignment with the light pointer.[6]

These dates, in April and August, are exactly fifty-nine days on each side of the summer solstice. This interval is two 29.5 day lunations. The ancient 'astronomer/ priests' could mark the April 23rd date by observing the light pointer's position on the marker glyph, then, noting the phase of the moon, they could wait until that same phase of the moon was repeated twice and know that the summer solstice was at hand. Then, other gauges could be observed to determine the solstice with even more precision. Many years of observation must have been necessary to confirm this prediction of the solstice. In years when the moon was a new crescent in the evening sky, this system would have been especially notable and distinct. It also obviated the necessity of having a number system or even having to make fifty-nine notches on a stick.

In order to verify the fifty-nine day summer solstice predictor theory, I drove to the site on April 21, 1993. The following day, April 22, was a bright, sunny day with small cumulus clouds sailing above, but with plenty of space between for sunlight. I began recording at 1600 hours with a 35 mm. camera and a video camera, taking pictures with both at five-minute intervals. The sunlight entering the chamber gathered itself into a more and more narrow shaft until it became a sharp spear of light that sliced across the rock wall until the point rested about one inch below the center of the middle lobe of the target glyph. This spear of light grazed the ridges of the 'sunset mask,' and, at the culmination of the sequence, it seemed to emanate from the eye of the 'mask,' and the point appeared to pierce the target glyph, almost to the center (Figures 28 and 29).

Crouching there in the rough-walled cave, I had the eery sensation that I was being glared at by the eye itself!

I had hoped to see on the following day, April 23, an even more precise verification of our prediction, but the morning showed low, heavy clouds, with snow squalls on the nearby mountain and the beginning of a major storm.

There was nothing to be gained by staying, so I headed home, certain that our theory was correct.

Figure 27 'TARGET GLYPH'

CONCLUSIONS

Our research demonstrates that the Willow Creek site is an observatory for determining the summer solstice, the equinox, and possibly other events; dramatic alignments allow a prediction of the summer solstice by marking the date fifty-nine days before and after the event. The ancient people who used this site were probably hunter-gatherers who developed an elaborate and sophisticated method of noting, measuring, and marking various celestial events.[7]

The natural configuration of the site lends itself to archaeoastronomical calculations. The ancient people found that the rock formations provided some unique alignments of sun and season. By a little modification and embellishment, they turned the natural rock caves into chambers to memorialize various events that they observed. The 'little embellishment' is not meant to disparage the tremendous amount of work and long years of observation that created this ingenious observatory, which still works today.

The oldest, or 'Classic,' petroglyphs are quite ancient, as evidenced by the depth of the carving, the similarity of

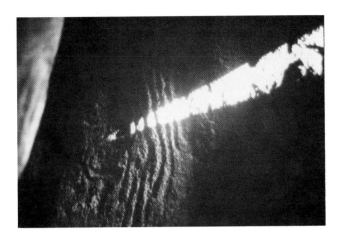

Figure 28 LIGHT SPEAR ON EYE OF 'SUNSET MASK'
Pointer touches the center of the 'Predictor Glyph.'

Figure 29 VIEW FROM INSIDE SUNSET CHAMBER
Near sunset, the angle of the roof rock and outer rock
form the light pointer.

patina to that of the untouched rock, and comparison with the other, newer-looking inscriptions. How old they are is yet to be determined. Dating might be achieved by cation-ratio techniques, or by determining the shift of alignments with the shift in the earth's obliquity, or by comparing the depth of weathering for bare rock with that of rock protected by red ochre. There is, apparently, a method being developed to measure the age of paint such as red ochre, and there may be other means unknown to this author. Various glyphs at Willow Creek should be dated to help determine when these glyphs were carved, who these ancient astronomers were and what they believed. While certain affinities to Old World sites, symbols, and observations suggest themselves, no definite conclusion can be drawn at this time about influences from other than indigenous cultures. However, with hints suggested by this site, these avenues should certainly be pursued.

We can also conclude that the Willow Creek site was used over a very long period of time, and it is reasonable to infer that more than one culture inhabited the area and used the observatory, or at least mimicked the inscriptions. Numerous metates and grinding holes in the neighborhood indicate longtime use of the area.

Because it was a natural happening, the event of sunlight penetrating the womb of the earth could have been more magical, and more significant, to the ancient people than if a human device or structure had been erected to accomplish the same ends of marking the changes in the seasons. Here, the Cosmos itself involved mankind in its miracles. These ancient people, immersed in nature, belonged to the earth and sky and its processes, and, with ritual, they could play a part in maintaining the balance, and in preserving not only their fragile culture, but the Cosmos itself. Hudson and Underhay, in *Crystals in the Sky* (1978), describe the beliefs and rituals of the California Chumash tribes, who carefully studied the heavens and conducted regular ceremonies in order to provide "ritual sustenance for the community and supply meaning meaning to life itself." They suggest that these beliefs were common to many, if not all, of the California tribes.

While this investigation is only beginning to reveal information about the use of the Willow Creek Observatory, it should demonstrate at the very least that some of the enigmatic glyphs throughout the western United States can be better understood if they are evaluated in an astronomical context. This new perception of the purpose of the site and its glyphs can move the appreciation and understanding of this ancient work from merely 'art' into the realm of functional astronomical symbolism and notation, which in turn can give us better understanding of the concept of the Cosmos in the minds of the ancient astronomers.

The author hopes that other investigators will take an interest in this and other sites used for seasonal or ritual observations.

NOTES

1. I wish to acknowlege both Rollin Gillespie and Nal Morris for their companionship and helpful suggestions and advice during the investigation of this site.
2. The expeditions of 1995 and 1996 revealed that this 'super-pi' glyph receives both sun and moon light-pointers. This discovery will be the subject of a future paper.
3. Experiments with a replica of the target stone during the expeditions of 1996 demonstrated that the light-triangle becomes an elongated light pointer as it strikes the sloping top of the target stone.
4. It was demonstrated during the expedition of 1996 that these wavy lines represent the Milky Way.
5. Careful observation and measurements during the 1996 expeditions have revealed that this glyph is indeed a gauge that marks sunlight and moonlight during part of the moon's 19 year cycle. We now call this glyph the 'Sun-Moon Gauge.'
6. This calculation was made with Nal Morris' expertise and his lap-top computer loaded with his astronomical program

SHAMOS. A cautionary note: The basalt at this site has magnetic properties which can affect compass bearings. Our bearings should be verified by observations of astronomical bodies and accurate timepiece before acceptance.

7. The probability of there being a winter solstice alignment seemed to be strong, and I did visit the site on December 21, 1992. I saw neither a sunrise nor a sunset alignment, which means either that there was none, or that it no longer exists, or that I missed it. There may be another explanation. Because the temperature was 17° F. and there was six inches of snow on the ground, my theory is that the ancient astronomers spent the winter in warmer parts, just as the Maidu were found to do. These hunter-gatherer people came together at their winter quarters in the lee of Diamond Mountain near Honey Lake and undoubtedly enjoyed the comforts provided by the nearby hot springs.

REFERENCES

Aveni, Anthony F.
  1980   *Skywatchers of Ancient Mexico*. University of Texas Press.
Beckenstall, Stan
  1986   *Rock Carvings of Northern Britain*. U.K.: Shire Publications Ltd.
Brennan, Martin
  1979   *The Boyne Valley Vision*. Mountrath, Ireland: Dolmen Press.
  1983   *The Stars and the Stones, Ancient Art and Astronomy in Ireland*. London: Thames and Hudson Ltd.
Calvin, William H.
  1991   *How The Shaman Stole The Moon*. New York: Bantam Books.
Connick, Robert E. and Frances Connick
  1990   Varieties of petroglyphs and implications for their use and chronology at Willow Creek near Susanville (CA-LAS-32). In *Rock Art Papers*, Vol. 7. K. Hedges, ed. San Diego: Museum Papers No. 26.
  m.s.   *A Summer Solstice Petroglyph Site*. Presented at the Australian Rock Art Research Association Symposium, Darwin, Australia, 1988. (To be published by AURARA.)
Cressman, L. S.
  1937   *Petroglyphs of Oregon*. University of Oregon Press.
Curtis, John S.
  1991   Little Blue Table revisited. *Utah Rock Art*, Vol. XI. Green River, Utah: Utah Rock Art Research Association.
Hadingham, Evan
  1974   *Ancient Carvings in Britain, A Mystery*. London: The Gainstone Press, Ltd.
  1984   *Early Man and the Cosmos*. New York: Walker and Co.
Heizer, Robert F. and M. A. Whipple
  1951,1971   *The California Indians, a Source Book*. University of California Press.
Heizer, Robert F. and Martin A. Baumhoff
  1962   *Prehistoric Rock Art of Nevada and Eastern California*. University of California Press.
Hill, Beth and Ray Hill
  1974   *Indian Petroglyphs of the Pacific Northwest*. University of Washington Press.

Hudson, Travis
  1984   California's first astronomers. In *Archaeoastronomy and the Roots of Science*. E. C. Krupp, ed. Papers presented at the AAAS Selected Symposium, 1980. Boulder: Westview Press.
Hudson, Travis and Ernest Underhay
  1978   *Crystals in the Sky: An Intellectual Odyssey*. Ballena Press/Santa Barbara Museum of Natural History Cooperative Publication.
Kroeber, Alfred L.
  1925   *Handbook of the Indians of California*. Washington: Bureau of American Ethnology, Bul.78.
Lindqvist, Cecilia
  1989   *China, Empire of Living Symbols*. Reading MA: Addison Wesley Press.
Lowell, John and Thomas C. Blackburn
  1976   *Native Californians: a Theoretical Perspective*. Menlo Park CA: Ballena Press.
Marshack, Alexander
  1972   Cognitive aspects of upper paleolithic engraving. *Current Anthropology* 13:3-4.
Mayer, Dorothy
  1975   Star patterns in Great Basin petroglyphs. In *Archaeoastronomy in Pre-Columbian America*. Anthony F. Aveni, ed. University of Texas Press.
  1977   An examination of Miller's hypothesis. In *Native American Astronomy*. Anthony F. Aveni, ed. University of Texas Press.
McGlone, William R., Phillip Leonard, and Rollin W. Gillespie
  1986   *Ancient Celtic America*. Fresno: Panorama West Books.
Moran, Hugh A. and David H. Kelley
  1969   *The Alphabet and the Ancient Calendar Signs* (2nd edition). Palo Alto: Daily Press.
Morris, Ronald W. B.
  1979   *The Prehistoric Rock Art of Galloway and the Isle of Man*. Dorset: Blanford Press.
  1981   *The Prehistoric Rock Art of Southern Scotland*. Oxford: England.
Saad-Cook, Janet
  1985   *Archaeoastronomy*, Vol. VIII(1-4).
Schmidt, Roderick L.
  1992   Swansea, a multicultural petroglyph site in Inyo County, California. *Epigraphic Society Occasional Papers*, Vol. 21. San Diego.
Steward, Julian H.
  1929   *Petroglyphs of California and Adjoining States*. Berkeley: University of California Press.
Thompson, Gunnar W.
  1989   *Nu Sun*. Fresno: Pioneer Publishing Co.
Voeglin, Ermine W.
  1942   *Cultural Element Distribution. Northeast California Records*, Vol. 7, No. 2. Berkeley: University of California Press.
Williamson, Ray A.
  1981   *Archaeoastronomy in the Americas*. California: Ballena Press.

Astronomical Alignments in the Newport Tower

WILLIAM S. PENHALLOW

PROLOGUE

A pre-Columbian origin for the Newport Tower cannot be dismissed at this time. AD 1492 is not that far from the 1500-1630 estimate recently reported (Siemonsen 1993). Astronomical alignments, Romanesque architecture, a stone with a runic inscription, and the possibility of a foundation to the northwest must all be satisfactorily explained first. Archaeoastronomy provides us with a powerful tool to study the most important artifact of all—the Tower itself. Who knows where it will lead us?

INTRODUCTION

Possible astronomical alignments in the Newport Tower were first reported as part of the *Vinland Revisited—1000 Years of Discovery* program that brought three Viking replica ships to Newport in September, 1991. Some of the results of this preliminary study were reported at the ABC Conference held at Brown University (Penhallow *et al.* 1992a), and at the 23rd Meeting of the Division of Dynamical Astronomy of the American Astronomical Society held in Chicago (Penhallow *et al.* 1992b). The possible alignments noted in these papers were based on Figures 5, 6, 7, 8, and 16 in Means (1942) and were known to be of limited accuracy. The reader should familiarize himself with these figures.

Mr. Jorgen Siemonsen of Denmark, Chairman of the Committee for Research on Norse Activities in North America AD 1000-1500, held a press conference in Newport on September 22, 1993, where he announced that the Tower had been built between AD 1500 and 1630 ± 50 years. This conclusion was based on radioactive carbon dating of the CO_2 trapped in the mortar, and other factors. Hence, Siemonsen concluded, the Tower was likely post-Viking, post-Columbus, yet pre-Colonial. That night at a special meeting of the Newport City Council, Mr. Siemonsen presented a copy of *The Newport Tower Photogrammetric Measurement* (*NTPM*) (1992), minus the detailed drawings, to the City of Newport for the benefit of future researchers. This study was done under the auspices of his committee by the Technical University of Denmark and the Danish National Museum to provide detailed measurements of the Tower. At a news conference held in Newport on December 2, 1995, Mr Siemonsen stated that "the result of this study gave the most probable dating of the mortar to the 17th century, but dating to the 16th is not completely ruled out" (Siemonsen 1995). Since there has been no refereed article in any journal relative to this study, it is difficult to assess the results.

For the *NTPM* study, forty-eight targets were placed on the tower, twenty-four on the inside and twenty-four on the outside. Using what they call 'total stations,' these targets, as well as references on the ground, were measured with a theodolite. The sun was also shot to establish the orientation of a three-dimensional coordinate system. Stereoscopic pairs of photographs of the tower were also taken. The position of each target was later determined to within 2 mm. The photos were then scanned under computer control and the positions of the features of the Tower determined to better than 1 cm.

The *NTPM* report as submitted contains a guide to the detailed drawings and depicts two cylindrical projections: one of the inside of the Tower using a radius of 2.79 m. and one of the outside with a radius of 3.53 m. The nomenclature of the features follows that of Means (1942). Tick marks clearly delineate north, south, east, and west on the top and the bottom of each projection.

The *NTPM* guide was carefully drawn, probably by a computer, and it provides accurate datum points for further analysis. For instance, it could be scaled in ninety degree segments to reconstruct a picture of the Tower which is more accurate than that provided by Means. Using this approach, we found pillars **1** and **5** in our analysis to be oriented three degrees west of true north. This result agrees with the three degree value reported in *NTPM*. A 'least squares' fit to all four pairs of pillars (assuming a perfect octagon) yields a standard deviation from the mean of 0.3 degrees. This shows how precisely the pillars were laid out. Means believed that pillars **1** and **5** were aligned to true north. Solar azimuths were also used to better define some of the openings in the Tower. See Appendix II.

Remember that the Tower is essentially a cylinder with arches, sitting on eight pillars. Our Figure 1 is a horizontal cross section and shows the location of the four windows **W1**, **W2**, **W3**, and **W4** on the first floor above the arches, as well as the niches **N1**, **N2**, **N3**, **N4**, and **N7**. In addition, the fireplace **FP**, ledge **2**, and indentations **S1**, **S2**, and **S6** are indicated. The location of the eight pillars, **P1** through **P8**, is also shown. Horizon alignments with their geodetic azimuths are superimposed. Also, see Figures 4 and 5.

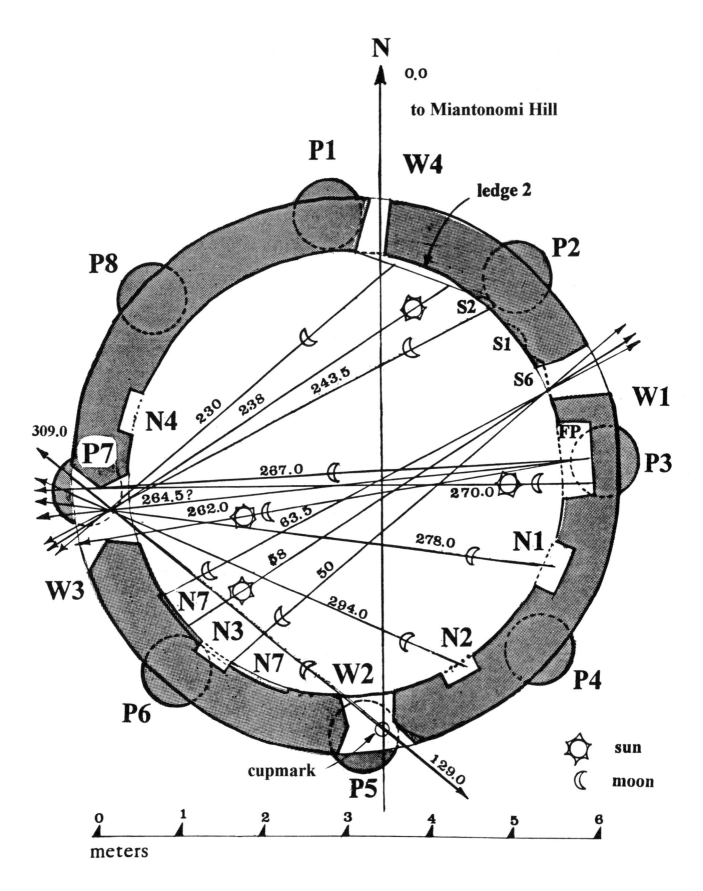

Figure 1 HORIZON ALIGNMENTS ON THE FIRST FLOOR

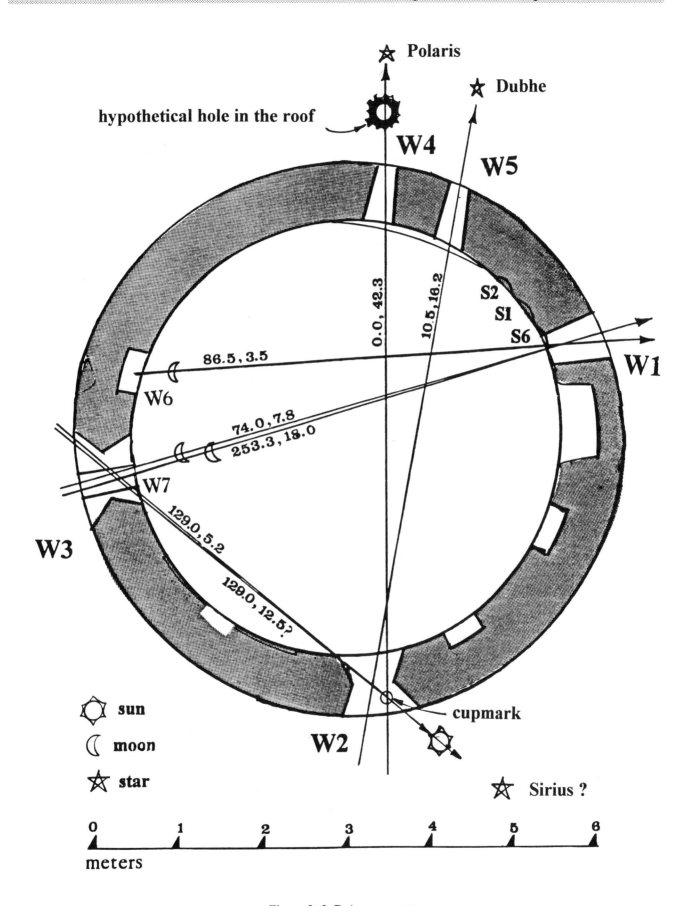

Figure 2 3–D ALIGNMENTS

Table I IDENTIFIED LUNISOLAR ALIGNMENTS

SIGHT	AZIMUTH (Geodetic)	ALTITUDE	DECLINATION (Measured)	DECLINATION (Theoretical)	TYPE of ALIGNMENT
BOTW2→W3	309.0	0.0	28.2	28.6	Lunar major
N7→W1	50.0	0.0	*	28.6	Lunar major
N7→W1	58.0	0.0	*	23.5	Summer solstice
N7→W1	63.5	0.0	19.5	18.4	Lunar minor
N2→W3	294.0	0.0	17.7	18.4	Lunar minor
W3→W1	74.0	7.8	17.8	18.4	Lunar minor
N1→W3	278.0	0.0	6.0	5.2	Lunar extreme
N4→W1	86.5	3.5	5.2	5.2	Lunar extreme
W1→W7	253.3	18.0	2.2	2.6	Lunar extreme
SFP→W3	270.0	0.0	0.0	0.0	Equinoxes
FP→NW3	267.0	0.0	-2.2	-2.6	Lunar extreme
FP→CW3→HOR	264.5?	0.0	-4.1	(Need to study horizon?)	
FP→SW3	262.0	0.0	-5.9	-5.2	Lunar extreme
S2→W3	243.5	0.0	-19.8	-18.4	Lunar minor
W3→W2	129.0	5.3	-23.6	-23.5	Winter solstice
L2→W3	238.0	0.0	*	-23.5	Winter solstice
L2→W3	230.0	0.0	*	-28.6	Lunar major
TOPW3→W2	129.0	0.0	-28.2	-28.6	Lunar major

*Simply drawn in where icons of the sun or the moon might have been located.

Our Figure 2 takes the openings **W5** and **W7** (which are at higher levels) and projects them down to the first floor level. The 3-D alignments with their azimuths and altitudes are shown. The **N4→W1** (86.5 [azimuth]; 3.5 [altitude]) sight was carefully determined and found not to be due east as one might judge from Figure 7 in Means. Pictures taken at a spring equinox sunrise show that the sun shining through **W1** does not extrapolate back to **N4** when allowance is made for a house obstructing the sun in the east. Using the results of our reconstruction, based on the accurate *NTPM* survey, this alignment turns out to be a lunar extreme of 5.2 degrees north declination. It can be observed in the early morning of April 4 and September 10 when the sun is at this declination shining through **W1**. The other sights were then determined from our reconstruction. Figure 3 shows the location in Touro Park from which to view sights involving pairs of windows. See Figure 6 for an aerial view of the park.

LUNISOLAR ALIGNMENTS

Lunisolar alignments are given in Table I. Column 1 gives the sight; column 2, the geodetic azimuth of the sight (north is 0.0); column 3, the altitude above the horizon, neglecting refraction; column 4, the declination determined (measured); column 5, the declination theoretical; column 6, the type of alignment. Taking each of the Table I alignments in turn:

BOTW2→W3 (309.0)

This alignment can be seen from the bottom of **W2** looking through **W3** as well as from Location **2** in the SE corner of Touro Park. See Figures 1 and 3. It represents the northern-most extreme of the moon's motion and is called a 'lunar major.' It will occur next in December, 2006, when the full moon will be seen setting through these two windows at dawn.

N7→W1 (50.0)
N7→W1 (58.0)
N7→W1 (63.5)

Niche **7** is a long groove in the SW sector of the inner wall at the same level as **W1**. See Figure 5. It might have had a shelf on which icons of the sun and the moon were placed. The lunar major moonrise, the summer solstice sunrise, and the lunar minor moonrise can be observed from this shelf. The next lunar minor moonrise will occur in December, 1996, and the next lunar major moonrise will occur in December, 2006. See Figure 1, as well as Tables VI and VII.

N2→W3 (294.0)

This alignment represents the lunar extreme called the 'lunar minor.' It will occur next in December 1996, when the setting full moon illuminates **N2** at dawn. The sun annually illuminates **N2** at sunset on May 14 and July 31. See Figure 1 and Table V.

W3→W1 (74.0; 7.8)

This is also a lunar minor and will next be seen early in the evening at the full moon in December 1996, from Location **5** in the park. Since the sun is at this declination on May 14 and July 31, it can be seen shining through these windows early in the morning from this location on those dates. See Figures 2 and 3, and Table V.

Nl→W3 (278.0)

This is a lunar extreme associated with the equinoxes. At such time the full moon would illuminate **Nl** at dawn. Since the sun is at this declination on April 4 and September 10, **Nl** will be illuminated at sunset on these dates. See Figure 1 and Table V.

N4→Wl (86.5; 3.5)

This is the same lunar extreme as **Nl→W3,** but the full moon would be seen rising early in the evening, illuminating **N4**. The sun can be seen illuminating **N4** early in the morning on April 4 and September 10. See Figure 2 and Table V.

W1→W7 (253.3; 18.0)

This is a lunar extreme at declination 2.6, which can occur when the sun is also at 2.6 declination. When this occurs, both the sun and the full moon will pass through this alignment (roughly 12 hours apart). Since the sun is at this declination on March 28 and September 17, it will shine through these windows in the afternoon on those days and be seen from Location **1**. See Figures 2 and 3, and Table V.

SFP→W3 (270.0)
FP→NW3 (267.0)
FP→CW3→HOR (264.5?)
FP→SW3 (262.0)

One notices that the azimuth defined by the center of the fireplace and the center of **W3** is 264.5 degrees, very close to the azimuth of the hill **BM120** on Jamestown (Conanicut) Island. In addition, one notices that the back of the fireplace is wider than the aperture defined by **W3**. This is the most complicated sight, probably involving both backsights and foresights. If one is located south of the center of the fireplace, the northern edge of **W3** would be at 270 degrees and mark the equinoxes. The illumination of the fireplace could, of course, be seen at sunset on March 21 and September 23. There could also be a feature on the horizon that might be used for this purpose. The sweep from one side of the fireplace to the other allows for a range of 0 to -5.9 degrees in declination to be observed either in foresight and/or backsight. A very interesting sight works as follows: when the sun is at -2.6 declination and the full moon is also at -2.6 degrees (at a lunar extreme), the moon will set at the same location on the horizon as the sun. Both the sun and the full moon will fully illuminate the fireplace when they set individually—a very auspicious occasion.

The usefulness of such an arrangement is suggested in the layout of the ground floor of the Österlars round church in Bornholm, Denmark, where the altar replaces the fireplace (Penhallow *et al.* 1992a). An astronomical alignment at

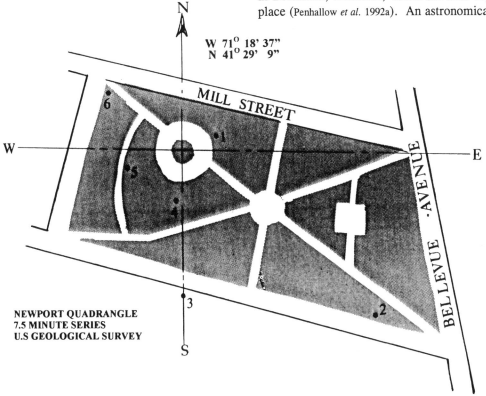

Figure 3 TOURO PARK LOCATIONS

an upper level of the Österlars church has already been videotaped (Whittall 1993a). The round churches on the island of Bornholm might be the prototypes for the Newport Tower.[1] The converts who built those 13th century churches may have incorporated in their architecture a long pagan astronomical tradition. Remember, Christianity was not well established in Scandinavia until quite late. Prytz (1991: 211) says that according to Rafn the ruins of three round buildings have been found on Greenland. We should not forget that Greenland had many churches, a bishop, a cathedral, and several monasteries by the 13th century. Perhaps the time may be ripe for a study entitled *Astronomy in the Service of Christianity* to borrow from King (1994).

When the sun is at -5.2 and the full moon is at 0.0 (a lunar extreme), each can be seen setting individually from the fireplace. The sun is at -5.2 degrees on March 8 and October 7. The sun illuminates the northern half at sunset and the full moon illuminates the southern half at sunrise. See Figure 1 and Table V.

Figure 4 VIEW OF THE TOWER LOOKING WEST
W2 is on the left and **W1** is on the right. (© John Hopf)

S2→W3 (243.5)

This is a lunar minor alignment and will next occur with the full moon setting at dawn in June, 1997. The sun can be seen illuminating **S2** on both January 28 and November 15 at sunset. See Figure 1 and Table V

W3→W2 (129.0; 5.3)

This is a winter solstice alignment that can be seen from

Location **6** on December 21. See Figures 1, 3 and Table V.

L2→W3 (238)
L2→W3 (230)

These alignments seem to mirror **N7→W1**. The ledge is probably used in the same manner as the shelf of **N7**. The winter solstice and the next lunar major with the full moon setting at dawn in December, 2006, can be observed from the ledge. See Figure 1 and Table V.

TOPW3→W2 (129.0)

This alignment can be seen from the top of **W3** looking through **W2**. It is a lunar major and can next be observed with the full moon rising in June, 2006. See Figure 1.

UNIDENTIFIED SIGHTLINES

The sightlines listed in Table II are a clear indication that more work needs to be done. Someone knowledgeable about practical astronomy might be able to shed some light on their significance. Two important astronomical instruments of the Middle Ages were the astrolabe and the Universal Ring dial. See Swarup, Bag, and Shukla (1987: 227); Waugh (1973:157); Toomer (1984:217); and Neugebauer (1975:866, 871). To construct such instruments out of wood with simple tools, see Fisher (1995:22, 55). Both instruments were invented in antiquity and improved upon by the Arabs. They were normally held so as to hang vertically (plumb) and be rotated in azimuth around the vertical axis. The astrolabe had sights so that vertical angles could be measured. The Universal Ring dial had a thin metal 'bridge' with a slit in it that allowed the sun to shine through and strike a ring where the time of day could be read. According to Pedersen (1993:231), an anonymous astronomer at Roskilde, Denmark in AD 1274 was one of the first people in Europe to measure the altitude of the sun at noon every day of the year by means of an astrolabe. By using trigonometrical methods garnered from the Arabs, the astronomer applied the data to compute the length of day, which he noted daily in a calendar. It might be interesting to mention here a statement due to a Harald Akerlund (Demerliac 1988:51):

> One saga mentions a man, Oddi Heldagon, who was known as 'Oddi the Star' and who served as long-distance pilot for an Icelandic magnate toward the end of the 900s. He left notes that included a complete table of the changes in declination of the sun throughout the year, expressed as the height of the sun on the meridian in semi-diameters. There is also a small table of azimuths giving the direction at different times of the year, of dawn twilight, defined as being a faint band of light on the horizon, visible before sunrise. We know nothing of the instrument used to measure the altitude of the sun.

Prytz (1991:14) also mentions astronomical 'Rim' tables associated with the old Norse navigational system dating

Table II UNIDENTIFIED SIGHTLINES

SIGHT	AZIMUTH	ALTITUDE	DECLINATION	TYPE of ALIGNMENT
N7→W5	40.0 to 19.5	0.0	56.1 to 62.0	?
N2→W4	350.0	0.0	47.5	?
N7→W4	46.5 to -11.0	0.0	40.0 to 47.3	?
N3→W1	53.0	9.2	34.7	?
N4→W2	142.0	0.0	-36.2	?
FP→W2	218.0	2.2	-34.1	?

back to the 900s. The astrolabe and the Ring dial may well have been used to determine the time to observe the canonical offices of the Church which date back to the seven prayers of early Syrian Christianity, which in turn were based on the Old Testament (Psalm 119, vs. 62, 164). See Whone (1990:32). The times of prayer for the Muslims have the same origin. To see the close ties between astronomy and religion, one should consult King (1994). Looking at **N3→W1**, **N4→W2**, and **FP→W2**, one notes an average value of declination ± 35 degrees. Could this have something to do with the observation of solar halos near the solstice? According to Minnaert (1954:190), if you keep a close watch on the sun, you can expect to see a halo every four days on the average. See Cyr (1997) for a discussion on halos associated with Stonehenge.

STELLAR ALIGNMENTS

Alignments **W3→W1** (74.0; 7.8), **N4→W1** (86.5; 3.5), **W1→W7** (258.5; 18.0), and **W3→W2** (129.0; 5.3) provided the first clues to the 3-D design of the Tower. See Figure 2. The alignment **W2→W5** (10.5; 16.2) to Alpha Ursae Majoris (Dubhe) at the time of upper culmination of Polaris was then discovered, and the connection with the horizontal north-south alignment **W2→W4→HOR** (0.0; 0.0) was appreciated. See Figures 1 and 2.

The perimeter of the **W2** and the center of **W5** define an area of the sky roughly 5.1 degrees by 5.7 degrees (azimuth x altitude) centered at 10.5; 16.2. Precession of the equinoxes affects Dubhe and Polaris in such a way that the azimuth of Dubhe when Polaris is at upper culmination changes by less than a degree in the period AD 1200-1600. During the same period, the altitude changes by less than two degrees. See Table III.

When Dubhe was seen through **W2→W5** by an observer at Location **4** (during the period AD 1200-1600), Polaris was at its highest point in the sky due north. A sighting of Polaris with an astrolabe would then establish the local meridian. An error of 1/3 the width of **W3** produces an error of twenty minutes in determining the hour/angle of Dubhe. With Polaris at four degrees from the pole in AD 1400, this method produced an error of less than 0.3 degrees in azimuth. Hence, the builders had an accurate method of establishing the meridian at night (they

Table III LOCATION OF DUBHE
FOR UPPER CULMINATION OF POLARIS

EPOCH (AD)	HOUR/ ANGLE	DECLINATION	AZIMUTH/ ALTITUDE (Geodetic)	
1200	13 47 40	65.9	11.3	19.4
1300	13 45 28	65.4	11.3	18.8
1400	13 44 11	64.9	11.3	18.3
1500	13 44 8	64.4	11.5	17.9
1600	13 45 58	63.9	11.9	17.5
1700	13 50 51	63.3	12.6	17.1
1800	14 1 33	62.8	14.0	17.1
1900	14 25 16	62.3	16.8	17.8
2000	15 28 7	61.8	23.6	21.5

probably used **W2→W4→Miantonomi Hill** in the daytime). Perhaps someone knowledgeable about medieval surveying or town layout could comment on this. Market crosses were located at the center of many English towns. One, octagonal in shape, with eight pillars, marks the center of Wymondham in Norfolk where wool merchants plied their trade. See Mottram (1948:190). Land surveyors and geodesists with modern theodolites use Polaris to determine azimuths with great accuracy. Tables for this purpose are found in the *Astronomical Almanac* (1992:B62).

It should be noted that an instrument known as a 'nocturnal' was developed in the 1200s. It made use of Polaris and the pointer of the Big Dipper to tell time at night. See Fisher (1995:60).

To test the visibility of Dubhe through **W2→W5**, a scale model of the Tower was used at a dark location. When the roof and a floor are added to the model, one immediately realizes that the interior of the Tower must have been jet black at night. The opening **W5** in the model, with night sky illumination, was clearly visible against such a background. When an observer and the model were properly oriented, Dubhe was readily seen. The limited size of the windows in the Tower also improved the chances of seeing the sun and the moon illuminate the various niches. As the Tower was once completely covered with a white plaster cement, observers may have closed shutters on the windows (those not being used) to enhance the contrast.

Table IV Alignments Associated with Stars

SIGHT	AZIMUTH	ALTITUDE	DECLINATION	OBJECT	TYPE
W2→W4→HOR	0.0	0.0	48.5	Miantonomi Hill	Due north (HOR)
W2→W5	0.5	16.2	62 to 67	Dubhe	Upper culmination of Polaris
W2→HI*	0.0	42.3 (1994)	89.2 (1994)	Polaris	Upper culmination
W3→TOPW2	129.0	0.0 to 13.8	-27.5 to -15.4	Sirius?	Calendar**

*HI = Hypothetical hole in roof

**Neugebauer (1975:598) states ". . . of astronomical criteria, equinoxes and solstices are not well defined for primitive means of observation; obviously the helical risings and settings of bright stars or conspicuous constellations provide a much better guide for the steady progress of the solar year." There is a good chance that Sirius was used to keep a check on the lunisolar calendar. Remember that a lunisolar calendar based on a 19-year intercalation scheme gets out of whack about one day in 310 years.

The hypothetical alignment **W2→HI** (0.0; 42.3) to the North Star through the roof of the tower was then added. Finally, it was realized that Sirius could be sighted through **W3→TOPW2** (129.0; 12.5) and that this might have been intentional. See Table IV.

DISCUSSION

The sun and the moon have played an important role in the lives of mankind for tens of thousands of years. Rock art, bone incisions, calendar sticks, standing stones, stone circles, stonehenges, stone chambers, kivas, earth lodges, ziggurats, temples, churches, mosques, and modern observatories all provide evidence of the universality of such a role. See Chapter VII, *Notation: Early and Late* in Marshak (1991) for a fascinating discussion of bone incisions. Where does the Newport Tower fit into the evolutionary sequence implied by this listing?

If one accepts the AD 1500-1630 dating of the Tower (*NTPM*), the astronomical concepts used in its design and construction would probably predate the influence of Tyco Brahe, Kepler, and Newton. The technology available to the builders is most likely that of the Middle Ages (AD 1100-1500). The astronomy of that time was primarily Ptolemaic with some improvement in practice from India and the Arab world. Ptolemy was indebted to the Babylonians who had complete lunar eclipse records going back to Nabonassar (747 BC). These records provided accurate data for Ptolemy's development of a theory of the moon's motion.

One should realize that the motivation for the development of a theory of the motion of the moon is the calendar (Neugebauer 1962:106). The month begins when the thin crescent moon is first seen in the west after sunset. Predicting when this important event will occur has been of crucial importance to many civilizations (King 1991:223). To solve the problem, an analysis of the motions of both the sun and the moon are required. The solution which the Babylonians produced (Neugebauer 1962:117) not only gave you first visibilities of the crescent moon, but lunar eclipse predictions as well! Hence, we see how closely

eclipses and the calendar are related. Jim Whittall (1995a) is studying the relation between astronomical alignments, calendar days, and saint days in the Tower. We look forward to his results.

In 1900, F. X. Kugler (Neugebauer 1962:142) showed that eclipses were computed in the Seleucid period (beginning in 331 BC) by the Babylonians from a careful analysis of the latitude of the moon (angle above or below the ecliptic) at the time of new and full moons. This angle results from the inclination of the moon's orbit to the ecliptic (yearly path of the sun seen against the background stars). The orientation of the moon's orbit regresses (moves westerly along the ecliptic) with a period of 18.61 years. The inclination and regression produce the extremes known as the 'lunar major' and the 'lunar minor' often associated with the solstices. We see alignments to these extremes in the Tower and at many other sites in the world. In Newport, alignments to the horizon and in 3-D allow the observer to view lunar extremes at and near the equinoxes as well.

If a full moon is observed at or near a lunar extreme, then an eclipse is likely to occur three months (or ninety degrees) later. See Brown (1976:115-136) for a discussion of eclipses from an archaeoastronomical point of view. The lunar extreme indicates the location of the antinode of the moon's orbit (the position along the ecliptic where the moon's latitude is ± 5.2 degrees) from which the location of the nodes can be inferred. In three months the full moon will be located near a node where the sun, the earth, and the moon line up in 3-D to produce an eclipse.[2] The location of the ascending node of the moon's orbit on December 31, 1991, according to the *Astronomical Almanac* (1992:D2), was 279.85 degrees west of Aries or in the center of Sagittarius and moving westward at .05295377 degrees per day, or about 1.5 degrees per lunation. This information was used to predict the next lunar major and lunar minor. See Tables VI and VII in Appendix I.

The presence of the hill (**BM120**) on Jamestown at an azimuth 265 degrees and Miantonomi Hill due north was pointed out by Mavor (1992). The former is associated with the alignment **FP→W3** and the latter with **W2→W4**. Jim Whittall (1993b) discovered a pattern of cup marks on the

Figure 5 SOUTHWEST SEGMENT OF THE TOWER INTERIOR **W2** is on the left and **W3** is on the right. (© John Hopf)

stone at the base of **W2**. The deepest cup mark (nine inches west of the east side) and Miantonomi Hill define the accurate north-south sight through **W2→W4**. The association of cup marks with solar alignments at ancient sites has been noted by a number of investigators: MacKie (1988:220); Simpson and Thawley (1972:99); Gelling and Davidson(1969:103); and Morris (1969:51). See Streit (1984: 47-50) for a discussion of sun signs, drill holes, and solstice fires. The use of this north-south alignment for meridian observations in all likelihood determined the location of the Tower and explains why it was not built at the top of the hill near the art museum, which is twenty feet higher in elevation. Had it been built there, it would not be due south of Miantonomi Hill.

If you held an astrolabe above the cup mark on the outer portion of the bottom of **W2** and sighted Miantonomi Hill, you could establish an accurate north-south line from the outside of the Tower. The sun at local noon could then be shot from the inside of the Tower. A Universal Ring dial might also be held there to determine the time of day. Reid (1993) suggested that the overhang at the top of the pillars on the outside might have supported a walkway around the Tower for observational purposes. At night when Alpha Ursa Majoris (Dubhe) was seen through **W2→W5**, Polaris was at upper culmination due north. Again holding the astrolabe above the cup mark, you could have sighted through a hypothetical hole in the roof to accurately establish the north-south line for meridian observations.

The use of the North Star for accurate alignment can be seen in the 14th century sundial depicted in Pedersen (1993:154). With Polaris at upper (or lower) culmination, the user sights through a hole on the north side of the device. When the north star is eclipsed by a plumb-line suspended from the top of the unit, the sundial is secured. It is then accurately aligned and ready for use the next day. Another example is depicted in *The Viking Compass*

by Vebaek and Thirslund (1992:39) where a bearing dial is oriented by the north star for navigation (setting a course) at night.

What could the purpose of the Tower have been? Possibly to provide the necessary information to determine the proper times and dates of religious observances. A religious building of this kind could have been the focus of activity for a group of Europeans seriously intent upon colonization since it represents a considerable expenditure of time and effort.

It is unlikely that Europeans arriving after AD 1500 would have erected a building to obtain information which was readily available in printed almanacs. Gutenburg had invented the printing press around AD 1450, and, by AD 1500, almanacs were available which provided religious calendars and other astronomical information. Moreover on his fourth voyage, Columbus forced the reluctant West Indian natives to supply him with provisions by threatening them with an eclipse of the moon on the night of February 29, 1504 (Liu and Fiala 1992:142). And, according to Morison (1942:654), Columbus had aboard ship a copy of Regiomontanus' *Ephemerides* printed in Nuremburg toward the end of the 15th century. Neugebauer (1975:185) states that Columbus used Abraham Zacuto's *Almanach Perpetuum* printed at Salamanca. Thus, it is far more likely that the Europeans arriving after AD 1500 would have built a typical 16th century church or chapel as a central focus for their activity. Without further investigation we cannot rule out the possibility that this Tower (structure) was part of a pre-Columbian settlement established by a determined group of northern European Christians.

I hope this paper will invite constructive criticism and open new avenues of research. Early Sites Research Society conducted a ground-penetrating radar survey of Touro Park where the Tower is located. The survey was used as a guide for test borings which located the foundation of a structure northwest of the Tower, according to Whittall (1995b). Hopefully someday, a comprehensive archaeological dig will be performed.

NOTES

1. *12th Century Round Churches*—Another possibility is the round church at Orphir on the Orkney Islands off the coast of Scotland. Ritchie (1993:113,114) shows a picture of what is left of this 12th century structure as well as a stone, with a runic inscription, that was taken from it and used in the construction of a later parish church. This inscription, like the one on the south side of the Newport Tower, might be a cryptogram. See Mongé and Landsverk (1967:127) and Landsverk (1974:158).

2. *The Role of the Nodes in Hindu Astronomy*—"In Hindu astronomy, the two nodes of the moon's orbit are personified as demons; they are handled in calculation and ritual like moving planets." They are depicted in Hindu temples. We again find close ties between astronomy and religion. See Krupp (1996:60).

Appendix I **AN EPHEMERIS FOR VIEWING ALIGNMENTS**

If one wishes to view the alignments, Tables V, VI, and VII should be consulted. The times are only approximate. Table V lists lunisolar sights, and on the dates given (plus or minus a day or two), the sun will show you where they are located. One should show up about an hour early to become acquainted with the Tower. Unfortunately, houses and trees complicate matters. When a house or tree gets in the way, you can extrapolate the illuminated area forward near sunset to see where it would go. After sunrise, you can extrapolate backwards in a similar fashion. A video camera is ideal to record these events so you can review them at your leisure. Remember that as the sun sets its light has to go through more and more atmosphere so that the brightness of the illuminated area decreases markedly even on a very clear day. For the external sights, go to the Touro Park locations shown in Figure 3.

Table V LUNISOLAR ALIGNMENTS VIEWED BY USING THE SUN

DAY	DECLINA-TION	SIGHT	SUN SHINING THROUGH	ILLUMIN-ATING	APPROX. TIME EST or (EDT)
Jan 28	-18.4	S2→W3	W3	S2	4:53 pm
March 8	-5.2	FP→SW3	W3	NFP	5:42 pm
March 14	-2.6	FP→NW3	W3	CFP	5:50 pm
March 21	0.0	SFP→W3	W3	SFP	5:56 pm
March 28	2.6	W7→W1	W7&W1	LOC #1	4:31 pm
April 4	5.2	N4→W1	W1	N4	5:51 am
April 4	5.2	N1→W3	W3	N1	6:12 pm
May 14	18.4	N7→W1	W1	WN7	(5:24 am)
May 14	18.4	W3→W1	W3&W1	LOC #5	(6:20 am)
May 14	18.4	N2→W3	W3	N2	(7:58 pm)
June 21	23.5	N7→W1	W1	N7	(5:07 pm)
July 31	18.4	N7→W1	W1	WN7	(5:35 am)
July 31	18.4	W3→W1	W3&W1	LOC #5	(6:31 am)
July 31	18.4	N2→W3	W3	N2	(8:05 pm)
Sept. 10	5.2	N4→W1	W1	N4	(6:42 am)
Sept. 10	5.2	N1→W3	W3	N1	(7:03 pm)
Sept. 17	2.6	W7→W1	W7&W1	LOC #1	(5:20 pm)
Sept. 23	0.0	SFP→W3	W3	SFP	(6:40 pm)
Sept. 30	-2.6	FP→NW3	W3	CFP	(6:28 pm)
Oct. 7	-5.2	FP→SW3	W3	NFP	(6:16 pm)
Nov. 15	-18.4	S2→W3	W3	S2	4:22 pm
Dec. 21	-23.5	W3→W2	W3 & W2	LOC #6	7:35 am
Dec. 21	-23.5	L2→W3	W3	L2	4:14 pm

Table VI NEXT LUNAR MAJOR

June 2006	TOPW3→W2	Full moon		Rising at sunset
June 2006	W3→L2	Full moon		Setting at dawn
Dec. 2006	BOTW2→W3	Full moon	From LOC #2	Setting at dawn

Table VII NEXT LUNAR MINOR

Dec. 1996	W3→W1	Full moon	From LOC #5	Rising early evening
Dec. 1996	W1→N7	Full moon		Rising at sunset
Dec. 1996	N2→W3	Full moon		Setting at dawn
June 1997	W3→S2	Full moon		Setting at dawn

Appendix II SOLAR AZIMUTHS

Accurate azimuths determined by sunbeams defined by the vertical edges of windows **W1**, **W2**, **W3**, **W7**, and the eight pillars were used to better locate some features of the Tower. By knowing the date and the time to the nearest minute, the following relation was used:

$$\tan Z = \sin(t)/[\sin(\text{ø})\cos(t)-\cos(\text{ø})\tan(d)]$$

where Z = sun's azimuth measured from the south
    t = sun's hour/angle
             measured westward from the south
    ø = your latitude
    d = sun's declination

See Waugh (1973:6-17, 139, 205-206) for details and the necessary Tables. To watch the sun peek out around an edge you can use inexpensive eclipse glasses made with aluminized mylar to protect your eyes. These can be obtained from Abelexpress (1994).

ACKNOWLEDGMENTS

The author would like to thank the following: Dr. Jurgen Stock of CIDA (Venezuelan National Observatory) and Dr. Arthur Upgren of the Van Vleck Observatory, Wesleyan University, for their useful suggestions and continued support; John Dawson, the Assistant Director of the Frosty Drew Observatory for his assistance; Cindy Ray, John Penhallow, and Joseph Dotolo for their help; Henry H. Anderson, Jr., for pointing out the usefulness of solar azimuths; Jim Whittall, III, for sharing his knowledge and enthusiasm; and finally, my colleague Mike Brennan of Newport for getting me into this.

REFERENCES

Abelexpress—Astronomy Division, 230-Y E. Main St., Carnegie PA 15106, 800-542-9001.

Astronomical Almanac, The
1992 Washington: U.S. Government Printing Office.

Brown, Peter L.
1976 *Megaliths, Myths and Men*. New York: Taplinger Publishing Company.

Cyr, Donald L.
1977 Hidden halos of Stonehenge. In *Stonehenge Viewpoint*, No 17. Santa Barbara CA.

DeMerliac, Antoine
1988 Sailors and astronomy. In *Stargazers, the Contribution of Amateurs to Astronomy*, IAU Colloquium #98. S. Dunlop, M. Gerbaldi, eds. Berlin: Sprenger-Verlag.

Fisher, Dennis
1995 *Latitude Hooks and Azimuth Rings*. Camden ME: International Marine.

Gelling, P. and H. E. Davidson
1969 *The Chariot of the Sun*. London.

King, David A.
1991 Lunar crescent visibility predictions in medieval Islamic ephemerides. In *Arabic and Islamic Studies in Memory of Malcolm H. Kern*. S. Seikaly, R. Baalbaki, P. Dodd, eds. Beirut: American University of Beirut.
1994 *Astronomy in the Service of Islam*. Brookfield VT: Ashgate Publishing Company.

Krupp, E. C.
1996 Merging traffic on the ecliptic. Pp. 60-61 in *Sky and Telescope*, April.

Landsverk, O. G.
1974 *Runic Records of the Norsemen in America*. New York: Irvington Press.

Lindberg, David C.
1992 *The Beginnings of Western Science*. Chicago: The University of Chicago Press.

Liu, B. L. and A. D. Fiala
1992 *Canon of Lunar Eclipses, 1500 B.C.-A.D. 3000*. Richmond VA: Willmann-Bell, Inc.

Marshak, Alexander
1991 *The Roots of Civilization*. Mount Kisco NY: Moyer Bell Limited.

Mavor, James W., Jr.
1992 Personal communication.

Means, P. A.
1942 *The Newport Tower*. New York: H. Holt & Co.

MacKie, E. W.
1988 Investigating the prehistoric calendar. Pp. 206-231 in *Records in Stone, Papers in Memory of Alexander Thom*. C. L. N. Ruggles, ed. Cambridge: Cambridge University Press.

Minnaert, M.
1954 *Light and Color in the Open Air*. New York: Dover Publications, Inc.

Mongé, A. and O. G. Landsverk
1967 *Norse Medieval Cryptography in Runic Carvings*. Glendale CA: Norseman Press.

Morris, R. W. B.
1969 The cup-and-ring marks and similar early sculptures of southwest Scotland, Part 2. Pp. 37-76 in *Transactions of the Ancient Monuments Society* 16.

Morison, Samuel E.
1942 *Admiral of the Ocean Sea*. Boston: Little Brown & Company.

Mottram, C. Henry
1948 Norfolk. Pp. 183-194 in *The English Counties Illustrated*. C. E. M. Joad, ed. London: Odhams Press Ltd.

Neugebauer, O.
1962 *The Exact Sciences in Antiquity*. New York: Harper & Brothers.
1975 *A History of Ancient Mathematical Astronomy*. New York: Springer-Verlag.

Newport Tower Photogrammetric Measurement, The
1992 Copenhagen: Technical University of Denmark, Danish National Museum.

Pedersen, Olaf
1993 *Early Physics and Astronomy*. Cambridge: Cambridge University Press.

Penhallow, William S., Michael J. Brennan, and Cynthia J. Ray
  1992a *The Archaeoastronomy of The Old Stone Tower, Newport, Rhode Island*. A paper prepared for distribution at the NEARA ABC Conference at Brown University, June 18-21. Physics Department, University of Rhode Island, Kingston, RI 02881.

Penhallow, William S., Michael J. Brennan, Cynthia J. Ray, A. Upgren, and J. Stock
  1992b (abstract) *The Archaeoastronomy of the Old Stone Tower, Newport, Rhode Island*. A paper presented at the 23rd Meeting of the Division of Dynamical Astronomy of the American Astronomical Society, Chicago IL, December, 1992.

Prytz, Kåre
  1991 *Westward Before Columbus*. Oslo: Norsk Maritimt Forlag A/S.

Reid, William
  1993 Personal communication.

Ritchie, Anna
  1993 *Viking Scotland*. London: BT Batsford, Ltd.

Siemonsen, Jorgen
  1993 Newport: Public press conference, September 22.
  1995 Newport: Public press conference. December 2.

Simpson, D. D. A. and J. E. Thawley
  1972 Single-grave art in Britain. Pp. 81-104 in *Scottish Archaeological Forum* 4.

Streit, Jakob
  1984 *Sun and Cross*. Edinburgh: Floris Books. Translation of *Sonne und Kruz* by Hugh Latham.

Swarup, G., A. K. Bag, and K. S. Shukla, eds.
  1987 History of oriental astronomy. In *IAU Colloquium #91*. Cambridge: Cambridge University Press.

Toomer, G. J.
  1984 *Ptolemy's Almagest*. New York: Springer-Verlag.

Vebaek, C. L. and S. Thirslund
  1992 *The Viking Compass*. Skjern: Gullanders Bogtrykkeri A/S.

Waugh, Albert E.
  1973 *Sundials. Their Theory and Construction*. New York: Dover Publications, Inc.

Whittall, James P. Jr.
  1993a Personal communication.
  1993b Personal communication.
  1995a Personal communication.
  1995b Personal communication.

Whone, Herbert
  1990 *Church Monastery Cathedral*. Longmead, Shaftesbury, Dorset: Element Books Ltd

Figure 6 AERIAL VIEW OF THE NEWPORT TOWER (© John Hopf)

COMMENTARY—SECTION I

Shadow and Substance

CURTISS HOFFMAN

I am delighted to have the opportunity to comment on the series of papers on *Artifacts, Sites, and Archaeoastronomy* from the ABC Conference. Since I transferred my area of specialization from the Near East to the Northeast, I have always remained sympathetic to the *idea* of transoceanic crossings before Columbus. This is not to say that I accept all, or even most, claims of diffusion and migration from the Old World to the New. I try to keep an open mind and to deal with the evidence on a case-by-case basis, using the conceptual tools of my trade.

I entitled the presentation I gave on this subject at the 1996 NEARA Fall Conference *Substance and Shadow* for several reasons. First, I am well aware of the importance to archaeoastronomers of observing the placement of shadows. Second, I believe that it is fair to characterize the history of neo-diffusionism in America as a gradual emergence of substantial evidence out of the shadows. But most importantly, I believe that the diffusionist position forms a useful foil for the isolationist archaeological orthodoxy. In the language of classical Jungian psychoanalysis, the Shadow is an archetype which carries all that the individual or the group wishes not to acknowledge about themselves (Jung 1969:20-24). I think that it would be fair to say that the neo-diffusionist movement, which now supports its own conferences, organizations, and publications, parallel but often antithetical to those of the mainstream, serves as a kind of shadow presence for orthodox archaeology.

For a long time, diffusionists and isolationists in American archaeology have been engaged in a kind of shadow-boxing, in which each refuses to acknowledge the validity of the other's claims or methods, and each identifies the other as the intellectual enemy. The isolationist mainstream accuses neo-diffusionists of implicit racism, in part because the early 19th century diffusionists like Adair are easy prey to charges that their ideas were formulated in a political climate which can best be characterized as government-sanctioned theft of Indian lands. The frequent claim that the existing native peoples had little time depth in the land, and that its ancient monuments were constructed by someone else—preferably someone of European or West Asian origin—was undeniably a rationalization for the seizure of property, displacement, and eventual interment of natives on marginal reservation lands by people of European descent (Willey and Sabloff 1974:30). Neo-diffusionists—especially those who approach the field on the basis of faiths like Mormonism—are often tarred with the same old brush. Sometimes, the tar sticks! We certainly all need to examine and deconstruct our beliefs, since they do not arise in an intellectual vacuum.

On the other hand, I have heard talks and read papers by diffusionists who exhibit a high degree of impatience with and disdain for the rather plodding methods of modern archaeology. The discovery of a connection, however speculative, appears to be tantamount to the truth for some people, and they do not feel they need any confirmation other than the pleasure of their own thoughts. Any attempt to 'disconfirm'—which is what science is all about—is met with overt hostility. Often enough, this is due to the failure on the part of mainstream archaeologists to present their findings to the literate public in a digestible form. Instead, they write in a highly specialized language of sampling universes and optimum foraging strategies. It is small wonder that more intuitive thinkers have become impatient with this and want to leap to conclusions which seem patently obvious without taking the time for more careful study.

Little of this posturing on either side has any relationship to the facts, and those who take extreme positions on either side and demonize their opposition are clearly incapable of coming any closer to the true substance of pre-Columbian history. They have projected their Shadows upon one another, and this makes communication next to impossible. The tragedy of this is that, while the opposing sides talk past each other, the sites are being rapidly destroyed, so that we may never know the truth.

It is for this reason that the opportunity to create a dialogue, which the ABC Conference and these conference papers present, is most welcome. I have read each of the eight papers in this section carefully and have provided the authors with a set of critical remarks. They have reworked their manuscripts so as to accommodate at least some of these. My comments below are the residuum of what I felt they did not fully deal with in their revisions. My opinions of the articles in their final form are very varied, and as I am not expert in all of the regions or technologies involved my remarks should certainly not be considered in any way as the last word on these matters.

Irving Rouse long ago (1958) suggested five criteria for determining whether diffusion had taken place (I paraphrase these below):

> 1. It is necessary to uncover the remains of one or more specific communities and to show that they are probably intrusive in the region where they occur.

2. These groups need to be traced back to their homeland, identifying the original group from which the migrants split off and discovering the traces of the group in the intervening areas through which the migration is presumed to have passed—though this may not necessarily be a continuous distribution, since people may have passed quickly through an area without leaving identifiable traces.

3. It is necessary to establish the contemporaneity (or near-contemporaneity) of the sites on either end of the migration route.

4. It is important to note whether the proper environmental and cultural conditions for migration are present.

5. It is incumbent upon the person who wishes to demonstrate migration to consider and eliminate the possibility that some other hypothesis may better fit the facts at his disposal. The differences as well as the similarities in culture between areas need to be considered, for if the differences are great enough they would favor diffusion of traits rather than whole peoples.

This is a very important basis for all diffusionist hypotheses to consider. Neo-diffusionists have been doing pretty well with the first two of these, though tracing movements through intervening areas remains a serious problem. They are beginning to present more credible evidence for the third and fourth criteria. But we should particularly pay attention to Rouse's last point, since there are at least three alternative hypotheses that can account for cultural similarities. These are: *common* (but ancient) *cultural heritage*, *psychic unity*, and *independent invention*. Blust (1981) has provided a useful typology for determining which of these is most likely in a variety of cases. We should also consider the likelihood that more than one of these mechanisms may have been operating at the same time: *e.g.*, a group of outsiders entering a previously occupied area with new technology may find that this technology can be adapted to local conditions because it squares with a preexisting set of ideas that derived from the common cultural heritage which the two peoples share, or because the society in question had independently reached a similar point of development, or because the people making contact share similar personality traits and are able to negotiate profitably with one another as equals—or any combination of these.

As I shall elucidate below, I take the position that it is no longer sufficient merely to demonstrate that diffusion has occurred. It is essential to place it within a social context. After the Paleo-Indians, whose entry into the hemisphere has recently been extended backwards from 11,200 BP (Dillehay 1989), no group of immigrants to the New World has encountered an empty land. All have had to negotiate their way with preexisting groups. In the course of this negotiation, individuals, artifacts, raw materials, traits, ideas, pathogens, and/or genes may have crossed the cultural divide. It is not always easy to tell from the archaeological evidence which, if any, of these we are dealing with. It is also most likely that the previous inhabitants will have done what they could to integrate the new inputs

into their existing cultural systems. No culture is a passive sponge; each is a vibrant, living collective entity with ideas, passions, and agendas of its own. A careful study of the historical record of post-Columbian contact makes this clear. Native peoples did not merely sit back and let themselves be conquered by 16th to 17th century Europeans; they fought back in as many ways as there were nations. Sometimes adopting the protective coloration of the conqueror over a covertly maintained set of beliefs worked best for them, as Mavor and Dix have shown for the Northeast. Sometimes a creative synthesis emerged, as in the peculiar Mesoamerican brands of folk Christianity. In a few cases, isolation or flight to reserved impenetrable areas served a people well. When the numbers of colonizers was small (as perhaps at Roanoke, or Columbus' first colony on Hispaniola), it was possible to eliminate the invaders, but not entirely their cultural influence. We may expect that all of the above strategies, as well as many others, would apply to pre-Columbian contacts as well. In every case, a study of exactly how incoming influences from the outside affected the local culture will provide rewarding insights into the nature of human cultural exchange. It is not enough to merely identify the outsiders as so many Kilroys, leaving their graffiti behind for future generations of archaeologists to ponder. In short, we need to turn the information into *anthropology* in order to make it useful. Once we are able to do this, I think we will succeed in getting beyond our Shadow-projections and providing each other and the public with some really substantive contributions to the understanding of America's rich pre-Columbian history.

MEGGERS

Of all the articles in this section, I felt that this one came the closest to the kind of study I am used to encountering in the archaeological literature. It is very substantive, well-referenced, cogently argued, and founded on a wealth of evidence. I have no trouble accepting her thesis, and am gratified that subsequent evidence has tended to bear it out.

1. The *entire list* of 32 dates does not extend Valdivia A back to 5620 ± 256 BP; only one date does that and it may be an outlier (*i.e.*, contaminated or otherwise nonrepresentative). It is standard practice in evaluating archaeological sites to discard outliers, or at least to refrain from accepting them as definitive, because there is so much that can go wrong in the radiocarbon process. It is significant that Meggers has extended the age of Valdivia I back into the 6th millenium, but it would be better to state that the list "extends Valdivia A back to *as early as 5620.*" More excavation might clarify the validity of the earliest date, as it has (finally) at Monte Verde.

2. What is known of the total distribution of different site types? This would be helpful in evaluating the function of Punta Conception vs. other sites.

3. What is the nature of the *co-occurrence* of various

stylistic motifs on Jomon and Valdivia pottery? Are there consistent iconographic *clusters* (this could be determined by computer analysis)? Also, what can be said about fine-grained technological comparisons? Are the designs produced with similar instruments? Are the *habits of production*—the characteristic and repeated manufacturing steps such as clay preparation, vessel construction, firing temperatures and atmospheres, etc.—and not only the final results similar? How about non-iconographic attributes such as ware thickness, vessel shape, paste, temper? Was it only the decorative attributes which diffused? If so, why? Has a double-blind test been tried, with scholars from both sides of the Pacific presented with a mixed sample of Jomon and Valdivia pottery to see whether they can reliably distinguish between them or not? (If the wares are radically different, this might have to be done with photos or drawings of the design elements only.)

4. Japanese pottery is traditionally made by male specialists, whereas New World pottery is often made by women. Is there evidence for gender specificity in the Valdivia pottery? This could be tested by examining the lengths of coils and mathematically reconstructing from them the characteristic size of the original clay balls—the smaller the ball, the smaller the hand which produced it (Philpotts 1993). If it was produced by women, what would account for the change in tradition? What has been so far inferred about the social context of pottery in Jomon culture, either in terms of gender or craft specialization? If it differs from that found in Ecuador, what could have caused this? Finally, were pots (not potters) typically taken on long sea voyages by Jomon fishermen? What was stored in them if they were?

5. Note that the argument for the priority of Puerto Hormiga is considerably weakened by the strong series of Valdivia dates which form an unbroken continuum from 5620 - 4330 BP. Is the author of the opinion that the San Jacinto ware was also introduced from outside the continent? Or that it diffused from the Ecuadorian coast? It is interesting to note that archaeologists in the Southeast seem to have little difficulty in concluding that Puerto Hormiga subsequently diffused rapidly across the Caribbean to the Carolina/Georgia coast (Sassaman 1993:24).

6. Provide a series of comparable dates for Jomon pottery. These should be available from Japanese published sources, or perhaps through a perusal of the volumes of the journal *Radiocarbon*. (Tedious, yes, but this is essential to establish Rouse's point 3.)

7. The dates from Colimas are late in the sequence, as is that from El Enciento. It looks as if the origins of the culture are on the coast, and that it spread southwards and then inland. This rebuts the argument for interior origins.

MAVOR AND DIX

This paper is my second-favorite article in the collection. I have great respect for the integrity and vision of the authors and for their knowledge of the universality of astronomical observation. Their thesis that some of the monuments in New England could have been the work of (both pre- and post-Contact) native peoples is eminently worthy of consideration, especially since the available chronological evidence places most of these structures at a time when horticulture first became an important food source in the region.

1. "Everyone watches the sky, and everyone sees mostly the same objects." Amen! This could be applied to many of the previous (and following) criticisms.

2. Domes arose spontaneously in some parts of the world as early as the 1st millenium BC (Mesopotamia). It is possible that this was an architectural experiment, since it isn't replicated elsewhere in the region.

3. It should be noted that the Nashoba earthworks are located on what is now a military reservation, where earth-moving is done as a matter of course during practice maneuvers. The 'donations' which I have viewed there are more likely surreptitious 'offerings' of trash by members of Euro-American culture.

4. Cite Patterson and Sassaman's work (1988) on the intentional aboriginal burning of forests in the Northeast.

5. Note the association of Chinese dragons with North.

6. Southwest social organization is very different from that in New England—there are permanent, hereditary ritual positions and sedentary agriculture. Most New England natives, even during the Late Woodland period, were transhumant and had a looser clan structure and no hereditary leadership (before the English created the 'Wampanoag Royal Line'). It would be better to look for more local sources for the horned figure (such as the Midewiwin Manibozho monster—the Ojibway also spoke an Algonquian language) rather than looking as far afield as the Southwest for parallels.

TOTTEN

The thing I like most about this article is that the argument is explicitly presented as an hypothesis. It is very important to separate speculation from fact, and Totten does a good job of this. He is also clearly aware of how much more work needs to be done to substantiate this hypothesis; he is essentially presenting it here and making some suggestions for future research. This is appropriately modest. The major drawback I find is in the lack of continuity; the article skips around from section to section and would benefit from some judicious reorganization.

1. Is there any evidence that Tiwanaku was built using iron tools?

2. It was Cieza's job to subdue the Inkas and other local natives and establish white (Spanish) rule. To accomplish

this, he may have had a political agenda which included the deliberate distortion of local histories by making the former occupants of Tiwanaku out to be *a*) white, *b*) peaceful, and *c*) very powerful. From what I know of the area (admittedly, little), it is usually considered that Tiwanaku was an incipient conquest state—that is, it dominated and exploited the labor of local and surrounding populations to support an elite ruling class (Clarke 1977:436-438). This does not fit well with the idealistic model Cieza cited, but it does fit well with the Realpolitik of the Spanish conquest.

3. How do we *know* what the eye-arrow motif meant to the various cultures who used it?

4. Give citations for the Carthaginean inscriptions found in the United States, etc.!

5. If the pot in question is unique in (apparently) having an inscription, what are the chances that it is in fact not an inscription at all but a set of ideograms or decorative figurings? How similar are its motifs/characters to others which the author considers to be non-inscriptional? What is the basis for considering this vessel to be older than the others, *independent* of its apparent inscription and the author's hypothesis that writing as a cultural institution broke down some time after colonization?

6. Why might the indigenous people of the Tiwanaku area have accepted Berber rulers? How "superior" in technology and education were the Berbers to the native people of western South America? Did the Berbers impose their rule on them by force? But I thought Cieza said they were peaceful!

7. The 'successor' pot to the Juba pot has not only lost its 'inscription,' it also appears to have lost its 'Berber' physical features and resembles a Native American.

8. The method of travel from the Caribbean to Peru posited by the author is questionable. The Cordillera is a formidable cultural barrier, even in Panama (Balboa had difficulty doing it because of both mountains and dense jungle; many of his men succumbed to jungle fevers). And going up the Orinoco, one runs into rather fierce and xenophobic peoples equipped with arrow poison, such as the Yanamamo—it's not too likely that a small group of elite Berbers would have gotten through. And even if they did, why did they preserve their script all the way to Peru, and then lose it?

9. How common is it for Berber inscriptions in North Africa to have the form on the pot of a twice-repeated name and title? Is Juba's name ever written there without the final 'A'?

10. How similar is the climate of Tiwanaku (not the Pacific coast) to North Africa? Why would it be attractive to North Africans to settle *there*, rather than remaining on the coast, which is rather dry and therefore somewhat similar to their homeland?

STEEDE

The Comalcalco site is clearly a fascinating one, with much room for further research into what has already been excavated. The article suffers by being rather under-referenced (this defect has improved since I first reviewed it), and there are some inconsistencies in the tables. I eagerly await the results of further radiocarbon dating at the site. Its position as well as its unique features make it a good candidate for Rouse's first point; it does look intrusive. More documentation is needed on the other points, however.

1. Since bricks can't be dated directly, mortar from the ruins was submitted for radiocarbon assay. There are several serious problems with using mortar for dates. First, one must have a good deal of information about the composition of the mortar and the proportion of shell it contains. If it is mostly composed of crushed limestone, the dates are likely to be wholly inaccurate due to the fact that what is being dated is the age of organisms which were alive many thousands (millions?) of years ago, not the age of the composition of the mortar or its incorporation into the site (Taylor:1987:34). Second, even if the mortar is all or mostly all from recent shell, one would need to know the species and sources involved, to account for the 'Reservoir Effect' produced by filter-feeders consuming carbon from marine microplankton at different rates, subject to the upwelling of ocean currents (Taylor 1987:127-131). Third, shell from the innermost part of the bivalve will also be older than the exterior because bivalves grow like trees, adding a ring each year. Fourth, because faunal rather than floral material is being dated, it is difficult to apply the Stuiver calibration curve to the dates to convert them into true years rather than AD/BC dates. This does not matter much when dating a site with a margin of error of, say 200 years; but it matters a great deal to Steede's argument for a Roman age for this site—or for it being antecedent to other sites in the region with similar architecture. A date (preferably several) from an associated charcoal deposit is really needed to confirm the mortar date. It would also be helpful to know the precise relationship of the sample to site stratigraphy, etc. (See McCulloch's article for levels of association.)

2. Discuss the "stages of brick construction."

3. Given that there is 82 percent comparability with Carthaginean bricks, and given the known maritime skills of the Carthagineans, why does the author think it was Romans and not Carthagineans who were the builders of Comalcalco? The latter would have had much more reason to flee the eastern Mediterranean after the Punic Wars, and they were well acquainted with at least the eastern Atlantic. (See Totten's article.)

4. The author questions why more technology didn't spread from the site to the surrounding area. This is a very good question. Perhaps a "near perfect" mix would

not be as near perfect in a tropical climate? Why assume degeneration rather than reinvention?

5. The statement that traits (*e.g.*, tombs) are "unique" without a specific demonstration of this is not satisfactory. The "Tomb of the Nine Lords" is a very specific Meso-american iconographic reference, one which is absent from Mediterranean cosmologies of the time. This suggests that, if anything, the site is a mix of intrusive and local ideologies, rather than being pure Roman.

6. Reference the "usual" Mayan system of linear measurement. What about mensuration at other Late Pre-Classic and Early Classic sites in the region—*e.g.*, Teotihuacan? It's hardly "amazing" that 99 percent of molded bricks conformed to the same set of sizes—that's what you get when you use brick molds! Granted that there were several modal sizes, that just means that they had several sizes of molds. Is there evidence for why certain sizes were used? Is there any chronology to this, or were bricks of different sizes incorporated into different parts of the same structure, perhaps for different purposes?

7. What are "measuring marks" on bricks *for*? How do we know they were for measuring?

BARRON

Once again we have an unusually challenging site, one which bears further investigation. To Barron's credit he does not make sweeping claims for the identity of the builders, but leaves the question open. I would also like to credit Nick Bellantoni, the Connecticut State Archaeologist, for his open-mindedness concerning this site. As with Steede's article, this paper is very under-referenced, but it relies more upon direct observation and therefore the omission is not as serious. I don't necessarily agree that the site was built by the Norse, but I confess that I haven't a really good idea who did build it.

1. When presenting radiocarbon dates, give mean, range, and lab number, and describe what was dated. Erving Taylor (1987:115) provides a framework for interpreting the likelihood of associations of cultural material with radiocarbon dates, ranging from "possibility" to "essential certainty," depending on how closely incorporated the material is with the dated substance. In this case, the Broadspear was within 1 m. of the dated feature, in the same stratigraphic horizon. A plan of the feature and its soil matrix should be provided; otherwise there is no conclusive evidence that there is a stratigraphic association. This would place the association in Taylor's 'possible' category, the least likely one he is willing to consider.

2. The cross is an ancient, universal symbol, sacred to many eastern Native Americans long before Christ. I have a co-authored article now in draft on this subject (Hoffman, MacLeod, and Smith in prep.). The *chi rho* is itself a pre-Christian symbol, found in ancient Mesopotamian and Syrian representations of the warrior goddess Ishtar/Astarte.

That's why the non-Christian barbarians fled when Constantine carried it into battle!

3. If early Christian adventurers exposed native populations to Christian symbols, what was the long-term effect on their cultures? The local Pequot-Mohegan beliefs point to a southwestern, not an eastern origin of their culture hero (Simmons 1986).

4. The absence of a pre-Viking explorers' settlement remains is only enigmatic if one presumes that they had a settlement in the vicinity of the site at all. It is far more likely that whoever built on the hill used it for only short-term occupations, such as hunting, shelter in storms, and ceremonial activities. This would fit the known cultural patterns of the region. Maybe even the late Colonial houses were marginal? A complete title search would be helpful.

HEIL

I had more difficulty with this article than any of the others, especially in its original form. It contains many unfounded speculations, based upon what seemed to me to be superficial similarities between Mesoamerican and East Asian cultures. While it was certainly interesting to learn of the skills of the Purhépecha metallurgists, I found the arguments for diffusion here to be unconvincing.

1. The identification of the Purhépecha with Buddhist monks is particularly absurd. Many peoples around the world are, or have been, nomadic, but this does not make them Buddhists! The Chichimecas were *also* the ancestors of the Aztecs, whose militarism, delight in human sacrifice, and ritual cannibalism bear no relationship to either Buddhist practice or doctrine. It was suggested to me at the NEARA meeting that there would have been closer similarities to Bon practice, and I agree with this—but Bon is part of a nearly universal shamanistic tradition (Eliade 1969:336), so this is not good evidence for diffusion. In Tibet, Tara is always a goddess, never a god, and there are several different Taras with different aspects (black, white, green, etc.). What was the role of the Chichimec god Taras?

2. The identification of the chief with the local Sun God is common to most chiefdom and state-level societies world-wide; *e.g.*, Heliogabalus, Louis XIV, the Natchez Great Sun, the Inca emperors, the Egyptian pharaohs. This is not just a Chinese trait. It is rather a natural metaphor that derives from the existence of a centralized political elite and its comparison to (and figurative assumption of) the solar power; it is not necessarily good evidence of diffusion. For a legitimate Chinese connection, one would want to show the presence of the entire Taoist/Confucianist cultural apparatus, especially the specific association of the North direction with royalty. Most Mesoamerican cosmologies begin with the East.

3. Bells used in Tibetan Buddhist monasteries are rather different in form and usage from those used in other

parts of the world—they are inverted, open-mouthed bronze vessels sounded by using a hand-held clapper after the fashion of a glass harmonica. They are not enclosed as jingles as in Figures 3 and 5.

4. Mirrors of polished magnetite and obsidian were used in Mesoamerica from Late Formative times onwards—long before the supposed date of diffusion (unless the author wants to resurrect the Olmec-Shang connection). They are associated with the dark trader-god Tezcatlipoca in Aztec cosmology—very different from imperial Japanese practice. The lack of a chronology for the supposed diffusion is a significant problem here.

5. Half-moon-shaped objects are, once again, very obvious, universal symbols, attested from as early as the Upper Paleolithic in Europe. Everyone can see the Moon!

6. In this article there is little sense of the internal chronology of Michoacán metallurgy.

7. The formula $x \sim y$ $\therefore$ $x \rightarrow y$ is unconvincing. Rouse's criteria for diffusion should be used instead. There is little sense of the *cultural context* of the status-oriented metal goods. Why should only high-status items have crossed the ocean? Is there any evidence for the priority of diffused forms followed by successive local adaptations?

RUDOLPH

As I am not an archaeoastronomer, I do not feel qualified to comment on the archaeoastronomy, except to say that it does seem to be present. As with the Heil article, Rudolph has a tendency to assume $x \sim y$ $\therefore$ $x \rightarrow y$. Again, it is important to place the site within its native cultural context, even if the native peoples at the time of European contact had, or claimed to have, no knowledge of it. The claim may have been protective coloration against invaders who demonstrated flagrant disrespect for their indigenous beliefs. And we do know something about the archaeology of pre-Contact northern California!

1. While the peoples of California (except the Mohave) were hunters and gatherers throughout the prehistoric sequence, they were *very prosperous* hunter-gatherers. During the Late Period, they organized huge intertribal fairs and festivals (Fagan 1991:206-209), and pre-Contact population densities are reckoned as being higher than anywhere else on the continent north of Mexico. Dealing with numbers like these required more complex political organization, and, maybe, better regulation of calendrics.

2. All peoples develop a cosmology, not just 'civilized' ones like the Aztecs and the Chinese. In Levi-Strauss' *The Raw and the Cooked*, he documents rather sophisticated astronomical observations among tribal societies in North and South America. For example, the Bororo of the Mato Grosso are able to accurately locate the planet Venus *during the daytime* (Levi-Strauss 1969:231).

3. Differential weathering is not necessarily a good indicator of age; it can be the result of different parent rock or degree of exposure. It is not at all surprising that the 'best' ideograms are in the most interior chambers, where they would be more protected from the elements.

PENHALLOW

Once again, I do not feel qualified to comment on the accuracy of the archaeoastronomical measurements in this article. But I do have difficulties in attributing any great antiquity to the Newport Tower. There is simply not enough evidence for a Norse presence anywhere in southern New England, let alone a rationale for the creation of a complex alien ceremonial structure in the very heartland of Wampanoag/Narragansett country without reference to what they might have thought of it. Quite simply, I regard the tower as a post-Contact, maybe post-King Philip's War construction—and the Carbon-14 date appears to support this conclusion. Maybe it was built by someone who had seen the similar structures in Europe?

1. Provide a proper citation for the Carbon-14 date. "Between AD 1500 and 1630 $\pm$ 50 years" is very difficult to interpret. Was the actual date AD 1565 $\pm$ 65 (splitting the difference between 1500 and 1630)? If so, there would be a 68 percent probability (1 sigma) that the age of the mortar fell between the endpoints. If there were two or more dates, it is possible that their ranges were averaged. Most archaeologists use dates at 2 sigma, because it gives 95 percent probability. In this case, the range would be double, allowing for the possibility of either a pre-1492 age (1430) or a post-plantation age (1695). The date is therefore very equivocal. I understand that this is a problem with the original Siemonsen report, but if the laboratory which ran the date could be determined, they would probably be willing to supply a copy of their report form to the author.

2. Why were the Danish churches not prototypes for later structures in Denmark also? The 13th century is a good deal too early for the radiocarbon date!

3. What evidence is there that market crosses or other monuments at town centers in Medieval Europe were used as astronomical markers? And if the Newport Tower were a monument situated at the center of a market town as claimed, *where is the occupational debris*? One would expect plenty of garbage around a market center!

4. Given that the tower required "a considerable expenditure of time and effort" to build, what sustained the builders while they were doing it? This would be a productive question for future research. Penhallow rather scornfully dismissed this critique in his response to my original comments, but the issue stands: no one spends that much effort on public construction without some form of material support—not at the pyramids of Egypt or

Mesoamerica, not at the mounds of the Ohio Valley, not anywhere. The study of *vernacular* cultures—the lives of common people, not kings or priests—has been the focus of archaeology for the past three decades. We ignore it at our peril.

5. Has any research been done into deeds and other documents to show the history of land use over the past 350 years? This might possibly yield references to the pre-existence of the Tower; it also might provide evidence on the affiliations of the early Colonial settlers and their successors which might suggest alternatives to pre-Contact construction.

REFERENCES

Blust, Robert
  1981 Linguistic evidence for some early Austronesian taboos. *American Anthropologist* 83(2):285-319.
Clarke, Grahame
  1977 *World Prehistory in New Perspective*. Cambridge, England: Cambridge University Press.
Dillehay, Thomas
  1989 Monte Verde: late Pleistocene settlement in Chile. Vol. 1: *Paleoenvironment and Site Context*. Washington DC: Smithsonian Institution Press.
Eliade, Mircea
  1969 *Yoga: Immortality and Freedom*. Bollingen Series LVI. Willard R. Trask, trans. Princeton NJ: Princeton University Press.
Fagan, Brian
  1991 *Ancient North America: The Archaeology of a Continent*. London: Thames and Hudson Ltd.
Hoffman, Curtiss, Maryanne MacLeod, and Alan Smith
  in prep. Symbols in stone: chiastolites at New England archaeological sites. Manuscript prepared for review for possible publication in the *Bulletin of the Massachusetts Archaeological Society*.
Jung, Carl Gustav
  1969 *The Archetypes and the Collective Unconscious*. Collected Works, Vol. 9. Bollingen Series XX. R. F. C. Hull, trans. Princeton NJ: Princeton University Press.
Levi-Strauss, Claude
  1969 *The Raw and the Cooked. Introduction to a Science of Mythology,* Vol. 1. John and Doreen Weightman, trans. New York: Harper and Row.
Patterson, William III and Kenneth Sassaman
  1988 Indian fires in the prehistory of New England. Pp. 107-136 in *Holocene Human Ecology in Northeastern North America*. George Nicholas, ed. New York and London: Plenum Press.
Philpotts, Anthony
  1993 *Petrofabric Analysis and Firing Temperature of a Late Woodland Ceramic Vessel from South Windsor CT*. Paper presented at the Annual Meeting of the Northeastern Anthropological Association, Western Connecticut State University, Danbury CT.
Rouse, Irving
  1958 The inference of migrations from anthropological evidence. Pp. 63-68 in *Migrations in New World Culture History*. Raymond Thompson, ed. Tucson AZ: University of Arizona Press.
Sassaman, Kenneth
  1993 *Early Pottery in the Southeast: Tradition and Innovation in Cooking Technology*. Tuscaloosa LA: University of Alabama Press.
Simmons, William S.
  1986 *Spirit of the New England Tribes: Indian History and Folklore 1620-1984*. Hanover NH: University Press of New England.
Taylor, R. Erving
  1987 *Radiocarbon Dating: An Archaeological Perspective*. Orlando FL: Academic Press.
Willey, Gordon R. and Jeremy Sabloff
  1974 *A History of American Archaeology*. San Francisco CA: W. H. Freeman Co.

BETTY MEGGERS

In general, I feel that the criteria stipulated by Rouse and accepted by Hoffman for assessing diffusion are unrealistic, particularly as they concern transoceanic movements of a few individuals. Most [of the criteria] could not be satisfied even for early European English colonies in eastern North America and are not required to demonstrate contacts within the hemispheres. With regard to alternative explanations, including independent invention and convergent adaptation, I have dealt with these at length in a book entitled *Prehistoric America* and have emphasized that they are complementary processes. We cannot place any contact in a social context, however, until we recognize its existence, and even then the mechanism may be impossible to reconstruct. The fact that "no culture is a passive sponge" is a large part of the problem, since elements may be adopted incompletely, incorporated into preexisting complexes, or modified in various ways. The resulting "mismatch" is seized upon by anti-diffusionists as evidence of independent invention.

With regard to comments directed toward my contribution, I should first say that many of the points have been discussed in our monograph, *Smithsonian Contributions to Anthropology Volume 1*, 1965. We provided 90 plates that show Valdivia motifs to be exclusive to a particular technique of decoration, as they are in Jomon, and 26 additional plates comparing the same types in the two complexes to document the use of the same techniques to produce the same motifs. Composition and vessel shape are less likely to be duplicated, the former because of differences in local raw materials and the latter because of the influence from traditional container shapes. Decoration is widely used by archaeologists to infer contact within hemispheres because it is free from such constraints. Whether Jomon pottery was made by males and Valdivia pottery by females is a matter of speculation. Prior to the advent of occupational specialization, pottery is typically (and perhaps exclusively) made by women. I doubt that reconstructing hand size, assuming that is possible, would solve the problem, since sex differences in physical dimensions vary among populations. This is not relevant in any case, because ethnographic evidence indicates that both sexes are capable of performing activities traditionally assigned to one when necessary. Whether or not Jomon men made pottery, they certainly would have known how to do it, and the existence of the Jomon-Valdivia similarities implies that whoever came had the relevant expertise.

The answer to the inquiry in point 5 is "Yes." Similarities between San Jacinto 1 and Early Middle Jomon pottery from Honshu are as striking as those between the contemporary Valdivia and Early Middle Jomon pottery from Kyushu, and I hope that someone will follow this up in the not-too-distant future.

CELIA HEIL

The Purhépecha is an entirely different culture from the Aztec or the Maya, and it is absurd for Dr. Hoffman to attempt to compare them. I based my paper on archaeological and anthropological research, and I found several Asian pre-Columbian cultural aspects (particularly Chinese and Japanese) in the Purhépecha, including symbols similar to those of the Buddhists. Supporting this possibility are two of the most important documents of the Purhépecha: the *Lienzo de Jucutácato,* and *La Relación de las ceremonias y ritos y población y gobierno de los indios de la provincia de Michuacan* (see my endnotes). Depicted in the *Lienzo* are long trumpets similar to those used by Buddhist monks in China and Tibet; also shown, in addition to metalworking, are mounds and pyramids which the Purhépecha called *yácatas,* similar to stupas where Buddhists place relics and show reverence as found in the *Lienzo.* In more recent studies such as Helen Perlstein Pollard's *Tariacuri's Legacy* are described a number of Asian similarities with the Purhépecha and their religious practices.

La Relación says that the michuaque, also known as Quaochpanme, which means 'people with shaved heads' (Buddhist monks shave their heads), wandered looking for metals; that may be the migration represented on the *Lienzo.* In addition, many of the figures drawn in *La Relación* are wearing clothing similar to that of Asian Buddhist monks.

Fray Bernardino de Sahagún wrote that: "*The god* (note that Sahagún said *god* and not *goddess* even though in Buddhism the deity is female) *they had was called Taras, from which the Michoaque took their name; it is said also to be Tarasca; and this Taras in the Nahuatl language is the same as Mixcoatl, that was the god of the Chichimecas*" (Sahagún, Book X, p. 610, para. 104) *La Relación* says that Chichimecas (nomads or wanderers) were the "*. . . people who didn't stay in one place; they were everywhere on the roads of the empire, working for Kurikaueri.*" This could mean that the chichimecas with shaved heads, on the move, working for their god Kurikaueri, may have been Buddhist monks. In recent years, historians have generally accepted the name *chichimeca* to be a word applied to any nomads and not a particular ethnic group. The Aztecs, therefore, may have been descendants of a nomad group of different ethnic and linguistic background from the Purhépecha. The Purhépecha were immigrants of unknown origin with a language that has no similarity to any other language in North America, and they were also called *chichimecas*. Sahagún did not describe any religious practices of the Purhépecha and their god Taras. This is the only reference found thus far regarding Taras and the Purhépecha.

The *Liang Shu*, a history of the Liang Dynasty, by Chinese historian Yao Si-Liang of the Tang Dynasty, records, in chapter 48, "Liezhuan," the voyage of Hui Sheng (Hoei-Chen) to the land of Fusang, accompanied by five Buddhist monks. He is the first person who reported to have visited Fusang (believed to be Mexico), in AD 458, returning to China forty-one years later, in 499. He died in a monastery after AD 500. Between 520 and 528, during the Liang Dynasty, his voyage was recorded by historians of the emperor Wu Di (Vargas 1990:159).

Although Asian cultural similarities I have found in the Purhépecha need further study, each is not an isolated cultural aspect but one more link in the chain of a cultural complex.

Neil Steede

1. We agree that better dating is needed for the Comalcalco site and, in fact, have several samples awaiting funding for such dating.

2. At this point, it seems that the first stage of brick construction was consolidation and conservation (stabilization) of existing clay structures. That is, flat surfaces, more prone to erosion, were first covered in brick; then other areas were covered or buildings built.

3. In fact, the argument for Carthaginian refugees is good, although Punic war refugees would be a little early, but possible. We *believe*, but cannot *prove* at this point, that Christians were the refugees in question. This belief is partially supported by the chronology and partially by the several Christian icons seemingly represented on several of the bricks. This belief is only theoretical at this point.

4. We *assume* "degeneration" because that position seems to fit the apparent facts. At earlier Maya sites (*e.g.*, Yaxchilan), we find very poor construction abilities or material, such as mortar. At later, Classic Maya sites (*e.g.*, Palenque) we find much better construction and much better materials. In the interlude between the building of such sites, we have the apparent intrusion of Comalcalco. Pre-Comalcalco construction is extremely poor, whereas post-Comalcalco sites show marked improvement but still not up to the standards of Comalcalco itself. This holds true from wing walls and buttresses to mortar mix. So, one may assume reinvention, but it does not quite fit the facts.

5. In fact, ideologies are mixed, and we have never suggested otherwise. It is the architecture, measurements, and the placement of the tomb which are unique. None of those factors has anything to do with ideology.

6. There are two other basic measuring systems in Mesoamerica; both are somewhat controversial. The more accepted of the two is the Teotihuacan unit, equal to 81 cm. or 31 7/8 inches. Refer to Ramon Almaraz 1985: Apuntes sobre las pyramides de San Juan Teotihuacan; pp. 349-358 in *Memoria de los trabajos ejecutados por la Comision Cientifica de Pachuca*; imprenta de J. M. Andrade y F. Escalante, Mexico.

The second system of Maya linear measurements is much more contoversial. Most Maya institutions say that the Maya had no lineal measuring system. On the face of it, this seems absurd to me considering all of their engineering feats. Nevertheless, this is the official claim of the Maya Institute of the National University of Mexico, per Drs. Victor Manuel Castillos and Lazaro Ocampa. Many other Maya scholars agree. However, several obscure studies all come independently to the same, but different, conclusion. They all agree that the Maya unit was 45 cm. or 17.7 inches. Refer to Daniel G. Brinton 1891: *Essays of an Americanist*; Porter and Coates, publisher. This rare work can be found in the library of the University of New Mexico; Athy, Linson, and Steede confirm Brinton.

7. On the subject of brick sizes and molds, I have apparently not expressed myself well, so allow me to change the terminology. Of the 4612 bricks used in our study, more than half, approximately 2750, were sufficiently intact to yield at least one measurement of either length or width because of having at least two opposing sides intact. From the appearance of these edges, one could see that the bricks had been made in one of three ways: molded (pressed into a wooden frame), rolled and cut (much like cookie dough), or hand-formed (patted by hand, leaving slightly less sharp edges, along with fingerprints). Previously, I had called this last type "hand molded." I think this term has led to confusion.

Of our sample (160 bricks), about 20 percent were molded in wooden frames, about 5 percent were rolled and cut, and about 75 percent were hand-formed. Of that same sample, 93-95 percent match Roman inch measurements to within 1/32nd of an inch. With such a high portion of bricks being hand molded, this consistency is incredible. For comparison, bricks made during the early Roman era were only true to size within one inch; late Roman bricks were true only to within 1/4 inch. Bricks from medieval through colonial periods were true only to within 1/2 inch, and often much more.

We have found no pattern of use relating to brick size. But we have found patterns relating to use and the inscription the brick carried. That is beyond the scope of this report.

8. We have 68 bricks which have 'measuring marks' on the edge. These marks seem to be neither tallies nor decorations. Of the 68, 64 are in Roman inches or fractional inches. The measuring marks fall into three groups. One we will call *systematic markings*, with one-inch Roman marks. All hash marks are the same length (true of all categories) and from 1/64th to 1/32nd of an inch wide, but measurements are true from the center of each hash mark (also true of all three categories). The second group is identical to the first except they display half-inch marks. The third group is what we call *incremental systematic markings*. In these cases, there are inches, half inches, thirds of inches, and fourths of inches, laid out incrementally in the bricks. In almost all the cases, the hash marks are of equal length. That is to say, the space between the marks may vary by the above-mentioned incremental fractions, but a 1/4 inch hash line is as long as a one inch hash line.

All cases have the following in common: all markings begin at the lower left corner—when the brick is oriented with the drawing upright and to the right; the first space is always a one-inch space followed by fractional spaces. Most marks are usually inches and half inches, or inches and quarter inches, or inches, half-inches, then quarter inches. Thirds of inches are always alone with one exception. In that case, all possible fractions are shown, with inch, two half inches, and four quarter inches in a row on the lower left edge. One full inch followed by thirds of inches run up the lower left side. All measurements are taken from the middle of the hash mark. All are exact with zero percent of error.

A few bricks have designs laid out with a 'straight edge.' Most of these use inch and fractional inch measurements. Beyond this, we do not know the intended use of these measurements. The combination of brick measurements and overall site measurements leads us to feel that the Roman measuring system was used.

Note: We would like to thank Dr. Hoffman for making this paper a great deal better through his constructive criticism.

DAVE BARRON

In paragraph one of Dr. Hoffman's critique of my paper, it is implied that we have suggested that the Gungywump site was constructed by Vikings. No; we are suggesting nothing of the sort. If anything, we are suggesting that our research and various findings point to a much earlier time frame for this site, *e.g.*, AD 500-600. This "window of opportunity" is reflected in the time range when the 'transitional style *chi rho*' symbols were used, in the radiocarbon date obtained at the so-called Tan Bark Mill, and in the given date of an identical crushing mill found on the Isle of Sark in the Channel Islands (AD 500-700). If these 'symptoms' are to be believed, they come some 500 to 300 years *before* the Vikings.

1. Under paragraph one, the Susquehanna broad point is referred to as a 'spearpoint,' and, although this is a common misuse, it is contrary to the actual identification. This item has an *off-center* shaft and has been identified by three independent researchers as a *knife*.

2. Yes, Constantine is given credit for having applied the *chi rho* symbol to his warriors' shields in AD 312, but the *style* of the several carvings in the Gungywump is identified as *transitional* and not of a pre-Christian era. This mere fact precludes an early British Colonial farmer, or modern Boy Scout, from having inscribed those symbols in two different locations in the North Gungywump.

3. The Pequots and the Mohegans differ markedly in their suggested origins. It all depends on whom Simmons (1986) spoke to. There are numerous tribal historians who insist that their origins were 'from across the waters,' not from the Southwest.

4. A fairly "complete title search" on the one extant Colonial ruins (1783) of an English half-house has been done by two separate parties, and its identification is probably correct. We agree, the absence of pre-Viking settlements in the Complex has been a frustration. Land masses have changed markedly even in the past one hundred years, including the flooding of Latham's Pond, the continued filling in of the so-called east ravine and brook, and the numerous housing developments in the area. Considering the several miles of rock walls which have been built in the Complex, we suggest that the parties involved spent several seasons in the area rather than simply coming and going on a short-term basis.

JAMES MAVOR

I thank Curtiss Hoffman for his kind comments and for focusing attention on two topics that are sensitive to Native Americans today and potentially important to archaeologists: modern Indian donations, and the Koshare fetish stone. They require more information than I provided in the article.

Item 3. The offering to spirits of bottles, pails, pans, tools, bicycles, bedsprings, and the like at Indian sacred places is known throughout America. It is believed to be akin to grave offerings. Byron Dix and I have published our observations and speculations over the past twenty years about the association of this type of material with stone rows, mounds, chambers, etc., in New England. Modern urban society sees these objects as waste, a concept foreign to aboriginal societies.

I agree with Dr. Hoffman that some material is likely to be "surreptitious 'offerings' of Euro-American trash." However, I believe that the site is more free of such trash than would ordinarily be expected, considering its location next to a river and a railroad bed and its openness to the public. Also, there is the presence of astronomical observation, types of material, and frequent association with earth and stone works to consider. These four factors lead me to believe that some of the 'trash' is more likely surreptitious Indian donations. Moreover, our article states, "we cannot be sure in every case whether or not such caches are Indian donations," and the study is a long-term work in progress.

Item 4. The Patterson-Sassaman reference to aboriginal burning of forest is cited as Reference No. 31 in the article.

Item 6. In my discussion of the differences between Southwest native social organization and known New England organization, it is noted that ancient astronomy in New England disappeared and/or went underground and so, probably, did the associated social organization. I believe that the comparison of horned figures at this stage is better made between cultures of the southwestern and northeastern parts of America than between more local sources.

On the one hand, we have two unique stone-horned figures, identical in shape, and nearly of a size. One was found among a pile of elongated stone slabs, some of which had been erected in holes in the bedrock at a place in Calendar One where Byron Dix and I suggest there was an astronomical focus of the site for observation from a stone shrine to horizon markers. The other was found during the excavation in 1919 of a prehistoric pueblo in New Mexico in the ruins of the ceremonial house of the Koshare Clan. It was identified as a Koshare fetish by an elder of the living pueblo associated by tradition with the prehistoric ruin. Members of the Koshare Clan are the sacred clowns and skywatchers. The pueblo has five principal circular stone shrines, suitable for horizon calendars, located on mesa promontories about the pueblo to the north, south, east, and west (Jeancon 1923: 67-73, Pl. 59). Interest in astronomy, the connecting tissue of this comparison, is truly universal. It is independent of distance and epoch and the presence or absence of cultural diffusion and independent invention. We see here specific and detailed similarities between the well-known and accepted practice of astronomy and its social organization in the Southwest and observations and artifacts in the Northeast.

On the other hand, comparison of the Calendar One stone with more local horned figures, such as the Ojibway demigod Manibozho, depends on a common language group, Algonquin, schematic petroglyphs, and a vague connection to a medicine society. In the future, it is possible that an astronomical connection may develop which might help to recover heretofore unknown meanings of northeastern petroglyphs and traditions such as Manibozho.

Jeancon, J.A.
  1923 *Excavations in the Chama Valley, New Mexico.* Smithsonian Institution, Bureau of American Ethnology, Bulletin 81.

JOHN RUDOLPH

Thank you, Dr.Hoffman, for your review and suggestions for improvements to my paper on "An Ancient Solar Observatory at Willow Creek, California."

I plead guilty to your observation that I tend to speculate, which, I know, can be irresponsible. I do hope that my pointing out possibilities that others may not have considered may be of value. In trying to shed some light on the purpose of the site, and by what culture it was used, I hope that other disciplines can become interested in the site and flesh out what are, at this point, only the bare bones of what the site was used for.

Since the time of writing this paper, I have visited the site almost every year and have been able to verify, with the help of a professional astronomer, that some of my guesses were very close to the mark. A subsequent version of this report of an on-going investigation was presented at the OXFORD V Conference on Archaeoastronomy and may be included in a volume of the papers presented there.

To date, there has been no dating of any of the glyphs at the site. It would be a great help to be able to determine when the various devices at the site were made and used. I am seeking funds to make this a possibility. The dating may help to determine what culture was involved as well.

Your comments in item 1 are much appreciated. I did not know of the work by Fagan; I plan to look up his work and your reference. There is a shadow that has fallen on the work of Hudson and Underhay, but, at the time I wrote the paper, I had no knowledge of it. Organizing large gatherings of people from distant places would possibly necessitate keeping a good calendar. I would like to point out that, at the Little Blue Table site in southwestern Idaho, which can be demonstrated to be another sun-watching site, I have found petroglyphs, in an astronomical context, that are very much like, if not identical to, the ones at Willow Creek near Susanville. This finding suggests that this calendric culture was indeed widespread.

I am sure that you are correct in saying that "not just 'civilized' ones like the Aztecs and the Chinese" developed a cosmology. I was trying to point out something that may not have been obvious to all: that *if* some of the circles connected by lines are asterism or constellation representations, then it is indeed interesting that both the Aztecs and the Chinese represented both in a similar way. It is entirely possible that this is coincidental, but the probability suggests otherwise. Again, I offered not a proof, but a suggestion. I will look up the Levi-Strauss book and read it.

Your third comment is certainly true. Too many variables enter into the weathering factor to use it conclusively. However, the well-made, carefully and deeply inscribed glyphs contrast strongly with the carelessly designed, shallowly scratched ones. I visited the site one year at the winter solstice, hoping to see some alignment of interest. I didn't find one, but this too is inconclusive. I did note that snow and ice lay in the petroglyphs carved into the rock that faced upward and that these glyphs looked much fresher and more recent than others that were of similar design but which were on vertical rock faces where lichen could take hold. The point I was trying to make about the "best" petroglyphs was not the erosion of them but that they seemed to be the ones that had been laid out most carefully and were pecked into the rockface most deeply and accurately. Some of the designs inside the "caves" were very much eroded, with the patina indistinguishable from the neighboring rockface. These matters are beyond my expertise, but not beyond my notice.

SECTION II

Botany, Biology, and People

SCULPTED FIGURE AT 13TH CENTURY HOYSALA TEMPLE, HALEBID, INDIA
Figure holds what appears to be an ear of maize (C. L. Johannessen, Figure 8 for text *ff*.)

PORTION OF THE HOYSALA TEMPLE AT SOMNATHPUR, INDIA
More than eighty sculpted figures hold large ears of maize. The figures are about three feet tall.

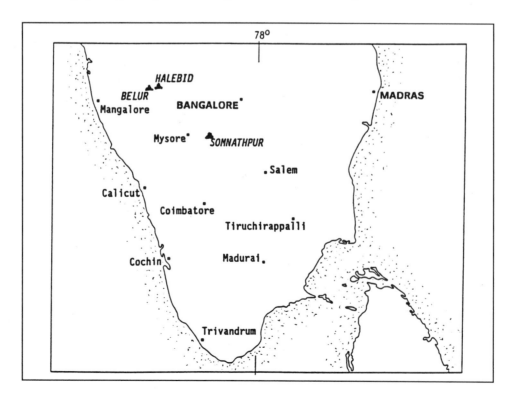

HOYSALA TEMPLE LOCATIONS IN SOUTH INDIA

Maize Diffused to India before Columbus Came to America

CARL L. JOHANNESSEN

INTRODUCTION

Social scientists have been struggling to understand better how the high civilizations arose around the earth in the pre-AD 1500 period, prior to the expansion of the European colonial powers. Many studies of technologies, religions, linguistics, etc., indicate that these developmental processes of civilizations were spread by exchanges across the oceans a millenium ago. Frequently, traditional and conservative researchers have demanded extremely high levels of substantiation for exchanges whose verification would threaten the prevailing belief that no significant contact across the oceans had occurred. Before evidence became available suggesting that dispersal of high cultures took place across the ocean 'highways', the traditionalists claimed that the homologous traits could have been developed independently. Therefore, it became necessary to conduct an active search for a trait, such as domesticated maize or some other crop, that could not be invented autochthonously twice.

HISTORICAL PERSPECTIVE

In the broad perspective, this research was initiated because of Stonor and Anderson's 1949 findings that the presence of maize varieties and cultural factors indicated considerable age of maize in Assam and adjacent India. Following up on this, Anderson's good friend Carl Sauer (1960) found evidence of maize in southern Europe prior to 1492. Others such as Carter (1963, 1974, 1988), Heyerdahl (1979, 1986), Jeffreys (1953, 1965, 1967, 1971, 1975), and Marszewski (1978, 1987) found data which indicated to them that maize was in Asia prior to Columbus' voyage. Against this background, when Hürlimann (1967) and Jett (1978) produced pictures of statues of maidens holding maize-like objects, in temples of south India, there seemed ample reason to start research on maize in the Mysore-Bangalore area of south India. This beginning of the study of maize in India was reinforced by over sixty photocopied pictures sent to me by Professor Donald B. Lawrence who, with his group, had photographed at three of these temples. Other photos of the temples were received from Dr. Jaweed Ashraf, who obtained his photos from the Photographic Library of the Archaeological Survey of India in New Dehli.

DATA GATHERING

A decade of research and seven trips to Karnataka State for the study of Hoysala Dynasty Temples in the region, have provided ample evidence (which includes crops) to support the thesis that there was early communication between the Americas and south Asia. Most of these Hoysala temples are dated to the 11th to 13th centuries AD (Narasimhachar 1977; Doshi 1981). Several papers relate to these data (Johannessen 1988, 1992; Johannessen and Parker 1989). In the process of this study I have been able to discover over thirty-five anatomical traits that indicate maize ears of considerable variety had to have been the models for the sculpted ears in the religious statuary in India. Every sculpted ear is distinctive. The ears are not copies of one another. No other plant has this much variability in its fruiting body. All of these anatomical features are found in both ancient and modern maize ears.

TRAITS INDICATING MAIZE

These traits that were sculpted during the 11th to the 13th century AD are homologous with real maize ears and are shown in the figures which follow:

Size and Shape of Ear
1. The relationship of size and shape of many sculptured maize ears to the anatomy of the sculptured human statues holding the maize ears appears subjectively to be inclusive of the range of real maize ears in relation to real human forms.
2. Sides of ears are: a) parallel; b) bulging at midway; or c) bulging at the base.
3. Tips of ears are: a) generally pointed; b) sometimes fasciated; c) occasionally rounded; d) knobbed.
4. Sculpted ears are sometimes warped, as real maize is when picked while still slightly moist and then dried fast. This could happen if they were originally given as offerings of the first-fruits harvest ritual, which is what was likely offered at the temples. However, sometimes maize ears grow in a warped condition when the water and sun relationships have not been optimum or when the 'silks' have exerted unevenly and have not been pollinated equally.

5. Straight ears are normal and indicate that some of the ears of first-fruits harvest offerings were fully mature, had been allowed to dry equally around the ear while still on the stalk, and were, therefore, unwarped.

Ears in Husks

6. Ears are usually shown with husks removed and kernels exposed. This could have happened when persons who grew the maize selected as offerings the most beautiful ears for the home or temple altars.

7. Husks only partly cover the ear in about three percent of the maize sculptures (in addition to that portion of the stone 'left' for sculptural, structural support) and therefore leave rows of kernels exposed.

8. Husks on the ears are relatively rare; still, some ears are entirely enclosed, and therefore generally have a smooth surface.

9. A smaller number of ears in the husk have a doubly-etched curl, representing 'silk,' from the top of the husk (the curl of which in Guatemala, among Mayan iconography, indicates the signature for the corn god).

10. Ears-in-the-husk in a very few cases have etched curls inside the curls of the silks.

11. Shape of ears in husk is similar to shape of ears that have been offered in a de-husked condition.

Rows and Ranks of Kernels

12. When dehusked, the rows of kernels generally are parallel and extend the full length of the ear. (Individual rows are not truncated as they are seen in basketry nodes where the rows shrink to form the tip of a cornucopia.)

13. Occasionally, rows of kernels are found also to be entirely jumbled in a condition called 'tessellate.'

14. Ears can be found that have parallel rows over the top two-thirds of the ear and also have: a) tessellate arrangement of kernels at the base; or b) the tessellate condition only at the small end of the ear; or c) the tessellate condition only on the front and bottom of the ear with the side rows of the same ear parallel.

15. Rows may be parallel on the basal three-quarters of the ears, and, in the upper one-fourth of the ear's length, the kernels in the row spiral around the tip end.

16. Rows are found that spiral gently towards the tip from the base.

17. Sometimes, where sculpturing was incomplete, sketches are found on the ears. In such cases, a) rectilinear scratches or grooves have been carved on the front of an ear with husks partly removed; or b) the ears may show normal kernels down the center rows of the ear, but only longitudinal grooves and ridges cut parallel to the rows with kernels. The maize kernels had not been carved individually into the bare continuous ridges at the time the sculpture was taken to be placed in the new temple walls. But the presence of ridges indicates by width and shape that they were designed to be carved upon to make kernels. Apparently, statues were not carved or touched up once

they were installed in the temple wall. Other evidence in the form of the details in the shapes of large blocks in the temple walls and foundations also similarly indicate there was probably an early prohibition against carving at the temple site once blocks were in place.

18. The compound female flower of maize is its ear, and on the cob the kernels develop as pairs of florets, each pair being in a single cupule. Normally, these cupules are stacked on top of each other to form rows of paired kernels called ranks. In both real and sculpted maize in India we find that: a) the pairs of kernels in a rank are at times exactly opposite the adjacent pair; but b) regularly they can also be offset by one-half a kernel's thickness up and down the cob; or c) individual cupules may be tilted on the cob with each kernel of each pair displaced half a thickness up or down the cob [creating near-tessellate conditions]; and d) the kernels' arrangements, relative to kernels at their sides, may change at various locations on the cob.

We find all of this variability on the sculptured maize ears. Although the 'textbook' pattern of displacements allows a nesting effect between ranks for closer packing of kernels, shifts in this sequence occur often too. Without the stimulus of a real maize ear as a model, it would be difficult to sculpt in this detail, and no sculptor could develop all these maize-specific details. Maize is idiosyncratic in this regard; no other grain has this feature nor most of the other traits detailed here either.

19. Knobs (of kernels and cob) at the end of the ear may occasionally represent a deformity caused by either lack of pollination, larval destruction of a part of the cob near the tip while it was immature, or some other unrecognized growth factor in the ear which is related to the availability of water in the soil.

Kernel Characteristics

20. Sculpted kernels are, on average, rounded rectilinear in shape, though they are somewhat more squared than is typical of modern maize. Archaeological maize kernels of a thousand years ago in America also show this Hoysala characteristic of smaller width to thickness (w/t) ratios, *i.e.,* about 1.0 to 1.5, though the range of shapes of modern maize spreads over a broader spectrum of w/t ratios, *i.e.,* from 1.0 to 2.3.

21. Kernels are often carved a) smaller at the tip of the ears; and b) sometimes rounder at the tip.

22. At least once, the upper 1/6 of kernels are tiny at the tip of the ear as though they were totally unpollinated.

23. Rows of mature kernels are parallel to rows of unpollinated kernels with partial husks on the sides. An artificial 'object' made by a person and copied into the stone would hardly have been arranged in this way.

24. A few kernels with dent characteristic are found in ears with otherwise flint or flour type of rounded-topped kernels.

25. 'Dog tooth' kernels, etched on an otherwise smooth, 'blank' ear, are similar to highland corn in the Americas.

Table I ANATOMICAL VARIATIONS OF MAIZE SHOWN IN PHOTOGRAPHS — Figures 1 through 20 *ff*

TRAIT   **FIGURE NUMBER**

TRAIT	1	2	3	4	5	6	7	8	9	10	11	12	13	14	15	16	17	18	19	20
1	X	X	X	X	X	X	X	X	X	X	X	X	X	X	X	X	X	X	X	X
2a	X	X	X	X		X		X		X				X	X	X	X	X		X
2b							X		X		X	X	X						X	
3a	X	X	X	X	X	X		X	X	X			X	X	X	X	X	X	X	X
3b							X													
3c		X	X									X								
4	X			X				X					X	X				X	X	X
5		X	X	X			X	X	X	X	X			X	X	X	X			
6	X	X	X	X	X	X	X	X	X	X	X	X	X	X	X	X		X	X	
7																X				
8																	X			
10																				X
11																X	X			X
12	X	X	X	X	X	X	X	X	X	X	X	X	X	X	X	X		X	X	
14a												X								
14b														X						
14c												X								
16																		X	X	
18a	X	X	X	X	X	X	X	X	X	X	X	X	X		X	X		X	X	
18b	X	X	X	X	X	X	X	X	X	X	X	X	X		X	X		X	X	
18c		X	X	X	X	X	X	X	X	X	X		X	X						X
18d	X	X		X	X	X	X	X	X	X	X	X				X		X	X	
19				X				X	X			X								
20	1.1	1.1-1.2	1.3-1.6	1.1	1.1-1.2	1.0-1.5	1.2	1.1	1.0	1.2	1.1	1.2-1.4	1.3			1.1		1.3	1.0	
21a	X	X	X	X	X	X	X	X	X	X	X	X	X			X		X	X	
21b	X	X			X			X			X					X			X	
23																X				
26													X							
27													X							
28																			X	

Traits discussed in the text but not illustrated in the photographs do not appear in the table.

26. 'Dog tooth' kernels at other temples are carved in the round with a point at the tip of the kernels on a few ears instead of the normal rounded-end. These shapes are found in certain flint-type kernels in locations such as high-elevation Mesoamerica and Peru.

27. Kernels which are imbricated (or overlapping) at the tip are also found in these same high-elevation areas.

28. Some very enlarged kernels are present, somewhat like 'Cuzco' variety maize from Peru. When this occurs, often the kernels are round and may not fit the modern Cuzco variety-type perfectly.

Color

29. Both Lakshmi, goddess of wealth and fertility, and Vishnu, god who protects earth, and even Kubera, earlier the god of wealth, had to be worshipped with golden objects. We obviously cannot tell from the sculptures what the color of maize was. However, we generally know that yellow maize is frequently golden in color; therefore, maize could have seemed an especially appropriate gift of gold for the gods when maize was viewed originally by Hindus. Perhaps they saw it as a sun symbol as well. The other colors of maize kernels—red, black, white, and yellow—would aid the Hindus' worship of the several compass directions, as well as the specific dates and numbered days of their calendric system. The Amerind, especially Mayan and Incan, have also used color in a similar manner to label directions.

PLATE I

Figure 1 HALEBID: Offset paired kernels

Figure 2 SOMNATHPUR: Large straight ear

Figure 3 SOMNATHPUR: Conical ear

Figure 4 SOMNATHPUR: Rows of paired offset kernels

PLATE II

Figures 5 and 6 SOMNATHPUR: Curving conical ear and elongate ear

Figure 7 BELUR: Fasciated tip of ear
(Figure 8, page 109)

Figure 9 HALEBID: Knobbed tip of ear

PLATE III

Figures 10 and 11 SOMNATHPUR: Left, offset paired kernels; Right, tessellate basal rows in front, parallel rows on side

Figure 13 SOMNATHPUR   Figure 13a WISCONSIN HERBARIUM
Compare 'dog tooth' kernels on a sculpted conical ear at left
with pointed kernels on a maize ear at right.

Figure 12 BELUR: Conical ear

PLATE IV

Figure 14 HALEBID: Tessellate middle, with *mudra*

Figure 15 HALEBID: Tessellate, knobbed, conical

Figure 16 SOMNATHPUR: Unpollinated kernels
Two rows of mature; four immature

Figure 16a ACTUAL AMERICAN MAIZE EAR
Bent tip, poorly pollinated
Compare with sculpted ear in Figure 16.
(Eugene OR 1995)

PLATE V

Figure 18 SOMNATHPUR
Rows spiral from base, normal for maize
Note *mudra.*

Figure 17 HALEBID: Ear in husk with silks pulled

Figure 19 HALEBID: Rows spiral from base

Figure 20 JAVAGAL TEMPLE
Ear in husk with curls of silk

ALTERNATIVE TO MAIZE

No other crop plant, or fruiting body, on any farm or at any market has this much all-inclusive variability and yet remains within the constraint of shapes that are correlated with maize ears. It is unlikely that, without an abundance of offertory maize ears grown by the community of religious farmers, the temple sculptors would have produced this much variability of artistic creativity at random. Perhaps the maize ear was imported as a simple trade good for religious purposes; this interpretation is unlikely, though a possibility. No other human-created objects have this much innate diversity.

Cornucopia

The horn-of-plenty made of basketry, does not correspond to the observed distributions of lumps—kernels in my analysis—nor would it be functional in the observed context due to the fact that the small end of these objects is up. If the object were a cornucopia, all its contents would spill out. In other Indian sculpture, the narrow, pointed end of cornucopia normally points down (Bussagli and Sivaramamurti 1971).

Purse

Purses decorated with stitched-on pearls or cowrie shells, as suggested by certain scholars, are also very unlikely models for these objects. Had such purses existed in the abundance suggested by the sculpted objects, surely some remains would have been found. Yet the Archaeological Survey of India has found no caches of pearls in any archaeological deposits.

Pomegranates

Pomegranates cannot have been the stimulus for these maize-like carvings held by an 8th century Kubera, as one Hindu scholar (Mundkur 1980) has suggested. The sculpted forms are neither round, nor do they have the calyx tips of the floral remnant of the pomegranate at the top. They are not carved in the way pomegranates are carved in other temple statuary found in northern India. Furthermore, if these sculptures were intended to represent pomegranates, they would have had to be *peeled* pomegranates, showing the juicy seeds and the blank spaces of the placenta as a pomegranate does when the outer skin has been removed. The Hindu priests would not have wanted someone else to peel the fruit and offer it in this perishable condition at the temple. It does seem likely that the pomegranate with its multi-seeded, red, round fruit may have been carved with its calyx protruding upward in a form reminiscent of a cross-section of the female symbol in the Siva temples.

The sculptured maize ear with its yellow-gold to white seeds and phallic shape, when used in a temple to Lord Siva, is most likely a multi-seeded symbol as is indicated by the traditional hand *mudra* of the attendants and goddesses holding the ears.

OBJECTIONS AND SUPPORT FOR THE MAIZE HYPOTHESIS

Maxwell's Objections

The anthropologist T. J. Maxwell (1979) has attempted to discredit the kind of investigation carried out here. In 1979 he had only the writings of Hürlimann (1967), Jett (1978), and Carter (1979b) that earlier had suggested the verity (but without the detail) of the maize represented at Halebid. Even though Maxwell acknowledges that he found no other fruit that really matched the objects held in the hands of the goddesses, he postulated the noni fruit (*Morinda citrofolia*) as a possible model. "Carved in stone it would look very much like an ear of corn." Nevertheless, he also says, "The noni looks nothing at all like maize in the flesh . . . ." It is strange what some are willing to do to support their previously held views.

Maxwell uses photographs in Coomaraswamy's (1927 [1965]) *History of India* as a source of the symbolism for lumpy objects that might have been used as the models for the maize-like objects or carvings. He postulates the following imagery of their origin: Buddha's hair curls, fluted stone stupas, coiled snakes and cobras, piles of balls, or heaps of gems. One can only assume that he never tried to pile balls on top of each other. Despite the impossibility of these explanations, Maxwell concludes that he has destroyed the interpretation of these objects as having been modeled from maize-like objects.

In an answer, Carter (1979b) points out that Maxwell did not make an effective case against maize, and I would certainly agree. In addition, Carter emphasizes that a multitude of potentially diffused cultural traits provides a matrix in which the other evidence of the presence of maize, such as the maize pollen discoveries, demonstrates that it is highly likely that diffusion across the oceans took place a long time ago.

The pollen studies appear to be too confounding for me to address here, because, apparently, the most important archaeological maize pollen that had been discovered was inadvertently discarded from Vishnu-Mittre's (1966) former laboratory when, on his retirement, the laboratory was cleaned of all its contents by a custodian. Vishnu-Mittre had been pressured to doubt the correctness of his former analysis of maize pollen from an early date.

Another reason for Carter's (1979b) rejection of Maxwell's article, referred to above, was a potsherd discovered by Vishnu-Mittre (1966) with what both men interpreted as possible maize kernel impressions on the curved pottery surface; but that bit of evidence for maize is in the process of being refuted (Johannessen 1989b).

Modern Replacement of Statuary

Some reviewers of the ideas about maize in India, such as Maxwell (1979), have suggested that the temples with the maize-like objects were simply the result of the replacement of AD 1529 temple carvings by more recent statues and friezes of women holding maize images that were thought to have been introduced by the Portuguese in the previous *three decades*. Maxwell's and others' inferences can hardly be valid because:

1. By this reasoning, the hypothetical carvers would have had to obtain, for the many models of maize, the ancient types of American maize, not the larger, later types available in the Americas in the 1490s.

2. The statuaries in the more than thirty-five temples I visited all have similar patina on their surfaces, the result of long exposure to weathering.

3. Statuary from temples that were destroyed or broken down and partly buried long before the Portuguese arrived have recently been unearthed, and these figures have the same maize representations. Moreover, these ruin excavations, carried out (*e.g.,* Halebid) over the last decade, are in the same general settings as five other temples, apparently of Hoysala Dynasty age.

4. Many of the sculpted maize ears have ancient 'pyramidal,' or conical, shape that are unlikely to have been available to serve as models in recent times.

5. Many of their kernels are frequently more roundish or squarish in plan outline than are the rounded-rectangular kernels that are normal for AD 1500 and the present. The old types of maize ears do still exist. It is unlikely that more recent sculptors, just to obfuscate modern scholars, could have recognized these more ancient shapes, which are largely absent in most modern maize near the temples.

6. As many as eighty ears of large size and several hundred smaller ones can occur in a single temple. At least eighty-two Hoysala temples are listed by the Archaeological Survey of India and many more are recognized. Each temple that I have visited has many sculptured ears of maize and often other American crop-plant representations as well. Maxwell (1979) apparently knew of only one temple at Halebid that had such carvings, yet there are at least five temples at that site alone, all with maize representations.

7. The sculptors of the original figures are identified by their signatures on these sculptures. The Indian archaeological community has compiled a history of the works of these master sculptors (Padmanabha 1989).

8. Since the Indians also value their antiquities and have limited economic resources, how can it be postulated that someone did all these carvings differently from the ancient heritage and did it for free, left no record, and inserted a new crop-plant into religious art of the many sects represented in the temples of the Hoysala Dynasty?

9. Look at the complexity of the statuary. Think about the labor of dismantling these interlocking bas-relief statues from their temple walls with their tons of stone roofs, and then reassembling the structures at eighty locations without leaving a record—just to tease scholars and the scientific community. In fact, even Maxwell (1979) wrote: "I suspect this frieze was not so remodeled."

Scholarly Resistance to New Research

The same arguments as Maxwell's have been advanced by others who were less objective, in communication as reviewers of manuscripts and grant applications, without recognizing that such arguments could not possibly constitute a valid reason for rejecting a grant proposal. Neither did the reviewers demonstrate that they understood the anatomy of the maize ears, but they remain anonymous.

However, the arch anti-diffusionist, E. D. Merrill (1954:373), in the fine print of the postscript to his book on Cook's voyages, accepts the evidence of maize in Europe in pre-Columbian times. Earlier in the same work, Merrill had berated the world-renowned diffusionists for suggesting exchanges across the oceans. He had claimed in the body of his book (already printed at the time he wrote the postscript) that the Portuguese had been the sole carriers of maize and the other crop-plants to Asia after the discovery of America by Columbus, even though he had no real basis in historical records to back it up.

The traditional Hindus do not accept a new crop easily into their religious heritage. Some of the temples have remained continuously active since their construction, according to what I am told. No one in archaeology at the University of Mysore, India, has suggested that the maidens have been tampered with in the way some critics claim. Patel (1990) did his doctoral dissertation on the temple at Somnathpur and found no evidence of this type of alteration, though reconstruction had occurred in places, but then neither did he mention the maize nor discuss what was in the maidens' hands that looked like maize. In the other dozen books on the Hoysala Dynasties, the possibility that these maize-like objects represented maize has been significantly ignored (Anand 1977; Collyer 1990; Foekema 1994; Narasimhachar 1977 [1917], 1919; Padmanabha 1989; Ramaswami 1984; and Settar 1991, 1992). In part, this results from the fact that we humans tend to accept authority figures, and for a long time, at least since the coming of the British, the professionals have been saying that no maize or other evidence of contact between New and Old World existed. Another reason is that not many people with Latin American experience of the high variability of maize have looked closely at the details of these maize carvings.

The climate of the eastern slope of the Western Ghats of Karnataka state produces moderate rainfall, and the stone in the temples has withstood weathering better than the random vandalism by humans. The Indian Government has been quite protective of their temples, but the randomness of the acts and the destruction from stones thrown over the outside walls protecting the temples are very difficult to control except by education stressing the world value of India's sculptural art, that surely matches anything on this scale in the world.

Critics of these data have objected to the dating of the temples. However, the Indians have sequential written records of the last 2,000 years of their history, and to challenge that record just to try to resist a shift in a scientific 'belief' system is not a productive activity. The data now discovered cause a shift to a new understanding of the history of world civilization. Both New and Old World civilizations are involved, and each influenced the other. The oceans were not a one-way route for culture.

Some scientists require that cobs and pollen be found in India before they will grant even a tentative acceptance of maize in that region. I agree that such discovery would be welcome, and I assume that ultimately ancient maize ears, cobs, and pollen will be found. But we cannot stop work on the problem that maize was being represented just because the archaeologists have not been able thus far to discover this better earth-borne evidence. They will find it. When they do, they can publish it without fear of retribution for further forcing a paradigm shift.

Phytoliths versus Pollen

A first step in the search for real maize in India should be an effort to find maize phytoliths—the little pieces of plant opal, or sand-sized quartz particles, that form in grass and maize leaves. These are likely to be located in the ground near the outer margins of excavated platforms of dated temples. Phytoliths are much more likely than pollen to have been preserved in the dry soil under the margins of these temples. Moreover, such excavation can be carried out with the cooperation of Indian government archaeologists and at no risk to the temples when they are already in the process of excavation for repairs. The temples provide their own dating by epigraphic stelae at the temples and written records.

Pollen, on the other hand, needs anaerobic storage in a reducing (not oxidizing) condition, which occurs in permanently wet clays of ponds and swamps that have remained wet for the last two thousand years. If we were to take pollen samples from bogs, we would also need to be lucky enough to find a source of carbon in the profiles (along with funds for carbon dating) in order to demonstrate the presence of maize.

Botanists versus Art Historians

Is not carving in the round, when excellently done, a better representation of a complex botanical object such as a maize ear than any written description of maize could be in pre-Columbian times? Yet, a few art historians and archaeologists have claimed that these carvings *should* not be interpreted as maize, as has been done by maize botanists and maize breeders. Instead some art critic has interpreted them as simply art objects that must have been created by religious sculptors with some unknown significance from some imaginary model. I am unable to give the critics' names because they were anonymous reviewers and each of the objections raised above has been offered. A reviewer even urged me, one assumes seriously, to soak an ear of corn in ocean water for a year and then test whether it would germinate. In fact, maize in aerated,

fresh moisture germinates within five days; moreover, it would take up ocean water and die in even less time. Modern sweet corn seed is relatively delicate.

It is the lack of botanical training that inhibits art critics and historians from seeing the totally idiosyncratic nature of the dozens of maize ear shapes in the carvings. None of the carvings is mass produced and none is 'regular' or 'normal.' In the temple sets of maizes, each is a distinctly different and individual case; they could not have been dreamed up if the sculptor or artist had never seen actual ears of corn. Nothing else like a maize ear exists in the world. No other grass grain, pandanus, or palm fruit has the distribution of kernels on a cob that maize has. If you do not believe, take this set of pictures to the corn breeders at their labs or to the maize-ear curator in an herbarium. By all means test the hypothesis, but use an expert on maize anatomy, not an art historian or a believer in a religious cult of false science.

PARADIGM SHIFT

What does it take to change the paradigm? Who better than botanical experts in classification of maize should judge the veracity of the carvings of maize? Maize experts recognize the diversity of maize anatomy, and they acknowledge that most variations of maize are represented by these carvings, with very few features in the carvings that are not presently found in actual maize ears. Maize is more variable than most other grain or fruit crops for the reason that maize is an outcrossing plant. Its genes continually mix due to the difficulty of controlling pollen blown on the wind. Normally, the wind pollinates the female parts of the maize plant at the tips of the silks, which then allows a nucleus from the pollen to grow down the silk to the developing kernel.

American Indians discovered some techniques (not breeding in the technical sense) which allowed them to maintain selected characters of maize. However, Asians, in general, have not bothered with sophisticated control of wind blown pollen for varietal maintenance because their other grain crops, such as rice, wheat, barley, and foxtail millet, are self-pollinating. Traditionally, they never tried to domesticate significantly outcrossing grains (Johannessen 1982, 1987). Sorghum outcrosses only 10-15 percent of the time.

Since maize was selected for increased length and was maintained genetically by special planting techniques, it developed into the vegetational monster that we find today in the Americas. This part of the process had to have been developed in the Americas before the large maizes could have arrived in India, probably over two millennia ago. This lack of selection and maintenance in India was not disastrously disruptive to maize's subsequent genetics, though at present there are fewer varieties of maize in India than in the Americas.

Much, and perhaps most, basic seed genetics for the modern production of maize in commercial agriculture in India have been imported from North America in the last half century as hybrid seed. Older maize types are nevertheless present.

We need field researchers to check on the varieties grown by the small farmers in the Hill Tribes as we hunt for the ancient kinds of maize. You may have to ask hundreds of people in the farmers' markets to find the very few old folk, especially the oldest women, who still grow a little of it for traditional reasons. This is also true in the Balkans and the Middle East—the old women have the seed banked.

TEMPLE AGE

The age of these Hoysala temples is fixed by records carved in stone—built-in documentation (Doshi 1981; Maity 1978; Chopra 1973). New aspects of research will involve mapping the location and age of an early series of sculptures of male Hindu gods that hold maize ears, carved in the 5th to 8th centuries AD (Bussagli 1971:192; Bhattacharya 1974). These are found in west central India and were sculpted three to six centuries before maize began to show up in Hoysala Dynasty sculptures to the south of this earlier Gupta realm. Dispersal of temples with statues holding maize continued to the south, but with the difference that, instead of maize being held primarily by males, most of the later, larger, and more intricate representations of maize are held in the hand of female statues, always with the new, distinctive *mudra,* or hand position. You can note the fertility aspects of this sign for yourself. Surely we have to respect the religious symbolism of maize and of God Siva in this representation. During the later Hoysala Dynasty temple-building, most, but not all, of the males and their corn had been relegated to carvings outside and on top of the roofs.

SUMMARY

We have shown that living maize had to have been used as the model for the sculptured, maize-like objects held in the hands of statues in early temples and in the outer-wall friezes in the Hoysala Dynasty temples. These maize-like objects are of an age that demonstrates subcontinent Indians or their trading associates must have had early sailing contact with the Americas or with seafaring traders such as the Arabs, Phoenicians, Africans, Chinese, or Malaysians who had had the contact. Maize is found to have been growing 5,000 to 7,000 years ago in America, where the ears were selectively elongated into what we can recognize as the maize of one to two thousand years ago.

This fact of sailing contact means that the hundreds of other homologous cultural and technological traits that are found on both sides of the Atlantic and Pacific Oceans are also likely to have been exchanged in this trading and missionizing process of the early sailors. Now we start the real work of deciphering the source regions in the New or Old World cultures for these many features. Which traits are sufficiently different from their 'match' that they probably developed independently in each hemisphere? This is a task for revitalizing the Social Sciences at a time when people in high civilization enjoy the detective processes so immensely. Other cultivated plants, such as sweet potato, lagenaria gourd, peanut, sunflowers, tomato, chili pepper, marigold, pineapple, kapok, yam, jicama or yam bean, moschata squash, grain amaranths, prickle poppy, tobacco, guava, construction bamboo, linted-cotton, and many more, should be seriously challenged with respect to their arrival dates on the other sides of the oceans. Western scientists need to recognize that sailors from the civilizations of the earth's relatively tropical regions were exploring the world before and during Europe's Dark Ages. If the many crops existed on both sides of the oceans in the 15th century AD, abundant sailing and exchanges must have occurred that help explain the many similarities in technologies, religions, and cultural traits of the peoples of the world's high civilizations

ACKNOWLEDGMENTS

As a result of a National Science Foundation grant (#2187) to study maize in the Himalayas with Dr. Anne Z. Parker, I subsequently continued research on the archaeological sculptures of maize in southern India with Dr. Parker and Doris Johannessen. I thank Prof. John Sorenson and the Foundation for Ancient Research and Mormon Studies (FARMS) at Brigham Young University for funding the continuation of this research. I am grateful for assistance from the University of Oregon Research Services and the University of Oregon Foundation. I thank the following people and organizations for their funding of part of the expenses for seven other maize research trips and activities: Prof. George Carter at Texas A&M University; Robert and Sharon Wilson and Caterpillar Tractor Co.; Gordon Swoffer and Brookhurst Mill; Robert Lewis and Alpine Map Co.; Jerry's Home Improvement Center; Furrow Building Materials Co.; Northrup Seed Co.; Lily Miller Seed Co.and Casey Dale. Invaluable help in the field was provided by Barbara Northrup, Grace Schneiders, S. G. Samak, and Bruce and Laura Johannessen. Thanks also to the Archaeological Survey of India: Drs. Mahadev N. Katti, C. Margabandu, J. C. Joshi, K. V. Ramesh, K. P. Poonacha, Shitala P. Tewari; University professors T. Dayananda Patel, P. D. Mahadev, Joginder Singh, Hugh Iltis; and students Greg Howard, K. Venkatesh, L. Ravi, Ananda Kumar, and a host of other helpful people. The map is provided by David Imus of Imus Cartographic Co.

REFERENCES

Anand, Mulk Raj
  1977 *In Praise of Hoysala Art.* Bombay, India: S. J. Bhabha for Marg Publications.
Bhattacharya, B. C.
  1974 *The Jaina Iconography.* Delhi: Motila Banarsidass.
Bussagli, Mario and Calembus Sivaramamurti
  1971 *5000 Years of the Art of India.* New York: Harry N. Abrams; Bombay: Tulsi Shah Enterprises.
Carter, G. F.
  1963 Movement of people and ideas across the Pacific. Pp.7-22 in *Plants and the Migrations of Pacific Peoples.* J. Barrau, ed. Honolulu: Bishop Museum Press.
  1974 Domesticates as artifacts. Pp.201-230 in *The Human Mirror.* Miles Richardson, ed. Baton Rouge: Louisiana State University Press.
  1979a Megalithic man in America? *Stonehenge Viewpoint,* 27:3-5.
  1979b Maize in Asia and elsewhere. *Stonehenge Viewpoint,* 32:26-27.
  1988 Cultural historical diffusion. Pp. 3-279 in *The Transfer and Transformation of Ideas and Material Culture.* Peter J. Hugill and D. Bruce Dickson, eds. College Station: Texas A & M University Press.
Chiba, Tokuji
  1968 *The Dispersal of Maize in Continental China.* 21st International Geographical Congress, pp. 293-294. Calcutta, India: National Committee for Geography.
Chopra, P.N.
  1973 *Gazetteer of India. Vol. II History and Culture,* p.479. India: Gazetteers Unit, Dept. Culture, Ministry of Education and Social Welfare.
Collyer, Kelleson
  1990 *The Hoysala Artists: Their Identity and Styles.* Mysore, India: Directorate of Archaeology and Museums.
Coomaraswamy, A. K.
  1927 [1965] *History of Indian and Indonesian Art.* London: Edward Goldston.
Doshi, Saryu
  1981 *Homage to Shravana Belgola.* Bombay: Marg Publications.
Foekema, Gerhard
  1994 *Hoysala Architecture: Medieval Temples of Southern Karnataka Built During Hoysala Rule,* 2 Vols. New Delhi: Books and Books.
Heyerdahl, Thor
  1979 *Early Man and the Ocean.* Garden City NJ: Doubleday & Co.
  1986 *The Maldive Mystery.* Bethesda: Adler & Adler.
Hürlimann, Martin
  1967 *India.* New York: Viking Press.
Jeffreys, M. D. W.
  1953 Pre-Columbian maize in Africa. *Nature,* 4386:965-966.
  1965 Pre-Columbian maize in the Philippines. *South African Journal of Science,* 61:5-10.
  1967 Who introduced maize into southern Africa? *Suid-Afrikaanse Tydskrif vir Wetenskap* (South African Journal of Science), 63:24-40.

Jeffreys, M. D. W.
  1971 Pre-Columbian maize in Asia. Pp.376-400 in *Man Across the Sea.* Carroll L. Riley, *et al.,* eds. Austin: University of Texas Press.
  1975 Pre-Columbian maize in the Old World: An examination of Portuguese sources. Pp. 23-66 in *Gastronomy, The Anthropology of Food and Food Habits,* Margaret L. Arnott, ed. The Hague: Mouton Publishers.
Jett, Stephen C.
  1978 Pre-Columbian transoceanic contacts. Pp.593-650 in *Ancient Native Americans.* Jesse Jennings, ed. San Francisco: W. H. Freeman.
Johannessen, Carl L. and Anne Z. Parker
  1989 Maize ears sculptured in 12th and 13th century AD India as indicators of pre-Columbian diffusion. *Economic Botany,* 43(2):164-180.
Johannessen, Carl L.
  1982 Domestication process of maize continues in Guatemala. *Economic Botany,* 36(1):84-99.
  1987 Domestication process: An hypothesis for its origin. Pp. 177-204 in *Carl O. Sauer: A Tribute.* Martin S. Kenzer, ed. Corvallis OR: Association of Pacific Geographers.
  1988 Indian maize in the twelfth century [AD]. *Nature,* 332:587.
  1989a Distribution of pre-Columbian maize and modern maize names. Accepted for *Phil Wagner Festshrift.*
  1989b *Maize Impressions on Pre-1400 AD Potsherd from Kaudinyapura, India Disproved.* Lecture and abstract for1990, Annual Meetings of Association of American Geographers.
  1992 Distribution of pre-Columbian maize and modern maize names. Pp. 313-333 in *Person, Place and Thing: Interpretative and Empirical Essays in Cultural Geography.* Shue Tuck Wong, ed. *Geoscience and Man,* Vol. 31. Baton Rouge LA: Louisiana State University.
Maity, S. K.
  1978 *Masterpieces of Hoysala Art: Halebid-Belur-Somnathpur.* Bombay: D. B.Taraporeyala Sons and Co.
Mangelsdorf, Paul C.
  1974 *Corn, Its Origin, Evolution and Improvement.* Cambridge: Harvard University Press.
Marszewski, Tomaz
  1978 The problem of the introduction of 'primitive' maize into South-East Asia. In *Folia Orientalia,* Tome XIX, Part II. Wroctaw: Publishing House of the Polish Academy of Science.
  1987 Some implications of the comparative studies of the vernacular names of maize and other cultigens from Southeast Asia, Part 1. In *Sprawozdania z Posiedzen Komisji Naukowych Polska Akademia Nauk. Oddjia w Krakowie.* Tome XXVIII/1-2, Styczen-grudjien, 1984, Wroctaw.
Maxwell, T. J.
  1979 Maize in India. *Stonehenge Viewpoint,* 30:3-7.
Merrill, E. D.
  1954 The botany of Cook's voyages. *Chronica Botanica,* 14(5/6):1-373.
Mundkur, Balaji
  1980 On pre-Columbian maize in India and elephantine deities in Mesoamerica. *Current Anthropology,* 21(5):676-679.

Narasimhachar, R.
  1919   Architecture and sculpture in Mysore, India. In *Mysore Archaeological Series,* No. III., Mysore.
  1977 [1917]   The Kesava Temple at Somanathapur. Pp. 1-12 and 22 plates in *Karnataka Archaeological Series,* No. 1,. Mysore, India: Directorate of Archaeology and Museums in Karnataka.

Padmanabha, K.
  1989   *Hoysala Sculptures: a Sculptural Study.* Delhi, India: Sundeep Prakashan.

Patel, T. Dayananda
  1990   *The Kesava Temple at SomnathaPura.* Delhi: Agam Kala Prakashan.

Ramaswami, N. S.
  1984   *House of God Select Temples of South India.* Madras, India: Maps and Agencies.

Sauer, Carl O.
  1960   Maize into Europe. In *Akten des 34 Internationalen Amerikanisten Konngress.* Vienna.
  1963   *Plant and Animal Exchanges Between the Old and the New Worlds.* Robert M. Newcomb, ed. and comp. Los Angeles: California State University at Los Angeles.

Settar, S.
  1991, 1992.   *The Hoysala Temples,* 2 Vols. Bangalore, India: Kala Yatra Publications.

Stonor, C. R. and E. Anderson
  1949   Maize among the hill peoples of Assam. *Annals, Missouri Botanical Gardens,* 36(3):355-405, incl. plates 18-22.

Vishnu-Mittre
  1966   Kaudinyapur plant economy in protohistoric and historic times. *Paleobotanist* 15:152-156.

The Zuni Enigma

Nancy Yaw Davis

INTRODUCTION

Accidental juxtaposition of ideas in 1960 led to what at first seemed to be a preposterous idea. A complex chart I had prepared based on Zuni directional orientation looked remarkably similar to a Japanese version of Chinese *yin-yang* (Abegg 1955:51). Inspection of words associated with the concepts revealed a number of cognates, or loan words, and subsequent research in each of the four main branches of anthropology contributed further specific data that support the original idea in many diverse and complex ways. This paper is a brief overview of the major findings, with references but without technical analysis.

The Zuni Pueblo of New Mexico has long been known as an unusual group of North American Indians. Although they are among the ten most documented peoples in anthropological literature (Murdock 1953:158-160, 322), questions persist about the relationship of Zuni to other Indians. Indeed, the complexities of the Zuni social, religious, and political system have "occupied scholars and defied interpretation by them since the 1890s" (Ladd 1979: 482). For example, religious rituals and detailed direction-based orientation are unusually elaborate, intense, and well-integrated (Cushing 1896:373; Eggan 1950:202; Underhill 1954:651). A mixed form of kinship terminology puzzles ethnologists (Schneider and Roberts 1956). The Zuni language has no close affiliation with any other language (Sapir 1929:171; Greenberg 1953:282; Newman 1954:630; Hale and Harris 1979:173; Woodbury 1979:468), although a remote tie to California Penutian has been proposed (Newman 1964). Zuni-like traits are found among Indians of Southern California, but these similarities have not been explained (Strong 1927; Hawley 1937; Parsons 1939).

There are also questions about Zuni prehistory, especially regarding what happened during Pueblo IV, *ca.* the 13th century AD (Seltzer 1944; Danson 1957; Jett 1964; Davis 1965; Ford, Schroeder, and Peckham 1972; Eggan 1972; Kintigh 1985; Adams 1991). Furthermore, the Zuni have distinctive tooth features (Scott *et al.* 1983, 1986; Sofaer *et al.* 1972) and certain blood-group frequencies (Workman *et al.* 1974; Scott *et al.* 1986; Spuhler 1979) that set this population apart from other North American Indians.

Why are the Zuni so unique, biologically, linguistically, and culturally? I propose that they are distinctive partly because of 13th century AD Japanese contact. Other important events certainly occurred before and after that time-frame, and those events also shaped and reshaped that which is now Zuni. As noted by Ortiz (1979:1), "the various peoples of the Southwest fashioned unique cultural syntheses from elements of diverse provenance," a creative on-going process. But in this paper I address only one period, a period significant enough to be reflected now in Zuni language, culture, and biology.

If the many different kinds of evidence presented here are ultimately proven to be examples of independent innovation, then we have a remarkable incidence of convergence and identical innovation. That in itself would warrant attention. Perhaps efforts to disprove the hypothesis will tell us something new about the state of our knowledge and our ability to explain human phenomena. If we can reach new understandings about this one, small, but many-faceted, Zuni puzzle, then we should come to a better general understanding of the processes that have occurred throughout our shared human history.

BIOLOGICAL EVIDENCE

The following briefly outlines questions in four biological areas: 1. Zuni human remains from the 13th century AD; 2. distinctions in dentition; 3. blood-group frequencies; and 4. the high, yet unexplained, incidence of a kidney disease, mesangiopathic glomerulonephritis.

1. *Skeletal Remains*

Studies of Zuni skeletal remains from the Pueblo IV period (AD 1250-1400) show significant change in physical characteristics during that period, such as shape of crania and body stature (Roberts 1932; Seltzer 1944). Roberts found the evidence strong enough to indicate "the arrival of a new element in the population" and added that the "stage immediately following the advent of this alien group was a period of transition and instability" (1932:8). Seltzer noted that the physical features of the Hawikuh Zuni of Pueblo IV "are in many respects highly distinctive in character, especially as reflected in the small-headedness" (1944:9). The new population was shorter and smaller than the population already there.

This leads to the question: if significant admixture occurred between two different populations during Pueblo IV, would that be reflected in the gene pool today?

Several studies suggest that close attention be given to contemporary evidence of possible prehistoric admixture with a non-Indian population. The Zuni do have genetic

Table I TOOTH MORPHOLOGY

	AMERICAN INDIAN [1]		PIMA [2]		ZUNI [2]		JAPANESE	
	N	%	N	%	N	%	N	%
Upper 1st Incisor Palatal Shoveling	342	100 %	325	97.5%	549	94.4%	725	94.6% [3]
							110	87.3% [4]
Upper 1st Molar Cusp of Carabelli	844	60.2%	322	53.3%	517	36.2%	339	35.4% [5]
							458	31.2% [6]
Lower 2nd Molar 5 or More Cusps	197	60.2%	258	45.5%	523	34.9%	40	25.3% [1]
							352	13.1% [6]

Source: 1. Sofaer *et al.* 1972:363; 2. Sofaer *et al.* 1972:360; 3. Suzuki and Sakai 1964:67; 4. Pinto-Cisternas and Figueroa 1968; 5. Tsuji 1958:24; 6. Turner 1987:313-314

features that set them apart from other Southwestern Indians including a cluster of tooth-cusp and blood-group frequencies.

2. *Dentition*

Tooth morphology is one way of distinguishing biological differences, distances, and admixture between populations (Sofaer, Niswander, MacLean, and Workman 1972(37):357-366; Pinto-Cisternas and Figueroa 1968(29):339-348; Turner 1969 (30):421-426). Teeth have many distinctive and durable properties that make them especially amenable to analysis of evolutionary changes through time and gene pool differences across space. For three tooth features shown in Table I—shoveling, Carabelli's cusp, and 5-cusp pattern on the lower second molar—the Zuni frequency lies midway between other American Indian groups and the Asian incidence, and perhaps closer to the latter. Scott, Street, and Dahlberg (1986) analyzed crown-trait frequencies of ten morphologic variables for ten Southwest Indian populations and found that the Zuni stand consistently apart from the other groups.

3. *Blood-Group Characteristics*

The Zuni are also set apart on a genetic distance graph based on seven blood-group frequencies (Figure 1). One of the inherited characteristics that is exceptionally unusual among North American Indians is type B in the ABO group. In general, B is absent in American Indians, but it is present and high (20%-40%) among East Asian populations and relatively low (15%) among Caucasian groups (Garn 1969:40). In one study, which included 1234 Southwest Indians (Navaho, Apache, Pima, Yuma, Mohave, Chemehuevi, Hopi, Tewa, and Maricopa), only two persons (0.0016%) had type B and one had type AB (Brown *et al.* 1958:177). But in a sample of 662 Zuni Indians, seventy-one (10.7%) were found to have type B; this was considered "the most

striking observation" by the research team (Workman, Niswander, Brown and Leyshon 1974:126.). And it remains unexplained. Since no specific Caucasian features were found in association with the type B individuals, early Spanish influence does not account for it. The Japanese frequency of type B ranges between 12.8% and 32.4% (Watanabe *et al.* 1975:77-84).

Other indications of possible biological admixture are suggested by the similar gene frequency of red cell acid phosphatase (AcP): .199 in a Tokyo sample (Watanabe *et al.* 1975: 110), and .208 in Zuni (Workman *et al.* 1974:125). In a technical report in *Nature* on highly specific blood features (HLA-B alleles), the Zuni were reported to have "the same B*3501 subtype as the Japanese" (Belich *et al.* 1992: 328). Clearly, much more comparative work among non-Zuni American Indians and other populations needs to be done, especially on genetic features that may be indicative of admixture.

Spuhler (1979), in a complex study of genetic, cultural, and linguistic trees of 53 North American populations, found that the Zuni gene frequencies placed Zuni closer to the California culture area than to the Southwest, a finding consistent with detailed migration narratives, and with linguistic suggestions of a remote link to California Penutian.

4. *'Zuni Disease'*

Finally, the Zuni population has an extremely high incidence of a kidney disease, mesangiopathic glomerulonephritis, which appears to have a genetic base and to be concentrated along family lines (Hoy, Megill, and Hughson 1987). The incidence among the Zuni is much greater than among White Americans, Black Americans, Hopi, or Navajo (Hughson *et al.* 1989). But this disease is "extremely common in some Oriental populations, the best described prevalences being in Japan and Singapore" (Hoy, Megill, and Hughson 1987:494).

In summary, evidence in several biological areas sets

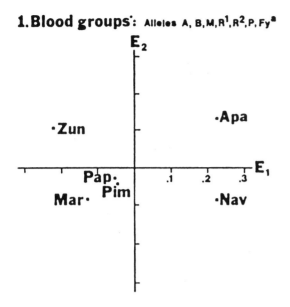

Figure 1 BIOLOGICAL EVIDENCE
Source: Scott, Street, and Dahlberg 1986:314

the Zuni population apart from other American Indians: skeletal changes, contemporary tooth morphology, blood type, and a particular disease so prevalent it is called locally 'the Zuni Disease.' Ultimate resolution of the biological questions may have to await genetic studies of admixed populations (Long 1991) and comparative DNA analysis of Zuni and many other populations, including Japanese. But this preliminary review suggests that careful attention should be given to evidence of possible prehistoric admixture of an American Indian group with a non-Indian population, and that the initial search should begin with genetic markers for kidney, teeth, and ABO polymorphism.

ARCHAEOLOGICAL RECONSTRUCTION

The next question is whether the archaeology of the Zuni area indicates a period of notable changes in the material culture. If significant admixture occurred with a population already there, it seems reasonable to consider archaeological evidence in an area that is exceptionally well documented (Woodbury 1979; Kintigh 1985). Pueblo IV, during the late 13th and early 14th centuries, may be the critical timeframe to consider; it is characterized by evidence of general abandonment of some areas, consolidation in other areas, increase in fortification, and a general decrease in Pueblo population. But, at Zuni, the population increased, and, as noted, the gene pool reflected changes in the direction of smaller stature and crania.

POPULATION

The question "Where and when did these Pueblo people originate?" continues to be asked. Eggan noted that there

is little agreement about the answers, but that "the twelfth and thirteenth centuries are the critical periods" (1972:290). His assessment leads him to state: "Today the evidence for diversity of origin for the prehistoric Pueblo cultures seems greater than ever" (Eggan 1972:305).

The population changes in the Pueblo areas during Pueblo IV are variously explained as the result of wars, drought, sickness, erosion, and/or Athapaskan or other 'enemy' invasion (Jett 1964). Wormington (1959:101) says the Zuni village was begun in the 11th century (now revised to be earlier), and "after a time, due to the arrival of new people, the community increased in size." Zuni continued to be occupied and grow in population (Woodbury 1956) while other Pueblo communities were abandoned.

Kintigh (1985) reviewed the extensive archaeological literature and characterizes the late prehistoric period (specifically AD 1250-1400) in the American Southwest by noting "dramatic changes in settlement patterns" (1985:1). He suggests that the changes were a result of new irrigation techniques and a greater concentration of population in fewer locations. Further, he indicates that the changes in size, location, and complexity of settlements may be related to a development of new institutions (Kintigh 1985:117).

POTTERY

In addition to changed settlement patterns and new irrigation systems, including terracing, the period of Pueblo IV is clearly marked by the appearance of glazed pottery. At least twenty classifications and fifty-three different types of pottery have been identified in the Southwest (Danson 1957:87), but one of the more unusual categories is the glazed ware, which was made in the Zuni area for about 100 to 150 years during Pueblo IV, beginning about AD

1250. Six sequential types of glazed ware have been recognized (Wormington 1959:112). Haury studied lead-glazed pottery techniques and reported that they occurred first in the Zuni area (1932:422). Reed's review of the sequences confirms the transition from St. Johns Polychrome to Zuni glazes at the end of the 13th century (1955:184). The timing and uniqueness of the glaze is distinct enough to be used as an indication of both time and contact between areas in the Southwest (Haury 1932; Danson 1957; Gladwin 1957; Wormington 1959).

Haury was convinced of the indigenous origin of the glaze technology (1932:418), but glazed pottery is most unusual in North America. Hough questions whether the glaze was an indigenous art (1928:245), and he also notes a religious preference for green glaze (1928:248). To my knowledge, this technique occurs only in the Zuni, and, later, the Rio Grande areas. This may be glaze-by-accident, or it may be part of a cluster of techniques that came into the area in the late 13th century. The earlier examples were more finely executed than the later ones, suggesting technical loss over time.

Japan also had a lead-glaze tradition, for a period earlier than the one that appears in the Southwest. Lead-glaze, originally from China, was introduced into Japan by Korean or Chinese pottery experts during the 7th century near the present-day city of Nara. From there the technology spread to other areas including southern Kyushu where green glaze continued until about the end of the 12th century.

The early glazes of the Nara period (AD 710-794) included three-color wares, usually green, white, and yellowish brown (similar to the Chinese Tang polychromes), but the green-glazed wares became more favored during the Heian period, AD 794-1185 (Mellott 1990:62). These glazes were painted on after the wares had been fired once; the second firing was at a relatively low temperature of about 750-800° centigrade. There was some association of green glaze with religious ceremonial use.

The lead glazes of Zuni may be an example of extremely rare independent innovation; or, alternatively, perhaps new pottery techniques reached Zuni during the late 13th century, along with the new irrigation methods, changed settlement patterns, and modified physical characteristics.

COSMOLOGY AND RELIGIOUS CONCEPTS

The 13th century may also have been a time for the introduction of new religious concepts, such as *kachinas*[1] (Adams 1991) and associated institutions. As suggested by Kintigh (1985:117), larger, more concentrated populations may have required "new institutions of social integration and control." Religion and its organizations provide powerful integrators *and* leadership. Here I briefly review the

possibility that ideological changes may have been part of the cluster of cultural complexes introduced from the west.

DIRECTION/ORIENTATION

Both Zuni and Japan have complex systems of directional orientation involving colors, seasons, elements, and many other characteristics. These systems are well-known, respectively, to students of American Indians (Smith 1952; Mallery 1893; Parsons 1939; Eggan 1950; Cushing 1882, 1896, 1920; Stevenson 1904) and to students of the Far East where they are usually called *yin-yang* (Anesaki 1930; Chamberlain 1932; Tsunoda *et al.* 1958; Abegg 1955).

Although a basic direction-color orientation is found among many American Indians, including the Navajo, Hopi, and Aztec (Table II), the idea is particularly pervasive and complex among the Zuni. Parsons (1939:959) refers to Zuni as the "cultural center" of religious ritual revolving around six directions. And Eggan states: "It is evident that the Zuni have tended to organize much of the world on a basis of six directions; not only were the clans so organized in Zuni thinking but also kivas, societies, seasons, corn, prey animals, and colors" (1950:202).

Table II DIRECTIONS AND COLORS

	Yin-Yang	Zuni	Aztec	Hopi	Navajo	Java
S	Red	Red	Blue	Red	Blue	Red
E	Blue	White	Red	Yel'w	White	White
W	White	Blue	White	Blue	Yel'w	Yel'w
N	Black	Yel'w	Black	White	Black	Black

Cushing (1896:325) notes that former Zuni towns were organized in relation to direction and ruled from a central tribe and town through priest-chiefs. The Zuni themselves believe they are in the middle of the world. Through their all-inclusive directional orientation they relate themselves to the rest of the world, or conversely, the rest of the world to themselves. It is one great interrelated life, oriented to the middle.

YIN-YANG

Long before the proposed time of contact with North America, Japan had assimilated Chinese concepts of Taoism, Confucianism, and Buddhism while also maintaining the traditional Shinto religion. For example, an account of *yin-yang* is found in the earliest Japanese record, *Kojiki*, dated AD 712. Through a government department of *yin-yang* established as early as AD 675, the teachings were spread to all levels of Japanese society (Chamberlain 1932; Tsunoda *et al.* 1958:60).

Yin-yang and Zuni religion (Table III) share concepts of avoiding calamities and keeping the right relations with the major elements (Tsunoda *et al.* 1958:60; Cushing 1920:19-20). In both systems the arrangement of houses and things within the house is influenced by direction orientation (Tsunoda *et al.* 1958:60; Stevenson 1904:432). Both *yin-yang* and the Zuni religion provide a dual organization of the universe. In Japan, the *yin* represents the 'kwei,' the female or material, substantial soul of the earth. The *yang* is the 'shen,' male or immaterial soul of heaven, the sky. *Yin* is dark and of the earth; *yang* is light and of heaven (Abegg 1955:76, 86). Accounts of Zuni also indicate a duality of sky and earth, male and female, light and dark (Parsons 1939:252; Eggan 1950:213). Frequent references to earth-mother and sky-father are made.

Table III ZUNI RELIGION AND JAPANESE YIN-YANG

SUMMER

Zuni:	South	Red	Fire	Husbandry/Medicine
Japan:	South	Red	Fire	Creativeness

AUTUMN

Zuni:	East	White	Earth	Magic/Religion
Japan:	West	White	Metal	Care

SPRING

Zuni:	West	Blue	Water	Hunting/War Cure
Japan:	East	Blue	Wood	Anger

WINTER

Zuni:	North	Yellow	Wind	War/Destruction
Japan:	North	Black	Water	Fear

OTHER RELIGIOUS PARALLELS

Both Shinto and Zuni religions include polytheism, ceremonies for fertility and harvest, ritual washing, and reverence for shrines and prayers to the sun (Parsons 1939; Ishaikawa 1936:319; Tsunoda *et al.* 1958; Buchanan 1935; Kato 1924:60). An additional aspect of Shinto with specific correspondence to Zuni is the idea of a three-dimensional universe: high, low, and middle (Kitagawa 1966:13-14). Zuni and Shinto religions further share a concern over the navel. This center point of the body is referred to as the 'source of life' in Zuni (Stevenson 1904:384).

'World view' may seem to be too broad a concept to allow comparisons. However, it should be noted that both the Zuni and Shinto/Buddhism have a theme of concern about totality, harmony, unaggressiveness, integration, and cohesion (Abegg 1955:101; Benedict 1934; Bellah 1957:15).

LOAN WORDS

These general ideas might be more easily dismissed as examples of independent innovation were it not for specific religious terminology which appears to include loan words. For example, of the words for basic directions, four sets appear to be related, as do two principal deities. For an example: one Zuni word for 'west' is *kalishi*; the Japanese word is *nishi*. The phonemic correspondence of \l\ and \n\ is also found in a word for 'south': in Zuni, *alaho*, and in ancient Japanese, *umanoho*. The Zuni word for 'east' is *temakoha*; the **koha** ending is derived from *kohakwa*, meaning 'white' which is also associated with 'east' in the Zuni system. *Tema* alone denotes 'east', as does *atuma* in Japanese.

Central in both systems is the concept of 'middle,' the center of the world. The current word in Zuni is *ittiwanna*, but in the old religious language, 'middle' is *wanakwin*; in Japanese, *mannaka*. This \w\ and \m\ correspondence is also found in the names of important gods concerned with the middle of the world. The Shinto 'Deity Master of the August Center of Heaven' is *Ame-no-mi-naka-nushi-no-kami* (Kato 1908:141). The Zuni 'Maker and Container of All, the All-father Father' (Cushing 1896) and the great 'He-She, the symbol and initiator of life, and life itself, pervading all space' is *Awo-na-wi-lo-na* (Stevenson 1904:22). The functions of these two deities are similar in the origin stories. The \m\ to \w\ occurs twice: *Ame-no-mi; Awo-na-wi.* The Japanese word for Shinto deities is *kami*; the Zuni word for 'divine ones' is *kowwituma*. Again the \m\ to \w\ shift. (The etymology of **tuma** is not known, but may be related to 'east.')

MORE PARALLELS

The high status Zuni clown and galaxy fraternity is *Newekwe* (Stevenson 1904). The Zuni word for 'clown', *newe*, also has an equivalent in a Japanese root for 'clown,' **niwa**. In Zuni, **kwe** refers to clan, society, or fraternity. A Japanese word meaning 'meeting' or 'society' is *kwai*, a word borrowed from Chinese. In Zuni, *Kokkokwe* means 'godclan' and *koko* is one word for *kachina*, or for a 'supernatural being or dead person' (Wright 1985:143). *Kogoshi* refers to 'god-like' in Japanese; *Koko*, the late Emperor.

A Zuni priest is *shiwani*; a Shinto priest is *shinkwan*. The Japanese word for Buddha is *Butsu*, which represents the Chinese word at the time it was borrowed by the Japanese, about AD 400; it has survived unchanged in the modern language (Sansom 1928:11). The Zuni phoneme \b\ in the initial position is most unusual; the foremost scholar of Zunian does not even include \b\ in the list of consonants

(Newman 1954; 1965), but Bunzel (1932:432) declares it is present, though rare and barely distinguishable from the unaspirated \p\. Perhaps it is part of the separate religious language (Newman 1955). In any case, \b\ definitely occurs in the name *Bitsitsi*, the great leader of the Galaxy (*Newekwe*) Fraternity. Stevenson observed that *Bitsitsi* is "held in high regard by the people" (1904:408); there is an aura of reverence and silence given his appearance. He speaks "with the heart," not the lips. He is the leader of the highest ranking religious organization. One of *Bitsitsi*'s characteristics is a topknot of hair tied with corn husks on his forehead (Stevenson 1904:277), a practice still continued today (Wyaco 1988).

As noted earlier, the Zuni consider themselves a composite of at least two different groups, one which long occupied the area and another, a new group which came from the west. If *Bitsitsi* is an American Indian *Butsu*, a reincarnated Buddha, this would explain his name, his authority, his leadership in the migration, and his continued recognition in the modern day. *Bitsitsi* is known and highly respected in modern Zuni also because he saved the Zuni from famine (Nahohai 1988); he found and returned The Corn Maidens.

These complex religious and cosmological concepts suggest that some Asian religious ideas may have come to North America relatively late in the prehistoric period. If the ideas and the lexicon came from Japan, they were already mixed; perhaps the people who later became the Zuni mixed those traditions further—with what they already had as American Indians.

LINGUISTIC PARALLELS

Basic to the enigma of Zuni-Japanese similarities is the question of language parallels.[2] But to date, no one has attempted a detailed comparison of Zuni and Japanese. Both Swadesh (1966) and Hockett (1987) reviewed a more extensive version of my linguistic analysis of 627 words, provided constructive suggestions, and encouraged further investigation. Here is a summary of some of my findings:

Newman, who published both a Zuni dictionary (1958) and grammar (1965), provided a weak demonstration of a possible genetic relationship between Zuni and California Penutian (Newman 1964:1-14). Still, a specific unresolved problem exists regarding the linguistic relationship of Zuni to other Amerind languages. In my comparison of Zuni with other Penutian languages (Greenberg's notebooks 1971), I found none of the Penutian nearly as strongly linked to Zuni as Zuni appears linked to Japanese.

However, the difficulties inherent in comparing Zuni and Japanese include problems such as differences 1. in orthography, 2. between the old language and the modern,[3] 3. between the written and the unwritten, and 4. between a large society and a small society, each with its own unique history.

GENERAL SIMILARITIES

Yet, despite these problems, some distinct similarities are clearly identifiable. For example, both languages have the same five basic vowels: **a, e, i, o,** and **u.** The twelve consonants that Japanese and Zuni share are: **ch, h, k, m, n, p, s, sh, t, w, y** and **z.** The only Japanese consonants definitely not found in Zuni are /r/ and /f/. The Japanese /**r**/ is the open '**r**,' close to /l/ in pronunciation, and /r/ seems to occur in a similar phonemic environment as the Zuni /l/ and /n/. The repetitive CV (consonant-vowel) pattern is pervasive.

In addition, both languages are agglutinative and synthetic; they share the same word order: subject, object, verb. In both, stems may function alone as nouns, or with suffixes as verbs, adverbs, or adjectives. Suffixes are also used to add mode, tense, and number to otherwise neutral root forms. Gender is not expressed in the grammar in either language. In both, conjunctions are rare. Postpositions and particles relate parts of a statement. Both languages have two pitches; the higher pitch and greater stress tends to occur in the first syllable of a word. Finally, age and sex dialects are found in both.

Specific words in areas of religious terminology, environmental features, and kinship appear so similar that recent borrowing may be the most likely explanation. Also, one wonders if words like *sale* in Zuni and *sara* in Japanese, both referring to a special category of dishware, could be related to new pottery techniques introduced in the 13th century. Owen (1965:685) suggested that a kind of hybridization of languages may occur when two social structures find themselves geographically or socially contiguous. One wonders how languages might change if the men spoke one language (Japanese) and the women another (Zuni, or a predecessor).

ZUNI-CALIFORNIA RELATIONSHIPS

If Zuni-Japanese contact occurred as postulated here, links between Zuni and Californian or other West Coast groups should be expected. Specific trade routes have been reconstructed (Figure 2), and as early as 1927 similar culture traits were noted between the Pueblo region and several coastal Indian groups of Southern California. The similarities included the groundhouse, priest complex, offering prayers for rain, feather sticks (or prayer plumes), offering or sprinkling of meal, and the bull roarer. Specific comparisons with the Kuksu cult might also be considered (Kroeber 1951:56;412).

Finding the ceremonial features so similar in detail, Strong stated "historical relationship is thereby implied" (1927:56-57). He suggests that the connection between the Southwest and Southern California was ultimately cut off by Yuman people of the Colorado River and again, later, by the Athapaskans.

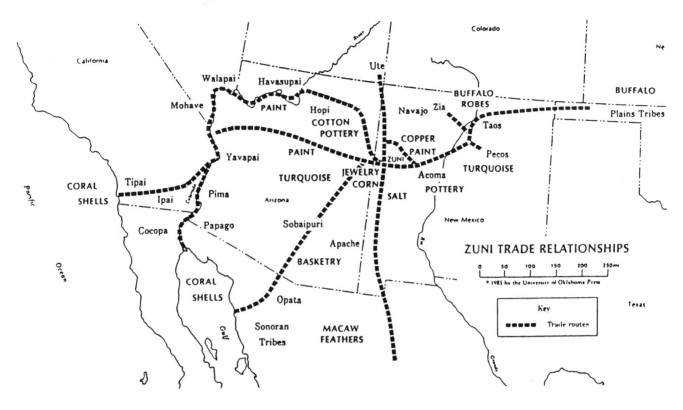

Figure 2 ZUNI TRADE RELATIONSHIPS
Source: Ferguson and Hart 1985:52

After Strong's proposal, a controversy developed as to whether Pueblo peoples with these particular traits moved west to the coast, whether some southern California Indians broke away and moved east to the Pueblo region, or whether a California-Pueblo continuum developed *in situ* and was only recently interrupted by intrusive groups.

Hawley (1937:506) supports Parsons' view (1939:989) that the western Zuni and Hopi had origins to the west, or to the south. After discussing Strong's theory of linkage with Southern California and the possibility of development of both groups *in situ*, Hawley states that both cases appear "... too simple an explanation to fit the data known at present. It seems more reasonable to postulate at least two different places of origins for the cultures we know as 'pueblo'" (Hawley 1937:520).

ZUNI MIGRATION TO THE MIDDLE PLACE

Hawley's statement most accurately reflects the Zuni's own concept of who they are and where they came from. The Zuni claim they have at least two origins, one in the Pueblo region, and another in a group that moved from the "ocean of the sunset world" looking for "the middle of the world" (Cushing 1920:216). They expressed to Cushing "terror of vague reference for the distant seas" (1920:217) and a belief in a "goddess of the ocean." The idea of oceans

survives in the modern oral traditions (Quam 1972: 112; Tedlock 1972:288, 291, 292).

In his detailed recording of Zuni narrations about their migrations, Cushing notes:

> The intrusive or western branch is, strange to say, although least numerous, the one most told of in the myths, the one which speaks throughout them in the first person; that is, which claims to be the original Shiwi or Zuni. Of this branch it is unnecessary to say much more here than the myths themselves declare, save to add that it was, if not the conquering, at least, and for a long time, the dominant one (1896:343).

Stevenson (1904), Cushing (1896), and Bunzel (1932) recorded in great detail the migration stories that tell how the people were instructed to move east, crossing mountains and rivers, passing lakes, valleys, and rows of springs, until they reached the middle. One motif in the stories reflects a definite religious motivation behind this search for the middle.

A sequence of earthquakes influenced the moves to the east (Cushing 1896:390-430). After each, the people "get up and move on," toward the east. After they arrived at the middle, there were no more earthquakes (Cushing 1896:429).

On their pilgrimage, the people gathered other groups, and the new members were impressed with the power of the Zuni gods (Cushing 1920:218). After generations of traveling, a great council of men and beings determined where the true middle was located. In the key passage referring to that decision (Cushing 1896:428-430), three themes dominate: six directions, concept of the middle of the earth-mother, and the navel. The final stopping place of the migrants at Zuni is about 700 miles from the west coast of California.

A map of the direction of migration in a more localized area has been reconstructed (Figure 3). Over thirty springs and resting places are mentioned in Zuni origin histories (Ferguson and Hart 1985:21-23); great detail remains in current knowledge about the search for the middle place, and many shrines are maintained marking the stops enroute.

Recent versions of finding the middle place appear in Quam's *The Zunis: Self Portrayals by the Zuni People* (1972:113) and in Tedlock's *Finding the Center* (1972:275-283). The Zuni People write in their book:

> To this day, there still rests in the heart of the village under a building, a rock that is the very place recorded as the middle place (Quam 1972:149).

Clearly, the middle place continues to be significant to the Zuni.

JAPANESE AND THE MIDDLE PLACE

Early Japanese literature reveals similar concern about the middle of the world, a concept perhaps borrowed from China. A speech by Emperor Jimmu is quoted in Japan's first book, *Kojiki* (AD 712):

> Now I have heard from the Ancient of the sea that in the East there is a fair land encircled on all sides by blue mountains . . . . I think that this land will undoubtedly be suitable for the extension of the Heavenly task, so that its glory should fill the universe. It is, doubtless, the center of the world. At present things are in a crude and obscure condition and the peoples' minds are unsophisticated. They roost in nests or dwell in caves . . . . Now if a great man were to establish laws, justice could not fail to flourish . . . . Thereafter, the capital may be extended so as to embrace all six cardinal points, and the eight cords may be covered so as to form a roof. Will this not be well?" (Tsunoda *et al.*1958:67-68).

Although I cannot establish a direct link between this statement and a mandated search east of Japan, perhaps such a venture did occur and will some day be documented.

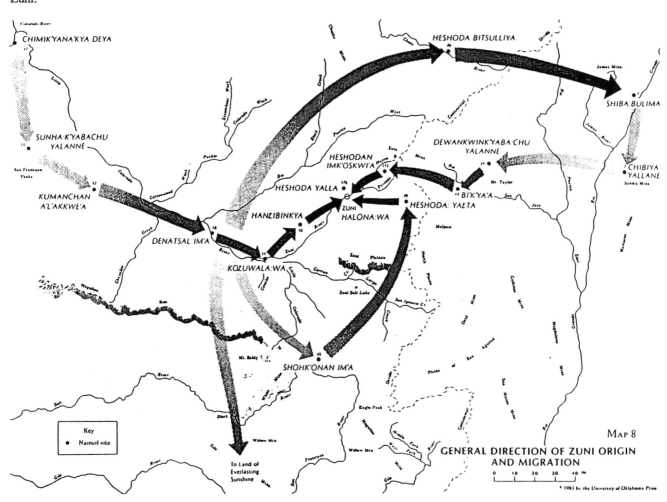

Figure 3 ZUNI ORIGIN AND MIGRATION
Source: Ferguson and Hart 1985:20

KINSHIP AND SOCIAL ORGANIZATION

Several curious characteristics of Zuni kinship terminology and social organization are not yet solved (Schneider and Roberts 1956; Fox 1972; Ladd 1979). I suggest that the confusion may result in part from relatively recent Japanese religious and patrilineal influence on an older, matrilineal, North American Indian base.

Certain changes in Zuni suggest a shift from formerly strong matrilineal clans and a clearly defined Crow lineage system, to a generational system with significant influence of the father's side in ceremonial and political affiliation (Eggan 1950). This kind of change seems consistent with what might be expected when a strong patrilineal system intrudes upon and mixes with a matrilineal system, especially if the new arrivals are Japanese men with new religious concepts who marry local Native American women with a land base.

The economic focus of Zuni society is still centered in the matrilineal household, which controls land usage, but the matrilineal clan does not function as a highly integrating entity, either economically or ceremonially. A Zuni man's more significant identity is through his father's side with fraternities, kivas, medicine societies and *kachinas* that cut across household and clan affiliations.

KINSHIP TERMS

If a new group moves into an area and establishes itself and its religion, would the kinship system and social organization of the original occupants alter in the ways suggested by Schneider and Roberts (1956)? A few kinship terms suggest such a mixing. A Zuni root word for 'woman' is **oka**. Oka also refers to 'woman' in Japanese, where frequently the honorific suffix **san** is added—*okasan*. Also, the words for 'wife' in each language are based on the same stem: *okassiki* (Z) and *okasama* (J). The Zuni word for 'man/male' is *otse*. An ancient Japanese word for 'man' is *osu* (Sansom 1928). A Zuni word for 'husband' is *oyemshi*. In Japanese, a term for 'father,' 'parent,' or 'boss' is *oya*. 'Older brother' in Japanese is *ani*; 'younger brother' in Zuni is *hanni*, which is also one of ten kinship terms used to designate ceremonial relatives (Ladd 1979:483).

JAPANESE SHIPS AND NAVIGATION

If Japanese contact occurred on the west coast of North America as postulated here, consideration must be given to Japanese knowledge of navigation and to the relative size of their ships at the time of the proposed trip, *ca.* late 12th century AD. Kidder (1959:165) found that boats played a prominent role in subject matter in several tombs dated about the 1st century AD. During the Nara period (AD 710-794), shipbuilding increased to facilitate many missions to China. During the following Heian period (AD 794-1185), such embassy traffic between Japan and China decreased, but shipping on the Japanese coast increased. Indeed, sea routes linked nineteen Japanese provinces (Furuta and Hirai 1967:9-11). Japanese maritime knowledge grew, as did piracy, and by the 12th century numerous Japanese-built-and-operated ships were traversing the unpredictable and frequently turbulent waters between Japan and China. Near the end of the Heian period "more than 120 Buddhist monks of Chinese and Japanese origins are known to have crossed the sea" (Hori 1967:81). The Chinese and the Korean ships were recognized as superior in size and construction, but the Japanese were honing their ocean-going skills (Sansom 1958:137-138).

SHIPWRECKS

Even the number of shipwrecks on the China coast at the end of the 12th century reflects something about the frequency of Japanese-initiated voyages to the mainland. Six wrecks on the China coast were reported for the 26-year period between 1176 and 1202. At least one of these ships was large enough for 100 men. Another carried 73 men (Tsunoda *et al.* 1958). If six ships of this size were lost during this period, how many might have made the voyage successfully? If the Japanese could navigate the notably difficult passage between Japan and China (Kakubayashi 1981:518), could they not also navigate the waters to the east, either by intent or by mishap?

Further, if the Japanese have operated relatively large boats for the last 1000 years, and if currents, including El Niño (Finney 1985), were the same during that period as they are now, it would seem that conditions were conducive to occasional shipwrecks on the North American west coast during prehistory. Japanese iron and steel have been found in Northwest Coast prehistoric sites (Quimby 1985). During early historic times, numerous Japanese shipwrecks on the west coast of North America have been documented, many with survivors (Quimby 1948:4:247; 1985; Brooks 1964; Kakubayashi 1981).

12TH-CENTURY JAPAN

Earlier we noted that Pueblo IV, AD 1250-1400, was a period of marked change in the Southwest. The 13th century was also a time of change in Japan, but it had been preceded by the turmoil of the 12th century. The end of the Heian period (1185) was a time of stress, characterized by the rise of military institutions and by the rise of many religious movements. For example, by the late 12th century, Honen (AD 1133-1212) had founded the Jodo sect of Pure Land Buddhism. Personal charisma in religious leadership grew, and Honen, who objected to formal religious leadership, was banished from Kyoto. His disciples then formed a religious society, and they, too, were persecuted and driven out of Kyoto. Among the concerns of Pure Land Buddhism was finding the center place of the world (Anesaki 1930:202).

If the concern for the center of the world by Amida Buddhism is related to the long, detailed migration narratives of the Zuni search for the middle of the world, led by Bitsitsi, then the time of possible departure from Japan, late in the 12th century, would allow for several generations of search from "the ocean of the sunset world" to the arrival some 700 miles inland in the 13th century at Zuni. Even today, the people who live there perceive Zuni to be the true center of the world. Certain environmental terms in Zuni suggest relatively recent loan words. For example, 'mountain' (Z: *yala*; J: *yama*); 'river' (Z: *kawina*; J: *kawa*); 'inside' (Z: *uchi*; J: *uchi*); 'badger' (Z: *tanushi*; J: *tanuki*); and as noted earlier, 'west' (Z: *kalishi*; J: *nishi*); and 'middle' (Z: *wanakwin*; J: *mannaka*).

Robert Lewis, Governor of the Zuni Pueblo, speculates that some Japanese, customarily expected to commit suicide in the face of a hostile military takeover (as at the end of the Heian period), may have chosen, instead, the slightly less risky option of fleeing east by boat (1988).[4]

In light of the several factors discussed above—12th century political turmoil in Japan; the rise of religious 'messiahs', especially Buddhas; and the persecution of certain sects—it would seem that conditions in Japan set the stage for a religiously-motivated pilgrimage to the Pure Land, a perceived center of the world to the east. After all, the ships were large enough for 100 persons, and general navigational knowledge was available; there is also growing evidence of Japanese shipwrecks on the North American coast. Hence, I suggest that a group, or groups, survived, and that the voyage or voyages may have been planned.

THE CHRYSANTHEMUM AND THE ROSETTE

Comparative analysis of Japanese and Zuni designs may provide additional insight, although this is a risky hypothesis to pose, both because human cultures are so creative, and because the Southwest is so rich in diverse motifs. Yet, consideration should be given to the possibility that the Zuni adopted, and elaborated on, an outside design, a many-petalled flower motif, which is referred to as a 'sacred rosette.' This distinctive design with a small center (unlike another motif, the Hopi 'sunflower') appears remarkably similar to the Japanese chrysanthemum (Figure 4).

In Zuni, the sacred rosette is found on Shalako robes (Kent 1981:48, 93), on many *kachinas* (Wright 1985), and on pottery (Hardin 1985). But only certain families use the design on pottery. Kenegy (1978) studied the medallion style as it appears on Zuni ceramics and reviewed previous efforts to explain its presence and prevalence. Some scholars consider the source to be European and recent. However, there is indication that the medallions may appear much earlier, as reflected on Pueblo IV kiva wall paintings (Smith 1952). Kenegy (1978:49) also reports that Carlson traces the medallions to St. Johns Polychrome on the upper Little Colorado, the site of the earliest glazed pottery.[5]

The Zuni Sacred Rosette[1]

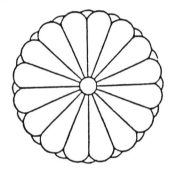

The National Arms of Japan[2]
(Chrysanthemum)

Figure 4 CHRYSANTHEMUM AND ROSETTE
Sources: 1. Hardin 1985; 2. Brooks 1964

Finally, Kenegy's analysis (1978:51-52) suggests that the design in Zuni today is associated with water, emergence, directions, and the center. In Japan it is associated with Buddhism, water, longevity, and the Royal Family (Arts 1983; Adachi 1972). With its extensive use on Zuni ceremonial and ceramic items, the medallion motif may be a local innovation, or alternatively, an example of creative cultural elaboration of an old Japanese crest.

SUGGESTIONS FOR FURTHER INQUIRY

To be consistent with anthropological ethics, I have invited the Zuni people to participate in this discussion. It is, after all, a part of their history we are exploring. My four meetings with the Pueblo of Zuni Council (May 26, June 1, and November 22, 1988; May 28, 1991) revealed their keen intellectual and objective interest in the enigma.

Together and individually, council members provided important insights and offered additional perspective. Several indicated a willingness to participate in further development of the study. Two members of the 1988 Zuni council had been Japanese prisoners during World War II (see Adair and Vogt 1949). One member who had been a prisoner for nearly three years noted, "I always wondered why I spoke Japanese so easily."

It is imperative that we consider the effects which these findings, so briefly summarized here, may have on living peoples—Zuni, other North American Indians, and Japanese. Perhaps what happened in the 13th century in the American Southwest is less important than how we manage new ideas now.

RESEARCH NEEDS

Certainly, the limitations of the information and explanation offered in this short overview must be acknowledged. And much work remains to be done, if only to resolve questions raised by this preliminary investigation. Some obvious considerations include:

1. The diversity of the evidence—from linguistics to dentition; from cosmology to genes—requires a theoretical framework to knit the pieces together and to identify gaps in the data.

2. This same diversity, and the extensive geography involved—Southwest, West Coast, and Asia—requires research by many specialists. No one person has the expertise to evaluate all the data. This implies a team effort.

3. This study does not yet include other Pueblo groups, such as the Tewa, Acoma, and Hopi, who share with Zuni some of the characteristics mentioned here. Nor has the literature on dozens of Indian groups located along the west coast been inspected for evidence of Japanese contact. Perhaps not just the people who became Zuni were influenced; Asian contact may have been much more extensive.

4. Additional Japanese data about the ancient language, religion, archaeology, history, lead-glaze pottery, tooth morphology, and blood factors are needed. The problem requires the attention of Japanese and other Asian scholars.

OTHER RESEARCH NEEDS

Future research might also consider other time periods. For example, evidence of much earlier Japanese contact in South America is documented in Estrada and Meggers (1961) and Meggers, Evans, and Estrada (1965). Moreover, a comparison needs to be made between, on the one hand, the structure and function of the excavated round dwellings of the Yayoi period in Japan, (250 BC-AD 250) (Kidder 1959:plate 34); and, on the other, the pit houses of Basket Maker III (AD 400-700) and the kivas of Pueblo I

(AD 700-900) in the American Southwest (Ferguson and Rohn 1987:26-33, 115). Further, a number of figures from the Yayoi period in Japan are also found in Zuni. For example, the dragonfly, crane, turtle, and heartline, which appear on a Japanese Dotaku bronze bell (Figure 5), also appear in shrines and on pottery in Zuni (Stevenson 1904: plates 34, 59, 104, 108, 114, 126, and 127; Hardin 1985).

Figure 5 PICTURES ON A DOTAKU BRONZE BELL, JAPAN
Source: Mallery 1893

Perhaps some day a specific Japanese group, and a precise time of departure, will be documented. Nobuhiro Yoshida, Executive Editor of the Petrograph Society in Japan, provides us with this challenge: "I am of the opinion that the Zuni tribe must have derived from A-Zumi, a seafaring tribe," a "powerful and distinguished people in ancient Japan before AD 600" (1992). Yoshida adds that the A-Zumi lost power and were forced out of the Yamato district by the Emperor's families in the 9th century. As mariners, might they have departed for the east?

SOME QUESTIONS

Many specific questions demand answers. How many words may be found to be related, especially in religious terminology? How frequently has an extensive, highly integrated system such as *yin-yang* developed independently? In what other North American and Mesoamerican groups do we find a system of directional orientation associated with fraternities, secret societies, clans, colors, seasons, gods, and elements? Would further comparison of Zuni and other American Indian beliefs with Shinto, Taoism, and Buddhism reveal other specific similarities in concept and lexicon?

Are there periods other than the 13th century at Zuni that suggest the introduction of a new population significant enough to modify genes, language, and culture? Can archaeologists prove that the glazed pottery was of indigenous origin? When and where else in North America was glaze applied? Is there evidence in the prehistory of California suggesting outside contact? How long would the proposed migration take for what size population?

In how many genetic features are the Zuni biologically distinctive from other southwestern groups? What additional information might be revealed through a complete analysis and comparison of Zuni and Japanese tooth morphology and blood features? Can DNA analysis ultimately resolve the biological questions?

What theoretical contributions could be provided by studies in acculturation, nativistic movements, migration, and resettlement? How might such theories add to an understanding of the social changes that contact might have stimulated?

Finally, what alternative explanations, equally well-researched, are there for the anomalies and questions raised here?

SUMMARY

Evidence suggesting Asian admixture is found in Zuni biology, lexicon, religion, social organization, and oral traditions of migration. Possible cultural and language links of Zuni to California, the social disruption at the end of the Heian period of the 12th century in Japan, the size of Japanese ships at the time of proposed migration, the cluster of significant changes in the late 13th century in Zuni, all lend further credibility to a relatively late prehistoric contact. Some details may ultimately be found to be coincidental, but I believe that additional research will support and expand the multi-faceted evidence presented here.

Whatever Japanese influence there may have been, the Zuni did not stop being American Indian; rather, they became a different kind of American Indian, mixing what came with what was—a creative process. Other surrounding groups probably responded in different and also distinctive ways. It may be clearer to think not of the 'diffusion' of Japanese culture and genes to Zuni, but rather of the acculturation and assimilation of a group of Japanese who mixed culturally and genetically with an American Indian group, or groups.

I end on the same challenge with which I began. The Zuni Indians of New Mexico constitute one of the most thoroughly documented cultures in the world, yet many unresolved questions remain concerning their origins and uniqueness. I maintain that the Zuni are distinct in biology, language, culture, and prehistory partly because of relatively recent Japanese admixture.

NOTES

1. *Kachina* refers to the general Pueblo idea of 'the masked spirit' or 'supernatural being,' and is sometimes associated with ancestor worship (Adams 1991:12). In Zuni, the term is *koko*, the ancestral spirits impersonated in religious ceremonies by masked male dancers.

2. For recent discussion and summaries of the history of attempts to place Zunian with other North American languages, consult Ruhlen (1987) and Greenberg (1987). For a statement on the history of Japanese language studies, see Shibatani (1990).

3. Yoshida (1990) provided a series of more closely related words than I had found in the Tokyo-based dictionary. He suggests that the rural dialects retain more of the older words. For a few examples: 'priest' is *shawani* (J), *shiwani* (Z); 'spleen' is *bari* (J), *pali* (Z); 'to become hot' is *karhi* (J), *kalhi* (Z); 'to become angry' is *ikachi* (J), *ikati* (Z); 'to be mean' is *sami* (J), *samu* (Z).

4. The 1992 council is familiar with this study but does not endorse the theory (Wilford 1992). There is no intent here by the author to question Zuni understandings of their origins; this paper just adds one more consideration to an already rich, diverse, and complex history—one more possible dimension for us to contemplate and research together.

5. St. Johns is 50 miles southwest of the present town of Zuni, just over the border in eastern Arizona.

General: The Zuni Pueblo, with about 8000 residents, is the largest of nineteen pueblos in New Mexico. The tribe is governed by an elected eight-member council and manages its own school district, police force, hospital, businesses, archaeological research program, and museum. Most residents, including the children, speak Zuni and maintain a vital traditional religious system with an annual cycle of complex ceremonies. The exceptional quality of Zuni art, especially jewelry and pottery, is recognized nationally and internationally.

A portion of an earlier version of this paper was presented at the Circum-Pacific Prehistory Conference, Session on Prehistoric Trans-Pacific Contacts, Seattle WA, August 5, 1989.

ACKNOWLEDGMENTS

Grateful appreciation is extended to many creative mavericks who have variously supported, and challenged, the writing of this paper. Leaders and friends in the Pueblo of Zuni have been most kind, and patient, with this effort. Scholars of the Southwest have been skeptical, and puzzled, and have raised questions I cannot answer. For over thirty years, my husband, Bill, has encouraged, and endured my curiosity about the questions raised here; he also edited earlier versions of the paper. The organizers and supporters of the ABC Conference provided a format for discussion, and Brown University provided an academic setting conducive to new ideas. Finally, the meticulous attention to detail and quality of suggestions provided by Don Gilmore and Linda McElroy, editors of this final paper, have made it possible to bring these ideas to print. Let the discussion and the fun continue!

REFERENCES

Abegg, Lily
1955 *The Mind of East Asia*. London: Thames and Hudson.

Adachi, Fumie, trans.
1972 *Japanese Design Motifs: 4,260 Illustrations of Japanese Crests*. Compiled by the Matsuya Piece-Goods Store. New York: Dover Publications, Inc.

Adair, John J. and Evon Z. Vogt
1949 Navaho and Zuni veterans: A study of contrasting modes of culture change. *American Anthropologist* 51(4):547-561.

Adams, E. Charles
1991 *The Origin and Development of the Pueblo Katsina Cult*. Tucson: The University of Arizona Press.

Anesaki, Masaharu
1930 *History of Japanese Religion*. London: Kegan Paul, Trench, Trubner and Co., Ltd.
1963 *History of Japanese Religion: With Special Reference to the Social and Moral Life of the Nation*. Rutland VT and Tokyo, Japan: Charles E. Tuttle Co.

Arts, P. L. W.
1983 *Japanese Porcelain: A Collector's Guide to General Aspects and Decorative Motifs*. Lochem-Poperinge: Uitgeversmaatschappij De Tijdsroom.

Belich, Monica P., J. Alejandro Madrigal, William H. Hildebrand, Jacqueline Zemmour, Robert C. Williams, Roberto Luz, Maria Luiza Petzl-Erler, and Peter Parham
1992 Unusual HLA-B alleles in two tribes of Brazilian Indians. *Nature* 357:326-329.

Bellah, Robert N.
1957 *Tokugawa Religion: The Values of Pre-Industrial Japan*. Glencoe IL: The Free Press.

Benedict, Ruth
1934 *Patterns of Culture*. Boston MA: Houghton Mifflin Co.

Brooks, Charles Wolcott
1964 *Japanese Wrecks Stranded and Picked Up Adrift in the North Pacific Ocean*. Fairfield WA: Ye Galleon Press. (Originally printed in 1876 by the California Academy of Sciences).

Brown, K. S., B. L. Hanna, A. A. Dahlberg, and H. H. Strandskov
1958 The distribution of blood group alleles among Indians of Southwest North America. *American Journal of Human Genetics* 10:175-195.

Buchanan, D. C.
1935 Inari: Its origin, development and nature. *Asiatic Society of Japan*. London: Kegan Paul, Trench, Trubner and Co., Ltd.

Bunzel, Ruth L.
1932 Zuni origin myths. Pp. 545-609 in *47th Annual Report of the Bureau of American Ethnology for the Years 1929-1930*. Washington DC.

Chamberlain, Basil Hall
1932 *Ko-ji-ki or Records of Ancient Matters*. Trans., 2nd ed., J. L. Kobe. Thompson and Co.

Cushing, Frank H.
1882 Zuni social, mythic, and religious systems. *Popular Science Monthly* 21.
1896 Outlines of Zuni creation myths. Pp. 321-447 in *13th Annual Report of the Bureau of American Ethnology for the Years 1891-1892*. Washington DC.
1920 Zuni breadstuff. Museum of the American Indian, HeyeFoundation. *Indian Notes and Monographs* 8. New York.

Danson, Edward B.
1957 An archaeological survey of west central New Mexico and east central Arizona. *Papers of the Peabody Museum of American Archaeology and Ethnology*, Harvard University 44(1). Cambridge MA.

Davis, Emma Lou
1965 Small pressures and cultural drift as explanations for abandonment of the San Juan area, New Mexico and Arizona. *American Antiquity* 30(3):353-355.

Eggan, Fred
1950 *Social Organization of the Western Pueblos*. Chicago: The University of Chicago Press.
1972 Summary. Pp. 287-305 in *New Perspectives on the Pueblos*. A. Ortiz, ed. A School of American Research Book. Albuquerque: University of New Mexico Press.

Estrada, Emilio and Betty J. Meggers
1961 A complex of traits of probable transpacific origin on the coast of Ecuador. *American Anthropologist* 63:913-939.

Ferguson, T. J. and E. Richard Hart
1985 *A Zuni Atlas*. Norman and London: University of Oklahoma Press.

Ferguson, William M. and Arthur H. Rohn
1987 *Anasazi Ruins of the Southwest in Color*. Albuquerque: The University of New Mexico Press.

Finney, Ben
1985 Anomalous westerlies, El Niño, and the colonization of Polynesia. *American Anthropologist* 87(1):9-26.

Ford, Richard I., Albert H. Schroeder, and Stewart L. Peckham
1972 Three perspectives on puebloan prehistory. Pp.19-39 in *New Perspectives on the Pueblos*. A. Ortiz, ed. Albuquerque: University of New Mexico Press.

Fox, Robin
1972 Some unsolved problems of pueblo social organization. Pp. 71-75 in *New Perspectives on the Pueblos*. A. Ortiz, ed. Albuquerque: University of New Mexico Press.

Furuta, Ryoichi and Yoshikazu Hirai
1967 *A Short History of Japanese Merchant Shipping*. Trans. and annotated by D. MacFarlane. Tokyo New Service, Ltd.

Garn, Stanley M.
1961 *Human Races*. (1969 ed.) Springfield IL: Charles C. Thomas.

Gladwin, Harold S.
1957 *A History of the Ancient Southwest*. Portland ME: Bond Wheelwright Co.

Greenberg, Joseph H.
1953 Historical linguistics and unwritten languages. Pp. 265-286 in *Anthropology Today*. An Encyclopedic Inventory. A. L. Kroeber, chair. The University of Chicago Press.
1971 *Notebooks. Vol. 8, Penutian*. Stanford University Library.
1987 *Language in the Americas*. Stanford University Press.

Hale, Kenneth and David Harris
1979 Historical linguistics and archaeology. Pp. 170-177 in *Handbook of North American Indians. Vol 9, Southwest*. Washington DC.

Hardin, Margaret Ann
1985 *Gifts of Mother Earth: Ceramics in the Zuni Tradition*, p. 32. Phoenix AZ: The Heard Museum.

Haury, Emil W.
1932 The age of lead glaze decorated pottery in the Southwest. *American Anthropologist* 34:418-425.

Hawley, Florence M.
1937 Pueblo social organization as a lead to pueblo history. *American Anthropology* 39(3):504-522.

Hockett, Charles F.
1987 Personal communication. Letter, 4 pp. June 17.

Hori, Kyotsu
1967 *The Mongol Invasions and the Kamakura Bakufu*. PhD dissertation. Political Science, Columbia University, ms.

Hough, Walter
1928 The lead glaze decorated pottery of the pueblo region. *American Anthropologist* 30(2):243-249.

Hoy, Wendy E., Donald M. Megill, and Michael D.Hughson
1987 Epidemic renal disease of unknown etiology in the Zuni Indians. *American Journal of Kidney Diseases* 9(6):485-496.

Hughson, Michael D., Donald M. Megill, Suzanne M. Smith, Kenneth S. K. Tung, Gerald Miller, and Wendy E. Hoy
1989 Mesangiopathic glomerulonephritis in Zuni (New Mexico) Indians. *Archives Pathological Laboratory Medicine* 113:148-157.

Ishaikawa, Michiji
1936 The Japanese concept of man. *Cultural Nippon* 5(4):317-328. Tokyo: Nippon Bunka Renmei.

Jett, Stephen C.
1964 Pueblo Indian migration: An evaluation of the possible physical and cultural determinants. *American Antiquity* 29(3):281-300.

Kakubayashi, Fumio
1981 Japanese drift records and the Sharp hypothesis. *Journal of Polynesian Society* 90(4):515-524.

Kato, Genchi
1908 The ancient Shinto deity Ame-no-minaka-nushi-no-kami. *The Asiatic Society of Japan Transactions* 36(1):141-162. Tokyo.
1924 A study of the development of religious ideas among the Japanese people as illustrated by Japanese phallicism.*Transactions of the Asiatic Society of Japan*. Second Series, Supplement to Vol. 1. Tokyo.

Kenegy, Susan G.
1978 Deer-and-medallion style pottery at Zuni Pueblo: Iconography and iconology. *New Mexico Studies in the Fine Arts* 8:46-52.

Kent, Kate Peck
1983 *Pueblo Indian Textiles: A Living Tradition*. Sante Fe NM: School of American Research Press.

Kidder, J. Edward
1959 *Japan Before Buddhism*. New York: Frederick A. Praeger.

Kitigawa, Joseph M.
1966 *Religion in Japanese History*. New York: Columbia University Press.

Kintigh, Keith W.
1985 Settlement, subsistence, and society in late Zuni prehistory. *Anthropological Papers of the University of Arizona*. No. 44.

Kroeber, A. L.
1951 Elements of culture in native California. Pp. 3-68 in *The California Indians: A Source Book*. R. F. Heizer and M. A. Whipple, eds. University of California Press.

Ladd, Edmund J.
1979 Zuni social and political organization. Pp. 482-491 in *Handbook of North American Indians. Vol. 9, Southwest*. A. Ortiz, ed. Washington DC: Smithsonian Institution.

Lewis, Governor Robert
1988 Personal communication. Pueblo of Zuni. November 22.

Long, Jeffrey C.
1991 The genetic structure of admixed populations. *Genetics* 127:417-428.

Mallery, Garrick
1893 Picture-writing of the American Indians. *Tenth Annual Report of the Bureau of Ethnology*. Smithsonian Institution.

Meggers, Betty J., Clifford Evans, and Emilio Estrada
1965 Early Formative Period of coastal Ecuador: The Valdivia and Machalilla Phases. *Smithsonian Contributions to Anthropology*, Vol. 1. Washington DC: Smithsonian Institution.

Mellot, Richard L.
1990 Ceramics of the Asuka, Nara, and Heian Periods (AD 552-1185). Pp. 56-66 in *The Rise of a Great Tradition: Japanese Archaeological Ceramics from the Jomon Through Heian Periods (10,500 BC-AD 1185)*. Agency for Cultural Affairs, Government of Japan. New York: Japan Society.

Murdock, George P.
1953 *Ethnographic Bibliography of North America,* 2nd Edition. New Haven: Human Relations Area Files, Inc.

Nahohai, Milford
1988 Personal communication. Pueblo of Zuni. May 27.

Newman, Stanley
1954 American Indian linguistics in the Southwest. *American Anthropologist* 56:4.
1955 Vocabulary levels: Zuni sacred and slang usage. *Southwestern Journal of Anthropology* 11:345-354.
1958 Zuni Dictionary. *International Journal of American Linguistics* 24(1) Part II.
1964 Comparison of Zuni and California Penutian. *International Journal of American Linguistics* 30(1)1-13.
1965 Zuni grammar. *University of New Mexico Publications in Anthropology*, No. 14. Albuquerque: The University of New Mexico Press.

Ortiz, Alfonzo, ed.
1979 Introduction. Pp. 1-4 in *Handbook of North American Indians*, Vol. 9. Washington DC: Smithsonian Institution.

Owen, Roger C.
1965 The patrilocal band: A linguistically and culturally hybrid social unit. *American Anthropologist* 67:675-791.

Parsons, Elsie (Clews)
1939 *Pueblo Indian Religion*. 2 Vols. Chicago: University of Chicago Press.

Pinto-Cisternas and Hernan Figueroa
1968 Genetic structure of a population of Valparaiso II: Distribution of two dental traits with anthropological importance. *American Journal of Physical Anthropology* 29:339-348.

Quam, Alvina, trans.
1972 *The Zunis: Self-portrayals by the Zuni People*. Albuquerque: University of New Mexico Press.

Quimby, George I.
1948 Culture contact on the northwest coast, 1785-1795. *American Anthropologist* 50(2):247-255.
1985 Japanese wrecks, iron tools, and prehistoric Indians of the northwest coast. *Arctic Anthropology* 22(2):7-15.

Reed, Erik K.
1955 Painted pottery and Zuni history. *Southwestern Journal of Anthropology* 11:178-193.

Roberts, Frank H. H., Jr.
1932 The village of the great kivas on the Zuni reservation, New Mexico. *Bureau of American Ethnology Bulletin 111*. Washington DC.

Ruhlen, Merritt
1987 *A Guide to the World's Languages, Vol. 1, Classification*. Stanford University Press.

Sansom, George
1928 *An Historical Grammar of Japanese*. Oxford: Clarendon Press.
1958 *A History of Japan to 1334*. Stanford CA: Stanford University Press.

Sapir, Edward
1929 Central and North American languages. Pp. 169-178 in *Selected Writings of Edward Sapir*. D. G. Mandelbaum, ed.,1958. University of California Press.

Schneider, David M. and John M. Roberts
1956 Zuni kin terms. *University of Nebraska, Laboratory of Anthropology Notebook 3*. Lincoln. (Reprinted, New Haven: Human Relations Area Files Press.)

Scott, G. Richard, Rosario H. Yap Potter, John F. Noss, Albert A. Dahlberg, and Thelma Dahlberg
1983 The dental morphology of Pima Indians. *American Journal of Physical Anthropology* 61:13-31.

Scott, G. R., S. Street, and A. A. Dahlberg
1986 The dental variation of Yuman-speaking groups in an American Southwest context. In *Teeth Revisited: Proceedings of the VIIth International Symposium on Dental Morphology*, D. E. Russell, J. P. Santoro, D. Sigogneau-Russell, eds. Mem. Mus. Natn. Hist. Nat., Paris (serie C) 53:305-319.

Seltzer, Carl
1944 Racial prehistory in the Southwest and the Hawikuh Zunis. *Papers of the Peabody Museum of American Archaeology and Ethnology* 23(1). Cambridge MA: Harvard University.

Shibatani, Masayoshi
1990 *The Languages of Japan*. Cambridge Language Surveys. Cambridge University Press.

Smith, Watson
1952 Kiva mural decorations at Awatovi and Kawaika-a, with a survey of other wall paintings in the Pueblo Southwest. *Papers of the Peabody Museum of American Archaeology and Ethnology*, Harvard University 37. Cambridge MA.

Sofaer, J. A., J. D. Niswander, C. J. MacLean, and P. L. Workman
1972 Population studies on southwestern Indian tribes, V: Tooth morphology as an indicator of biological distance. *American Journal of Physical Anthropology* 37:357-366.

Spuhler, James N.
1979 Genetic distances, trees, and maps of North American Indians. Chapter 7, pp. 135-183 in *The First Americans: Origins, Affinities, and Adaptations*. W. S. Laughlin and A. B. Harper, eds. New York: Gustav Fischer.

Stevenson, Matilda (Coxe)
1904 The Zuni Indians: Their mythology, esoteric fraternities, ceremonies. Pp. 3-634 in *23rd Annual Report of the Bureau of American Ethnology for the Years 1901-1902*. Washington DC.

Strong, William D.
1927 An analysis of Southwestern society. *American Anthropologist* 29(1):1-61.

Suzuki, Makoto and Takuro Sakai
1964 Shovel-shaped incisors among the living Polynesians. *American Journal of Physical Anthropology* 22:65-72.

Swadesh, Morris
1966 Personal communication. Letters dated February 20 and March 18.

Tedlock, Dennis, trans.
1972 *Finding the Center: Narrative Poetry of the Zuni Indians*, from Performances in Zuni by Andrew Peynetsa and Walter Sanchez. New York: Dial Press.

Tsujii, Tadashi
1958 Incidence and inheritance of the Carabelli's cusp in a Japanese population. *Japanese Journal of Human Genetics* 3:21-31.

Tsunoda, Ryusaku, William T. de Bary, and Donald Keene
1958 *Sources of the Japanese Tradition*. New York: Columbia University Press.

Turner, Christy G., II
1969 Microevolutionary interpretation from the dentition. *American Journal of Physical Anthropology* 30:421-426.
1987 Late Pleistocene and Holocene population history of East Asia based on dental variation. *American Journal of Physical Anthropology* 73:305-321.

Underhill, Ruth
1954 Intercultural relations in the greater Southwest. *American Anthropologist* 56:645-656.

Watanabe, S., S. Kondo, and E. Matsunagi, eds.
1975 Anthropological and genetic studies on the Japanese. *Human Adaptability*, Vol. 2. Japanese Committee for the International Biological Program. Tokyo: University of Tokyo Press.

Wilford, John Noble
1992 Case for other pre-Columbian voyagers. *The New York Times*. Science B10, July 7.

Woodbury, Richard B.

1956   The antecedents of Zuni culture. *Transactions of the New York Academy of Sciences*, 2nd. series, Vol. 18 (6):557-563.

1979   Zuni prehistory and history to 1850. Pp. 467-473 in *Handbook of North American Indians*, *Vol. 9, Southwest*. A. Ortiz, ed. Washington DC: Smithsonian Institution.

Workman, P. L., J. D. Niswander, K. S. Brown, and W. C. Leyshon

1974   Population studies on Southwestern Indian tribes IV: The Zuni. *American Journal of Physical Anthropology* 41:119-132.

Wormington, H. Marie

1959   *Prehistoric Indians of the Southwest*. Denver: The Denver Museum of Natural History (4th printing).

Wright, Barton

1985   Kachinas of the Zuni: Original paintings by Duane Dishta. Northland Press, Southwest Museum.

Wyaco, Virgil

1988   Personal communication. May 26.

1988   Personal communication. Pueblo of Zuni. November 22.

Yoshida, Nobuhiro

1990   Personal communication. December.

1992   Personal communication. January 5 and April 1.

Dyestuffs and Possible Early Contacts
Between Southwestern Asia and Nuclear America

STEPHEN C. JETT

He is trained to work in purple, blue, and crimson fabrics . . .
—Hiram, King of Tyre, to Solomon, King of Israel, *2 Chronicles* 2:14

For these garments they [the Incas] *had such perfect dyes*
—red, blue, yellow, black, and other colors—that they truely excell those of Spain.
—Pedro Cieza de León, 1553 (Hagen 1959)

INTRODUCTION

The historical hearths of sophisticated pre-industrial textile manufacturing are Southwestern Asia, especially in what today are the Indo-Iranian- and western Turkic-speaking areas, and the Central Andean region of South America (Donkin 1977b:847). Many structural and esthetic characteristics are shared by textiles of these areas, as is the practice of resist-dyeing by the plangi (tie-dye), ikat, and batik methods (also known from Southeast Asia and Mesoamerica [*e.g.*, Johnson 1959:464, 468; Williams 1964:5; Rowe 1977; King 1979; 1980; Bühler 1972]).

Of interest for the present paper are the following dyestuffs that were shared in pre-Columbian times by Southwestern Asia, on the one hand, and Peru and Mesoamerica, on the other: madder red, indigo blue, scale-insect scarlet, and shellfish purple (*cf.* Spinden 1924; Hagen 1959:177). These dyestuffs are somewhat obscure and are not easy to use, for they are not obvious in the environment and generally require that complex procedures be effectively applied in order to fix the colorants. Therefore, it is important to examine both the materials and the technologies as possible items of transfer by humans, via early sea voyages (*e.g.*, Marschall 1979:135-43).

MADDER

Old World *Madder and* Morinda

A red dyestuff derived from the roots of shrubs of the *Rubiaceae*, found wild and also cultivated widely, is dyer's madder. Known as *Rubia tinctorum* and *R. perigrina* in Southwest Asia, it is *R. cordifolia*, called *manjit* or *munjeet*, in South and East Asia; in India, there is also a similar Indian madder or *chay* root, *Oldenlandia* (or *Hedyotis*) *umbellata* (*chayaver*, or 'color-fixing root'). (For additional native names, see Mohanty, Chandramouli, and Naik 1987:18, 100, 148-149.) Madder's earliest known use was at the Harappan city of Mohenjo-daro in the Indus Valley, *ca.* 3000 BC, by which time weaving was already a mature craft (Allchin and Allchin 1982:191-192); madder was also employed in ancient Persia, the Levant, Egypt, Greece,

and Rome. The name appears to have been *ponikija* (adjective) in archaic Greek, *p*w*t* in Ugaritic (for madder-dyed cloth), *puwwa* in Hebrew (adjective, *puni*), and *fuwwa* in Arabic (Astour 1965: 348-349; Knapp 1991:27, 38). In Sanskrit and Pali, madder is *manjistha* and *mañjitta*, respectively, and in Persian *run*[i]*as* (Dhamija 1990:841); it is often called [*a*]*lizari* in the East (Forbes 1956:143). (For native names, see Mohanty, Chandramouli, and Naik 1987: 149, 212; Buddhatta Mahathera n.d.:317.) The roots of another shrub genus in India, *Morinda* or Indian mulberry (*al*, *ach*, or *suranji*), also yield the same coloring matter, known as 'alizarin.' (For native names, see Mohanty, Chandramouli, and Naik 1987:50, 67, 207; Gittinger 1982:21; Ploss 1963a:24-25; Gerber 1978:4; Morton 1992:244-247; Rosenberg *et al.* 1993:93.)

Madder, a direct dye, is prepared by unearthing, drying, cleaning, and pulverizing the roots; then soaking the product overnight and steeping it for a short time at about one hundred and fifty degrees. The yarn or fabric to be dyed is briefly mordanted (*para karavo* in India) with aluminum sulfate (alum, *pitakadi* in Pakistan, *zaj* in Persian) or iron sulfate, and is then gently cooked in the dye bath, following which it is rinsed in water containing wood ash (Forbes 1956:104-105; Leggett 1944:3-4; Wulff 1966:190; Robinson 1969:26; Donkin 1977a:6-7; Peterson 1991:7; Mushak 1991:25; Dhamija 1990:841-842; for other recipes, see Mohanty, Chandramouli, and Naik 1987:18-20, 37, 56-59, 148-150, 168-171). Mordanting—which fixes, and sometimes enhances, the color (Ortiz 1968:20)—is attested at Mohenjo-daro from at least about 2000 BC, as well as in ancient Egypt, but was supposedly not reported in the western ecumene until the 1st century AD (Forbes 1956:132-133; Gittinger 1982:31, 33; Barber 1991:236-237; Barnes 1993:1, 30; but see Faber 1938:287).

Madder and Indian mulberry were never used in many areas where wild *Rubia* and *Morinda* were available (Robinson 1969:26; Morton 1992:47).

Relbun *(New World Madder) and* Morinda

Alizarin and/or pupurin and pseudopupurin occur in close *Rubia* relatives *Relbunium nitidum*, *R. galium microphyllum, R. ciliatum, R. hirsutum*, and *R. hypocarpium*, which are small, inconspicuous, subtropical, rubiacious shrubs found from Mexico to Argentina (*e.g.,* Ortiz 1968:41; Robinson 1969:26; Reid 1991:62). Aluminum-mordanted alizarin (probably from *R. niditum*) is attested at pre-ceramic La Galgada, in Peru's northern highlands, dating to the 3rd millennium BC (Grieder 1988:181), as well as at coastal Ancón and Paracas Necrópolis and in northern Argentina in later prehistory (Donkin 1977a:7; Paul 1990: 12). Aluminum mordant has been identified at Paracas, and iron was also used ('mordant' = *millu* in Aymara; *kollpa* or *alcaparosa* in Quechua); other mordants included oxalic acid, tannin, and ashes (Fester 1954; Young 1957; Antúnez 1989:182-183, 188; Girault 1969:26, 29; Schweppe 1986: 158; Jakes 1991:228-230, 235; Saltzman 1978:179; 1986:32-34, 36; 1992:478; Reid 1991:64). Relbun red is "difficult to gather and use," and in most places was largely replaced by cochineal during Peru's Early Intermediate Period beginning about 200 BC (Dwyer 1979:75). Since wild cochineal insects existed in Peru (Diguet 1909:78; Fester 1954:243-44), and since cochineal is easier to dye with than is relbun (Saltzman 1992:478), the former's late use suggests that even a people who are sophisticated in dye utilization don't automatically discover and employ good, available dye sources.

Relbun red is called *chapi-chapi,* or *puka chchapi*, in Peru (Dwyer 1979:75; Reid 1991:62). This name *chapi* is reminiscent of the word *chaili* for *Morinda* in India's Santhal language and *chayaver* for the madder-like root of *Oldenlandia umbellata* (Mohanty, Chandramouli, and Naik 1987:207, 209). Further, *puka* reminds one of the Old World words for madder, *i.e., ponikija, p*w*t*, and *puwwa* (and of purple, *e.g., popureja*).

There is no evidence that the ancient Maya used relbun (Carsen and Wenger 1991:370), despite the presence of wild *Relbunium* (Robinson 1969:26), but this may simply reflect incomplete information. Two species of *Rubiaceae* are reported as ethnographically known dyestuffs in Guatemala and El Salvador: *Calderonia salvadorensis* and *Exandra rhodonclada* (Osborne 1942:89). An American species of *Morinda* apparently was used to produce yellow to orange dye in Yucatan and the Cayman Islands (Morton 1992:244).

INDIGO

Classic Indigo

As its name implies, classic cultivated indigo originated in India, and northwestern India remained the center of production. There, and throughout Southwest Asia, to where its use spread, the dye is called *nil[ah]* or *nili*, an Indian term for blue that apparently predated the Aryan invasion. It is also known as *rang*, blue, in Persian (Dhamija 1990:842), and *ram* in Tibetan (for native names, see Mohanty, Chandramouli, and Naik 1987:37, 52, 166, 204). Indigo, in one form or another, also spread to Egypt by about 2500 BC, and to various parts of Asia and beyond.

However, large-scale trade in Indian indigo, apparently from the Indus region, seems to have awaited the conquests of Alexander (Forbes 1956:111-112; Ploss 1963b:65-66; Robinson 1969:24; Rao 1985:686).

"Of all the natural dyestuffs, indigo is among the oldest in use [and] most complicated technologically . . ." (Gerber 1984:xiii). The dye is produced from the leaves of *Indigofera tinctoria*, which contain small amounts of indican. To obtain high-quality dye, the plant must be very carefully cultivated. Even in primitive dyeing, the fresh-cut leaves (*lank* in India), whole or ground, must be steeped in heated water for nine to fourteen hours, during which time fermenting occurs (with a highly unpleasant odor), thereby reducing the insoluble indican to the water-soluble leuco-compound, indoxyl. The resultant liquid is clear, and the soaked yarn or cloth turns blue only upon oxidization of the indoxyl to indigotin upon exposure to the air (Wulff 1966:192; Bühler 1948:2494; Balfour-Paul 1992:99-100; Gittinger 1982:22, 23; Gerber 1984). "To obtain depth in coloring, the dyeing process must be frequently repeated, and sometimes it takes months, even years . . . to produce the effects desired" (Bühler 1951:3091).

Dyeing procedures are considerably more complicated in their developed form (*e.g.,* Mohanty, Chandramouli, and Naik 1987:27-36, 83-100). For example, the water may have quick-lime added to enhance solubility and may be beaten for aeration, in which case oxydized indigotin precipitates; the sludge is heated to stop fermentation, and is filtered through cloth. When shaped and dried, it yields cake indigo for trade (Leggett 1944:19-20; see also, Forbes 1956:134-135). In India, such cake is known as *buttis* or *guttis* (Mohanty, Chandramouli, and Naik 1987:28). "[I]ndigo and murex purple . . . produce colorfast dyes all by themselves [without mordants, though they may be used], although the process of reduction by fermentation and later oxidation make the 'vat-dye' procedure long, complicated, and far from obvious" (Barber 1991:235). Middle Eastern "indigo dyeing has always remained in the hands of experts due to the unusual complexity of the chemical processes involved . . . dyers have jealously guarded their trade secrets . . . until a mystique came to surround the process" (Balfour-Paul 1992:101; see also, Heringa 1989:115). "It is remarkable, almost beyond coincidence, that the technologies involving indigo have been virtually constant in all cultures through all time" (Gerber 1984:xiv).

American Indigo

In the Americas, additional shrub species of *Indigofera* and other indigo-producing plants existed. Especially used for dyeing in pre-Columbian times were *I. suffruticosa* (*xiquilite* in Peru) and *Fuchsia parviflora* in Central and South America, as well as *Cybistax antisyphilitica* and *Muehlenbakia hastiuta rupestris* (*mullaka*) in Peru (Osborne 1942:88; Leggett 1944:18; Towle 1961:46-47; Williams 1964:11; Robinson 1969:24; Johnson 1971:314; Gade 1975:89, 167; Antúnez 1989: 183; Reid 1991:62). In Guatemala, where indigo was in use pre-Contact (Carlsen and Wenger 1991:368), in contemporary usage sacatinta (*Fuchsia*) leaves are steeped for two days, and ground cake indigo and wood ash added to the cold water. Yarn is immersed after five days and bathed for twelve hours. Ash and lime are employed as solubility-enhancers (O'Neale 1945:25-29). In Bolivia, leaves of four local plants are boiled, and cake indigo is added, and the mixture boiled for fifteen minutes and then left to sit for two hours. Wool and separately-prepared alum are added, boiled for two hours while being stirred, and then allowed to cool. When the wool is removed, it turns blue in the sunlight. The process is repeated until the desired shade is obtained (Girault 1969:26-27). Indigo has been identified at 7th-century-BC Nazca and at Paracas Necrópolis, *ca.* 450-175 BC (Fester 1954:239; Jakes 1991:228-230, 235; Young 1957; Paul 1990:4, 12; see also, King 1965:1).

INSECT DYES

Kermes and Lac

The use of female wild scale insects of the species *Kermococcus vermilio* to produce a carmine or vermilion dye (kermesic acid), called *kermes* (Ziderman 1986a:419-20), < Persian *qermes*, < Old Persian *qerema*, 'worm,' goes back to prehistory (*i.e.*, Neolithic times) in the Mediterranean and Southwest Asia. The dyestuff was traded by Phoenicians (the main producers, who called it *thola*) to Iraq in the mid-2nd millennium BC; its use was recorded in 1727 BC (Donkin 1977b:860; Forbes 1956:102; Dhamija 1990:841; Laudermilk 1949:117; Robinson 1969:25). It "was introduced into Assyria about 1100 BC and spread to Greece, Rome, and Spain in classical times" (Wulff 1966:190; also, Born 1938:206, 210; Ploss 1963a:25). The tiny insects, which show scarlet or vermilion when crushed, are harvested by being scraped off oak leaves with the fingernails at a rate of about a kilogram per day. The insects are killed by a vinegar bath or fumes, which gives them a reddish-brown color. When crushed, they yield the direct dyestuff, which is dissolved in water or alcohol and fixed with alum or urine. Dried grain, or cake kermes, was traded and, because of the labor involved, was expensive (Born 1938:206, 208, 209, 211; Forbes 1956:102-104). It became a symbol of sun, fire, deity, and royalty (Dahlgren 1961:387-388).

Another red dye, occurring in South and Southeast Asia from Sind eastward, is *lac* (laccaic acid), from wild or domesticated scale insects of the genus *Kerria* (*Lakshadia*), parasitic on various trees. Twigs to which the insects adhere are broken off, sun-dried, and scraped or dropped into a hot soda solution, from which the evaporite is molded into cakes for sale. The complex dye is known in Sanskrit as *alaktaka* (Monier-Williams 1899:891), *laksha*, or *raksha* (< *raga*, dye); in Pali as *lakha* (Buddhadatta Mahathera n.d:296); and in Dravidian as *tuppu* = 'redness' (Burrow and Emeneau 1984:287); other names in India include *rung*, *rungia*, *jhuri*, and *cha* (Mohanty, Chandramouli,

and Naik 1987:21, 50-52, 56-59). Lac is mentioned in a 5th-century-BC Greek treatise, *Indika*; the dye was noted as being obtained (in small quantities) from Barugaza (Broach) on India's Gulf of Cambay (Forbes 1956:104-106; Robinson 1969:25; Krochmal and Krochmal 1974:18-19; Donkin 1977a: 10-11; 1977b:864-865; Schweppe 1989:200-201).

Cochineal

The principal New World equivalent of the kermes and lac insects is the female of the scale insect *Dactylopius coccus* (*Coccus cacti*), parasitic on *Opuntia* and *Nopalea* cacti, on which it envelopes itself in a cottony white secretion (Gade 1972:59). In contrast to kermes, but like lac, there is a protected, domesticated form; it is twice the size of the wild one, *D. tomentosus* (Brand 1966:3; Donkin 1977a:14-16; Dahlgren 1961; Ross 1986:67; Born 1938:216). *D. coccus* displays its scarlet color when crushed, producing cochineal carmine (carminic acid), ten times richer in dyestuff than kermes, which it fast replaced in the Middle East after AD 1550 (Laudermilk 1949:118; Donkin 1977b:865; Ziderman 1986b:190; Dahlgren 1961:388; Gerber 1978:5). The traditional production center is in southern Mexico (Oaxaca, Chiapas, Puebla, and Guerrero) (Williams 1964:11; Brand 1966:5; Johnson 1971:312; Ross 1986:67-68), where use is known to be pre-contact (Diguet 1909:75-79; Donkin 1977a:20-23) and where production is thought to have originated. Tradition attributes the rise of domesticated cochineal to pre-Aztec, Toltec times. As in Asia, the color is associated with royalty (Dahlgren 1961:388-91). The Mixtec name for the substance is *n'duce*; in Nahuatl, it is *nacheztli*, *i.e.*, 'nopal blood' (Diguet 1909:80; Laudermilk 1949:114; Dahlgren 1961). Born (1938:214) felt that New World cochineal use suggested early contacts with Old World coccoid-insect dyers.

Some have thought that cochineal-dyed textiles in ancient Peru reflect dyestuff trade from Mexico (Gade 1972:60). Genus *Opuntia* (but not the Mexican host species for domestic cochineal) is attested as far back as the pre-ceramic period (Pearsall 1978:406-410), and Diguet (1909: 78) stated that nopal and wild cochineal insects were also native to South America. However, Gade (1972:60; 1979: 354; personal communication 1992) pointed out the lack of evidence of *Nopalea* there and the unresolved question of just which species of Cactaceae can host which species of cochineal insect. It is probable that domesticated cochineal insects *were* eventually raised on the Peruvian coast (Towle 1961:70-71), the practice perhaps being introduced from Mesoamerica. Not only *D. coccus* was employed but also the wild *D. ceylonicus* (Fester 1954:243-244). Present in Paracas Necrópolis times, *ca.* 450-175 BC, cochineal dye (*makhnu*, in Quechua) has also been identified for Peru's Classic Nazca, Classic Mochica, and Post-Classic Chimú cultures, and in Bolivia and northwestern Argentina (Fester 1954; Young 1957; Paul 1990:12; Saltzman, Keay, and Christensen 1963:245, 247; Gade 1975:192; Donkin 1977a: 35; Saltzman 1978: 179-180; 1986:32, 36; 1992:478). It seems largely to have replaced relbun starting at the beginning of the Early

Intermediate Period, *ca.* 200 BC (Dwyer 1979:75; Saltzman 1992:478).

"The exploitation of [domesticated] cochineal involves much care and no few risks" (Dahlgren 1961:388). The cactus must be farmed, protective 'nests' provided, and caution used in the harvest. Domesticated cochineal insects are brushed off the cactus, and two kilograms a day, representing some 310,000 insects, is the usual quantity collected. The insects are killed by suffocation in containers, by toasting on comals or in ovens, or by immersion in boiling water or steam. They are then sun-, pan-, or oven-dried, which results in their turning rose color. Typically, they were traded in pellets, as was also done with kermes. For dyeing, leaves of *Miconia argenta* and limejuice mordant are boiled and the ground-up insects added; the yarn is boiled for an hour and a half; sometimes, cakes of dyestuff mixed with the mordant alum were prepared for commerce, as with kermes and lac (Diguet 1909:92-93, 96-97; Osborne 1942:89, 90; Gade 1972:62; Donkin 1977a:17-20; O'Neale 1945:30; Dahlgren 1961:390; Ross 1986).

Use of insect dyes in the two hemispheres has been pointed to as a possible indicator of transoceanic contacts (*e.g.*, Ferguson 1958:68). True (Mexican) cochineal is generally thought to be post-Columbian in the Eastern Hemisphere, although Mertz (1972:72-73) thought it possibly pre-Columbian in South Asia. According to Wulff (1966: 189), true cochineal was mentioned as early as the time of Sargon II of Assyria, in 714 BC, as coming from Armenia and northern Persia. This would seem likely to refer to the native grass-parasitic 'Armenian-red' coccid, *Porphyrophora hameli* (Donkin 1977b:851), as pointed out by Dhamija (1990:841), which was preferred over kermes (Forbes 1956:102). Robinson (1969:25) stated that "Cochineal made from . . . *Coccus cacti* . . . came to Europe from the New World, but recent discoveries in the Ararat Valley and adjacent areas suggest it was known and used by the Assyrians before the 7th century BC, being produced in the Armenian mountains," although the evidence is not specified. Forbes (1956:102) wrote, "We also have hints in later Jewish documents that the cactus cochenillefera was grown near Nablus, and the insect producing the red dye was fed on it."

Abrahams and Edelstein (1964:20, 21), reporting on Bar Kokhba-period textiles from *ca.* AD-135-Judea, Israel, identified not only madder and indigo but also carminic acid, the dye chemical in cochineal. (*Cf.* the Bar Kokhba-period coin finds from Kentucky and environs and the Hebrew-inscribed Bat Creek Stone of Tennessee, from the same period [Gordon 1971:175-187; McCulloch 1988].) Before jumping to transoceanic conclusions here, however, note must be taken of Dhamija's (1990:841) statement that Armenian red (*vortan*) "is chemically similar to New World cochineal." In fact, the primary colorant in Armenian cochineal has proven to be carminic acid (Schweppe 1989:188-189, 200). Early Palestinian cactus-raising remains unproved, although today at least two *Opuntia* species are naturalized in the Mediterranean Basin (Groves and di Castri 1991:7, 68).

An interesting and perhaps relevant aside is the discovery (apparently, in Egypt) of an early medieval Gujarati Indian textile containing cochineal. This location is far outside the Eastern Anatolian-Caucasian area where Armenian red was produced (Rosenberg *et al.* 1993:92), but trade in this dyestuff between the two areas is not impossible.

SHELLFISH DYES

Royal (Tyrian) Purple

Certain marine snails produce a purple vat dye. The earliest archaeological evidence, in the form of shell middens of *ca.* 1700 BC, is from the Minoan Aegean region. However, garments dyed with shellfish purple there seem to have been called *popureja*, a term apparently derived from the Semitic word for 'boiling,' which was a part of the process required for the manufacture of the dyestuff. This suggests that Phoenicia—whose very name in Greek means 'purple' or 'crimson' (*phoinix* < *ponika*)—was the source (Astour 1965:348-350; but see Aubet 1993:5-11); the name *Canaan* is also associated with purple (*cf. kinahhu*, 'red-colored wool' in Akkadian [Aubet 1993:9]). "[O]ne of the chief [Canaanite (Phoenician) enterprises] . . . was the manufacture of purple dye. . . . The color [ranging from scarlet to violet] was derived from the shellfish or mollusk, *Purpura* [*Thais haemastoma*, *Murex* spp., and *Helixianthina* spp.], native to the eastern Mediterranean coast. Tyrian purple was the most celebrated of all colors for dyeing. Since it was very expensive, only the wealthy could purchase it, and robes of this color became a mark of high rank . . . ." (Wright 1943:3; also, Jackson 1917a:7-9; 1917b:8-9; Born 1937a:107, 1937b: 111, 114-117; Faber 1938:284-285; Forbes 1956:112-121, 139-141; Jensen 1963:105; Möhres 1963: 16; Robinson 1969:25; Safer and McLaughlin 1981:26; Ziderman 1986b:188; Knapp 1991:27, 38-39, 43-44). "Since antiquity, the colors purple and scarlet possessed special esteem in the Mediterranean world. The magico-religious thought of the epoch associated them with the sun and fire and took them as symbols of divinity and royalty" (Dahlgren 1961: 387, S. C. J. translation). Purple-dye factories were ultimately established as far west as Morocco and Spain, as well as in the Red Sea (Jackson 1917a:9-19; Jensen 1963:107; Donkin 1977a:7).

"Whoever [discovered *Purpuridae*-shellfish dyeing] . . . was intimately acquainted with the creatures of the sea, for the dye substance as it comes out of the mollusk is not purple but yellowish-white (the so-called leuco-base), and becomes purple only after it has been oxidized somehow" (Barber 1991:228). The precursors of Mediterranean shellfish dyes are found in minute amounts in the hypobranchial mucous glands of these murex and rock-shell snails. Primitive use apparently involved direct application from shellfish to cloth, but this must have been extremely inefficient. In the advanced industry, according to Pliny, the smaller-shelled species were crushed whole, and the larger dye murex had its shell opened and the gland removed.

> Mixed with salt [to steep for three days] and [then mixed with] water, the mass was simmered in lead cauldrons for about ten days [and then strained], after which raw wool was soaked [five hours, carded, and dipped again] in the still-clear liquid which turned purplish red [and emitted a fetid odor] when exposed to sunlight. . . . Enormous quantities of mollusks were necessary to produce a tiny amount of dye: twelve thousand specimens of the larger Dye Murex produced a mere 1.5 grams of pure dye (Safer and McLaughlin 1981:27-28; also, anonymous 1872:396; Jackson 1917a: 1-4; 1917b:3-4; Forbes 1956:114-117; Jensen 1963:108-109; Gerhard 1964:177).

Forty thousand individuals of a smaller species yielded only one gram of dyestuff (Möhres 1963:16). Alum was sometimes used as a dressing (Born 1937b:112, 114) but was not required. "Everywhere the purple dyers formed their own professional bodies . . . carefully guarding the secrets of their tested recipes" (Möhres 1963:18; also, Forbes 1956:118). Following Islamic conquest of the Levant, shellfish-purple-making declined and, after the fall of Byzantium in AD 1453, largely ceased in the Mediterranean region. "The [developed] technique of purple-dyeing was one of the most closely guarded industrial secrets of all time. . . . As the centuries passed, not only were the dyeing processes themselves lost but also [knowledge of] the species of snails . . . ," and these things were not rediscovered until after the middle of the 19th century (Ziderman 1986a:419-420; also, Jensen 1963:104, 108, 117-118; Möhres 1963:18-19).

American Shellfish Purple

"[S]hellfish purple was also known to ancient Peruvians and is still used as dye in Mexico, Guatemala, and Japan" (Safer and McLaughlin 1981:26; also, Jackson 1917a:19-27; 1917b:19-20; Carter 1976); in Mesoamerica, it is known as *caracol* (snail) in Spanish. In the New World, shellfish purple was produced by Indians, mainly from Michoacán to Ecuador (Osborne 1942:88; Gerhard 1964; Donkin 1977a:8), and especially on the Pacific coasts of Oaxaca and Costa Rica, where it was documented as early as AD 1535 and is known to be pre-Columbian (Dahlgren 1961:389; Williams 1964:11; Feldman 1985:58).

As early as 1898, shellfish purple was remarked upon as a possible indicator of transoceanic contacts, a notion that has been repeated since (Nutall 1909; Jackson 1917a:28; 1917b:28); Johnston (1913:211) asserted that "There is probably no stronger evidence of the presence of the Phoenician in the New World [specifically, Mexico] than can be drawn from the use of dyes [especially purple]," and Born (1937c:127) wrote, "there is no doubt that the purple industry of Central America is derived from that of the

Mediterranean people." Even Mayanist J. E. S. Thompson (1928:167), in an anti-diffusionist tirade, acknowledged purple as implying Asian contacts.

In Middle America, the leucocompound of the living mollusk *Pupura patula pansa* was capable of being freely 'milked' onto individual threads, thus obviating the necessity of elaborate extraction procedures, as in the Mediterranean. Still, this method was highly laborious, and use of expensive purple-dyed clothing was a sign of status in indigenous Mexico (Nutall 1909; Jackson 1917a:21-24; 1917b:24; Gerhard 1964:180-185; Donkin 1977a:8). It is, of course, possible that more elaborate methods were used in pre-contact times to produce purple in greater quantity (Dahlgren 1961:390). *P. patula*, gathered in spring (as in the Levant [Forbes 1956:114]) at the full moon, was also used in Guatemala, Nicaragua, and Costa Rica (Osborne 1942:88; Carlsen and Wenger 1991:365-67). Another species used was *Thais kiosquiformis*, which had to be killed and the soft parts extracted prior to painting on cloth (Feldman 1985:58).

On the coast of northwestern South America (Jackson 1917a:24-27; 1917b), the dye-producing species include *T. kiosquiformis* and *T. chocolata* (Donkin 1977a:8; Saltzman 1978:183). In Peru, molluscan purple, probably from *Concholepus concholepus*, has been identified on fabrics from the Paracas and Ica valleys, dating to about 450-100 BC, as well as on more recent textiles (Saltzman, Keay, and Christensen 1963:243-246; Gerhard 1964:179; Williams 1964:11; Donkin 1977a:8; Saltzman 1978:175-176, 179, 183; Safer and McLaughlin 1981:29; Paul 1990:12). This dye seems not to have been greatly used in that country and appears no longer to be employed. It was locally applied to fabric rather than to yarn (Saltzman 1986:27, 32), being rubbed or painted onto the cloth and then oxided to purple in the air and sunlight (Antúnez 1989:182).

It is worth noting that in both Eastern and Western hemispheres, shellfish purple has fertility and status associations (Jackson 1917b:6; Gerhard 1964:178, 186).

CONCLUSIONS

It is easy to imagine independent discoveries that crushing rubiaceous roots and scale insects would yield red. And although indigo and shellfish purple develop their colors only upon oxidization in the air, multiple accidental discoveries of this phenomenon among users of wild plants and eaters of shellfish were probably inevitable (*e.g.*, Jensen 1963:104-105). Yet, in many areas where the step of applying these substances as colorants might have occurred, it didn't, and sophisticated application of them to fiber is so involved that it seems remarkable that it developed at all, not to say multiple times. In fact, recent attempts in Turkey and Iran to revive the use of forgotten vegetal dyes have required the efforts of chemists to reinvent recipes.

Diffusion was not a casual matter, either. At least in the Middle East, "Dyeing has always been in professional

146   *Section II — Botany, Biology, and People*

hands" (Wertheimer 1992). "In most Persian towns there are professional dyers . . . , whose secret recipes have been handed down . . . for generations. The dyeing trade was highly regarded in earlier times, and . . . dyers traveled to many parts of the world in order to train others and to prepare special dyes for large workshops . . ." (Dhamija 1990:842). "[T]he master dyers of an earlier age protected their recipes in order to keep competitors from using them" (Peterson 1991:4, 7; also, Forbes 1956:101; Donkin 1977b:849; Opie 1992; Balfour-Paul 1992:101). Thus, when we find several of these dyestuffs, together with use of mordants, shared by distant regions, we must consider the possibility of historical contact, and rather intimate, repeated contact at that—especially in light of a host of other shared, and often arbitrary, traits (e.g., Jett 1971:33-40; 1983:372-374; 1992a: 66; 1992b). Born (1937c) baldly stated that "It is impossible that so many similarities should be accidental; a common source of the two civilizations [Central American and Mediterranean] must therefore be assumed . . . ."

Although reliable data are scarce, indigo, madder, and insect dyes appear to be traceable back to before 2500 BC in South and Southwest Asia, seemingly centered on the northwestern Indian subcontinent, where dyers' vats have been recognized at Mohenjo-daro (Allchin and Allchin 1982: 179). Shellfish dyes, on the other hand, are not attested before about 1700 BC and are associated particularly with the eastern Mediterranean, although extending ultimately at least to the Red Sea as well as to the Atlantic.

Information on these dyes' antiquity in America is even spottier than for the Eastern Hemisphere, but relbun use goes back to the 3rd millennium BC. Thus, if its employment, including employment of metallic-salt mordant, was a transfer from Asian madder and mordant use, it would have occurred much earlier than previously-suggested southwestern Asian influences. (The other dyes are so far not attested to in the Americas before the 1st millennium BC.) But use of madder, indigo, and insect dyes could be seen as possible imports from the greater Indus region, perhaps via Gulf of Cambay (Khambhat) ports in present-day Gujarat State, where these kinds of dyestuffs were also produced (for Harappan overseas trade, see Rao 1985: 685-688; Allchin and Allchin 1982). "Gujarat . . . has been one of the foremost textile-producing areas of India for many centuries" and very involved in long-distance Indian Ocean trade. "The Indian traders obviously had the maritime skills to travel over vast areas of ocean and the diplomatic or coercive skills to be accepted as trading partners" (Barnes 1993:5, 9-11).

Rather recently, recognition of early 2nd- and 3rd-millenium-BC large-scale adobe construction and cotton-raising and -weaving on Peru's desert coast (e.g., Pozorski and Pozorski 1992; Guillermo 1991)—as in the Indus region—has given rise to thoughts, by George Carter and others, of a possible Indus connection (cf. Heyerdahl 1986:109, 294-295), where these things are early—cotton going back to the 5th millenium BC (Allchin and Allchin 1982:191-192). One may

note that New World domesticated cottons are hybrids between wild New World species and some African cotton (Hutchinson, Silow, and Stephens 1947).

Shellfish purple is not known to be associated with the Indian Ocean (although the Red Sea is, in fact, if not in name, an arm of that ocean), but its known Old World dates are later than those for the other dyes. If purple involved a transoceanic transfer, it could have been a separate one. The fact that the dye precursor is much more copious and easy to extract from American shellfish than from Old World ones could argue for shellfish purple's discovery in the Americas and, by presently unidentified means, subsequent introduction of its use to the Mediterranean. Or, Old World purple use could have been introduced to the Western Hemisphere at an early, primitive stage of technical development.

The hints of true cochineal production in ancient Southwestern Asia call out for further investigation.

REFERENCES

Abrahams, David H. and Sidney M. Edelstein
1964   A new method for the analysis of ancient dyed textiles. *American Dyestuff Reporter* 53(1):19-25.

Allchin, Bridget and Raymond Allchin
1982   *The Rise of Civilization in India and Pakistan.* Cambridge: Cambridge University Press.

anonymous
1872   Purple dyeing, ancient and modern. *Smithsonian Institution Annual Report*, 1863:385-403.

Astour, Michael C.
1965   The origin of the terms 'Canaan,' 'Phoenician,' and 'Purple.' *Journal of Near Eastern Studies* 24(4):346-360.

Atúnez de Mayolo, Kay
1989   Peruvian natural dye plants. *Economic Botany* 43(2):181-191.

Aubet, Maria Eugenia
1993   *The Phoenicians and the West: Politics, Colonies and Trade.* Cambridge: Cambridge University Press.

Balfour-Paul, Jenny
1992   Indigo in the Arab world. *Hali* 61:98-105, 140.

Barber, E. J. W.
1991   *Prehistoric Textiles: The Development of Cloth in the Neolithic and Bronze Ages, with Special Reference to the Aegean.* Princeton: Princeton University Press.

Barnes, Ruth
1993   *Indian Block-Printed Cotton Fabrics in the Kelsey Museum: The University of Michigan*, Kelsey Museum Studies 8. Ann Arbor: The University of Michigan Press.

Born, Wolfgang
1937a   Purpura shellfish. *Ciba Review* 4:106-110.
1937b   Purple in classical antiquity. *Ciba Review* 4:111-118.
1937c   The use of purple among the Indians of Central America. *Ciba Review* 4:124-127.
1938   Scarlet. *Ciba Review* 7:206-227.

Brand, Donald D.
1966   Cochineal: Aboriginal dyestuff from Nueva España. *Congreso Internacional de Americanistas* 36(2):77-91.

Buddhadatta Mahathera, A. P.
n.d.   *English-Pali Dictionary*. Colombo: The Pali Text Society.

Bühler, Alfred
1948   Dyeing among primitive peoples. *Ciba Review* 68:2478-2507.
1951   Indigo dyeing among primitive races. *Ciba Review* 85:3088-3091.
1972   *Ikat Batik Plangi: Reservmusterungen auf Garn und Stoff aus Vorderasien, Zentralasien, Sudosteuropa und Nordafrika*, 3 Vols. Basel: Pharos-Verlag Handudolf Schwabe.

Burrow, T. and M. B. Emeneau
1984   *A Dravidian Etymological Dictionary*, 2nd ed. Oxford: The Clarendon Press.

Carlsen, Robert S. and David A. Wenger
1991   The dyes used in Guatemalan textiles: A diachronic approach. Pp. 359-378 in *Textile Traditions of Mesoamerica and the Andes: An Anthology*. Margot B. Scheville, Janet C. Berlo, and Edward B. Dwyer, eds. New York and London: Garland Publishing.

Carter, George F.
1976   Shells as evidence of the migrations of early culture. *The New Diffusionist* 6(23):50-57.

Dahlgren de Jordan, Barbara
1961   El Nacheztli o la Grana de Cochinilla Mexicana. Pp. 387-399 in *Homenaje a Pablo Martínez del Río en el Vigésimoquinto Aniversario de la Primera Edición de Los Orígenes Americanos*. Ignacio Bernal *et al.*, eds. Mexico City: Instituto Nacional de Antropología e Historia.

Dhamija, Jasleen
1990   Raw materials and dyes. Pp. 839-843 in *Encyclopaedia Iranica 4, Bayju—Carpets*. Ehsan Yarshater, ed. London and New York: Routledge & Kegan Paul.

Diguet, Léo
1909   Histoire de la Cochenille au Méxique. *Journal de la Société des Américanistes de Paris* 6(1):75-99.

Donkin, R. A.
1977a   *Spanish Red: An Ethnogeographical Study of Cochineal and the Opuntia Cactus*. Transactions of the American Philosophical Society 62(5).
1977b   The insect dyes of western and West-Central Asia. *Anthropos* 72(5/6):847-880.

Dwyer, Edward B.
1979   Early horizon tapestry from south coastal Peru. Pp. 61-82 in *The Junius B. Bird Pre-Columbian Textile Conference*. Ann P. Rowe, Elizabeth P. Benson, and Anne L. Schaffer, eds. Washington: The Textile Museum and Dumbarton Oaks.

Faber, G. A.
1938   Dyeing in Greece. *Ciba Review* 9:284-294.

Feldman, Lawrence H.
1985   *A Tumpline Economy: Production and Distribution Systems in Sixteenth-Century Guatemala*. Culver City: Labyrinthos.

Ferguson, Thomas Stuart
1958   *One Fold, One Shepherd*. San Francisco: Books of California.

Fester, G. A.
1954   Some dyes of an ancient South American civilization. *Dyestuffs* 40(9):238-245.

Forbes, R. J.
1956   *Studies in Ancient Technology*, Second Revised Edition 4. Leiden: E. J. Brill.

Gade, Daniel W.
1972   Red dye from Peruvian bugs. *The Geographical Magazine* 45(1):58-62.
1975   *Plants, Man and the Land in the Vilcanota Valley of Peru*. The Hague: Dr. W. Junk B. V.
1979   Past glory and present status of cochineal. *The Geographical Review* 69(3):353-354.
1992   Personal communication.

Gerber, F. L.
1978   *Cochineal and the Insect Dyes*. Ormond Beach FL: published by the author.
1984   Introduction. Pp. xiii-xiv in *Indigo: From Seed to Dye*. Dorothy Miller, ed. Aptos CA: Indigo Press.

Gerhard, Peter
1964   Shellfish dye in America. *Congreso Internacional de Americanistas, Actas y Memorias* 35(3):177-191.

Girault, Louis
1969   *Textiles Boliviens: Région de Charazani*. Catalogues du Musée de l'Homme, Ser. H, Amérique 4.

Gittinger, Mattiebelle
1982   *Master Dyers to the World: Technique and Trade in Early Indian Dyed Cotton Textiles*. Washington: The Textile Museum.

Gordon, Cyrus H.
1971   *Before Columbus: Links Between the Old World and Ancient America*. New York: Crown Publishers.

Grieder, Terence, Alberto Bueno Mendoza, C. Earle Smith, Jr., and Robert M. Malina
1988   Fiber arts. Pp. 152-181 in *La Galgada: A Preceramic Culture in Transition*. Austin: University of Texas Press.

Groves, R. H. and F. di Castri, eds.
1991   *Biogeography of Mediterranean Invasions*. New York: Cambridge University Press.

Guillermo Lumbreras, Luis
1991   Textiles in ancient Peru. Pp. 17-23 in *The Textile Arts of Peru*, James W. Reid, ed. Lima: Industria Textil Piura.

Hagen, Victor Wolfgang von
1959   *The Incas of Pedro de Cieza de León*. Norman: University of Oklahoma Press.

Heringa, Rens
1989   Dye process and life sequence: The coloring of textiles in an East Javanese village. Pp. 106-130 in *To Speak with Cloth: Studies in Indonesian Textiles*. Mattiebelle Gittinger, ed. Los Angeles: Museum of Cultural History, University of California.

Heyerdahl, Thor
1986   *The Maldive Mystery*. London: George Allen & Unwin.

Hutchinson, J. R., R. A. Silow, and S. G. Stephens
1947   *The Evolution of Gossypium and the Differentiation of the Cultivated Cottons*. Oxford: Oxford University Press.

Jackson, J. Wilfrid
1917a   *Shells as Evidence of the Migrations of Early Culture*. Publications of the University of Manchester, Ethnological Series 11.
1917b   The geographical distribution of the shell-purple industry. *Manchester Literary & Philosophical Society, Proceedings* 60(6):1-25.

Jakes, Katherine A.
　1991　Physical and chemical analysis of Paracas fibers. Pp.
　　222-239 in *Paracas Art & Architecture: Object and Context
　　in South Coastal Peru*. Anne Paul, ed. Iowa City: University
　　of Iowa Press.
Jensen, Lloyd B.
　1963　Royal purple of Tyre. *Journal of Near Eastern Studies*
　　22(2):104-118.
Jett, Stephen C.
　1971　Diffusion versus independent development: The bases
　　of controversy. Pp. 5-53 in *Man across the Sea: Problems of
　　Pre-Columbian Contacts*. Carroll L. Riley, J. Charles
　　Kelley, Campbell W. Pennington, and Robert L. Rands, eds.
　　Austin & London: University of Texas Press.
　1983　Pre-Columbian transoceanic contacts. Pp. 337-393 in
　　Ancient South Americans. Jesse D. Jennings, ed. San
　　Francisco: W. H. Freeman and Company.
　1992a Asian contacts with the Americas in pre-Columbian
　　times. *NEARA Journal* 26(3 & 4):62-68.
　1992b Hypotheses of Mediterranean/Southwest [Asian]
　　influences on New World cultures. *NEARA Journal* 26(3 &
　　4):82-85.
Johnson, Irmgard Weitlaner
　1959　Hilado y Tejido. Pp. 439-478 in *Esplendor de México
　　Antiguo 1*. Mexico City: Centro de Investigaciones
　　Antropológicas de México.
　1971　Basketry and textiles. Pp. 297-321 in *Handbook of
　　Middle American Indians 10, Archaeology of Northern
　　Mesoamerica 1*. Austin: University of Texas Press.
Johnston, Thomas Crawford
　1913　*Did the Phoenicians Discover America?* London: James
　　Nisbet
King, Mary Elizabeth
　1965　*Ancient Peruvian Textiles from the Collection of the
　　Textile Museum, Washington, D.C.,* The Museum of
　　Primitive Art, New York. New York: New York Graphic
　　Society.
　1979　The prehistoric textile industry of Mesoamerica. Pp.
　　265-278 in *The Junius B. Bird Pre-Columbian Textiles
　　Conference, May 19th and 20th, 1973*. A. P. Rowe, E. P.
　　Benson, and A. L. Schaffer, eds. Washington: The Textile
　　Museum and Dumbarton Oaks.
　1980　Possible Indonesian or southeast Asian influences in
　　New World textile industries. Pp. 365-373 in *Indonesian
　　Textiles*. Mattiebelle Gittinger, ed. Irene Emery Roundtable
　　on Museum Textiles, 1979 Proceedings. Washington: The
　　Textile Museum.
Knapp, A. Bernard
　1991　Spice, drugs, grain and grog: Organic goods in Bronze
　　Age East Mediterranean trade. Pp. 20-68 in *Bronze Age
　　Trade in the Mediterranean*. Papers presented at the
　　conference held at Rewley House, Oxford, December 1989.
　　N. H. Gale, ed. *Studies in Mediterranean Archaeology 90*.
Krochmal, Arnold and Connie Krochmal
　1974　*The Complete Illustrated Book of Dyes Made from
　　Natural Sources*. Garden City NY: Doubleday & Company.
Laudermilk, Jerry
　1949　The bug with a crimson past. *Natural History*
　　58(3):114-118.

Leggett, William F.
　1944　*Ancient and Medieval Dyes*. Brooklyn: Chemical
　　Publishing Co.
Marschall, Wolfgang
　1979　*Influencias Asiáticas en las Culturas de la América
　　Antigua: Estudias de su Historia*. Mexico City: Ediciones
　　Euroamericanas Klaus Theile.
McCulloch, J. Huston
　1988　The Bat Creek inscription: Cherokee or Hebrew?
　　Tennessee Anthropologist 13(2):79-123.
Mertz, Henriette
　1972　*Gods from the Far East: How the Chinese Discovered
　　America*. New York: Ballantine Books. [Originally published
　　in 1953 as *Pale Ink: Two Ancient Records of Chinese
　　Exploration in America*. Chicago: privately printed.]
Mohanty, B. C., K. V. Chandramouli, and H. D. Naik
　1987　*Natural Dyeing Processes of India*. Ahmedabad: Calico
　　Museum of Textiles.
Möhres, Franz Peter
　1963　Purple. *The BASF Digest* 63(1):15-19.
Monier-Williams, Monier
　1899　*A Sanskrit-English Dictionary*. Oxford: The Clarendon
　　Press.
Morton, Julia F.
　1992　The ocean-going noni, or Indian mulberry (*Morinda
　　citrifolia, Rubiaceae*) and some of its 'colorful' relatives.
　　Economic Botany 46(3):241-256.
Mushak, Paul
　1991　Dye analysis in miscellaneous rugs and trappings of the
　　Central Asian group. *Oriental Rug Review* 11(67):24-27.
Nutall, Zelia
　1909　A curious survival in Mexico of the purpura shellfish
　　for dyeing. Pp. 368-384 in *Putnam Anniversary Volume*.
　　Franz Boas, ed. New York: Stechert.
O'Neale, Lila M.
　1945　Textiles of highland Guatemala. *Carnegie Institute of
　　Washington, Publication 567*.
Opie, James
　1992　Vegetal dyes, Iran restores an ancient tradition.
　　Oriental Rug Review 12(6):26-29.
Ortiz Garmendia, Juan
　1968　*Plantas Tintoreas de las Zonas del Desierto y la Estepa
　　Septentrional Chilenas*. Museo de la Serena, Contribuciones
　　Arqueológicas 7.
Osborne, Lilly de Jongh
　1942　Materias tintoreas indígenas. *América Indígena* 2(1):86-
　　91.
Paul, Anne
　1990　*Paracas Ritual Attire: Symbols of Authority in Ancient
　　Peru*. Norman: University of Oklahoma Press.
Peterson, Jane
　1991　A passion for color. *Aramco World* 42(3):2-9.
Ploss, Emil
　1963a Purple dyeing in the ancient world. *The BASF Digest*
　　63(1):24-27.
　1963b Indigo. *The BASF Digest* 63(2):65-69, 71.
Pozorski, Shelia and Thomas Pozorski
　1992　Early civilization in the Casma Valley, Peru. *Antiquity*
　　66(253):845-870.

Rao, S. R.
1985 *Lothal: A Harappan Port Town, 1955-1962* 2. Memoirs of the Archaeological Survey of India 78.

Reid, James W.
1991 *The Textile Arts of Peru*. Lima: Industria Textil Piura.

Robinson, Stuart
1969 *A History of Dyed Textiles*. London: Studio Vista.

Rosenberg, Amy, Mary W. Ballard, Agnes Timár-Balázsy, and Norman Indicator
1993 *Indian Block-Printed Cotton Fabrics in the Kelsey Museum: The University of Michigan*. Pp. 91-97 in Appendix: Technical Notes. Kelsey Museum Studies 8, Ruth Barnes. ed. Ann Arbor: The University of Michigan Press.

Ross, Gary N.
1986 The bug in the rug. *Natural History* 95(3):66-73, 104.

Rowe, Ann Pollard
1977 *Warp-Patterned Weaves of the Andes*. Washington: The Textile Museum.

Safer, Jane Fearer and Frances McLaughlin
1981 *Spirals from the Sea: An Anthropological Look at Shells*. New York: Clarkson N. Potter, in association with the American Museum of Natural History.

Saltzman, Max
1978 The identification of dyes in archaeological and ethnographic textiles. Pp. 172-185 in *Archaeological Chemistry II*, Giles F. Carter, ed. Advances in Chemistry Series 171.
1986 Analysis of dyes in museum textiles or, you can't tell a dye by its color. Pp. 27-39 in *Textile Conservation Symposium in Honor of Pat Reeves, 1 February 1986*. Catherine C. McLean and Patricia Connell, eds. Los Angeles: The Conservation Center, Los Angeles County Museum of Art.
1992 Identifying dyes in textiles. *American Scientist* 80(5):474-481.

Saltzman, Max, A. M. Keay, and Jack Christensen
1963 The identification of colorants in ancient textiles. *Dyestuffs* 44(8):cover, 241-251.

Schweppe, Helmut
1986 Identification of dyes in historic textile materials. Pp. 153-174 in *Historic Paper and Textile Materials: Conservation and Characterization*. H. L. Needles and S. H. Zeronian, eds. ACS Symposium Series 212. Washington: American Chemical Society.
1989 Identification of red madder and insect dyes by thin-layer chromotography. Pp. 188-219 in *Historic Paper and Textile Materials II: Conservation and Characterization*. S. H. Zeronian and H. L. Needles, eds. ACS Symposium Series 410. Washington: American Chemical Society.

Sorenson, John L. and Martin H. Raish
1990 *Pre-Columbian Contact with the Americas across the Oceans: An Annotated Bibliography*, 2 Vols. Provo: Research Press.

Spinden, Herbert J.
1924 New World correlations. *International Congress of Americanists, Proceedings* 21(1):76-86.

Thompson, John Eric S.
1928 The 'Children of the Sun' and Central America. *Antiquity* 2(6):161-167.

Towle, Margaret A.
1961 *The Ethnobotany of Pre-Columbian Peru*. Viking Fund Publications in Anthropology 30.

Wertheimer, Ellen
1992 Some thoughts on dyes. *Oriental Rug Review* 13(1):44.

Williams, Gerald
1964 *Textiles of Oaxaca*. Hanover and Manchester NH: Hopkins Center, Dartmouth College, and the Currier Gallery of Art.

Wright, G. Ernest
1943 How did early Israel differ from her neighbors? *The Biblical Archaeologist* 6(1):1-20.

Wulff, Hans E.
1966 *The Traditional Crafts of Persia: Their Development, Technology, and Influence on Eastern and Western Civilizations*. Cambridge MA: The M.I.T. Press.

Young, William J.
1957 Appendix III: Analysis of textile dyes. Pp. 53-54 in *Late Nazca Burials at Chaviña, Peru*. S. K. Lothrop and J. Mahler, eds. Papers, Peabody Museum of Archaeology and Ethnology, Harvard University 50(2).

Ziderman, I. Irving
1986a Biblical dyes of animal origin. *Chemistry in Britain* 22(5):cover, 19-21, 454.
1986b 3600 years of purple-shell dyeing: Characterization of hyacinthine purple (*Tekhlet*). Pp. 188-198 in *Historic Paper and Textile Materials: Conservation and Characterization*. H. L. Needles and S. H. Zeronian, eds. ACS Symposium Series 212. Washington: American Chemical Society.

ACKNOWLEDGMENTS

I wish to acknowledge the extreme usefulness of Sorenson and Raish's (1990) bibliography as well as bibliographic suggestions by Roslyn Strong, Daniel W. Gade, Howard L. Needles, Lucky Kaiser, and James L. Guthrie.

Figure 1 HEADS AND TAILS AND BODIES

Details differentiate the classes of chickens: the differences in combs and wattles are striking; bodies vary greatly, as do tails; legs range from average in the Mediterraneans to short among the Cochins and very lengthy among the Malays; spurs vary from long and up-curved among the Mediterraneans to short and blunt among the Cochins.

Figure 2 THE MEDITERRANEAN, CHINESE, AND MALAY
These three assemble the traits for strikingly differentiated birds.

The Chicken in America:

Spanish Introduction or Pre-Spanish?

GEORGE F. CARTER

BACKGROUND

If the Spanish brought the first chickens to America, then the chickens in the hands of the Amerinds must be of the basic Mediterranean class. By class is meant a large regional type of chicken. Mediterranean chickens are not at all like Chinese or Malay chickens. Further, the chicken should be known among the Amerinds by names based on the Spanish *gallo* or *gallina* if the Spanish brought the chickens to America, but they are not. The chicken, by the Spanish in the 16th century, was used for food, but this was not true of many Amerinds. The chickens should have been spread at some reasonable rate after introduction, but that is not true either. In every category, when one looks at the chickens in Amerind hands, the requirements to fit the Spanish introduction are not met. The chickens in Amerind hands are Asiatic, not Mediterranean; Amerind names for the chickens are not based on Spanish models; chickens were not eaten but were used only for sacrifice, divination, and healing.

KINDS AND DISTRIBUTION OF CHICKENS

The differences between the Mediterranean chickens and chickens in Amerindian hands will be listed below. Briefly, in combs, tails, feathering of legs, dispositions, feathering of the body, and so forth, the chickens in the Amerind hands are not at all like those of the Mediterranean class. Instead, they are much more like the Asiatic classes of chickens. Traits listed below should make this clear. I will include illustrations, one picture being worth a thousand words.

The Spanish were not breeding chickens in 1600 in the manner that was characteristic of the time after 1850. In recent time, careful breeding has resulted in the breeds so well known today; for example, the Black Minorcas of Spain, and the Leghorns of Italy. The heavy and large chickens of China, the Cochin, the related Black Langshans, and the Brahmas, must be the result of similar selection, but we do not know when the Chinese began selecting for large chickens—perhaps, as in the West, in the 19th century, but perhaps earlier. Whatever characteristics they sought in the breeding process would have been based on chickens then present in Asia.

Prior to the onset of selective breeding, Europe had mongrel chickens commonly called Dung Hill Fowl. In feathering and coloration, they often have reverted back toward their wild progenitors. These birds are notably nervous and easily take to flight. They are single-combed, tight-feathered, and bare-legged. The cocks have showy tails held up at a 30-degree angle, and up-curved, long, sharp spurs. These were the kind of chickens the Spanish would have brought to America. See Figures 1 and 2 opposite.

There is another trait which differentiates types of chickens, and that is whether they are setters or non-setters. Today, Mediterranean class chickens do not set, *i.e.*, they do not stop laying to incubate their own. But Asiatic chickens lay a few eggs, then quit and take to incubating their chicks. Along with other features, these traits are related to sets of cultural practices. Europeans eat eggs and chickens. To an astounding degree, the rest of the world does not, even today. (On this see Simoons, *Eat Not This Flesh* 1966; and Johannessen 1981; and Johannessen and Fogg 1982.)

What the Asiatics would have brought is less easy to specify, for we know less about the history of chicken breeding in Asia. The Malay class was very tall, males being able to eat off a dinner table. They had a distinctive head, often lacked paired wattles, instead had a bare throat and a bare strip running down the breast. Survivors in something like a pure state are to be found in the Philippines today where they are the preferred chickens because they need very little care. The cocks have showy tails which are held down, not up, as with the Mediterranean class. They are notable fighters, but they do fight on the ground while the Mediterranean chickens fight in the air. In recognizable pure-state they are unknown in Amerind hands. They are common in Brazil but Finsterbusch (1929) considers them late Portuguese imports for cock fighting.

The Chinese type chickens today are noted for their great size, heavy bodies, feathered legs, fluffy body feathering, and relatively short wings and legs. The cocks have short tail feathers and short blunt spurs. I am using the Cochin chicken here as the type. They are notably tame, and poor flyers. In pure selected form, they are not known in Amerind hands, but some of their traits are found everywhere in Mexico. Chickens resembling the Rhode Island Red, an Asiatic derivative, are commonly seen. My direct knowledge comes from travel in Mexico and, for the rest, gleanings of the sparse information in the literature. The greatest recent help has been the publication of the *Catalogue of the Native Poultry of Southeast Asia* (Bay-Peterson 1991). One finds therein color illustrations and data on names, size, and probable age in the regions covered: Korea, Japan, the Philippines, and Malaya. The absence of data on China is a sad gap. Another source is *The Standard of Perfection* published by the American Poultry Association. I have a 1942 edition.

There is a seldom-described small chicken to be found in Asia, in a line running from India through the Philippines, to Japan. In India, it is described as having about as much meat as a pigeon. China also has small chickens. In Japan, they are described and named. The name *dori* is attached to birds of this type and not to the later introductions, and the Japanese consider them the original type in Japan. Every district had variants of this one type of chicken. Bantams and Malay types were introduced after 1500, and the Chinese chickens did not reach Japan until the very end of the 19th century and then from, of all places, England. They had first reached America via the China Clippers, thence to England, and thence to Japan. Today, small chickens are found everywhere in Eurasia, Polynesia, and Latin America.

In Asia, one finds specialty breeds that were unknown to the Mediterraneans in 1600. There is the silky-feathered melanotic chicken. Silky feathers are like the down feathering on chicks. 'Melanotic' refers to the black feathers, skin, flesh, and bones of this odd fowl. These chickens are today bred for white feathering, and, in mixed breeding, these traits are lost; white feathering first, then silky feathering, then black feathering, then black skins, then black flesh, and, finally, black bones. In America, careful breeding is not done by the Amerinds today, and the result is that melanotic chickens are found throughout Latin America but in every stage of loss of the melanotic traits.

In Johannessen's study of the melanotic chickens in America, he had a separate category for the black-feathered and black-skinned birds and another for those that had only black bones. An example of their presence is supplied by the fact that in 1828 an American warship in Peru was supplied with enough chickens to feed the crew. This implies a hundred men or more (crew, gun crews, and marines). The crew refused to eat the black-meated chickens! This story caught Carl Sauer's attention and was one of the reasons he suggested to Carl Johannessen that he look into melanotic chickens.

There is the odd trait of Naked Necks of Southeast Asia. In this fowl there is no feathering of the neck. It is said to be the most disease-resistant of the chickens, and this is also said of the Malay type chicken which has a bare throat, but not a totally naked neck. As late as 1920, the poultry specialists had no idea where this strange chicken came from. They knew it only from eastern Europe and called it the Transylvanian Naked Neck. It is very

common in Amerind hands throughout Mexico. When one asks about chickens in Mexico this is the one trait noted, for it is a striking sight. It is usually thought to be due to some disease, but it is purely genetic. (Comments on genetics are taken from Crawford 1984.)

Figure 3 MELANOTIC SILKIE (above)
FRIZZLE FOWL (below)

From Aldrovandi, *ca.* 1600, a great naturalist who had never seen such chickens. He borrowed the Silkie illustration from a cosmographic map. He considered the Frizzle Fowl to be a freak. Both chickens are Asiatics found all over Latin America.

The Frizzle Fowl is another interesting case. This, like the Naked Neck chicken, points back to India or Southeast Asia. All feathers on this fowl are recurved instead of lying flat. There is no evident adaptive value in such chickens as the Frizzle Fowl and the Silky. They testify to an early interest in chicken breeding. Early, for these chickens were introduced into America before AD 1500, if we are to judge by their distribution in America, and, for the Silky, by their enormous importance in religion among the Maya and others.

The chickens in Amerind hands have an abundance of added feathering on their heads in the form of topknots, sideburns, and beards. Chickens in Mexico in Amerind hands may have one or several of these odd, added featherings. This trait in the Old World reaches its greatest development among the Russian Orloff breed. They have bearding all over the head, leaving only the eyes and beak peeking out, along with feathering down to the toes. It is seemingly a good adaptation for life in Russia, and added feathering would also be adaptive in northern China. I have not seen it illustrated in China except for the Silkies where one finds feathering as extensive as on the Orloffs. We know very little about the chicken, its origin, variation and distribution. Beyond the biology of the chicken, its significance as a valuable cultural, historical item has been unrealized, least of all by the poultry men. The exceptions are the Japanese poultry men.

In Chile, there is a strange assemblage of traits. The problem with this is that we have a spurt of descriptions of chickens from Chile stimulated by the strange blue egg trait that is found in America and nowhere else in the world. Actually, blue-egg layers are found all the way up to Costa Rica. Blue-egg laying is associated strongly with peacomb. Another unique trait is the feathered loops on the side of the head. This is genetically separate from the tufting of head feathering described above. The tendency of those interested in the blue trait has been to lump all of the eccentricities of the region into an Araucana race, but what the actual assemblage was is really unknown. The melanotic chicken is found all over Latin America, being even more widely distributed than the blue-egg layers.

Also present in this area is tailessness—the absence of the terminal part of the skeleton. This, too, is common in Mexico and is probably widespread over Latin America. The presence of melanotic chickens, and very probably even the silky feathering, survived here until recently in the Chile-Argentina area. The usual assumption is that some of these traits originated in Chile, but this may be due only to the better reporting we have for that area. Actually, most of these traits, except the loops of feathers on the head, are widespread in chickens in the hands of the Amerinds in Latin America, and, given the poor reporting, loops may be more widespread than we know.

The natural range of egg color is from pure white through creamy to a reddish-brown. Pure white, rare among the wild Gallus, is characteristic of Mediterranean chickens today. In Asia, the tinted (cream-colored) and reddish-brown eggs are characteristic. In Amerind hands, one sees tinted and reddish-brown eggs associated with the many Asiatic traits mentioned above. I am told that cream-colored eggs are commonest in Peru. In Mexico, the tinted and reddish-brown eggs are both found. In Mexico, the white eggs today are associated with the recently-introduced egg-layers, the White Leghorns, and with the Mediterranean-type fighting chickens. According to Finsterbusch (1929), the fighting chickens in Brazil are all Asiatics and, as illustrated, are close to the Malay types. He considers them recent introductions. It is notable that cock fighting is not characteristic of the Amerinds but is the sport of the Ladinos, those no longer in their Amerind cultures.

A note needs to be added on the recentness of brown-egg preference in New England today. This dates to the time when the large Asiatic chickens were introduced. These chickens are not only large and succulent, but they do not stop laying eggs with the first onset of cold weather. They were promptly adopted in New England and, with some crossing that changed the types little, became known as Rhode Island Reds, Plymouth Rocks, and Wyandottes. The New Jersey Black Giants are simply the Chinese Langshans. The Langshans are single-combed, and melanotic in wattles, comb, and legs. They share the deep, heavy bodies of the classic Chinese chickens. Note that the names here are most deceptive. It has been called to my attention that in Europe, traditionally a region of white-egg layers, brown eggs are today favored. I assume this to be late, the adoption being for the same reason as in America.

The very small chickens mentioned for India and Japan are probably in all intervening areas but are rarely described. The Japanese have done an exceptional job on the chickens in Japan. The indigenous chicken is described as a nondescript type, the equivalent of the European Dung Hill Fowl. There are many local variants. These chickens are illustrated and described as single-combed, or pea-combed. The tails are showy and held up at a 30-degree angle. They are noted as looking much like the wild jungle fowl and very small (Bay-Peterson 1991). They are described as laying brown-shelled eggs. This chicken was almost certainly carried to America, for very small chickens virtually indistinguishable from the wild Gallus chickens are found in the archaeology at Picuris and Pecos in the American Southwest. The Mexican Amerinds say that their original chickens were small. The wide spread of the heavy-bodied Chinese chickens in Amerind yards today could be early or late, but the Rhode Island-like chickens mentioned above for Mexico suggest the possibility that some of the heavy-bodied chickens were brought to America before AD 1500.

To summarize: If the Spanish brought the common Dung Hill Fowl, they would be bringing chickens of the Mediterranean class—tight-feathered, single-combed, fancy-tailed, with long spurs on the cocks, and with hens laying white-shelled eggs. They would not be bringing fluffy-feathered, very large heavy chickens with abbreviated tails and short blunt spurs. Nor would they be bringing the large Malay-type chickens. Much less would they be bringing melanotic chickens, Frizzle Fowl, Silky Fowl, or Naked Neck chickens. Or chickens that laid blue-green eggs, with feathered loops on their heads. Nor the diminutive chickens best described for Japan. It seems probable that, back in time, China also had these diminutive chickens. It is these many Asiatic kinds of chickens that are to be found widely in varied degrees of mixture throughout Latin America.

Since the Asiatic chickens are very different from the Mediterranean chickens, and most of the traits that reappear in the flocks of the Amerinds are found in Asia, the obvious conclusion would be that the Amerind chickens were first introduced from Asia and not from the Mediterranean. Further evidence will be presented below.

EARLY SOURCES

Acosta and Capa

Acosta, one of the earliest to study the Spanish introductions to America, wrote in 1590; his work must have been based on lengthy prior study. He returned to Spain about 1580. He is writing, then, within the 1st century following the Columbian discovery of America. He commented that it is peculiar that Indian names for the chicken are not based on Spanish names, but that the Indians have their own names for the chicken. He cites the Quechua *hualpa* for chicken and *ronto* for egg. He finds this odd, for items such as the 'horse' and 'cow' have names obviously derived from the Spanish (Acosta 1590).

Capa, writing centuries later, observes: "In the first accounts of the conquest we frequently hear of hens, and the names lead one to believe that they were like our own; this, however, is not so, and only the birds of Paraguay and Tucumn were somewhat similar to ours" (Capa 1915). The Spanish would use *gallina* for chicken, and that could lead to the expectation of Spanish chickens, but Capa is saying they were not like Spanish chickens.

Aldrovandi

Aldrovandi, an Italian, in 1600 wrote a book on the chicken. This is one hundred years after the discovery of America by the Spanish and within a decade of Acosta's work, and Aldrovandi refers to this, noting that Acosta said that the Indians worshipped the chicken. Aldrovandi had little interest in the local chickens of Italy. He obviously felt that everyone knew them. He has much more on the Greek and Roman chickens. The relevance of Greek-Roman times for the 16th century will not be discussed here beyond noting that descriptions from antiquity have limited value. There were huge changes brought

about by conquests, collapses of empires, plagues and so forth, in post-Roman times. Probably Christianity suppressed many pagan practices. It is usually stated that all selective breeding stopped with the Romans. This is surely an overstatement, for breeding was maintained by the Abbeys and Monasteries during Medieval times. But very probably there were losses.

Aldrovandi knew that there were Silkies in China but had obviously never seen one, for he thought that they were hairy rather than feathered. Aldrovandi illustrates a Frizzle Fowl, but labeled this drawing a 'freak' chicken. This is very odd, for he had heard that there were chickens with strange feathering in India. Other than a passing mention that he heard there were very big chickens in Asia, he says nothing about them, mentioning neither the very leggy and tall Malays nor the very heavy and large Chinese chickens, nor the Naked Necks, nor the diminutive chickens of India, the Philippines, and Japan. One finds what is clearly meant to be a peacock labeled 'The Indian Chicken.' That raises the question whether Aldrovandi is mixing reports of the peacock with the chickens of Asia (Aldrovandi 1963/1600).

If that is all that a learned naturalist of 1600 knew of chickens, there is very little chance that the Spaniards a hundred years earlier were rushing chickens to their new-found lands—Silkies, Frizzle Fowl, Melanotic chickens, or chickens that had much tufting on their heads, and special loops of feathers on their heads, or naked necks, or layers of blue eggs, or reddish-brown or tinted eggs, but not the white-shelled eggs characteristic of the Mediterranean.

We may safely conclude that Acosta was correct. The chickens in the Amerind land were not like the Spanish chickens, and this means that the Spanish did not introduce the wide array of chickens seen in Amerind yards nor the melanotic chickens so deeply rooted in Amerind religion.

Wafer

In the 1690s, an Englishman living in Panama noted that the Indians had two kinds of chickens (Wafer 1903). One was "our common Dung Hill Fowl" and the other was a smaller chicken that did not flock with the Dung Hill Fowl. Wafer added that the Indians did not engage in cock fighting. Johannessen, 290 years later, wrote of the Mayan chickens in the same terms. They have a very different small chicken that does not flock with the Mediterranean chickens. This is a very useful note for it documents the persistence of poultry types.

NAMES FOR CHICKENS

We have variable material on names for the chicken: spotty in Mexico and Central America, but considerable for South America, thanks to Nordenskiöld (1922) who was interested in the European introductions and plotted the spread of these items. The chicken and the plantain (the banana that needs cooking before eating) were assumed to be Spanish-Portuguese introductions along with steel knives, scissors, and guns, etc. Everything spread uniformly except the chicken and the plantain, both of which must have spread with lightning speed if the Portuguese or the Spanish introduced them. Sauer (1952) considered the plantain to be a pre-Columbian introduction and gave his reasons. Here I will deal with the chicken.

Nordenskiöld assumed an introduction of the chicken by Cabral in 1500 when he bumped into Brazil on his way to India. He is known to have put two mutineers ashore instead of hanging them. Nordenskiöld (1922/1979) makes the flat assumption that the mutineers were supplied with chickens. These would, of course, be Mediterranean-type chickens. Sauer noted that there is no mention of chickens in this episode. For that matter, I suspect that there is no evidence that chickens were aboard. A possibility, of course, but of factual evidence there is none. The same argument is true for the other early explorers who contacted Brazil.

The matter is fraught with difficulties. A cock and some hens would have to have been supplied. The mutineers must not have eaten them, but taught the Indians to raise them. The Indians then invented their own names for the chicken; actually, a wide range of names. The Amerinds also would have to decide not to eat the flesh or eggs of the chicken. There are a lot of assumptions here and a lot of unreality. Nordenskiöld was driven to accepting some such scenario, for he knew from his study of names for the chicken in South America that, when Pizarro reached Peru in 1532, the Inca emperor was named Atahualpa. The latter also had an uncle named Hualpa, and usually your uncle is older than you.

This name matter is complicated, and informative. *Ata* is the word in Ecuador for chicken. *Hualpa* is the name for the chicken throughout the Inca empire. So, the last head Inca was named 'Chicken-Chicken.' Obviously, it was an honorific name. Something of this sort must underlie Acosta's statement (according to Aldrovandi) that the Indians worshipped the chicken. More on this below. Ecuador was the last addition to the Inca empire, and this had just been completed by Atahualpa's father. He wanted to divide the empire between the brothers, but they fought, and it was Atahualpa who prevailed. Thereafter, he did his very best to exterminate every relative, close or distant. Losing a battle could be fatal for many. The significance of this is discussed further below.

Nordenskiöld knew that the chicken was an Old World item, but it alone was subject to instantaneous diffusion in America. In a study of this question, I found that, from the alleged giving of the chickens to the mutineers, it took only about thirty years for chickens to spread across the continent, a distance of about 3000 miles, or at a rate of 100 miles per year. Comparable spread of the chicken in the Old World was at a rate close to one mile per year. One has to add time for the adoption of the chicken as a

royal symbol and to invent a name for the bird. This becomes highly unlikely. (For a lengthy treatment of rates of spread of names for the chicken from India into western Europe, see Carter 1971, *Pre-Columbian Chickens in America*).

Nordenskiöld lived at times among the Brazilian Indians and knew that they kept and raised chickens with considerable difficulty, for the vampire bats would bleed them to death if they were not very carefully housed. Yet, as Nordenskiöld recorded, these people ate neither chickens nor their eggs. He knew that the Indians did not use any word derivable from Spanish. The Amerinds were keeping chickens with great difficulty but not eating them or their eggs. Why? Did he have no curiosity about kinds of chickens, uses of chickens, and so forth? Was he simply avoiding a subject too hot to handle?

Given the knowledge that the kinds of chickens common in Latin America were not in the possession of the Portuguese or the Spanish; that the names are not Spanish or Portuguese; that all of the attitudes and beliefs concerning chickens are not at all like those of 16th century Mediterraneans; and that the chickens in Amerindian hands were not at all like Mediterranean chickens and were found everywhere well before the first-recorded introductions of Mediterranean chickens, one should begin to wonder about the axiomatic acceptance of the Spanish being the first to bring chickens to America.

MORE ON NAMES

Names are most interesting. The name for the chicken amongst the Arawak of northern South America is clearly from India. In India, melanotic chickens are named *karaknath, karnatak, chogakara*. Among the Arawak, the chicken names are closely related to the names in India: *karaka, kalaka, kanka*, etc. The Caribbean Arawak names for the chicken are unknown, for those people became extinct too early. The wide spread of the Arawaks and their obvious preceding of the Caribs suggest at least modest age for them in America or at least for their obtaining chickens.

Table I NAMES FOR MELANOTIC CHICKENS IN INDIA
AND NORTHERN SOUTH AMERICA

INDIA		ARAWAK
kharcha	small fowl	karaka
karaknath	melanotic	garaka
karnatak	melanotic	'takara
chogakara	melanotic	

Karaknath and Karaka are especially notable. In addition, melanotic chickens are specifically meant in India, and melanotic chickens were present in the Arawak area. This would not seem significant to the American ethnologists, so the evidence of special names for varieties, including the melanotic chicken, has not been investigated.

The other names for the chicken in India fall into a *murgh, kuk,* and *pilij* series. These names went west with the chicken, giving rise to the cock and gallus series in Europe (Carter 1971). They supply the model for rates of diffusion of names and the longevity to be found in names. Note that the word 'cock' has now circled the globe and with its *kuk* root has persisted for about 3500 years.

The name for the chicken among the Tarahumar in northwest Mexico is *tori,* and variants are *otori, totori,* etc. The startling correlation is to Japanese: *nihua tori,* meaning 'chicken,' or 'yard-bird'; *ondori* meaning 'cock'; and *mendori* meaning 'hen.'

Table II OTHER CHICKEN NAMES

JAPANESE		TARAHUMAR
nihua tori	yard bird	tori
ondori	cock	totori
mendori	hen	'otori

CHINESE	MAYA
ke, ki, kai	ke, ki, ek
	ik (among the K'echi Maya)

Sahagun's name for one of the many birds for sale in the Aztec market is *cihuatotolin.* M. R. Key, Emeritus Professor of Linguistics at the University of California, Irvine, and familiar with Aztec, says that this translates as 'female chicken.'

Table III MORE NAMES FOR COMPARISON

NAHUATAL	cihuatotolin	female chicken
YAQUI	totoi	
PIMA	totowa	
ZUNI	toko-ko	

Here, I may have gone too far. The linguists can decide.

The names for the chicken in Latin America are well known, but relationship to other languages outside America is not obvious, and I mention here only the very obvious overseas relationships. One negative is worth mentioning. The word all over Polynesia is *moa,* but that name never appears in America. On the other hand, Wallace gives a list of names for Malaysia including small islands east of Celebes. Relationships there are unclear in any direction except for a series such as *mona* and *muna,* which are identical to terms in the Phillipines and obviously related to the Polynesian *moa.*

Johannessen supplies the following Maya names for chicken: *Cambuja, ik, kec, ak, xie, bac, boc, cax,* and *cayaywick.* This is an intriguing list. How would one get so varied a set of names? The Chinese names for chicken

are all based on **k** and a vowel. Note the K'echi Maya *kec, ik* (the consonant reversed), and perhaps *cax.* But that also is a problem for the linguists. Maori at times uses *heihei* suggestive of the Chinese with typical Polynesian duplication, and perhaps late. The Carib of Brazil use *hehehe* and a mixture of other names. *Xep rix* plus *bot cuex* means 'speckled with boot-pants.' *Petz* means 'dwarf.' What one finds are specific native names for Asiatic type chickens. I am not a linguist and have been criticized for such very obvious name relationships as *tori* and *totori,* so I avoid the more tenuous possibilities.

From Michael Wilson, University of Saskatchewan, I have a list of chicken names used by the K'echi Maya (personal communication). He recorded nine descriptive names by color, including *benk* for the melanotic chicken. The body and feather form names are mostly specific for the Asiatic races.

Table IV MICHAEL WILSON'S LIST OF K'ECHI MAYA NAMES FOR THE CHICKEN

This list is important because the kinds of chickens noted duplicate the kinds of chickens in the hands of Indians in South America.

By COLOR

saq	white
aplomad	yellow/brown mottle
sep ris	speckled black/white
kokos	speckled black/white
xasmin	speckled, mainly white
s-po'ot	yellow-throated
c'eo	black
benk	black skin & bones
c'an ci kaq	yellowish red

By BODY and FEATHER FORMS

cit	5 toes per foot
pec	short-legged
xolin	tailless
turu'kus	naked-necked (Spanish *Pelona*)
bot wes	feathered legs & feet; often combined with *cit*
kok'wes	same as *bot wes*
sil	flight feathers reverse curved
mor	all feathers recurved
tuntu ris	same as *mor* but lacks *kis*
sutu	puffy feathers on top and sides of head

JOHANNESSEN'S RESEARCH

Carl Johannessen, following up a suggestion by Carl Sauer, investigated the melanotic chicken in America. He found the melanotic bird to be deeply involved in religion. This was particularly true of the Maya and their linguistically close relatives the Huastec. He finds a bewildering list of religious practices. With the aid of a Chinese-American

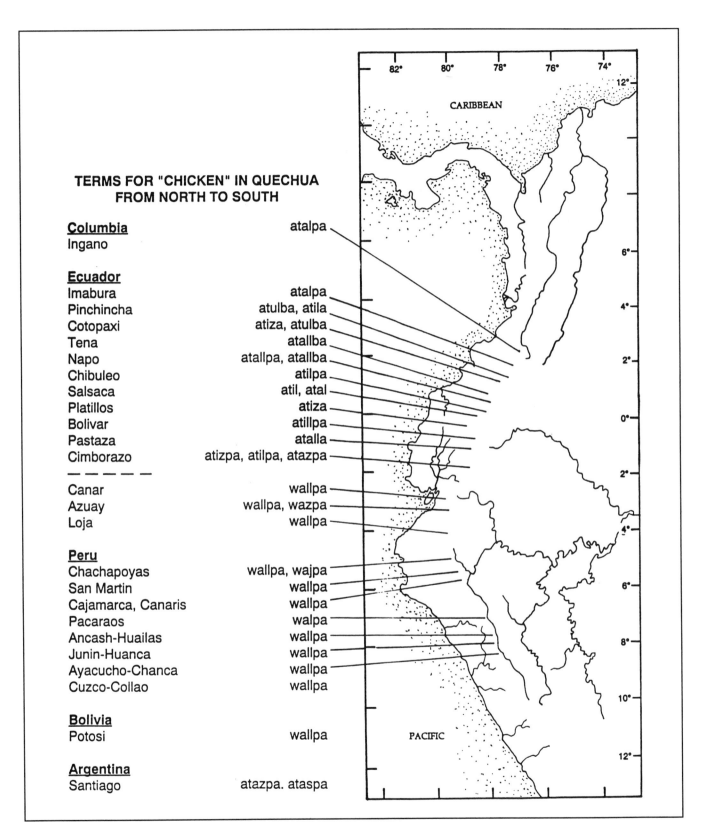

**TERMS FOR "CHICKEN" IN QUECHUA
FROM NORTH TO SOUTH**

Columbia
Ingano — atalpa

Ecuador
Imabura — atalpa
Pinchincha — atulba, atila
Cotopaxi — atiza, atulba
Tena — atallba
Napo — atallpa, atallba
Chibuleo — atilpa
Salsaca — atil, atal
Platillos — atiza
Bolivar — atillpa
Pastaza — atalla
Cimborazo — atizpa, atilpa, atazpa

Canar — wallpa
Azuay — wallpa, wazpa
Loja — wallpa

Peru
Chachapoyas — wallpa, wajpa
San Martin — wallpa
Cajamarca, Canaris — wallpa
Pacaraos — walpa
Ancash-Huailas — wallpa
Junin-Huanca — wallpa
Ayacucho-Chanca — wallpa
Cuzco-Collao — wallpa

Bolivia
Potosi — wallpa

Argentina
Santiago — atazpa. ataspa

Figure 4 DISTRIBUTION OF NAMES FOR CHICKEN ON THE WEST COAST OF SOUTH AMERICA
(Modified from Langdon 1980)
The high variability in Ecuador suggests some antiquity. Note also *atallpa*, from which *wallpa* and *ata* could easily be derived. See earlier discussion of the name of Inca Atahualpa.

scholar, May Chen Fogg, he extended his work to comparison with China. Chinese practices are found widely in Southeast Asia and are present as far back as the Chinese sources go. The comparisons are precise and detailed. They leave no doubt that a whole set of beliefs and practices, like the chicken itself, derives from Asia. Examples include divination with eggs, dripping chicken blood on bark paper and then burning the paper, the belief that a melanotic chicken in the yard protects the household from evil spells, etc.

Among the Maya, the great variation suggests either much time or plural introductions. Johannessen found that the Huastec, while geographically distant from the main body of the Maya, share their linguistic traits concerning melanotic chickens and show linguistic divergence in the name for the chicken that suggests to him quite large time intervals. He also found the Maya-Asiatic ritual traits in Western Bolivia and in the Mapuche people in Chile, but absent elsewhere. A linguistic relationship with the Maya is also suggested for these distant people. Everything in this great variability of language, language differences over time and distance, and the wide dispersal of the people of similar language, suggests that rather great time is involved. If some of this is not hard knowledge, that is true. That is the state of the field at the moment, and it invites further inquiry.

ANTIQUITY OF THE CHICKEN IN AMERICA

The date when the Spanish first brought chickens to America is AD 1520. This date is disputed by some. One German argued that all references to domestic birds were to turkeys (Franz Termer, *Die Huhner de Azteken*, 1962). Abundant evidence is presented in this article that that is not true. Another German reached the conclusion that the Spanish were the first to introduce chickens and that they spread so fast that the notion arose that they had preceded the Spanish. Mere nonsense, Termer thinks. And again, if the Spanish brought them, where did *they* get these remarkable chickens? Even a 1495 introduction of chickens, a date that Termer reports, would not affect any of the data above.

First, why would the Spanish bring chickens to a land already well provided with chickens? The probable answer is that the Spanish wanted eggs and the native chickens produced few. The Spanish non-setting chickens were virtual egg factories. One might object that egg factories would not reproduce themselves. However, the chickens already present were setters, and the melanotic chickens notably good setters and mothers, and so that problem was simply solved. Put the Spanish eggs under the native chickens to incubate and raise the chicks. This is well known in northwest Mexico for the wild turkey eggs. If a clutch of eggs is found, it is placed under a broody hen.

There have been surveys of the literature on the early Spanish records. Ricardo Latcham of Chile sought the answer to the problem of whether it was Spanish chickens first or chickens from some other source already present (Latcham 1922). He concluded firmly for a pre-Spanish chicken and, with less certainty because of a lesser survey of the North American literature, that the chicken probably preceded the Spanish chicken introduction there as well. Carl Sauer saw the blue eggs in Chile, met Latcham, read his material, and checked on the Cabral account. Sauer concluded that the Spanish did not introduce these melanotic chickens and blue-egg laying chickens because they did not have them. Why that astute scholar never followed up those clues is a mystery (Sauer 1952).

I have had access to a manuscript by John Kilgore, one chapter in a projected book on the chicken in the Americas. Kilgore went back to the original accounts and read them in Spanish to be sure of the translations. Kilgore finds the earliest accounts filled with references to chickens. In several cases, the chickens are listed along with turkeys, ducks, pheasants, and other birds. He concluded for a pre-Columbian presence of chickens but cautions that words are always subject to interpretation

An interesting case concerns Magellan's voyage. In 1519, when in the vicinity of Rio de Janeiro, they were supplied with chickens. On December 13th of 1519, Pigafetta recorded: " . . . where we picked up a great store of chickens, ... For one fishhook or a knife, they gave me six chickens, fearing even so that they were cheating me" (Pigafetta 1985). As mentioned, there are many such accounts with very specific mention of chickens, often right along with references to turkeys, in Mexico or to ducks in South America.

OTHER TIME CONSIDERATIONS FOR INTRODUCTION OF CHICKENS

First, without going into reasons other than those already mentioned indicating Japanese, Chinese, and Indian introductions, much of the evidence suggests early and plural introductions perhaps at widely separated times. The linguistic divergence is large, only some of which can be due to separate introductions. The Maya/Huastec/Mapuche language relationships seem to point to quite early divergence from some early introduction.

Truly explosive recent discoveries may come to bear on all of this. Dr. H. Mike Xu, a native of Shanghai who teaches at the University of Central Oklahoma, has now read the carvings on celts found by Heizer and Drucker at La Venta, Mexico (Xu 1996). This is a pure Olmec site, and considered to date to around either 800 BC or 1100 BC. The writing on celts at the site reads in Shang Dynasty Chinese. Well-known Chinese people are named in these dedicatory tablets. Xu relates this to the historic accounts of the defeat and death of the last Shang ruler in 1122 BC, whereupon thousands of loyalists took to the 'Eastern Ocean' (the Pacific). Recall that, when Atahualpa defeated his Inca brother in Peru, all relatives were hunted down and executed, and we can be sure that this practice would also have been applied to loyal supporters of the defeated. It was flee or die.

It is at that exact time that the Olmec civilization appears, full blown, on the shores of Mexico. The landing seems to have been near Acapulco, from which point they expanded across Mexico. Xu mentions 250,000 refugees, but thinks that only some of them reached America; obviously, large numbers were involved.

Now, if only we knew whether the Olmec already had the ceremonial rituals of China! The Maya are obviously the direct descendants of the Olmec. From May Chen Fogg's work with Johannessen we know that the ritual and the melanotic chicken practices and beliefs are ancient in China. They document accounts as early as 196 BC. We need an Olmec or Mayan account! The possibilities are slight, given the limited Olmec material, and only slightly better for Mayan material. We have at best an outside chance of finding a reference relevant to the chicken question. The hope is that Xu's amazing discoveries will stimulate inquiry. If the melanotic chicken was so important to the early Chinese, we would have an explanation why they might bother to bring chickens across the great Pacific and not eat them nor their eggs.

I will add that there is some skeptical reaction to Xu's findings. I think that Xu is probably correct because I am aware of very specific art resemblances to China and of palm prints like Chinese, and blood groups like China in Mexico. Then there are the lengthy comparisons with China and Mexico made by Needham and Lu Gwei-Djen (1985). The evidence is startling in detail and most of the overall knowledge has long been available. Xu's work is enormously important in explanation power for solving the puzzle of the sudden appearance of civilization in America.

CONCLUSION

When one considers the total data available on the chicken in America, a conclusion for a Spanish or Portuguese first introduction of chickens into America is simply counter to all the evidence. The Mediterraneans, as late as 1600, did not have, and did not even know of, the galaxy of chickens present in Amerind hands. How could they have introduced them? The names are all wrong and a program to have the Amerinds invent such a vast array of specialties, including names, religious practices, and so on, in some short time, related to some introduction by the Manila Galleon or another such event for which there are no data at all, is simply to engage in obscurantism. If a scholarly and scientific approach to the subject is taken, an approach that pays attention to the data instead of the clichés

of the past, then the only possible conclusion is that chickens were introduced from across the Pacific, probably repeatedly, long before the Mediterranean discoveries of America.

I will end this paper, as I did with the *Man Across the Sea* paper in 1971, by saying that those not acquainted with the field may conclude that this is the final word. Far from it. I have left masses of data undiscussed, and I shudder at my gross ignorance of the genetics of the chicken. A man with a PhD in poultry science and a life at work in the field will find lapses and errors and wrong emphasis. Historians will click their tongues and point out that I did not include so and so. The anthropologists and archaeologists will be even rougher, for I am challenging their fundamental beliefs concerning the American Indians, their origins, and their civilization. They will call for Carbon-14 dates for chicken bones, but they have thrown away all the chicken bones found, or stored them under conditions guaranteed to make dating impossible. We do have a book-length treatment of the subject that we hope to get out some day. Those that call for more detailed reporting will have to wait for the book.

In discussing our effort with Charmion McKusick, one of the authors in the proposed book, she commented: "We are introducing the subject and not the definitive and final work. There is an infinity more to be done."

I wish to acknowledge John Sorenson's continuing support of the study of the chicken in America. Despite our setbacks and disappointments, John Sorenson has continued to aid us financially with grants through the New World Archaeological Foundation. I also want to acknowledge that throughout this short article I have used material from the more extensive work by my co-authors: John Kilgore on the Spanish sources; Carl Johannessen on the melanotic chickens; and Charmion McKusick's broad studies in the Southwest with special attention to the osteology of the few chicken bones preserved from the archaeological sites. The late Herbert Dick also contributed to work on the Picuris site, virtually the only site in the American Southwest to preserve the chicken bones found.

REFERENCES

Aldrovandi, Ulisse
  1963 *Aldrovandi on Chickens: the Ornithology of Ulisse Aldrovandi (1600),* Vol. 2, bk. 4. L. K. Lind, trans. Norman: University of Oklahoma University Press.
Acosta, Jose de
  1590 *Historia Natural y Moral de las Indias.* Number 34.Cronic, Series Histori a 16. Madrid: Edición José Franch.
Bay-Peterson, Jan, ed.
  1991 *Catalogue of the Native Poultry of Southeast Asia.* Taiwan, Food and Fertilizer Technology Center. This is a most useful work. For the first time, we have pictures of Chinese chickens as well as invaluable pictures of Japanese chickens, plus the Malays in the Philippines.

Bolton, H. E.
1932 *Spanish Explorations in the Southwest*. New York: Charles Scribners Sons. This contains the accounts of the earlier entradas, *e.g.*, Coronado.

Capa, Rev. P. Ricardo
1915 Estudios críticos acerca de la dominación española en América. Vol. 5: *Industria agrícola-pecuaria llevada a America por los españoles*, 4º edición. Madrid: Imprenta del Asilo de Huérfanos. (Critical studies concerning the Spanish domination in America. Vol. 5: The cattle-farming industry carried to America by the Spanish.)

Carter, George. F.
1971 Pre-Columbian chickens in America. In *Man Across the Sea*. Carroll L. Riley, *et al.* eds. Austin: University of Texas Press.

Crawford, R. D.
1984 Domestic fowl. Pp. 298-304 in *Evolution of Domesticated Animals*. Jon L. Mason, ed. London: Longman. Crawford is a careful scholar and impressed with the evidence suggesting that Asiatics carried chickens to America, but he demands an archaeologically-dated bone before he is convinced. He is my authority on genetics.

Finsterbusch, C. A.
1929 *Cock-Fighting All Over the World*. Gaffney SC.

Hargrave, Lyndon L.
1972 Comparative osteology of the chicken and the American grouse. In Vol. 2: *Studies in Biology*. Prescott AZ: Prescott College. Hargrave identified the chicken bones found at the Picuris Pueblo site. When I pointed out the fact that chicken bones came from before 1490, according to the stratigraphy and the sherds, he undertook a study to test the identification of chicken and grouse bones. The chicken bones remained chicken and still at 'unacceptable' levels. That is where the matter remains in archaeologists' opinion: unacceptable.

Johannessen, Carl L.
1981 Folk medicine uses of melanotic Asiatic chickens as evidence of early diffusion to the New World. *Social Sciences and Medicine* 73-89.

Johannessen, Carl L. and May Chen Fogg
1982 Melanotic chicken use and Chinese traits in Guatemala. *Revista de Historia de América* 93:427-434. México.

Jull, Morley
1927 The races of domestic fowl. *National Geographic* 4:379-452. Excellent pictures, and the record shows that this poultry expert had no idea where the Naked Neck chicken came from.

Latcham, Ricardo E.
1922 *Los animales domesticos de la América pre-Colombiana*. Santiago: Museo Etnological Antropological. Publication 31:1-199.

Langdon, Robert
1980 When the blue egg chickens come home to roost. *The Journal of Pacific History* 24:24-36 and 164-192. An interesting paper about the chicken on Easter Island. There was a large input from Peru of plants and animals. The blue-egg laying chicken could only have come from America.

Meggers, Betty J.
1975 The transpacific origin of mesoamerican civilization: A preliminary review of the evidence and its theoretical

Meggers, Betty J., continued
implications. *American Anthropologist* 77:1-27. This was 'not acceptable' at the time and has given her considerable difficulty. Xu's work, and much more, supports her fully.

Menghin, Oswald
1962 Vorkolubischer Hauhuhner in Sud America (International Symposium on Domestication). *Zur Domestikation Der Haustier Verlag*. Hamburg: Paul Parey. Menghin had access not only to Latcham but also to Sauer and so was alerted to the problem. He recorded seeing hundreds of blue-egg laying chickens in Argentina.

Needham, Joseph and Lu Gwei-Djen
1985 *Trans-Pacific Echoes and Resonances: Listening Once Again*. Singapore and Philadelphia: World Scientific. Needham also has an interesting account of his conversion to a diffusionist position in his great study of Chinese Civilization. See volume 4, Nautics.

Nordenskiöld, Erland
1922 Deductions suggested by the geographical distribution of some post-Columbian words used by the Indians of South America. Vol. 5 of *Comparative Ethnographical Studies*. Goteborg: Pehrssons. Reprinted 1979, New York: AMS.

Pigafetta, Antonio
1985 Primer viaje alrededor del Mundo. Edición Leoncio Cabrero Fernández, Historia 16, Madrid.

Sahagún, B. de
1950 General history of the things of New Spain: Florentine Codex. A. J. O. Anderson and C. E. Dibble, trans. and eds. *School of American Research Monograph* No. 14, Santa Fe. Sahagún has a lot to say about the turkey and the chicken, using a name for the turkey that is totally different from that for the chicken. He even gives recipes for chicken.

Sauer, Carl O.
1952 *Agricultural Origins and Dispersals*. American Geographical Society, Bowman Memorial Lectures. New York. A stimulating look at the evidence by the dean of cultural historical geography. Of the blue-egg laying chickens and melanotic chickens, he says that the Spanish could not have brought them, for they did not have them.

Simoons, Frederick J.
1966 *Eat Not This Flesh: Food Avoidance in the Old World*. Madison: University of Wisconsin Press. Simoons finds that, world-wide, there is surprisingly little interest in eating chickens or their eggs. He includes virtually all of Latin America in the listing of where chickens are avoided as food. Simoons' book is one of the great resources.

Stephenson, Martin
1987 The role of poultry husbandry in the medieval agrarian economy 1200-1400. *The ARK* 1987:378-381. In this paper, he destroys the cliché that chicken breeding stopped with the Romans.

Wafer, Lionel
1903 *A New Voyage and Description of the Isthmus of America*. New York: B. Franklin.

Wilson, Michael
n.d. Personal communication.

Xu, H. Mike
1996 *Origin of the Olmec Civilization*. Edmond: University of Central Oklahoma Press.

The Yuchi, American and Asian

JOSEPH B. MAHAN [‡]

THE 'AMERICAN YUCHI'

The Yuchi have been the most mysterious of all the tribes of eastern North America since the general subject of the origin and history of the American Indians became of interest to antiquarians and the literate public early in the 19th century. Their presence in the upper drainage of the Savannah River and among the foothills of the Appalachian mountains was first noticed by the colonial South Carolinians about 1690. They are presumed to have migrated into that area from somewhere to the north not long prior to that time. Whence they came has remained uncertain, as their language was unlike any other known to 19th century linguists and the speakers of other Indian languages as well. There were two recorded exceptions to the latter assertion, however: William Bartram, 18th-century botanist widely acquainted with southeastern Indians, and Thomas Woodward, a militia general of the War of 1812 and afterwards, who knew the Creek and Yuchi on a personal basis. Both said the Yuchi language was the same as that of the Shawano. This information only compounded the issue, as all scholars involved in the matter assumed that the Shawano were the same people as the Shawnee. They knew that the Yuchi and Shawnee languages are completely unrelated!

I once had the rare opportunity to ask the elderly hereditary chief of the Yuchi, Samuel W. Brown, Jr., to explain to me the relationship between the Yuchi and the Shawnee. He responded that he would have to think about the answer. In a few days, I received the following taped statement:

> These people were the Choyaha or Yustafa Wano, or better known today as Yuchi. And their original name was Zoyawahano, which was the governing word, as it is of today, from their starting point.
>
> And their leader had many nations. Spiritually, they inherited instilled in them their lineage for generations to come. They had a tribal town, a big one, at Coshafa. That is a Yuchi word. And it was said by the old people that was what they called Shalala Wano or Shawano, that they called themselves Shawanogee. That is not a Yuchi word.
>
> They traveled and branched off in different branches and from Shawanogee became known to the public and to the world as Shawanees. There was a big tribe of them, and one bunch called itself Ispogogee, another Kispogogee, and another Iste Muscogulgee, and the last Muscovee.

Recent historians studying the reports and journals of the earliest French missionaries and explorers into the region south of the Great Lakes (translated by James Gilmary Shea and Reuben Goldthwaits) are now aware that the Shawano were a peaceful, populous people who resided in some forty large towns in the Ohio River drainage and controlled the vast region from the Lakes to the Gulf of Mexico and the Savannah River valley. These historians know much that has not been within the ken of the ethnologists, linguists, and archaeologists who have been involved during the past century and a half in making sense of southeastern Indian history. They know that the Shawano were slaughtered and their town destroyed during the period 1645-1670 by the Seneca and other Iroquois from New York and New Jersey using firearms they obtained in trade from the Dutch and Swedes.

It was not merely the Shawano who were destroyed. So were many of their allies. The Erie were so decimated that the tribe ceased to exist. The Miami, Illinois, Shawnee, and Sac and Fox were severely weakened and fled westward into the upper Mississippi valley. The surviving Shawano, Yuchi, and Abihka moved south to live among kinsmen and allies who were principal components of both the Creek Confederacy and the Cherokee Nation. A few of these and a people called the Canas took refuge in William Penn's new colony and remained for a couple of generations before they too moved south.

So thorough was the destruction of the Shawano that their home territory and town sites lay abandoned for a half century or more before the Shawnee and Sac and Fox returned to claim their old towns on the Wabash and upper Ohio rivers.

South of the Ohio, the twin valleys of the Cumberland and Tennessee, in what is now Kentucky and middle Tennessee, were never reoccupied by the native peoples and continued to be known as the 'Dark and Bloody Land' until the time of the American Revolution.

The mystery surrounding the Yuchi involved much more than simply their language, which they never taught to anyone outside their tribe, and about which they encouraged the idea among other people that it was too difficult to learn in less than a lifetime. The further mystery involved their physical and political relationship to other tribes among whom they resided for many generations without physical admixture or political integration. Because of their separatism, the Yuchi maintained their tribal identity for some three centuries while at the same time regularly holding positions of leadership in the Creek Nation.

My own research has been directed to the problem of identifying the role of the Yuchi in cooperation with other peoples, for example, the diverse peoples of the Creek Confederacy. I have drawn the following conclusions: The Yuchi are themselves an ancient confederation of earth people led by Sun and Moon people, the Zoyaha and the Yustafa Wano. At some time in the more recent past they united with another earth-sky people they called the Sha people (wano). *Sha* means both 'serpent' and 'eagle' in the Yuchi language. The Shawano, then, was a confederation of the original Yuchi and the Eagle-Serpent people.

The Creek Confederacy maintained until this century a dual monarchy with a king of the moon and another of the sun, each of whom had well-defined responsibilities and restrictions. The moon king presided in the ceremonial 'peace' or 'white' towns, and the sun king was the leader of the 'war' or 'red' towns. Both positions were hereditary through the women of the dynastic line. The white king, named *Fushudgee,* or 'Birdtail' king, was supreme and acted for the entire confederation in times of peace and in all matters relating to peace. *Zopathla,* the sun king, reigned in time of war or in matters relating to war.

This was the protocol which governed the Shawano, whose white kings were priests in the Order of the Four Roads and whose red kings were *miccos,* or medicine men, in the Great Medicine Society. The sun king of the Shawano held sovereignty over the sun kings in the confederated towns, thereby earning the title 'emperor,' which European colonists gave to persons of this position. Their emblem was the peacock. Their totem was the falcon; that of their mothers and sisters was the crane or goose.

The Creek Confederacy duplicated this arrangement exactly as did the Cherokee tribe prior to their successful revolt against Shawano dominance about 1750.

There is only one more thing to be said about the Yuchi and that is that they came south in the latter 17th century and settled among their kinsmen, the Tukabatchee and the Apalachicola. The former was a red town, and the latter, a white town. These became the head towns of the Creek Confederacy. The emperor known to history was Yuchi. This was a *Cu,* or 'bird,' town. It was also a *Sha* town, hence the name *Cusha.*

THE 'ASIAN YUCHI'

In Pakistan and India a few years ago, I researched another people with the same name, Kushan, who were also Yuchi. They were the people the Chinese called the *Yueh-chih,* meaning 'Moon People.' According to them, these people were a branch of the Tungu, or eastern Tartars, who, several centuries before the Christian era, had passed into western Tartary where they founded an extensive empire, the limits of which enclosed the Chinese provinces of Tangut and West Kansu, with a part of South Thiangshan.

About 200 BC, they were defeated by the Hiungnu and driven from their country. Fifty years later, they were again defeated and driven farther westward, separating into two divisions. The smaller of these moved southward into Tibet, and the larger division, called the Great Yuchi, moved still farther west and south, and eventually into Bactria, the present northeastern Afghanistan.

Earlier, there were the Shakyas who moved into northern India. Buddha's mother belonged to this people. His father's people were the Koshala, 'Man-Bird.' They were absorbed by the Magdha, who became the undisputed masters of India by the turn of the 5th century BC. The Magdha rulers, themselves relatively new in the region, were able to ignore the Brahmans and to court the allegiance of new social classes, the merchants and bankers. With their support, the Magdha rulers were free to turn to the newer religions with their emphasis upon the individual rather than family or caste heritage. I believe it is easy to detect here a return to the more ancient teachings of the people we have called the Cosha, or Cusha, who were certainly represented in the Kingdom of Kosha, as the name proves, and of the Shaya, ('inseparable from Sha'), the Buddha's own tribe.

The ruling family of the Magdha were the Maurya, a variant of the Sanskrit word *Mayura* meaning 'peacock.' It is not surprising that this family had a member with the name *Chandragupta,* 'Son of the Moon,' or another whose name was *Asoka,* pronounced 'a-choka,' meaning 'sun' and 'spirit' in the Yuchi religious language. It is also not surprising that these men became, respectively, followers of the non-violent, learned orders of Jains and of Buddha. Chandragupta was reared to adolescence as a peasant and then adopted and educated at Taxila by a learned man, a Brahmin, named Kautalya. In this way, Asoka had access to knowledge dating from long before the time of Buddha or of the Jain movement, but which influenced both. This was the source from which the Brahmins had sprung also; it was the religion taught by the followers of Sha.

Asoka's conversion to Buddhism was effected by a monk called Upagupta, whose name incorporates a Yuchi word we have already met: *yupa,* meaning 'above.' *Gupta,* in this context, means 'descended from,' so this man had 'descended from above,' in the manner of the Shawano. Asoka died about 232 BC, and his dynasty slowly declined until 73 BC when it was replaced by the Sungas.

Meanwhile, the Yuchi were in the process of moving towards the borderlands of the Indian empire. A new dynasty, that of the Kushans, had been founded by one of the five chieftains among whom Bactria was divided. The Kushan kingdom extended its power southward and eastward into India. There, they headed a great empire until about AD 400, when it was replaced by another dynasty, itself of Yuchi origin.

The third and greatest of the Kushana kings was *Kanishka,* 'Peacock's-eye man spirit.' His name and policies as emperor prove that at least a cultural heritage had come to him from the Mauryas and Asoka. Kanishka embraced the Buddhist religion, and it was during his reign that a Buddhist shrine and monastery were built on the already ancient citadel at Mohenjo-daro, the great city of the Indus abandoned about 1500 BC. Kanishka most certainly considered Buddhism to be a worthy successor of the ancient religion practiced there or this would not have been done. His name clearly indicates that he was part of the ancient Earth-Sky religion for the purposes of which the structures on the artificial mound in the ancient city were intended.

Kanishka's personal heritage is revealed in a letter from a monk who had been invited by Kanishka to discuss Buddhist doctrines with him. The historian John Rosenfield tells this story:

> Being too old to travel, the monk put his advice into the form of a poetic epistle. He urged the king, for example, to give up hunting of wild beasts, exhorting him to live an exemplary Buddhist life: 'Train yourself in the way of your own people; born in the Kusa race, do not impair the household law of your ancestors, the sons of the Arya.' And, urging Kanishka to refrain from any killing, to be compassionate, the letter says, 'Since we cannot look upon the hurtful sun, act, Oh Moon of Kings, like the Moon.'

As we know that Kanishka, being a Kushan, was a follower of the Sun and the Moon, we suspect also that he believed all of the religions he permitted to be practiced in his empire pertaining to the worship of the one god. This was essential to the teachings of his own religious heritage as well as of the Buddhism he adopted.

Kanishka's empire had two capitals, one of which was Taxila, in what is now northern Pakistan. Its original form, *Tuckasila*, indicates the Tuka people as the dominating element of the population. Much archaeological work has been done there in this century both by the British and by the present Pakistani government. There is a museum in which is housed an extensive collection of art work in stucco and stone from the ruins of Asoka's reign as well as that of Kanishka. In addition, there are many artifacts and a collection of magnificent gold jewelry found in the ruins. I made several visits to this museum and studied the items it houses with great interest.

A few miles away in the museum at Peshawar is a relic casket from a nearby Buddhist stupa which was made to contain some of the physical remains of the Emperor Kanishka. It is an urn less than a foot tall and is beautifully carved from the hard gray schist of that region. On the lid, in the place of a handle, stands a three-inch tall figure representing the emperor. He is flanked by figures personifying the Sun and Moon.

This seemed appropriate. Here were the symbols representing the great sky-god in the two aspects the old monk mentioned in his letter to the king. The implication was that Kanishka was descended from both. This would have told the story of the Kushan emperor's identity even if I had not looked at a freize in low relief which circles the rim of the vessel. When I found that it consisted of a row of geese with their necks stretched as though they were asleep or dead, I knew that Kanishka, although a mighty king, a son of the Sun and a follower of Sha, also belonged to his mother the Earth, represented here by the geese. His people were the *Shalalawano*, 'Goose People,' just as Chief Brown said the Yuchi were. That day, I realized that the Asian Yuchi were indeed the same people as the Yuchi of North America.

NOTE

‡ This paper is reproduced with the kind permission of Dr. Katherine H. Mahan, Executor, Estate of Joseph B. Mahan, Jr. The text is essentially as it was delivered at the June 1992 ABC Conference and as published in *ESOP* (The Epigraphic Society Occasional Papers), Vol. 21. In a letter received by the editors a few days before he passed away in September 1995, Dr. Joseph Mahan expressed his intention to make slight revisions to this paper, noting, "and certainly with an added reference to information on the Asian Yuchi which Ethel G. Stewart included in [the 1992 edition of] her book, *The Dene and Na-Dene Indian Migration to America, 1233 AD*." Readers will have to search the reference volume, as, regrettably, Joe did not complete that task.

REFERENCES

Appert, Gustav
  1893 *On the Original Inhabitants of India.* Westminister: Archibald Constable & Co.
Cunningham, Alexander, ed.
  1872 *Archaeological Survey of India: Four Reports Made During the Years 1862, 1863, 1864, 1865.* 2 Vols. Delhi: Indological Book House.
Gokhale, Balkrishna Govind
  1966 *Asoka Maurya.* New York: Twayne Publishers.
Hackin, J., et al.
  n.d. *Asiatic Mythology: A Detailed Description and Explanation of the Mythologies of All the Great Nations of Asia,* T. M. Atkinson, trans. New York: Crowell.
Mahan, Joseph B.
  1983 *The Secret: America in World History Before Columbus.* Columbus GA: Privately published.
Marshall, John, ed.
  1931 *Mohenjo-Daro and the Indus Civilization, Being an Official Account of Archaeological Excavations at Mohenjo-Daro Carried Out by the Government of India Between the Years 1922-1927.* 3 Vols. London: Arthur Probathain.
Rosenfield, John
  1967 *The Dynastic Arts of the Kushanas.* Berkeley and Los Angeles: University of California Press.
Stewart, Ethel G.
  1981[1992] *Dene and Na-Dene Indian Migration 1233 AD, Escape from Genghis Khan.* Columbus GA: ISAC Press.
Unknown author
  1968 *The Indus Civilization: Supplementary Volume to the Cambridge History of India.* 3rd ed. Cambridge: University Press.
Wheeler, Mortimer
  1961 *Early India and Pakistan.* Oxford: University Press.

COMMENTARY—SECTION II

Peregrination of the Organic

DANIEL W. GADE

Theories of early diffusion impel us to consider possibilities beyond conventional understandings by examining spatially disjunct patterns. When the object of diffusion is a biologically defined organism, the odds are overwhelming that no repeat inventions exist to cloud the narrative. The same plants and animals and also many human genetic traits are arguably not invented twice. The case for diffusion of an organic entity is the concern of the papers in this section. Some of these essays have a fuller grasp of the variables and a more persuasive argumentation than do others, but all of them propose bold configurations that merit open-minded consideration. Although none of them gives any real attention to the actual mechanisms of possible transfer, they offer by implication reconstructions of what might have happened.

Carl Johannessen hypothesizes that maize was the inspiration for 11th to 13th century stone sculptures found in several out-of-the-way Hindu temples of southern India. Was maize found in India at that time? Noone, of course, supports the idea that this plant could have also originated outside the Western Hemisphere, for its wild progenitor, teosinte, is not found outside Mesoamerica. After the European transoceanic explorations, maize was carried hither and yon. The prevailing orthodoxy of scholarly opinion still denies the presence of maize in the Old World before the European discoveries.

The crux of Johannessen's argument revolves around the evidence that maize was the model for what we see in these sculptures. With an eye well trained to taxonomic variation of maize and its morphological sinuosities, Johannessen scrutinized the carved motifs found in these temples in a way that no historian of Hindu art could have done. Certainly these sculptured designs look like ears of corn, for no other plant, cultivated or wild, has such a striking individualistic appearance. The question is whether there are mythic associations in Hindu art and representations still to be probed that suggest a different interpretation. To bolster his case, Johannessen (1992) assembled in a previous paper a formidable "armoire des mots" which provides linguistic evidence of a bevy of non-European and non-American names for maize that supports the spread of maize over much of the tropical world before the European discoveries.

Stephen Jett, who first studied cultural-geographical diffusion with George Carter at Johns Hopkins University, presents a more nuanced package of diffusionary ideas. Substitution of the original diffused item with one readily available is called stimulus diffusion. Jett asserts that dye technology spread between the Old and New Worlds when species, closely enough related to those introduced to make substitution obvious, were found and used. Thus, it was the knowledge of how to dye with certain colors—madder red, indigo blue, scale-insect scarlet and shellfish purple—that became the durable diffused trait. Presenting an unusually rich documentation, Jett argues that because dye procedures are so complicated, the likelihood of their multiple invention is greatly reduced.

George Carter, long known for his intrepid perspectives on prehistory, offers his latest thinking on Old World domesticated poultry in pre-Columbian America. The possibility of a domesticated chicken before Columbus had earlier intrigued Raymond Gilmore and Carl Sauer, but it has been Carter to whom we owe its elaboration and refinement. Chickens with blue eggs and/or black meat and bones and/or absence of feathers on the neck were not known then in Europe; therefore Carter asserts, the presence of these exotic chickens in the Western Hemisphere raises the intriguing possibility that they were early, pre-Columbian, introductions from Asia. He elaborates especially the linguistic evidence to make this case. Alternative explanations get no attention in this paper. However, I have long wondered whether the Manila galleon trade which linked the Philippines and thus much of Asia with the Western Hemisphere beginning in the 16th century, might not have offered an early, though post-Columbian pathway for transoceanic spread. A particular Asian breed of pig reached Peru in the early colonial period by that means. The archaeological evidence for the pre-Columbian chicken suffered a setback when the chicken bones found at Las Colina, a Hohokam site near Phoenix, AZ, dated AD 1100-1450 were found in association with the domestic pig and the domestic cat, neither of which are considered to be pre-Columbian in the New World. Rea (1986) acknowledged this as a site error. Yet Carter has developed a battery of evidence which commands close attention.

Nancy Yaw Davis presents a multi-faceted case for Japanese influences in Zuni human biology and culture. In addition to skeletal remains, she also considers bloodgroups, a genetic propensity toward kidney disease, as well as art, cosmology, apparent loan words and other linguistic parallels, which together make for intriguing similarities. That much of Zuni culture differs from that of its southwestern neighbors is certain. If at one time the

Zuni had been a coastal people, the cultural connection with Japan would be easier to grasp. A deeper linguistic analysis is called for to solidify this fascinating hypothesis.

Joseph Mahan also offers a putative connection between North America and Asia. The American Indian tribe called the Yuchi and the Yuchi of India have both been historically known as migratory. The former, displaced from Pennsylvania to South Carolina in colonial America, are poorly known as a culture, but their apparent distinctiveness from neighboring native peoples has received enough comment to raise questions about their origins. The peripatetic Yuchi of India, who have a long history on the subcontinent, share with their North American namesakes a sky-god cult focused on the moon and sun. Given these and other parallels, might some Yuchi of India have migrated to North America? Mahan's evidence is somewhat meager, and many other trait comparisons would be needed to develop a convincing case for contact between them. Greater attention to the Yuchi in India would seem to be in order in developing a strong case for transfer.

The rich bundle of diffusion studies in this section as well as in the whole volume will intrigue anyone who follows clues to solve a puzzle and who likes to ponder not-yet-accepted, maybe even offbeat, possibilities. However well-argued the studies are, a vociferous core of opposition will always insist the data presented do not support diffusion to explain the parallels presented. From that, they assert that early movements could not have happened. Diffusionist scholars must develop a thick skin against the naysayers. As Professor Alice Kehoe states in her essay in this volume, the dogma of the oceans as an "impassable barrier" is based on a belief that 'science' is somehow undermined by these assertions. However, science is increasingly asked to defend what it has always taken for granted. Conclusive 'proof' for just about anything is a grand illusion of modernist thought. Learning to live with uncertainty is the first diffusionist commandment. At the same time, one thing is certain: the power

of diffusion in the cultural transformation of the world cannot be denied (Hugill and Dickson, 1988).

To those of eclectic and receptive minds, these studies open unorthodox vistas. All of these papers question the canon of separate development between the Old and New Worlds before AD 1492 and, taken as a group, they enhance the plausibility of transoceanic contacts before the Europeans initiated their explorations. To me, none of them represents closure, and each may be said to offer ideas in process. They all use logical inference from rather slim data. Greater use of counterfactual evidence would build stronger cases. As ideas, they are likely to remain in limbo for decades before some of them receive general acceptance. New techniques, some still undreamed of, may provide new understanding. Let's hope that other scholars will be stimulated by these essays and will build upon the foundations laid by the authors of this volume.

REFERENCES

Hugill, Peter J. and D. Bruce Dickson, eds.
  1988 *The Transfer and Transformation of Ideas and Material Culture.* College Station: Texas A&M University Press.
Johannessen, Carl L.
  1992 Distribution of pre-Columbian maize and modern maize names. In *Person, Place and Thing*, *Geoscience and Man*. Vol. 31. S. T. Wang, ed. Baton Rouge: Louisiana State University.
Kehoe, Alice B.
  1998 Vestiges of the natural history of archaeology: Setting up the Americas as a scientific experiment. Pp. 267–271 in *Across Before Columbus?*. D. Y. Gilmore and L. S. McElroy, eds. Proceedings of NEARA Columbian Quincentenary Conference, Brown University, 1992. NEARA Publications.
Rea, Amideo
  1986 Verification and reverification: Problem in archaeofaunal studies. *Journal of Ethnobiology* Vol. 6, pp.9-18.

AUTHOR RESPONSES—SECTION II

CARL JOHANNESSEN

Professor Gade has failed to use his own experience with maize in Latin America. Instead, he seems willing to accept an alleged mythic association in Hindu art (which no one has actually found) as the equivalent of proved evidence of more than forty different features of the maize ear that are carved into the suppporting walls of over a hundred Hoysala Dynasty and earlier temples spread throughout the state of Karnataka. In fact, the evidence goes back to the 6th century AD at Cave temple three, Badami, Karnataka, India. These temples are only 'out of the way' for Western scholars. The non-diffusionist authorities either do not know Latin American corn with its morphological details in their homeland, or they have not been to see the thousands of maize ears, large and small, that adorn these temples. Maize is only one of several American species that moved across the oceans long before the Europeans. Granted, Gade recognizes this too.

He seems to give credence to " . . . the data presented do not support diffusion to explain the parallels presented. From that, they assert that early movements could not have happened." This is like arguing that you have to see both sides of the sheep leaving the shearing shed before you can accept the fact that sheep are sheared on both sides in that process. The data on maize in India are accepted by the archaeologists and corn breeders in India, China, England, and the United States every time that they have seen the evidence. Super objectivists may not learn: there have been three archaeologists in the United States who did not.

Mahan cannot answer any more, (deceased, September 1995) but it should have been known by Gade that Mahan had found peach pits in the early archaeology of South Carolina, and those had to have come by sail from across the ocean before Columbus. Mahan's posited Yuchi arrival may be slim, but diffusion was proved by the peach pit.

George Carter and other authors, including me, are in the process of writing a book on the history of the chicken in the New World. The data needs to be presented critically, I admit. Because of the super objectivists it is significantly difficult to find publishers for this material. Just to keep the chicken record straight, I was the researcher who found the black-boned, black-meated chicken (BB-BMC) in Latin America from Mexico to Chile and across Brazil. The use of the BB-BMC by the Mayan Indians and the Huastecans (who speak Maya) in the fashion of 15th century AD South Chinese in medical cures, by very esoteric treatments, demonstrates that the chicken came to America a few thousand years before the Spaniards.

The Manila galleons are suggested by friend Gade for the transportation of the BB-BMC. I find this an excuse not to think clearly on this subject. Imagine, if you will, a Spanish ship captain in the Philippines allowing a group of Chinese witch doctor teachers to board his ship in Manila with a flock of BB-BMC and white-boned chickens laying blue eggs. Remember, the King of Spain had specifically excluded anyone who was not a Catholic from New Spain and his New World. Do you think the crew was going to let that cargo stay on board for the Pacific crossing, let alone what the informants—the snitches—in the crew would have enjoyed doing to the Captain on return to New Spain for breaking the king's edict?

Besides, the Huastecs and the Maya have been separated by 800 km. for over 2000 years, yet they have the similar, 'weird' (to the Spaniards) 15th century Chinese treatments with the BB-BMC chickens. The 'medical' treatment procedures using BB-BMCs are not utilized effectively in Mexico between these separated Maya-speaking cultures. The Olmecs were probably the people who originated the Maya language. Of itself, this way of reasoning is a method of dating the presence of the chicken that has not been used by others. It is tremendously unlikely that witch doctors from one half of this split Mayan language group journeyed and trained the other half in the intricacies of medical (and somewhat dubious scientific) treatments only after the Spaniards had introduced these melanotic chickens, which they did not know about prior to leaving Spain. How is the scientist to feel, when he comes back with foreign field experience and is met by objectivists who would rather follow tradition than allow someone else to lead in scientific discovery?

GEORGE CARTER

Gade's opening and conclusion have interesting and sage comments, but there are a few points that need sharpening.

There is criticism of lack of discussion of mechanisms for transoceanic diffusion. Surely more than navigation and shipping is meant, for that has long been shown to be a non-problem. The term 'nuances' is introduced and is perhaps meant to cover the horde of such things as how many of what kinds of people and the necessary predispositions that are needed to facilitate diffusion. All of us have discussed these items elsewhere. Here, I focused on the chicken; Johannessen, on maize. I would think it regrettable to construe this focus as evidence of our lack of awareness of such problems.

Johannessen's data on maize in India are called 'hypothetical.' I consider them fact and not unexpected facts. Stephen Jett first noted the probability of maize representation in Indian temples, and at that same meeting a Chinese scholar gave a paper documenting the widespread use of maize in the 1400s in South China. Stoner and Anderson, Anderson, Sauer, Jeffreys, and Carter, to mention a few, have presented varied data suggesting the pre-AD 1500 presence of maize in the Old World. Pliny the Elder, who died in the explosion of Vesuvius in AD 79, had described maize as a new grain appearing in Rome in his day. Maize is such an unusual plant that any adequate description becomes definitive, and Pliny gave the essential traits: a big stalk, ear at the side of the plant, tightly wrapped leaves, and with threads coming out at the top of the ear. In the face of all that, it is odd to suggest the possibility that some mythic Indian discovery yet to come might supplant the maize evidence now on the record.

We have equally good data for the pre-Spanish chickens in America. Several scholars have seen the chicken problem as indicating the probability of Asiatic chickens early in America. Acosta and Nordenskiöld both commented on the strange fact that the Indians never used a Spanish-derived name for the chicken, but had their own names for it. Three of these names are clearly Asiatic: *arawak* from India and specific for the melanotic chicken, a Chinese word among the Maya, and another is from Japan. Capa also noted that there is much in the letters of the conquistadors about chickens but that the chickens in America were not much like the Spanish chickens. Sauer's conclusion is worth fuller reporting than Gade gave it. Sauer found Latcham correct in concluding that the chicken was long pre-Spanish in America, and that the kind of chicken was a greatly aberrant form unknown elsewhere. "The Europeans could not have brought it for they did not have it. . . . It survives vestigially as a marker of vanishing Indian cultures." (Sauer 1952, 57-60, with more than I can cover here). Sauer lumped melanotic and blue eggs and was seemingly unaware of naked neck, frizzle fowl, silkies, feather puffed heads, feathered legs, and other Asiatic traits widespread among Amerind fowl and which, in total, suggest plural introductions of Asiatic fowl.

To suggest the Manila Galleon as an alternative explanation to early Asiatic chickens in the Americas runs into a shoal of facts. Consider my discussion in the paper of the name of Atahualpa—'chicken-chicken,' obviously an honorific title and certainly not Mediterranean. Atahualpa died in 1533. The first Manila Galleon set sail in 1565, too late to explain any of this case. I am not opposed to alternative explanations, but they should square with the known evidence. Otherwise, they simply muddy the waters.

There is the interesting question of closure, the final conclusive bit that clinches the case, here, of culturally significant Asiatic contact of great import. The cultural evidence is convincing to many: Needham, Meggers, Covarrubias, Ekholm, Jett, Kelley, and others. I have stayed with the biological evidence (47 papers) only because it totally obviates the independent invention argument.

The final bit in the Chinese contact puzzle is to be found, as I discussed in the paper, in Mike Xu's 1996 work, *Olmec Origins*, published by Central Oklahoma State University Press. A linguist with a deep interest in Chinese history, Xu finds that the Olmec material carries Shang dynasty glyphs. The time is 1100 BC, and that is the date of the appearance of the fully-developed Olmec civilization in Mexico. The lack of developmental stages for the Olmec has vexed the archaeologists for decades. This influx brought the whole gamut of learned men and skilled people, as is evident in the architecture and in the beliefs implied in the art. Here we find the answers to many questions. In this case, it means navigation and shipping capable of transporting thousands of people across the greatest sea that exists, with enormous cultural impact. Professor Xu will have an expanded volume out shortly.

Just such migratory impacts have been suggested at various times, notably by Thor Heyerdahl, David Kelley, Betty Meggers, and, more speculatively, by Harold Gladwin.

It is possible that these Shang dynasty people brought the melanotic chicken ritual so prevalent in the Chinese areas. The identical Mayan beliefs associated with the melanotic chicken have been developed by Johannessen and his Chinese-American colleagues. It is clear that the chicken was a ritual bird of great importance to the Chinese and could have been carried as a necessary religious item. While I think it likely that the chicken-Olmec-Maya-Chinese ritual practices link up, at the moment this is hypothetical but, in my view, not unreasonable.

It is important that the chicken case be seen in the much wider context of other data supporting Asiatic contacts with America, beginning at the time of formative civilizations. A sizable bibliography of relevant papers could be listed, but Sorenson and Raish's enormous bibliography on transoceanic diffusion makes all of this and much more easily available, and no one with any interest in this topic can afford to be without a copy of the new expanded and more critical edition.

SECTION III

Linguistics, Inscriptions, and Glyphs

KENSINGTON STONE
(Courtesy of Runestone Museum, Kensington, Minnesota)

Figure 1a PETROGLYPHS UNDER COVER AT PETROGLYPH PROVINCIAL PARK
Near Peterborough, Ontario

Figure 1b DETAIL OF THE PETROGLYPHS
(Photos courtesy of Ontario Ministry of Natural Resources)

The Identification of the Proto-Tifinagh Script
at Peterborough, Ontario

DAVID H. KELLEY

BACKGROUND

In a presentation at Brown University and in a subsequent long paper, still unpublished, I attempted to show similar problems and difficulties, together with some differences, between decipherment of Proto-Sinaitic of the ancient Near East, well summarized by Benjamin Sass (1988), and the identification and decipherment of Proto-Tifinagh in Ontario, Scandinavia, and northern Italy. I also attempted to appraise particular claims of decipherment and iconographic parallelism among the three areas. In the present paper, I am limiting myself largely to the identification of the Proto-Tifinagh script. The recognition of the existence of a Proto-Tifinagh script in inscriptions near Peterborough, Ontario, and in Scandinavia is entirely the work of Barry Fell (1982a; 1982b; 1984; 1985a; 1985b; 1986; 1987; 1989).

This identification has at least four major implications for culture history. First, it demonstrates that there was a phonetically sophisticated alphabet in existence in Scandinavia in the Bronze Age. Second, it reveals that, although the alphabet virtually died out in its homeland, it was somehow introduced to North Africa where the Tifinagh form is still in use among the Tuaregs and other North African tribes. Third, it shows that users of this alphabet reached the New World. And fourth, analysis of this alphabet as found in all three locations produces little indication of derivation from Proto-Sinaitic or its kin. It now seems to me that the inscriptions at Peterborough probably date between 1000 and 700 BC, much later than Fell thought, but we do not yet have good evidence as to how much earlier the script appears in its presumed Scandinavian homeland. It could even be as early as Proto-Sinaitic, especially if the later date for Proto-Sinaitic is preferred.

Any one of these implications alone is shattering enough to scholars having a strong interest in the specific problem. Taken together, they must either be dismissed as rubbish, or they must be recognized as a substantial contribution to our knowledge of the past, which requires some drastic changes in our perceptions, and perhaps even in our theoretical orientations.

All of these inferences stem from the identification of Proto-Tifinagh at Peterborough and in Scandinavia. They depend in no way upon the decipherment of the script, which requires a very different level of inference. Fell's contention that the script was being used to write some

form of ancestral Germanic depends, in part, on repeated letter sequences (a standard way of recognizing the presence of a script) and on the association of repeated sequences with iconographically similar figures, both at Peterborough and in Scandinavia.

In preliminary decipherments, I think that one is doing well to be correct one time in ten. In *Bronze Age America* (1982:282-287), Fell proposed 94 decipherments of particular words, of which 82 were phonetically read (or reconstructed). I would not be surprised if eight or ten of these were correct. Validation of these would be more than enough to prove that the texts are Germanic. I understand the term 'decipherment' to mean both the first correct recognition and demonstration that a particular script was being used for a particular language, and the continuous process by which scholars determine the details of reading a particular script. Remember that the decipherment of Proto-Sinaitic as Semitic rested for many years upon the decipherment of a single deity name. If any considerable number of Fell's readings of mythological names is correct, then we must suppose not only that a language ancestral to some or all of the present Germanic languages was present in Scandinavia in the Bronze Age, but we must also suppose that the Scandinavian mythology of AD 1000 has amazingly detailed prototypes at about 1000 BC or even substantially earlier.

Of scholars who have worked on these problems, only Colin Renfrew (1987) is apt to be pleased with the linguistic implications of this decipherment. Orthodox linguists and comparative mythologists must be added to the list of scholars outraged by the implications of Fell's work, if Fell is correct not only about the identification of the script, but also about the decipherment. I think that he probably is correct and will shortly attempt to show why.

A third level of interpretation is represented by Fell's attempts at translation. Here, I think, he falls into the errors of a William Foxwell Albright or a Herbert Grimme and furnishes ammunition in abundance to his critics. In Maya studies, it took us about 120 years to get to the point where we could read simple sentences adequately and consistently, despite having perhaps 100 times more material in inscriptions and books and systematic access to meaning. In Proto-Sinaitic studies, it took about 30 years to get to the stage of the useful but error-laden translations which seem to me comparable with what Fell has provided for us. It is time now for competent specialists in the Germanic languages to take over and work on the hundreds of petty details which will have to be resolved before genuinely adequate translations can become available. For myself, I am more interested in what I perceive as massive accomplishments, rather than in criticizing Fell's work. There were some very important defects in Fell's knowledge and understanding of comparative linguistics and in his 'any clue will do' approach to translation. Such an attitude, which slides over inconsistencies and difficulties, is valuable in preliminary decipherment, but becomes increasingly a handicap in later stages of work. Until the importance of the work is recognized, however, these defects will not be corrected.

Fell's work has been met with scholarly vituperation and accusations of racism. It seems to me very unfortunate that scholarly problems about the identification of inscriptions in an ancient script should become associated with matters of academic dogma about the absence of Old World influences in the New World, on the one hand, and with modern problems about the mistreatment of some human beings and groups, on the other. People of European origin have systematically exploited and robbed indigenous people of Asia, Africa, Australia, the Pacific Islands, and the Americas, as well as each other, and there has sometimes been retaliation in kind. Among academicians, however, it is regarded as improper to suggest that such a process occurred in the Americas before the time of Columbus—or to argue that not all relationships between groups of humans must be inimical or exploitative. One can understand that to some people it seems an ultimate theft or indignity to propose that symbols, ideas, and art in the Americas derived, even in part, from external sources. However, the process of adopting and modifying information from other cultures is utterly normal in all other parts of the world, and the evidence suggests to me that the same process occurred, equally normally, in the Americas.

I think that we are all thoroughly mixed biologically and culturally. At AD 800, the number of our ancestors would, except for overlap, exceed most estimates of the total population of the world. It is my personal conviction that, at 500 BC, everyone then living who left descendants surviving to the present is the ancestor of everyone living today. We descend even from such relatively isolated groups as African Bushmen, Australian aborigines, or Congo pygmies, and their ancestors included Europeans and Chinese. Only the number of times that we descend from a particular individual will vary. I would be very surprised if the Scandinavians who came to Peterborough were not among the ancestors of the present Algonquians of the area. I have a possibly naive view that it is good to know as accurately and truthfully as possible what has happened in the past. To be sure, it is possible for vicious and unprincipled people to twist any data away from its proper implications, but I don't think that we

should avoid interpretations because of the possibility that they may be misused by someone else. To me, the fact of contact between different peoples implies nothing about the innate capabilities of members of the two groups.

The Peterborough site has an extensive series of depictions of a wide range of animal and human figures, depictions of artifacts, including watercraft and probable weapons, and a wide range of more arbitrary symbols which are the principal topic of this paper. The inscriptions at Peterborough were carefully drawn by Joan Vastokas, who has kindly allowed me to use her drawings on the condition that I make it clear that she is not convinced that the inscriptions are alphabetic. At the time of the first extensive publications of the materials, by the Vastokases, they thought that all of the carving had been done by Algonquian Indians, a supposition which was certainly the most probable explanation *a priori*, and which seemed to agree with the use of equivalents of some of the symbols by modern Algonquians. Fell's later contention that the site had been produced by Bronze Age Scandinavians seemed, and still seems to most anthropologists, so improbable that it could be dismissed essentially without examination.

Some people have objected that the Peterborough inscriptions are not sufficiently weathered to be as early as the Bronze Age (ending between 900 and 700 BC in Scandinavia). The problem of estimating how fast erosion occurs is a difficult one and may vary greatly even between two parts of a single inscription. Unfortunately, the surface of the rock at Peterborough is very eroded and the degree of accuracy of the Vastokas drawings is visually virtually impossible to check. The technique used was a careful one which should have produced good results. The fact that the many symbols produced by Vastokas match so closely with Proto-Tifinagh can hardly be due to chance, and I do not think that the generic identity of the set can reasonably be challenged, whatever doubts there may be about individual symbols. In Scandinavia, inscriptions on 'hogback' surfaces quite comparable in a generic way to those at the Peterborough site are routinely assigned to the Bronze Age and sometimes to the Neolithic. Some inscriptions show minimal erosion while others are greatly worn. Differences seem to reflect micro-environmental conditions and individual histories much more than chronologically regular factors. Earth cover during any part of the history may offer a substantial protection against erosion. In any case, it seems to me futile to argue that 'can't be' is a stronger position than 'is'. Empirical reality takes precedence over theoretical objections, however strong the latter may seem *a priori*.

It will be shown that there is at Peterborough a restricted symbol set approximating 31 forms, some very rare, that many are repeated with frequency, and that some sequences are repeated. A few repeated sequences seem to be associated with similar representations, but these will not be considered here. These circumstances

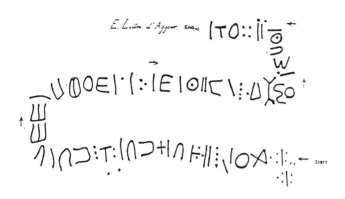

Figure 2 A TIFINAGH LETTER, NORTH AFRICA
Late 19th century
The letter was turned as it was read (Fell 1989:188).

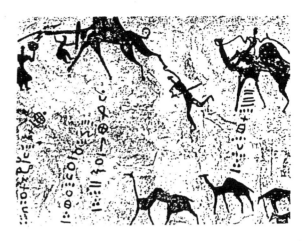

Figure 3 TIFINAGH INSCRIPTIONS, TASSILI, ALGERIA
(Fell 1987:26)

by themselves strongly suggest that the symbols form an alphabet. Of known alphabets, only Tifinagh and Libyan show marked similarities to the Peterborough set. Since the Tifinagh alphabet is little known, I should explain that it is in use at present among Berbers and some other groups in northern Africa, including the Sahara. It is closely related to the ancient script variously referred to as Libyan or Numidian, the most striking difference being the extensive use of dots in Tifinagh where Libyan has bars. In this and other characteristics, the Peterborough set is more like Tifinagh than Libyan. It seems to represent the alphabet from which both Tifinagh and Libyan derived, and the name Proto-Tifinagh strikes me as appropriate for this alphabet.

There are not evident at Peterborough any close similarities to the letters of any of the Mediterranean alphabets derived from Proto-Sinaitic, except in the few cases where Tifinagh itself shows such similarities. Despite what I now perceive as massive evidence for the presence of Proto-Tifinagh at Peterborough, I would not have seen it without Fell's work, and it seems to me entirely understandable that most scholars interested in the site still resist this idea.

Our knowledge of Tifinagh is, of course, crucial to any interpretation of Proto-Tifinagh. But, for a number of factors, Tifinagh is a difficult script even at the present time. Figure 2 shows a modern Tifinagh letter (Fell 1989) and Figure 3, an African rock painting (Fell 1987). The letter is more organized than any Proto-Tifinagh inscription, but it helps to make clear that the rules governing such things as the direction of writing are quite flexible. The painting is, like the carvings at Peterborough, a combination of graphic figures and text, here in clearly delimited columns. Fell suggests that the inscriptions may be later than the scene, but does not give his reasons. Note that three of the columns end in a three-dot triangle and a bar. This is the sort of evidence which is extremely helpful when one is in the preliminary stages of decipherment.

The modern Tifinagh script contains seven letters written entirely with various patterns of dots. It used to be assumed that Tifinagh developed from Libyan, which generally has bars where Tifinagh has dots. I have arranged the letters in Figure 4 (next page) to bring out this substitution between the two series and to show that Tifinagh, rather than Libyan, more closely resembles the prototype. The Tifinagh drawings in Figure 4 are from David Diringer (1948). Barry Fell knew much more about these two scripts than do either Diringer or I, but in presenting new material, I think it is desirable to draw on some neutral source. This figure also shows the forms of the Proto-Tifinagh letters as given by Fell, in two slightly different versions. Fell suggested that the letters are derived acrophonically from the names of objects, but these names for the Tifinagh letters are entirely hypothetical. Though they provide a fine demonstration of Fell's ingenuity, they have little relevance to decipherment and can safely be ignored for present purposes.

Besides Diringer's versions of the Tifinagh and Libyan alphabets, and Fell's two versions of Proto-Tifinagh, Figure 4 includes a column with drawings by Joan Vastokas of symbols from the Peterborough site which seem to me equivalent to the Tifinagh forms, and also to forms from Italy and Scandinavia which will be discussed shortly. The variant forms in the column of symbols drawn by Joan Vastokas include virtually all such symbols known from Peterborough. It should be emphasized that they are not a random collection from a much larger series of geometric forms. I could have included the 'hammer' glyph as a possible letter, and there are one or two other forms which show up once or twice in contexts which are not clearly textual. Possibly some forms which I regard as insignificant variations will eventually be shown to be important.

A more analytical comparison is shown in Figures 5a and 5b. I made a reasonably careful count of the recurrence of the 31 symbols distinguished in Figures 5a and 5b at a 'most probable' level, which came to about 850 letters. This count includes complex forms which look like several letters eroded together, and it omits other forms which look, subjectively, as if intended as complex forms. It also includes judgments about whether series of dots or lines form single letters or are merely parts of letters.

Figure 4 PROTO-TIFINAGH, TIFINAGH, AND LIBYAN ALPHABETS.

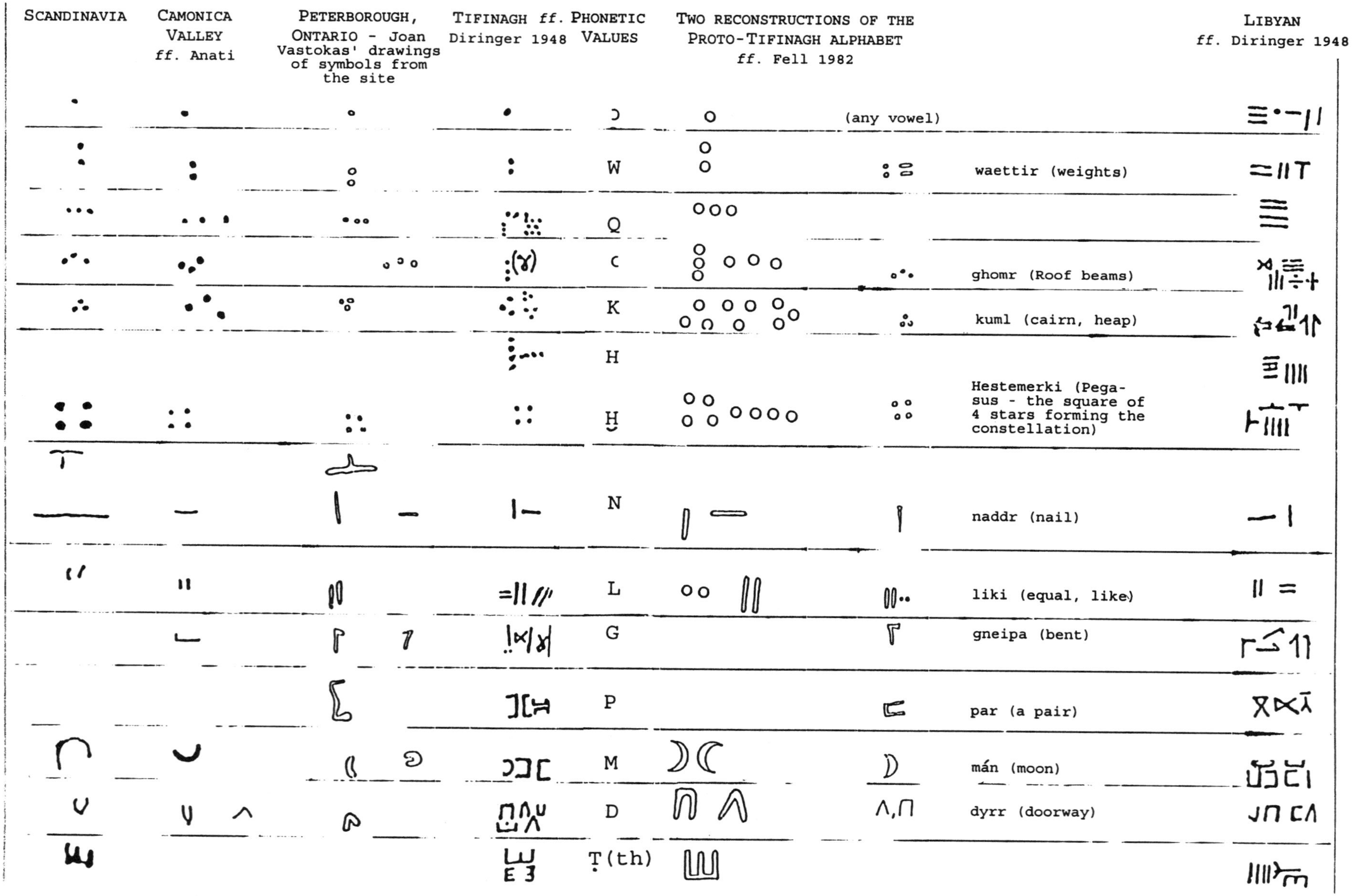

SCANDINAVIA | CAMONICA VALLEY ff. Anati | PETERBOROUGH, ONTARIO – Joan Vastokas' drawings of symbols from the site | TIFINAGH ff. Diringer 1948 | PHONETIC VALUES | TWO RECONSTRUCTIONS OF THE PROTO-TIFINAGH ALPHABET ff. Fell 1982 | LIBYAN ff. Diringer 1948

⊃ (any vowel)

W waettir (weights)

Q ghomr (Roof beams)

C

K kuml (cairn, heap)

H Hestemerki (Pegasus - the square of 4 stars forming the constellation)

N naddr (nail)

L liki (equal, like)

G gneipa (bent)

P par (a pair)

M mán (moon)

D dyrr (doorway)

T(th)

Tⁱ

				Meaning		Phonetic			
		thili (planks, partition)							
		rifa (to split)				T			
		tagg (barbed arrow)				Z (ts)			
		zaun (railing, fence)				Š (sh)			
		Yorsa (Cassiopeia) (the W-shaped group of stars that form the constellation)				Y			
		hringr (ring) also written				R			
		sol (sun)				S			
		bukla (shield, buckler)				B			
						Ẓ, Ṭ			
						Ṣ			
		far (ferry boat)				F			

Some items were omitted because of erosion, probably with some inconsistency. However, even if one takes only the clearest items, I doubt if the count would fall much below 600 letters. This corpus ignores the Scandinavian and Italian Bronze Age materials, where even a casual examination shows texts which were not considered by Fell. I shall be very surprised if future study of those materials does not provide us with a corpus at least four or five times larger than the corpus of Proto-Sinaitic texts of which the total is only about 400 letters. Moreover, these texts are frequently found in association with depictions to which, judging by repetitions which are already apparent, the texts refer. This situation is ideal for semantic decipherment. Fell proposed readings for just under 400 letters at Peterborough. About one fourth of these are items which I did not include in my count. If he is right about any substantial number of these, then my original count could have been well above 1000 letters.

In linguistic studies, it is conventional to mark reconstructions of unattested sounds, words, or meanings with an asterisk, *. For phonetic values of an alphabet, I think it is always acceptable to write either the equivalent modern values without an asterisk, or the postulated earlier values with an *. In this case, it is also desirable to mark in some way those letters which differ in their forms from later Tifinagh and Libyan; I suggest a circled asterisk for this purpose. There is, in such studies, an initial presumption that the phonetic values of the prototype are those of the modern derivative letters. This is not a strong presumption and may be easily refuted by any substantial body of contrary data. Sometimes there seem to be two similar derivatives with different values. Sometimes there are two different forms given the same phonetic values. These factors raise problems which must be considered. There is also a presumption, sometimes easily refutable, that any consistent difference in form probably represents a phonetic difference. Sometimes there is free variation over a rather wide range of slightly differing forms, as seems to be the case with Proto-Tifinagh letter **M**. Sometimes there may be some stabilization into two or three substantially different forms which, nevertheless, seem to have originated as free variants of a single earlier form. A useful place to start the analysis is with the dots of Tifinagh and the corresponding bars of Libyan, as these enter into several other problems.

The discovery of Proto-Tifinagh now reveals that the dot forms are original and the bar forms are systematic substitutions in Libyan. However, Proto-Tifinagh had, besides the dots, a single bar form (presumably for **N**, which is its value in both Tifinagh and Libyan) and a two-bar letter which was **L** in both Tifinagh and Libyan. When the substitution occurred, a two-bar letter replaced the two-dot **W** of Tifinagh. Hence, Libyan had both a two-bar **W** and a two-bar **L**. I think that this factor led to orientation as a distinguishing device between the two letters. In a horizontal text, two horizontal bars became **W**

Figure 5a

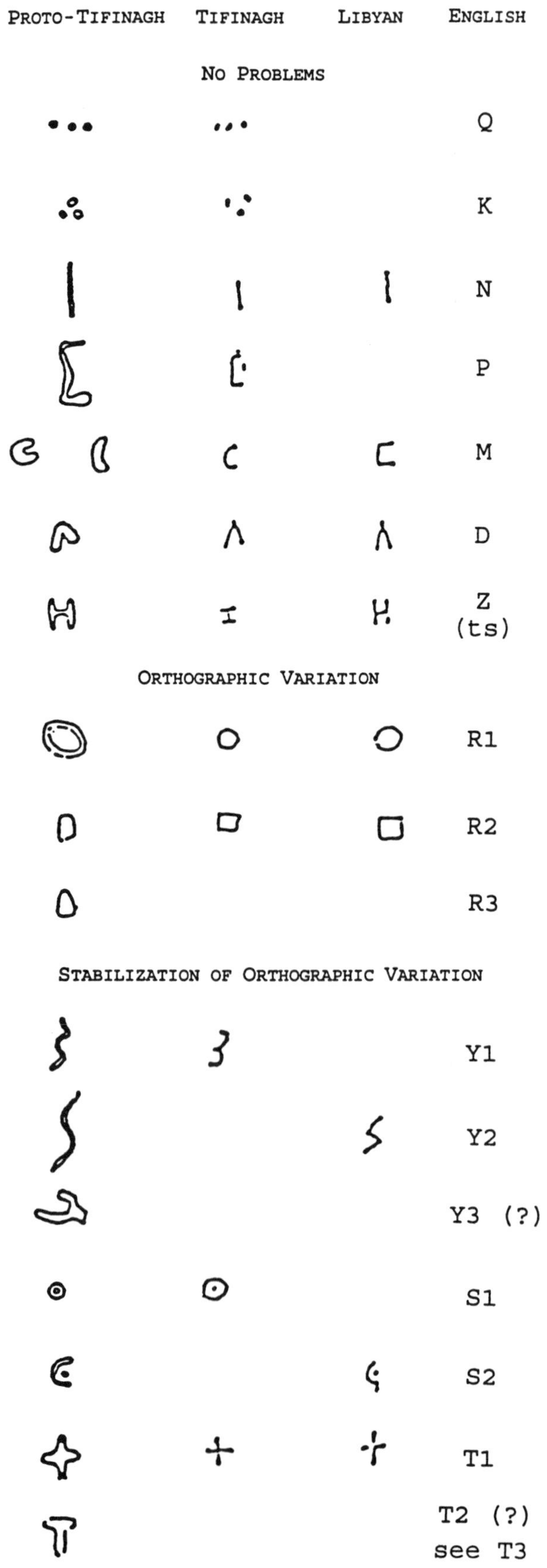

PROTO-TIFINAGH	TIFINAGH	LIBYAN	ENGLISH
	NO PROBLEMS		
•••	•••		Q
•°°	•°°		K
|	|	|	N
ʃ	˙ᴄ		P
ᴄ	ᴄ	⊏	M
ᴇ	ᴧ	ᴧ	D
ᴴ	⊥	ᴴ	Z (ts)
	ORTHOGRAPHIC VARIATION		
⊙	○	○	R1
◖	◻	◻	R2
◖			R3
	STABILIZATION OF ORTHOGRAPHIC VARIATION		
ʒ	ʒ		Y1
ʃ		ʅ	Y2
ᴕ			Y3 (?)
◉	◉		S1
ᴇ		ᴕ	S2
✦	+	ᐟ	T1
⍕			T2 (?) see T3

and two vertical bars became **L**. In a vertical text, two horizontal bars became **L** and two vertical bars became **W**. In some texts, both dots and bars were preserved (though this is not indicated by Diringer). Apparently, two dots, one above the other, in a horizontal text read **W**, in a vertical text **L**; two dots, one beside the other, read **L** in a horizontal text, **W** in a vertical text, thus:

	W	**L**	**W**	**L**
horizontal text	=	||	:	..
vertical text	||	=	..	:

A number of Fell's readings depend upon the presumption that this distinction was already present in Proto-Tifinagh (although even these show some inconsistencies). On *a priori* grounds, I tend to think it more likely that originally two dots, however oriented, were reserved for **W**, and two bars were reserved for **L**. This remains a problem for further investigation.

This brings up a further consideration. It seems probable that there was some sort of basis for replacing dots by bars. In a substantial number of cases, Fell has read a single short bar, clearly drawn as such by Vastokas, as one of the dots of a two- or three-dot letter, and this is certainly what the distribution seems to suggest in some cases. If there were no later substitution of bars for dots, one would think that Fell was simply wrong in these cases; however, at the moment, I think this issue must also be left open.

In later Tifinagh, three dots in a horizontal line (relative to a horizontal text) were read as the stop, ᶜ. If I am correct in thinking that this orientation device is secondary in Tifinagh, perhaps a back derivative from Libyan, where the bars had made it necessary, then **Q** and ᶜ must have been distinguished in a different manner at an earlier date. The Libyan form of ᶜ actually shows a bar between two dots (very like the occasional substitution of a short bar for a dot alluded to earlier) or a long bar between two shorter bars. This suggests the frequent Proto-Tifinagh three-dot letter in which the dots are arranged in a low triangle (.·.), which would be distinguished by form rather than by orientation from three dots in a line (···), or three dots in a high triangle (.˙.). Fell proposed that the vertical line of three dots found in later Tifinagh derives from the low triangle (not found in later Tifinagh); this derivation seems to me virtually certain. Fell read the letter as *Gh, perhaps intended as an equivalent for ᶜ, but he seems to treat this letter as a simple **G**. Linguistic justification for this procedure is thus far lacking.

Effectively, there seem to be no problems (save the practical ones caused by individual cases of sloppy writing) in the identification of the letters **Q, K, N, P, M, D,** and **Z** (Figure 5a). For orthographic variations, the letter **R** recurs in three partially stabilized forms, an open circle,

a rectangle, and a rounded near-triangle shape. These have been designated **R1**, **R2**, and **R3**. The first two occur, apparently, in free variation in both Tifinagh and Libyan, according to Diringer, and the third occurs on a Swedish monument showing Thor fishing for the Midgard serpent. I see no reason to suppose that they are other than free variants at Peterborough. It should be pointed out that the differences between **R**, **S**, and **B** depend upon rather minor interior differences, and that the **S** and **B** likewise show circular and rectangular variants. Erosion may make it very difficult to distinguish among these letters. I believe that all three are present at Peterborough, but am not entirely certain of this.

The Tifinagh letter **Y** is distinct from the Libyan **Y**. The typical form of the latter looks like an orthographic variant of the former with a stroke eliminated. Both forms are present at Peterborough. It seems reasonable to assume that they were in free variation and that one stabilized into the conventional form for Tifinagh, the other into the Libyan form. I have called these **Y1** and **Y2**. **Y1** also appears in Libyan with the value š (**sh**). This is its value in the Mediterranean alphabets derived from Proto-Sinaitic, and is a good example of how such scripts have influenced Libyan and, to a lesser extent, Tifinagh. There is a third form which Fell has identified as **Y**, which could be an orthographic variant of the middle section of **Y1**. I am not entirely convinced of this, but have labelled it **Y3**. I think that **Y1** and **Y2** are certainly identified, but that some doubt should be maintained with respect to **Y3**.

Like **Y1** and **Y2**, the case of **S1** and **S2** shows a partially stabilized variation between a circle or rectangle with a dot in the center, and a half-circle or crescent partially enclosing a dot—an incomplete form of the prototype. The Tifinagh variants for **S** correspond to **S1**; the Libyan variants for **S** correspond to **S2** and a number of other forms. The **S1** version appears in Libyan for **B**, adding to the confusion. **S2** certainly occurs at Peterborough, and I think that **S1** does as well, though the clearest apparent example of this could be intended for an **R1**, with a double circle outline, rather than an interior dot.

The simple cross is very rare at Peterborough, but it does seem to occur, although with some erosion on all examples. I have identified it as **T1**. A tau-shaped form, which could be regarded as a cross with one arm truncated, appears rarely at Peterborough. It is not an attested variant of **T** in Tifinagh or Libyan, but I have called it **T2** on purely orthographic grounds. It is quite possible that it is not a **T** at all and even possible that it is some sort of ideograph or depiction of a tool. It is formally like a Libyan version of **W**, but if my understanding of how bars replaced dots in Libyan is correct, this must be presumed to be an accidental convergence which has nothing to do with the presence of **T2** at Peterborough.

Now, some phonetic problems must be considered (Figure 5b). The stop, ᵓ, appears as a single dot in Tifinagh. It seems to me that there is no reason not to accept this, but Fell read it variously as **I**, **A**, or 'any vowel.' I cannot understand why he did this. Fell repeatedly emphasized that Tifinagh and Libyan are consonantal scripts. The stop, ᾿ , is a perfectly good phonemic consonant. It appears and disappears in texts rather erratically but not in any way which remotely suggests to me that it was substituting for a vowel, either a specific vowel or as a generic vowel indicator. Even if some such usage had developed later, it would be exceedingly unlikely for it to extend back to the prototype. This reading of Fell's must be rejected.

The letter **G** is given the value ***GN** by Fell, based on various proposed decipherments. It would be at least mildly surprising if two phonemes in combination were written by a single letter, but I do not think that the suggestion can be rejected *a priori*. In at least one case, Fell has written this as representing the **NG** of long-(boat); however, English **ng** is a single phoneme, neither **N** nor **G**, and has only an orthographic relationship with them. This letter *might* stand for ***GN**, or might stand for ***NG**. It is exceedingly unlikely that it stands for both, and I see no very good reason for supposing that it doesn't stand for **G**, although this would mean that certain of Fell's interpretations would have to be rejected. For the moment, it may be written either **G** or ***GN** or ***Ng**, but with the clear understanding that the latter two interpretations are unproven and can't both be correct.

One of the most interesting problems is posed by the fact that Tifinagh **Ḥ** is composed of four dots in a rectangle, while Libyan **Ḥ** is formed of a bar with a line in the center at a right angle. The forms are utterly distinct, and I cannot believe that they arose by orthographic variation; yet, both are almost certainly present at Peterborough. It is hard to be absolutely certain that four dots, somewhat carelessly grouped into a rectangle, are not two groups of two each, or a group of three accompanied by a single separate dot, but the four-dot rectangle does seem to be present. If both this letter and the bar with line attached are present at Peterborough, there is a very strong presumption that they represent two distinct consonants. However, both four dots in a line and the four dots in a rectangle of Tifinagh correspond to four bars drawn in the same way in Libyan. This suggests that four dots in a rectangle are an orthographic variant of four dots in a line, which is, indeed, how they appear in Fell's first table. In that case, one may presume that the differentiation of four dots in a line for **H** in Tifinagh and four dots in a rectangle for the phonetically similar **Ḥ** was a secondary development and that both were originally ***H**. The form which survived in Libyan for **Ḥ** must be presumed to have preserved the original consonantal value of that letter. I think, therefore, that we should always write ***H** for the four dots in a rectangle, that four dots in a line may be written **H**, and that the Libyan form may be written **Ḥ**.

Fell interpreted a wrench-like letter as an ***R**, presumably on the basis of some proposed decipherments. I think it corresponds fairly well to a Libyan letter used for **T** (Th).

Figure 5b

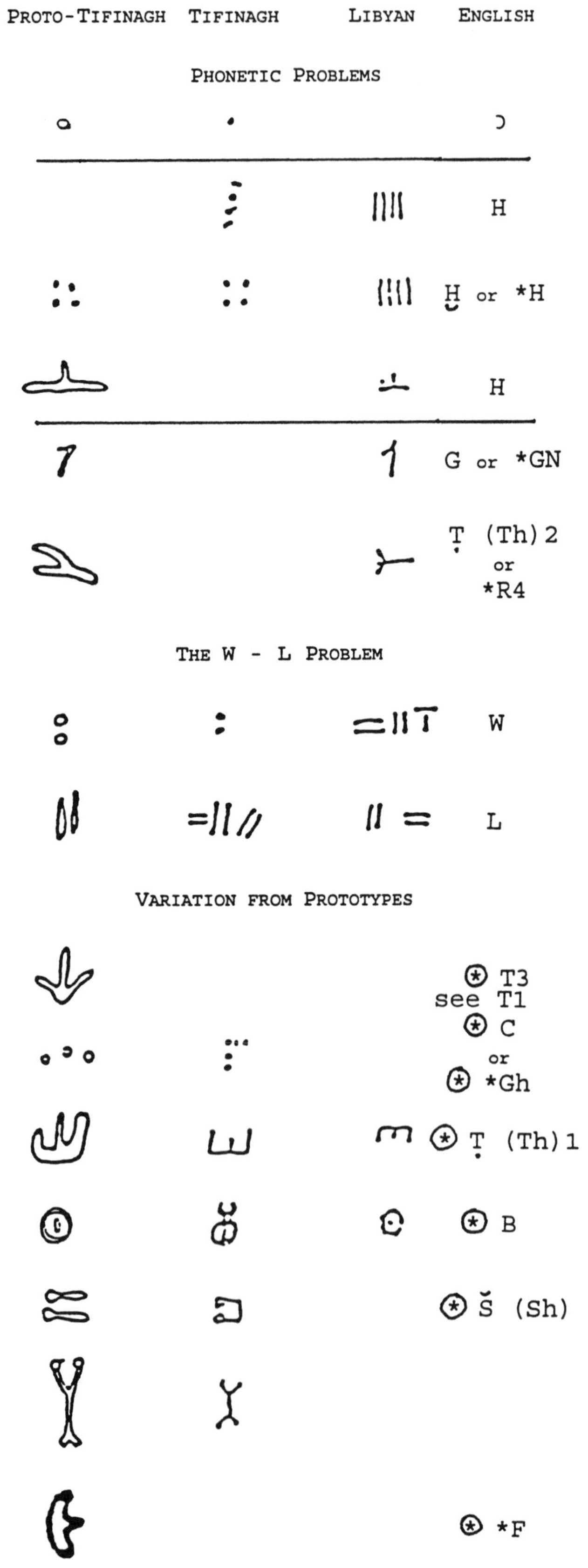

PROTO-TIFINAGH	TIFINAGH	LIBYAN	ENGLISH

PHONETIC PROBLEMS

It does not seem to me likely to be an orthographic variant of the usual form of Libyan and Tifinagh Ṭ; if not, then it should represent a sound close enough to Ṭ so that the two might fall together. The letter is orthographically distinct from the series **R1**, **R2**, **R3**, and Fell maintained that it represents a phonemically distinct **R**. He assigned the **R1**, **R2**, **R3** series to the sound represented in Scandinavian orthography by **Hr**, and this wrench-like letter to the 'other' **R**. For reference, I suggest that it might be referred to either as ***R4** or as Ṭ**2**. It could be a dental **R**, which could appear in conventional script as **Tr** or **Dr**.

The Libyan second **Z**, sometimes read Ṭ, is structurally identical to the one occurrence I have noted at Peterborough where, however, it seems to be part of an amalgamated series of letters. Although it is inconvenient not to have a reference name for this letter, I am reluctant to assign one without a better understanding of the phonetic value.

The Tifinagh letter Ṭ (Th) is absent from Peterborough (though present in a Scandinavian text (Figure 4). It, however, shows a close formal resemblance to the letter shown as ***Ṭ** (Th) 1, which I regard as the prototype of the Tifinagh and commonest Libyan forms, as identified by Fell.

I am again in agreement with Fell that the probable prototype for the barred circle and crescent, which is Tifinnagh **B**, is to be found in the Scandinavian barred circle. The Peterborough form which I have equated seems reasonable to me, but could be **R1-N**.

Fell's ⊕ ***F** is surely present as a letter at Peterborough and is the only one which has no certain or probable derivative in Tifinagh or Libyan. It has a vague similarity to the Libyan second **Z/Ṭ**, but that seems to be a borrowing from the Punic **Y**, assigned to a different phonetic value.

The doubled bars with dots on the end could conceivably be read as two bars, **L**, plus two dots, **W**—or as one bar, **N**, plus one dot, ͻ, plus **N**, plus ͻ, but it looks like a unity. In that case, it must be the prototype of Tifinagh **š** (sh), and the bar joining the two parts of the Tifinagh letter may have been added to make sure that it was read as a single letter. Although there are no extremely good parallels for **Y3**, **T2**, or ⊕ ***F**, the match seems otherwise far more clearcut than the match between Proto-Sinaitic and its modern derivatives.

Figure 6a SOME PROTO-TIFINAGH INSCRIPTIONS
Peterborough, Ontario

These inscriptions were not considered by Barry Fell in his published work. Texts are from Joan Vastokas; transcription into Tifinagh letters as given by Diringer; English transcription by DHK.

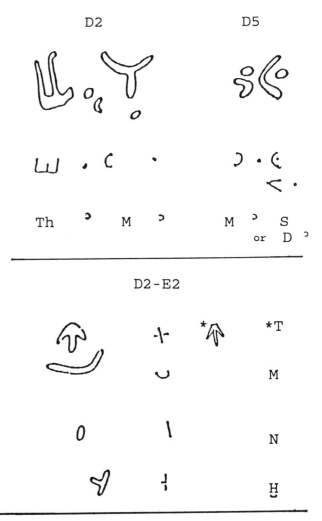

Figure 6b SOME MORE PROTO-TIFINAGH INSCRIPTIONS
Peterborough, Ontario

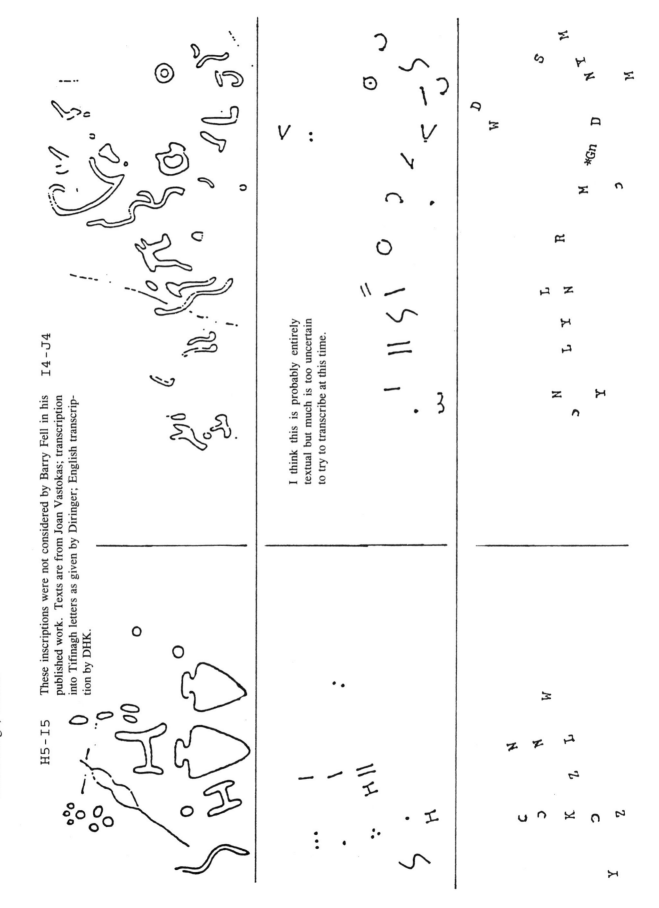

H5 – I5   These inscriptions were not considered by Barry Fell in his   I4 – J4
published work. Texts are from Joan Vastokas; transcription
into Tifinagh letters as given by Diringer; English transcription by DHK.

I think this is probably entirely
textual but much is too uncertain
to try to transcribe at this time.

In Figures 6a and 6b, I show a number of texts from Peterborough, as drawn by Joan Vastokas, which occur in relative isolation. None of these was considered by Fell. I have shown a transcription of these into the forms of historic Tifinagh letters, as drawn by Diringer, and a further transcription into our letters. By themselves, I think that they provide utterly convincing evidence that the inscriptions of Peterborough are written in the Proto-Tifinagh alphabet.

Fell drew parallels, both linguistic and iconographic, between the carvings of Peterborough and many carvings of Scandinavia, especially Bohuslan (in Sweden, near the Norwegian border). I have placed in Figure 4 a column of Proto-Tifinagh letters derived from the two Scandinavian

inscriptions in Figure 7, which have not been mentioned in any of Fell's publications. When this degree of correspondence can be found so easily, the presence of the Proto-Tifinagh script in Scandinavia must be accepted, completely aside from any questions of parallel texts and decipherments. Fell has also pointed out generic similarities of composition between Peterborough and the great carved rock panels of the Camonica Valley in the Italian Alps, near the amber route from northern Europe.

Examination of Anati's popular book (1961) on the Camonica Valley reveals a host of additional parallels both to Scandinavia and to Peterborough. Many of these are extremely arbitrary and extend to style as well as iconographic content. A quick examination of Anati's book showed

Figure 7 PARALLEL INSCRIPTIONS FROM ONTARIO, SCANDINAVIA, AND ITALY

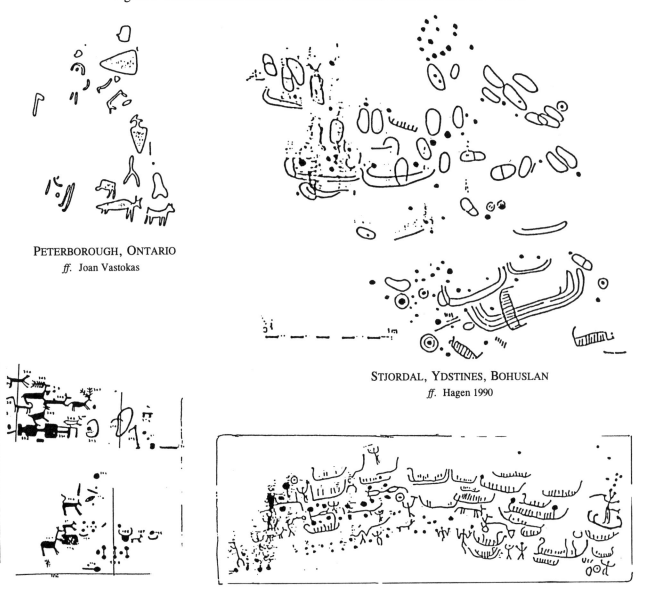

PETERBOROUGH, ONTARIO
ff. Joan Vastokas

STJORDAL, YDSTINES, BOHUSLAN
ff. Hagen 1990

CAMONICA VALLEY
ff. Anati

SOLBERG, SKJERBERG, OSTFOLD
ff. Hagen 190:164

the presence of at least eighteen of the Proto-Tifinagh letters, some in rather helter-skelter compositions with tools, animals, and people, like some of the less orderly texts at Peterborough and in Scandinavia. These have been included in Figure 4. No attempt has been made to complete the alphabetic set from other works on the Camonica Valley. To show the rather haphazard way in which the texts, animal and human figures, and tools tend to be interspersed, Figure 7 shows a brief segment from Peterborough with comparative material from Italy and Scandinavia.

CONCLUSIONS

What we have in the Proto-Tifinagh inscriptions of Peterborough, Scandinavia, and Italy are the consonantal skeletons of words, normally without word boundaries, which may be read left to right, or right to left, or up and down, or in more complicated word orders, such as *boustrophedon*. We could understand the texts so much better if the scribes had marked word boundaries and always used a similar reading order. Vowels would have made interpretation so much easier and less ambiguous. The absence of these characteristics which we value may be deplored, but something as complex as a script is not invented immediately at the highest level of perfection, nor were the scribes' values necessarily ours. Some ambiguity may have been not merely tolerated, but desired. Writing was a mystery with magical powers, and it was designed for people who knew the language which was being written and knew probably, or certainly, the topics of discussion. It was not intended to be immediately intelligible to everyone. Under these conditions, even determining approximately what language was being written is a major achievement.

The discovery of the existence of alphabetic texts of the Bronze Age in Scandinavia and Italy and Peterborough, Ontario, is a major break-through in our knowledge of culture history. It is natural to want to move immediately from a knowledge of the literacy of Bronze Age people to a knowledge of what the texts say. This requires a very different level of inference. Specialists may be happy to say 'it says **S-L-D-R**'—in three different places—but non-specialists want more. Fell gave them more, in abundance. At the moment, nobody can be reasonably sure of how much of that 'more' is valid. The contribution would still be a major one if none of the additional interpretations were valid. I think that some of the additional interpretations *are* valid and that the decipherment as Germanic is reasonable and even probable, but the conclusions will need a great deal of testing by competent specialists before that conclusion can become validated with enough assurance for general acceptance. In subsequent work, I shall attempt to appraise suggested decipherments of individual words in considerable detail. Here, I will only say that, after careful examination, none of the suggestions seems to me absolutely compelling, but that there are a few sequential repetitions of letters and some contexts which seem to me to accord very well with suggested interpretations. These do not constitute a large enough proportion of the texts to be more than highly suggestive.

REFERENCES

Anati, Emmanuel
    1961   *Camonica Valley*. New York: Alfred A. Knopf, Inc.
Diringer, David
    1948   *The Alphabet*. New York: Philosophical Library, Inc.
Fell, Barry
    1982a   *Bronze Age America*. Boston and Toronto: Little, Brown & Co.
    1982b   The Bohuslan Culture (Bronze Age Norse) in North America. *Epigraphic Society Occasional Publications* (ESOP) 10:17-29.
    1984   The Bronze Age cult of thunder gods. *ESOP* 12:65-70.
    1985a   The Tifinagh coinage of King Offa of Kent. *ESOP* 14:102-3.
    1985b   Tifinagh legends on Hiberno-Danish coins. *ESOP* 14:134-5.
    1986   Tifinagh letters on coins of the ancient Britons (Letter of Lionel H. Atkinson with brief comment by Fell). *ESOP* 15:16.
    1987   A Tifinagh text at Tassili, Algeria. *ESOP* 16:26-7.
    1989   Deciphering the Easter Island tablets, Part 1. *ESOP* 18. (Tifinagh letter, p.188).
Hagen, Anders
    1990   *Helleristnigar i Noreg*. Oslo.
Renfrew, Colin
    1987   *Archaeology and Language*. Cambridge University Press.
Sass, Benjamin
    1988   The genesis of the alphabet and its development in the second millenium B.C. *Aegypten und altes Testament* 13. Wiesbaden: Otto Harassowitz.
Vastokas, Joan M. and Romas K. Vastokas
    1973   *Sacred Art of the Algonkians*. Mansard Press.

American Indian Languages before Columbus[1]

MARY RITCHIE KEY

INTRODUCTION

The American Indian cultures comprise vast groups of peoples on two continents from Alaska to the tip of South America. This impressive array includes hundreds of languages still spoken today throughout the Americas. In South America, the languages can be grouped into more than a dozen different language families, though many have not yet been classified or are dubiously classified. Much of history has been lost or unknown in the past 500 years, and we can only make educated guesses about the number of languages and the population size of the Indian groups who lived in the Americas in 1492. Presently, the Indians of South America live in a variety of altitudes, from sea level to 12,000 feet above; and in a variety of climates: dry and wet, desert and jungle, icy cold and blistering hot. In this amazing ecological diversity, outstanding thinkers and inventors had been building Indian civilizations of a very high order, long before Columbus was born.

This presentation will treat languages of South America for the most part, with occasional reference to the Uto-Aztecan family of Mexico and the United States. I believe that one of the reasons that language relationships have not been discovered, or established effectively, is that the data are too scattered. The South American linguistic material available nowadays is published all over the globe, in various publications, and in various alphabets and scripts. When I worked with one South American language recently, I had to deal with four orthographies that were used in the publications, including a PhD thesis, a practical dictionary for use in literacy classes, and technical articles written with different phonetic symbols for various audiences.

PROPOSITION FOR ORIGINS

Concerning the origins of American Indian languages, I assume that important migrations affecting the New World took place before writing was invented in the Old World. Intercontinental migrations could have continued after writing was invented, without being recorded. It was more important for seafarers to know how to read the movements of the stars and the currents of the sea than it was to know how to write. Pizarro conquered Peru, but he was not reputed for his education. It is also possible that information about migrations might have been archived in libraries that have been burned throughout history.

I assume multiple migrations, and layers of migrations.

The result to linguistics is confusion. When the same language migrates at different times, the changes that occur may seem to be sporadic, making it appear that there is no pattern. The obvious and easiest explanation for this kind of 'mess' is that similarities between languages are due to chance or coincidence. When there is historical or archaeological evidence, scholars may correctly identify the disturbing variations. For example, English has two words that are similar: 'wine' and 'vine.' Historical documents show that both words derive from a common source, but at different times, and through different languages, with resultant differences in both pronunciation and meaning. The spectacular differences in the vocabularies and linguistic structures among families of languages in South America would seem to defy any such satisfactory explanation. In my view, the impressive array of variation indicates that migrations took place over a long period of time.

I propose, further, that in prehistorical times migrations took place by various routes across the Atlantic Ocean, in addition to the Bering Strait route, and that evidence can be found in ancient languages of the Old World. Examples from Hittite and Sumerian suggest that their predecessor(s) were the same as the ancestor(s) of at least some American Indian languages. Finally, I propose that large quantities of data are not needed as evidence for common origins. The perseverations which are evidence of historical relationships from pristine times can be discovered in a small inventory of basic building blocks which are maintained as the core of a semantic system.

METHODOLOGY: SOUNDS AND MEANING

Three principles have guided my thinking in my linguistic research and in my teaching. In linguistic classes I have repeated these principles often, particularly when we dealt with solving problems and encountering new data. The answer to a problem, or a theoretical explanation must: 1. cover all the data; 2. not be contradictory; and 3. be the simplest explanation possible. The first principle keeps one honest. It is not necessary to have an answer for everything, but one must not sweep things under the rug. What cannot be explained is humbly filed in 'Residue.' The second principle is obvious: the explanatory proposals must not be contradictory. The third, the principle of simplicity, is difficult to apply sometimes, because one may be dealing with a type of situation that is six of one, or half-a-dozen of another. Nevertheless, we should remind ourselves that the most elegant statement is a simple one.

I don't have to remind readers that all research should be done with careful judgment and great humility. One can unwittingly misunderstand or misuse even sound principles. Take an example from biology. The wings of birds and the wings of insects appear to be similar. So much similarity could lead one to conclude that the simplest explanation, the third principle, is that the two items compared are from the same origin. But, alas, the wings of birds and insects are analogues which do not have common origins and structures. Yes, research is fraught with pitfalls.

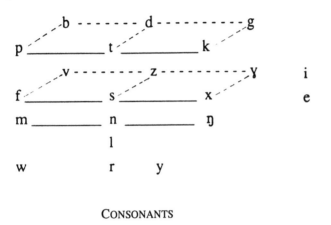

CONSONANTS

VOWELS

Figure 1 BASIC PHONETIC CHARTS

The raw data for linguistics center around sounds, grammar, and meanings. Early phonetic charts based on scientific principles were crude, of course, as all first attempts of theory are rough around the edges. It took a century or so to develop the science of sounds and come to a reasonable theory of phonetics, and we now have a rigorous way to describe the sounds of any language in the world. The phonetic chart in Figure 1 is based on this development; such a model can be used to discuss languages in general. There are some languages which actually have fewer sounds than are on this chart. There are also, of course, languages which have more. In such cases, the basic sounds shown here are modified, expanded, and distributed in various ways, exhibiting more complex systems. But a basic chart such as that in Figure 1 can be modified and used to describe and compare all languages of the world.

Note that the arrangement of the symbols on the chart is asymmetrical in places, but one can still see *system* in the framework of series (horizontal) and orders (vertical) of the entities. One can also see relationships in the system when one observes that all the consonant sounds in the first column are *labial* sounds, produced with the lips. At the opposite side of the consonant chart, in vertical arrangement, are sounds produced in the back of the mouth, the *velar* area. There is another kind of relationship holding

the system together that has to do with how the sounds are produced, that is, the manner of articulation. The upper two horizontal lines are made up of sounds that are produced with a stoppage of air, and these are called 'stops.' The next two lines display *fricative* sounds, those produced with friction. Following are *nasals*, *liquids*, and *semivowels*. Another dimension is represented on the chart, showing that voiceless /**p t k**/ are related to their counterparts /**b d g**/ by voicing, or vibration of the vocal cords.

A chart of vowels is also a part of the linguist's equipment, and it is constructed on the basis of articulation. Essentially, the proofs that comparative linguistics engenders are based on: 1. inventory of sounds, and 2. how the sounds operate together in a system. That is, we don't deal with sounds in an **ABCDEFG** fashion, which is useful for compiling dictionaries or playing the piano. This is not a complete course in phonetics, but it is enough to illustrate that every language has an inventory of sounds, and these sounds relate to each other in a systematic network that can be rigorously documented and tested. I have been explicit in explaining this phonetic network, because it is crucial to understanding my next point.

SEMANTIC MODEL AND PERCEPTION

The analysis of a semantic system should also expect to find relationships among the entities. In linguistics this can be illustrated easily in phonology, as we saw above in the model for sounds: /**p**/ is to /**m**/, as /**t**/ is to /**n**/, and /**k**/ is to /**n**/ (Figure 1). This kind of interdependency can also be seen in the analysis of social and political systems when the investigator ferrets out connections or networks.

The discipline of Historical or Comparative Linguistics was built upon the predication that words to be compared must be similar in both sound and meaning. But I want to take it further than that and say that the comparisons must be compatible with a semantic theory that attempts to explain how the lexical entities are intermingled in a network. The analysis, then, deals with the inventory, or 'building blocks,' if you please, and it also makes statements such as the above: **A** is to **X**, as **B** is to **Y**, and **C** is to **Z**. With the givens of the predictable/unpredictable human being, this goal is easier stated than achieved. We have seen that such a goal has been realized in phonetics and phonology for the most part, but there is not anything like it to apply to the analysis of *meaning* in languages of the world, to say nothing of comparative studies dealing with semantic structures of two or more languages. I believe that eventually we will see that the semantic network can be mapped through languages that are related, in much the same way that phonological patterns can be mapped among languages that are related.

In a series of papers presented since 1986, I have set forth some premises and considerations that such a theory might contain. It comprises a model based on perception, that is, how human beings perceive themselves and their world. The linguistic output reflects the built-in neurological hardware that controls the senses: how people see, hear, and feel. Anatomical configurations are a part of all human beings' consciousness, no matter what language they speak, and these concepts figure in the network of meaning. The 'head' is 'on top' in every language of the world; the 'feet' are 'below, under' in every language of the world. These corporeal markers are inextricably intermingled with the perceptions of *space* and *time*; together they provide a cognitive rationale for human beings to view each other and their environment. Linguistically, the *corporeal* morphemes (or words) are extended to natural elements, and to psychological needs. Thus, the 'top, peak' of the mountain may be referred to with the morpheme for 'head,' and 'below' is the 'foot' of the mountain. The 'head' or chief of the clan is uppermost; subordinate members provide the 'hands' so the community can function.

These corporeal labels are seen throughout the American Indian languages, and indeed our own language, if we stop to think about it. Such elements of a semantic system are universal in that all human beings have the same kind of brain, with the same senses, that make speech and interaction possible among people. The brain is very efficient and controls a tight, cohesive system that works!

An example of the close connection of *space* and *corporeal* vocabulary is often seen in location markers, such as 'behind, inside, center,' which are also used for body parts. Words that deal with space, such as 'hole, covering,' are often anatomical vocabulary. In Sumerian, this is illustrated in the following sets, where the same morpheme (or word) is used for labels on both sides of the equal sign: behind = body; front = eye; inside = heart; middle, center = waist; hole = body orifice.

A similar concept and design can be observed in American Indian languages, and one concludes that the reference to body parts is a principal way that human beings perceive space. The term 'shape morpheme' is often used in descriptions of American Indian languages, and this term is also useful to explain the glosses in one of the Hittite dictionaries (Güterbock and Hoffner 1980:21). Hittite /**lala-**/ is given seven meanings, grouped around the glosses, *tongue,* meaning 'speech, slander,' and *blade,* meaning 'knife, ingot,' presumably because of the blade-like shape. Giuseppe Verdi's *Rigoletto* captures the essence of this juxtaposition in bringing together the tongue and the dagger in a masterful use of simile with a complex basis of analogy. The librettist puts words in the mouth of the tragic character of the hunchback jester, suggesting the common

denominator of the tongue, *lingua,* and the dagger, *pugnale*:

> We are equal!
> I, the jester, and he the murd'rer!
> I stab with cold derision,
> He with the dagger.[2]

From this quite marvelous little speech we can infer the cognitive processes that underlie 1) function: they both can kill—by gossiping or by stabbing; and 2) shape: they both have a similar form. We could learn much from the instincts of poets and artists.

The spatial arrangement of the human body figures in how people view the world, and it also may figure in mythical or supernatural beliefs. A simple formula can be used to show how pristine concepts are adapted and applied in the linguistic labeling of the world we live in:

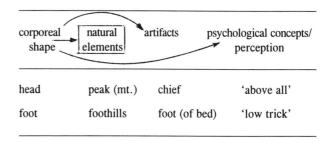

head	peak (mt.)	chief	'above all'
foot	foothills	foot (of bed)	'low trick'

Figure 2 FROM CORPOREAL SHAPE TO PERCEPTION

The Incas used the metaphor of the human body to understand their community and belief system (Bastien 1987: 68). They used toponyms relating the mountain to the body: the upper level of the mountain has an /**uma**/ 'head,' /**nawi**/ 'eyes,' and /**wayra**/ 'mouth'; the central level has a /**sixa**/ 'stomach,' and /**sonko**/ 'heart'; and the lower level has /**čakis**/ 'legs,' and /**silʸus**/ 'toenails,' which are indentations on the river. In a similar manner, the Hittites deified their mountains, which had backs like humans. This is illustrated in Gurney (1952 [1966]:143). The term for 'back' or 'mountain ridge' /**iškiš-**/ was also used for the 'ridgepole' of the house in Hittite (Hoffner 1967:60).

COMPARATIVE LINGUISTIC APPROACH

Comparative linguistics is a well-established discipline that has developed a reliable methodology over the last two centuries. No one doubts its validity and competence when applied to recognized language families. Essentially, it deals with the relationships of sounds and meanings as they are exhibited in two or more languages. Languages can be shown to be genetically related when lexical items exhibit sounds which occur in the same phonological space (according to the phonetic chart) and meanings which are similar enough to be considered in the same semantic space. An example is the word for 'foot' in Indo-European languages—English, German, and Spanish:

/**foot** : **fuss** : **pata**/, which provide the consonant formulas: **f** : **f** : **p**; and **t** : **ss** : **t**. These formulas must recur over and over again in the vocabularies in order for them to be included in the rules of language change between the Germanic languages, English and German, and also between the Germanic family and the Romance family, which includes Spanish. When comparative linguists analyze the similarities that they observe in the data at hand, they must note whether or not the similarities exhibit the formulas found among the cognates, or whether the similarities are spurious. The key to establishing the formulas is the word 'recurring.' Complete predictability is not possible, because languages are always in a state of flux. Dialects, for example, may by-pass the expected formulas. Loanwords present problems: at times they follow the formulas, and at times they do not. Note again the words 'wine' and 'vine'; one reflects the results of common origin, while the other reflects the results of borrowing. Comparative linguistics is one of the best examples of order and randomness working together to show system on the one hand, and variability on the other hand. At times, we can explain the rule change; at other times the change is not explainable, at least by our present techniques.

History and archaeology corroborate what comparative linguists tell us about the derivation of closely-related languages from the same origin. Such relationships are accepted without doubts among scholars. The questions that I have been dealing with have to do with distant relationships, and with lesser-known languages, and this moves into areas of uncertainties and unknowns. As comparativists, we know too little about language change from a global perspective, that is, how theories of Historical Linguistics may apply to non-Indo-European languages. We have not had much time to put the methodology to the proof and to examine the outcomes. Is it reliable at the level of stocks or phyla? How many millennia can it go back to show historical relationships?

In a study of Hittite and English, and Hittite and Spanish, I have shown that one can find evidence that structural features have remained intact for 4,000 years (Key 1988). Hittite is known to be genetically related to these European languages. Now, is it possible to do such a study with languages that are not known to have a common origin? I propose that it is possible, and I present here some of the evidence I have accumulated that can be scrutinized, in the same way that we can examine ancient Hittite and present-day English.

Briefly, the principles for comparative work state:

1. Words to be compared must have something in common, though exact meaning is not required. A cognate set may include, for example, 'foot-words' that group lexical items of that part of the body, such as 'leg, ankle, heel,' or functional items such as 'path, trail, walk.' Cognate sets of 'water-words' include a long list of such labels as: 'liquid, river, rain, urine, tears, juice, bathe' and others.

2. Onomatopoeic vocabulary is not useful for showing relationships; it simply shows how the brain reacts to the world. Symbolism may be in the area of sound, in words that typify repeated sounds: 'laugh, suckle.' Symbolism may also represent movement, in words such as 'earthquake, lightning, butterfly.'

3. A good comparative study may have a list of cognates that is made up of something like 600–800 sets. One of the tenets I hold in attempting to show relationships is that large masses of data or hugely complicated statements are not needed. Only a few crucial formulas in both phonetics and semantics are necessary to meet the scientific requisite of simplicity. It is more important to reveal the semantic network than it is to display huge quantities of data. The core vocabulary avoids the 'brie and chablis' vocabulary and deals with basic cheese and wine.

South America is several times closer to the Old World than it is to the Bering Strait. Seaworthy sailors of the Mediterranean would not have been intimidated by the wide-open ocean to the west. The Mediterranean Sea was the Center of the Universe to several cultures in ancient times. The Hittites had an expression that referred to the 'Four Corners of the World'—a word that was based on angles of the shoulder. The Inca empire also incorporated the concept with their term *Tawantinsuyu*, 'Four Corners of the World.'

Migrations between continents have to contend with ocean currents and air currents, and these reverse themselves under certain conditions, as we know, for example, from the tricky behavior of the El Niño phenomenon. It remains that we are fairly ignorant about what actually flowed across the natural highways of ocean currents in prehistorical times. Moreover, we know little about maps that might have secretly existed. Along with map makers, it seems that sea captains, fishermen, spice-traders, and gold-hunters didn't want to advertise their finds to others. Undoubtedly they had knowledge of distant or obscure lands that were not drawn on maps produced for the public.

Figure 3 GEOGRAPHY AND LANGUAGE MIGRATION

From a linguistic point of view, the realistic picture about migrations to the Americas and to the Pacific Ocean areas can be diagrammed as follows. Questions remain, of course, about the original place(s) of the birth of language.

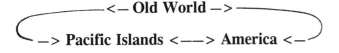

Figure 4 FLOW OF WORLD MIGRATIONS

In this presentation I am assuming that migrations might have moved across the Atlantic into North America as well as South America. I am also assuming that people might have gone both north and south across the Panamanian bridge, as well as along both coasts. Therefore, in the following linguistic examples, I may refer to North America, using data from my Aztec dictionary, and also from the Uto-Aztecan database which has been accumulating since 1959 and is by now a very reliable resource (Miller 1988).

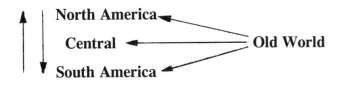

Figure 5 DIAGRAM OF NEW WORLD ENTRANCES

Five locations are noted on the following map of South America (next page): The capital letters **A B C D E** identify areas where examples from my linguistic studies show similarities between American Indian languages and Hittite, Sumerian, and ancient Indo-European. The letter **A** represents any or all of North America and borders of South America. The letters, **B**, **C**, **D**, **E**, are placed at the mouths of river systems which have been chosen for their potential as entrances into South America. The mouth of the Amazon, at the letter **C**, appears to be the most likely path into the interior, and its drainage area is subdivided roughly into three areas: C_1, C_2, C_3.

Several languages and language families have been identified with entrance locations. Onward travel would have been regulated by difficulty of access, with regard to barriers such as mountain ranges and swamps. Locations must be regarded tentatively and with discretion, as one would do with a pilot study. In fact, we do not usually know the prehistorical movement of these groups. If a linguistic group is now located between rivers, we may not know which river was the place of entrance.

Roughly, the languages are located as follows:

A. North American Aztec and Uto-Aztecan; Chocoan and Barbacoan, the coastal languages of Colombia and Ecuador.

B. Languages of the Orinoco River basin, and river pathways reaching up into the foothills of Colombia. Also languages of eastern Venezuela (some neighboring with Brazil) and languages of the Guianas.

C. Amazon River basin:

C_1 covers the area directly across the continent and into northern Peru, where some Tucanoan languages (bordering on Colombia) and some Arawakan languages are spoken.

C_2 includes the area of rivers running through northern Bolivia and incorporates the Panoan and Tacanan languages along the Purus and Madre de Dios Rivers. This grouping reaches up into the Andes and includes Quechuan, Aymaran, and Chipaya languages, which have many similarities with Tacanan languages. (Old Inca ruins are found in the Tacanan areas.)

C_3 covers the Brazilian jungle areas of rivers flowing into the Amazon from south of it.

D. Languages of the Paraná River system, in Paraguay, including Guaranían. Also Kaingáng of Brazil, and languages of the Chaco area.

E. Languages of the tip of South America, including those that might have moved up rivers and even across the mountains to Chile.

VOCABULARY EVIDENCE

I present here some of the core of basic building blocks that can be thought of as potential evidence for common origins of American Indian and Old World languages, with access across the Atlantic Ocean. The examples of distant relationships cited in this paper are drawn from my comparative files which have been accumulating since 1975. The following represents a fraction of the hundreds of basic vocabulary similarities. Additional evidence has been offered by many others, as I have noted in my 1991b article, "A World Map of Hypothesized Language Affiliations." I feel certain that many of us will continue to amass the significant evidence. The data will be tested and tried; they will be winnowed and refined over time. As happens in research, some examples will be discarded as not viable. If the general thesis holds up, we will move on to determine classifications.

Migrant people immediately claim new land by naming it; and place-names around the great Amazon River basin include many occurrences of the morpheme /**pa**/,

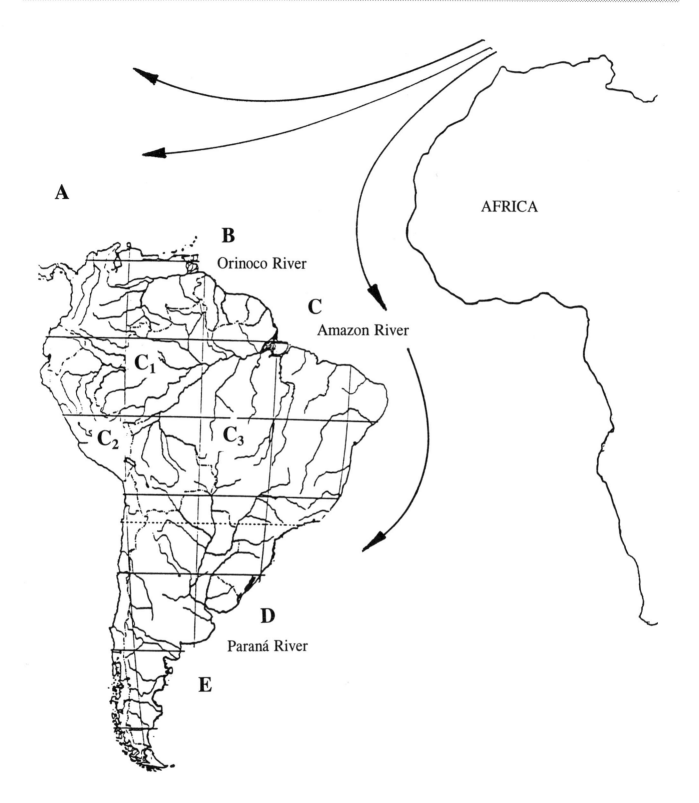

Figure 6 POSSIBLE LANGUAGE MIGRATIONS TO SOUTH AMERICA

which means, variously, 'water, river, sea' etc. Present-day languages still widely exhibit the morpheme in words that imply the presence of water, such as 'swamp'. The morpheme is used in combinations with other morphemes to construct 'water-words,' such as /**pará**/ 'sea, river' in Guaraní (map **D**); /**paraña**/ 'sea,' also in Guaraní; /**palaa**/ 'sea' in Guajiro (Arawakan, map **A**); /**pʰaran**/ 'ocean' in Wapishana (Arawakan, map **B**); /*****paro**/ 'river' in Proto Panoan (map **C₂**); /**pania**/ 'water' in Epena-Saija (map **A**); /**palaxa**/ 'rain' in Yagan (map **E**).   The morpheme is probably very ancient. I do not believe that it is an accident or coincidence that the Sumerian language also had a morpheme /pa/ that means 'river.' Thousands of years ago, this label was widespread in Europe; it is known to have been used in ancient times in hydronyms, in combination with other morphemes, in the same way that similar constructions occur in the Amazon region. The morpheme /pa/ also occurs in North America; it is well-known as the proto form for 'water' in the Uto-Aztecan languages. It is found in place-names in San Diego county, California, in such Indian sites as *Pala* and *Pauma*.

Water-words are important to an agricultural people, as were the Sumerians in the 'Cradle of Civilization,' who dominated and controlled the flooding of the Tigris and Euphrates rivers with canals and masterful waterworks. There was also remarkable agricultural engineering in South America, where superior earthworks are still held in awe by geographers and archaeologists. In Bolivia and Colombia, among other places, ancient history has left its mark. When flying over the area, one becomes aware of aboriginal earthworks built up to form ditches that fill with water during the rainy season. Long causeways, mounds, and tens of thousands of ridged fields are still visible, evidence of large Indian populations who controlled the seasonal flooding by digging ditches and raising the land for passageway and planting.

Agricultural people have many uses and labels for 'grain, seed.' The word was /še/ in Sumerian. A similar form occurs in South America, for example: /šixe/ in Eseexa (Tacanan, of Bolivia, map **C₂**); /*šiki/ in Proto Panoan (Peru and Bolivia, map **C₂**); and /*zɨ/ 'seed' in Proto Jê (Brazil, map **C₃** and **D**). Proto Aztecan (North America, map **A**) has /*s n-/, a form that occurs in several related vocabulary forms.

Another marker of place-names is a morpheme which occurs in Quechua names, and is found on maps, in the form of *-marca*. In Proto Quechua (map **C₂**), the term /*marka/ means 'town, place.' It also occurs in Aymara of Bolivia and Peru. The Uru-Chipaya people lived in the region of Lake Titicaca, where drained fields and causeways are still identifiable. This was the area of the marsh-dwellers who constructed boats with high curled prows. The Chipaya people of Bolivia call the related Uru people who lived south of Lake Poopo, the *Marcamaz*, 'fellow countrymen.' In Hittite, the morpheme /mark-/ means 'boundary' and is used in many lexical items with the meaning of dividing or separating or setting apart.

Many South American kinship terms are similar to Old World forms, such as: /na/ 'female (relative)'; /tata/ 'father, grandfather'; /koko/ 'grandfather, uncle'; /baba/ 'grandparent, grandchild'; /toto/ 'uncle'; /dom(o)/ 'ancestor'; /kena, kina/ 'relative'. The terms are glossed variously, according to the particular kinship system represented. For example, /koko/ may mean 'grandfather' in one language and 'uncle' in another language.

The importance of the sexual dynamic is seen throughout semantic structures. It is not unusual in languages in general, for the sex organ to symbolize the person; thus the morpheme or word for 'male' or 'female' may also serve for the body part. Hittite does this, as noted below. In American English, the word *man* can occur as a euphemism for the body part, as it did recently in a television comedy show, with the right intonation pattern and expression of wide-eyed innocence: "I had never *seen* a man before!" Some South American languages also function in this way, as illustrated here, though not because of the Victorian inhibition, of course. Cayapa is a Barbacoan language of Ecuador (map **A**); and their term for *man* is /lʸu-pu/, which is analyzed, literally, as 'penis-is'. Other forms for *man* in South America are: /lukkunu/ in Lokono (Arawakan, map **B**); /*runa/ in Proto Quechua (map **C₂**); /*ulʸu/ 'penis' in Proto Quechua (map **C₂**); /lu-/ 'father' in Wayapi (Tupian, map **B**). Chipaya (Bolivia, map **C₂**) uses this morpheme for several male kinship terms: /luktaka/ 'man'; /luko/ 'husband'; /lukmaxč/ 'boy.' In Sumerian the word for 'man' is /lu/. Significantly, the term for 'female' has parallels in both Sumerian and in South American languages. The Barbacoan languages of Ecuador (map **A**) have several examples of the morpheme /su, so/ 'female, vagina' in the kinship vocabulary: in Cayapa /su-pu/ 'woman'; in Colorado /so-na/ 'woman (*lit.*, 'vagina-is'); and also in the entries for 'girl, sister, daughter-in-law, widow.' These are comparable to Sumerian /sal/ 'pudendum/a.'

The term for 'tongue' is often related to 'penis,' undoubtedly because of the shape characteristics also noted by the hunchback jester in *Rigoletto*. In the Chocoan languages of southern Colombia, the same morpheme /-me/ serves for 'tongue' and 'penis.' The Sumerian term for 'tongue' is /eme-/. In Hittite, the same connection is made, though the similarity is a cognitive one, not a phonological one. In Hittite, 'tongue' is /lala-/; and '(erect) penis' is /lalu/. Resemblances are found in several South American languages, particularly in Chipaya (Bolivia, map **C₂**) /las/ 'tongue'; in Proto Quechua /*kalʸu/ 'tongue'; in Proto Quechua /*lani/ 'penis.' Similar examples occur in other languages.

Terms for body parts are known to be especially useful in comparative linguistic studies because they comprise a semantic group of words that maintain with vitality throughout the millennia. Everyone has them! Such terminology is not likely to be borrowed. An example from Hittite is the word /pata/ 'foot,' which compares readily with Spanish /pata/. Several language families of South America have a morpheme for 'foot' which can easily be compared with Hittite: /pata/ in Panare (Chibchan of Venezuela, map **B**); /*-pɨ/ in Proto Tupi Guaraní (map **D**); /*par/ in Proto Jê (map **C₃** and **D**); /padi/ 'footprint' in Araona (Tacanan family of Bolivia, map **C₂**).

Some vocabulary items show a cross-over in meaning

when words reflect the mythology or belief system of a people. The words for 'sun, moon, star' are particularly variable, because of their potential for functioning with supernatural connotations. 'Sun' and 'moon' also may have temporal associations, and thus can mean 'day' and 'month' respectively. 'Sun' is associated with warmth, shining, and fire, providing another network of cognates that challenge the linguist thousands of years after the connections were established. In South American languages, the morphemes /ti/, /ra/, and /ta-ta/ appear to figure in the associations of 'god (Dios)' and 'fire.' In Kaingáng, a southern Jê (= Gê) language (map **D**), the word for 'sun' is /rã/.

In presenting these examples, I am working from the premise that all South American languages can eventually be shown to be related, although this evidence has not yet been definitively established. The actual linguistic material contains hundreds of examples of American Indian vocabulary represented by the ones presented here. The Sumerian and Hittite material is limited to some extent because of the state of research and time-consuming publication in these unfolding fields. Moreover, the comparative linguistic study of language migrations to the Americas is hampered because so few scholars of ancient languages are conversant with American Indian languages and vice versa.

HISTORY OF IDEAS

There is an important history concerning studies that have attempted to show linguistic and cultural relationships between the American continents, as well as between the Americas and the Old World (Key 1991b). The amount of evidence is an embarrassment of riches, a cornucopia of interesting data. I looked at some of these references a few years ago and was impressed with the plausible data that had not been thoughtfully considered in a scholarly way. These attempts have not been taken seriously; they have been repeatedly rejected, but not always for valid reasons. The studies have been treated with derision and suppressed so effectively that textbooks and reputable scholars in general do not refer to any viable global connections. Nonetheless, it is not a reasonable assumption that there were no historical connections between the American continents and between the Americas and other parts of the world, and the substantial data call for further research. If linguistics cannot give definitive answers, at least it can suggest hypotheses that can be further explored to reconstruct something about the origins, history, and migrations of the American Indians.

The overwhelmingly dominant position regarding the connection of the American Indian with the Old World has been the assumption that they all came over the Bering Strait from Asia. It would appear that the exclusive stance of the one-route migration theory grew out of our justifiably revered, and otherwise noteworthy, Smithsonian Institution,

where this inflexible position was held earlier in this century. Gordon (1990:76) tells how he met the influential "dean of American archaeology," Ales Hrdlicka. In Gordon's own words:

His dogma was that Old World man entered pre-Columbian America by only one route: across the Bering Strait. Unless a young anthropologist subscribed to that view, it was virtually impossible for him to get a museum or university job in American anthropology or archaeology.

The authoritative stance discourages other perspectives.

CONCLUSIONS

There is evidence to be dealt with, which until recently had not entered the main stream of linguistic research. Each time a wave of migration took place, a new culture was born. This is the history of mankind; and it continues today. We can speak of cross fertilizations of cultures, fruitful fusions that often caused creative spurts and produced new cultures and new languages.

This is why it is difficult to label the language families, stocks, and phyla(s), and even more difficult to label the prehistorical languages that we suspect are part of history. We don't have names for the people and languages that preceded the known history of Sumerian, Hittite, Akkadian, Assyrian, Ugaritic, Eblaite, Etruscan, Egyptian, and other ancient cultures of which we know only a little.

Here I will relate a little parable about Red Marbles. Primitive morphemes act as particles that become scattered throughout the semantic system of a single language, and, with time, become dispersed throughout all the languages that derive. It is as though a large bag of colored marbles is held in the possession of the original language. Half of the marbles are colored red, the basic marble-color, and the other half are of various colors. The marbles are mixed well, and by handfuls the marbles are scattered abroad in different directions. A new language emerges from each handful. Because there were so many red marbles, each language receives a portion of red, along with varying mixes of other colors. If there were just a few turquoise marbles in the original bag, then some languages would not receive any turquoise marbles. If there were quite a few blue marbles, several languages would receive a generous portion of blue. All the lanuages would continue to reflect something of the original red. It is possible that this is what we see now in languages: vestigial remnants of the red in some languages, and a vast array of combinations of shadings and colorings in the sister and cousin languages (Key 1989:70).

There will be those who disagree with my conclusions. I don't regret this; an atmosphere of debate will give balance to our research and our discussions. Indeed, doubt is one of the healthiest characteristics of the work of a careful scholar. It is not to be feared, but welcomed, as we were reminded by the late Richard Feynman. Absolutely essential in our work is to maintain a tentative attitude in our 'conclusions.' Anyone who regularly reads the newspaper knows that we keep discovering something else about 'Eve.'

The quincentenary is a good time to take a hard look at the information that has been gathered in the last five hundred years. We now can reappraise what has been said about the languages and peoples of the Americas.

Finally, I would like to depart slightly from the usual ending of a technical paper and leave you on a poetic note. I believe that one of the beautiful things about our lives in academia is that we can blend poetry, music, and the arts with a rigorous scientific approach to our data. So I will present a little poem called *Security* written by William Stafford.[3]

SECURITY

Tomorrow will have an island. Before night
I always find it. Then on to the next island.
These places hidden in the day separate
and come forward if you beckon.
But you have to know they are there before they exist.

Some time there will be a tomorrow without any island.
So far, I haven't let that happen, but after
I'm gone others may become faithless and careless.
Before them will tumble the wide unbroken sea,
and without any hope they will stare at the horizon.

So to you, Friend, I confide my secret:
to be a discoverer you hold close whatever
you find, and after a while you decide
what it is. Then, secure in where you have been,
you turn to the open sea and let go.

END NOTES

1. This paper was first proposed for *America Before Columbus*, the Columbian Quincentenary Conference sponsored by the New England Antiquities Research Association (NEARA), with George F. Carter as Honorary Chairman. The celebration of Professor Carter's 80th birthday brought forth an expanded version, presented at the Association of American Geographers in San Diego, California, April 1992, in a session arranged by Stephen C. Jett. This paper complements the other, which has additional examples of Sumerian and Hittite and further rationale of comparative linguistics.

2. *Rigoletto,* 1957, music by Giuseppe Verdi; libretto by Francesco Maria Piave. New York:G. Schirmer, p. 5.

3. From the book *Passwords* by William Stafford. Copyright 1991 by William Stafford. Reprinted by permission of Harper Collins Publishers.

REFERENCES

Bastien, Joseph W.
1987 *Healers of the Andes: Kallawaya Herbalists and Their Medicinal Plants.* Salt Lake City: University of Utah Press, 198 pp.

Buck, Carl Darling
1949 *A Dictionary of Selected Synonyms in the Principal Indo-European Languages: A Contribution to the History of Ideas.* Chicago: University of Chicago Press, 1515 pp.

de Barenton, Hilaire
1932 Les radicaux primitifs des langues: Conservés dans le Sumérien: ou lexique Sumérien-Français. *Etudes Orientales, No. 7: L'Origine des Langues: des Religions et des Peuples.* Paris: G. P. Maisonneuve, 116 pp.

Gordon, Cyrus H.
1990 A Hebrew inscription authenticated. Pp. 67-80 in *By Study and Also by Faith,* Vol. I. J. M. Lundquist and S. D. Ricks, eds. Provo UT: Deseret Book Company.

Gostony, Colman-Gabriel
1975 *Dictionnaire d'Étymologie Sumérienne et Grammaire Comparée.* Paris: Editions E. de Boccard, 204 pp.

Gurney, O. R.
[1952] 1966 *The Hittites.* Baltimore MD: Penguin Books, 240 pp.

Güterbock, Hans G. and Harry A. Hoffner, eds.
1980-1989 *The Hittite Dictionary: of the Oriental Institute of The University of Chicago,* Vol. 3, fascicle 1, pp. 1-96(1980). Vol. 3, fascicle 2, pp. 97-224(1983). Vol. 3, fascicle 3, pp. 225-352(1986). Vol. 3, fascicle 4, pp. i-xxx; 353-477(1989). Chicago IL: The Oriental Institute of the University of Chicago.

Hoffner, Harry A., Jr.
1967 *An English-Hittite Glossary.* Paris: Klincksieck, 99 pp.

Key, Harold and Mary Ritchie Key
1953 *Vocabulario Mejicano de la Sierra de Zacapoaxtla, Puebla.* México, D. F., Instituto Lingüístico de Verano, and Dirección General de Asuntos Indígenas, 232 pp.

Key, Mary Ritchie
[1963] 1968 *Comparative Tacanan Phonology: With Cavineña Phonology and Notes on Pano-Tacanan Relationship.* The Hague: Mouton, 107 pp.

1979 *The Grouping of South American Languages.* Tübingen: Gunter Narr, 170 pp.

1980-1981 South American relationships with North American Indian languages. *Boletín de Filología* 31:331-350, Part I, Homenaje a Ambrosio Rabanales. Santiago, Chile: Universidad de Chile.

1981 North and South American linguistic connections. *La Linguistique* 17.1:3-18.

1984 Polynesian and American linguistic connections. *Edward Sapir Monograph Series in Language, Culture, and Cognition 12. Supplement to Forum Linguisticum* 8.3 (April), 80 pp.

1986 *A Semantic Study of Basic Morphemes in Comparative Linguistics.* Paper presented at the Third Biennial Symposium on Linguistics and Semiotics, Genetic Classification of Languages. Houston TX: Rice University, 32 pp.

Key, Mary Ritchie
 1988 The cockroach syndrome: Phonological and semantic
      stability throughout the millennia. Pp. 43-64 in *The Four-
      teenth LACUS Forum.* S. Embleton, ed. Lake Bluff IL: Lin-
      guistic Association of Canada and the United States
      (LACUS).
 1989 Language origins and the red marble theory. Pp. 67-72
      in *Studies in Language Origins,* Vol. 1. J. Wind, E. G.
      Pulleyblank, E. de Grolier, and B. H. Bichakjian, eds. Am-
      sterdam: John Benjamins.
 1991a *Language Change in South American Indian Languages.*
      Philadelphia: University of Pennsylvania Press, 297 pp.
 1991b A world map of hypothesized language affiliations. Pp.
      159-173 in *Studies in Language Origins,* Vol. 2. Walburga
      von Raffler-Engel, J. Wind, and A. Jonker, eds. Amster-
      dam: John Benjamins.
Key, Mary Ritchie, ed.
  In preparation. South American Indian languages, Vol. I, of
      the *Intercontinental Dictionary Series.*
Kramer, Samuel Noah
 1963 *The Sumerians: Their History, Culture, and Character.*
      Chicago: University of Chicago Press, 355 pp.

Miller, Wick R.
 1988 *Computerized Data Base for Uto-Aztecan Cognate Sets.*
      Salt Lake City UT: University of Utah, 382 pp.
Puhvel, Jaan
 1984 *Hittite Etymological Dictionary,* Vols. 1-2. Berlin:
      Mouton, 504 pp.
 1991 *Hittite Etymological Dictionary,* Vol. 3. Berlin: Mou-
      ton, 461 pp.
Sjöberg, Åke W., ed.
 1984 *The Sumerian Dictionary: of the University Museum of
      the University of Pennsylvania,* Vol. 2 "B". Philadelphia:
      Babylonian Section of The University Museum, University
      of Pennsylvania, 220 pp.
Walker, C. B. F.
 1987 *Cuneiform.* Berkeley: University of California, and
      British Museum, 64 pp.
Weeks, David Michael
 1985 *Hittite Vocabulary: an Anatolian Appendix to Buck's
      Dictionary of Selected Synonyms in the Principal Indo-
      European Languages.* PhD Dissertation. Los Angeles
      (UCLA) CA: University of California, 279 pp.

Early Eurasian Linguistic Links with North America[1]

ROGER WILLIAMS WESCOTT

The 'early links' referred to in the title of this paper are connections that preceded the Viking visits and the Spanish colonization of the past millennium. And the 'linguistic links' are primarily lexical, rather than typological or graphonomic, in nature: that is, they consist of vocabulary rather than of speech-structure or of writing systems. Our discussion will therefore exclude the western European vernaculars that now dominate the Western Hemisphere and the Yupik Eskimo vernaculars that make it easy for Yupik speakers on opposite sides of the Bering Strait to understand each other.

The polemic context of the paper is one that contrasts two divergent schools of linguistic thought as regards linguistic genealogy. The more conservative school is one that I term isolationism. Linguistic isolationists generally recognize a large number of so-called 'linguistic isolates'—that is, individual languages (such as Basque in Europe, Sumerian in Asia, and Meroitic in Africa) which cannot be consensually subsumed under any of the conventionally recognized familial rubrics, like Indo-European, Semitic, or Cushitic. In addition, isolationists usually regard these language-families as being themselves isolated, in the sense that they cannot be subsumed under yet higher taxonomic categories. From an isolationistic standpoint, Indo-European, for example, cannot be combined with Uralic or Altaic to form the supra-familial category which, almost a century ago, Danish linguist Holger Pedersen called 'Nostratic' (1903).

The converse of isolationism may be called phyleticism. Phyleticism is the view that language groupings, even when they consist of many languages and cover extensive territories, can usually be included in still larger groups, known as phyla, as is the case with organic taxa, both plant and animal. The most extreme form of phyleticism is called monogeneticism (or monogenism, for short). Monogenists, following Alfredo Trombetti, hold that all of the world's spoken languages have a common source—a single language which eventually differentiated to yield thousands of languages (Trombetti 1905). This position is termed 'extreme' by linguists only because most of them do not hold it. In biology, monogenism is not only 'moderate' but standard: most biologists assume that the millions of species known today were once a single species.

When the vocabularies of two or more languages resemble each other on a large scale, the resemblances are almost certainly due either to common inheritance or to borrowing. Common inheritance implies that the languages are descendants of a single 'mother tongue' which,

in time, gave rise to daughter tongues. In some cases, such as that of French and Spanish, the ancestral language, Latin, is documented. In other cases, such as that of German and English, the ancestral language, usually called Proto-Germanic, has to be reconstructed. But either way, the ancestral tongues are 'dead languages'—that is, vernaculars which are no longer colloquially used. The acquisition of inherited vocabulary is analogous to the more general process that anthropologists call enculturation, the acquisition of culture by children. In each case, the acquisition fills a behavioral void rather than altering behavioral patterns already established.

Lexical borrowing is invariably due to culture contact between speakers of different languages. The apparent cause of the borrowing is a perception on the part of the speakers of the receiving language that the borrowed vocabulary, whose components are termed 'loan-words,' expresses ideas or labels objects more effectively than does the inherited vocabulary. The most dramatic influx of borrowed vocabulary in English came with the Norman invasion of Britain in the 11th century. While Old French words like *chair* and *table* or *beef* and *pork* did not entirely replace the native Anglo-Saxon words *stool* and *board* or *cow* and *pig*, they succeeded in conveying an air of mobiliary and culinary sophistication that the inherited words did not. The acquisition of borrowed vocabulary is analogous to the process that anthropologists call acculturation, the adoption of elements of one culture by members of another culture.

When lexical borrowing is so heavy that it enters not only the technical periphery but also the basic core of a people's vocabulary, it is sometimes called creolization (Anttila 1972:176). Some historical linguists think that the best explanation of the huge difference between the Old English of the 'Dark Ages' and the Middle English of the 'Middle Ages' is that Middle English was essentially a creolized—that is, simplified and 'foreignized'—form of Old English, adapted for speakers of Norman French.

The only hypothesis in terms of which some Native American vocabulary can be regarded as having been inherited (rather than borrowed) from Eurasia is that of monogenesis, proposed, as noted above, by Trombetti. Monogenists find some basic word-roots to be universal, appearing widely in both the Eastern and Western Hemispheres. Among these are:

tek	finger	**kun**	dog
man	hand	**mek**	big[2]
pet	foot		

These lexical items stand out not only because they are elemental in nature but also because they appear both in Amerind[3] and in Indo-European languages including English. English derivatives of these roots are indicated below:

tek	*cf.* English	*teach*
man	*cf.* "	*manual*
pet	*cf.* "	*foot*
kun	*cf.* "	*hound*
mek	*cf.* "	*much*[4]

The means by which this basic vocabulary reached the New World is almost certainly migration from Eurasia to a North America devoid of human population. The migrants were probably hunters and gatherers who left the Old World well before the advent of farming. The most likely route that they took was across the Bering Strait between Siberia and Alaska. Because this population movement presumably took place during the Pleistocene Ice Age, the consensual view is that these first Americans then traveled southward, down an ice-free corridor between the Cordilleran Glacier Complex to the southwest and the Laurentide Ice-Sheet to the northeast (Wenke 1990: 199). In keeping, however, with my own 'ponticism' (the hypothesis that early man was drawn to large bodies of water) (Wescott 1995), I prefer the minority view that the migrants kept to the Pacific shore of North America—at least until they reached unglaciated regions that permitted them to follow river courses into the interior of the continent.

Eventually, these newly native Americans occupied most of the land from the Pacific to the Atlantic coast. Whatever Eurasian vocabulary they acquired after this time must be regarded as borrowed rather than as inherited.

Of the various Amerind language families, the two which seem to me to provide the most convincing evidence of linguistic borrowing are the Penutian and the Uto-Aztecan. The Penutian languages are spoken from Alaska to New Mexico. The Penutian subfamily, which seems to contain diffused Eurasian vocabulary, is the California group consisting of Wintun, Maiduan, Yokuts, Miwok, and the extinct Costanoan.

Many linguists maintain that, of all semantic clusters, the one which is most fundamental is composed of personal pronouns (whether morphologically free, as words, or morphologically bound, as affixes). If they are right, we should look first at the personal verb endings in Miwok, which have the meanings 'I,' 'thou,' 'we,' and 'ye.' In Central Sierra Miwok (spoken due east of San Francisco Bay and due south of Lake Tahoe), these forms are (Callaghan 1980:35):

1st person singular	**-m**
2nd person singular	**-s**
1st person plural	**mas**
2nd person plural	**-tos**

In Proto-Indo-European, as consensually reconstructed (and held to have been spoken no later than 3000 BCE), the corresponding forms are:

1st person singular	**m(i)**	1st person plural	**-me(s)**
2nd person singular	**-s(i)**	2nd person plural	**-te(s)**

Although Catherine Callaghan regards this four-fold paradigmatic correspondence as coincidental (Callaghan 1980:39), I consider such extensive coincidence unlikely.

On the other hand, this apparent pronominal cognation need not oblige us to conclude that a group of prehistoric Indo-Europeans crossed the Pacific in the 4th millennium, landing in San Francisco Bay. Another name for Nostratic, the more inclusive rubric under which 'long rangers' classify Indo-European, is Mitian (Ruhlen 1987:259). The reason for this synonym is that the first person pronoun is reconstructed as **mi** and the second person pronoun as **ti** in Proto-Nostratic (Bomhard and Kerns 1994). And it may be that the pronominal infusion into Miwok was made not by Indo-Europeans but by more easterly Nostratians, such as the Manchu, the Chukchi, or the Japanese.[5]

Personal pronouns, however, though they form a tight lexical complex, are few in number. A more extensive semantic field is provided by the hunting lexicon of the California Penutians generally—not only the Miwok but the Wintuan, Maiduan, Yokutsan, and Costanoan peoples as well (comprising a total of about 20 tribes). This lexicon exhibits a broad emphasis on shamanism and a more specific focus on the institution of the sweat-lodge (von Sadovszky 1983:516-530). Representative examples of this lexical complex are these Proto-California Penutian forms:[6]

not	arrow
tolt-	spiritual power
kel	sweat-lodge

In Otto von Sadovszky's view, California Penutian, despite its largely Amerindian vocabulary, is essentially a displaced Uralic language, genealogically related to Finnish, Estonian, and Hungarian. More precisely, he holds that California Penutian belongs to the Ob-Ugric sub-branch of the Uralic family, a Siberian group that includes Ostyak and Vogul (von Sadovszky 1989).[7] And it must be admitted that there are striking lexical correspondences between California Penutian and Ob-Ugrian. In fact, the correspondence between lexical sets in California and Siberia often constitutes identity, as in the case of the triad just cited, compared with the one below:

Ostyak	**not**	arrow
Ostyak	**tolt-**	shamanic power
Vogul	**kel**	sweat-house

Where Sadovszky sees cognation, however, I am inclined rather to see linguistic borrowing. Were California

Table I POSTULATED COGNATES (von Sadovsky)

Miwok	mi	what?	Proto-Uralic	mi	what?	Turkish	-mi	what?
Wintun	'el	no!	Proto-Uralic	el-	no!	Mongolian	ül-	no!
Wintun	qol	tongue	Proto-Uralic	kel-	tongue	Mongolian	kel-	tongue
Costanoan	saw-	sing	Proto-Uralic	saw-	sing	Uighur	sav	sing
Nisenan/ Maidu	di	louse	Proto-Finno- Ugric	täj-	louse	Turkish	ti-	louse
Costanoan	ur-	husband	Proto-Finno- Ugric	ur-	male	Old Turkish	ur-	male
Nisenan/ Maidu	bun-	hair	Proto-Finno- Ugric	pun-	hair	Manchu	fun-	hair

Penutian languages actually Ob-Ugrian in a genealogical sense, one would expect them to exhibit extensive Ob-Ugrian vocabulary in semantic core-areas such as demonstratives, body organs, and kin terms. But little such vocabulary is evident.

During the past year, in fact, Sadovszky himself has blurred his earlier focus on Ob-Ugric by postulating what he believes to be cognates shared by California Penutian with Ugric generally (including Hungarian), with Finno-Ugric generally (including Mordvin), with Uralic generally (including Samoyed), and with Altaic generally (including Turkic, Mongolian, and Tungus). Examples of these postulated cognations are found in Table I above.

Now that the 19th century idea of a special connection between the Uralic and the Altaic languages has been generally abandoned, Sadovszky's findings point to a different conclusion. This conclusion (even though he himself does not draw it) is that California Penutian is cognate not merely with Uralic or Altaic but with Nostratic as a whole—including Indo-European. Of these form-sets, at least three can be derived from Proto-Nostratic (Bomhard and Kerns 1994):

Proto-Uralic	mi	what?	< Proto-Nostratic	mi	what?
Wintun	'el-	no!	< Proto-Nostratic	'al-	no!
Mongolian	kel-	tongue	< Proto-Nostratic	kal-	speak

If it should turn out that both the Indo-European and the Uralic forms in California Penutian are Common Nostratic, then it may be that we are dealing with linguistic material which antedates any specifically Uralic or Indo-European migration or visit to North America. Its antiquity could well be more than half of that of the human habitation of the Western Hemisphere.

Nevertheless, the question remains: Is this Eurasian lexicon inherited or borrowed? Sadovszky, who previously insisted that California Penutian inherited its vocabulary exclusively from Ob-Ugric, now seems to concede that some of this vocabulary, while Eurasian rather than Amerindian, is "most likely due to borrowing" (von Sadovszky

1993). He derives this borrowed vocabulary, however, not from Uralic but from Altaic—more specifically, from the most northeasterly of the Turkic languages, Yakut. Examples of this derivation are:[8]

Maidu	palík	fish	< Yakut	balik	fish
Costanoan	katak	nape	< Yakut	ketex	nape
Maidu	k'ym'ýk	sand	< Yakut	kumax	sand
Costanoan	sarka	blind	< Yakut	soxxor	blind
Costanoan	xak-	mussel	< Yakut	xax	shell

Perhaps the most surprising of all Eurasian-American linguistic connections, at least in geographic terms, is that proposed by Brian Stubbs: a strong link between the Uto-Aztecan and Afro-Asiatic (or Hamito-Semitic) languages. The Uto-Aztecan languages are, or have been, spoken in western North America from Idaho to El Salvador. One would expect that, if Semites or their linguistic kinsmen from northern Africa were to reach the New World by water, their route would be trans-Atlantic. Indeed, what graphonomic evidence there is indicates exactly that: Canaanite inscriptions are found in Georgia and Tennessee as well as in Brazil; and Mediterranean coins, some Hebrew and Moroccan Arabic, are found in Kentucky as well as in Venezuela (Gordon 1971).

But we must follow the evidence wherever it leads. And, lexically at least, it points to the Pacific rather than to the Atlantic coast. Stubbs finds Semitic and (more rarely) Egyptian vocabulary in about 20 of 25 extant Uto-Aztecan languages. Of the word-bases in these vernaculars, he finds about 40 percent to be derivable from nearly 500 tri-literal Semitic stems. Despite this striking proportion, however, he does not regard Uto-Aztecan as a branch of Semitic or of Afro-Asiatic. Instead, he treats Uto-Aztecan Semitisms as borrowings. But, because these borrowings are at once so numerous and so well 'nativized,' he prefers to regard them as an example of linguistic creolization—that is, of massive lexical adaptation of one language group to another (Stubbs 1988). (By way of analogy, we may recall, as noted above, that historical linguists regard the heavy importation of French vocabulary into Middle English as a process of creolization.)

Of the various Afro-Asiatic languages represented in Uto-Aztecan vocabulary, the following occur in descending order of frequency:

1. Canaanite (cited in its Hebrew form[9])
2. Aramaic
3. Arabic
4. Ethiopic
5. Akkadian (usually in its Assyrian form)
6. Ancient Egyptian

Among the many Semitic loan-words in Uto-Aztecan, the following, listed by Stubbs, seem unexceptionable as regards both form and meaning:

Hebrew	**baraq**	lightning	> Papago	**berok**	lightning
Aramaic	**katpa**	shoulder	> Papago	**kotva**	shoulder
Hebrew	**hiskal**	be prudent	> Nahua	**iskal**	be prudent
Hebrew	**yešïväh**	sitting	> Hopi	**yesiva**	camp

Lest sceptics should attribute these correspondences to coincidence, however, Stubbs takes care to note that there are systematic sound-shifts, analogous to those covered in Indo-European by Grimm's Law, which recur consistently in loans from Afro-Asiatic to Uto-Aztecan. One of these is the unvoicing of voiced stops in the more southerly receiving languages. Another is the velarization of voiced labial stops and glides in the same languages. Examples of these two processes in co-occurrence follow. (The presumptive stages of phonic shift are: b > gw > kw.)

Hebrew	**ben**	son	> Nahua	**kon-**	son[10]
Hebrew	**bar**	field	> Tubar	**kwir-**	field[11]
Hebrew	**bor**	well	> Tarahumara	**kor**	well
Hebrew	**basar**	penis	> Hopi	**kwasi**	penis[12]

Before we leave the subject of early Semitic influence on the Americas, it may be of interest to note that the very name 'America' is of uncertain origin. The conventional etymology, which derives it from the name of the cartographer Amerigo Vespucci, is questionable for several reasons. First, it is not certain that Vespucci ever visited the Western Hemisphere. Second, the precedent of Columbia (or Colombia), derived from the name Christopher Columbus (or one of its national variants), suggests that 'Vespuccia' would have been a more appropriate name for the New World (Bailey 1973:246). And finally, even if the place-name had been derived from the forename Amerigo, one would expect it to be only minimally altered to 'Ameriga' or 'Amerigia,' with the word accent on the syllable **-ri-**, as in Italian. But if America is not a name of European origin, where else may it have come from? James Bailey ingeniously suggests that it may come from *Amurru*, the Akkadian (that is, Assyrian and Babylonian) word for 'west' (Bailey 1973:246). The Hebrews called the people of this western region *Emörï*, and we call them *Amorites*. Their language seems to have been an early Mediterranean form of West Semitic. Beyond this, relatively little is known

about them. It would have been relatively easy, however, to Europeanize the name of the overseas locale of this mobile people by adding the suffix **-ica**, as in Armorica (the old name for Brittany and Normandy) or Africa, to their ethnic appellation.

From such a diachronic survey as this, what can be concluded? My own conclusion is that much of the early North American vocabulary is Eurasian in origin. What I cannot say is how much of that vocabulary was inherited and how much borrowed. Nor can I confidently determine how much of this lexical accretion belongs to this or that stratum of acquisition. Some is probably derived from a global vocabulary, some from a later Nostratic vocabulary, and some from a still later and more specifically Afro-Asiatic, Uralic, or Indo-European vocabulary. But, whatever the lexical sequences and proportions turn out to be, there is little likelihood, I believe, that North America ever experienced a prolonged period of complete linguistic isolation.

END NOTES

1. A written version of the second segment of an oral presentation entitled "Varieties of Diffusionism, with Special Reference to Early Eurasian Influence on North America," given at the NEARA Conference on *America Before Columbus*, Brown University, Providence RI, June 1992.
2. John D. Bengtson and Merritt Ruhlen, "Global Etymologies," forthcoming in *The Genetic Classification of Languages,* Vitaly Shevoroshkin, ed., University of Texas Press; and Merritt Ruhlen, *The Amerind Phylum and the Prehistory of the Old World*, a paper presented at the Symposium on the Genetic Classification of Languages, Rice University, Houston TX, March 19, 1986. (The form of their reconstructions is here adapted to fit that of the primal reconstructions found in *Language Origins*, Roger W. Wescott, ed., Linstok Press, Silver Spring MD, 1974.)
3. The term *Amerind* is here used to refer to a genealogical linguistic group that excludes Eskimoan and Athabaskan but includes all more southerly Native American families. (See Joseph H. Greenberg, *Language in the Americas,* Stanford CA: Stanford University Press, 1987.)
4. In this series of English glosses, the word *manual* is borrowed from Latin. All the other words are directly inherited from Proto-Germanic.
5. Of these three peoples, the Manchu are the only one whose language is accepted as Nostratic by all Nostraticists. Yet, of the three, the Manchu seem least likely to have crossed the Pacific.
6. The reconstructions themselves, though based on Sadovszky's data, are mine.
7. Ostyak is also called Xanty. Vogul is also called Mansi.
8. In his article *Preliminary Data on the Relation of California Penutian to Uralic and Other Nostratic Languages* (Proceedings of the Academy of Sciences of the Estonian Soviet Socialist Republic, Vol. 7, No. 2, Tartu, 1971), the Estonian scholar Tiit-Rein Viitso relates California Penutian to Uralic generally, without confining that relationship to the Ugrian branch of Uralic. He does not specify whether this relationship is one of inheritance or borrowing, although one may infer that he intends the former.

9. Phoenician, Ugaritic, and Moabite are other dialectal variants of Canaanite.

10. In the Uto-Aztecan languages of Mexico, **kw** becomes **k** before back vowels.

11. Tubar, a Uto-Aztecan language of Mexico, is the only extinct vernacular from which Stubbs cites forms.

12. Semitic **r** becomes **y** in all Uto-Aztecan languages except the Pimic group (consisting of Papago and Tepehuan). If an adjacent vowel is deleted, this **y** is then vocalized as **i**.

REFERENCES

Anttila, Raimo
  1972 *Historical and Comparative Linguistics*. Amsterdam: Benjamins.

Bailey, James
  1973 *The God-Kings and the Titans: The New World Ascendancy in Ancient Times*. New York: St. Martin's Press.

Bomhard, Allan R. and John C. Kerns
  1994 *The Nostratic Macrofamily: A Study in Distant Linguistic Relationship*. Berlin and New York: Mouton de Gruyter.

Callaghan, Catherine A.
  1980 An 'Indo-European' type paradigm in Proto-Eastern Miwok. In *American Indian and Indoeuropean* [sic] *Studies*. K. Klar *et al.*, eds. The Hague: Mouton.

Gordon, Cyrus H.
  1971 *Before Columbus: Links Between the Old World and Ancient America*. New York: Crown Publishers.

Pedersen, Holger
  1903 Tuerkische Lantgesetze. Band 57, 560 in *Zeitschrift der deutschen Morgenlaendischen Gesellschaft*.

Ruhlen, Merritt
  1987 *A Guide to the World's Languages: Vol. 1, Classification*. Stanford: Stanford University Press.

Stubbs, Brian
  1988 *A Creolized Base in Uto-Aztecan*. Privately published at the San Juan campus of the College of Eastern Utah, Blanding UT.

Trombetti, Alfredo
  1905 *L'Unità d'Origine del Linguaggio*. Bologna.

von Sadovszky, Otto J.
  1983 The new genetic relationship and the paleolinguistics of the central California Indian ceremonial houses. In *The Lacus Forum*. A. Manning *et al.*, eds. Columbia SC: Hornbeam Press.

  1989 Linguistic evidence for the Siberian origin of central California Indian shamanism. In *Shamanism*. M. Hoppal *et al.*, eds. Los Angeles: ISTOR Books.

  1993 *Altaic Elements in the Central California Indian Languages*. Paper presented at the Yakutsk Conference on Arctic Peoples, Yakutsk, Siberia, June 13, 1993.

Wenke, Robert J.
  1990 *Patterns in Prehistory*, 3rd ed. New York: Oxford University Press.

Wescott, Roger W.
  1995 Types of cultural diffusion. *NEARA Journal,* Vol. XXIX, Nos. 1 & 2.

An Inscribed Stone:

The Anatomy of a Decipherment

DONAL B. BUCHANAN

There are two inscriptions in North America which are in scripts that most nearly resemble the Iberic variant of the Pan-Mediterranean alphabet: one on the New Hampshire Dagger (found in 1870 near Concord NH) and the other on the Grand Traverse Stone (once called the Kent County Stone). I am concerned here with the Grand Traverse Stone.

The Grand Traverse Stone was found sometime prior to 14 January 1878 (perhaps as early as 1876) on a farm in Grand Traverse County about twelve miles east of Grand Traverse Bay. It was picked up by a small boy walking behind his father in the freshly plowed furrow as the land was being plowed for the first time. The finder gave the stone to a Judge Ramsdell, who gave it to a Dr. Parker who was on the Board of Trustees of the Kent County Institute in Grand Rapids, Michigan.

The stone eventually became part of the holdings of the Kent County Institute (hence its previous name). In a letter dated 14 January 1878, W. L. Coffinberry of Grand Rapids, Chairman of the Committee on Archaeology for the "RST" (not further identified) and Curator of the Kent County Institute, reported on the stone to P. P. Cherry of the District Historical Society. He described the stone as:

> a sort of argillaceous slate, rather rhomboid in shape, one-half inch thick and about two and one-half inches on the sides, engraved on both sides; the characters on one side seem to be much more ancient than the other. The lines seem to be sharp, with fine edges, and appear to be more recent on one side, and more weather-worn and disintegrated on the other (Coffinberry 1878).

Dr. Parker admitted that he had cleaned the stone of dirt and clay to make casts (no casts are known to exist at present). If the stone had lain in the dirt for some time however, one side would have been protected and the other weathered, just as noted above.

It was reported that a Mr. Bates had found a similar stone (perhaps the same one) in Grand Traverse County, but lost it. That stone, however, was said to be inscribed on one face only.

W. L. Coffinberry gave a photograph of the stone to C. C. Baldwin, Secretary of the Western Reserve Historical Society, probably in January 1878. That photo is reproduced here in Figure 1. The Kent County Institute turned over all of its material at some point to the Grand Rapids Museum, which has yet to find the stone among its holdings of about 200,000 artifacts.

Figure 1 GRAND TRAVERSE STONE

I do not recall exactly when I first became acquainted with this inscription, but I suspect that it was in the mid-seventies, courtesy of the late Dr. Paul Cheesman of Brigham Young University in Utah. I filed it away among 'things to tackle someday.' Finally, I got to it, and it has proved to be a fascinating problem indeed.

The first thing an epigrapher does with a new inscription is make some attempt to identify the script and the language involved. This inscription is very clearly in a variant of the Pan-Mediterranean alphabet. Some of the known variants of that alphabet are: Greek, Italo-Celtic (including Etruscan), Punic, and several forms of Iberic.

The Inscription Database (in which I have recorded most Iberic, many Italo-Celtic, and some American inscriptions) was consulted. Each character in this short inscription was run through the Character Dictionary portion of that database. One particular character established itself very quickly as special: $\triangledown$. I found it in four inscriptions from two areas of Spain, not widely separated: numbers 4, 13, 30, and 31 in the Database (30 and 31 are two sides of the same lamina). Number 4 was sepulchral, on a stele; 13 was a lamentation for Carthage written on a votive tessara shaped like a horse (a symbol for Carthage); and 30 and 31 were inscribed on a bronze lamina containing a prayer to the Household Gods (Penates) on one side and instructions for the care of the Penates on the other. In all cases, the language was a form of Vulgar Latin. A tentative date of between 200 and 100 BC had been assigned to all four inscriptions.

So, there was a tentative identification of the script and language. Just to be sure, however, a check was made of Greek and Italo-Celtic scripts. In terms of the characters of the alphabet, all of the characters on the Grand Traverse Stone could be found in one or the other of these variants of the Pan-Mediterranean alphabet. The character second from the right in the bottom line of the graphic (here represented by ‡ —ultimately derived from the Semitic *samek*) was common in Greek, which, with Latin, strongly influenced the Iberic alphabet.

It was early determined that this inscription was inscribed boustrophedon, 'as the cow walks.' It starts at the top right reading right to left; the second line reads left to right; the third, right to left; the fourth, left to right; and the fifth, right to left. The final character in line 3, ▷ , was carved incorrectly for an R-L line, so the scribe tied it to the first character of the next line to indicate that it was rendered in a L-R form. The first character in the fifth line is a known variant of a reversed N.

When Greek sound values are applied, we get:

LUOPsLKh
AKhNL-I
LXKhISLA
KhRUAL
NXTKhI?

The question mark denotes the last character, which was not Greek, but seemed to appear only in Roman monetary documents. The sound values did not feel right, and no decipherment in Greek or any other language was forthcoming. Similar results were obtained using the accepted sound values for the Italo-Celtic alphabets.

I therefore returned to the Iberic variant and applied my own sound values, derived from twenty years of study. There was a problem, however, relating to the character ∨ . Depending on when the inscription was written, this symbol would have had either of two different sound values. In the early alphabet, it was a Category IV character carrying a **G/K** sound **GA**. In later inscriptions, probably under the influence of Greek and Latin, it became a Category III sound **VEE**. I tried it first as a Category IV sound. As for the ‡ character, it appears in Libyan Punic as an **'ain**. Since Punic affected Iberic, I tried that value. I got:

LGRTLD
ADNL-N
L'ADNSLA
DRGAL
N'ATDN?

If the inscription was a very late form of Vulgar Latin (almost Spanish), we could get from the first line: *Llegar tal* . . . meaning 'amounting to talents(?) . . . '. What if we were dealing with a financial document? This supposition would tie in with the strange concluding symbol. Perhaps ✕ did not appear as a Category II (**D/T**) character,

but as a Category N (Numeral)! That would explain the use of ✛ (another form of ✕ . Perhaps | also appeared as a numeral. Following these suppositions, I arrived at this interpretation: and this possible reading:

LGRTL(X)	*Llegar tal 10*
A(X)NL-(I)	*a 10 nulla-1*
L'A(XI)SLA	*. . . 11 sola*
(X)RGAL	*10 regalo*
N'AT(XI)?	*. . . 11 . . .*

Regalo could mean 'donation.' It began to look as if I might be on the right track.

But, suppose the ‡ character was not a Punic **'ain** after all? That character shared characteristics of both Category IV (**G/K**) and Category VII (**S/Z**) in Greek. What would happen to it if it entered Iberic from Greek? Perhaps it would shift more towards Category IV (**GO**).

Then, what about the ∨ character? Perhaps this inscription was relatively late; in that case it would read as Category III (**VEE**). Making these two changes gave me the following: which read:

LVRTL(10)	*Llevar tal 10*
A(10)NL-(1)	*a 10 nulla-1*
LG(11)SLA	*lego 11 sola*
(10)RVAL	*10 reval*
NGT(11)?	*negotio 11 . . .*

It looked like a bastard mixture of Spanish and Latin (which is what you would expect from a Vulgar Latin developing in Iberia), but it was beginning to make sense. What about the final character? It appeared to be a ligature of a known Punic **D**, often used in Iberic, ⊓ and the numeric character ✕ , which would carry a **T/D** reading. What if that is just what it was in this special symbol, a **T** plus a **D**? What would we get?

We would get this: and my final reading:

LVRTL(10)	*Llevar tal 10*
A(10)NL-1	*a 10 nulla-1*
LG(11)SLA	*lego 11 sola*
(10)RVAL	*10 reval*
NGT(11)TD	*negotio 11 todo*

We can translate this:

(I am) carrying (in accounts) 10 talents.
To 10 (add) 1 voided (or useless).
I am collecting (or sending) 11 only,
10 (of which) I can confirm.
Transaction (is) 11 in all (or total).

I went back to the Iberic Database to see if I could find further matches. Again, the database came through. Inscriptions 17, 18, 21, and 22 in the database—all from Yatova, Spain—were financial documents that used many of the same characters and often sounded eerily like our present document. Line 1 of 22 for instance: *Yo llevar que: ya 2* . . . is equivalent to: "That which I am carrying (in accounts) is 2." Note that the nature of the unit the scribe' is speaking about is not given, just as in the Grand Traverse inscription. That is understood (portions, cash?) between the scribe and his master. Inscription 17 uses the term *Negociada* meaning 'business or profit,' echoing the *Negotio* of our example here. Virtually all the characters used on the Grand Traverse stone appear in the Yatova inscriptions (the ≢ character, however, is rendered as X , while ▽ becomes ▷, and ⊓ appears as a numeral). The Yatova inscriptions, in my opinion, probably date to sometime after AD 100.

I conclude that the Grand Traverse inscription is a financial document, possibly a household account or a report from an overseer to a landlord. I suggest a date for it between 100 BC and AD 100. The stone was reported to have been inscribed on both faces. We have only one face recorded. We hope that the Grand Rapids Museum (which may have the stone in its holdings) will eventually provide good photographs of both faces so that work on this fascinating artifact can continue.

VOCABULARY

(*F, L, LS, P,* and *V* denote authors in the References.)

Llevar: (Lat: *levare/levo; levatio*) (OSp: *F*243A; Sp: *V*417C; Lat: *LS*1055B, *L*274A) = to carry, bear, produce; carry in accounts (to raise, levy [dues]).

Tal: a short form of *talentum* (Lat: *LS*1835A) = talent, a Grecian coin equal to about 60 *mine*. Note also Spanish *talla* (*V*607B) = dues paid by vassals to the lord of the manor.

A: (Lat: *ad*) (OSp: *F*177A; Sp: *V*1A; Lat: *LS*26C) = to, toward; at, in; by, for; of.

Nulo, -la: (Sp: *V*461A; Lat: *LS*1124A) = null, void of effect, of no force; of no value.

Legar: (Sp: *V*407A; Lat: *LS*1047B) = to send, bequeath; to gather, collect.

Solo, -la: (Sp: *V*594A; Lat: *LS*1724B) = alone, only, single, sole.

Reval: probably a form of *revalidar* (Sp: *V*559B) = to ratify, confirm, which makes more sense than *revelar* (Sp: *V*559C) = to reveal, manifest.

Negocio: (Lat: *negotium/negotio*) (Sp: *V*436B, *P*352B; Lat: *LS*1199A) = business, transaction, trade, profit.

Todo: (Lat: *tot*) (Sp: *V*621C; Lat: *LS*1881B) = all, entire, whole (total, altogether).

REFERENCES

Buchanan, Donal B.
  1985/6 The decipherment of Late Iberic. *Epigraphic Society Occasional Publications* (ESOP), 13, 14, 15 (Inscriptions #4, 13, 17, 18, 21, 22, 30, and 31 from the Inscriptions Database).
  1994 An inscribed Roman dagger from New Hampshire. *NEARA Journal* XXVIII (3&4).
Coffinberry, W. L.
  1878 Letter to P. P. Cherry, 14 January 1878. In *District Historical Society Tract #3*. P. P. Cherry, ed. Wadsworth OH: Steam Printing House.
Ford, J. D. M.
  1967 *Old Spanish Readings*. New York: Gordian Press.(*F*)
Latham, R. E.
  1983 *Revised Medieval Latin Word List*. London: Oxford University Press.(*L*)
Lewis, Charlton T. and Charles Short
  1980 *A Latin Dictionary*. Oxford: Clarendon Press.(*LS*)
Pei, Mario A.
  1968 *The New World Spanish-English and English-Spanish Dictionary*. New York: Signet.(*P*)
Velazquez de la Cadena, Mariano
  1952 *A New Pronouncing Dictionary of the Spanish and English Languages*. Englewood Cliffs NJ: Prentice-Hall.(*V*)

Figure 1a THE BAT CREEK STONE
(Photo © Warren W. Dexter)

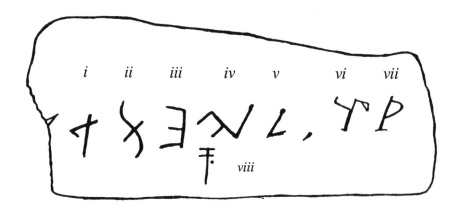

i = D   *ii* = W   *iii* = H   *iv* = Y   *v* = L   *vi* = Q?   *vii* = R?
viii = ?

Figure 1b FACSIMILE OF THE BAT CREEK INSCRIPTION
Numerals correspond to those used in the text to identify individual characters discussed.
It is proposed that the inscription be read from right to left.

The Bat Creek Stone:
A Reply to the Critics[4]

J. Huston McCulloch

INTRODUCTION

In their recent article, *The Bat Creek Stone: Judeans in Tennessee?* (1991), Robert C. Mainfort, Jr. and Mary L. Kwas comment on my own earlier article (McCulloch 1988) on the Bat Creek stone (National Museum of Natural History 134902). This small inscribed stone (Figure 1a) was found in 1889 in a burial mound on the lower Little Tennessee River by a technician working for the Smithsonian Bureau of Ethnology under Cyrus Thomas (Thomas 1894: 392-4). Although many professional archaeologists and Semitists have privately expressed doubts about the antiquity and/or authenticity of the stone, or about Cyrus Gordon's (1971, 1972) identification of the exotic characters on it as a 1st or 2nd century AD Paleo-Hebrew graffito, they have, at least until Mainfort and Kwas's article appeared, allowed Thomas's account and Gordon's analysis to go virtually unchallenged in print. Whatever case there may be against the claims that have been made concerning this unusual artifact deserves to be presented out in the open, as Mainfort and Kwas have done, rather than behind closed doors. Mainfort and Kwas are particularly to be congratulated for having elicited comments from Frank Moore Cross on the Paleo-Hebrew aspects of the artifact.

The principal arguments presented by Mainfort and Kwas are: 1. the brief inscription on the stone is not Paleo-Hebrew, as identified by Cyrus Gordon; 2. the brass bracelets found with the stone are in all probability modern trade artifacts; 3. the association of the Carbon-14 dated wood fragments with the inscribed stone is tenuous; 4. in 1898 Cyrus Thomas discreetly denounced his own 1894 Mound Explorations report as containing imaginary earthworks and fraudulent artifacts, and the Bat Creek stone was one such fraudulent article that Thomas had in mind; and 5. the Smithsonian agent who excavated the stone was particularly unreliable.

The present reply to Mainfort and Kwas's comments refutes these arguments one by one, and goes on to add some new material concerning the patina on the inscription, and regarding the word divider.

THE INSCRIPTION

Mainfort and Kwas readily concur with Joseph Mahan (1971) and myself that Cyrus Thomas (1894:393) and Marshall

McKusick (1979) were wrong to identify the inscription on the Bat Creek stone as Cherokee. In 1991, McKusick was still alluding to the inscription as "a scrap of 1820s Cherokee syllabary" (1991:156). However, he gave no new information to support this claim, and made no mention of my 1988 article which had extensively and expressly refuted his 1979 position. A consensus may therefore be said to have formed, at least among informed parties, that the inscription is not Cherokee.

If it is not Cherokee, then what is it? According to Cyrus H. Gordon, recently retired Professor of Hebrew and Other Oriental Languages at New York University, and a leading expert on the pre-Hebrew Semitic inscriptions of Ugarit and Ebla, the inscription is in Paleo-Hebrew script of the 1st or 2nd centuries AD. Although not entirely clear, it contains the word *lyhwd*, or 'for Judea,' in the Hebrew language.

In their critique of Gordon's interpretation of the inscription as Paleo-Hebrew, Mainfort and Kwas disclaim any knowledge of the Hebrew language or scripts, and instead rely entirely on the views of Frank M. Cross, Hancock Professor of Hebrew and Other Oriental Languages at Harvard University. Cross was a logical person to approach, since he is a leading authority on ancient Hebrew scripts, and since he has crossed pens with Gordon in the past concerning other allegedly pre-Columbian Semitic inscriptions reportedly found in the New World (Cross 1968). Cross gave his considered opinion on the Bat Creek inscription in two related letters, one to Mainfort (1989a), and one to myself (1989b), with copies of each to both of us. Mainfort and Kwas quote extensively from the letter they received. They report that Cross read and commented on an earlier draft of their paper, so we may assume that his views have been represented accurately, and with his permission.

Unfortunately, Professor Cross makes no less than three elementary and readily documentable errors of Hebrew paleography, both in his letters and as accurately quoted and paraphrased by Mainfort and Kwas.

Cross's first clear-cut error is his statement that the E-like letter I designated in my article as letter **iii**, (see Figure 1b) and which Gordon identifies as a Paleo-Hebrew **he**, "is impossible as Paleo-Hebrew in the period 100 BC-AD 100, based on shape and stance." In his letter to

Mainfort, Cross praises Mark McLean's Harvard doctoral dissertation (1982) as "the best treatment of the Palaeo-Hebrew script" available. Indeed, Cross served on McLean's committee and signed off on the cover page. However, if we open McLean's dissertation to his Plate 13, we find the letter reproduced in Figure 2a, which is essentially identical to the Bat Creek letter **iii**, identified as being a **he** from a bulla (seal impression) of a King Jonathan. Furthermore, according to McLean's source, Avigad (1975), this particular King Jonathan would have to be Alexander Jannaeus, whose Hebrew name was Jonathan, and who ruled Judea from 103-76 BC. Bat Creek letter **iii**, far from being "impossible," as Cross assured Dr. Mainfort, is therefore in fact a perfectly acceptable Paleo-Hebrew letter for the late Second Temple period, including, specifically, the 1st century BC expressly denied by Professor Cross.[1]

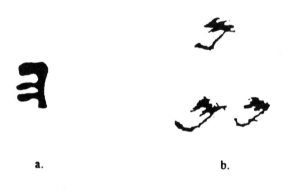

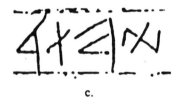

a.   b.

c.

Figure 2a PALEO-HEBREW **HE**
From a Bulla of King Jonathan, 103–76 BC
(McLean 1982:Plate 13)

Figure 2b SPECIMENS OF PALEO-HEBREW **MEM**
From *11 Q Paleo Lev*, *ca.* 100 BC
(Freedman and Mathews 1985:Plate 19)

Figure 2c THE ARAMAIC WORD **YHWD**
Paleo-Hebrew letters, from the 'Abba' inscription
(Naveh 1982: Plate 15)

The letter **he** appears with essentially the same stance as the Bat Creek letter on the coins of the 1st century AD that I cited already in my Table III (1988:90), though with a very formal and inessential (as demonstrated by Figure

2a) overhang of the top crossbar, and with purely ornamental dots or 'pearls' at the ends of the lines. The Bat Creek letter is rather sloppy, but is just as readily identifiable as **he** in this orientation as it would be as an English **E** or Cherokee **gun** when inverted. The reason the Bat Creek letter looks so much like a backwards **E** is that our **E** was originally just a backwards Canaanite **he**. The Bat Creek form would be out of place in a much earlier period, such as the 9th century BC, but works fine as Paleo-Hebrew *ca.* the 1st century AD.

Cross's second clear-cut error is his assertion that "The broken sign [to the left of the letter I designate as **i**] cannot be **mem** in the designated period [which in his letter is the 1st century BC – 1st century AD] . . . " (1989a). Now, in his other letter, Cross urged me to consult Freedman and Mathews' book (1985) on *11 Q PaleoLev* (the Paleo-Hebrew Leviticus Dead Sea scroll from Qumran cave 11), which he describes as "the largest script in Paleo-Hebrew and the best preserved MS." However, if we turn this volume to its Plate 19, we find the three specimens of **mem** reproduced in Figure 2b. These are particularly clear examples of the **mem** used throughout this scroll, as indicated in the volume's summary Table III. A **mem** of this type would fit the broken Bat Creek letter very well. Furthermore, Richard Hanson dates this particular scroll to approximately 100 BC (Freedman and Mathews 1985, p. 23). The same form of **mem** also appears on coins of Hyrcanus II, 63 – 40 BC (Birnbaum 1971:Chart 51*). The broken letter is therefore a perfectly good **mem** for the period Prof. Cross designates, contrary to his assurances to Dr. Mainfort.

Cross's third clearcut error is his statement that "if we limit the 'deciphered' text to Gordon's **lyhwd**, ignoring the following broken sign, the reading would be anomalous. In Palaeo-Hebrew, Judah (Judea) is spelled **yhwdh**, not **yhwd**. The latter is the Aramaic designation and appears only in Aramaic scripts" (Cross 1989a).

In fact, however, Paleo-Hebrew is a script, not a language, and it was used to write both Hebrew language and Aramaic language, as evidenced by the 'Abba' inscription, a 7-line tomb inscription found carved into the bedrock of Jerusalem (Naveh 1973; 1982:120-21, plate 15). Despite the fact that the script of the Abba inscription is Paleo-Hebrew, Joseph Naveh identifies its language as Aramaic, not Hebrew. There is therefore no reason why the word **yhwd** could not appear in Paleo-Hebrew letters on the Bat Creek stone, even if it is a purely Aramaic idiom.[2] Indeed, the very word does appear, in Paleo-Hebrew letters, in line 6 of the Abba inscription, as reproduced in Figure 2c. In the Abba inscription, the word **yhwd** is used as a personal name. However, it is a matter of little consequence whether the reference on the Bat Creek stone is to a *person* named Judah, to the *land* of Judah, or to the *people* of Judah, or whether its language is Hebrew *per se* or Aramaic. Any which way, it indicates a Roman-era contact between the Old and New Worlds.

In addition to the above three points, Cross also objects to my own use (1988:93) of a 4th century BC text that he himself had documented (1969:Fig. 35) to strengthen Gordon's identification of letter **ii** as **waw**. It should be noted that Naveh (1973:87) uses this same specimen to identify the unique **waw** of the Abba inscription, shown in Figure 2c, as the third letter when read from right to left. This is despite the fact that the fit is much worse than in the Bat Creek case, and even though he has to stretch to 3rd century AD and even later Samaritan inscriptions for parallels to some of the other letters. Naveh's best guess for the date of the Abba inscription is the 1st century AD or late 1st century BC.

Cross raises several other, basically valid objections to the letters and orthography of the Bat Creek inscription. However, *every one* of these problems has already been noted and, in some cases, even resolved by Gordon in his definitive 1972 treatment. Cross has therefore added nothing to Gordon's interpretation, other than his overall assessment (which admittedly deserves note) that the specific problems Gordon had already identified are too serious for the inscription to be Paleo-Hebrew.

Mainfort and Kwas, quoting Cross (1989a), object that "Gordon's interpretation of the Bat Creek inscription could justifiably be criticized on the grounds that his zeal to make a case for the radiation of higher culture from a single Near Eastern center caused him to relax the disciplines of historical linguistics, paleography, and historical orthography" (1991:6). I have demonstrated above that it is Cross, not Gordon, who is shooting from the hip, at least when it comes to the Bat Creek inscription. Gordon's 1972 claims about Bat Creek generally check out, while what Cross says often does not. Gordon did make a few outright errors, that I have already pointed out, such as his reading of the shape of letter **ii** and his assumption that the two vertical strokes were part of the original inscription, but these errors actually weakened the case for Paleo-Hebrew. Where he disagrees head-on with Cross (as on the above three points), Cross is documentably wrong.

If anyone has permitted himself "to relax the disciplines of historical linguistics, paleography, and historical orthography" in the present instance, it is therefore Cross himself, and not Gordon. Cross's errors do not, of course, reflect directly on Mainfort and Kwas themselves, since they were justifiably relying on what they could reasonably have expected to have been an authoritative outside opinion. Given the numerous and demonstrable elementary errors in Cross's response, however, readers would do well to seek out additional qualified opinions before leaping to any conclusions about this unique artifact.

One additional expert who has looked at the stone is Professor P. Kyle McCarter of the Johns Hopkins University Department of Near Eastern Studies. McCarter, an expert on the ancient Hebrew 'Copper Scroll' from Qumran, has given me permission to quote him to the effect that while he reserves final judgment on the inscription, he believes that it looks too much like Paleo-Hebrew to be a mere coincidence. At the same time, he finds that it lacks the sophistication found in most forgeries (personal communication).[3]

In their concluding remarks (p. 14), Mainfort and Kwas add the astonishing statement that their conclusion that "the inscription is not a legitimate Paleo-Hebrew inscription" is "based on assessments by two Near Eastern language specialists," one of whom is Cyrus Gordon. In fact, Gordon is clearly on record that *despite its admitted problems*, he is *confident* that the Bat Creek inscription is Paleo-Hebrew. This is as much a misrepresentation of Gordon's views as it would be of Cross's to take his admission that letter **iv** bears a "striking resemblance to Paleo-Hebrew script," and that letter **v** is "normal," as an assessment on his part that the inscription as a whole *is* Paleo-Hebrew.

THE BRASS BRACELETS

Mainfort and Kwas (pp. 7-9) also readily concur with me that the composition of the brass bracelets (NMNH 134898) found with the Bat Creek stone is not by itself conclusive as to whether they are ancient or modern. Brass is an artificial alloy of copper with zinc that became common in the Old World after 45 BC, but which is not believed to have been made in the New World before Columbus. Even if there had been no inscription found with the Bat Creek burial, the brass bracelets, together with the Carbon-14 date discussed in the next section, therefore constitute conclusive evidence of a pre-Norse Old World contact with the New World, or else, equally remarkably, of the independent invention of brass in the New World.

Mainfort and Kwas object, however, that "importantly, no documentation regarding the production and use of comparable artifacts by 1st or 2nd century AD Mediterranean peoples has been presented" by either myself or others, and deduce that "application of Occam's Razor strongly suggests a relatively recent European origin for the bracelets from Bat Creek" (p. 9).

While it is true that I did not actually cite any evidence for C-shaped bracelets being used in ancient times, they were in fact a popular ornament in the Mediterranean world, from the early Iron Age down to Byzantine and Islamic times; (see Richter 1915:336-7, #1115; Comstock and Vermeule 1971:188, #222; Davidson 1952:263, Plate 112, #2133, #2134; Holum *et al.* 1988:210, Fig. 151). Richter (1915:336) notes that simple types such as her #1115 were in use for a long time, and that in the absence of ornamentation they provide no clue as to date. The ancient specimens I have been able to find to date are all bronze, silver, or gold, though as noted above, brass was also available after 45 BC.

Mainfort and Kwas concede that most modern brass trade bracelets were cut from mass-produced drawn wire rather than being laboriously hand-wrought as were the

Bat Creek Bracelets. Indeed, the 'Tunica Treasure' of 18th century trade goods from Louisiana that they cite even contains rolls of the uncut wire (Brain 1979:193-4). They conjecture that some of the heavier Tunica bracelets may have been wrought. If this were true, it would by no means prove that the Bat Creek bracelets are modern, but it would be an interesting consideration. However, they do not cite a single one that is actually known to have been wrought and not drawn or cast.

Mainfort and Kwas make a point of attempting to exonerate Cyrus Thomas for mistakenly identifying the brass bracelets as merely 'copper.' For some purposes it may make little difference whether an object is brass or pure copper, *e.g.*, the modern kettle lugs they cite from Fort Michilimackinac. A major issue that was to be addressed and resolved by the Smithsonian's Mound Survey, however, was whether or not the builders of the ancient North American mounds had access to advanced metallurgy, including the ability to smelt and alloy copper and iron. Thomas concluded, on the basis of the mass of evidence his project found, that there was no evidence of such advanced metallurgy, and that all copper and iron artifacts in the mounds could be explained away as native copper, meteoric iron, or modern intrusions. The Bat Creek bracelets prove, if nothing else, that in at least one instance Thomas misidentified brass as unalloyed copper. This legitimately casts doubt on his identification of the many other 'copper' artifacts his study found. Note that had it not been for Gordon's identification of the script on the stone as Paleo-Hebrew, the Bat Creek bracelets would never have been analyzed, and would have remained 'copper' to this day.

Robert N. Anderson of the San Jose State University Materials Engineering Department has further developed the copper alloy age-dating methods I mentioned in my original article (p. 107), and now reports success using merely the electrical conductivity of the article, in place of PIXE spectrometry (personal communication). His current method is completely non-destructive, except for two pinpricks made by the electrodes through the patina. If Mainfort and Kwas wish to demonstrate that the bracelets are somehow modern, despite their mound context and the Carbon-14 date, they could evaluate the reliability of Anderson's method, and then have it applied to the Bat Creek bracelets. Since I have obtained the Carbon-14 date, however, the burden of proof is now with them.

THE CARBON-14 DATE

In my article (pp. 107-110), I reported a new AMS Carbon-14 date (Beta-24483/ETH-3677) on wood fragments (NMNH 134899), shown in Figure 3, that were found with the inscribed stone and brass bracelets. The dendro-calibrated date was AD 427, with a 2σ band (corresponding to a 95 percent confidence interval) of AD 32 – AD 769. These

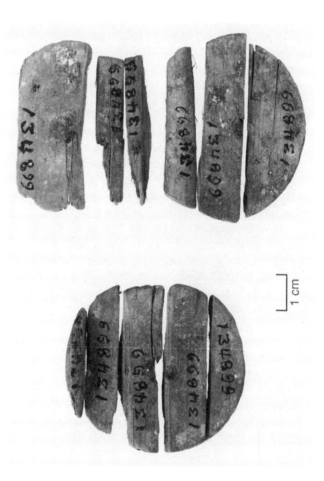

Figure 3 THE BAT CREEK WOOD FRAGMENTS
(NMNH 134899)
(Courtesy of the Smithsonian Institution, photograph 89-13231)

disks are apparently portions of earspools, similar in style to those worn by the Etowah figures (Thomas 1894:304-307).

As Mainfort and Kwas would have it, this date "was obtained on fragments of preserved wood that were recovered during the removal of the burial with which the inscribed stone was *allegedly* associated [emphasis added] (McCulloch 1988)." Note that my own paper is the only source they give for this "alleged" association. They continue that

. . . while it is possible that the recent AMS determination accurately dates the burial, McCulloch's claim that the date 'rules out the possibility of a modern origin for either the inscription or the bracelets' (1988:116) is not only erroneous, but also represents a characteristic, non-skeptical, cult-archaeology assertion about a topic in which he has no expertise.

They cite an authority of which I was admittedly unaware, namely Wendy Hanford Arundale (1981), who

has offered a number of precautions relative to the interpretation of radiocarbon dates. Many of these are pertinent to the Bat Creek stone, but of particular importance is the degree of association between the dated material (in this case, the 'polished wood' fragments) and the cultural event to be dated (in this case, the burial of an individual with which the inscribed stone was *purportedly* associated) [emphasis added], as well as the age association between the dated material and the associated remains. In the case of the former, the primitive excavation and recording techniques employed render the certainty of association between the wood fragments, the inscribed stone, and the skeletal remains indeterminant (or at best very tenuous) (1988:9).

Mainfort and Kwas thus make it appear that although the wood fragments were "recovered during the removal of the burial," there is an "indeterminant (or at best very tenuous)" association between them and the burial itself, and that it is only *I* who "allege," and "purport," as they put it, that the inscribed stone and/or bracelets were in any way associated with the wood fragments and/or burial.

In fact, Cyrus Thomas's official *Report on the Mound Explorations of the Bureau of Ethnology*, which constitutes the bulk of the *Twelfth Annual Report of the Bureau of Ethnology to the Secretary of the Smithsonian Institution, 1890 – 1891*, is perfectly clear as to the degree of association between the dated material, the burial, the bracelets, and the inscribed stone:

[Bat Creek] Mound 3 was of small size, measuring but 28 feet in diameter and 5 feet in height. Some large sassafras trees were standing on it, and the owner, Mr. Tipton, stated that he had cut trees from it forty years ago, and that it had been covered by a cluster of trees and grapevines as long ago as the oldest settler in the locality could recollect. At the time the excavation was made there was an old rotten stump yet on the top, the roots of which ran down to the skeletons. It was composed throughout, except about the skeletons at the bottom, of hard red clay, without any indications of stratification. Nothing of interest was discovered until the bottom, where nine skeletons were found lying on the original surface of the ground, surrounded by dark colored earth. These were disposed as shown in Fig. 272. No. 1 lying at full length with the head south, and close by, parallel with it, but with the head north, was No. 2. On the same level were seven others, all lying close side by side, with heads north and in a line. All were badly decayed. No relics were found with any but No. 1, immediately under the skull and jaw bones of which were two copper bracelets, an engraved stone, a small drilled fossil, a copper bead, a bone implement, and some small pieces of polished wood. The earth about the skeletons was wet and the pieces of wood soft and colored green by contact with the copper bracelets. The bracelets had been rolled in something, probably bark, which crumbled away when they were taken out. The engraved stone lay partially under the back part of the skull and was struck by the steel prod used in probing. This stone is shown in Fig. 273 [on Thomas's p. 394] (Thomas 1894: 392-4).

Thomas did not just make up this description of the excavation five years after the event. Rather, he lifted it, almost word for word (without attribution, as was his custom), from the first-hand account of John W. Emmert, the Bureau agent who actually excavated the stone. This account

(Emmert 1889c) was written the month after the discovery. Thomas deleted a few sentences from Emmert's report, and I have already quoted (1988:104, 108) a few of these. For the sake of completeness, the following should be added: Emmert, in his then extensive experience excavating mounds, found it "a little Singular that all [the skeletons] were lying with heads north but No. 1 whose head was to the South." Furthermore, although he admitted that "I punched it [the stone] on the rough side with my steel rod in probing before I came to the skeletons," he added that "the other side of the stone is exactly as it was taken from the skeleton at the bottom of the mound about five feet deep." There is indeed a still fresh-looking gash on the back side of the stone. Emmert included a sketch of the burial, shown in Figure 4, which was the basis for Thomas's Figure 272.

Figure 4 EMMERT'S SKETCH OF THE BAT CREEK BURIAL
(1889C) (National Anthropological Archives, MS 2400)

Emmert added at the end of his report, "I have packed the Specimens carefully and put the engraved stone in a box Separate as you directed and have made two Catalogues one to you and one to Maj. Powell." Immediately upon receipt of the artifacts, Emmert's catalog numbers, which clearly identified which artifacts in the shipment were the ones described as having come from Bat Creek Mound No. 3, were assigned NMNH catalog numbers. The number 134899 assigned to the wood fragments (Emmert's #7) is clearly legible, eleven times over, in Figure 3. It was from one of these pieces that Carolyn Rose extracted a sample to send to Beta Analytic, Inc. for testing. In the color slide of 134899 that is available from Smithsonian Photo Services, the green copper salts from the bracelets, as noted by Emmert and that preserved the wood over the centuries, are clearly visible. (See also McCulloch 1993a:52.)

In letters dated 2/15/1889 and 2/25/1889, Emmert had already announced the find to Thomas, and indicated that it had aroused considerable excitement locally. There is therefore no possibility that Emmert inattentively mixed up the artifacts found with the stone with those from any other burials.

Unfortunately, the National Anthropological Archives did not save the actual field notes of Emmert or of any of the other Mound Survey agents in its MS2400, so we have no record of how accurate or primitive they may have been. However, Emmert wrote Thomas (1889b) that "I am taking full notes as I go along," so we at least know that they at one time existed, and that he did not simply write his report from memory a month after the excavation. Given Thomas's interest in, and puzzlement over, the stone (1890:35-37; 1894:714), we may be certain that he examined these notes most carefully for any discrepancies. As I have already noted (1988:113), Thomas actually took the unusual precaution of sending another agent, James Middleton, to the field to check the details of Emmert's report. His investigation "confirmed the statement by Mr. Emmert in every particular."

In a complex earthwork such as the Citico Mound, which Emmert excavated in January through March of 1885, reference to accurate and detailed field notes would be essential in order to be confident of the relationships among the 91 interjected burials and all of the associated artifacts (Thomas 1894:373-77). However, Bat Creek Mound No. 3 had none of this complexity. It would of course be ideal if we could see Emmert's actual field notes, but even without them the association of the artifacts of interest is adequately clear from his report. There is no reasonable possibility that the wood fragments Carbon-14 dated in 1988 were not the same ones reported to have been found 99 years earlier, under the same skull as the inscribed stone and bracelets, and preserved by corrosion that appeared to have come from the bracelets.

As for the age relationship between the dated material and the associated remains, which Mainfort and Kwas would have me neglecting, I in fact clearly stated (1988:109) that "the carbon date refers, of course, to the tree-growth represented by the wood fragments, and not to the inscription or the contact itself." The tree-growth could well have been several decades, or conceivably even a century or two old, if the wood was taken from the heart of a very old tree at the time of the burial. But even if we add two hundred years to the upper end of the 2σ band, we are still left with a pre-Norse, not to mention pre-Columbian, date for the burial. (Vikings began raiding England in the 790s, but Leif Erickson is not said to have reached 'Vinland' until approximately AD 1000.)

R. A. Taylor (1987:108-15) classifies Carbon-14 dates into three major confidence categories, according to the reliability of the association of sample material with the archaeological feature of interest. In our case, we are interested in the date of burial of the inscription and brass bracelets, as an upper bound to the date at which knowledge of the script and the bracelets themselves were presumably brought over from the Old World. His highest category, #1, has two sub-categories, which he designates as "Essential certainty," and "High probability." We do not have his "Essential certainty" for the inscription or bracelets, since this would require a direct date on the inscription or bracelets themselves. We do, however, have his "High probability" for the burial, which he defines as "^{14}C analysis on organics in direct functional relationship with [the] object/event for which temporal placement [is] sought." As an example, he gives "^{14}C analysis of textile used to wrap [a] burial to obtain [an] age estimate on [the] burial." Grave goods, such as earspools placed with a skeleton in the Bat Creek case, have a comparable degree of association with the burial. We may, therefore, say that according to Taylor's classification, the Bat Creek Carbon-14 date has a "High probability" of providing an upper bound on the date of the contact. This degree of association is far superior to his category #2, "Reasonable probability," an example of which would be a date on charcoal in sediments adjacent to the burial to obtain a date on the burial itself.

The article by Arundale, which Mainfort and Kwas found to contain "a number of precautions relative to the interpretation of radiocarbon dates," "many of [which] are pertinent to the Bat Creek Stone" is in fact concerned with the special problems archaeologists confront in dating Arctic sites, where "the skin, bone, fat, ivory, or baleen from a sea mammal may be the only available organic substance." As she points out in her introduction, "Arctic researchers face difficulties with radiocarbon dating *not shared by Temperate zone colleagues*" [emphasis added] (Arundale 1981:224). These special problems are irrelevant to the Bat Creek burial.

Mainfort and Kwas do make the valid observation that the 'dark soil' at the base of the mound may have been an occupation midden or old humus zone, and add the interesting suggestion that the wood fragments may have derived from this midden or humus rather than being grave goods actually placed with the burial (pp. 5, 9). However, in a midden or humus zone in the Temperate climate of Tennessee, small pieces of wood lying on or near the surface would not last for more than a few years without some artificial means of preservation. It is only the fact that the wood fragments were in direct contact with the cupreous bracelets and entombed in the mound from the time of the burial that they survived at all. In any event, earspools such as those shown in Figure 3 are much more likely to be intentional grave goods, particularly when found under a skull with other fancy items, than village refuse.

Mainfort and Kwas correctly note that the soil at the base of the mound was wet, and suggest that this "raises the possibility of contamination from groundwater" (p. 9). However, the cover letter on the report from Beta Analytic Inc., signed by Dr. Murry Tamers and dated May 2, 1988, certifies that

> Your wood was pretreated by first examining for rootlets. The sample was then given a hot acid wash to eliminate carbonates. It was repeatedly rinsed to neutrality and subsequently given a hot alkali soaking to take out humic acids. After rinsing to neutrality, another acid wash followed and another rinsing to neutrality.

Contamination by either calcium carbonate or humic acid from groundwater has therefore already been eliminated as a possibility, to the best of the laboratory's ability. The real problem with the radiocarbon date, one which Mainfort and Kwas did not mention, but which I have already raised on p. 108 of my 1988 article, is its unusually large standard error, namely one hundred and seventy years on the uncalibrated date, whereas one hundred years or less would be more usual. Using the Gaussian probability distribution, a 95 percent confidence interval for the true date extends 1.96 standard errors on either side of the point estimate.

The reason for the large standard error was that, although 30 mg. of material was reportedly submitted for testing, an unusually small amount of pure carbon remained after the above-described pretreatment. The reasons for this in turn are unclear, but may include: 1. much of the mass of material submitted may have been the very copper salts from the bracelets that preserved the wood; 2. the wood may have been partially fossilized, further reducing its carbon content; 3. the laboratory admittedly "hit the sample pretty hard" with pre-treatments, knowing its potentially controversial nature.

The existing test used up less than 1 percent of the total 5.5 gm. of material that was available. I personally would favor AMS retesting with as much as 10 percent of the available material, *e.g.*, one of the larger disk segments shown in Figure 3. This should be more than adequate to obtain a date in which we can have more confidence, while at the same time leaving enough behind for further study and/or display. Again, however, the burden of proof is on Mainfort and Kwas or others to have this done if they wish to discredit the existing test date.

One pertinent recommendation that Arundale did make (and which Mainfort and Kwas did not mention) is that carbon-dated wood should routinely be identified as to species if at all possible. In the Arctic, for example, willow almost surely rules out driftwood, which can be quite old when used. This should be done (by someone other than myself) with the Bat Creek wood fragments. This may not tell us anything, but if by chance they turned out to be

the heartwood of a burr oak, some adjustment for this could be appropriate.

FANTASTIC ARCHAEOLOGY

Mainfort and Kwas's least tenable argument is that in 1898, Cyrus Thomas personally denounced his own *Mound Explorations* report as having presented certain fictitious earthworks and recently fabricated artifacts as if they were authentic and ancient, and that the Bat Creek stone in particular was one of the artifacts he thus repudiated. They base this claim on the following passage from Thomas's *Introduction to the Study of North American Archaeology*:

> It is safe therefore to base important conclusions only on monuments in reference to which there is no doubt, and on articles whose history, as regards the finding, is fully known, except where the type is well established from genuine antiquities. One of the best recent works on ancient America is flawed to some extent by want of this precaution. Mounds and ancient works are described and figured which do not and never did exist; and articles are represented which are modern productions [*sic*] (Thomas 1898:24-25).

From this they deduce:

> We believe that the "best recent work" alluded to by Thomas is his own final report on mound explorations (1894), and that the "articles whose history . . . is fully known" is a reference to the alleged discovery of the Bat Creek stone. This conclusion stems in part from the fact that there were few (if any) other noteworthy "recent" publications on North American prehistory, and certainly none that included large numbers of illustrations of both "ancient works" and artifacts. Moreover, Cyrus Thomas was never shy about naming names, whether by way of praise or criticism. Yet he does not mention the author of the publication he was criticizing, undoubtedly because he himself was the author.
>
> This of course begs the question of why Thomas did not admit to the failings of his *magnum opus* in a more direct manner. With respect to the Bat Creek stone, which we have now demonstrated beyond a reasonable doubt was one of the "modern reproductions" [*sic*] alluded to by Thomas, we believe that the answer is quite straightforward—Thomas had placed himself in a position such that he could not really afford to pronounce the Bat Creek stone a forgery.

Note that Thomas did not really allude to "the 'best recent work'," as misquoted by Mainfort and Kwas, but rather merely to "*one of the best* recent work*s*." In Thomas's view, "the best recent work" could of course only be his own *Mound Explorations*, whereas "one of the best recent works" at least potentially embraces the efforts of other authors.

Furthermore, Thomas's words, "mounds and ancient works are described and figured which do not and never did exist" echo his own earlier attack on certain illustrations in Squier and Davis (1848): "Some of the singular works described and figured in *Ancient Monuments* and elsewhere are to a large extent imaginary. Of these we may name Nos. 1 and 2, Pl. XXXIV of that work. The wing to No. 1 is not only imaginary, but, according to the Bureau assistant who visited the locality, was made impossible by the topography" (1894:566).

In 1898, Squier and Davis's 1848 volume, although extensive and still authoritative, could not have been considered "recent." However, had Mainfort and Kwas done their homework, they would have checked Silverberg's extensive bibliography (1968), and found that in 1898 there was indeed *another* recent publication on North American prehistory besides Thomas's own work, containing many illustrations of both "ancient works" and artifacts, namely the first (1892) edition of Rev. Stephen D. Peet's *The Mound Builders*. And indeed, if we turn to p. 78 of Peet's book, we find an illustration of the very Squier and Davis earthworks that Thomas had earlier denounced as "imaginary." Furthermore, on pp. 13 and 41 of the same volume, we find illustrations of the famous Davenport, Iowa tablets and elephant pipes, which Thomas was well on record (1894:632-643) as believing were fakes. Peet not only failed to deny the authenticity of the tablets and elephant pipes, but actually had the temerity to cite new evidence in favor of the pipes.

It was Peet's book, *and not his own*, that Cyrus Thomas was denouncing in 1898. The Mound Survey was precisely intended to have the very virtues he cites as having been to some extent absent in the unnamed book to which he so delicately alluded. The "modern productions" (misquoted by Mainfort and Kwas as "reproductions") alluded to by Thomas were clearly the Davenport artifacts, and not his own Bat Creek stone, however enigmatical he may have found the latter. If he did not call Reverend Peet a fool by name, it was perhaps merely out of deference to the clergy.

In an article approvingly cited by Mainfort and Kwas, Stephen Williams (1988:17) defines 'Fantastic Archaeology' as, "when you try to track down the actual sources for the story, it dissolves into nonsense." Mainfort and Kwas are thus indulging in some 'Fantastic Archaeology' of their own when they interpret Cyrus Thomas's veiled attack on Peet's book as pertaining to the Bat Creek stone. It is most unfortunate that Mainfort and Kwas's absurd claim was too recent to have been included in Professor Williams's new book by the same name. Williams himself praises Thomas's 1894 volume, Bat Creek stone and all, so it would appear, as having "for all intents and purposes shut the door, from a scientific standpoint, on the Mound-builder question" (1991:74).

Nor are Mainfort and Kwas on much stronger ground when they claim (p. 10) that "an extensive review of roughly contemporary and later professional literature contradicts [my own] assertion" that "authoritative contemporaries, who knew the circumstances better than anyone today, accepted the tablet as genuine" (p. 113). I had cited Thomas

and Fowke, who clearly regarded it as a genuine, though Cherokee, artifact. To "contradict" me, as they put it, Mainfort and Kwas cite a string of archaeologists and Cherokee ethnologists who *make no mention of it at all*, one way or the other! Silence is hardly the equivalent of denunciation.

Mainfort and Kwas do deserve credit for having unearthed one actual reference to the Bat Creek stone of which I was unaware, by the same Rev. Peet whose book they so carelessly overlooked:

> In another mound on the Little Tennessee, two miles from Morgantown, were found nine skeletons, and with one were two copper bracelets, copper beads, a small drilled stone, an engraved stone which had some of the characters of the Cherokee alphabet on it. The argument which Dr. Thomas makes in connection with these finds [in Thomas 1890] is that the mound-builders were Indians, and the particular tribe who built these mounds were Cherokees. The argument is, however, misleading. It may be forcible as proving the migration and the modern character of the Cherokees, but it begs the question as to the other tribes of mound-builders . . . The value of the finds consists in the fact that the record of the Cherokees is carried back into prehistoric times and the record of mound-building brought up to modern times; but to make the Cherokees the mound-builders of the Mississippi Valley is absurd (1891:146-147).

Like Fowke in 1902, however, Peet was simply taking Thomas's word for it that the Bat Creek inscription is genuine and Cherokee. If Fowke in 1907 denied the existence of any "ancient article," as quoted by Mainfort and Kwas, north of Mexico with other than pictographic writing, it was simply because he continued to accept Thomas's misguided verdict that the inscription was Cherokee and therefore modern.

JOHN EMMERT

Mainfort and Kwas go on to accuse Emmert himself of having forged, or at least planted, the Bat Creek inscription (pp. 12-13). This is implausible on several grounds that I have already enumerated (1988:112-5), but its major problem is that there is absolutely no indication that the inscription is a forgery in the first place, other than the circular, and therefore unscientific, argument that being Hebrew, it must surely be fake.

They argue that Emmert's motive was

> that he felt the best way to insure permanent employment with the Mound Survey was to find an outstanding artifact, and how better to impress Cyrus Thomas than to 'find' an object that would prove Thomas' hypothesis that the Cherokee built most of the mounds in eastern Tennessee? . . . As to the specific signs on the Bat Creek stone, several are passable Cherokee, and the inspiration for the remainder could have been any number of published sources, including illustrations of the Grave Creek stone and the Davenport tablets.

In 1889, however, there was no prospect of "permanent employment with the Mound Survey," since the project was almost completed except for a little mop-up work (Smith 1985:18-19). Furthermore, as Bruce Smith has pointed out, Cyrus Thomas "was not an easy person to work for" (1985:12). He was tight with expenses, and in one letter to J. W. Powell actually prided himself on driving his staff, including specifically Emmert, "day and night" (1887). Emmert's first assignment as a regular assistant, in January through March of 1885, was to excavate the Citico Mound in snow and freezing rain, a task that left him gravely ill with ague, a malaria-like fever. If he had just wanted employment, he could easily have found a less demanding job.

As for ingratiating himself with Thomas by producing a Cherokee mound inscription, I have already demonstrated (1988:113) that in February of 1889 Emmert could easily have done a fine job of Cherokee if that was what he intended. Yet Mainfort and Kwas themselves readily admit (p. 7) that the Bat Creek inscription is *not* intelligible as Cherokee. Grasping at straws, they claim that the Bat Creek letters that do not work as Cherokee may have come from the Grave Creek stone and the Davenport tablets, but do not specify which Bat Creek letters come from which Grave Creek and/or Davenport letters. In fact, of the letters that do not work even fairly well as Cherokee, specifically **a**, **c**, **d**, **e**, and **h** in my Table I and **iv**, **vi**, and **viii** in my Table II (1988), only one would rate even a 'fair' on my scale when compared to either the Grave Creek stone or the principal Davenport tablet. (This is the very simple letter **d**, which has a fair match on the upper panel of the Davenport tablet.) And even if these letters could be matched, how could Emmert have pleased Thomas by finding a tablet with letters drawn from artifacts which Thomas openly regarded as frauds? Once again, when we try to check their story out, it "dissolves into nonsense."

Mainfort and Kwas do point out (pp. 10, 13) that Whiteford (1952) expressed some doubts as to the accuracy of Emmert's work in Tennessee for the Mound Survey. Whiteford, as quoted by Mainfort and Kwas, specifically questioned certain "non-typical" artifacts, in particular the Bat Creek Stone itself, and four burial types that were either "unique," or never "duplicated" by any "recent investigation."

In a discussion of the Bat Creek stone, it is circular to use the Bat Creek stone itself as evidence against Emmert's, and therefore the stone's, credibility. As for the burial types, it should be noted that the "stone domed vaults or 'stone hives'" from Sullivan Co., Tennessee (Thomas 1894:352-353), that were excavated by Emmert and to which Whiteford objected, far from being unique, are in fact very similar to those found by Emmert's colleague John Rogan, in Caldwell Co., North Carolina (Thomas 1894:334). Furthermore, Peet (1903:223) illustrates yet another such vaulted burial in a mound on the Iowa River. If

Emmert's 'stone hives' have never been duplicated (or quadruplicated, to be precise) by more recent investigations, does this mean that Rogan's famous (and unique) finds at the Etowah group (Thomas 1894:292-311) should not be taken seriously either?

Or does it just mean that the Mound Survey excavated and reported on more mounds than any study before or since (over two thousand, according to Thomas 1894:23), and therefore had a higher probability of finding unique artifacts and structures? Mainfort and Kwas themselves admit (p. 12) that Emmert alone "personally directed a truly amazing number of excavations at sites in eastern Tennessee and adjacent areas." Yet the rapidity with which these mounds and earthworks were disappearing forever was noted already in 1884 by F. W. Putnam:

> The opportunities offered by these excursions for comparing the present condition of these wonderful monuments of antiquity with their condition when first described have shown how rapidly they are becoming obliterated. A generation of men has not yet passed away since most of these earthworks were in a good state of preservation; our children's children will look for them in vain unless something is done at once to preserve them . . . Every year that passes without action is one more year allowed for ploughing over and destroying these wonderful works (1884:350).

If Whiteford and his contemporaries did not observe anything like some of the structures and artifacts reported by the Mound Survey, it is most likely because there were simply none left.

The Patina

An important part of the case against a forgery by Emmert, or any one else, however, comes from a careful examination of the patina of the letters, in conjunction with the unusual, comma-shaped word divider that appears between letters **v** and **vi**.

I have already demonstrated (1988:96) that two vertical strokes now clearly present on the stone were not on it when it was found. These strokes were added by an unknown party while the stone was in the National Museum of Natural History, at some time between 1894 and 1970. They are clearly visible in the modern photograph reproduced by Mainfort and Kwas (p. 4), but are conspicuously absent in Emmert's 1889 sketch (1889b), in Thomas's 1890 drawing (reproduced in McCulloch 1988:84), and in Thomas's 1894 photograph (1894:394).

Gus Van Beek, Curator of Old World Archaeology at the Smithsonian Institution, was aware that these two strokes were modern, and was quoted in *Science Digest* (Ford 1972) to the effect that they appeared to him to have the same patina as the rest of the inscription. He concluded that the original inscription must therefore also be modern, and could not date to the 1st or 2nd century AD, as claimed by Cyrus Gordon. When I wrote my 1988 article, I had not yet had an opportunity to check this out, but on the basis of the new Carbon-14 date concluded (p. 108) that Van Beek must somehow have been mistaken. I have since had a chance to actually examine the stone with Van Beek's considerations in mind.

On examination with the naked eye and with a 2X magnifying glass, there are indeed no obvious differences between the vertical strokes and the brighter portions of the original inscription. In particular, they are of roughly the same brightness in contrast with the dark surface of the stone, and therefore seemed to be about as fresh. (This is apparent in the photograph reproduced by Mainfort and Kwas in their Figure 1.)

Under a low-power (20X) microscope, however, the two groups of marks look very different. To understand these differences, it should be recalled that the stone itself is light-tan colored, but that it is coated on the inscribed face and edges with a thin, dark gray-brown, almost black, crust. According to a tag from the USNM Department of Paleontology that accompanies the stone, the stone is an iron-rich siltstone, and the crust is an iron oxide. The tag does not indicate which oxide of iron this is, but it is presumably limonite, goethite, or hematite, chemically similar minerals composed of ferric oxide with varying degrees of oxidation, with yellow to red streaks.

Ferric oxide is semisoluble, so that in a wet environment like that of the Bat Creek burial mound molecules of it will slowly dissolve into the water. After the solution becomes saturated, the ferric oxide will continue to dissolve, but an equal amount of material from the solution will redeposit on the solid mass. In this manner, any sharp corners will slowly become rounded over time, and separate but adjacent pieces may become fused together.

The original letters are, for the most part, cut entirely through the crust into the light siltstone beneath, making the letters stand out very brightly against the dark face of the stone, even without special lighting. In a few places (notably the heads of the letters I identify in my article as **ii** and **vi**), the crust was either thicker or the scribe lost patience, and the letters do not penetrate the crust. In these places the original letters are very hard to read without oblique lighting, and indeed Gordon actually misread the shape of letter **ii** as a result.

Under the microscope, it becomes clear that the two vertical strokes do not penetrate the dark crust, and are bright only because they are the red-orange color of freshly pulverized iron oxide. In the original characters, on the other hand, the red-orange coloration that must have been originally present along the edges of the grooves and in the heads of letters **ii** and **vi** has entirely reconsolidated into the same dark brown finish as the rest of the encrusted face. If the new strokes had patinated under the same wet conditions as the stone, and for as many centuries, they would be as difficult to see without oblique lighting as are the non-penetrating heads of letters

ii and **vi**. The relevant comparison for brightness is therefore between the new strokes and the heads of **ii** and **vi**, not between the new strokes and the rest of the letters.

The siltstone bottoms of the grooves in the letters that penetrate the crust have beads of dark brown oxide on them, which must have reconsolidated since the letters were made. One letter actually has a tiny concretion in it, evidently a speck of silica or other foreign matter that became fused into the groove by the iron oxide dust as it reconsolidated. This concretion (near the base of letter **vi**) is on top of the strokes that made the letter.

Emmert, as quoted above, reported that he struck the stone, but only on its back side, with a steel probe before he actually dug down to it, and indeed there is a small gash in the siltstone on the back. This gash looks much fresher under the microscope than do either the back of the stone or the bottoms of the penetrating grooves.

As Gordon originally noted (1972), three of the Bat Creek letters have small dots or 'pearls' at the end of the line segments, an inessential detail which is common in Greek and Paleo-Hebrew coin inscriptions. Under the microscope it became apparent that these were not drilled in, as Gordon assumed, but rather were nicked in with small knife strokes. Thus, the top of letter **v** looks like a mace head under magnification. Interestingly, the microscope revealed a heretofore unsuspected pearl shallowly cut onto the end of the left leg of the **yod** (letter **iv**). This would originally have been as visible as the new strokes, but now has patinated to where it is quite unapparent to the naked eye.

I would not venture to say just how old the patination on the original characters is, but it certainly gives the impression of great antiquity in comparison with the two modern strokes. This patination is not a mere stain, as might be obtained by soaking the stone for a few months in iron-rich water, but is actually a partial healing of the disturbance to the surface. Van Beek was therefore clearly wrong to have claimed that the patina itself indicates the Bat Creek inscription is modern.

THE WORD DIVIDER

In Paleo-Hebrew, words are ordinarily separated by small marks rather than by spaces as in English, Cherokee, or standard Square Hebrew. In the Bat Creek inscription, there is a small mark between the letters I designate as **v** and **vi**, which Cyrus Gordon has identified as a Paleo-Hebrew word divider. The Bat Creek form is rather distinctive, however, being comma-shaped, instead of a simple dot.

In my earlier article, I erroneously indicated that the distinctive Bat Creek word divider was completely unknown in Paleo-Hebrew before the 20th century discovery of the Qumran manuscripts (p. 115). However, the recent correspondence with Frank Cross prompted me to take a closer look at the Siloam Tunnel inscription, which was found in Jerusalem in 1880, and subsequently removed to Istanbul. In Lidzbarski's 1902 drawing, which I had consulted before writing my article, the word divider in this inscription is shown as a simple dot. Under magnification, however, Birnbaum's photograph (1954:Plate 14) shows that the Siloam inscription in fact consistently uses a comma-like mark that is set at about 60° from the vertical, just as is the Bat Creek word divider. I was therefore wrong to have stated that this was entirely unknown in 1889. Nevertheless, it would still appear that no source for it was known prior to 1880. The famous Mesha Stele, found in 1868, for example, uses the simple dot form to separate words, along with a tall vertical stroke to separate clauses or sentences.

The Bat Creek word divider, therefore, does rule out the possibility that an 18th century or early 19th century prankster such as James Adair or John Haywood placed the stone in the mound at any time prior to 1880. Furthermore, the state of vegetation on the mound when Emmert excavated it in 1889 rules out the possibility that anyone who had been to Jerusalem or Istanbul to scrutinize the Siloam inscription placed the stone in the mound between 1880 and 1889. Therefore the stone, if a forgery, must have been introduced by Emmert as he dug, and so was never in the mound for the letters to patinate at all. The fact that they are, in fact, well patinated, therefore provides independent evidence that the stone is not a forgery.

CONCLUSION

Although Mainfort and Kwas have raised some interesting issues concerning the Bat Creek stone, their three principal conclusions concerning this interesting artifact are seriously defective.

First, their conclusion that the inscription on the stone is not Paleo-Hebrew, as identified by Cyrus Gordon, is based entirely on correspondence with Frank M. Cross, who makes no less than three elementary and documentable errors. The jury is therefore still out (if, indeed, it has ever been seriously empaneled) as to whether the inscription is really Paleo-Hebrew. No one has ever made a better or even equally good suggestion as to what it might be instead.

Second, their conclusion that the brass bracelets found with the stone "are in all probability relatively modern European trade items" is contradicted by the Carbon-14 date on the wooden disk fragments found, according to the official record, in intimate association with the bracelets and inscribed stone. Indeed, even if the inscribed stone had never existed, the bracelets, together with the Carbon-14 date, in themselves provide solid evidence of some kind of a pre-Norse contact between the Old and New Worlds, unless we are to believe (equally remarkably) that

the cementation process for making brass was independently invented in the New World.

And third, when we investigate their claim that in 1898 Cyrus Thomas backhandedly repudiated his own 1894 *Mound Explorations*, including in particular the Bat Creek stone, it turns out that what he really was attacking was an 1892 book by his arch-rival, Stephen D. Peet, and Peet's inclusion of the Davenport tablets and elephant pipes as potentially authentic mound artifacts.

Many real questions concerning the Bat Creek stone do remain unanswered: If the inscription is indeed Paleo-Hebrew, as identified by Cyrus Gordon, what are the unidentified letters and what do they say? Or, if it is not Paleo-Hebrew, as maintained by Frank Cross, then what is it instead? Philology should be able to tell us what it meant, and to whom.

Retesting of the wood fragments with a larger sample of material would in all likelihood pin down the Carbon-14 date to a narrower interval. Furthermore, a new technique for age-dating copper alloys may soon make it feasible to date the bracelets directly. However, the burden of proof now rests on Mainfort and Kwas or others to have these tests performed if they wish to discredit the existing Carbon-14 date.

NOTES

1. It is unclear why Cross, in his letters, shifted the time frame under discussion from the 1st or 2nd century AD, which Gordon and I (without intending to be rigid) had identified as the best fit for the letters, to the period 100 BC – 100 AD. Nevertheless, Cross's claim is false as stated.
2. The finer issues of whether **yhwd** eventually became the Hebrew word for Judea and whether it is the same word as **yhd** that frequently appears on Paleo-Hebrew coins are beyond the scope of the present paper.
3. Since the above was written, Prof. McCarter has been much more negative about the Bat Creek stone in his comment on my article in the July/August 1993 *Biblical Archaeology Review*.
4. This article, which was presented at the ABC Conference, originally appeared as "The Bat Creek Stone: A Reply to Mainfort and Kwas," in *Tennessee Anthropologist* 18 (Spring 1993), pp. 1-26.

REFERENCES

Arundale, Wendy Hanford
  1981 Radiocarbon dating in eastern Arctic archaeology: A flexible approach. *American Antiquity* 46:244-271.
Avigad, Nachman
  1975 A bulla of King Jonathan. Pp. 245-6 and Plate 26 BC in *Israel Exploration Journal* 25. Reprinted in *IEJ Reader*, Vol. II, pp. 1204-6.
Birnbaum, Solomon A.
  1954 *The Hebrew Scripts*, Part Two: Plates. Leiden: E. J. Brill.
  1971 *The Hebrew Scripts*, Part One: Text. London: Paleographia.

Brain, Jeffrey P.
  1979   *Tunica Treasure.* Cambridge: Peabody Museum.

Comstock, Mary and Cornelius Vermeule
  1971   *Greek, Etruscan and Roman Bronzes in the Museum of Fine Arts, Boston.* Greenwich CT: New York Geographic Society.

Cross, Frank Moore
  1968   The Phoenician inscription from Brazil: A nineteenth century forgery. *Orientalia* 37:437-60.
  1969   Papyri of the fourth century BC from Dâliyeh. Pp. 41-62 in *New Directions in Biblical Archaeology.* D. N. Freedman and J. C. Greenfield, eds. Garden City NY: Doubleday & Co.
  1989a Letter to Robert C. Mainfort, Jr., 6/19/1989, cc: Author.
  1989b Letter to Author, 6/21/1989, cc: Robert C. Mainfort, Jr.

Davidson, Gladys R.
  1952   *Corinth: Results of Excavations: Vol. XII, The Minor Objects.* Princeton NJ: The American School of Classical Studies at Athens.

Emmert, John W.
  1889a Letter to Cyrus Thomas, 2/15/1889. Tennessee: Smithsonian National Anthropological Archives, MS 2400.
  1889b Letter to Cyrus Thomas, 2/25/1889. *Loc. cit.*
  1889c Letter to Cyrus Thomas, 3/7/1889. *Loc. cit.*

Ford, Barbara
  1972   Semites in America. *Science Digest* 71 (Jan.):43-53.

Fowke, Gerard
  1902   *Archaeological History of Ohio.* Columbus OH: Ohio Historical Society.

Freedman, D. N. and K. A. Mathews
  1985   *The Paleo-Hebrew Leviticus Scroll (11Q Paleo Lev).* Winona Lake IN: American Schools of Oriental Research.

Gordon, Cyrus H.
  1971   *Before Columbus: Links Between the Old World and Ancient America.* New York: Crown Publishers, Inc.
  1972   The Bat Creek inscription. Pp. 5-18 in *The Book of the Descendants of Doctor Benjamin Lee and Dorothy Gordon.* C. H. Gordon, ed. Ventnor NJ: Ventnor Publishers.

Holum, Kenneth G. *et al.*
  1988   *King Herod's Dream: Caesarea on the Sea.* New York: Norton.

Lee, Larry
  1991   Mystery of the Bat Creek stone. *Knoxville News-Sentinel,* Feb. 18, p. B1.

McCarter, P. Kyle
  1993   Let's be serious about Bat Creek. *Biblical Archaeology Review* 19 (July/August):54-55 *et seq.*

McCulloch, J. Huston
  1988   The Bat Creek inscription: Cherokee or Hebrew? *Tennessee Anthropologist* 13(2):79-123.
  1991   Isaac Roberdeau on the East Fork, Milford, and West Milford Works. Unpublished MS, Ohio State University.
  1993a The Bat Creek inscription—did Judean refugees escape to Tennessee? *Biblical Archaeology Review* 19 (July/August):46-53 *et seq.*
  1993b McCulloch replies to McCarter. *Biblical Archaeology Review* 19 (November/December):14-16.

McKusick, Marshall
  1979   Canaanites in America: A new scripture in stone? *Biblical Archaeologist* 42:137-40.

McKusick, Marshall
  1991   *The Davenport Conspiracy Revisited.* Ames IA: Iowa State University Press.

McLean, Mark
  1982   *The Use and Development of Paleo-Hebrew in the Hellenistic and Roman Periods.* Unpublished Harvard University dissertation.

Mahan, Joseph B., Jr.
  1971   The Bat Creek stone. *Tennessee Archaeologist* 27(2):38-44.

Mainfort, Robert C., Jr. and Mary L. Kwas
  1991   The Bat Creek stone: Judeans in Tennessee? *Tennessee Anthropologist* 16(1):1-19.
  1993   The Bat Creek fraud: A final statement. *Tennessee Anthropologist* 18 (Fall 1993):87-93.

Naveh, Joseph
  1973   An Aramaic tomb inscription written in paleo-Hebrew script. *Israel Exploration Journal* 23:82-91.
  1982   *Early History of the Alphabet: An Introduction to West Semitic Epigraphy and Paleography.* Jerusalem: Magnes Press.

Peet, Rev. Stephen D.
  1891   The migrations of the Mound-Builders. *The American Antiquarian and Oriental Journal* 13 (May):131-150.
  1892   *The Mound Builders: Their Works and Relics,* Vol. 1, 1st. ed. Chicago:Office of the American Antiquarian. Photocopy reprint edition available from Ancient Earthworks Society, 104 Lathrope St., Madison WI 53705.
  1903   *The Mound Builders: Their Works and Relics,* 2nd. ed. Chicago:Office of the American Antiquarian.

Putnam, Frederick W.
  1884   *17th Annual Report.* Cambridge: Peabody Museum.

Richter, Gisela M. A.
  1915   *Greek, Etruscan and Roman Bronzes.* New York: Metropolitan Museum of Art.

Sariandi, Victor
  1985   *The Golden Hoard of Bactria.* Leningrad: Aurora Art Publishers.

Shimada, Izumi and John F. Merkel
  1991   Copper-alloy metallurgy in ancient Peru. *Scientific American* 265 (July):80-86.

Smith, Bruce D.
  1985   *Introduction to Reprint Edition of Thomas (1894).*

Squier, Ephraim G. and Edwin H. Davis
  1848   Ancient monuments of the Mississippi Valley: Comprising the results of extensive original surveys and explorations. *Smithsonian Contributions to Knowledge,* Vol. 1. Washington: Smithsonian Institution.

Stieglitz, Robert R.
  1976   An ancient Judean inscription from Tennessee. *The Epigraphic Society Occasional Publications* 3(2,#65):1-5.

Stieglitz, Robert R., Mainfort and Kwas, Marshall McKusick, *et al.*
  1993,1994 Letters to the Editor. *Biblical Archaeology Review.* November/December and January/February.

Thomas, Cyrus
  1887   Letter to J. W. Powell, 1/20/1887. Smithsonian National Anthropological Archives, BAE Letters Received, Thomas, Cyrus.
  1890   *The Cherokees in Pre-Columbian Times.* New York: N. D. C. Hodges.

Thomas, Cyrus

  1894   Report on the mound explorations of the Bureau of Ethnology. In J. W. Powell, *Twelfth Annual Report of the Bureau of Ethnology to the Secretary of the Smithsonian Institution, 1890-'91*. Washington:Government Printing Office. (Reprinted in facsimile, Washington:Smithsonian Institution Press, 1985.)

  1898   *Introduction to the Study of North American Archaeology*. Cincinnati: The Robert Clarke Company.

Whiteford, Andrew H.

  1952   A frame of reference for the archaeology of eastern Tennessee. Pp. 207-225 in *Archaeology of Eastern United States*. James B. Griffin, ed. Chicago: University of Chicago Press.

Williams, Stephen

  1988   Fantastic archaeology: Fakes and rogue professors. *Symbols* (December):17-23. Cambridge: Peabody Museum and Department of Anthropology, Harvard University.

  1991   *Fantastic Archaeology: The Wild Side of North American Prehistory*. Philadelphia: University of Pennsylvania Press.

ACKNOWLEDGMENTS

The author is grateful to Curtiss Hoffman and Timothy Gregory for invaluable suggestions.

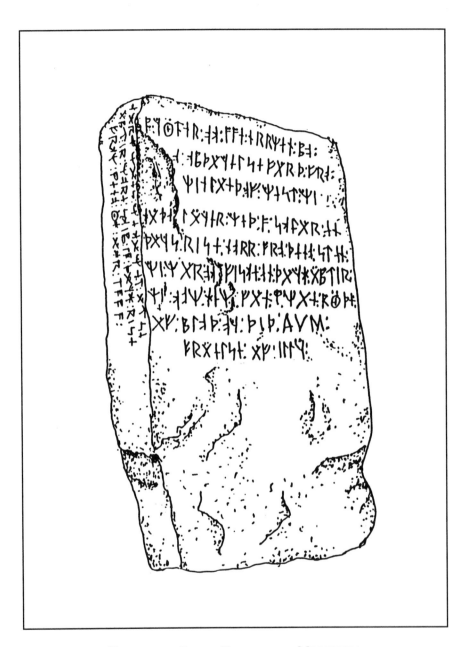

KENSINGTON STONE, KENSINGTON, MINNESOTA

The Decipherment of American Runestones

SUZANNE O. CARLSON

The Hanged God Finds The Runes

I know that I hung
in the wind on the gallows tree
all nine nights
wounded by a spear
and by Odin given
myself to myself
on that tree
which nobody knows
where its roots run

None blest me with a loaf
nor with the drinking horn
I peered down
I grasped up the runes
crying, yet grasping
I fell from that tree

from the Poetic Edda, Hávamál – translation by S. Carlson

That is what the Norse believed. Later scholars have sought other origins for these mysterious signs.

The consensus is that Gothic warriors who had been in contact with the Romans, or the Greeks, had learned about writing and had borrowed and adapted alphabet forms into stick-like forms easily carved on wood or bark. Caesar reported that the Goths cast lots using twigs carved with strange signs. Others contend that the Germanic Odin carried the runes west.

The thousands of 'rune stones' dotting the Swedish countryside are lovingly conserved by a stalwart fan club. The Swedes have grown accustomed to their silent witness of ancient times. The Danes, however, and even less so the Norwegians, were not as enthusiastic about raising runic memorials, but merchants' tallies and wall graffiti attest to their common use. The Icelanders, being mostly of Norwegian stock, carried little interest in runic inscriptions with them to their new home. Barren Iceland is also barren of runic inscriptions.

RUNES IN AMERICA

Carl Christian Rafn, Danish archaeologist, scholar, professor, and Royal Councilor, possessed a formidable knowledge of the repertoire of old Norse literature and, in 1837, produced his *Antiquae Vinlandicum*. In it he presented a forceful case for Norse presence along the New England Coast, specifically Dighton Massachusetts, near the mouth of the Taunton River, in Massachusetts. Rafn had been sent drawings of the Dighton 'Writing Rock' and, in collaboration with scholar and runologist Finn Magnussen, had concluded that **THORFINN** was indeed written on the rock in runic letters of the 11th century.

Rafn's enthusiastic support of an early Norse presence in America set off a flurry of interest, explorations, discoveries, theories, and proofs in an endless search to locate Leif's Vinland. Armed with this or that theory, amateurs and professionals alike scoured the countryside for clues, searching especially for runic inscriptions.

The secret hope of a 'North Atlantic First' believer is finally to find carved in stone the words LEIF WAS HERE or THIS STONE MARKS THE BORDER OF GREAT IRELAND. Since the days of C. C. Rafn and his discovery of **THORFINN** on the Dighton Rock, words, phrases, pleas, and prayers have been discerned carved on stone in a myriad of languages from a myriad of times to bolster the faith of diffusionists.

The longest journey and the longest debate centers on a stone found in 1898 in Douglas County, Minnesota. Olaf Ohman and his son said they had extracted a marked stone from between the roots of a poplar tree while grubbing land. The newly settled Scandinavians of the area were quick to recognize the marks as the runic letters of their forefathers, and a translation soon appeared. It tells of eight Goths and twenty-two Norwegians, out on a voyage of discovery from Vinland, who returned to camp after a fishing trip and found ten of their fellows red with blood and dead. It also states that they had another ten men by the sea looking after the ship which was fourteen days' journey from the site. This translation was dated 1362.

This inscription, on what is now known as the Kensington Stone, was soon declared to be a fake by notable runologists and linguists on both sides of the Atlantic. The prime candidate for hoaxer was the Swede Ohman himself. Disgusted by the publicity, Ohman placed the stone face-down as a doorstep in his barn. A young journalist, Hjalmar Holand, became interested and, in 1907, acquired the stone from Ohman. Holand devoted the rest of his life to defending the authenticity of the inscription. The most likely tie to this inscription is the expedition of Paul Knutson,

DECORATED RUNES

who embarked for Greenland and lands west at the behest of King Magnus of Norway in 1357. The theory is that Knutson's crew made its way through Hudson Bay and up the Nelson River where a reconnaissance party traveled overland to meet its fate.

The notorious stone now has its own museum in Alexandria, Minnesota, but its authenticity is still fiercely attacked or stoutly defended by a new generation of stone watchers.

As the years passed, enthusiasm for finding 'runic' records ran high, and dozens of purported 'rune stones' surfaced. Olaf Strandwold prepared a fairly complete catalogue with translations in his thick pamphlet *Norse Explorers in America*, published in 1948. The East Coast has its share of these candidate runes, including the sought-after name LEIF ERIKSON on the remote little Noman's Island at the mouth of Narragansett Bay.

Debate on the authenticity of these possible testimonials to Norse presence simmers on, with advocates appearing for this or that particular inscription, and detractors ready with a rebuttal. A new angle on interpretation made its debut in 1967 when Alf Mongé, a Norwegian by birth, but a World War II U.S. Navy cryptographer, in collaboration with O. G. Landsverk, a retired engineer, began publishing their claims that coded messages were cleverly concealed within plaintext in runic inscriptions found in Norway and in America. According to Landsverk and Mongé, the messages usually included the name of the author and the date, and they maintained that this encoding was a pastime engaged in by medieval clerics with a penchant for puzzle-making. Mainstream Scandinavian-

ists and runologists were appalled at the very idea, and denunciations were loud and clear.

The battle was still raging in 1971 when three mysterious stones were found on state land at the edge of Spirit Pond, in Phippsburg, Maine, not far from Popham Beach. About six by eleven inches, one stone clearly featured a rough map and runic 'words' placed randomly on one side, while other runes and some images were carved on the other side. The second stone bore a dozen letters on one side, and the third contained a long message of sixteen lines inscribed on both sides.

The finder, a Maine carpenter named Walter Elliott, took the stones to the Bath Marine Museum where director Harold Brown   FORWARDS
suggested the markings might be runic.   BACKWARDS
Subsequently, the stones found their way   UPSIDE-
to Einar Haugen, the distinguished Harvard   DOWN
Professor of Scandinavian Languages and History. In his published evaluation, Haugen was adamant in crying fraud, hoax, modern artifact, "a few Norse words in a sea of gibberish."

Next to study these artifacts were Landsverk and Mongé. Not surprisingly, they found concealed in the "gibberish" a coded message revealing the date as 1123 and the puzzlemaster none other than Bishop Eric Gnupson of Greenland, who had set out in search of Vinland in 1123 and was never heard of again.

The rank and file of runic and Scandinavian scholars stood behind the Haugen pronouncement that these inscriptions were fakes. Only Dr. Cyrus Gordon, orientalist from Brandeis and New York Universities, joined the cryptography side in his book *Riddles of the Past*. The stones remain sequestered and labeled 'fake' in the Maine State Museum, while a few committed researchers continue to probe the meaning of the inscriptions.

A unique school of epigraphy (the study of inscriptions) was born with the publication in 1976 of *America B.C.* by Barry Fell, a marine biologist at Harvard University.

Fell (1919-1995) developed an ardent following, and the Epigraphic Society which he founded has carried the torch for acceptance of a wide range of inscriptions allegedly proving pre-Columbian transoceanic contact with the Americas from the world over. The *Epigraphic Society Occasional Publications* (ESOP) has reported on a number of runic inscriptions.

BACKWARDS

Several researchers, myself included, continue the quest for authentic runic inscriptions in the Americas. Presented herewith is an inventory of all purported runic inscriptions that have come to my attention. I welcome additions to this inventory.

INTRODUCTION:
FORM OF RUNES AND THEIR USE

Futharks: Freyr's Eight, Hagel's Eight, Tyr's Eight

The elder, or earliest, runic alphabet known to us is composed of twenty-four letters arranged in three groups of eight, each group being dedicated to one of the Norse Gods. Transliterated their order looks like this:

Freyr's eight   **f u t h a r k g w**
Hagel's eight   **h n i j p e R s**
Tyr's eight   **t b e m l n g d o**

As Odin saw them:

Sometime during the 8th century, the parsimonious Norse shortened the group to sixteen letters, modified some, eliminating **g, j, e, d, ng, w,** and **p,** and rearranged the order, leaving:

Freyr's 'eight'   **f u t h o r k**
Hagel's 'eight'   **h n i a s**
Tyr's 'eight'   **t b m l R**

They were further modified by the Swedes, who changed the letters **a, h, s, r, b, m,** and **R** into 'short twig' runes.

Numerous variations developed responding to the differing dialects that were evolving into the modern Scandinavian languages. A curious variation was found in the Swedish Province of Hälsingland which gave its name to this 'shorthand' form of runes. For the most part, the vertical staff is omitted, making for quick writing but odd-looking runes. This form seems to have been used throughout the Norse world for more temporary messages written on wood or bark and appears only on a few monumental rune stones. The alternative name of 'staveless' runes is also used.

Another form of shorthand evolved using the same vertical stave for two letters. These are called 'bind' runes.

After some centuries, the Norse realized that their sixteen-rune alphabet was inadaquate for expressing the full range of Nordic sounds and augmented them with dots to differentiate similar letters. These are the later 'stung' runes.

AS THE OX PLOWS

The ancient Greeks often wrote one line left to right and the next right to left, then left to right, and so on. They called this manner of writing *boustrophedon,* or 'as the Ox turns' (as he plows). The early Norse often followed the ox in their runic inscriptions. In addition to boustrophedon and the conventional left to right arrangement, the Norse also wrote right to left in mirror image. In the lushly decorated monumental stones, the messages were contained within the bounds of wonderful interlocking serpentine shapes. Occasionally, random 'graffiti' are found carved in stone, although graffiti *per se* is more apt to be found hastily carved on soup bones or church walls.

THE MURKY ART OF DECIPHERMENT

After determining that a certain set of incised marks might indeed be some form of the runic futhark, or its later form futhork, the first step is to transcribe the runic symbols into Latin letters. Particularly, in the case of the sixteen-rune systems, this process may be quite tricky. For example, an **a** rune could be considered an ordinary 'a', an 'ae', 'au', 'ou' or any number of somewhat 'a'-sounding vowels. Runic **i** represents 'i' and 'e' as well as 'j'. Runic **b** can stand as well for 'p'. **k** is also 'g', while **t, d,** and **th** are occasionally jumbled. As we have seen, there are many variations, with different rune masters adopting their own conventions to represent sounds in different dialects in different regions at different times. The intent in transliterating the runes into Latin letters is to attempt to recognize Old Norse or later Scandinavian words. Many of the symbols in the runic row are common to most alphabets or numbering systems, and the translator must look for diagnostic symbols that are unique to Norse runic writing. These are:

f th R j p b e m o

in the elder futhark, and

f th r b m and capital **R** (actual sound unknown)

in the younger.

The Old Norse of the sagas was written down during the 12th and 13th centuries, often based on a long oral tradition and fairly conservative linguistic development. Before the printing press put order into orthography, spelling varied a great deal according to the whim, mood, and local dialect of the scribe. Modern scholars have codified this into a form called normalized Old Norse. This practice became necessary because northern dialects developed a wide range of vowel sounds in adaptation to frigid northern air. This range of sounds became part of a shifting vowel system called 'mutation' or the rules of umlaut we encounter in modern German and in the other Scandinavian languages.

FRONTWARDS

Runes, however, are not often written in normalized Old Norse, and so the would-be translator faces a major challenge in decipherment.

But runic words alone do not make for coherent translations. As a branch with solid Indo-European tap roots, Norse evolved as a highly inflected language (*i.e.*, one in which words change their form to show case, gender, time, person, etc.). The level of inflection of Old Norse is about the same as Byzantine Greek, which makes sense, given the corresponding centuries of use. Thus, it is a little less inflected than classical Latin, with nouns and adjectives characterized by inflected nominative, accusative, genitive, and dative cases. Verbs are also inflected, with person and number endings, but, like English, use auxiliaries to form the more complex tenses. The subjunctive is separate and very much in use, as is a middle voice. A firm grasp of grammatical structure and syntax is necessary for any translation, and the translator must be prepared to adjust to changes as the differentiation into the modern Scandinavian languages emerges.

GRAFFITI

INVENTORY OF AMERICAN RUNIC INSCRIPTIONS

The Fletcher and Bayview Stones, Yarmouth, Nova Scotia
Reported by Philips, 1875; Jones and Raddall, *ca.* 1920

The first of these stones was found on the shore of Yarmouth Harbor about 1790 by a settler named Fletcher. This four-hundred-pound curio remained a mystery until 1875 when Henry Philips, Jr. of Philadelphia published a pamphlet proclaiming the inscription Old Norse. In 1896, a second stone was discovered on the shore of Yarmouth Harbor at Bay View but has since disappeared. The Fletcher stone may still be seen in the Yarmouth Public Library.

Philips	Transliteration:	**HARKUSSEN MEN VARU**
	Translation:	HARKO'S SON ADDRESSED THE MEN
Carlson	Comments:	The marks on this stone appear to be intentional and some form of writing, but there are no diagnostic runes that would label it as a runic carving.

The Ellsworth Stone, Ellsworth, Maine
Reported by Willoughby, 1898; Strandwold, 1948

Strandwold reports that this stone was taken from the bottom of a grave near Ellsworth, Maine and was reported by Charles G. Willoughby in 1898. Examination of the Willoughby material may help determine the date and provenance of the burial. Strandwold bases his interpretation on a code he devised to translate vertical strokes into letters which he then translates as 'Steinar rules.'

Strandwold	Transliteration:	**STHANAR RAITH**
	Translation:	SThANAR RULED
Carlson	Comments:	There are no diagnostic runes on these stones and no indications that they might be runic.

The Sebec Stone, Sebec, Maine
Reported by Strandwold, 1948

Strandwold gives no background other than that a "Mr. Chatfield, who visited the locality in 1940, says that it is a sportsman paradise." The two lines intersected by vertical strokes do not resemble any known runic symbols. Strandwold managed to extract the words **AUTH REKR** by contriving a combination of 'code' runes and 'regular' runes.

Strandwold	Transliteration:	**AUTH REKR**
	Translation:	TO DRIFT ALONG EASILY

Manana Inscription, Manana Island, Maine
Reported by Strandwold, 1948; Fell, 1976; Whittall, 1976; Carlson, 1993

In 1855, Dr. Augustus Hamlin noticed these mysterious markings on a face of ledge on Manana Island. The 'inscription' is located near the center of the upper plateau on the vertical face of an outcrop 40 or 50 ft. long. The main lines are restricted to a small stripe of intrusive rock (perhaps basalt). Many of the vertical lines continue in a weakened form up and down into the base rock, and the whole thing appears to be natural cracking, perhaps resulting from differential expansion/contraction pressures in the two types of rock. Although the cracks may have been enhanced to form strokes and look as though they could be some form of writing, there was nothing I could interpret as runes.

Strandwold reproduces Malcolm Pearson's fine photograph in conjunction with his own reading of the runic symbols and an English transcription below.

In *America B. C.*, Fell shows a picture of a cast of the intrusive section only, losing all sense of the lines continuing into the base rock. His translation is part 'Norse' and part Celtic-Goidelic. The runes come out **L-NG-B-T** or *langa bata* meaning 'longboat.' The remaining Celtic section is interpreted **B F-N-C C-D-H-H L-B-D**. The whole phrase is translated SHIPS FROM PHOENICIA; CARGO PLATFORM.

Strandwold	Transliteration:	**IK VAGLI LA SIAU ARA AR IUA IIU**
	Translation:	I VEIGLE, LAY (at anchor or remained) SEVEN YEARS, YEAR OF JESUS 32 (1031 AD)
Fell	Transliteration:	**L-NG-B-T B F-N-C C-D-H-H L-B-D**
	Translation:	SHIPS FROM PHOENICIA CARGO PLATFORM.
Carlson	Comments:	First hand observation convinced me that the markings are natural differential weathering on an intrusive band of dissimilar stone on the rock face and that the various 'translations' are the result of enthusiastic partisans of any number of theories.

Popham Beach Stone, Popham Beach, Maine
Reported by Strandwold, 1948

No background is given on this stone, which appears to have random scratches.

Strandwold	Transliteration:	**AR 19 ILIRI ER**
	Translation:	YEAR 19 (1018 AD) IS AN ILL (famine) YEAR
Landsverk	Cryptography:	Advent Sunday 1114 AD

Spirit Pond Stones #1, #2, #3, Phippsburg, Maine
Reported by Haugen, 1972; Whittall, 1972; Buchanan, 1972, 1992; Trilling, 1972; Gordon, 1974; Landsverk, 1976; Syversen, 1979; Chapman, 1981, 1993; Nielsen, 1988, 1992; Carlson, 1993

Stone #1
The first stone depicts a map on one side and a short inscription with primitive drawings on the other. Early investigators considered the map to represent the Popham Beach, Atkins Bay, Spirit Pond area where the stones were found in 1971. The words have been identified as **VINLANT, HOOB, TAKH, TUAU, DAGH, J(EL)AK** and the

numbers **10, 1, 1**. Rendered as VINLAND, HOP TAKE TWO DAYS, this has been construed as a direction map to or from Vinland. **JAK** remains controversial.

Paul Chapman presents an alternative theory, placing the origin and explanation of the map in the Hare Bay, L'Anse aux Meadows area of northern Newfoundland based on navigational directions and other information in the Vinland Sagas.

The reverse side transcribes variously as **MILTIAKI**, or **MILTIAGI**, or **MILDIAKI**, or **MILDIAGI**. Haugen dismissed this word as meaningless. Landsverk and Mongé rearrange the letters according to cryptographic rules and discover the plaintext **LIT A MIK**, translated as BEHELD BY ME, presumably referring to the items depicted on the rude drawings below. This seemingly logical translation is inconsistent with grammatical requirements, however. BEHELD (seen) would need the past participle **LITINN**; BY would be commonly rendered as **AF**; and ME would require the dative **MER**, producing **LITINN AF MER**. It would be easier to say I SAW THESE (things) or **EG LIT THESSUM**.

Reconsidering the plaintext, I select **MILD I AKI** as representing good Norse. In this context **MILD** means 'generous.' With a dative object, phrases such as **MILD I MAT**, 'generous with food,' or **MILD I FE**, 'generous in (giving) money' or goods, are common and represented as such by Haugen in *Scandinavian Language Structures*. Norse **AKI** is a defective dative form of **AKRI** (nominative **AKR**) meaning 'field,' 'meadow,' 'cropland,' or 'pasture' located outside the walls of the home field. Therefore, **MILD I AKI** can comfortably be interpreted as 'generous in (giving of) the fields,' or in English, 'bountiful land.'

Stone #1: OBVERSE

Passim	Transliteration:	**VINLANT, HOOB, TKA, TUAU, DAGH, JAK** and the number **10, 1, 1**
	Translation:	VINLAND, HOP, TAKE TWO DAYS
Carlson	Comment:	**JAK** may refer to the Old Norse word **jak** meaning 'pack-ice.'

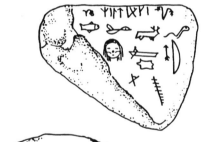

Stone #1: REVERSE

Mongé/ Landsverk	Transliteration: Translation:	**MILTIAKE** (LIT A MIK) BEHELD BY ME
Carlson	Transliteration: Translation:	**MILD I AKI** BOUNTIFUL FIELDS

Stone #2

The second stone bears ten letters on one side, **NORKOLK SJA**, which has defied translation by most researchers. Landsverk transposes the letters and renders the name of 'Henrikus,' the Latin name of Bishop Eric Gnupson of Greenland, who set sail for Vinland in 1117 AD.

Passim	Transliteration:	**NORKOLF SJA**
	Translation:	possible error for NORFOLK
Landsverk	Cryptography:	Henrikus

Stone #3

The third and most impressive stone contains a long message of sixteen lines inscribed on both sides.

Most of the runic symbols on these stones are from the 'normal' sixteen-rune futhark, with groups of letters separated by double dots. The inscription has been criticized for its anomalous letters, namely the 'stung **A**,'which only appears on the Kensington Stone (and now on the Narragansett Stone), its use of double vowels, intrusive **H**, and the introduction of Arabic numbers.

Dr. Einar Haugen was first to analyze the stones. After thorough examination, he found very little Old Norse, the previously cited "few words in a sea of gibberish." Despite his excellent advice on the proper way to translate old inscriptions, he gets stuck in a rut of assumptions that limits his scope of inquiry. He assumes that the double φφ with φ standing for ten, translates into the year 1010, the period of the Vinland voyages; he then examines the runes for examples of grammar and usage from that period, declaring the double vowels and other usages inappropriate to the 11th century. His article in *Man in the Northeast* (1972) is a detailed rebuttal of any possible claims as to the authenticity of the stones.

Accepting Haugen's dictum of 'no understandable Old Norse,' Landsverk and Mongé approached the stones with their usual zeal for cryptology and found hidden in the incomprehensible plaintext another message from Bishop Henrikus, which reads HENRIKUS SAILED 68 DAYS, OCTOBER, 1123 AD.

Dr. Cyrus Gordon entered the debate in 1974 with the publication of *Riddles of the Past* in which he gave serious study to the possibility of a cryptographic message.

In 1988, Dr. Richard Nielsen posited a later date, 14th century, and suggested that the inscription on stone #3 was a list of names, and that the anomalous runes, the double vowels, and the intrusive 'helping' **H** were entirely consistent with 14th century usage.

Haugen held that double dots indicated word dividers. First, examination of rune stones, parchments, and such evidence as the Bayeux Tapestries indicates that word division was, at best, arbitrary and not necessarily indicative of every word separation. This indication allows a great deal more latitude for determining the actual word structure. Leaving few Norse words discernible between dividing marks, Haugen concludes that not only are there few Norse words, but no identifiable grammar, another proof of fraud. He also points to the anomalous letters and numbers as being reminiscent of the Kensington Stone and probably copied from it. In fact, there is only one letter, the troublesome stung **A,** that is unique to both inscriptions. The words which were supposedly copied from the Kensington stone, **NOR, VIST,** are made with different runes or are spelled differently. In comparing the two inscriptions carefully, I find exact replication in the words **FAN** (FOUND), **AHR** (YEAR), and **ThETh** (DEAD), words which I would not consider highly specialized.

In close examination, a significant part of the inscriptions can be broken down into meaningful Norse words, with inflected grammatical patterns evident. But word order is confused and apparent meaning obscure. It reminded me of the difficulties associated with translating the complex and esoteric poetry of the Eddas. It is interesting to note that Stone #3 consists of sixteen lines. Norse poetry is conventionally made up of eight-line stanzas with strict rules, though varied for different types of verse, for the number of stressed and unstressed accents, and for the formation of alliterative phrases and end rhyme. The beat and rhyme control the verse. The inflected nature of the language allows for great variety in word order.

The poetic rhythm, stresses, accents, and alliteration in Stone #3 suggest a poetic meter. The early or Eddic Poems were crisp and demanded strict adherence to the rules. The later Skaldic poetry was more contrived and convoluted in its many forms. In the section of the 13th century prose Edda called the Hátatál, Snorre Snurlusson, the premier medieval scholar in Iceland, presents one hundred and two different metric forms. The possible poetry on this part of Stone #3 has thus far defied translation, and only prose renderings in English have been published.

If the letter forms, some of the spelling, apparent dialectical usage, and the use of numbers suggest a later date for the inscriptions, it would not be inconsistent for it to reflect a later and degraded form of poetic meter. In the wake of the Black Death, toward the end of the 14th century, the Common Scandinavian language began to evolve into the separate languages we know today.

This hypothesis poses a major challenge to eventual translation, but all indications convince me that these stones cannot be a 20th century hoax.

SPIRIT STONE # 3

Stone # 3

Note: Each transliteration varies somewhat. I will present my own and Syversen's to indicate the range of possible transcriptions:

Carlson Transliteration:

SEGAT UM OThIN GELSA SJA
1/7 ThETh HALAThIR ME BAIN BATh
HUM AHR 10/10 —LESA SVEIT L-G
1/2 RISE VEST 1/2 NOR 10 SAGAM J
UNG SKEGHEILMAN HAAKON FAN
HRINIGIN AT VEST PAA LAAGA
SELGA GISL REKN ME BAIN BAThH
UM AHR 10/1/1/ SKVALA LJOISA
PA MAR OI R MAT THAT
SIGLA SHIPI
RI

NA EK JAKTA PAA
MB VINA SHIP VITHH
AGI 1/7 ROIHTHA HOIGVA
GOILSA GANG BANINA HALATHHIR
ME BAIN BATHHUM AHR M/1/1

Syversen Transliteration:

SIKATUMOThIN KELSA SLEA
17 ThIThHALAThIR MIBAINBATh
HUM AHR 1010 IUULISASUITNR
12 RISI VIST 12 NOR 10 SAGAM EL
UNK SKIKHILMAN HAAKON FAN
HRINIKIN AT VIST BAALAAKA
SILKA KIRSLRIKN MIBAINBATh
UM AHR 1011 SKRALALELOOSA
BAMAROOMAT THAT
SIKLA SHIBI
RI
R

NAIKELAKTA BAA
MB UINA SHIP UIThH
AKI 17 BOIHThAHOIKUA
KOISAKANK BANINA HAIAThHIR
MIBAINBAThHUM AHR M 11

Landsverk   Cryptography: Henrikus sailed 68 days, 1117 AD.

Spirit Pond Stone #4

Reported by Whittall, 1974; Keeler, (no date)

The fourth stone was found by Walter Elliott some months later not far from the discovery site of the first three. This small pierced 'pendant' features a Norse-style Christian cross on one side and the word **VIN** and two **M,** or 'ten' symbols, on the other. The cross on the reverse is typical of Norse Christian crosses with serifs at the end of all arms. The markings are consistent with the other stones and should be considered part of the same collection.

Clyde Keeler sees in this a Norse crypto-puzzle attributed to the ubiquitous Henrikus. Keeler speculates that it is clumsy in its craftmanship and may be a poor copy of Henrikus' original.

Carlson   Transliteration: **VIN 20 (10 + 10)**
            Translation: WINE 20 (units)
Keeler   Cryptography: Kirie E(leison) and/or Erik E

The Byfield Inscriptions, Byfield, Massachusetts

Reported by Strandwold, 1949; Mongé and Landsverk, 1967; Pohl, 1972; Landsverk, 1974

This series of marked stones was discovered between 1930 and 1948 in the localities of Byfield, Groveland, and West Newbury along the Merrimac River by Olaf Strandwold, Malcolm Pearson, and Magnus Bjorndal with the help of local residents such as Lawrence Rogers of Byfield.

Strandwold and Bjorndal were enthusiastic backers of early Norse presence and seemed determined to find evidence to support their theories. Random scatterings of lines and curves are picked apart, lined up, and interpreted as letters, mixed and matched from normal, short-twig, and staveless runes, with 'coded' runes introduced from time to time. To my eye, there are no diagnostic runes and nothing conclusive to suggest that these are runes. Both Strandwold and Bjorndal had knowledge of Norwegian. The translations are an interesting mix of words plucked from Cleasby and Vigfusson's *Icelandic Dictionary,* with a few modern Norwegian words used to bridge the gaps. Most of the phrases are too short to indicate the syntax, so grammatical structure is arranged to suit the rich imagination of the translator.

These markings are available for study through the photos in Strandwold's book and in drawings shown in the works of Mongé and Landsverk. From the resolution of the reproduced photos it is impossible to ascertain if they are natural or to determine the technique used to incise the characters.

All of the markings are extremely random in their placement and not consistent with a regular letter placement that would be expected in a written word, nor consistent with any of the forms of word or phrase placement common in runic inscriptions. Few of the marks can be recognized as uniquely runic. Single stroke letters, **V** and **X**, I discount as being diagnostic because they appear in nearly all alphabets and numbering systems. I have not located any examples of similar runic forms and conclude that these marks served another purpose.

Continuing to assume Norse origins for these markings, Mongé and Landsverk pick up on the cryptography of them, discerning the random lines as a different set of letters by rearranging them according to complex rules of numerical and spatial transcription; they manage to extract dates and sometimes days of the week from the puzzle. Fred S. Pohl accepts the cryptography of Mongé and Landsverk.

Øn's Marker

Strandwold	Transliteration:	**JARTAR VAGR ØN SITI**
	Translation:	OVERLAND ROUTE, ON SET THE STONES
Landsverk	Cryptography:	Advent Sunday, December 1, 1118 AD

Iwaf's Grave Stone

Strandwold	Transliteration:	**KUML IWAF Ø**
	Translation:	(the cairn) HOLDS IWAF

Crane Neck Memorial

Strandwold	Transliteration:	**† RISTU THAU**
	Translation:	RISE YE, MEN AND WOMEN, BY THE CROSS

Ijis's Memorial

Strandwold	Transliteration:	**I † RAIS IJIS**
	Translation:	IN THE CROSS RAISE IJUS

Alu's Memorial

Strandwold	Transliteration:	**ALU † RAITH**
	Translation:	ALU PREACHED OR RULED BY THE CROSS
Landsverk	Cryptography:	Advent Sunday, December 1116 AD

Ari's Memorial

Strandwold	Transliteration:	**I SIØI UTHI ARI I ISA VØK**
	Translation:	IN THE SEA OUTSIDE (is) ARI IN AN ICE WAKE

Christian Memorial

Strandwold	Transliteration:	**† RAIS THA I SIU O, JASUI**
	Translation:	† RAISE THE MEN ON SEA ISLAND, JESUS

Øn's Memorial

Strandwold	Transliteration:	**A ISS ØN TIV, RAIS (H)AN AT LIUSI**
	Translation:	ICE OWNS ON, GOD RAISE HIM TO HEAVEN

Aptucxet Stone, Bourne, Massachusetts
Reported by Strandwold, 1948

The stone was found face down, which has preserved the carvings. It is now a feature in the tiny Aptucxet Museum in Bourne, at the heel of Cape Cod. Strandwold continues to mix and match various runic alphabets to concoct his reading. Although some of the marks appear to be runes, no coherent consistency is obvious. The larger marks bear no resemblance to runes. I suspect that these are Native American glyphs.

Strandwold	Transliteration:	**JUI US LIUSOM AUTHI KIRI**	
	Translation:	JESUS AMPLY PROVIDES FOR US HERE AND IN HEAVEN	

Dighton Rock, Taunton River, Dighton, Massachusetts
Reported by Rafn, 1837; Beamish, 1840; Strandwold, 1948; da Silva, *ca.* 1970

Begining in 1630, when Rev. John Danforth copied these carvings, American antiquarians had long been interested in the 'remarkable monument.' But no conclusive explanations were found. In 1830, a committee was appointed by the Rhode Island Historical Society to examine and report on the stone. As part of the inquiry, facsimile drawings were sent to Professor Rafn in Copenhagen for study. In collaboration with the eminent runologist Finn Magnusen, Rafn produced an elaborate dissertation 'proving' its Scandinavian origins. The jumble of marks yielded the name **ThORFINN** (presumably for Thorfinn Karlsefni) and the number **CXXXI** (recorded according to the Old Norse use of 'hundred' as 120 units). The number may represent the number of comrades in Karlsefni's colony at Hop.

Strandwold doesn't disappoint us and extracts his own runic version.

Professor Edmund Delabarre said of this tangled palimpsest of carvings: "It constitutes one of those rare objects where everyone sees something definite, but sees it differently from everyone else." In his 1923 article in *Old Time New England*, Delabarre saw the faded hints of **MIGV...CORTER...**, leading quickly to the name MIGUEL CORTEREAL. The Cortereals, father and sons, were early 16th century Portuguese explorers who very likely found their way to the North Atlantic. Manuel da Silva continued Delabarre's work and discerned additional Portuguese heraldic symbols and crosses of the Portuguese 'Order of Christ' giving further evidence of purported Iberic contact.

Rafn	Transliteration:	**ThORFINN CXXXI**	
	Translation:	THORFINN 151	
Strandwold	Transliteration:	**THYGSTHI HRING O: AAAU 10A AR**	
	Translation:	THYGESTHI THE RING OF SHORE OWNS: 50TH JESUS YEAR	

Pool Whittier Inscription, West Newbury-Groveland, Massachusetts
Reported by Strandwold, 1948

The original drawing was submitted by John G. Whittier to the New England Historical and Genealogical Register in 1854. This remarkable inscription which echoes the early drawings of Dighton Rock is probably a palimpsest of inscriptions by many authors. Strandwold extracts a runic message, Christian in the top row and heathen on the bottom. He jockeys them into old Norse using a combination of staveless, short twig, and, when convenient, normal runes. I find no diagnostic runes evident in the drawing.

Strandwold	Transliteration:	**IS ERU KAA I U, KUTH THURRU EROIUL D THURO FR (U) R TH MAT**	
	Translation:	ON DRY LAND IS CHRISTMAS TIDE, or ON THE ICE ARE 34 MEN ON AN ISLAND. GOD ON DRY LAND IS YULE TIDE	
Carlson	Comment:	The bottom line is given as an appeal to Thor for the stranded mariners.	

The Narragansett Stone, Greenwich, Rhode Island
Reported by Devine, 1985; Buchanan, 1986; Chapman, 1986; Carlson, 1990

In December 1984, a quahogger digging in the mud flats along Narragansett Bay noticed a series of incised marks on a large sandstone boulder located not far from the mouth of a small river emptying into the Bay and presented a sketch to NEARA's Jon Woodson. Later, in April 1985, Charles Devine and Thomas Hardie located the landowner and, with his help, located the stone.

Photos were sent to several authorities soliciting comments. O. G. Landsverk suggested that the inscription "appears to be a genuine Norse runic carving . . . . However," he noted, "I have been unable to find a hidden date in your inscription." At the same time, Donal Buchanan presented his reasons why the inscription could not be runic and offered a pan-Mediterranean translation as the more likely solution. In 1986, Paul Chapman rejoined with his runic translation.

The marks are clearly runes, cut crisply into the rock. The nine letters in two rows are mostly from the normal sixteen-rune futhork, with several anomalous runes. Transliterated, the runes yield: **SHROMLI AO**. Consolidated into a whole phrase, allowing for the modification of transcribing **H** as **K**, the inscription can be: **SKROMLI AO**.

The top word seems to relate to the verb **skramsa**, to 'scream,' in the masculine form of the adjective **skraumi**. I consider the **L** to be part of the derivational component **lig**, or **ligr**, which is a common suffix in many adjectives, and is related to our 'ly' suffix. It seems to convey the sense of 'state of being.' Although it is not shown as such in the dictionaries, it is not far-fetched to expect a variant form **skraumligr**. The missing **gr** doesn't seem far-fetched either. In Modern Icelandic, and in other Scandinavian languages, it is not clearly pronounced. So, this could well be a variant, or dialectic adjective, meaning 'in a screaming state.' The form of the ending would depend on the noun which it modified.

That leaves **AO** as the modified noun. **A** is the feminine Norse noun for 'river,' with an old form **AO** declined thus: nominative, accusative, and dative—**AO**; genitive—**AR**. Thus, **skraumli(gr) ao** would mean something like 'in a screaming state river,' or 'screaming river.' The Cleasby and Vigfusson Icelandic dictionary has: the feminine noun **Skrauma-u**, and **Skraumu-hlaupa** a., the name of a river in Iceland taken from the Landnamabok, roughly 'the river of screaming leaps,' denoting turbulence, probably (in Iceland) from glacial ice melt. A bridge was built in the 1920s over the Skrauma Ao, also in Iceland. I considered several variations of the verb **skrama**, 'to scare away,' but none of them made sense either in context or grammatically.

Don Buchanan's interpretation of the inscription as pan-Mediterranean languages does not address the rigorous inflectional grammatical systems of those languages, which to my mind, makes his translation dubious.

Chapman considered an initial mark which showed in early photos, and reads it as a **Th** coming up with **thes(s)** meaning 'thus.' His transliteration differs from mine somewhat. In **HRAMDI** he transposes the **O** to an **A**. The switch from a **T** to a **D** is possible. He derives this word from **hrammdyr**, meaning 'beast of prey,' but without the **r** nominative ending, he leaves us with a dative ending having the sense of 'for,' or 'of' the beast of prey. I don't know how he gets **ᚠ** to represent **j**, but I'm sure he has some precedent, and I'll accept that as well as the transposition into **ag**.

In summation, the arguments in favor of authenticity seem to be that: 1. It is reported to have been known before 1972 so it couldn't have been copied from the Spirit Pond stones. 2. After its discovery, it was reported to and examined by a team of reputable NEARA members. 3. A similar, or cognate, name is attested for a river in Iceland. 4. Marker stones are common at fords or crossing points of rivers, though usually with memorial inscriptions. 5. No forger with a motivation has been suggested or accused.

It can also be argued that the **gr** ending is my assumption and not attested and that the anomalies in letter form and spelling, particularly the vowels, suggest something amiss.

A search of the historical record to ascertain any knowledge of the stone before 1972 (or 1898) is necessary to determine whether this stone is a candidate for an authentic Norse inscription.

Buchanan	Transliteration:	Th S/Z C/K R B TO L I
		DON/TON/DUEN/TUEN A/O/E
	Translation:	REGISTERED BOUNDARY LINE, THE OWNER
Carlson	Transliteration:	SKROMLIgr) AO
	Translation:	SKREAMING RIVER or SCREAMING RIVER
Chapman	Transliteration:	HROMDI AJ
	Translation:	THUS BEAST OF PREY TERROR

Newport Tower Inscription, Newport, Rhode Island
Reported by Landsverk, 1974; Syversen, 1979; Chapman, 1981; Hahn, 1989

Initial study suggests random placement of a few short strokes with no resemblance to runic characters. However, if they are viewed as being written with a severe backhand slant and translated into vertical forms, they are consistent with short-twig runes. Because of the non-diagnostic nature of one-line vertical stroke letters, we are left with very little on which to base a firm conclusion.

The letters could spell **ALKRS** which has no apparent meaning to me. It could be a mason's initials, date, or some other message. The long, thin, attenuated letters bear a resemblance to the forms of graffiti found in Norwegian churches. It is not unlikely that a mason scratched a quick message for posterity before the stonework was covered with plaster. This sort of hidden thing is often uncovered in old construction. I hope that these marks will be examined more carefully as part of any detailed study of the Newport Tower.

Landsverk, Mongé, Syversen, and Hahn found the ubiquitous cryptographic name 'Henrikus' hidden in these marks.

Carlson	Transliteration:	**ALKRS**
	Translation:	Possible initials or mason's marks
Landsverk/	Transliteration:	**HE N IK R S** with a /U above
Syversen/Hahn	Cryptography:	December 10, 1116
Strandwold	Transliteration:	**UN AR S**
	Translation:	ØN YEAR 11 (1010 AD)
Keeler	Dedication mark:	IN HOC SIGNO and/or IHS
Pohl	Accepts Landsverk	

Northman's Rock, Mount Hope, Rhode Island
Reported by Strandwold, 1948

This rock appears to have another series of random marks wishfully teased into runic form using the same techniques of analysis and interpretation used on the Byfield Stones.

Strandwold	Transliteration:	**DAR RAN AS A RUTH**
	Translation:	THERE IS A HOUSE IN THE CLEARING

Noman's Island Inscription, Noman's Island, Rhode Island
Reported by Strandwold, 1948; Gray (date unknown)

This inscription on a remote little island in Narragansett Bay was known to Delebarre and published in Edward Gray's book, *Leif Eriksson, Discoverer of America, A.D. 1003*. Mr. Gray apparently chalked the inscription with a slight adaptation to make it read *Lief Eriksson*, which was sent to Magnus Olsen in Oslo for interpretation. Strandwold presents his transliteration as a mix of elder, normal, and short-twig runes, reading **LEIFS ERIKSSUNAR EY THIRTIKIR MEN** or LEIF ERIKSSON'S ISLAND, 30 MEN. 'Erik' would probably have been written 'AErikr' at that time. It is intriguing to imagine an authentic Eriksson autograph in Narragansett Bay, but more conclusive evidence is needed.

Strandwold	Transliteration:	**LEIFS ERIKSSUNAR EY THIRTIKIR MEN**
	Translation:	LEIF ERIKSSON'S ISLAND, 30 MEN

Ax, Pemberton, New Jersey
Reported by Nadaillac, 1895; Strandwold, 1948

Other than saying that this ax was found near Pemberton, New Jersey, and copied from "manners and monuments of prehistoric people," there is no comment on context, date of find, or other specific information. From the poor resolution of the photo it is difficult to discern any diagnostic runes, and Strandwold takes considerable license with his transliteration, which is a combination of twig and staveless runes. The translation is without grammatical context.

Strandwold	Transliteration:	**SVEAR TUKU UR LEN**
	Translation:	THE SWEDES TOOK OUT CHARTER

The Potomac Inscription, Washington, DC — Not illustrated
Reported by the Chicago Tribune, 1867

On July 16, 1867, the Chicago Tribune reported "an extraordinary discovery," "A remarkable runic" inscription, and "America discovered by the Irish." The remains of an Icelandic woman buried in 1051 with trinkets, Roman coins, etc., was exhumed below the Great Falls of the Potomac.

In the flamboyant style of the period, the article describes the Norse discovery of America as told in the Skalholt Saga, and the Potomac discovery. The Saga, claimed to have been written in 1117 and found in the runes of the Skalholt, Iceland, Cathedral in 1863, tells of the voyage of Hervardr southerly from Vinland along the coast of Hvitramannaland (Great Ireland), who travelled up a river to a succession of falls, called Hvidsaerk from their foamy appearance. It also tells of the death of a natural daughter of Snorri Thorfinnsson. Snorri was the first Norse baby born in Vinland.

In pursuit of evidence, an expedition consisting of Thomas C. Raffinnson, M. Louis Lequereux, a distinguished geologist, Professor Brand, and Dr. Boyce of Boston, set out June 28, 1867 and found to their awe and astonishment not only the burial but a runic inscription. Unfortunately, the article does not show us the form of the runes, only a transcription into Latin letters with some signs and indistinct letters in brackets.

Rafinnsson was a fellow of the Royal Society of Northern Antiquities, Copenhagen, and was the runic scholar in the group. He presents his English translation "as nearly literally as possible," and, omitting the signs.

The translation as given follows a common formula for epitaphs on memorial and grave stones, particularly in late Medieval Iceland. Raffinnson's translation is accurate, although Norse forms are more cryptic. For example, there is no English equivalant for **SAMFOThRE**, denoting children of the same father (but not mother). A number of assumed fillers are included in brackets. Their use would be consistent with widespread use of abbreviations in Norse writing. The author comments that the form of the runes is an ancient style known as *Narvok* found in the Orkneys and the Isle of Barljof, which, by his description, seem to use bind runes extensively. I'm not familiar with this type of rune and am truly sorry that drawings are not given to confirm the possible authenticity of this inscription.

Raffinnson	Transliteration:	**HER HVILLIR SYASY** (sign **T**) **FAGRHARDR** (sign **X**)
		AUS[TFIR] THINGR [IK]IA KILDI
		SY[ST]R TH[OR]G SAM[FETh]RA (word or sign obliterated)
		HALFTHRIT[UGR] (sign **X**)
		GLEDA GUD (sign **X**) **SJAL HJENAR** (sign **X**) **MLI** (unknown sign)
	Translation:	HERE RESTS SYASY (SUASU) THE FAIR HAIRED,
		A PERSON FROM THE EAST OF ICELAND,
		THE WIDOW OF KJOLDR, SISTER OF THORGR,
		CHILDREN OF THE SAME FATHER..25 YEARS OF AGE.
		MAY GOD MAKE GLAD HER SOUL, 1051.

Grave Creek Stone, Grave Creek, West Virginia

Reported by Schoolcraft, 1824; Strandwold, 1948; Fell, 1976

By 1775, westward explorers took note of the Grave Creek Mound. Initial investigation in 1819 promised to reveal "thousands of skeletons," and in 1838 an impressive tomb was found, inviting interpretation as a "royal burial." Five years later, Henry Rowe Schoolcraft found the curious relic, now known as the Grave Creek Stone, lying among the debris. Schoolcraft termed it an "intrusive Antiquity" not of native origin, and various scholars have tried to decipher it as Libyan or Numidian. His assertion occasioned more controversy on the origins of the Adena culture, which continues today, most recently with Barry Fell's contribution in *America B. C,* in which he describes it as an Iberian inscription written in Phoenician, 1st millennium BC.

Meanwhile Strandwold, in his runic quest, brought this curious relic into the Norse fold by his usual methods and produced a lengthy translation.

Strandwold	Transliteration:	**IK HNA A U ØNAR IULRA,**
		A A—NG Ø: H Ø DD
	Translation:	I KNELT ON THIS ISLAND ØN'S
		YULE SITE ON MEADOW ISLAND.
		NOW THE ISLAND IS A SANCTUARY,
		WHERE HOLY THINGS ARE HOARDED

Braxton-Wilson Tablet, Central West Virginia

Reported by Strandwold, 1948

Unfortunately, Strandwold gives no background material on the date or context of the find. Of the twenty-two letters, none can be construed as diagnostic. He considers the 'cross' at the bottom a Christian symbol which indicates a date between 1000 and 1050 AD. Without any other characteristic features, I consider this horizontal line with one vertical stroke to be too universal to be diagnostic. I suspect the roots, as in the case of the Grave Creek Stone, are to be found either in Mediterranean contact or in Native American symbols.

Strandwold	Transliteration:	**RIKAR O Ø KURI VERI ERIK**
		NU ØLE
	Translation:	RICHARD OWNS THE ISLAND; GURI
		(GUDRID) HAD HUSBAND IN ERIK;
		NOW OLE

Rushville Ohio Stone, Rushville, Ohio

Reported by Syversen, 1979; McCulloch, 1990

This small roughly triangular stone was discovered in 1972 in an uncultivated field or on a mound near Rushville, Ohio. Comprised of three lines and twelve symbols, the letters transliterate from twig runes into **HA? KR**. The **L** or **T** could be interpreted as one letter **E**, from the elder futhark. Syversen offers a number of possible translations but settles on "in this mound is Haukr buried." He focuses on deciphering a dated cryptogram, solved as Advent Sunday, December 1112.

J. Huston McCulloch shed new light on this inscription when he discovered its prototype buried in Nevil Shute's 1940 novel, *An Old Captivity*, where Leif Erikson carves the names of the young lovers, **HAKI** and **HEKIA,** on a stone so that their love shall last as "long as this stone shall endure."

This innocent copy of a declaration of love should caution us to investigate each stone. Perhaps all modern artifacts are not frauds created to befuddle the minds of scholars.

Syversen	Transliteration:	**IS, HA'KR, HEKIA**
	Translation:	IN THIS MOUND IS HAUKR BURIED
	Cryptography:	Advent Sunday, December 1112
McCulloch	Transliteration:	**HAKE HEKJA**
	Translation:	HAKE and HEKJA

Piqua Stone, Piqua, Ohio
Reported by Morehead, (date unknown); Landsverk, 1974

According to Landsverk, the Piqua tablets had been discovered some time before 1910 when they were illustrated and discussed by Warren G. Morehead in his *Archaeological Encyclopedia*. They had been excavated from a mound near Piqua, Ohio, and have since been lost. It is impossible to tell if the sketch is reliable.

However, as drawn, the majority of the symbols bear a strong resemblance to runes, and the transliteration is fairly straightforward. Half of the symbols are missing on the second tablet making translation impossible. It would be worth additional study.

Landsverk   Transliteration: U K T ANG G - - L L ? U
U ? L K I K - - - - I K
- - - A NG F

Spruce Hill Stone, Ross County, Ohio
Reported by Mallery, 1951

Shown in a photo and mentioned as an aside in his description of the Spruce Hill iron smelting furnaces, Mallery notes "near the Nordic furnace there is a circular stone-covered mound on a high promontory. Set deep in top of this mound is a stone engraved in runes." He likens the accompanying cist to Scandinavian "passage graves." It is impossible to tell if these are natural marks, but if it is engraved, there are no diagnostic runes. Also, Swedish passage graves predate runecarving by more than a thousand years.

Mallery   Transliteration: None given
Translation: None given

Kensington Stone, Kensington, Minnesota — Illustrated on title page for this section
Reported by Flom, 1910; Holand, 1932/40/46/56/59/62; Hennig, 1938; Thalbitzer, 1946/47; Jansson, 1949; Hagen, 1950; Pohl, 1952; Wahlgren, 1952; Liestol, 1964; Mongé and Landsverk, 1967; Hall, 1982/94; Neilsen, 1987/88/89; Nilsestuen, 1994

Since it first came to the attention of the press in 1898, this stone has triggered both heated debate and boiling emotions on the part of partisans and detractors.

The inscription of sixteen lines and sixty-five words and numbers is not difficult to translate. In fact, its ease of translation has led to the conclusion by some that it is written in a dialect of 19th century Swedish (*Dalcarian*, from finder Olaf Ohman's home district).

Early investigators, particularly the scholars back in the Old Country, tended to expect Old Norse to be Old Norse, classically correct in grammar, spelling, and syntax. Any deviation from the classical norm was tendered as proof of fraud. Professor O. J. Breda of the University of Minnesota, the Norwegian philologist, Olaf Rygh, and historian Gustaf Storm, along with George T. Flom, discounted its authenticity.

A great deal of argument surrounded an assumed 'Viking' date for the inscription. The Roman-Arabic date on the stone was unrecognized or ignored in the early debates.

Journalist Hjalmar Holand took up Ohman's cause and stoutly defended his position, with occasional support from scholarly circles. The German geographer Richard Hennig, together with Hjalmar Lindroth (1938), Danish Eskimologist William Thalbitzer (1946), and American S. N. Hagen (1950), supported the authenticity of the stone.

The noted Swedish don of runes, Sven Jansson, and Norwegian runologist, Aslak Liestol, were ready with a counterattack, joined by Wahlgren (1958) and Blegen (1968) who were entrenched in a view of flat denial. The objections seem based largely on character attacks on Ohman or Holand, or on circular reasoning contrived to prove points not always logical. Some accusations are just plain silly, for example, that Ohman carved the stone, dug up a tree, bent the tap-roots around the stone, reburied it, and waited until the roots took hold of the stone and the time was right for him to perpetrate his hoax.

Holand studied runes and the evolution of the modern Scandinavian languages and presented forceful arguments in favor of the inscription language being a dialect of 14th century Swedish.

In 1967, Mongé and Landsverk added their cryptographic solution to the evidence.

Richard Nielsen has pursued the case for authenticity for some years, doing meticulous research in Scandinavian museums and libraries, and presenting lengthy arguments for the precedent and usage of each individual letter, number, word, and phrase, as appropriate usage for the year 1362, leaving little doubt as to the authenticity of the language.

In 1982, Dr. Robert Hall, Linguistics Professor at Cornell University, published a well-reasoned, clear-headed review of the whole Kensington Stone debate in a slim volume titled the *Kensington Stone is Genuine*. A reworked version was published in 1994 as *The Kensington Runestone, Authentic and Important*. These studies should convince all but the most obstinate that Ohman was no hoaxer and that the inscription is authentic. After following the debate for many years and studying the runes and the language, I, too, am convinced that this stone is genuine and that it reports actual events as interpreted by Holand, Hall, and Nielsen, and recently published new work by Hall and Nilsestuen.

Passim   Transliteration:

8 GOTER OK 22 NORRMEN PA
O OPTHAGELSFARTH FRO
WINLANTH OF WEST WI
HATHE LAGER WETH SKJAR EN
THAGS RISE RISE NORR FRO THENNO
STEN
WI WAR OK FISKE EN THGH APTIR
WI KOM HEM FAN 10 MAN ROTHE
AF BLOTH OG THETH AVM
FRAELSE AF ILLY
HAR 10 MANS WE HAWET AT SE
[APTIR WORE SKIP 14 THAGH RISE]
FROM THENO OH AHR 1362

Translation:

8 GOTHS AND 22 NORWEGIANS ON
(THIS) DISCOVERY – VOYAGE FROM
VINLAND OVER (THE) WEST WE
HAD CAMP BY 2 SKERRIES ONE
DAYS JOURNEY NORTH FROM THIS STONE

WE WERE AND FISH(ED) ONE DAY AFTER
WE CAME HOME FOUND 10 MEN RED
WITH BLOOD AND DEAD AV(E) M(ARIA)
PRESERVE FROM EVIL
HAVE 10 MEN BY THE SEA TO SEE
AFTER OUR SHIPS 14-DAYS JOURNEY
FROM THIS ISLAND YEAR 1362.

Mongé/	Cryptography:	**HARREK IVNE ME(K) TOLLIK HOAAR M(EK) 1362 AD**
Landsverk/ Syversen		
Carlson	Comment:	See my earlier comments. I generally accept the translation above.

Ludlow Cave, South Dakota
Reported by Fell, 1986

As part of the petroglyph assemblage in Ludlow Cave, three marks below the neck of the cow appeared to Barry Fell to be runes. Using Strandwold's table of variant runes, he deciphered the letters **M-L-T** as signifying MALTA in Old Norse, or milk, and he presumed an 800-year-old date for this textbook message that cows give milk. **MALT** is 'malt' for brewing; 'milk' is **mjólk**.

Fell	Transliteration:	**M-L-T**
	Translation:	MILK
Carlson	Comment:	I see no diagnostic runes here, and it
		seems the scratches have another relationship to the petroglyphs.

Heavener Inscription, Heavener, Oklahoma
Poteau Stone, Poteau, Oklahoma
Shawnee Stone, Shawnee, Oklahoma
Reported by Farley, 1951/90/94; Mongé and Landsverk, 1967; Pohl, 1972; Syversen, 1979; Landsverk, 1974; Nielsen, 1987

Local tradition has it that a Choctaw hunting party in the 1830s discovered the eight mysterious signs that make up the Heavener inscription. It was reported to have been seen in 1874, and an eyewitness, Luther Capps, reported seeing it in 1898. In 1913, the inscription was rediscovered by Carl F. Kemmerer of Heavener, who sent a copy of it to the Smithsonian for evaluation. The Smithsonian confirmed that the characters were runic, but guessed that the carver had a Scandinavian grammar as a guide. Gloria Farley was first taken to the site in 1928, but it was not until 1951 that she found it again and dubbed it the 'Heavener Runestone.' After years of effort, Mrs. Farley's persistence paid off, and the stone, 12 feet wide and 10 feet long with eight six to nine inch high letters, was fenced for protection. The Heavener Runesone State Park was dedicated in October 1970.

The runes were correctly recognized by early analysts as from the elder futhark, spelling out **GAOMEDAL** or **GNOMEDAL**. Alf Mongé read **GAOMEDAT** and extracted the date of November 11, 1012 from a cryptographic message. In 1967, another incised stone was found in Poteau, 10 miles away. A third similar inscription was found in Shawnee, Oklahoma in 1969. These three inscriptions bear enough resemblance to each other to be considered together.

In 1986, Richard Nielsen offered a transliteration of **GLOMEThDAL**, translated as Glome's valley, for the Heavener Stone, and **GLOI ALLW**, magic or protection to Gloi, for the Poteau Stone. The Shawnee stone is transposed as **MEDOK** with no translation given.

The elder futhark was replaced by the shorter 16-rune version in the 9th century or so. If authentic, the language would be a form of common Scandinavian. Due to the limited number of inscriptions from this period, linguists are dependent on reconstructions to unravel the structure and meaning of this early language.

My transliteration varies slightly from the others: Heavener, **GAOMEDAL**; Poteau, **GAOIEALTH**; Shawnee, **MLDOK**. But I can offer no translations that would vary substantially from Nielsen.

Without question, these inscriptions are runic. If reports of their early discovery are accurate, it is difficult to imagine Swedish or Norwegian pioneers carrying J. T. Liljegren's *Runlärabok* (1832) into the wilderness for consultation when carving runes, and the 9th-century date suggested by the letters offers intriguing evidence of early contact.

In 1987, Paul Chapman offered a reverse reading for the Heavener inscription, producing **LADEMONG**, with a translation TO INVITE BARTER. He presents no reading for the Poteau Stone and transcribes the Shawnee Stone as **MYRDOK**, 'to conceal a murdered body.'

Heavener Inscription:

Mongé/ Landsverk/ Syversen	Transliteration:	**GAOMEDAT**
	Cryptography:	(year) 1012
Nielsen	Transliteration:	**GLOMEThDAL**
	Translation:	GLOME'S VALLEY
Chapman	Transliteration:	**LADEMONG**
	Translation:	TO INVITE BARTER
Carlson	Transliteration:	**GAOMEDAL**
	Translation:	None given
Pohl		Accepts Mongé and Landsverk

Poteau Stone:

Syversen	Transliteration:	**G A NG I E A L Th**
	Translation:	GOING TOGETHER ALWAYS
	Cryptography:	October 3, 1016
Nielsen	Transliteration:	**GLOIE ALLW**
	Translation:	MAGIC OR PROTECTION TO GLOI
Carlson	Transliteration:	**GAOIEALTh**
	Translation:	None given
Landsverk	Transliteration:	**GAOIEA (17) Th**
	Cryptography:	November 11, 1017
Pohl		Accepts Mongé and Landsverk

Shawnee Stone:

Syversen	Transliteration:	**MEDOK**
	Translation:	November 24, 1024
Nielsen	Transliteration:	**MEDOK**
	Translation:	None given
Chapman	Transliteration:	**MYRDOK**
	Translation:	CONCEAL A MURDERED BODY
Carlson	Transliteration:	**MLDOK**
	Translation:	None given
Pohl		Accepts Mongé and Landsverk

Tulsa Stone, Tulsa, Oklahoma
Reported by Landsverk,1974; Syversen, 1979

This inscription shown by Landsverk and Syversen is clearly a carved inscription of some sort, but, as the forms are not runic, I will turn them over to students of other alphabets and other languages for interpretation.

Landsverk	Transliteration:	GI (SAS) (KI) SSI
	Cryptography:	December 2, 1022
Mongé	Cryptography:	Advent Sunday, December 2, 1022
Syversen	Comment:	Does not consider it runic
Pohl		Accepts Mongé and Landsverk

The Colorado Stone
Reported by Hahn, 1992

The late Albert Hahn suggested that this stone was a likely candidate for a runic inscription, but added that there are "some strange features about these letters" that keep their true identity up in the air. He considers their transliteration as possible runes, or as possible Greek letters, or as possible rune 'magic' in the form of cryptography. He presents his evidence and leaves the question open.

Hahn	Transliteration:	E T L U
	Translation:	None given
	Cryptography:	Not solved

Deer Lake, Ontario — The published photo is not clear enough to interpret.
Reported by Strandwold, 1948

This enigmatic marking is apparently found in association with ancient stone foundations, chimneys, and other structures. Strandwold thinks the area is one of great promise. The jumble of random marks does not suggest much promise to me. I can find no hint of runes in these marks.

| Strandwold | Transliteration: | BUA ARA IUJ ERU ThRIR |
| | Translation: | DWELLING-YEARS OF JESUS ARE 3 (1002 AD) |

Runes you will find
the letters will counsel
great mighty letters
strong magic letters
which the wise one painted
and the holy gods made
carved by Hroftar-Odin

from the Poetic Edda, Hávamál – translation by S. Carlson

REFERENCES

Agrell, Sigurd
1920 *Runornas Talmystik och Dess Antika Forebild*. Lund: C. W. K. Cleerup.
(1920) *Rokstenens Chiffergator och Andra Runologiska Problem*. Lund

Beamish, North Ludlow
1841 *Discovery of North America by the Northmen in the Tenth Century*. London: T. & W. Boone.

Bjerrum, Anders
1966 *Grammatik over Skanske Lov*. Kobenhavn: Gyldendal.
1967 *Grammatik over De Sjaellandske Love*. Kobenhavn: Gyldendal.

Blegen, Theodore C.
1968 *The Kensington Rune Stone: New Light on an Old Riddle*. St. Paul: Minnesota Historical Society.

Brink, Thorgunn Snaedal
1983 *Igul ok Bjorn Lato resa stenen, Runstenar och runinskrifter i Sigtuna Musseer*. Uddevalla.

Buchanan, Donal B.
1985 Report on the Narragansett Inscription. *NEARA Journal*, 20(1&2).
1993 Spirit Pond Runestones. *ESOP*, Vol. 21.

Carlson, Suzanne O.
1990 The Narragansett Stone reconsidered. *NEARA Journal*, 25(3&4).
1993 Manana revisited. *NEARA Journal*, 27(3&4).
1994a The Spirit Pond inscription stone, rhyme and reason, Part I. Pp. 1-7 in *NEARA Journal*, 28(1&2).
1994b *Ibid*., Part II. Pp. 74-82 in *NEARA Journal*, 28(3&4).

Chapman, Paul H.
1981 *The Norse Discovery of America*. Atlanta: One Candle Press.
1986 Narragansett Bay runestone translation. *NEARA Journal*, 21(1).
1987 Oklahoma runestones. *ESOP*, Vol. 16.
1993 An in-depth examination of the Spirit Pond Runestones. Pp. 114-137 in *ESOP*, Vol 21.
1994 Spirit Pond Runestones. *ESOP*, Vol. 22.

Cleasby, Vigfusson and Craige
1957 *Icelandic-English Dictionary*. Oxford: Oxford University Press.

da Silva, Manuel Luciano
1970s *Portuguese Pilgrims and Dighton Rock*. Private Publication.

Devine, Charles, Tom Hardie, and Jon Woodson
1985 A newly-located inscription from Narragansett Bay, Rhode Island. *NEARA Journal*, 20(1&2).

Farley, Gloria
1990 The Ohio runestone. *ESOP*, Vol. 19.
1994 *In Plain Sight: Old World Records in Ancient America*. Columbus GA: ISAC Press.

Fell, Barry
1976 *America B. C.* New York: Quadrangle/New York Times Book Co.

Flom, George T.
1910 *The Kensington Runestone*. Transactions of the Illinois State Historical Society.

Fries, Ingegerd
1990 *Nutida Islanska*. Stockholm: Biblioteksförlaget.

Glendening, P. J. V.
1961 *Teach Yourself Icelandic*. London: English University Press, Ltd.

Goodwin, William B.
1946 *Ruins of Great Ireland in New England*. Boston: Meador.

Gorden, E. V.
1957 *An Introduction to Old Norse*. New York: Oxford University Press.

Gordon, Cyrus H.
1974 *Riddles in History*. New York: Crown Publishers.

Hagen, S. N.
1950 The Kensington runic inscription. *Speculum, 25*.

Hahn, Albert G.
1990 What lies behind the Spirit Pond rune stones? *NEARA Journal, 24*(1&2).
1992 What magic do the Colorado runes work? *Western Epigraphic Society Newsletter*.

Hall, Robert A., Jr.
1982 *The Kensington Stone is Genuine*. Columbia SC: Hornbeam Press, Inc.
1994 *The Kensington Rune Stone. Authentic and Important*. Lake Bluff IL: Jupiter Press.

Haugen, Einar
1972 The runestones of Spirit Pond, Maine. *Man in the Northeast, 4*.
1982 *Scandinavian Language Structures*. Minneapolis: University of Minnesota.

Holand, Hjalmar R.
1940 *Norse Discoveries and Explorations in America*, pp. 982-1392. 1969 Reprint. New York: Dover Publications.

Horsford, Eben N.
1892 *The Landfall of Leif Erikson, A. D. 1000*. Boston: Damerell and Upham.

Ingstad, Helge
1966 *Land Under the Pole Star*. New York: St. Martins Press.

Jacobsen, Lis og Erik Moltke
1942 *Danmarks Runeinskrifter* Ejnar Munksgaards Forlag. Kobenhavn.

Jansson, Sven, trans. Peter Foote
1968 *The Runes of Sweden*. (1990) Stockholm: AWE/Geber.

Jansson, Sven
1949 *Runstenen fran Kensington I Minnesota*. Norsk Tidskrift för Vetenskap, NS 25.

Jones, C. H. L. and Thomas H. Raddall
(1920) *The Markland Sagas*. Private publication.

Keeler, Clyde
1974/75 A Latin inscription on the Newport Tower. *NEARA Newsletter, 9*(4).
1985 The Newport round church. *ESOP*, Vol. 13.

Lagman, Svante
1990 *De Stunga Runorna*. Uppsala: Institution för Nordisks Språk.

Landsverk, O. J.
1974 *Runic Records of the Norsemen in America*. *USA*: Erik J. Friis.

Larsson, Mats G.
1990   *Ett Odesdigert Vikingtåg, Invars den Vittfarnes Resa*,
pp. 1036-1041. Södra Sandby: Bokförlaget Atlantis.

Liestol, Aslak
1963   *Runer Fra Bryggen*. Bergen: Bergens Privatbank.

Liljegren, Joh. T.
1832   *Runlärabok*. Stockholm: P. A. Norstedt & Soner.

Maling, Joan and Annie Zaenen
1990   *Syntax and Semantics: Modern Icelandic Syntax*, Vol.
24. San Diego: Academic Press.

Mallery, Arlington and Mary Roberts Harrison
1979   *The Rediscovery of Lost America*. New York: E.P.
Dutton.

McGee, Robert
1987   The Vinland Map: Hoax or history? *The Beaver*,
April/May, p. 37.

Means, Phillip Answorth
1941   *The Newport Tower*. Boston: Henry Holt & Co.

Mongé, Alf and O. J. Landsverk
1967   *Norse Medieval Cryptography in Runic Carvings*.
Glendale CA: Norseman Press.

Nadaillac, Marquis de, trans. N. d'Anvers
(1890)   *Customs and Monuments of Prehistoric People*. New
York: G. P. Putnam's Sons.
1895   *Prehistoric America*. New York: G. P. Putnam's Sons.

Neukomm, Edmond
1896   *Rulers of the Sea: The Norsemen in America from the
Tenth to the Fifteenth Century*. Boston: Estes and Lauriat.

Nielsen, Richard
1986   An Old Norse translation of the Heavener Runes.
ESOP, Vol. 15.
1986   The Arabic numbering system in the Kensington
Runestone. *ESOP*, Vol. 15.
1987a   The runestones of Oklahoma. *ESOP*, Vol. 16.
1987b   The Kensington Runestone, part 2: Aberrant letters.
ESOP, Vol. 16.
1988/89   The Kensington Runestone, part 3: Evidence for its
authenticity. *ESOP*, Vol. 17, 18.
1993   The Spirit Pond Runestones of Maine: A proposed
dating and tentative translation. Pp. 92-113 in *ESOP*, Vol. 21.

Nilsestuen, Rolf M.
1994   *The Kensington Runestone Vindicated*. Lanham MD:
University Press of America.

Page, R. I.
1987   *Reading the Past: Runes*. Berkeley: University of
California Press.

Palson, Hermann, and Magnus Magnusson
1965   *The Vinland Sagas, the Norse Discovery of America*.
New York: Penguin Books.

Percy, Bishop
1847   *Northern Antiquities*. London: Henry G. Bohn.

Pohl, Frederick J.
1952   *The Lost Discovery: Uncovering the Track of the
Vikings in America*. New York: W. W. Norton & Co.
1966   *The Viking Explorers*. New York: Thomas Y. Crowell Co.
1972   *The Viking Settlements of North America*. New York:
Clarkson, N. Potter, Inc.

Rask, Lars
1990   *Runläsaboken*. Stockholm: Utbildningförlaget
Brevskolan.

Silliman, Horace
1979   *The Newport Tower: The English Elizabethan Solution*.
NEARA Special Publication.

Skelton, R. A., Thomas E. Maston, and George Painter
1965   *The Vinland Map and the Tartar Relation*. New Haven:
Yale University Press.

Snurlusson, Snorre
1924   *Edda*. Kobenhavn: Arnamagense.

Strandvold, Olaf
1948   *Norse Inscriptions of American Stones*. Weehauken NJ:
Magnus Bjorndal.

Valfells, Sigrid and James E. Cathey
1981   *Old Icelandic: an Introductory Course*. New York:
Oxford University Press.

Wachtmeister, Ingegerd, ed.
1984   *Runstenari Sodermanland*. Nyköping: Sodermanlands
Museet.

Wahlgen, Erik
1958   *The Kensington Stone: A Mystery Solved*. Madison:
University of Wisconsin Press.

Williams, Stephen
1991   *Fantastic Archaeology: The Wild Side of North
American Prehistory*. Philadelphia: University of
Pennsylvania Press.

Zoega, Geir T.
1984   *Old Icelandic Dictionary*. New York: Oxford
University Press.

AUDIO CASSETTES

Audio-forum cassette course; *Icelandic Conversations*.
1990   Audio-forum, Guilford CT.

Sveinsson, Einar O.
1990   Reading *Brennu Njals Saga*. Reykjavik: Almenna
bokafelagith hf.

The Transmigrations of Tanit[1]

GLORIA FARLEY

Wherever people go, they take their gods. This was true of the Old World people who traveled in ships all over the known and unknown world, centuries before Columbus and even well before Christ. It appears that the goddess Tanit (Tanith, Nith), who was the principal goddess of Carthage in North Africa, was one of the most traveled deities of all. We can deduce this from the profusion of places in which her images have been found.

TANIT IN CARTHAGE

The 'Sign of Tanit' (Soren, Khader, and Slim 1990:133), as principally used in ancient Carthage, was simple: a triangle for a skirt or body, a circle at the apex for a head, and a horizontal line for arms stretched out at the juncture (Figure 1). The forearms were often angled upward.

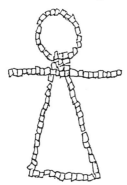

Figure 1 TANIT IN MOSAIC (after Matthews)

There were many variations of this simple sign, however. As Tanit was a lunar goddess (Harden 1962:88), above her head could appear the crescent moon, or the crescent plus a circle to represent the sun, since she was also the spouse of Baal the Sun God. In her hand, or nearby, could appear variants of the caduceus (the wand carried by Mercury, messenger of the gods, usually represented with two serpents entwined around it), symbol of healing. She could be on a pedestal, she could have legs, she could have a decorated skirt (Figure 2).

Over the centuries there was a rumor that babies had been sacrificed to Tanit; unfortunately, this was proven true when excavations were begun in the 1920s at the Tophet area of Carthage (Soren and Khader 1987:40-43). The site yielded thousands of clay jars containing bones and ashes of young children, many accompanied by steles with inscriptions to Tanit. In contrast, she was also considered to be a beneficent Mother-Goddess, with arms raised in blessing. A ceramic baby bottle, or *biberon*, (*Ibid.* 1987:45) from Carthage, with an amusing face using the nose as a nipple, bears on it the image of Tanit (Figure 3).

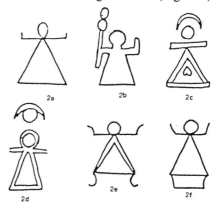

Figure 2 VARIATIONS OF THE IMAGE OF TANIT
(after Harden)

Figure 3 CARTHAGINIAN CERAMIC BABY BOTTLE
Shows Sign of Tanit (after Soren)

For many decades scholars have argued about her origin: whether she first appeared in Carthage after this colony was established by Phoenicians from Tyre, presumably in 814 BC (Edey 1974:10); whether she originated in Egypt; or whether she existed in Phoenicia and was taken from there to Carthage.

TANIT IN EGYPT

The scholars who favor Egypt as her origin, point out the close similarity of the 'Sign of Tanit' to the Ankh, symbol of life in Egypt (Figure 4). This is especially noticeable in the shape of Pharaoh Tutankhamen's mirror case. Eleven trapezoidal objects of sandstone, incised with a circle on a crossbar over a triangle, and topped with a floral sprig, were found in upper Egypt at the site of the Buchem near Thebes. Although not found in a datable context, they are thought to be of the Ptolemaic period (305 to 30 BC). There was a colony of Phoenicians near Memphis as early as the mid-5th century BC (Korr 1981:95-96).

Figure 4 THE EGYPTIAN
ANKH

Figure 5 EGYPTIAN PETROGLYPH
Recorded by Hans Winkler
(after Cervicek)

In 1936 to 1938, Hans Winkler recorded many petroglyphs in Egypt and published most of them. However, some were not published until 1986 (Cervicek 1988). A very interesting one he called an *ankh*. Found near the Valley of the Kings on the vertical face of a stone, it closely resembles the image of Tanit. It has a radiating head (Figure 5) which, to my knowledge, is never found on an ankh. A stele from Carthage (Soren and Khader 1987:180) does show a Tanit with a radiating head (Figure 6).

Figure 6
CARTHAGINIAN STELE
Tanit with radiating head
(after Soren)

TANIT IN PHOENICIA

Evidence has been accumulating since the 1970s that there was a Tanit cult in the Phoenician area of the Levant, which preceded her appearance in Carthage. Figurines were found off the coast of Shave Zion, and lead weights with her image at Beirut and Ashdod. A broken sherd from an amphora (Figure 7) excavated at Tel Akko showed two-thirds of a Tanit image (Dothan 1974:45).

Figure 7 POTTERY SHERD
Ancient Phoenicia
(after Dothan)

In excavations begun in 1984 at Ashkelon on the coast south of Tyre and Sidon (Stager 1991:17), three 5th century BC images of Tanit in bronze and bone were found (Figure 8). Excavations at Sarepta (Matthews 1974:158), the 7th century BC Phoenician city eight miles south of Sidon, yielded the 'Sign of Tanit' on a small amulet, a glass disc (Figure 9). But most important, proof that Tanit was the same as the Semitic goddess Astarte was found on a small tablet with an inscription in Phoenician script, identifying her as 'Tanit-Ashtart' (Stager and Wolff 1984:50).

Figure 8 TANITS FROM ASHKELON (after Stager)

Figure 9 TANIT ON GLASS
Amulet from Sarepta
(after Matthews)

TANIT IN THE MEDITERRANEAN

The fact that Tanit traveled by ship is attested by a Carthaginian stele (Massa 1977:77) which shows two images of her in a boat. Between them is a form of the caduceus (Figure 10). She must have sailed to Crete as well (Wood 1988:73), for her image appears as a syllabogram in the linear B alphabet (Figure 11).

The Mediterranean islands of Sicily and Sardinia both bear evidence of the presence of Tanit. Three cities in Sardinia have yielded a temple to Tanit and two Tophets. Motya in Sicily also has a Tophet (Guido 1963:194-95). At a museum in Sardinia, a mosaic of Tanit and the caduceus was photographed by Ella Footman (Figure 12).

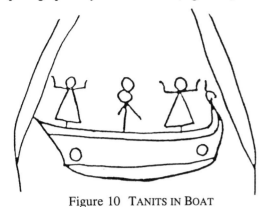

Figure 10 TANITS IN BOAT
Carthage (after Massa)

Figure 11 TANIT AS SYMBOL
IN LINEAR B ALPHABET
(after Wood)

Figure 12 TANIT IN MOSAIC
Sardinia (photo by Footman)

TANIT IN AFRICA

It is my own theory that Tanit traveled by ship with the expedition ordered by Pharaoh Necho, a Libyan, to circumnavigate the continent of Africa. About 600 BC, he sent his ships, with navigators from Tyre, down the east coast. They returned to Egypt three years later via the Mediterranean Sea (Kushaim 1980). The crews would have docked at many ports along the way and could have introduced the goddess to the natives. Illustrated are wooden

Tanit-like figures from Ghana on the western coast and Kenya on the eastern coast (Figure 15).

Figure 13 TANIT ON GRAVESTONE
Bosnia (after Engler)

Figure 14 TANITS IN MUSEUM
Madrid (after photo by Dexter ©)

Figure 15 WOODEN TANIT-LIKE EFFIGIES
Kenya (left) and Ghana (right)
(photo M. Farley)

A friend from South Africa reports that even now the native craft shops in Johannesburg are filled with images of Tanit, called fertility emblems, ranging from small stone pendants to figures two feet tall (Sullivan 1979).

The concept of Tanit seems to have been passed down through the Zulu tribe of South Africa. In 1986, when Warren Dexter of Vermont visited Credo Mutwa, the Zulu Shaman and educated author, he photographed a ten-inch verdite figurine of a woman which Mutwa had inherited from his grandfather. An image of Tanit was incised across the back of the lower legs. She had the crescent moon above her head, a triangular decorated skirt, legs and feet, and her arms were outstretched like wings (Figure 16). Above Tanit was an Ogam inscription, translated by the late Dr. Barry Fell as "A token to obtain the object of desire from Tanith." A co-authored article about this artifact was published in *ESOP* (Fell, Dexter, and Farley 1988:101-2).

Tanit apparently penetrated the Adriatic Sea also. In Bosnia there is a gravestone (Engler 1962:203) bearing her image, with a design of Celtic influence (Figure 13). A museum case in Madrid contains three figurines of Tanit, photographed by Warren Dexter (Figure 14).

Figure 16 TANIT AND HER CRESCENT MOON
On effigy from South Africa
(after photo by Dexter ©)

As Necho's expedition proceeded homeward, north up the west coast of Africa, they would have hugged the coast-line. Many Tanit-like images considered as fertility emblems are found in these west African countries. The Ashanti people of Ghana call them "Akus'ba" dolls (Smithsonian 1983). An intricately carved image from western Africa is in Dr. Fell's collection (Figure 17).

Figure 17 TANIT STATUETTE
West Africa (photo by Fell)

Algeria has its share of Tanit images on monuments, although they may have diffused overland from the east (Constantine Librairie 1854-55:14). One grave marker photographed in Constantine shows two small children under the 'Sign of Tanit,' which is reminiscent of the Tophet grave-stones of Carthage (Figure 18).

TANIT IN AMERICA

I have personally recorded images of Tanit in America from Vermont to California, and have been assisted by contributions of her image from others. Labor Day of 1975 found me with Dr. Fell and friends in a megalithic chamber

in Vermont. When I called his attention to a plainly abraded figure on the ceiling, he identified it as Tanit, with round head, skirt, and outstretched arms like wings (Figure 19). Later, his identification was verified by an inscription on the then-buried portal, in Celtic Ogam, reading **B–Y–N,** meaning 'Byanu' the Mother Goddess, also known as Tanit (Fell 1976:236-37).

Figure 18 GRAVESTONE FROM ALGERIA
Shows children and Sign of Tanit
(photo by Dexter ©)

Figure 19 TANIT IMAGE FROM VERMONT
(photo by Dexter ©)

Proceeding east to west across America, there is a plain Tanit found by Jeff Jolley on a vertical stone surface in North Carolina, near the confluence of two rivers (Fell and Myers 1989:259; Jolley 1990) (Figure 20).

Tanit apparently found her way up the Mississippi River and into its tributaries both east and west. She must have made friends with the Indians, for her image is plainly incised on one side of an Indian stone pipe, which was

Figure 20 TANIT FROM NORTH CAROLINA
(photo by Taylor)

Figure 22 TWO SHEET-COPPER IMAGES
From Ohio Mound and stele from Carthage
(after Bitsko and Massa)

Figure 23 TANIT IMAGES FROM FARLEY COLLECTION
a) Oklahoma; b) Kansas; c) Nevada

found on the Tennessee River (Figure 21). On the opposite side appears the agricultural grid, an Egyptian hieroglyph often found in the American west in association with Old World inscriptions (Fell 1991:154-55).

Two artistic images of Tanit cut from sheet copper were found in Ohio in a Hopewell Indian mound (Bitsko). One has a heart-shaped skirt which compares closely to a stele (Massa 1977:110) from Carthage (Figure 22). Other small images of her have been found: one in eastern Oklahoma in a dry creek bed, one on a cliff-side in Kansas north of the Arkansas River, and a third in a Nevada petroglyph (Figure 23).

In western Arkansas near a small tributary to the Arkansas River, a treasure hunter using a metal detector unearthed an ancient Carthaginian coin, with the standard stylized portrait of Tanit copied from Syracuse on the obverse, and the symbols of Carthage, a horse head and palm tree, on the reverse (Figure 24). Identified by Dr. Fell and numismatist Dr. Norman Totten (Totten 1976), it finally proved to be only one of seven very similar coins discovered in America all the way from Connecticut to Nebraska. One was buried five and one-half feet deep.

Figure 24 STANDARD TANIT ON CARTHAGINIAN COIN
Found in Arkansas (photo by Pruitt)

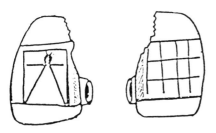

Figure 21 INDIAN STONE PIPE FROM TENNESSEE
Tanit on obverse;
Egyptian hieroglyphic grid on reverse
(photo by M. Farley)

Figure 25 a) INDIANS IN BOAT: Incised on conch shell
from Spiro Mound, Oklahoma
(after Phillips and Brown)
b) BOAT FROM ANCIENT SARDINIA
Note similarity of figures (courtesy Gimbutas)

According to Dr. Fell, a conch shell from the Spiro Mounds in eastern Oklahoma, engraved with two men paddling a native Indian boat, bears three symbols of Tanit (Fell 1980:56-59; *Ibid.* 67; Phillips and Brown 1984:160). A painting of a boat from ancient Sardinia shows four figures in a boat, one of which on the far right (Gimbutas 1989) is an exact replica of the Spiro figures (Figure 25).

The first image of Tanit found and recorded in America was my own discovery in 1973, in Picture Canyon, Colorado. The twenty-eight-inch petroglyph (Figure 26a) seemed important because the figure wore a skirt, had breasts, and held up a symbol in her right hand. There was lettering at her knees (Farley 1976:69). Identified by Dr. Fell as Tanith, with the inscription "Nith protect us" (Fell 1978), she held the Phoenician word for 'Sun-disc,' according to Fell. Very near this image in Picture Canyon were two more with triangular skirts; these have since been destroyed, probably by tourists (Figure 26b). The square skirt shown in Figure 26a compares with those in images from Algeria, one of which also has breasts (Figure 27).

Figure 26a, 26b Colorado Petroglyphs of Tanit
(tracings by G. Farley)

Figure 27 Tanits with Square Skirt
Algiers (after Constantine Abadie Library)

Almost any Mississippi tributary to the west will lead to the same general area in southeastern Colorado and the Oklahoma panhandle. The entire area is carved with ancient scripts and related petroglyphs. In 1978, I recognized on the bank of the Cimarron River in Oklahoma a lovely petroglyph of Tanit with feet and legs, named by me 'The Walking Tanit.' Radial marks from her skirt and other marks nearby are Ogam script, translated by Donal Buchanan, which identifies her as the good wife of Bel, the Sun God, and also implies a lunar eclipse (Farley 1995:174-176) (Figure 28).

Figure 28 'Walking Tanit'
Cimarron River, Oklahoma
(tracing by G. Farley)

Continuing westward into New Mexico, there is an image of Tanit within a radiant circle, photographed at my request by Carol Patterson. On the same boulder is the stylized image of a bird. Tanit with birds appears on a stele from Libya (Figure 29).

Figure 29 a) Tanit and Bird
New Mexico (after photo by Patterson)
b) Tanit and Birds: Algiers (after D'Alviella)

A small petroglyph of a Tanit-like figure was photographed on a stone facade at the Joshua Tree National Park in southern California. Her arms hung downward, and she had feet and a dot on her skirt. A stele from Libya (Constantine 1854-55:14) has the downward-hanging arms, and monuments from Algeria (D'Alviella 1891:91) have a dot on the skirt, while some from Carthage have legs (Figures 30 and 2).

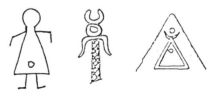

Figure 30 a) Tanit from California (after Amos)
b) Tanit with Arms: Libya (after D'Alviella)
c) Tanit with Dot on Skirt: Algiers
(after Annuaire de Constantine)

In 1988, I found two petroglyphs of Tanit in Owens Valley, California. A twelve-inch one wearing a paneled triangular skirt was pecked on a basalt boulder (Figure 31). At another site in Owens Valley, the petroglyph on marble is so old and eroded that it can be seen only in the slanting rays of the setting sun. A four-inch image of Tanit wearing a crescent-decorated skirt is only three inches away from a lovely ship-petroglyph in a Mediterranean style, with an incurving bow (Figure 32).

Figure 31 CALIFORNIA
PETROGLYPH
(tracing by G. Farley)

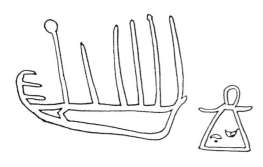

Figure 32 PETROGLYPH OF TANIT
Found near image of Mediterranean-style ship
Owens Valley, California
(tracing by G. Farley)

TANIT IN LOUISIANA

In 1995, a photograph of another image of Tanit on stone was sent to me by Max Norris of Dallas, who said it was found about 1980 by Troy Sandell. It had been sticking out of a reservoir clay bank (since eroded away) near Hornbeck, Louisiana. The stone bears the standard image of the Carthaginian Goddess Tanit, with round head, triangular skirt, and outstretched arms. Below the figure is a very dim line of ancient script, three consecutive letters of which, in the Punic alphabet, have been transliterated by Texas linguist Mike Skupin as **T–N–T**, without vowels. The stone measures 12 x 8 x 3 inches (Figure 33).

The Louisiana reservoir site is near the Sabine River, which leads directly into the Gulf of Mexico; it is also about thirty-seven miles from the Red River, which leads upstream to the Oklahoma and Colorado images of Tanit and downstream to the Mississippi. This latest find lends

support to the theory that worshippers of Tanit traveled that great river in ancient times.

And Tanit indeed seems to have traveled far and wide in the New World.

Figure 33 TANIT IMAGE ON A STONE
Louisiana (photo by Norris)

NOTE

1. The original presentation of this material at the ABC Conference consisted of eighty slides with comments. Later, written in narrative form with line drawings and photographs, it was published in Volume 21 of *Epigraphic Society Occasional Papers*, 1992. With the permission of René Fell and The Epigraphic Society, it is published here in revised form.

REFERENCES

Bitsko, pub.
  Undated   Postcard from Mound City Group National
    Monument. Chillicothe OH.
Cervicek, Pavel
  1988   *Rock Pictures of Upper Egypt and Nubia*. Institute
    Universitario Orientale, Supplemento n. 46 agli ANNALE,
    Vol. 46, Figure 174. Napoli.
D'Alviella, Eugene G.
  1891   *The Count Goblet: The Migration of Symbols*. New
    York: Burt Franklin.
Dothan, M.
  1974   A sign of Tanit from Tel'Akko. *Israel Exploration
    Journal*, 24/1.
Edey, Maitland A.
  1974   *The Sea Traders: Emergence of Man Series*. Time-Life
    Books, Inc.
Engler, H. Rudolf
  1962   *Die Sonne Als Symbol*. Zurich, Switzerland:
    Helianthus-Verlag Kusnacht.
Farley, Gloria
  1976   Inscriptions from mid-America. *ESOP*, Vol. 3, Part 2,
    No. 69.

Farley, Gloria
1995 *In Plain Sight: Old World Records in Ancient America*, pp. 174-176. Columbus GA: ISAC Press.
Fell, Barry
1976 *America BC*. Quadrangle: The New York Times Book Co.
1978 Personal communication, January 27.
1980 *Saga America*. The New York Times Book Co.
1991 An ogam solution to the agricultural grid symbol. *ESOP*, Vol. 20.
Fell, Barry, Warren Dexter, and Gloria Farley
1988 Tanith with two scripts from South Africa. *ESOP,* Vol. 17.
Fell, Barry and R. B. Myers
1989 Tanith in North Carolina. *ESOP,* Vol. 18.
Gimbutas, Marija
1989 *The Language of the Goddess*. San Francisco: Harper and Row.
Guido, Margaret
1963 Sardinia. In *Ancient People and Places Series*. New York: Frederick A. Prager.
Harden, Donald
1962 The Phoenicians. In *Ancient People and Places Series*. New York: Frederick A. Prager.
Jolley, Jeff
1990 Personal communication, May 23.
Kansas State Historical Society
1981 *Kansas Rock Art*. Topeka KA: Historic Preservation Department.
Korr, Craig S.
1981 Evidence of the sign of the Goddess Tanit in the Theban region of Egypt, pp. 95-96. *Israel Exploration Journal,* Vol. 31, Nos. 1-3. Jerusalem.
Kushaim, Ali F.
1980 On Libyan contributions to the Mediterranean cultures. *ESOP*, Vol. 8, Part 2.

Massa, Aldo
1977 *The Phoenicians*. Geneve, Switzerland: Minerva.
Matthews, Samuel W.
1974 The Phoenicians, sea lords of antiquity. *National Geographic*. Washington DC, August.
Phillips, Phillip and James Brown
1984 *Pre-Columbian Shell Engravings from the Craig Mound at Spiro, Oklahoma, Part 2*. Cambridge: Peabody Museum of Archaeology and Ethnology, Harvard University.
Smithsonian Catalog
1983 Spring. Washington DC.
Société Archéologique de la Province de Constantine
1854/55 *Annuaire de la Société*. Constantine: Abadie Librairie.
Soren, David, Aicha Ben Abed Ben Khader, and Hedi Slim
1990 *Carthage: Uncovering the Mysteries and Splendors of Ancient Tunisia*. New York: Simon and Schuster.
Soren, David and Aicha Ben Abed Ben Khader
1987 *Carthage: A Mosaic of Ancient Tunisia*. New York: W. W. Norton & Co.
Stager, Lawrence E.
1991 Why were hundreds of dogs buried at Ashkelon? *Biblical Archaeology Review,* May/June.
Stager, Lawrence E. and Samuel R. Wolff
1984 Child sacrifice at Carthage—religious rite or population control? *Biblical Archaeology Review,* January/February.
Sullivan, Brenda
1979 Personal communication, January 22.
Totten, Norman
1976 Carthaginian coins found in Arkansas and Alabama. *ESOP*, Vol. 4, Part 2.
Wood, Michael
1988 Scripts and writing in the Aegean world. Foreword in *The World Atlas of Archaeology*. New York: Portland House, distr. by Crown Publishers.

COMMENTARY—SECTION III

BRIAN D. STUBBS

INTRODUCTION

Near the beginning of most books dealing with historical linguistics can be found a reference to the famous words of Sir William Jones:

> The Sanskrit language, whatever be its antiquity, is of a wonderful structure; more perfect than the Greek, more copious than the Latin, and more exquisitely refined than either, yet bearing to both of them a stronger affinity, both in the roots of verbs and in the forms of grammar, than could possibly have been produced by accident; so strong indeed, that no philologer could examine them all three, without believing them to have sprung from some common source, which, perhaps, no longer exists (Beekes 1995).

The accuracy of Jones' observation has since been abundantly verified. However, Jones did none of the verifying. He merely observed striking similarities and stated his general observations. Later scholars, following his lead, looked more closely at the data relevant to his proposal and saw patterns that provided keys to unlock the basic principles of language change, thereby giving birth to the science of linguistics.

The papers in this section are like Sir William's lead: they are observations of unusual similarities (though treated in a more thorough and scholarly fashion). Though Jones did not establish any facts with irrefutable documentation, his astute observation led to a subsequent flood of insights and knowledge about language, linguistics, Indo-European, and other language families of the world. Likewise, these papers are not the final word either, but only a very important first word that may someday be looked upon as the tip of later-to-be-discovered masses of evidence that eventually sank the ships of skepticism which are presently secure in their attachment to supposedly unsinkable theories.

Unfortunately, less informed scholars perpetuate the standard biased views in the university systems, so that students who are prospective scholars are not made aware of the evidence for pre-Columbian transoceanic contact. The irony is that many professors take pride in their openmindedness, their careful consideration of all evidence, and their courage in challenging established ideas. Yet, in the face of a growing body of evidence for transoceanic diffusion, the self-styled academic adventurers get cold feet at the water's edge. Regarding diffused cultural traits, genes, and language, they have rejected data inconvenient for established theories.

If the evidence discussed in these articles had been found in locations more convenient to convention, that is, in more 'appropriate' Old World settings, their validity would more likely be accepted. Although unusual settings raise more questions than do expected ones, they do not negate the existence or importance of the evidence. Therefore, let not continents obscure the contents of these papers.

I have organized my remarks into three areas of discussion: comparative linguistic evidence (Wescott, Key); inscriptions (Kelley, Buchanan, McCulloch); and the Semitic or Phoenician evidence in the Americas (Farley, McCulloch, Wescott, Gordon).

COMPARATIVE LINGUISTIC EVIDENCE

Comparative linguistics seems to be the least utilized of all the available research tools. First, there are relatively few linguists. Second, as Key has noted, among those there are even fewer who know well the languages in both arenas—the Old World and the New. A third reason may be that the strength of comparative linguistic evidence is simply overlooked. By its nature, comparative linguistic evidence provides large bodies of data (several thousand words per language) that cannot be forged. Archaeological ruins and buildings reveal some facts about themselves, but who built them is not always clear. Visual similarities are often at the mercy of subjective judgment. And inscriptions are nearly always branded as forgeries initially, if not indefinitely. However, it would be imposssible to fabricate several Native American tribes speaking a variety of related languages.

It is true that in the early stages of research (which characterizes most comparative projects of transoceanic possibility), some linguists may argue that the data are being stretched to imply more than they really do. Linguists know such stretching often happens and, understandably, this makes them a generally suspicious and critical lot. If, on the other hand, the quality and quantity of comparative data accumulate to irrefutable proportions, coincidence can no longer serve as a viable explanation for the similarities. The crux of the matter is that if so much of non-linguistic evidence points to transoceanic activity, and from a variety of sources, then some linguistic evidence should parallel at least a few of those sources. We should not expect to find parallel evidence in many cases necessarily, since ancient groups could arrive, leave an inscription and then travel on, eventually to return home, or die, or be killed, or be assimilated into indigenous populations without maintaining their original language. Nevertheless, some linguistic evidence should remain for at least a few groups, though that evidence may never reach the proportions needed to convince everyone.

Pursuing the line of transoceanic comparative investigation, Roger Wescott and Mary Key have each presented brief summaries of possibilities deserving continuing research. Besides being a knowledgeable Indo-Europeanist, Roger Wescott has been a key watchman for transoceanic possibilities surfacing on comparative linguistic research. Moreover, I have met no one who maintains a more thorough awareness of the comparative linguistic research occurring worldwide than Roger Wescott.

Wescott presents a few instances from among scores of parallels that Sadovszky has noticed between California Penutian and Ob-Ugric—the tip of another iceberg. I am not knowledgeable in Penutian nor in Ob-Ugric, and thus I feel unqualified to evaluate fully Sadovszky's proposal; nevertheless, in light of the number of striking similarities, such as these cited by Wescott and others, the matter clearly merits further investigation and should not be automatically dismissed on geographic grounds.

We ought to keep in mind that the existence of Penutian itself is still a hypothesis. Though most linguists studying Penutian languages see enough similarities to consider them a related group, no one has yet produced a satisfactory system of sound correspondences and other linguistic features necessary to establish Penutian as a language family.

Newman (1964) has produced a list of similarities between some Penutian groups and Zuni sufficient to convince many of a distant relationship, though I notice that a sizeable portion of those items which are common to both Zuni and Penutian are also common to Uto-Aztecan.

So, which of all these proposals is/are correct? Linguists who assume a phylum of one single large tree limit the possibilities. What of the possibility that several mixtures coming from different directions occurred, so that Zuni, Uto-Aztecan, and Ob-Ugric may all be related to Penutian, but in different ways, either by substantial language mixtures at different times in the past, or one or two possibly by remote genetic forks in trees? To explain apparently distant relationships among Native American languages, Americanists tend too often to think in terms of the family tree, supposing that all seemingly remote relationships are due to tremendous time-depths according to the calculations of glottochronology (rates of vocabulary replacement), when in reality multi-layered mixtures may be the culprit. These mixings would not only have nothing to do with family trees, but would also result in relationships appearing to be more distant glottochronologically than is actually the case. Mary Key's words say it well (as they often do), "multiple migrations, and layers of migrations" have occurred so that the "result to linguistics is confusion."

(See M. R. Key, *American Indian Languages Before Columbus,* this volume).

A leader in South American linguistics, Mary Ritchie Key has produced an exceptional amount of work. In addition to raising here the possibility of linguistic ties across the Atlantic, she has pioneered research into possible Pacific contributions to American languages (1984). As she mentions, a primary obstacle to progress in transoceanic comparative linguistic research is that few minds are able, or care, to master both American languages and those from across either ocean. Most linguists specialize in a language family or two, in one hemisphere or the other, but seldom more. A second obstacle is the short, or simple, shape of morphemes in most of the languages associated with these relationship possibilities. This is not the fault of the investigator, but it does provide opponents with ammunition, since smaller canonical shapes and phonological inventories offer less resistance against claims for coincidence. Both the Atlantic and Pacific arenas that Key has touched upon are perfectly logical first considerations, in light of both the geography and the known nautical abilities of the Polynesian and Mediterranean peoples.

Even if skepticism may be understandable regarding transoceanic crossings from other areas of the world, the probability that Polynesians reached American shores seems logistically beyond doubt. If the ancient Polynesians were such expert seamen that they could find and people every inhabitable island of the Pacific, how could they miss a land mass that runs from the north pole to the south pole? The islands are but specks in the huge oceanic expanse, yet none was missed. The dimensions of the 'so-called' Polynesian triangle are such that each side is of greater length than is the distance from the eastern side of that triangle to the Americas. In other words, the distance from Hawaii to either New Zealand or Easter Island is twice the distance from Hawaii to California. And from Easter Island, both New Zealand and Hawaii are twice as far away as the coast of South America. To accept the Polynesian discovery of the Polynesian islands (which is irrefutable) without accepting the probability of Polynesian arrivals in America is comparable to trying to roll as many thousand marbles as needed to hit all of a group of one hundred marbles randomly placed in the center of a gym, without ever having a stray marble roll to the opposite wall.

The question of whether or not oceanic peoples arrived at American shores seems less significant than other questions: How many times did they arrive? In which centuries did they arrive? What are the relative numbers of those who stayed versus those who returned? Were those who stayed sufficiently numerous to leave a perceptible cultural or linguistic impact (Key 1984)?

One item that some favor and others dispute as evidence for contact between the Americas and Oceania is the sweet potato and one of its names—*kumar* in a dialect of Quechua and *kumara/kumala* in some islands of Polynesia.

Although it was widely cited in earlier decades, most scholars now caution that this item of possible evidence for contact may be due only to the fact that chance similarities do indeed occur.

In a random comparison of any two unrelated languages chance similarities can range from one to five percent of the vocabulary, depending on the basic stem and morpheme shapes, phonological inventories, etc., of the respective languages. However, the chances of identical words of the length of *kumar* and *kumara/kumala* occurring by coincidence are very, very small, in the range of one in twenty-five thousand. (With the minimum phonemic inventory being about ten consonants and five vowels in Polynesian, the probability of coincidence would be *ca.* 1/10x1/5x1/10x1/5x1/10 = 1/25,000.) Despite such odds, the transoceanic implications of this term put it under attack from both directions.

Although some Austronesianists question the word's validity perhaps because of the possible American tie, Ross Clark (1979) vouches for Polynesian **kumala* to be as valid a proto-Polynesian lexeme as any. From the American side, almost every reason given for discarding this term could as easily strengthen its case. For example, even if the term *kumar* was not originally Quechua, and even though it occurs as a loan word in only one dialect of Quechua, the possibility or probability of oceanic transport of the term is not problematic. That the sweet potato is most likely of American origin and the term **kumala* of oceanic origin only strengthens the case for repeated contact. Other and more prominent terms for the sweet potato, including Quechua *apichu*, are cited in the literature along with evidence that the Quechua dialect containing *kumar* was not coastal. In my view, these factors do not adversely affect the probabilities of this loan, since terminology in neighboring or competing languages or dialects is constantly shifting, expanding, and contracting (Brand 1971).

Whether the term died out in the coastal dialects/ languages, or a Pacific group carried the term past coastal peoples in joining a highland group, or any of innumerable possible scenarios, the facts surrounding **kumar(a)* are entirely consistent with a pattern of interaction between different cultures and languages which originally had different terms but ultimately shared one of the terms for this tuber.

One chance in twenty-five thousand is formidable odds against this being mere coincidence, yet many authorities seem inclined to discard what is 99.996 percent probable (oceanic diffusion) in order to side with what is .004 percent probable (its coincidence). I share Baker's "twinge of regret" (1971) that various authors can think the term coincidental and set it aside; however, I do not share their "missing it," because I am not discarding it, just yet. No doubt, the Polynesian language and genes clearly derive from Southeast Asia, as is the case for all Austronesian peoples. Nevertheless, Yen (1971) cites genetic evidence in Simmons suggesting a tripartite ancestry for the Polynesians,

one of the three being a South American element. If an American element is thick enough in the Polynesian blood to be perceptible, why so many flags about a word that is linguistically 99.996 percent probable and aligns with genetic evidence as well?

Yen (1971) recounts the evidence suggesting an American origin for the sweet potato and brings out other evidence that could bear on answers to some of the questions raised above. A number of factors point to probabilities for Pacific-American contact between the 9th and 14th centuries: 1. The settlement of Easter Island dates to at least the 9th century, if not earlier (possibly AD 400) (Irwin 1992; Yen 1971) and regular contact with America is more likely after that time than before. Polynesian explorers were not likely to ignore nor forget such a magnificent land mass and its resources after a successful round trip to America. 2. Given the apparent American origin for the sweet potato, its presence in pre-Columbian Polynesia, but absence in the far western Pacific, suggests American contact in the more recent pre-Columbian centuries; otherwise, earlier contact would have spread it throughout the Pacific. 3. Despite efforts of some to discard the equivalent Quechua and Polynesian terms for sweet potato, the constancy of the word, which shows no sound change at all, speaks not only for contact but also for its being a fairly recent loan.

DECIPHERMENT AND INSCRIPTIONS

David Kelley was a key player in the decipherment of the Mayan glyphs, and he continues to impress his colleagues with the variety and scope of subjects in which he surfaces as a knowledgeable authority. His analysis, in this section, of the petroglyphs at Peterborough, Ontario, typifies the extent of his knowledge and the thoroughness of his method.

Yale's Michael D. Coe has perhaps said it best, that in professional meetings Kelley ". . . can always be expected to present a paper that may be unusual and even outrageous, according to one's lights, but is usually grounded in the most impeccable scholarship" (Coe 1992). Kelley's carefully reasoned scholarship is displayed here as he argues well for Barry Fell's recognition of patterns in the Peterborough glyphs suggesting that Old World proto-Tifinagh, dating from centuries BC, is indeed also in the New World. "I would not have seen it without Fell's work," writes Kelley. (See David Kelley, *The Identification of the Proto-Tifinagh Script at Peterborough, Ontario,* this volume.)

The scholarly bent, all too often, is to pick tenaciously at the incorrect ten percent of a published piece, while ignoring the meritorious ninety percent, so that a reader of the critique concludes that the work is entirely amiss. No doubt, Fell erred or overreached in much of what he did, and much more than ten percent of the time. Who would not, in attempting so much requiring so many specialties? Nevertheless, Kelley's view of Fell's work is a more reasonable and useful approach: "I am more interested in what I perceive as massive accomplishments, rather than in criticizing Fell's work" (*idem*). Again we see the tremendous importance of the simple first noticing of similarities, thereby bringing the possibility to the attention of specialists who can subsequently carry the investigation through a more sophisticated analysis.

As I read Buchanan's very competent treatment of the Grand Traverse Stone, I am impressed by his initiative in collecting a database of inscriptions and applying his multifaceted background to deal with them. Buchanan's skillful and methodic approach to the Grand Traverse Stone is exemplary. As Kelley has stated, in translating rare inscriptions one cannot expect one hundred percent certainty, but even a partially correct translation is a wonderful first step. In this light, Buchanan's results with the stone are reasonable and very plausible.

An unusual context for a lone inscription does test the tolerance of the international scholarly community, but the context alone cannot invalidate the existence of the anomalous item. If the Peterborough inscriptions and the Grand Traverse Stone had been found in the Mediterranean arena, their authenticity could be more easily accepted, and the respective treatments by Kelley and Buchanan might be more widely received.

THE ANCIENT NEAR EAST AND AMERICA

It is common knowledge that for hundreds of years Phoenician mariners sailed all about the Mediterranean Sea—a place as familiar to them as a large harbor. It is also recorded that the Phoenicians ventured beyond their Mediterranean home, out into the Atlantic—both southward along the African coast and northward about Europe. The shortest width of the Atlantic—from Africa to Brazil—is less than the length of the Mediterranean Sea. Thus, a transatlantic journey should not be deemed so incredible nor unlikely. Similarly, Mary Ritchie Key reminds us in this volume that, "South America is several times closer to the Old World than it is to the Bering Strait."

Gloria Farley's years of research have brought together an impressive accumulation of Tanit figures and symbols which she and others have found at many American sites. Her work is entirely consistent with Gordon's observations of Phoenician or Northwest Semitic inscriptions found in eastern areas of the Americas.

McCulloch meticulously delineates and clarifies the trail of differing opinions among scholars regarding the authenticity of the Bat Creek Stone. The unusual New World location and context for a Hebrew inscription could understandably arouse suspicion, yet, when all the evidence is weighed, the authenticity of the inscription seems more probable than not. If the Bat Creek inscription had been found in Palestine, what would have been the response of the academic community? Or if Farley's collection of Tanit symbols had all been found in African or Mediterranean areas? So why should problematic geography be automatic grounds for dismissing evidence?

It is especially appropriate for Wescott to reference Cyrus Gordon's work. First, Gordon is no amateur; he is an internationally renowned Near Eastern scholar, among the world's most knowledgeable in matters Semitic. So, when Gordon finds enough evidence to write a book about Semitic groups in ancient America, it should not be lightly discarded (1971). Second, it is not solely inscriptional or archaeological evidence that is emerging. In addition to the many kinds of evidence presented by Gordon that suggest Near Eastern arrivals in ancient America (which include sculpted images, writings by ancient authors, coins, and inscriptions), now some comparative linguistic evidence is also emerging that is consistent with the inscriptional discoveries, as noted by Wescott.

Beyond the similarities mentioned by Wescott, two more sound correspondences are pertinent to data presented by Cyrus Gordon. One is that the **aleph** or glottal stop of Phoenician/Hebrew/Northwest Semitic corresponds to or appears in Uto-Aztecan (hereafter UA) as a form of rounding **w, o, u**. This also happens in Semitic on occasion. For example, Arabic *sa'ala* in conjugation V is *tasawwala*, where a doubled glottal stop changes to **w**. Consider some similarities illustrating this sound correspondence:

	HEBREW/SEMITIC		**UTO-AZETECAN**	
1.	'ari:	lion	wori/wari	mountain lion[1]
2.	'adam	man	otam	man, tribesman, person[2]
3.	'i:š	man	wïsi	person, someone[3]
4.	qr'/qara'	call, cry	koyoa	howl[4]
5.	pl'/pala'	be wonderful	palaw	be pretty[5]
6.	pa'r	mouse (Arabic)	puwe-/pu'i-	mouse[6]
7.	r'y/ra'a	see	tïwa	find, see[7]
8.	kam'	truffle (Arabic)	kamo'-tli	sweet potato (Nahuatl)
	kama'a:tu(m)	truffles (Ugaritic)	kamwah	sweet potato (Cora)
9.	ya-'ami:n	he believes	yawamin	believe
10.	ya-'ami:n-o	he believes it/him	yawayno	believe it

The match of all three consonants in 8) is intriguing; even though the truffle and potato are not exactly the same thing, they are both fleshy edible nodules appended to a root system growing in the ground.

The last two items form a remarkable pair: 9) is a Serrano form, *yawamin*, which parallels the Northwest Semitic imperfect verb form, with the third person masculine singular prefix appearing fossilized into the form, and contains seven segments. In light of thirteen proto-UA consonants and five proto-UA vowels, the probability of a word of that length matching by chance is $1/13 \times 1/5 \times 1/13 \times 1/5 \times 1/13 \times 1/5 \times 1/13 = 1/3,570,125$, or less than one in three and a half million. Number 10) is a Gabrielino form *yawayno*, which is only missing the **m** (since **y = i** for practical purposes); however, it has an extra **-o** suffix and a meaning that includes a direct object. To add a third person masculine singular object to a verb in Hebrew, an **-o** suffix can be added, which means 'he believes him/it.' And in Gabrielino we have both the meaning 'believe it' and the **-o** suffix to match the meaning that includes an object. If one were to figure the probability of that Gabrielino form matching Hebrew in both form and meaning, and then multiply the result by the probability of the Serrano form, the resulting probability of that pair occurring as they do by coincidence is one in several millions—so miniscule that it approaches non-existence. Then multiply that factor by the other nine hundred plus similarities between UA and Northwest Semitic, and it becomes very difficult to attribute the whole of it to chance.

These data, and dozens of others which I will not take the space to cite here, serve as background for consideration of Cyrus Gordon's observation (1971) of the similarity of Egyptian **sbk** 'crocodile-god' (Egyptian shows only consonants) to Nahuatl *sipak-tli* 'crocodile.' First of all, note that Gordon's comparison aligns exactly with my observation of a general devoicing of voiced stop consonants (**b, d, g > p, t, k**) to merge generally with the voiceless stops of UA, as mentioned in Wescott's article, though intervocalic exceptions exist. Second, it is not a short word. Given thirteen proto-UA consonants, finding three consecutive consonants corresponding as expected yields a chance probability of one in over 2,000 ($1/13 \times 13 \times 13 = 1/2197$), a probability which is quite unlikely, though remotely possible.

If Gordon's suggestion is correct—that the Nahuatl word is somehow tied to the Egyptian word—then it is not likely to be the only such word. When one language influences or imparts loans to another, then normally more than a single word evidences that fact. So, if Nahuatl *sipak-tli* is the only word similar to an Egyptian word, then the transfer could be barely possible, but it would be much more suspect as a rare linguistic oddity bordering on the unbelievable indeed; however, if it is one of several or one of a group of words found in both language groups, then the items in this group of similar words mutually strengthen each other exponentially. Other similarities between Egyptian and UA do exist, among which are:

EGYPTIAN

11.	nmi	travel, traverse	nïmi	walk, travel about
12.	rn	young (of animals)	rana	brood, litter, child [8]
13.	ḫt (Coptic kuht)	fire	ku/kut	fire [9]
	q'hd	to smoke (meat)		
14.	m'i (Coptic mui)	lion	mawiya	mountain lion
15.	di/ti	give, causative (of verbs)	-ti	causative (of verbs)

UTO-AZTECAN

Note that the Coptic form of 'lion' shows rounding (**u**) at the glottal stop as UA (**w**) does. So, Gordon's observation is not alone; more examples exist, but these will suffice for our space and purposes, to show that Gordon's item is only one of a group of similarities between Egyptian and UA. And that set is small compared to the much larger set of similarities (1000) between Northwest Semitic and UA. We should not discount the possibility that a Phoenician vessel with a Mediterranean mix aboard, such as Phoenicians (Northwest Semitic speakers), Egyptians, and whoever else, could have reached the Americas somewhere, and a splinter group from that or another group could have contributed to the UA language family.

As Wescott points out, the location of the UA language family initially appears to be something of a geographic enigma, since the Phoenicians roamed the Atlantic, while UA is found on the Pacific coast. That apparent contradiction initially puzzled me too. However, a larger picture paints a clearer one.

Some preliminary evidence may suggest possible ties between UA and South American or Mesoamerican groups.[10] In addition to other proposals, I have noticed many more similarities than have appeared in print. For example, consider Wescott's mention of 'lightning' taken one step further:

HEBREW	baraq	lightning
UTO-AZTECAN	berok	lightning
YAQUI and MAYO		
ARAWAKAN	eeno iperoka	lightning
(CURRIPACO)	(eeno = thunder)[11]	

This set is phonologically compelling. The consonants are near identities, and the vowels have changed exactly as one might expect. The liquid **r** is pronounced near the front of the mouth, which would explain the raising and fronting of the first vowel **a** to **e**; and uvular **q** is pronounced near where **o** is pronounced in the back of the mouth, which would explain the backing of the second **a** to **o**. This and several other sets appearing in Hebrew, UA, and South American languages, though they provide nothing close to a tight case yet, certainly suggest possibilities meriting further investigation.

Let me clarify that I doubt that UA necessarily holds a full genetic relationship with any South American group (nor with Semitic), but rather that Near Eastern elements did arrive in the Americas, splintering in various directions to affect various Native American groups, which might or might not be genetically related otherwise. Such a scenario does greatly complicate the linguistic unraveling, which may ever remain too opaque in any particular language family to be convincing to the linguistic community at large. Nevertheless, pockets of data are scattered about that test the coincidence argument severely. One must keep in mind that much more remains to be learned and sorted out among South American languages generally, as South American linguistics is still to some degree, in its infancy.

Uto-Aztecanists consider the UA 'unity homeland' most likely to have been in areas straddling the western Mexico-U.S. border. Nevertheless, if a contributing element to UA populations had migrated from Middle or South America, it would explain many things: 1. It would explain a number of similarities between UA and South American language groups. 2. It would explain the apparent puzzle of the west coast. In Mesoamerica, the geography is thin enough and both the Atlantic and Pacific oceans close enough to each other, so that, if a segment of pre-UA peoples traveled from or through the Middle America funnel, then a spread up either coast is equally likely, regardless of which coast received the original landing. In other words, the problem of an Atlantic landing and a present Pacific residence is defused. 3) It would also explain Gordon's note of the similarity between the Nahuatl and Egyptian words for 'crocodile.' In all present UA areas, except Nahuatl, there are no crocodiles. If all segments of the pre-UA peoples originated or landed in their present locations in the greater Southwest, they would not have known nor retained a word for crocodile beyond one generation. But if a Mediterranean element arrived in tropical American climates, then came northward to mix with early UA peoples, the retention of 'crocodile' only in the most southern of the UA languages (Nahuatl) is explainable.

CONCLUSIONS

1. I would like to see four items become required reading for every student's general education: Stephen Jett's

"Precolumbian Transoceanic Contacts" (Jennings, ed. 1983); Cyrus Gordon's *Before Columbus* (1971)*;* the precurser to the present volume, *Man Across the Sea* (1971)*;* and the present volume itself, *Across Before Columbus?* Then let each weigh the evidence in his or her own mind.

2. Whether pursuing leads touched upon by Key and Wescott or following other possibilities, increased resources and personnel in comparative linguistic research are needed. Even in global terms, there are few trained linguists. And within that small subset of humanity, most focus on Old World languages, a small minority contribute to comparative research in Native American languages, and very few are interested and knowledgeable in both Old World and New World language families, as Key noted.

3. DNA research is a relatively new field which has considerable potential. Though still in its infancy, this branch of genetic research, whose methods will be refined with time, should eventually be able to reach into spheres of evidence destined to help answer many questions. For example, recently disclosed DNA evidence shows that the Southwest Athapaskans (Navajo and Apache) are more closely related genetically to their present geographic neighbors than they are to their linguistic relatives in Canada and Alaska (Cavalli-Sforza, Menozzi, and Piazza 1994). This suggests considerable mixing since their arrival in the Southwest. Massive mixing probably underlies many of the complexities in American prehistory. Is there DNA evidence for oceanic peoples reaching America, or Mediterranean peoples reaching America? There is a host of possibilities.

It is becoming less necessary that each piece of evidence be an island or fluke out of context. Many kinds of evidence are beginning to fit together to support one another, for some combinations. For example, Gloria Farley's Tanit figures, Cyrus Gordon's inscriptional identifications and his other observations, and the 1,000 similarities found between Uto-Aztecan and Northwest Semitic are all consistent with Phoenician or Northwest Semitic arrival(s) in ancient America. When these are considered against the background of Phoenician seafaring capability, the evidence should not seem so strange. Time will tell.

END NOTES

1. For all the Uto-Aztecan and Semitic forms, see the bibliography in Brian Stubbs, "A Curious Element in Uto-Aztecan," to appear in *The Epigraphic Society Occasional Publications;* and Brian Stubbs, *A Comparative Vocabulary of Uto-Aztecan Languages*, in preparation. All cognate forms in this set appear in the Sonoran branch: *wori* 'mountain lion' in Guarijio; forms from **wari* in three other Sonoran UA languages. See *The Comparative Value of Tubar in Uto-Aztecan* to appear in a memorial festschrift volume for professor Wick R. Miller.

2. These forms again appear in the Sonoran branch of UA: **otam(i)* in Northern and Southern Tepehuan languages; *o'odham* in Papago; and complex reductions in three other languages.

3. Hebrew *'iš,* meaning 'man' with negatives, is a common way of saying 'no one' (no man); likewise, Tarahumara *wesi* (< *wïsï), 'someone,' with negatives means 'no one.'
4. Nahuatl *te-koyoa,* 'howl,' *koyo-tl* 'coyote'; keep in mind that in most UA languages we see *r > y; only in the Sonoran branch, as in the first item in the table, 'lion,' does **r** often remain **r**.
5. Cahuilla *palaw.*
6. In the following words, all meaning 'mouse,' some UA languages show rounding (**w, u**), some show glottal stop, and some show both for an original glottal stop in Arabic *pa'r* 'mouse': Mono *puwe-;* Southern Paiute *pu'i-;* Serrano *pa'i-s;* Hopi *pöhsa.*
7. Initial Semitic **r** corresponds to **r** in Tarahumara and **t** in most UA languages (7, 12); thus, reflexes of UA *tïwa* 'find,' 'see' match Semitic *r'y/ra'a* 'see,' and are found in no less than ten UA languages.
8. Tarahumara *raná* 'child,' 'offspring'; Guarijio *taná* 'child,'

'little one.'
9. Egyptian *ḫt* becomes Coptic *kuht* 'fire,' which aligns well with UA *ku-t* 'fire' in many UA languages. Though the final **t** is also an absolutive suffix, the fact that it is **t** instead of **l** in some UA languages (*e.g.* Tubatulabal) suggests another final consonant which could easily be *t:* *kut-ta > ku-t.*
10. Beyond those in print thus far, numerous other similarities between UA and South American languages exist; nevertheless, a start is Lila Wistrand-Robinson, "Uto-Aztecan Affinities with Panoan of Peru I: Correspondences," in Mary Ritchie Key, ed. *Language Change in South American Indian Languages.* Philadelphia: University of Pennsylvania Press, 1991.
11. See Randall Q. Huber and Robert B. Reed, *Comparative Vocabulary: Selected Words in Indigenous Languages of Colombia.* Bogotá: Asociación Instituto Lingüistico de Verano, 1992, p. 70.

REFERENCES

Baker, Herbert G.
    1971 Commentary: Section III. Pp. 428-444 in *Man Across the Sea.* Carrol L. Riley *et al.,* eds. Austin: University of Texas Press.
Beekes, Robert S. P.
    1995 Comparative Indo-European Linguistics, p. 13. Amsterdam: John Benjamins Publishing Company. The words quoted were part of a speech delivered to the Asiatic Society in 1786, when Jones was the Chief Magistrate in Calcutta, India.
Brand, Donald D.
    1971 The sweet potato: An exercise in methodology. Pp. 343-365 in *Man Across the Sea.* Carrol. L. Riley *et al.,* eds. Austin: University of Texas Press.
Cavalli-Sforza, L. Luca, Paolo Menozzi, and Alberto Piazza
    1994 *The History and Geography of Human Genes,* pp. 323-325. Princeton: Princeton University Press.
Clark, Ross
    1979 Language. Pp. 249-270 in *The Prehistory of Polynesia.* Jesse D. Jennings, ed. Cambridge: Harvard University Press.
Coe, Michael D.
    1992 *Breaking the Maya Code,* pp. 156-7. New York: Thames and Hudson.
Gordon, Cyrus H.
    1971 *Before Columbus: Links between the Old World and Ancient America.* New York: Crown Publishers.
Irwin, Geoffrey
    1992 *The Prehistoric Exploration and Colonization of the Pacific,* p. 76. Cambridge: Cambridge University Press.
Jett, Stephen C.
    1983 Pre-columbian transoceanic contacts. Pp. 337-93 in *Ancient South America.* Jesse D. Jennings, ed. San Francisco: W. H. Freeman and Company.
Key, Mary Ritchie
    1984 *Polynesian and American Linguistic Connections.* Edward Sapir Monograph Series in Language, Culture, and Cognition 12. Lake Bluff IL: Juniper Press.
Newman, Stanley
    1964 A comparison of Zuni and California Penutian. *International Journal of American Linguistics,* 30(1):1-13.
Riley, Carol L., J. Charles Kelley, Campbell W. Pennington, Robert L. Rands, eds.
    1971 *Man Across the Sea: Problems of Pre-Columbian Contacts.* Austin: University of Texas Press.
Yen, Douglas E.
    1971 Construction of the hypothesis for distribution of the sweet potato. P. 340 in *Man Across the Sea.* Carrol L. Riley *et al.,* eds. Austin: University of Texas Press.

SECTION IV

Diffusion and Voyages

TUMULUS OF KERCADO, BRITTANY, FRANCE
(P. Ferryn, Figure 3 on page 263)

Types of Cultural Diffusion[1]

ROGER WILLIAMS WESCOTT

The term 'diffusionist' was first used in 1893 to denote a scholar who believed that most folklore was borrowed from an Old World center of high culture, such as Egypt, Mesopotamia, or India (Oxford English Dictionary 1971). The term initially contrasted with it was 'evolutionist,' meaning, in this context, a folklorist who maintained that most traditional oral narratives originated in the area in which they were current. But, because the term evolutionist was more often employed to designate someone supporting a non-theistic theory of biological speciation, the word 'inventionist' came to replace evolutionist as the label for a believer in predominantly autonomous local cultural development.

The distinction between diffusionism and inventionism became progressively sharper as the two positions polarized. Increasingly, adherents of each school saw themselves as defensively compelled to refute the misinterpretations of the other school. In this respect, the relation between diffusionism and inventionism was much like that between evolutionism and creationism with regard to the origin of species, or that between uniformitarianism and catastrophism with regard to the history of the earth. In all three cases, polemics grew at the expense of mutual understanding.

Fortunately, however, there are usually some farsighted thinkers who find ways to bridge the widening gulfs between theoretical positions. In the case of evolutionism and creationism, two such thinkers were the French philosopher Henri Bergson and the British biologist St. George Mivart. In his book *Creative Evolution* (1911), Bergson argued that evolution is itself a continuing process of creation; while, in his book *Nature and Thought* (1871), Mivart held that God's creation, once in existence, had an inherent tendency to evolve higher forms.

In the case of uniformitarianism and catastrophism, it is not so much individual thinkers who bridge the gulf between conceptual extremes, as the schools themselves, which exhibit unexpected overlaps in the specific concepts advanced by each. Uniformitarians, who hold that the changes in our planet and its surroundings have been predominantly incremental over eons, nonetheless maintain that the universe originated in a gigantic explosion nicknamed the 'Big Bang.' In other words, they accept an initial catastrophe but deny most subsequent catastrophes. Catastrophists, on the other hand, attribute biotic extinctions, like those of the dinosaurs and the mammoths, to disasters of global scope. Yet they maintain that, between disasters, organic groups experience stasis, or complete cessation of collective change, speciation being restricted to the same brief periods of intense disruption that produce die-offs. The seemingly paradoxical character of these mutual overlaps is well expressed both in the title and the contents of a recent anthology of evolutionary theory, *Catastrophes and Earth History: The New Uniformitarianism* (Berggren and Van Couvering 1984).

Analogously, I would argue that inventionism and diffusionism are neither monolithic theories nor mutually exclusive positions. Both viewpoints are conceptually complex. And each not only permits elements of the other but, in some cases I would say, actually requires them. To clarify this claim, however, I must distinguish among various types of cultural diffusion.

Perhaps the first step in creating a typology of diffusion is separation of individual from collective effects. Each human being is born without culture but becomes a culture-bearer by the time he learns to talk. This process is referred to by anthropologists as enculturation and by sociologists as socialization. Although culture as a whole is necessarily post-natal, some of its components may be pre-natal. Evidence for this suggestion comes from the fact that the three chief ingredients of speech as an acoustic system—consonants, vowels, and prosody—are not learned with equal facility by infants. Prosody, or speech-rhythm (consisting of pitch, tempo, and stress), is usually mastered during the first year of life, whereas vowels and consonants are usually not mastered till the second year. The most plausible explanation of this discrepancy is that speech-rhythm is audibly transmitted to fetuses through maternal body-tissues that muffle more discrete speech sounds.

Transmission of culture from one community to another is known as acculturation. Acculturation differs from enculturation in the same way that second-language learning differs from first-language learning. Infants have no language or culture prior to what they acquire from their families and communities. But adults have both language and culture. So, when an adult community adopts new cultural (including linguistic) traits, these traits must be superimposed on traits already in place. Such superimposition is not mere addition but accommodation: what is adopted must also be adapted to what preceded it.

As commonly understood, acculturation is usually the result of either or both of two transmissive processes: migration and exchange. Migration, as permanent relocation of a community, is to be distinguished from nomadism, whereby hunting peoples follow game in a roughly circular pattern, and transhumance, whereby pastoral peoples alternate their herds between seasonal pastures. Of apparent prehistoric migrations, two of the most extensive were the overland expansion of the Indo-Europeans from Ireland to Tocharia (in

Chinese Turkestan) and the transoceanic expansion of the Austronesians (or Malayo-Polynesians) from Madagascar to Hawaii.

Most archaeologists regard overland migrations as typical and transoceanic migrations as exceptional. As analogs of the Indo-European expansion, they cite Turkish expansion from Siberia to the Balkans and Bantu expansion from Nigeria to Natal, treating the Austronesian pattern as unique. Few archaeologists, however, have had extensive maritime experience or have engaged in underwater explorations. They are consequently predisposed to regard bodies of water, especially large ones, as obstacles to travel rather than as pathways to potential new homelands (Doran 1971). But, if anything, deserts like the Sahara and mountain ranges like the Himalayas are probably greater impediments to migration than are seas and oceans. A case in point is the body of water which we call the Black Sea and the Ionian Greeks called the Euxine (eúk-seinos), or the 'Hospitable One.' Most classicists, knowing this sea to be subject to sudden storms, assume that its Greek name was a euphemism, intended to placate aquatic furies. Yet, since virtually all the Euxine shores were colonized by Greeks before the mid-6th century BC, I am disposed to take its laudatory name at face value.

In an earlier article (Wescott 1993a), I referred to willing traversal of large expanses of water as *thalassophilia*, and, in the oral presentation on which it was based, I described the view that our species has a predominantly positive orientation toward seas as *thalassicism* (Wescott 1993b). While my position on this matter has not changed, my choice of terms has. I now prefer the words *pontophilia* and *ponticism* as replacements for thalassophilia and thalassicism. Although the Classical Greek nouns *póntos* and *thálassa* both meant sea, only the former was also used to mean seacoast, particularly the northeastern coast of Anatolia, fronting the Black Sea. Moreover, only *póntos* has cognates in related languages that suggest travel over land as well as over sea. Among these are Latin *pons* (genitive *pontis*), 'bridge,' and Old Prussian *pintis*, 'road.' The mutual convertibility of land and water travel is underscored by the derivation, from Latin *pons*, of Latin *ponto*, 'flat-bottomed boat,' from which comes the English verb *punt*, 'to propel water craft with a pole.'

The probability that human pontophilia is of long standing is enhanced, I think, by Elaine Morgan's Aquatic Ape hypothesis (1982). According to Morgan, our species' striking divergences from the hominoid norm, represented by the great apes, are best explained as the consequence of a prolonged pre-Pleistocene sojourn in the shallow waters of lakes, rivers, and estuaries. Although this hypothesis was generally dismissed when advanced by her predecessor, Sir Alister Hardy, it has gained increasing attention in the past decade, becoming the focus of scientific conferences in both Europe and North America.[2] In any case, a swimming-prone primate seems to me to be a far more likely candidate for a seafaring life than one which, like both the Asian and the African apes, exhibits an aversion to all bodies of water.

The other major means of acculturation is exchange. Like migration, exchange may be of several kinds. Of these, the simplest is one that may itself require a kind of small-scale migration. This most basic form of exchange, according to French ethnologist Claude Lévi-Strauss, is sister-exchange between men of different families, who intend thereby to avoid the danger of incest (Lévi-Strauss 1967). The further the incest prohibition extends (as to distant cousins), the greater the distance between exchanging families is likely to be.

When commodities rather than persons are exchanged, the exchange is more commonly called trade. The simplest form of trade is probably exchange of food-stuffs, as when Congolese Pygmy hunters provide meat for local villagers who, in turn, provide garden produce for the hunters. Trade need not always involve verbal agreement. Silent trade, or 'dumb barter,' prevailed among many pre-industrial peoples, a representative example being foodstuff exchange between Canadian Amerinds and Eskimos. Nor need trade involve quantitative or even qualitative equivalence of goods exchanged. The celebrated kula ring of Melanesia is a system whereby sailors from island **A** present a boatload of body-ornaments to the inhabitants of island **B**. The **B** islanders, however, do not give anything to their benefactors. Instead, they make their prestation to the inhabitants of island **C**—and so on until the last islanders in the ring make a delivery to island **A** and the circle is completed (Malinowski 1922). Overall, such exchange is more like holiday gift-giving in our society than like interstate commerce. But it is no less effective in the dissemination of artifacts.

On the other hand, exchange can be purely verbal or ideational. Such exchange was termed 'stimulus diffusion' by anthropological theorist Alfred Kroeber (1948:368-370). A good example of it is provided by the Cherokee syllabary, a writing system devised by a tribesman named Sequoyah (or John Guest). Sequoyah knew that whites wrote, and he had seen alphabetic letters. But he was illiterate and did not know the phonemic principle on which alphabetic writing is based. What he did was adapt letters—some borrowed and some invented—to a system whereby each Cherokee syllable was represented by a single sign. In appearance, his syllabary resembled the Latin alphabet. In principle, however, it resembled Japanese kana—to which, in all probability, he had never been exposed.

A special form of stimulus diffusion, which usually involves behavior as well as ideas, is proselytism, or the deliberate dissemination of beliefs. Some of these beliefs are religious, as in the case of Christianity; others secular, as in the case of Marxism. The earliest missionary ideology of which we have extensive knowledge is Buddhism, which may be regarded either as religious (though it initially lacked supernaturalism) or as philosophical (though it was sometimes dogmatic). Prior to Buddhism, which became a missionizing creed by the 3rd century BC, proselytic activity is harder to establish. But the existence of what appears to be a world-wide pre-urban megalithic complex strongly suggests an ideological underpinning. And missionary zeal is implied by the Quetzalcoatl cult of Mexico and the Viracocha cult of Peru, both of which center on the tradition of an alien teacher who came from across the sea and then departed, promising to return.

The reality of telepathy, or direct mind-to-mind transmission of thought, remains in dispute. Most parapsychologists accept it, while most psychologists reject it. To the extent that it is real, telepathy presumably resembles enculturation in being a primarily individual, rather than a collective, process. An interesting aspect of the telepathy debate is that the telepathic experience seems to depend not only on one's attitude but also on one's state of consciousness. It is hardly surprising that an attitude of acceptance, or at least of open-mindedness, facilitates direct transmission of thoughts. But it is not so generally realized that telepathic reception can apparently occur during sleep for people who never have the experience while awake. This finding has been supported by sleep-laboratory experiments carried out at Maimonides Hospital in New York and described by Montague Ullman (1972).

The fact that the dream state may facilitate telepathy—imaginal as well as verbal—reminds us that, in antiquity, 'dream incubation' was a common practice. In the east Mediterranean area, the religiously devout periodically slept in pagan Greek or Egyptian temples in the hope and expectation that deities would visit them by night and counsel or enlighten them.

The line between such visitations, human or divine, and hypnosis is difficult to draw. The very word 'hypnotic,' derived as it is from the Greek word for sleep, implies that suggestion is more effective when it occurs in a mental state other than that of ordinary waking consciousness: preferably in a trance state. In the Introduction to his book *Consciousness and Reality,* Charles Muses (1972) remarks that "acculturation is slow hypnosis." By the same token, hypnosis may be thought of as rapid acculturation. Under hypnoid conditions, one can perhaps absorb more ideas and images more easily than would otherwise be possible.

As if psychic phenomena were not already controversial enough, British biochemist Rupert Sheldrake takes us a step further toward ontological dissension with his concept of 'morphic resonance.' In his book *The Presence of the Past,* he argues that every innovation in thought and behavior creates a pattern which, if it lasts long enough, constitutes a zone of influence affecting all within it (Sheldrake 1988). This zone, he asserts, need not be verbal or pictorial. It is, in effect, a "climate of opinion" transmitted by "winds of doctrine." If he is right, the notion of pyramid building could have diffused from the Old World to the Americas even in the absence of human travel from one hemisphere to the other.

Having seen how capacious the concept of diffusion is, we will, I think, soon find that the concept of invention is equally so. The English word 'invention' comes from the Latin verb *invenio,* best translated as 'find' or 'discover.'

Literally, however, it means 'come upon,' suggesting that when we invent, we do so more by accident than by intention. This, of course, is the principle which we now know as serendipity: that happy accidents favor the prepared mind.

But, if invention is not the best example of unqualified creativity, what is? Many perceptual psychologists would say that it is hallucination—the subjective construction of an appearance based on no objective stimulus. Leonard Zusne and Warren Jones (1982:133), however, argue that even such "bodiless creations" are simply delayed or rearranged presentations of objective realities previously encountered.

The ancients saw things differently. If an individual saw a figure that others did not, it was, they often held, because that individual had been favored with a divine visitation not vouchsafed to others. And, if a poet wrote or sang more beautifully than others, it was because he was inspired in the most literal sense—that is, 'breathed into' by a muse or other agent of creativity. Preliterates today take much the same position: if dancers move with extraordinary beauty and passion, it is probably because they are possessed by ancestral spirits.

The very notion of inventiveness is, in fact, a relatively modern one. It has been said that the greatest invention of the 19th century was that of the profession of the inventor. Students of the history of civilization, who generally credit the Sumerians with having invented the literate urban way of life, are perennially amazed that the Sumerians themselves took no such credit. Instead, the Sumerians insisted that civilization had been brought to them by an articulate fish-like being named Oan, who emerged from the Persian Gulf. According to their various predilections, modern Westerners have so interpreted this ancient Mesopotamian tradition as to make Oan an aquanaut, an astronaut, or a ufonaut. Yet, however the tradition is reworded, its central import remains the same: the earliest civilized society of which we have knowledge did not regard itself as the creator but rather as the receiver of civilization.

When inventors and other creative people are asked where they got their 'break-through' ideas, most reply, "I don't know. It just came to me!" The question that inevitably arises then, of course, is, "Where did the idea come *from?*" Until recently, most of the world's peoples would unhesitatingly have replied that the inspiration to innovate comes from preternatural—or at least supra-individual—sources. Since the advent of psychoanalysis, however, most students of the creative process have assumed that the source of any major invention is the inventor's unconscious mind. In these terms, invention is usually an exclusively individual procedure: after all, inventions are rarely produced by committees—or even by research teams.

The individualism underlying this assumption is typical of the modern West. Paradoxically, however, the very independence of mind fostered by our individualistic society has led some of its members to question a psychology that hermetically seals off minds from one another. Carl Jung, the earliest and most prominent psychoanalyst to secede from orthodox Freudianism, held that an individual's ideas may stem from any one of three sources: his conscious mind, his unconscious mind, or the collective unconscious mind (Jung 1964). Of these three, it is the last that is most distinctively Jungian and most relevant to the question of the diffusion of concepts.

Discussion of diffusion may be either source-oriented or destination-oriented. Focus on invention highlights sources. But attention can just as well be focused on destinations, leading us to ask who accepts cultural innovations and why. We may also ask whether acceptance of innovation is a predominantly active process, whereby receivers solicit new ideas and products, or a predominantly passive process, whereby receivers accept such innovations only because they cannot indefinitely resist doing so.

Perhaps the most common form of diffusion within a society is imitation. In the field of mythology, one of the strongest advocates of the Diffusionist School of interpretation was folklorist Fitzroy Somerset, Lord Raglan, who argued that the transmission of traditional narratives is overwhelmingly imitative and that invention of such narratives is minimal (Somerset 1965). Furthermore, he extended this argument to other matters of cultural transmission, holding that most peoples, like most individuals, are mere imitators. In response to the implied derogation here, one is tempted to quote P. G. Wodehouse's hero Bertie Wooster, who, when described by his aunt Agatha as "a mere popinjay (parrot)," responded, "What, may I ask, is mere about a popinjay?" Good imitation requires considerable skill, if not creativity. Ethologists are well aware of the fact that, in the animal world, imitative ability is rare and restricted to such higher animals as insects, birds, and mammals. Foraging honey-bees, for example, when they have discovered a source of nectar, do a 'honey dance' in the hive which orients other workers to that source by drawing what is, in effect, a map with indications of direction and distance. Most songbirds can reproduce the vocalizations of others, particularly of conspecific adults. And all apes and monkeys observe each other's actions, mimicking many of them.

At least among vertebrates, moreover, imitativeness and inventiveness are not mutually exclusive. On the contrary, in fact, they appear often to be mutually reinforcing. The European song-thrush *Turdus philomela*, for example, not only mimics melodies when young but improvises them when adult. And Japanese macaques have been observed both introducing new behavior patterns to their troops and imitating patterns introduced by others.

Let us return now to our initial concern: that of the relation between cultural invention and cultural diffusion. To be effective, I should say, every invention must be diffused by its inventor to others. Yet diffusion itself, even in its receptive aspect, is far from being a sheerly automatic process. When diffused, each invention has to be, to some extent, reinvented in the minds of the receivers. Furthermore, to the degree that an invention is a theme, most

inventions permit—perhaps even invite—variations. And, when a theme is diffused, most of its variations are invented by those receptive to the invention.

For centuries, Western thought has been constricted by European dualisms. One of these is the Aristotelian distinction between celestial and terrestrial mechanics, which undoubtedly delayed the Newtonian synthesis. Another is the Cartesian distinction between mind and body, which similarly impeded psychosomatic thinking about questions of health. Ironically, these dualisms seem to have been imposed on an older and more unitive tradition, variously known as the Hermetic Tradition,[3] or the Rule of Correspondence. In its best-known formulation, this rule was: As above, so below. A variant formulation was: As without, so within. In either case, the essence of the Rule seems to have been one of ultimate connectedness—a welcome antidote to the fragmentation characteristic of our overspecialized age.

END NOTES

1. A written version of the first segment of an oral presentation enitled "Varieties of Diffusionism, with Special Reference to Early Eurasian Influence on North America," given at the NEARA Conference, *America Before Columbus*, Brown University, Providence RI, June 1992.
2. Conferences: "The Aquatic Ape: Fact or Fiction?" Valkenburg, Netherlands, August 1987; and "The Aquatic Ape Theory," Sonoma CA, June 1994.
3. A Greek phrase, derived from the Egyptian "Law of Thoth."

REFERENCES

Berggren, W. A. and John A. Van Couvering, eds.
  1984 *Catastrophes and Earth History: The New
    Uniformitarianism.* Princeton: Princeton University Press.
Bergson, Henri
  1911 *Creative Evolution.* Arthur Mitchell, trans. New York:
    Henry Holt & Co.
Doran, Edwin, Jr.
  1971 The sailing raft as a great tradition. In *Man Across the
    Sea.* C. L. Riley *et al.*, eds. Austin: University of Texas
    Press.
Jung, Carl G.
  1964 *Man and His Symbols.* New York: Dell.
Kroeber, Alfred Louis
  1948 *Anthropology*, 2nd ed. NewYork: Harcourt, Brace and
    Co. Esp. Section 154, Invention by Stimulus Diffusion, pp.
    368-370.
Lévi-Strauss, Claude
  1967 *Structural Anthropology.* Claire Jacobson and Brooke
    Grundfest Schoepf, trans. Garden City: Anchor/Doubleday.
Malinowski, Bronislaw
  1922 *Argonauts of the Western Pacific.* New York: Dutton.
Mivart, St. George Jackson
  1871 *Nature and Thought.* London: Macmillan & Co.

Morgan, Elaine
  1982 *The Aquatic Ape: A Theory of Human Evolution*. New York: Stein & Day.
Muses, Charles and Arthur Young, eds.
  1972 Introduction. P. 3 in *Consciousness and Reality*. New York: Outerbridge/Dutton.
Oxford English Dictionary, The
  1971 Compact (unabridged) Edition. Oxford, England: Clarendon Press.
Sheldrake, Rupert
  1988 *The Presence of the Past: Morphic Resonance and the Habits of Nature*. New York: Times Books.
Somerset, Fitzroy, Lord Raglan
  1965 The hero of tradition. In *The Study of Folklore*. A. Dundes, ed. Englewood Cliffs: Prentice Hall.

Ullman, Montague
  1972 Vigilance, dreaming, and the paranormal. In *Consciousness and Reality*. C. Muses and A. Young, eds. New York: Outerbridge/Dutton.
Wescott, Roger Williams
  1993a Civilization in context. P. 19 in *The Comparative Civilizations Review*, No. 29, Fall 1993. Rolla MO.
  1993b *The Presidential Address to The International Society for the Comparative Study of Civilizations*. University of Scranton, Scranton PA. June 3, 1993.
Zusne, Leonard and Warren H. Jones
  1982 *Anomalistic Psychology: A Study of Extraordinary Phenomena of Behavior and Experience*. Hillsdale NJ: Lawrence Erlbaum Associates.

CHINESE ADMIRAL ZHENG HE'S HUGE SHIP (140 m. long) COMPARED TO COLUMBUS' SANTA MARIA (30 m.)

A European View of Diffusion and Transoceanic Contacts before 1492

PATRICK FERRYN

BACKGROUND

As a Belgian who is also a European, I have been given the charge of opening this initial session. I don't know whether the organizers, in taking this decision, wanted to underline the contribution of the Old World to the New. Nevertheless, it is a great honor for me to be here among you for this occasion.

Before moving to the substance of my presentation, I can't resist the pleasure of briefly telling you about a delightful coincidence. A few hundred meters from where we are meeting at this university there lived, until 1937, a famous resident of Providence. His name was Howard Philip Lovecraft. He was a poet and a writer of weird fiction whose works are full of the ruins of cities which vanished well before man appeared, at the time when the earth belonged to the 'Ancient Old Ones.'

The group to which I belong, in Brussels, is basically composed of friends who share a passion for archaeology and ancient history. It happens that we also enjoy reading Lovecraft's books, which we discovered at the beginning of the 1960s. That is why, when we created our group twenty-three years ago now, we naturally called it *KADATH*, a name that symbolizes in Lovecraft's fantastic mythology the 'City of the Ancient Old Ones.' We do not, of course, seriously believe that there really was a primordial civilization, as described by Lovecraft, but in our minds this idea perfectly illustrates our quest: to understand what happened at the dawn of the major human achievements in the world.

In the 1970s, wild archaeomania in the Von Daniken style caused a great loss of interest among the diffusionist thinkers in our French-speaking countries. In order to achieve a better understanding, we created an association named *KADATH, CHRONICLES OF LOST CIVILIZATIONS*. *KADATH* aims to elucidate the real enigmas of archaeology, retaining on the one hand the results of Establishment science (which is essential, of course), while concurrently drawing attention to other well-documented research that might challenge the prevailing theories. So it is that we find ourselves on a 'third path,' one which is most uncomfortable because we are constantly in the awkward middle position, yet are considered by many to be on the periphery.

At *KADATH*, we took an early interest in diffusionist theories, not only those related to the Ancient World, but also those concerning the New World. And it is to Professor Marcel Homet (author of *The Sons of the Sun* and, under the pseudonym of Pierre Honoré, *In Quest of the White God*), that we owe our interest in transoceanic contacts. He first put us in contact with the late Charles Hapgood, who became a member of the Honorary Committee of *KADATH*. This committee is composed of other well-known persons, among whom are Alexander Von Wuthenau, Maria Reiche, Charles Herberger, John Carlson, George Carter, and the late Alexander Thom. As you may readily understand, some of our favorite subjects are megalithism, archaeoastronomy, ancient Kings of the Sea, America before Columbus, mythologies, and ancient traditions. So, I wish to pay homage to H. P. Lovecraft, who, in a way, brought me here today!

OVERCOMING ACADEMIC BIAS

As the title of my paper is *A European View of Diffusion and Transoceanic Contacts before 1492*, I'll start with a brief explanation and will then proceed to a series of reflections, proposals, and ideas which I hope you can indulgently consider as you might weigh ideas put forth in a brain-storming session. Remember that even the craziest ideas could lead, one day, to an interesting achievement!

From my contacts with many 'official' archaeologists and researchers, including those from universities, as well as from other European institutions, I have to tell you that the subjects to be discussed during these four days are not really popular across the Atlantic. In fact, I should say at the outset that these subjects are nearly unknown to most researchers. Only a minority have a few bits of information, very fragmentary at that.

The papers of some European researchers reveal either extremely biased views, or ignorance of the subject, or even disdain for any work which runs contrary to the theories they have been defending all their lives.

When Thor Heyerdahl presented his theory on the populating of Easter Island to a prestigious assembly gathered in the fifties at the Sorbonne in Paris, one of the most distinguished French specialists of that time, Dr. Paul Rivet, then Director of the Musée de l'Homme, was in the audience. Well aware that his reactions were being observed, Rivet proceeded to open his newspaper on the desks of the amphitheatre and began to read it in order to demonstrate how much he wanted to ignore the new ideas of the famous Norwegian navigator! This attitude clearly shows the lack of interest in academic circles in the work undertaken by independent or non-mainstream researchers. Nevertheless, in defense of Paul Rivet, I should add that a few years later he became a fervent diffusionist! But Rivet still has imitators; in 1980, a small book dealing with the problem of Native American origins was published in France by another famous specialist, Professor Annette Lemaing-Emperaire. In her book, which is still a reference work today in French academic circles, she qualifies Thor Heyerdahl with a kind of disdain, saying that he is a "mere sportsman" whose achievements have nothing to say to serious historians!

However, there may still be signs of hope, and we think it is fair to say that mindsets are slowly changing. For example, we notice that, at the modest level of our journal, more and more students and young teachers are becoming interested in *KADATH*'s content, while many of their older teachers cannot stand reading it!

The nay-sayers with whom I am acquainted, as well as the few more or less interested skeptics, mostly regret the lack of serious publications or detailed reports issued by official authorities. I'm sure you have encountered the same objections, so allow me to make some suggestions in order better to inform and sensitize the international academic community, because I remain convinced that we have to succeed in expanding public interest in the matters with which we are dealing. Respected specialists belong to that community, and we need their knowledge and competence.

Although I always read with utmost interest such excellent publications as the *New England Antiquities Research Association Journal*, or the *Early Sites Research Society Bulletin* (from James Whittall), the *Epigraphic Society Occasional Publications* (ESOP), *Stonewatch*, *Stonehenge Viewpoint*, and several others, I can foresee a unique publication that would be devoted to the study of diffusionist theories. It could be an annual document like John Carlson's *Archaeoastronomy*, issued by the University of Maryland, that would assemble the best research and most interesting documentation. A report of this nature should be sent to all universities as well as to all other relevant institutions.

In the same way, I also envisage a conference similar to this one, which would take place every two, three, or four years, perhaps like the famous Congress of the Americanists. We would invite prominent specialists from various disciplines—and even opponents—and we would draw upon their competence, if, of course, they were willing to cooperate. Remember the example of the *Ancient Vermont Conference*, organized in 1977 at Castleton State College by the late Dr. Warren Cook. He had invited two recognized British specialists, Peter Reynolds and Ann

Ross; although they did not share the opinion of most of the participants concerning the non-indigenous, pre-Columbian origin of the Vermont lithic structures, neither did they adhere to Giovanna Neudorfer's reductionist thesis which concluded that these stone chambers were colonial constructions!

Finally, I would continue my vision by advocating more excavation work, properly carried out by specialists, and detailed reports thereon.

Figure 1 ER-GRAH, THE GREAT BROKEN MENHIR
Locmariaquer, Brittany, France, 21 m. long

LITHIC FEATURES

I had the good fortune, in 1988, of visiting several sites in New England in the company of Roslyn Strong and several friends of NEARA and other groups. I was struck by the impressive number of remains that you have here, and by the dearth of excavation effort. For example, a monument such as the so-called dolmen, 'Balanced Rock,' in New Salem, New York, known for more than two hundred years, has never been the subject of any excavation work! Considering the fact that the Establishment regards that stone as being nothing more than an ordinary extravagance of nature, a souvenir of the Ice Age, I assume that it should be easy enough to obtain a permit to undertake geological surveys and excavations. In my opinion, that would be an excellent project to suggest to a university and a team of archaeology students.

If that heavy New Salem stone really was placed on its support pillars by men, it should be possible to find evidence in the subsoil around the stone. A few years ago, near Carnac in France, archaeologists started excavation around the largest megalithic standing stone ever put up by man—about 21 m. long and over 300 tons—the Grand Menhir, called 'Er-Grah,' in Locmariaquer (Figure 1). (It now lies in four pieces on the ground.) Although there had been disturbance of the site over the centuries, including decades-long use as a parking lot, fantastic things were discovered there. For example, we now know that Er-Grah was part of a system made up of sixteen other aligned monoliths, the wedging holes of which have been discovered, and that it was a gigantic grouping, certainly as important as Stonehenge, erected some six thousand years ago!

In like manner, I realize that there have been decades of discussion about a possible European, pre-Columbian origin for the famous Newport Tower. It is a fascinating subject deserving research.

Figure 2 ONE OF THREE STANDING MONOLITHS
These stones form a triangle at the top of the French River stone chamber.

You probably know that there is another comparable structure in France, at Lanleff (near Saint-Brieuc, Brittany), dated late 11th century. I had the pleasure of visiting Lanleff with Roslyn Strong, Sue Carlson, and Bett Peterson in 1989. Several French authors have noted the striking resemblance between these French and American structures, always cited by tourist guides. My suggestion is to create a committee and ask the authorities of Newport and Lanleff to officially twin the two cities, a move which would favor numerous exchanges. Both communities would benefit, from a touristic point of view, and, most of all, it should encourage more detailed research on the history of these structures. While this is a long-term project, it should, nevertheless, alert scientists to the enigmas, and enable us to learn more from the knowledge they gather.

Let me repeat and emphasize: more geological surveys and professionally directed excavations would be the desirable starting point before hypothesizing about the possible origins and meaning of many New England stone structures. Meanwhile, one can always engage in comparative archaeology, which is intellectually interesting but will not satisfy the Establishment.

Among other things that struck me during my trip through New England was the stone chamber located in French River near Grosvenordale, Connecticut, to which Jim Egan took us (Figure 2). At the top of the mound covering this structure were three standing stones arranged in the shape of a nearly equilateral triangle. This feature immediately reminded me of an important megalithic monument of the Carnac area of Brittany, the tumulus of Kercado (Figure 3). At the top of that burial mound is a standing monolith, and remarkable astronomical alignments have been observed at that monument, which is at least 6800 years old. The French River site, in my opinion, also deserves some study, which could be undertaken at little cost.

Figure 3 THE TUMULUS OF KERCADO
Note the monolith on top of the chamber.

I would also like to draw the attention of researchers to the particular shape of some of the standing stones found at Mystery Hill, in Salem, New Hampshire (*e.g.*, the so-called 'Stone J'). In the good work they have undertaken at this site, Robert Stone and his team have discovered interesting astronomical data involving the setting and rising sun, not only at the solstices and equinoxes, but also on the occasion of the traditional Celtic cross-quarter days, Beltane, Samhain, Imbolc, and Lugnasad.

In Belgium and, more generally speaking, in Celtic Gaul, we have several examples of standing stones of similar shape for which sacred geometry and/or astronomical data have been observed. They are called 'beveled menhirs' because their tops have been cut to form an oblique edge, as seen in Figure 4. It would be interesting to investigate similar details in the case of Mystery Hill.

Let's not forget the remarkable lithic features of the American Southwest. Among some people I know in Europe who are interested in these subjects, there is a desire to learn much more about Native American stone construction. Their intent is not to avoid or to deny the possibility of pre-Columbian transoceanic influences, but rather to explore this field more deeply than has been done. That was the main idea developed by Byron Dix and Jim Mavor in their book *Manitou*. Personally, I think there is still a lot to be learned about this topic.

Figure 4 THE FAMOUS 'BRUNEHAULT STONE'
Hollain, Belgium

Figure 5 does not show a standing stone from New England nor from Brittany, but a monolith raised at the Yellow Jacket ruin, a site of the 11th or 12th century Anasazi, sun-watchers of the Montezuma Basin. The ruin is located near one of the major springs of the high plains between the Abajos of Utah and the San Juan mountains of Colorado. In their book, *Prehistoric Astronomy in the Southwest*, Malville and Putnam see the Yellow Jacket monolith as obvious evidence of ceremonialism on that site. Pointing out that the stone's wedge-top is aligned toward Wilson Peak near where the sun rises on June 21, they observe that:

> On the morning of summer solstice, the pointed shadow of its top falls across the ruined wall of the room just to the west of the monolith. Throughout the weeks before solstice the position of the sharp top of the shadow could have been marked on the wall and would have provided an accurate calendar. To the west and east are four additional fallen monoliths of similar size . . . . (See end note 1.)

The site was studied in 1954 by Professor Joe Wheat of the University of Colorado.

RED OCHRE

Now for the problem of red ochre, another topic deserving of more detailed study. As you know, numerous Maritime Archaic archaeological sites in the northeastern part of North America have revealed burials and other features containing red ochre. One of the more unique discoveries, that of the cairn at l'Anse Amour on the coast of Labrador, has been compared to Norwegian and French sites on the Atlantic coast, particularly at Teviec, in Brittany, which are nearly as old; that is, they date back at least seven thousand years.

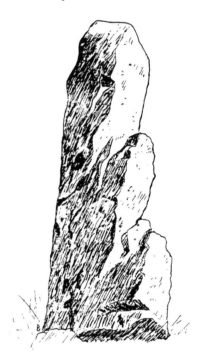

Figure 5 MONOLITH
Yellow Jacket Anasazi ruin site
The stone is about 5 ft. high and shaped into a wedge
at its top.

Many similarities can be observed among these sites; they seem to belong to communities that had comparable life styles and economies. We can also see some similarities in burial practices and, even more curious, in the habit these cultures had of smearing the bones, and sometimes also the burial goods, with red ochre, as well as often spreading red ochre at various places on the grave. For several years now, I have been comparing prehistoric burial practices of both the ancient world and the new world, mostly during what constitutes the Upper Paleolithic and Mesolithic Ages in Western Europe. Personally, I think that what we are seeing is an example of diffusion; at least this has been my working hypothesis. However, the research is not easy, and it is difficult to prove anything in that field today. Because we find red ochre marking in graves on both sides of the Atlantic Ocean is insufficient reason in itself for us to assume that there has really been diffusion of this practice.

Interesting discussion of that topic has already appeared in, among others, three issues of the prominent review, *Current Anthropology*, back in 1980 and 1981. I realize that, for excavations dating back more than thirty years from the present, reports referring to the presence of red ochre in a burial are not precise enough. Too often the finding is summarized in a laconic sentence such as, "We found red ochre in the tomb," or, "The skeleton showed marks of red ochre," etc. The skeptics will, with reason, object that the people who carried out the excavations forgot to describe the nature of the soil, whether there was red ochre elsewhere around the burial, or if, for example, anyone had noticed the presence of *yellow* ochre.

Indeed, there could be deposits of natural ochre at the place where the body was buried. One should also take into account the fact that all that is red is not automatically red ochre! Moreover, the earth of the gravesite, the artifacts buried, as well as the bones, might show the reddish color simply due to the dissolving of iron salts in the soil. Of course, if one discovers red ochre in a burial located in the middle of a shell heap, as was often the case for the Maritime Archaic populations of the Atlantic, this becomes interesting! It could also be that prehistoric man used red ochre, not for ritual purposes at all, but simply for practical reasons: to tan hides, for example; or because of its antiputrid, antiseptic, and waterproofing properties. Perhaps, in the use of red ochre, there was no magic, no idea of 'survival' in an afterlife, but merely just good common sense.

Many important points of information about the use of red ochre can be found in the remarkable book by Fabienne May, *Les Sépultures Préhistoriques* (Prehistoric Burials) from which a significant abstract was published in issue 25, Nos. 3&4 of the *NEARA Journal*. To conclude discussion of this topic, I would like to draw the attention of researchers to the utmost importance of reporting as much detail as possible about the presence of red ochre in any burials they might excavate.

KENSINGTON STONE

The controversy about the famous Kensington Stone also inspires me with the following idea: for nearly a century we have debated the authenticity of this stone and its runic inscription; supporters and opponents quarrel through repeated publication. Enough! There must be a way for the city and the museum that own the precious relic, with the help of a foundation or other sponsor, to set up a study commission that would bring the best experts together. Let them start the work, taking into account all the factors already included in the files. With a little good will and financial help, they should be able to see it through to a reasonable conclusion. An exhaustive publication, presenting the stone's history as well as the principal opposing studies thus far carried out, together with the commission's own new work as the final step in this undertaking, could then be sent to the concerned institutions throughout the world.

Figure 6 TWO INSCRIPTIONS FROM ARGENTINA

Above: 'Hyperborean Runic' inscription
Palancho, La Rioja Province
Below: 'The Medina Stone' with runic inscription,
according to the late Professor J. de Mathieu

SOUTH AMERICA

Finally, I would like to add a few words concerning the discoveries made in South America by Professor Jacques de Mahieu. This French anthropologist and archaeologist lived in Buenos Aires, Argentina, and devoted many years to the study of remains of what he was convinced was proof of Viking and Mediterranean presence in South America before Columbus. That is why he undertook extensive research on the 'white indians' of Paraguay (the Guayakis) and on unexpected inscriptions found in Brazil, Argentina, Paraguay, Uruguay, and elsewhere, which he considered as runic (Figure 6). He also studied the artifacts, of typical Trojan inspiration, in the unexpected collection gathered by the Wagner brothers in the thirties in Santiago del Estero, Argentina (Figures 7a, 7b). This is a long story and, if by chance someone has a particular interest in these subjects and would be able to undertake some research work, I would be more than glad to meet for a deeper discussion. Professor de Mahieu died in 1991, and there are numerous pieces of information that should be taken into account.

Figure 7a TWO EXAMPLES OF OLD WORLD POTTERY
Note characteristic 'Owl-Mask' and eyes with three tears.
Left is from Egypt; right is from Boetia.

Figure 7b POTTERY FROM SANTA MARIA CULTURE
Catamarca Province, Argentina
Note 'Owl Mask' and eyes with three tears.
(Museo del Instituto de Antropologia)

CONCLUDING COMMENTS

I realize that I will end my paper belaboring an obvious point—but I would like to address this last remark to the hypercritical ones among you. Last year (1991), the French navigator Gerard d'Abboville performed an exploit by rowing across the Pacific Ocean all *alone*. Of course, before him others had crossed the Pacific and Atlantic Oceans by other means. Alice Kehoe has already tackled this subject in her chapter, "Small boats upon the Atlantic," published in the excellent work *Man Across the Sea*. More recently, eleven Frenchmen rowed across the Atlantic and reached the West Indies on April 30th, 1992, after a thirty-six day trip. The interesting thing about that last exploit is that none of those Frenchmen was a real sailor! For most of them, it was a first experience! (See end note 2.) Which should be sufficient evidence to demonstrate how easy it really is to cross an ocean.

An illustration that has always amused me is the drawing opposite the start of this essay. It represents, to the same scale, the Santa Maria of Cristopher Columbus, which was barely thirty m. long, and the extraordinary vessel of the Chinese explorer, Zheng He, who sailed across the seas nearly sixty years before Columbus in his vessel—about one hundred and forty m. long!

Strabo said the following some two thousand years ago: "One day man will discover that the Ancients made longer journeys on the earth and across the seas than their descendants ever did."

NOTES

1. More information can be found about the Anasazi site mentioned in the text in *Prehistoric Astronomy in the Southwest* by J. McKim Malville and Claudia Putnam. Boulder CO: Johnson Publishing Company, 1989.
2. Another Frenchman has very recently succeeded in swimming across the Atlantic. On arrival in Barbados less than sixty days after his start, he admitted that it was quite easy to drift along in the current!

Vestiges of the Natural History of Archaeology:
Setting up the Americas as a Scientific Experiment[1]

ALICE B. KEHOE

INTRODUCTION

Science as we know it is part of modern Western culture. Its beginning is traditionally ascribed to Sir Francis Bacon, Lord Chancellor of England in 1621 under King James I (&VI). In his *Great Instauration* of 1605, Bacon advocated the experimental method for discovering Truth. Bacon's contemporaries understood him to say that only "the Light of Reason" and the "Testimonie of [the] Sense[s]"—of course, under "the Guidance of God"—could reveal true knowledge (Popkin 1992:106). The first Director of our Smithsonian Institution, Joseph Henry, echoed his forebears in science when, in the 1840s, he told an audience, " . . . there are three great divisions of human knowledge . . . founded on the three sources . . . Sensation, Consciousness, Revelation" (Henry 1980:25). The 'Baconian method' requires, first, direct observation of the natural world; next, gathering together and classifying these observations; then, inducting general principles from these classified data; and finally, validating these principles by subjecting new data to a test of consilience (whether they are in accordance). Bacon and his followers supposed an omnipotent God who offers two complementary sources of knowledge to mankind: the direct Word of God in the Bible; and nonverbal revelation in the Book of Nature.

Half a century after Bacon, following a Puritan-led Civil War and a Restoration of the established aristocracy, the Royal Society of London for Improving Natural Knowledge was founded to "assemble about some *calm*, and *indifferent* things, especially experiments" (Sprat 1667, quoted in Morrell and Thackray 1981:246; Sprat's italics). "Matters of fact" are to be established within "a disciplined space, where experimental, discursive, and social practices were collectively controlled by competent members" (Shapin and Schaffer 1985:39, 51-72, 78). When accredited "competent members" such as the men elected to the Royal Society were formally met to witness a controlled scientific experiment, a "matter of fact" was judged to have been substantiated. The 'Baconian method,' with its emphasis on direct personal observation of natural phenomena, supposedly fostered a calm, reasonable, gentlemanly approach to knowledge in contrast to the bitter wrangling attending the assertion of unattested private opinion.

By the latter part of the 18th century, the 'Baconian method' had become one of the supports for the Common-Sense philosophy developed by Thomas Reid in Scotland (Laudan 1981, esp. ch. 7). God, Reid asserted, ordained a universe embodying principles of order and endowed men with capacity, and the responsibility, to search to discover these principles. In its time, this philosophy was a revolutionary metaphysic deeply implicated in the English, American, and French Revolutions (Jacob 1976; Shapin and Schaffer 1985). American science and engineering have been strongly influenced by the Scottish Enlightenment and especially by Reid's Common-Sense Realism (Bozeman 1977). In recent years, the 'Scientific Creationists' of the Christian far right have been using a century-old version of science drawn from Reid's philosophy.

1844—ROBERT CHAMBERS

Slowly, science based on observation made obsolete the historicism of a Biblical universe. In 1844, a Scottish publisher, Robert Chambers, introduced, "as far as I am aware . . . the first attempt to connect the natural sciences into a history of creation" (Chambers 1847:199). Guessing that he would provoke cries of scandal, Chambers never openly acknowledged that he was the author of *Vestiges of the Natural History of Creation*. Chambers argued, "The inorganic has one final comprehensive law, GRAVITATION. The organic, the other great department of mundane things, rests in like manner on one law, and that is—DEVELOPMENT" (Chambers 1847:185). *Vestiges* describes the law of development as a continuum from the formation of stars and planets by gravitational attraction toward nuclei within nebulae, through the formation of rocks and of organic life in geologic time, all

to be regarded as a series of *advances of the principle of development*, which have depended upon external physical circumstances, to which the resulting animals are appropriate (Chambers 1847:105). . . . The probability may now be assumed that the human race sprung from one stock, which was at first in a state of simplicity, if not barbarism. . . . *The leading characters . . . of the various races of mankind are simply representations of particular stages in the development of the highest or Caucasian type* (Chambers 1847:157-158; his italics).

(Chambers, like Herbert Spencer after him, used von Baer's embryology as described in English by Carpenter, who wrote for W. and R. Chambers [Secord 1989:180-181; Gould 1977:109]). Chambers' final chapters on human development are not particularly original, adopting without citation the conjectural history of the 18th-century philosophers (*v.* Meek 1976) (*cf.* Piggott 1976:151) and citing James Prichard's *Researches into the Physical History of Man* as a primary source (Chambers 1847:143); the blatant racism in these sources was unchallenged.

Chambers followed the principle articulated only a few decades earlier by Lamarck (Barthlémy-Madaule 1982:80), when he wrote that:

> The style of living is ascertained to have a powerful effect in modifying the human figure in the course of generations. . . . it would also appear that nature has a power of producing new varieties. . . . We are ignorant of the laws of variety-production; but we see it going on as a principle in nature. . . . The tendency of the modern study of the languages of nations is to the same point . . . physiology and philology seem . . . decidedly favorable to the idea of a single origin . . . that the human race is *one*. . . . Civilization does sometimes rise in a manner clearly independent amongst a horde of people generally barbarous. A striking instance is described in the laborious work of Mr. Catlin on the North-American tribes (Chambers 1847:144-154; his italics).

In an earlier version, Chambers had written:

> *Variety-production*—that law by which nations of superior have sprung from nations of inferior endowments—may be considered as the highest that affects the natural history of our species. It produces great leaps in improvement, but these may be at long intervals. . . . It is also seen that, in the domesticated tribes of animals, and in cultivated shrubs, new varieties are constantly arising (*Chambers' Edinburgh Journal* No. 538, May 21, 1842:137, "Thoughts on Nations and Civilisation," unsigned but surely by Robert Chambers; his italics).

Chambers had not hesitated to combat England's leading philosopher of science when he declared "Dr. Whewell's views condemned" in *Explanations* (1847:265):

> . . . in Dr. Whewell's *History of the Inductive Sciences* . . . this writer (Whewell) halts when he comes to consider the origin of language and of arts, the origin of species and formation of globes. These he calls palaetiological sciences, because, in his opinion, we have to seek for an *ancient and different class of causes*, as affecting them, from any which are now seen operating. "In . . . palaetiological sciences," says he, ". . . philosophers have never demonstrated, and . . . probably never will be able to demonstrate, what was the primitive state of things from which the progressive course of the world took its first departure. . . . its starting point . . . becomes not only invisible, but unimaginable."

Can Chambers—the anonymous 'Mr. Vestiges'—*prove* the formidable Dr. Whewell wrong? Can he *demonstrate* by the 'Baconian method' of observation, classification, and

replication of results that "the human race sprung from one stock, which was at first in a state of simplicity [and that] Civilization does sometimes rise in a manner clearly independent amongst a horde of people generally barbarous"?

1851—DANIEL WILSON

Enter young Daniel Wilson, a poor but intelligent and hardworking Edinburgh engraver. Like Chambers himself, Wilson had not been able to afford a university degree. Like Chambers, Wilson read avidly and had enough artistic talent to prepare attractive sketches of the historic buildings in his native city. Again like Chambers, who was sixteen years older than he, Wilson brought his visual and accompanying lively narrative sketches to a more successful older man: for Chambers, it had been the aged, socially prominent Sir Walter Scott (whose favorite of all his novels was the 1815 *The Antiquary*); for Wilson, it was Chambers the publisher.

Robert Chambers engaged Daniel Wilson in 1846 to assist in the reorganization of the collections and programs of the Society of Antiquaries of Scotland. With the bookseller David Laing, Chambers and Wilson changed the Society from a gentlemen's club dallying in antiquities to a serious research group that in 1851 would turn its collections over to the new National Museum of Scotland for which Chambers had lobbied. Marking the new era was the publication of Daniel Wilson's *The Archaeology and Prehistoric Annals of Scotland*, the first use in English of the word 'prehistoric.'

Early in the summer of 1851, Chambers and Wilson walked out to a new subdivision on the outskirts of Edinburgh to look at a burial unearthed in construction. Wilson's description sounds like that of a Beaker grave. The two men took the skull and pot from the stone cist, walked back home, and relaxed together, as Wilson recalled:

> . . . our evening's talk led us through many a curious speculation on ethnical affinities, evolutionary development, perpetuated peculiarities, backward to the very origin of man. I still recall the startled interest with which I then listened to glimpses of Lamarckian and Darwinian views, now very familiar to all (Wilson 1878:147).

1862—WILSON'S *PREHISTORIC MAN*

That 1851 event was the genesis of Wilson's book *Prehistoric Man*, which would be published in 1862. In the intervening years, he had emigrated to Toronto to become a professor of English literature and history at University College. He wrote to one friend:

> When I left Edinburgh, I had sketched out a work partly historical, partly ethnological relating to Scotland on which I fancied I had something new to say. But transported here I

found not only that I had no books or other needful facilities for the task; but that I was in an uncongenial atmosphere for such work; and if I would be both useful and happy I must find my work in my new sphere. . . . I have been for some time collecting materials, and meditate some time or other trying to dip behind the historic dawn of America as I have already attempted for Scotland. There were great men before *Columbus* as well as Agamemnon! (Wilson 1860; his italics).

To another friend he wrote that he had been traveling through the Great Lakes

to observe thus the manners and habits of a people probably closely resembling those of Scotland's primitive eras, which constitutes one of the favourite themes on which I used to bore you, at our S. A. S. meetings (Wilson 1855).

Prehistoric Man, the second of Daniel Wilson's pioneering works in developing a new science of prehistoric archaeology, utilized the model of science presented by geology to expand Robert Chambers' ideas of human origins and development. Fieldworkers had observed that stratigraphic exposures reveal a series of increasingly sophisticated artifacts that compare to the series of increasingly complex organisms revealed in geologic history. In like manner, the study of living organisms elucidates the life processes of similar ancient specimens; study of living primitive humans should elucidate the ways of life of ancient races. Wilson's emigration to Canada broadened the range of his primary research without materially altering the plan of his new work (Wilson 1862:456-458). He queried:

Whence is man? What are his antecedents? What—within the compass of this terrestial arena, with which alone science deals—are his future destinies? Does civilisation move only through limited cycles . . . ? The history of civilisation is . . . an inquiry into the development of society, and the progressive growth of man (Wilson 1862:3-4).

Serious political consequences hinged on the question of the origins of the various human races. If monogenesis, a single origin for all humans, were true, then governments should have recognized inalienable human rights for all their subjects, American Indian, Asian, and African as well as European. If, on the contrary, the polygenesists were correct and the several acknowledged races had been separately created, gross inequities between members of different races might have been supportable. A politically liberal, humane person such as Daniel Wilson, or Robert Chambers, would have been inclined to favor monogenesis. The apparently parallel development of complex societies in different parts of the world seemed to them to be proof of our common human nature.

Wilson would argue scientifically from what he would claim has been a natural experiment: once the Bering Strait land bridge had closed, impassable oceans separated primitive Americans from the Old World. The presumably wholly independent evolution of culture in the New World was a *replication* of evolution in the Old—that is, the Americas were a laboratory for 'Baconian science,' beginning with the collection of observational data, then their classification and the derivation of general principles from them, and finally their validation by observing the experiment replicated.

Wilson's book *Prehistoric Man* was successful. Its first edition sold out quickly, and the London publisher asked him to prepare a second, which was printed in 1865. That same year, a rival publisher brought out Sir John Lubbock's *Prehistoric Times*, a collection of four reports on archaeological researches published between 1861 and 1864, and a long review of North American archaeology published in 1863. The latter includes paragraphs cribbed without acknowledgment from Wilson's *Prehistoric Man*, a fact that did not escape Wilson's notice (Wilson to Charles Lyell 1865). *Prehistoric Man* had one more substantial revised edition, in 1876, an edition bought by most university libraries. Wilson died in 1892. Sir John Lubbock lived to 1913, a year later than his book's last (sixth) edition in 1912. Standard histories of archaeology credit Lubbock with inaugurating a science of prehistory, but I believe I have demonstrated (Kehoe 1991) that it was Daniel Wilson who has clear priority—and it was Wilson, not Lubbock, who wrote the magisterial article on "Archaeology" for the Ninth *Encyclopaedia Britannica*.

CONSEQUENCES OF THE NEW SCIENCE

We now move to the consequences of the science of prehistory constructed by Daniel Wilson. He had followed 18th-century Enlightenment armchair historians who described the earliest humans as savages living like unreflecting animals in forests (Kehoe 1990). They claimed that examples could still be observed in

America . . . no Civil Government, no Religion, no Letters; the *French* call them *Les Hommes des Bois*, or Men-Brutes of the Forrest: They do not cultivate the Earth by planting or grazing: Excepting a very inconsiderable Quantity of *Mays* or *Indian Corn*, and of *Kidney-Beans* . . . which some of their *Squaas* or Women plant; they do not provide for To-Morrow, Hunting is their necessary Subsistence not Diversion; when they have good luck in Hunting, they eat and sleep until all is consumed and then go a Hunting again (William Douglass 1755, quoted in Meek 1976:137).

John Locke had said, "In the Beginning, All the World was America" (Meek 1976:3). This imperial propaganda—Locke was Secretary of the British Board of Trade—was repeated not only in the 1755 cant I quoted just above, but also by Lewis Henry Morgan in his 1877 *Ancient Society*, where he rejected Bancroft's history of New Spain on the argument that "the Aztec monarchy should be dismissed from American aboriginal history, not only as delusive, but as a misrepresentation of the Indians, who had neither developed nor invented monarchical institutions" (Morgan 1985 [1877]:196).

Daniel Wilson accepted, in common with most educated people in the 19th century, that world histories are histories of "progress" (Mink 1978:140). He differed from his politically powerful competitor Sir John Lubbock, and from Lewis Henry Morgan, in acknowledging that the great native nations of America had achieved "progress"; his adherence to his mentor's Law of Variety-Production supported such very liberal ideas. Lubbock and Morgan believed in a unilinear evolution in which only Europeans had the ability to create the fourth stage of human history, the Age of Commerce. In a century that took seriously the notion of manifest destiny and the white man's burden, Lubbock's and Morgan's relatively simplistic unilinear evolution prevailed in popularity over Chambers' and Wilson's Law of Variety-Production.

We do have a legacy from Daniel Wilson. There is still, as he noted in his article "Archaeology" in the Ninth *Britannica*, "the alliance of archaeology with geology . . . [that] largely contributed to its expansion. . . . It has thus been developed into a systematic science . . . the desultory and often misdirected labours of the antiquary have given place to researches characterised by scientific accuracy" (Wilson 1878:333-334). Wilson constructed archaeology on principles of universal applicability, and his widely-read 1851 and 1862 (-1876) books significantly popularized the scientific approach in place of capricious antiquarianism.

We have another component of Wilson's legacy with us still: the now dogmatic insistence that the oceans were an impassable barrier to intersocietal contacts before 1492. In back of that contemporary dogma lies the unexamined conviction that a scientific understanding of human nature is jeopardized unless a natural experiment independently replicated cultural development on the two sides of the 'impassable' oceans. The many documented crossings of the oceans by small craft (Kehoe 1971; Boehm, Topping, and Smith 1983:352) should be enough to prove the probability of pre-Columbian ocean crossings. That probability is resisted out of an obsolete belief that replication of experiments is the essence of science. This is a 19th century supposition necessary neither to Bacon or Reid, nor to present-day philosophy of science. If this, minor, element in Wilson's construction of a scientific archaeology is dropped, his substantial contribution is enhanced. Geology has been revolutionized by the admission of the once-rejected concepts of plate tectonics and continental drift; archaeologists can similarly reformulate basic positions to better accommodate accumulating data.

1. Copyright 1992, Alice B. Kehoe

REFERENCES

Barthlémy-Madaule, Madeleine
1982 Lamarck the mythical precursor. Trans. (no translator given) from *Lamarck ou le mythe du précurseur*, 1979. Paris: Éditions du Seuil; Cambridge: Massachusetts Institute of Technology Press.
Boehm, David A., Stephen Topping, and Cyd Smith, eds.
1983 *Guinness Book of World Records*. New York: Sterling.
Bozeman, T. D.
1977 *Protestants in an Age of Science*. Chapel Hill: University of North Carolina Press.
Chambers, Robert
1847 *Vestiges of the Natural History of Creation*. American edition. New York: Harper; bound with *A Sequel: Explanations*. (British editions, 1844 *et seq.*, London: Churchill.).
Gould, Stephen Jay
1977 *Ontogeny and Phylogeny*. Cambridge: Belknap Press of Harvard University.
Henry, Joseph
1980 *A Scientist in American Life: Essays and Lectures of Joseph Henry*, A. P. Molella, N. Reingold, M. Rothenberg, J. F. Steiner, and K. Waldenfels, eds. Washington: Smithsonian Institution Press.
Hudson, K.
1981 *A Social History of Archaeology*. London: Macmillan.
Hunter, Michael
1975 *John Aubrey and the Realm of Learning*. London: Duckworth.
Jacob, M. C.
1976 *The Newtonians and the English Revolution*. Ithaca: Cornell University Press.
Kehoe, Alice B.
1971 Small boats upon the North Atlantic. Pp. 275-292 in *Man Across the Sea*. C. Riley *et al.*, eds. Austin: University of Texas Press.
1989 'In fourteen hundred and ninety-two, Columbus sailed . . .': The primacy of the national myth in American schools. Pp. 201-216 in *The Excluded Past*. P. Stone and R. MacKenzie, eds. London: Unwin Hyman.
1990 Points and lines. Pp. 23-37 in *Powers of Observation: Alternate Views in Archeology*. S. M. Nelson and A. B. Kehoe, eds. Washington: Archeological Papers of the American Anthropological Association, No. 2.
1991 The invention of prehistory. *Current Anthropology* 32(4):467-476.
Kristiansen, Kristian
1985 *Archaeological Formation Processes*. Lyngby: Nationalmuseet.
Laudan, Larry
1981 *Science and Hypothesis*. Dordrecht: D. Reidel.
Levine, Joseph M.
1987 *Humanism and History*. Ithaca: Cornell University Press.
1991 *The Battle of the Books: History and Literature in the Augustan Age*. Ithaca: Cornell University Press.

Levine, Philippa
    1986 *The Amateur and the Professional*. Cambridge:
    Cambridge University Press.
Lubbock, John
    1863 North American archaeology. Pp. 318-336 in *Annual
    Report of the Board of Regents of the Smithsonian Institution
    for the Year 1862*. Washington: Government Printing Office.
    (Reprinted from *Natural History Review*, January 1863.)
    1865 *Pre-historic Times*. (Sixth ed., revised, 1912.) London:
    Williams & Norgate.
Lurie, Elizabeth
    1974 *Nature and the American Mind*. New York: Science
    History Publications.
Meek, Ronald L.
    1976 *Social Science and the Ignoble Savage*. Cambridge:
    Cambridge University Press.
Mink, Louis O.
    1978 Narrative form as a cognitive instrument. Pp. 129-149
    in *The Writing of History*. R. H. Canary and H. Kozicki,
    eds. Madison: University of Wisconsin Press.
Morgan, Lewis Henry
    1985 [1877] *Ancient Society*. Tucson: University of Arizona
    Press.
Morrell, Jack and Arnold Thackray
    1981 *Gentlemen of Science*. Oxford: Clarendon Press.
Needham, Joseph and Lu Gwei-Djen
    1985 *Trans-Pacific Echoes and Resonances: Listening Once
    Again*. Singapore: World Scientific.
Piggott, Stuart
    1976 *Ruins in a Landscape*. Edinburgh: Edinburgh University
    Press.

Popkin, Richard H.
    1992 *The Third Force in Seventeenth-Century Thought*.
    Leiden: E. J. Brill.
Secord, James A.
    1985 Darwin and the breeders: A social history. Pp. 519-542
    in *The Darwinian Heritage*. D. Kohn, ed. Princeton:
    Princeton University Press.
    1989 Behind the veil: Robert Chambers and *Vestiges*. Pp.
    165-194 in *History, Humanity and Evolution*. J. R. Moore,
    ed. Cambridge: Cambridge University Press.
Shapin, Steven and Simon Schaffer
    1985 *Leviathan and the Air-Pump*. Princeton: Princeton
    University Press.
Wilson, Daniel
    1851 *The Archaeology and Prehistoric Annals of Scotland*.
    Edinburgh: Shetland and Knox; London: Simpkin, Marshall
    and J. H. Parker.
    1853 Letter of April 29 to Albert Way. Ms. in National
    Library of Scotland.
    1855 Letter of September 8 to David Laing. Ms. La. IV. 17
    in Edinburgh University Library.
    1860 Letter of 19 March to John Stuart Blackie. Ms. in
    National Library of Scotland.
    1862 *Prehistoric Man*. Cambridge and London: Macmillan.
    (1865 and 1876 eds., same publisher.)
    1863 Letter of April 2 to John Stuart Blackie. Ms. in
    National Library of Scotland.
    1865 Letter of December 13 to Charles Lyell. Ms. Lyell 1 in
    Edinburgh University Library.
    1878 *Reminiscences of Old Edinburgh*. Edinburgh: David
    Douglas.

The Hebrew Presence in Pre-Columbian America

CYRUS H. GORDON

All of us are survivors and mobile. If our ancestors had not adjusted to changing conditions and moved by land and sea in order to survive, none of us would be here today. I have never come across any segment of the human race—past or present—occupying its original home. None of us is an aborigine in the land we call our own.

The Hebrews, whose history is unusually well documented for over three thousand years, have been especially mobile. One of the reasons is their will to be different, not only *vis-à-vis* their neighbors, but even amongst themselves. The Hebrews are portrayed by their own Prophets in the Old Testament as a rebellious people dissatisfied with the prevailing order (whatever it might be) and with themselves.

While Moses was leading his stubborn 'stiff-necked' people from slavery to freedom, instead of being grateful for their liberation, they complained about the inferiority of their diet as contrasted with the rations they had been receiving from their task-masters in Egypt. Such is the Hebrews' account of themselves. Any people so critical and severe, even in judging itself, is not likely to win popularity prizes in its dealings with others.

During the centuries of independent nationhood in Israel and Judah (*ca.* 1000-586 BC), the Hebrews lived in a world of idolatrous polytheists. The pagans generally behaved with at least outward civility toward each other's gods. But some of the Hebrew Psalmists, *e.g.*, Psalm 115:4-8, scorned their neighbors' deities as lifeless idols who had feet but could not walk, hands that could not feel, throats that could utter no sound, and so forth. This attitude became particularly serious in the Roman period.

THE ROMAN EMPIRE AND JEWISH REBELLIONS

Imperial Rome ruled the world from the Atlantic Ocean to the Parthian border, in an Empire that included Jewish Palestine plus a large Jewish Diaspora. Many Jews enjoyed Roman citizenship. Paul of Tarsus, for example, was both a committed Pharisaic Jew and a proud Roman citizen.

The Empire consisted of many peoples worshipping various gods in accordance with the rites of different cults. All cults were tolerated, and everyone was expected, overtly at least, to respect his neighbors' religious beliefs and practices. One cult was to be honored by all subjects of the Empire; namely, the cult of the divine Emperor, whose statues required universal adoration.

Roman citizens generally regarded reverence for the deified Emperor as a reasonable price to pay for the protection and other benefits provided by Rome. However, the Jews made a major issue of this requirement and refused to accord divine honors or to offer sacrifices to the Emperor. They excluded his, or anyone else's, statue from their Temple or synagogues. In AD 66, the Jews rebelled and for four years defended Jerusalem against the Roman legions. When Jerusalem finally fell in AD 70, the Temple was destroyed, the Jews were banished from their Holy City, and the mainstream of Jewish leadership turned to Scripture and rabbinic teaching for solace and survival. But the rebellious activists remained, albeit underground.

In AD 132, the Second Jewish Rebellion against Rome was begun under a charismatic leader named Bar Kosiba, who was hailed by his followers as the Messiah. He set out bravely to liberate Israel from Roman oppression, which would necessitate defeating the mighty legions of Rome. This would-be Messiah was undaunted by the overwhelming odds against him and took on the Roman legions at a time when the Empire was nearing its height, under Hadrian. For three long years, the 'Messiah' waged war and held out, to the chagrin of the Romans. Among his backers was the renowned Rabbi Akibah. Bar Kosiba became generally known as *Bar Kokhba*, 'Son of the Star,' (in fulfillment of an interpretation of Numbers 24:17). His inevitable defeat in AD 135 discredited him as the Messiah; however much Judaism still regards him as a hero, it has relegated him to its list of 'false Messiahs.'

The Second Rebellion made the Jews thoroughly odious to Rome. They were so harassed that they welcomed any conceivable avenue of escape. The sea provided such an avenue, though it was fraught with danger and uncertainty.

THE JEWS AND THE SEA

The Jews had a long naval history. Three of the twelve tribes are referred to in the Bible as maritime. Judges 5:17 describes the Tribe of Dan as living in ships and the Tribe of Asher as located on the sea shore, while Genesis 49:13 refers to the Tribe of Zebulon, bordering on Phoenician Sidon, as a haven for ships.

In the 10th century BC, both David and Solomon had a treaty with Hiram of Tyre enabling the Hebrews and Phoenicians to engage as partners in bold naval ventures (up to three years long). (See I Kings 10:22.) This marine partnership between the Hebrews and Phoenicians endured for many hundreds of years. In the 5th century BC, Herodotus (7:89) records that the largest contingent of the Achaemenian navy on the Mediterranean consisted of the three hundred triremes manned jointly by Phoenician and Jewish sailors. Herodotus (2:104) always calls the Jews "the Syrians of Palestine," whom he singles out for their practice of circumcision.

Josephus (Jewish War 3:141 *ff.*) records that during the First Rebellion (AD 66-70), the Jewish navy suffered such a disaster at Jaffe that the bodies of forty-two hundred Jewish sailors were washed ashore. Though that round figure can not be taken literally, the event was important enough for Vespasian and his two sons, Titus and Domitian, to strike coins celebrating the 'VICTORIA NAVALIS' over 'JUDAEA NAVALIS.'

In the Byzantine period, Theodosius I, 'the Great,' wrote into Roman law (AD 390) a provision exempting poorer members of the Jewish and Samaritan community from the obligation of supplying the state with ships. However, affluent Jews and Samaritans were required to provide the ships. Theodosius thus made it clear that these communities possessed a well-known naval capability (Gordon 1995). (Samaritans are not Jews, but both considered themselves Israelites, kindred members of different denominations, but of the same people and of the same faith.)

Figure 1 THE PHYLACTERY STELA
This stone stela from Tepatlaxco, Veracruz, Mexico, is in the National Anthropological Museum, in Mexico City. Some scholars date it *ca.* AD 100, while others attribute it to the Early Classical period, *ca.* AD 300.

ARCHAEOLOGICAL EVIDENCE IN THE NEW WORLD

By the middle of the 2nd century AD, shortly after the Second Rebellion (AD 132-135), Rome reached its maximum extent. At that time, a large number of artifacts of Mediterranean origin reached the Western Hemisphere.

A sculptured clay head professionally excavated at Calixtlauaca near Toluca, Mexico, was identified as Roman, dated *ca.* AD 200 by the distinguished Classical archaeologist, Robert Heine-Geldern. Dr. Heine-Geldern felt certain that the head had been either imported from Rome, or at least made by an ancient Roman sculptor in pre-Columbian America. (See Gordon 1971:195, note 35.)

A stela from Tepatlaxco, Veracruz, is dated by Maya archaeologists as AD 100-300 (Figure 1). It is on permanent display at the National Anthropological Museum in Mexico City. It portrays in relief a Mayan dignitary wearing phylacteries[‡] like those still worn during morning prayers on weekdays by Orthodox Jewish men. They are called *tefillin* in Hebrew. The stela portrays a phylactery fastened to an arm by a thong that is wound seven times around the arm and terminates below the wrist in windings around the fingers. The seven arm-windings followed by the finger-windings is practiced to this day. The rite is prescribed in the Old Testament, but it is probably pre-Hebraic in origin. In any case, the Tepatlaxco Phylactery Stela embodies a specific Jewish connection. (See Gordon 1974:151-152.)

COINS IN KENTUCKY

Three Bar Kokhba coins have turned up in Kentucky: one in 1932, in Louisville; another in 1952, in Clay City; and the third in 1967, in Hopkinsville. It is most unlikely that these are the work of a prankster because of the long time-span (thirty-five years) between the discovery of the first and last of the three coins and the distances between the three find-sites. Finding such a coin in Clay City is particularly significant because Clay City is an unsophisticated community of about five hundred inhabitants in the mountains of eastern Kentucky, far from the intellectual urban centers (with universities), such as Louisville and Lexington, in the western part of the state. During the ABC Conference at Brown University, I heard from a Kentucky member of NEARA that the coin is kept as a local treasure in the bank at Clay City.

The Bar Kokhba coins were not found by professional archaeologists nor taken seriously by the Establishment. However, they take on real significance in the light of unassailable evidence of a pre-Columbian and pre-Viking Jewish presence in the adjacent state of Tennessee.

BAT CREEK STONE

In 1889, the Smithsonian Institution of Washington, DC, excavated a burial designated by the expedition as Mound #3 at Bat Creek in Loudon County, Tennessee. Cyrus Thomas, who was in charge of the project, which involved many Indian Mounds in southeastern United States, was not present at Mound #3 while it was being excavated.

An assistant named John Emmert was left in charge. Emmert was a dedicated and careful excavator whose handwritten notes on the dig are kept in the Smithsonian. He recorded that the grave had not been rifled, nor in any way broken into, prior to his excavation in 1889. The soil had not been previously disturbed by anybody, a fact correctly stated in Cyrus Thomas' report published in 1894.

Cyrus Thomas was committed to the theory that the Mound Indians were the same stock of people traceable from the earliest archaeological times to the arrival of the first white settlers. Accordingly, he assumed that an inscription on the stone (Figure 2) found under the head of one of the nine skeletons in the grave had to be Cherokee, the only known written language of the local Indians. As the Cherokee script was invented by Sequoya in 1821, Thomas regarded the burial as less than a century old.

A few individuals with minds of their own observed that Thomas had published the inscription upside-down; for, right-side-up, they recognized a couple of letters in the ancient Phoenician-Hebrew alphabet. The late Dr. Joseph Mahan, who felt that their observation was correct, then consulted me. On studying it, I found that it was Hebrew in letter-forms of about AD 100, closely related to the script on the coins of the First and Second Rebellions. Moreover, the inscription, though short, contained the translatable phrase "for Judea."

The Bat Creek Stone is of special significance. This lapidary text is the first pre-Columbian inscription, in an Old World script and language, excavated by archaeologists in the Americas. It proves the antiquity of Mound #3 and all of the objects in it, because the undisturbed soil shows that everything found in the tomb had been buried at the same time. It is quite possible that the Stone had been handed down for several generations before the interment, but the inscription is definitely not a modern forgery. What should have been clear in 1889, from the inscription itself, or knowledge of its script, was that this constituted evidence of an Atlantic crossing *ca.* AD 100.

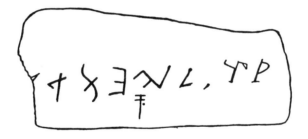

Figure 2 THE BAT CREEK INSCRIPTION

THE BRASS BRACELETS

An attempt was made to interpret a pair of brass bracelets from Mound #3 as products of modern manufacture. I promptly pointed out that the Romans made brass, in addition to the more common and better-known Roman bronze, in antiquity. (See Gordon 1972:7-18; *cf.* footnote 5, on Roman brass.)

The Smithsonian kindly allowed me to see the entire assemblage of objects found in Mound #3 and to publish color photographs of them. I also requested that a Carbon-14 test be made on wood and bone fragments from the tomb. The Smithsonian staff refused, telling me that because varnish had been applied to those organic materials for preservation, no Carbon-14 test would be of any use. I did not pursue the matter further.

However, J. Huston McCulloch of Ohio State University was interested in the Cherokees and had come across the publications on the Bat Creek Stone. His investigations had acquainted him with my Hebrew interpretation, as well as that of Cyrus Thomas, which had been tacitly accepted by the Establishment. It is greatly to McCulloch's credit that, though he was looking for Cherokees and not Hebrews, his careful and objective scrutiny of the evidence led him to the conclusion that the inscription was indeed Hebrew of *ca.* AD 100.

CARBON-14 TESTS OF BAT CREEK MATERIAL

McCulloch, after nine years of dogged perseverance, succeeded in having wood-fragments from Mound #3 put to a state-of-the-art Carbon-14 test at the same Zurich laboratory that the Smithsonian depends on for its general lab work. According to the results of the test, which were reported on May 2, 1988, the wood could not be older than AD 32 nor younger than 769. Thus, the burial could be of Imperial Roman date (*ca.* AD 100), but in any case it has to be pre-Columbian and pre-Viking.

McCulloch also looked into the problems posed by the brass bracelets, which contained about 3.3 percent lead. Such an alloy was used by the Romans from *ca.* 45 BC to *ca.* AD 200, whereupon it went out of use until its modern reappearance *ca.* 1400. All of this evidence favors a Roman date of *ca.* AD 100 rather than a Byzantine or medieval date.

THE DECALOGUES

In New Mexico is a site, in the Belen district, that visitors have for several generations been reaching from the town of Los Lunas, which is located about thirty miles south of Albuquerque. The artifact that has attracted the visitors is a large, heavy, inscribed rock in the Old Phoenician/Hebrew script containing an abridged version of the Ten Commandments. The Samaritans, who still use a variety of that script, place such Decalogues on stone at the entrance to areas such as synagogues. The Los Lunas Decalogue is at the base of a ravine leading up to a site at the top of a height called 'Hidden Mountain' (Gordon 1995).

The authenticity of the inscription is indicated by all criteria, *e.g.,* 1. the five-by-six-foot stone slab is part of the mountainside; 2. both the Indians and the white people of the locality say "it was always there"; 3. references to its presence among the whites go back into the early 19th century; 4. an outstanding archaeologist (who does not wish to be named) assured me that he had seen, on nearby Taylor Mountain, texts in the same script.

Thus, we know that Samaritans reached the site of the Los Lunas Decalogue, but by what route they traveled to such a distant location may forever remain a mystery.

But the most interesting discovery reflecting the fusion of Jews and Samaritans in pre-Viking America was made in 1860 near Newark, Ohio, where inscribed stone objects were unearthed by David Wyrick. Among them is a Decalogue abbreviated in much the same manner as the Los Lunas Decalogue, with differences. The Newark Decalogue, only seventeen cm. long, is not in the Samaritan script but in a strange, though unmistakable, variety of the Jewish letter-forms; it shortens the Fifth Commandment more than does the Los Lunas stone, omitting the reward for honoring father and mother. But this does not contraindicate the Samaritan connection, because the reward is also omitted in the Shechem Samaritan Decalogue reproduced by Montgomery (1907; Gordon 1995).

The facts, therefore, point to a pre-Viking crossing of the Atlantic. Since the Establishment has hitherto denied *a priori* the validity of all evidence pointing in that direction, each individual piece of evidence will have to be re-evaluated on its own merits.

COLUMBUS, SPAIN, AND THE JEWS

The five hundredth anniversary of Columbus' historic crossing of the Atlantic in 1492 occurs at a time when the scholarly atmosphere is more conducive to understanding what led up to that event than was the atmosphere a quarter of a century ago. Since Thor Heyerdahl's crossing of the Atlantic in *Ra II*, it has been difficult to insist (though Admiral Samuel Eliot Morison did) that, before the caravel, crossing the Atlantic was technologically impossible. Moreover, although Admiral Morison was also a Professor of History at Harvard, he had little understanding of Spanish society of the 15th and 16th centuries. Salvador de Madariaga, as demonstrated in his 1940 *Christopher Columbus: Being the Life of the Very Magnificent Don Cristóbal Colón*, had a far better knowledge of Spain in the time of Columbus than did Morison. (See his 1942 *Admiral of the Ocean Sea: A Life of Christopher Columbus.*) The mindset of most western scholars prevented them from taking the facts in stride. Now that Morison's commanding position in the Establishment is a thing of the past, we are better able to appreciate the knowledge and insight of Madariaga.

Columbus was not a Jew; he was a Catholic as were probably his parents, and perhaps also his grandparents. But his secretiveness, his interests, and his supporters typify many of the *Conversos* or 'New Christians.' The Inquisition had made the position of Jews so difficult that many, indeed most, of them sought escape in conversion. The Jews of Spain were talented and cultivated. After conversion they frequently attained high positions in church and state, as well as in the learned professions and in finance. Their success aroused resentment among the Old Christians. The Inquisition increasingly sought out the New Christians on charges of adhering to Jewish practices in secret. Those charges not infrequently had some truth to them. Indeed, the name of *Marranos* was applied to 'crypto-Jews' who overtly professed to be Christians but covertly clung to as much of Judaism as they could.

For a long time before 3 August 1492, when Jews and all other non-Catholics were expelled from Spain, the New Christians could see the handwriting on the wall. With no more real heretics left, the Inquisition would turn with all its fury on the New Christians. Columbus' backers and friends included many New Christians, who had a stake in the quest for discovering any overseas haven where New Christians might escape from the tyranny of the Inquisition.

It was not merely a coincidence that Columbus set sail on his first trans-Atlantic voyage on the very day of the Expulsion (Wiesenthal 1973). It is also no accident that Columbus sailed south to the Canary Islands before heading westward, but returned to Spain by a northern route via the Azores. Columbus knew much about winds and currents, and he had maps. In the forefront of nautical mapmaking and instrumentation were the Jews of Majorca. Columbus had useful connections, as well as friends and backers who shared his concerns.

Américo Castro (1954) understood the Jewish factor; Madariaga even more so. Any student of Sephardic Jewry is familiar with the state of affairs. But Morison was so opposed to the very thought of Jewish connections, that his only mention of it in his widely-read and acclaimed book on Columbus is the following entry in the index: "Jew. C. C. not one," which means "Christopher Columbus was not a Jew." There is no need for psychoanalysis to expose Morison's prejudices.

JEWS SEEKING A HAVEN

During the life of Columbus and throughout the Age of Discovery that directly followed, Jewish preoccupation with global geography and with the quest for a haven is documented.

A well-informed Jewish geographer of that period is Abraham ben Mordechai Farissol (or Ferizol) who was born in Avignon in 1451 but migrated to Italy where his career unfolded well into the 16th century. He reports that an exotic Jew (often identified as the colorful David Reuveni) had created quite a stir in Italy by telling how he had come from the Arabian shores of the Red Sea where there was a large and vigorous Jewish population. Those Arabian Jews, however, were separated into groups that could not unite because of Muslim Arab tribes wedged between them.

The presence of armed Portuguese ships at Yemenite ports, however, showed the Arabian Jews that the Christians of Europe were sufficiently advanced in the arts of war, and equipped with artillery, to level the shore fortifications of the Muslims.

The mission of the exotic Jew from Arabia, according to Farissol, was to request that Pope Clement VII (1523-34) dispatch European military technicians and materiel to the Arabian Jews, who would vanquish the Muslims and drive them out of the Holy Land. In exchange, the Jews would protect Roman Catholic interests in the Holy Land, including access to the Christian shrines. Farissol goes on to state that the Pope instructed the King of Portugal to send to the Arabian Jews a ship laden with the armaments and personnel needed to accomplish the mission. How true the story may be is uncertain, but in any event it shows that Jewry was seeking havens on different fronts.

Columbus was not the only explorer with Hebrew connections. It has been estimated that a third of the Conquistadores were New Christians who sought havens across the Atlantic in their attempt to get as far away as possible from the Inquisition.

CONCLUSIONS

The Hebrews were not the first people to cross the Atlantic to the New World. Nor were the Judeans who left their inscription in Bat Creek Mound #3 the first Hebrews to arrive here. This ABC Conference has brought out the evidence for the arrival of many different Old World people who reached the Americas via both the Pacific and the Atlantic in pre-Columbian antiquity. The Hebrews, who were among them, have left imprints on the Native American population who were already here when Columbus first sighted land in 1492.

Some of the American Indian tribes still preserve much of that part of their pre-Columbian heritage which they brought with them across the Atlantic. Assembling and preserving what is left of it constitutes a vast undertaking in itself. I had the good fortune in 1969 to witness the Green Corn Festival of the Yuchi Indians in Sepulpa, Oklahoma. The detailed correspondences with the Hebrew Feast of Tabernacles, now called Succot, or 'booths', cannot be accidental. Both the Old Testament Hebrew and the Yuchi holidays are eight-day pilgrimage festivals cele-

brating a harvest. During both holidays, the people dwell in flora-covered structures, through the roofs of which one can see the sky. Both have a ritual, whereby the ·men shake leafy branches as they make clockwise circumambulations of a sacred area. (For still other details, see Gordon 1971:89-90.)

The material for the study of the pre-Columbian Hebrew legacy to the Americas is vast and many-sided. Much of it is perishable and must be salvaged before it disappears. This holds true for artifacts, entire sites, and the recording of Indian languages and institutions. The evidence is fragile, and time is running out.

NOTE

‡ A phylactery is either of two small, black, leather cubes containing a piece of parchment inscribed with verses 4-9 of Deut. 6; 13-21 of Deut. 11; and 1-16 of Ex. 13. One is attached with straps to the left arm and the other to the forehead, during weekday morning prayers, by Orthodox and Conservative Jewish men. (Random House Dictionary of the English Language, 2nd ed., 1987.)

REFERENCES

Castro, Américo
1954 *The Structure of Spanish History*. Princeton: Princeton University Press.

Gordon, Cyrus H.
1971 *Before Columbus*. New York: Crown Publishers.
1972 The Bat Creek Inscription. Chapter I in *Book of the Descendants of Doctor Benjamin Lee and Dorothy Gordon*. Ventnor NJ: Ventnor Publishers.
1974 *Riddles in History*. New York: Crown Publishers.
1995 Diffusion of Near East culture in antiquity and in Byzantine times. *Orient*, Vol XXX-XXXI. The Society for Near Eastern Studies in Japan (Nippon Oriento Gakkai).

Herodotus
1946-1957 *Herodotus*, with an English translation by A. D. Godley, in four volumes. The Loeb Classical Library, Cambridge MA: Harvard University Press; and London: Wm. Heinemann, Ltd.

Madariaga, Salvador de
1940 *Christopher Columbus: Being the Life of the Very Magnificent Lord Don Cristóbal Colón*. New York: Macmillan.

Morison, Samuel Eliot
1942 *Admiral of the Ocean Sea: A Life of Christopher Columbus*. Boston: Little Brown.

Wiesenthal, Simon
1973 *Sails of Hope*. New York: Macmillan.

Ancient Chinese Maps of the World

DONALD L. CYR

To state that ancient Chinese maps of the world are controversial is an understatement. Yet, as many as twenty variations of these maps exist, some in museums, one in America, some in other places. The maps are not identical in all respects, but they have great similarity, nonetheless. How old are the maps? Their dates, according to who is making the estimate, are anywhere from 2250 BC up to AD 500. Whatever the date of a given map, it may well be only one in a long series of copies from some long-lost original. The problem becomes one of deciding, on the basis of internal information, what date the map represents in terms of Chinese exploration.

The matching of today's known geography with locations identified on these Chinese maps was begun by the late Hendon Harris, a skilled translator of Chinese, who made translations of one map and comparisons with two others (Harris 1975). So, without deciding what is true, let us examine research that continues his efforts.

The maps indicate rivers and mountains, as well as the names of countries and lands. About one hundred and fifty names occur on the maps. China is indicated clearly and so is Japan. The problem is to assign the remainder of the names to various other present-day locations. To give you the flavor of the nomenclature and the speculative game that can be played, I will mention some of my interpretations of names on the controversial circular 'Harris Map,' illustrated here (Figure 1). The character and style of the calligraphy indicate that this is a copy of an ancient map.

While the group of maps with which the Harris Map was found in Seoul, Korea, date to the 17th and 18th centuries, the maps were identified as dating back to the 5th century as copies of copies. Harris conjectured that the maps may even date back to 2200 BC (Harris 1975; L. C. Harris 1988). The tabulated lists of countries on the Harris Map which appear in *The Diffusion Issue* (Cyr, ed. 1989a: Tables 1-4)

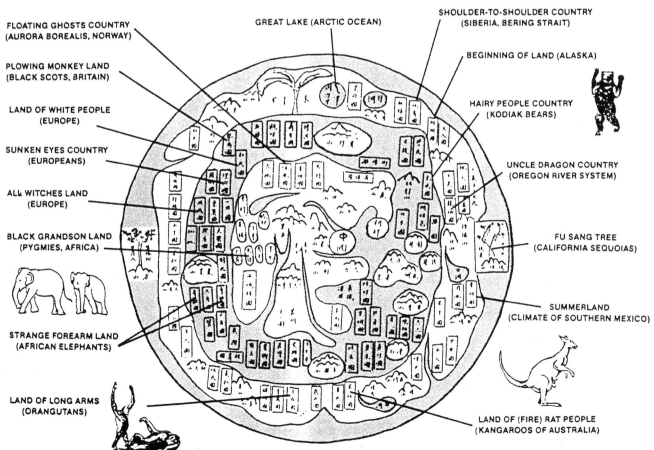

FLOATING GHOSTS COUNTRY
(AURORA BOREALIS, NORWAY)

PLOWING MONKEY LAND
(BLACK SCOTS, BRITAIN)

LAND OF WHITE PEOPLE
(EUROPE)

SUNKEN EYES COUNTRY
(EUROPEANS)

ALL WITCHES LAND
(EUROPE)

BLACK GRANDSON LAND
(PYGMIES, AFRICA)

STRANGE FOREARM LAND
(AFRICAN ELEPHANTS)

LAND OF LONG ARMS
(ORANGUTANS)

GREAT LAKE (ARCTIC OCEAN)

SHOULDER-TO-SHOULDER COUNTRY
(SIBERIA, BERING STRAIT)

BEGINNING OF LAND (ALASKA)

HAIRY PEOPLE COUNTRY
(KODIAK BEARS)

UNCLE DRAGON COUNTRY
(OREGON RIVER SYSTEM)

FU SANG TREE
(CALIFORNIA SEQUOIAS)

SUMMERLAND
(CLIMATE OF SOUTHERN MEXICO)

LAND OF (FIRE) RAT PEOPLE
(KANGAROOS OF AUSTRALIA)

Figure 1 THE HARRIS MAP

also indicate some alternatives suggested by my colleague James Brett. Actually, any number can play the game—a creative game of cryptography.[‡]

My favorite is 'Land of the (Fire) Rat People.' I identify the word 'fire' as being red, and the name 'rat people' as being kangaroos. Hence, since the land is located southward of China, the land of the red kangaroos is (to me) clearly Australia (Cyr, ed. 1989b).

In a similar vein, the 'Land of Long Arms' seems to be the Land of Orangutans, likely an island near Malaysia. The ancient mapmakers seem to have enjoyed naming countries for their animal inhabitants.

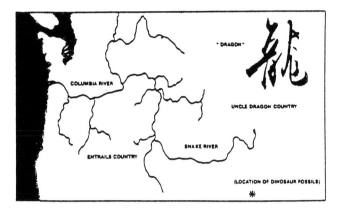

Figure 2 SIMILARITY OF RIVER PATTERN TO CHINESE
CALLIGRAPHY

The 'Strange Forearm Land' seems to me to be a country inhabited by elephants. Here I choose Africa. To see an elephant's nose characteristically in operation would, to the first-time viewer, cause this appendage to be classified as a very strange forearm indeed.

Another favorite of mine is the 'Floating Ghosts Land' suggested to be descriptive of northern Norway. If you don't believe in ghosts, you probably believe in the aurora borealis. Floating ghosts is a fair description of the northern lights.

Northward from China is Great Lake, 10,000 *li* around, which I take to be the Arctic Ocean. The unit of measurement called *li* is about a third of a mile, so the lake shore was indicated to be about 3300 mi. in length, certainly not an insignificant body of water.

'Shoulder-to-Shoulder Country' is nearby, and my first thought is that one shoulder was Siberia and the other was Alaska, thus being the Bering Strait location. One of my friends thinks the nomenclature is descriptive of yaks forming a defensive circle, shoulder-to-shoulder. Or maybe the thought concerns herds of caribou charging along, shoulder-to-shoulder. You can see how the game works.

'Land of Beginning' is clearly the Alaska Peninsula, although 'Beginning of Land' would be the proper word order. As the Japanese current carried the Chinese explorers eastward, the Aleutians would appear first, but the

Alaskan Peninsula would be the logical 'Beginning of Land.'

Further along, the ancient Chinese map indicates 'Hairy People Country,' which might be the location of the Ainu people of Japan, except that Japan is clearly indicated elsewhere. Since the land appears to be near Alaska, my conclusion is that the hairy 'people' were Kodiak bears.

When the Chinese explorers reached the Columbia River and made a map of its tributaries, they were amazed to note its similarity to the Chinese calligraphy for the word 'dragon' (Figure 2). Those who are familiar with Tristan Jones' work *ICE* (1978) will better understand how the Chinese explorers could have been helped in their map-making. For instance, Jones describes how modern Danish sailors can use the image reflected from a cloud layer (of ice crystals) to orient themselves with respect to stretches of land and water for miles around. The Chinese could very well have used the same surveying system when they explored the Columbia River basin. Hence, what is now the United States, specifically the northwestern states of Washington, Oregon, and Idaho, was purportedly written down as 'Uncle Dragon Country.'

When the Chinese explorers reached Colorado, someone recorded their expedition with petroglyphs, including what appears to be a standard-bearer and the symbol for the Middle Kingdom (Figure 3).

Figure 3 COLORADO ROCK ART
Shows a Chinese visitor with Symbol of China

I read the meaning as, "We are a peaceful group of explorers from the Middle Kingdom (China)." I must say that I part company with others who see this petroglyph as showing a hunter about to release an atlatl.

Gunnar Thompson has seen a similar image in a tomb painting that indicates that such standards were being carried in processions by Chinese 1500 years ago (Thompson 1989) (Figure 4). This illustration shows the banner identified as a 'China symbol' similar to the one shown on rock art in Colorado. The *Nu Sun* banner was found on a 6th century AD bas-relief in a Chinese tomb. Thompson's reason for showing it was that the banner also shows scroll motifs representing germinating plants. He has found similar motifs in Aztec illustrations (in the Vatican Codex) attesting to Chinese-Aztec diffusion.

The nomenclature 'Middle Kingdom' follows from the actual circular shape of China (Figure 5). The calligraphy for China (Middle Kingdom) (Figure 6), a circle with a dividing line, became a bisected rectangle long before the Han dynasty. Yet, every Chinese student knows that a circle is schematically portrayed as a rectangle in the present version.

Figure 4   SACRED BANNER FROM A BAS-RELIEF
6th century AD Chinese tomb
(Drawing courtesy of Gunnar Thompson)

Did the Chinese explore North America? Their name for North America was 'Fu Sang,' discussed at length by Henriette Mertz in *Pale Ink* (1958). There are Chinese and Japanese scholars today who study the *Shan Hai Ching*, an ancient Chinese story of travels to foreign shores. Of the original thirty-two books, sixteen have been lost; and perhaps four have been translated into English. One of the lands described was Fu Sang. Likely, it was North America. It was described as a fabulous land and was even thought by Asian scholars of the time to be a hilarious fairyland. They wrote that, in Fu Sang there was a bird that flew backward—we know of it as the hummingbird. Their documents state that Fu Sang is 10,000 *li* in size. That's 3300 by 3300 mi., rather accurate dimensions for North America that most of our European ancestors didn't know five hundred years ago.

Fu Sang is a common theme in Chinese poetry. One important mention occurs in a poem about the Chinese goddess, Hsi Ho, who each day hangs the ten suns out to dry in the Fu Sang tree, 300 *li* (100 mi.) high. One suggestion that I like is that the Fu Sang tree was located in California and that the term describes either the redwoods or the majestic sequoias (Cyr 1989a, 1989b; Stone 1979, 1982).

Others believe that the Fu Sang tree is maize in America. The concept of ten suns is an important meteorological record of atmospheric conditions a few thousand years ago. *The Crystal Veil* reviews this concept in great detail, describing a great layer of ice crystals that produced elaborate halo patterns recorded in archaeological motifs (Cyr 1995).

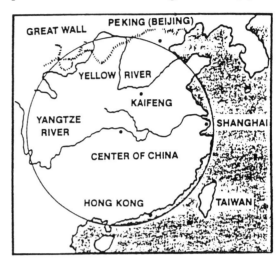

Figure 5   THE CIRCLE FOR CHINA, MIDDLE KINGDOM

'Summerland,' located further southward, certainly indicates a summer-like climatic zone. The description would fit parts of southern Mexico, perhaps even Acapulco.

Some of the Chinese map names are descriptive of observed racial characteristics that are at times clearly identifiable. 'Land of White People' could refer to the inhabitants of parts of Europe, as might 'Sunken Eyes Country.' Chinese eyes are typically located up front, compared to the depth (sunken appearance) of most European eyes.

Figure 6   CHINESE IDEOGRAMS, MIDDLE KINGDOM

'Black Grandson Land' could be that of the Pygmies of Africa; if so, the name indicates that tribes of Pygmies were visited by the Chinese explorers. Certainly, great expeditions proceeded from China to Africa in historic times.

The maps give some indication of having information that is thousands of years old. In what time frame would some part of Europe deserve the nomenclature of 'All Witches Land?' Try 3000 or 4000 years ago.

Or when would the name 'Plowing Monkey Land' have been appropriate for Britain? This term would be considered racist and unkind today. But there is a possible answer. Some 4000 years ago, Britain was inhabited by what today are called Black Scots. As pointed out by my friend James Brett, himself a descendent of Black Scots, these were the people who, like the Basques, spoke a non-Indo-European language and preceded the Picts, Celts, Norse, Danes, Saxons, and Normans, who at different times invaded the British Isles. Brett suggests that Chinese explorers might have recognized the short stature and darker complexion of the relatively hirsute Black Scots. Another possibility, Brett speculates, is that the explorers might have witnessed an ancient springtime ritual plowing by a Black Scot dressed in a bearskin. The name *Arthur* derives from the Old Welsh word for 'bear.' To this day, in rural Britain, boys compete annually in hand-pushed plowing contests.

Indicative of the ongoing nature of this exercise in cryptography is a case which came to our attention in 1995. One of the names on the Harris Map translates as 'Wagon Builders Country.' When we first saw it, it did not make sense, out in the middle of nowhere. And then we encountered the work of Victor Mair in the *Journal of Indo-European Studies* telling of 4000-year-old 'mummies' which were Tartan-wearing Caucasoids, found far out beyond the Gobi Desert with respect to China. They lived in the Tarim Basin, and they were wagon-builders.

Their location was noted as 'Wagon Builder Country' on the map of the world allegedly drawn up by Emperor Yu, who built the first great flood prevention projects in China. He also sent out expeditions to explore the world, about 2250 BC. Harris believed those maps were supposed to illustrate the *Shan Hai Ching*, alleged to have been written at the same time. Wagon-building in the Tarim Basin was a total fantasy until this 1995 discovery. Now it is a fact.

Some map nomenclature still needs further analysis. China, Korea, and Japan are clearly identified. Less than twenty more names have been listed in this cursory text. Yet the total of the names on three known maps is something like one hundred and fifty in all, including rivers and mountains. An ongoing exercise in cryptography purports to be able to find locations for dozens more (see references). You are invited to try your hand at this fascinating game.

NOTE

‡ Harris never claimed that all his place-name locations were beyond reproach. He invited others to join in the analysis. Cyr and Brett have taken up the challenge. Cyr believes that some of his answers are more likely than those of Harris, while acknowledging that Brett, whose work followed, has had many new insights.

REFERENCES

Brett. James S.
  1995   Personal communication.
Cyr, Donald L., ed.
  1989a *The Diffusion Issue*. Santa Barbara: Stonehenge Viewpoint. See particularly "Chinese Ancient World Mapping" by James S. Brett and Donald L. Cyr.
  1989b *Dragon Treasures*. Santa Barbara: Stonehenge Viewpoint. See particularly "Treasure Maps of Fu Sang" by Hendon M. Harris, and "Chinese Ice Blink Survey Map" by Donald L. Cyr.
  1995   *The Crystal Veil*. Santa Barbara: Stonehenge Viewpoint.
Harris, Hendon M.
  1975   *The Asiatic Fathers of America*. Taipei: Wen Ho Printing Company.
Harris, Lillian Craig
  1988   The Church and the world, the West and the wider world. In *Sins of the Fathers*, Vol. IV. Cyriac K. Pullapilly, series ed. Notre Dame IN: Cross Cultural Publications, Inc.
Jones, Tristan
  1978   *ICE*. Mission KA: Sheed, Andres and McMeel.
Mair, Victor
  1995   Prehistoric Caucasoid corpses of the Tarim Basin. *Journal of Indo-European Studies*, Vol. 23(3, 4).
Mertz, Henriette
  ca., 1958 *Pale Ink: Two Ancient Records of Chinese Exploration in America*. Privately printed, 2nd ed., 1972. Chicago: Swallow Press.
Stone, Merlin
  1979, 1982 *Ancient Mirrors of Womanhood*. Boston: Beacon Press.
Thompson, Gunnar
  1989   *Nu Sun*. Fresno CA: Pioneer Publishing Company. The author compares art motifs, particularly architecture, to date rather exactly voyages from Asia to Central America.

Columbus Was 100% Portuguese!

MANUEL L. DA SILVA

The many thousands of books and articles written about Christopher Columbus emphasize the mysterious and emotional aspects of this great navigator, how many women there were in his life, and the various places where his bones may be buried. I discard all this circumstantial information because it has no direct bearing on the correct and precise diagnosis of the true identity of the Navigator. I am interested in analyzing both Columbus' 'biopsies'— the ciphers written by the Navigator's own hand, as well as certain relevant documents residing in the Library of the Vatican.

For many centuries, the largest and most important library in the western world has been the Library of the Vatican, still today the largest in the world. Logic dictates that anyone researching the history of exploration and discovery should go to the archives of this famous library.

THE PAPAL BULLS

Five centuries ago, the Pope was considered the highest, most official, and most powerful authority in the European world. He was the referee who approved division of the New World between Portugal and Spain by sanctioning the Treaty of Tordesillas, in 1494.

Four Papal Bulls were issued by Pope Alexander VI in the year 1493, all of them in Latin, relating to the discovery of America. I discovered them, in the Vatican Library, on February 21, 1992. Only the first two Papal Bulls include the name of the Navigator, but the name that appears is not *Columbus*, but *Colon*.

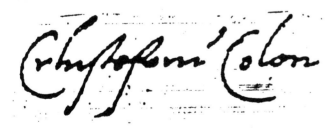

Figure 1 NAME IN THE FIRST PAPAL BULL

In the Bull of May 3, 1493, on the second page, line eleven, we read in the Latin, *dilectum filium Crhistophom Colon*—'my beloved son Crhistofom Colon.' Note that the name is *Colon*, not *Columbus* (Figure 1). We shall explain why below.

The second Papal Bull, issued by Alexander VI and dated the following day, May 4, 1493, repeats the name *Colon*. On the first page, line thirty-one, we can read the Navigator's name written in Portuguese: *Cristofõm Colon*! (Figure 2).

Figure 2 NAME IN THE SECOND PAPAL BULL

The entire texts of the First and Second Bulls are written in Latin. We would expect the name of the Navigator to appear in Latin as *Christopher Columbus*. But it does not. We might also expect the name to be spelled out in Italian, because the Bulls were published in Rome. But it is not. It could also be in Spanish,. But it is not. In Spain, and in all Spanish-speaking nations, the name of the Navigator has always been *Christóval Colon*. This is the same form in which his name appears on the cover of his *Book of Privileges,* in 1502 (Figure 3).

Dõ Xpõval Colon
Don Cristoval Colon

Figure 3 FORM OF THE NAVIGATOR'S NAME

The name that appears on the Second Bull, as we have noted, is *Cristofõm Colon*, as written in Portuguese. We should note that the name *Cristo* does not have the letter **h** and that there is a tilde over the letter **õ**. No other language in the world uses a tilde over **õ** except Portuguese.

HIS SIGLA

The word *sigla* is the plural of the Latin *siglum*, which means 'signal.' A sigla always has a secret meaning, making it difficult to interpret. Yet our world is loaded with siglas.

A sigla is sometimes formed by the initial letters of various words and is then called an acronym. The best known example of a sigla is *INRI* on the top of the cross, meaning *Iesus Nazarenus Rex Iudaerorum*—'Jesus of Nazareth, King of the Jews.'

The Columbus sigla is composed of two parts, top and bottom (Figure 4).

The upper part has seven letters **SSAS XMY**. The letter **X** means 'cross breed,' hence 'son of,' and, because the letter **J** did not exist in the Roman alphabet five hundred years ago, the Greek **Y** was used for the initial letter of the name *Joseph*. With this information, the top part of the sigla, which is a salutation to Christ, is read as *Sanctus Sanctus Altissimus Sanctus*—'Son of Mary and Joseph.'

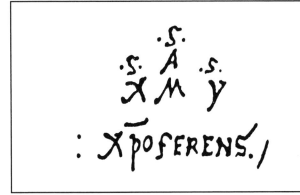

Figure 4 COLUMBUS' SIGLA

The bottom part of the Navigator's sigla is composed of [: **XpōFERENS** ./]. Analysis of this part reveals the following:

1. [:], a colon, is the Greek sign of punctuation that means 'member' or 'part.' Indeed, when we use a colon in punctuation, it divides or separates the sentence into parts or members.

2. [**Xpō**], with a tilde over the **ō,** is composed of the Greek letters **chi, rho,** and **omicron**. **Xpō** is a standard abbreviation of *Christo* in Greek, meaning 'Christ.' **Omicron** is the fifteenth letter of the Greek alphabet, and the tilde over the vowel **ō** is a Greek sign called a 'macron,' indicating that the main accent of *Cristo* should be on the letter **ó** and that the name should be pronounced as *Cristó*.

3. [**FERENS**] is the Latin word meaning messenger. **FERENS** in Spanish became 'val'; *Cristo + val* produces 'Cristoval.' In Portuguese, it became *vão*, producing *Cristó + vão*, or 'Cristóvão.'

4. [./] is the Greek semicolon.

Why colon and semicolon? Five centuries ago in Portugal and Spain, colon and semicolon were both called 'colons,' or separators, of sentences. The colon [:] was called the 'perfect colon,' and the semicolon [;]was called the 'imperfect colon.'

For many centuries in Portugal and Spain (and until very recently in France also), an interrogatory sentence was always signaled at its beginning with an inverted question mark, alerting the reader to the nature of the sentence,

which ended with an upright question mark [?]. The same rule was applied to exclamation marks and colons and semicolons. When a sentence started with a colon, the reader knew that it would end with a semicolon, and vice versa; but only one of these punctuation marks would affect the meaning of the sentence, as happens with the question mark.

With the above explanation, it should be easier to read the bottom part of the sigla, [: **XpōFERENS** ./] as 'colon' + 'Cristó' + 'vão' + 'semicolon.' The first colon serves as the alert sign to the reader that the second colon (semicolon) is coming. *Cristóvão Colon* was the trade name of the discoverer. His natural name was *Salvador Fernandes Zarco*.

We have stated above that a sigla has a secret meaning. Now we will show that the Navigator's sigla has a double meaning. The bottom part of the sigla contains his other name, Salvador Fernandes Zarco. How?

We should know that Christians commonly called Christ the *Savior*. *Savior* in Portuguese and Spanish is 'Salvador.' The letters '**pō**' of **Xpō** are small letters. Why? Because the name *Salvador* is the name of a person and does not stand for 'Christ,' or 'God;' otherwise, all letters would have been capitalized.

In addition to its meaning as messenger, **FERENS** has an encoded meaning. It is the abbreviation of the name *Fernandes* in Portuguese.

So far, we have two names, *Salvador Fernandes*. Where in the sigla is the last name *Zarco*? Taking another look at **FERENS**, we note that the final **S** differs from the **S**s in the upper part of the sigla—its upper extremity is raised. Although similar to an upper case **S**, it is not an **S**. Rather, it is the inverted Hebrew letter called a **lamed**. In its normal, upright position, this letter has the same meaning as the Greek word *colon* [:] or [./], meaning 'member' or 'parts' (Figure 5).

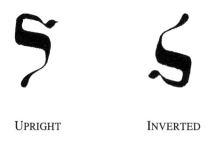

UPRIGHT   INVERTED

Figure 5 HEBREW LETTER **LAMED**

But there is a rule in the Hebrew alphabet that when a letter is upside down or inverted, it alters the meaning of what follows: "It looks like, but is not. It is the other one." And it is the other meaning of [./], *colon,* in Greek, that should be read instead of the meaning in Hebrew of the inverted **lamed**, and that is the name Zarco.

This sensational discovery was made by Major Santos Ferreira, in Portugal, in 1930. The conclusion is that the sigla contains two secret names: *Cristóvão Colon*, his trade name, and *Salvador Fernandes Zarco*, his real name. This requires further explanation.

His Monogram

Was the Navigator Portuguese? Our analysis of his monogram is going to answer this question clearly. Cristóvão Colon never signed his name on his documents or letters. He always used his sigla. In fifteen extant documents, to the left of his sigla, he placed his monogram, which no historian or investigator had noticed, let alone deciphered, until January 1989 (Figure 6).

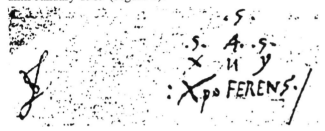

Figure 6 MONOGRAM BESIDE THE SIGLA

My wife, Silvia da Silva, is an excellent embroideress. Because she has executed many monograms in needlepoint, I asked her to unscramble the letters contained in the monogram to the left of the sigla. She easily obtained the three letters, **S, F, Z**, which are the initials of the Navigator, **S**alvador **F**ernandes **Z**arco, born in the southern Portuguese town of Cuba, son of Isabel Gonsalves Zarco and Dom Fernando, Duke of Beja, son of the King of Portugal (Figure 7).

Figure 7 THE NAME, SALVADOR FERNANDES ZARCO

Isabel was the daughter of João Gonsalves Zarco, a Portuguese Jew from Tomar, Portugal, who discovered the island of Porto Santo in 1418. The future navigator was born in 1448 and, at the age of six, accompanied his mother to the island of Porto Santo after she had married Diogo Alfonso Aguiar. He started his maritime life at the age of fourteen in the Portuguese caravels to Africa. He later married Filipa Moniz de Perestelo, daughter of Bartolomeu Perestelo, Governor of Madeira Island. They had one legitimate son, Diogo Colon, born in Portugal.

Salvador Fernandes Zarco (the future Cristofõm Colon) was a sailor for more than ten years in the Portuguese caravels. By decree of King John II, only Portuguese citizens could serve on the Portuguese ships—"All foreigns were thrown overboard, by order of the King."

His Blessing

The other cipher of Cristóvão Colon that we should study is his *Blessing*, which appears on all of the last twelve personal letters the Navigator wrote to his legitimate son, Diogo Colon, from November 12, 1504 to February 24, 1505.

This peculiar sign or cipher, according to Simon Wiesenthal (1973), appears on all of those letters in the upper left corner. This cipher consists of two Hebrew characters **beth** and **hei**, which stand for *baruch hashem*, meaning 'God bless you.' The letters **beth** and **hei** are intertwined like a monogram (Figure 8).

Figure 8 COLUMBUS' BLESSING WITH MONOGRAM

All dozen letters to his son, Diogo Colon, are consistent in having the three ciphers: the Blessing in the upper left corner, the monogram in the lower left corner, and the sigla on the right third of the bottom of each letter.

Obviously, the great discoverer, Cristóvão Colon, was a learned man, not only in the science of navigation, but also in knowledge of languages—Spanish, Portuguese, Greek, Latin, and Hebrew, including the Bible. Testifying to that fact are the intrinsic values of his sigla, his monogram, and his blessing. His mother, Isabel Gonsalves Zarco, was a Portuguese Jew from Tomar, central Portugal, where there is a Synagogue of Arco or Zarco, open to the public.

Forty Portuguese Names

Attesting to the fact that Cristóvão Colon, or Salvador Fernandes Zarco, was 100% Portuguese is a list of more than forty Portuguese names the Navigator gave to locations in the Greater or Lesser Antilles of the Caribbean area during his four voyages. Some of these are: *S. Vincente, Sta. Luzia, Guadiana, Ponta de Santo António, S. João Baptista, Porto Santo, Mourão, Isabel, Sanctus Spiritus, Sta. Clara, S. Nicolau, Conceição, Cabo de S. João, Cabo*

Alfa, S. Domingos, Cabo Roxo, S. Miguel, Cabo Omega, S. António, Sta. Catarina, S. Jorge, Ponta Galera, S. Bernardo, Bocas das Serpentes, Boca do Dragão, Margarida, Ponta de Faro, Boca de Touro, Cabo Isabel, Ilha dos Guinchos, Salvador, Santarém, Cuba, Curaçao, Brasil, Belém.

Some of the names on this list are common to both Spanish and Portuguese, but some can only be Portuguese: *Brasil, Santarém, Curaçao, Faro, Belém, Touro, Ponta, and Porto.*

Cristóvão gave the name *Salvador* to the first island he encountered because it was his own first name. He gave the name *Cuba* to the second island because it was the name of his birthplace in Portugal.

The list of these Portuguese toponyms was first compiled by Mascarenhas Barreto and can be found in his book *Portuguese Columbus* (Barreto 1992).

HIS COAT OF ARMS

The Coat of Arms of Cristofõm Colon also gives us interesting information. It takes the shape of the letter **U** divided in four parts: upper left has a castle; upper right a lion, symbol of strength. In the lower left is a blue sea with many islands—the Caribbean; and the lower right has five small anchors.

Figure 9 CRISTOFÕM COLON'S COAT OF ARMS

Why five anchors? The anchors represent five coins, and it is interesting that, in Hebrew, small anchor is *anchorote* or *angoroth*, also meaning 'coin.' But the Coat of Arms of Portugal also has five coins. Historians Henry Harrisse (1969) and Mascarenhas Barreto (1992) have both stated that these five small anchors stand for the five coins, or *Quinas*, of the Portuguese Coat of Arms (Figure 9).

CONCLUSIONS

1. The Navigator chose the name *Colon* because of its religious and mystic power. In addition to its meaning in punctuation and in anatomy, the word *colon* has religious or spiritual meaning and serves to ward off the evil eye. It equates with making the sign of the cross 'to protect us from evil' or 'to ward off the evil eye.'

Cristóvão may have chosen *Colon* because he foresaw that he would face bad weather and tempests on the high seas during his long and arduous voyages. Highly religious, he wanted to take with him all the protection he could by using the meaning of the colon signs. In his sigla [: XpõFERENS ./], his name in the center is shielded on either end by the protective colon and semicolon.

2. Historians failed to discover the name *Cristofõm Colon* because they were transfixed on the name *Columbus* or *Colombo*, a major mistake. *Colombo* means 'pigeon' or 'dove,' and the Navigator was never a pigeon.

3. All the documentation referring to the Genovese Columbus is false. The name *Cristoforo Colombo* is false, the Codicilio Militar is false, and the so-called last will in Italian is false. Fifteen different places in Italy claim to be Columbus' birthplace!

4. We find no single instance of an Italian place name in the Caribbean. Why? Because the Navigator did not know how to speak or write Italian!

5. Nobody has the right to transpose the Navigator's name into some other name. His true name, as it appears on two Papal Bulls, is *Cristofõm Colon*.

REFERENCES

Barreto, Mascarenhas
  1992 *The Portuguese Columbus, Secret Agent of King John II.* New York: St.Martin's Press.
da Silva, Manuel Luciano
  1971 *Portuguese Pilgrims and Dighton Rock,* N. Martins, ed. Privately published: Bristol RI.
  1989 Columbus wasn't Columbus. *Massachusetts Academy Magazine,* Fall/Winter 1989-1990, Vol. III, No. 3, pp. 3-10.
Harrisse, Henry
  1969 *The Discovery of North America.* Amsterdam: N. Israel Publishing Dept.
Thacher, John Boyd
  1967 *Christopher Columbus: His Life, His Work, His Remains,* 3 Vols. New York: AMS Press Inc.
Wiesenthal, Simon
  1973 *Sails of Hope.* New York: Macmillan.

The Brendan-Columbus Connection

PAUL H. CHAPMAN

Despite all the controversy about him during this era of 'political correctness,' it is a recognized fact that Christopher Columbus opened up the dreaded 'Sea of Darkness' and brought the peoples of the old and new worlds into communication with each other.

Columbus did this with the help of a pioneer who had preceded him by some nine centuries, an explorer who gets little credit for his achievement even today. This man was an Irish Abbott who, in the year AD 564, took to sea with a crew of seventeen monks intent on reaching "The Land Promised to the Saints" across the ocean, to where the sun sets. His name was Brendan, and for his exploits he became known as Saint Brendan the Navigator. He found his way to the promised land by trial and error, and his voyages were recorded in ancient manuscripts called the *Navigatio Sancti Brendani Abbatis* (Selmer 1959).

But Brendan lives only in legend. There is apparently no place for him in the history books. In fact, historians of record have gone out of their way to deny him (Morison 1971). This backhanded attempt to show superiority of the author through ridicule of the subject may be popular in some quarters of academia, but it evades the truth of the matter and is destructive rather than constructive.

While Columbus himself did not deny Brendan or the role he played, neither did he acknowledge the man or his feat. It is only through Columbus' son Ferdinand, who wrote his father's biography (Colon 1959), that we learn of his knowledge of the *Navigatio*.

In the case of Columbus this is understandable. In his day the possession of territory was accorded by the Pope, who acted on the basis of discovery. If some prior Christian Prince had discovered a land (the Pope's stipulation), then there could be no further claim. The Pope was interested in spreading the faith, and his stipulation was the inducement to help get the job done.

Columbus' knowledge of the *Navigatio* is revealed in statements made by Ferdinand, who accompanied his father during the fourth voyage to America when the boy was thirteen years old. For instance, Ferdinand wrote, "We could not learn the reason for this strange custom but judged it was caused by [the natives'] fear of the griffins that inhabit that country . . . " (Colon 1959:249).

The Griffa (or griffin) is an eagle-headed lion monster with wings that comes from Greek mythology and was known to the Irish monks who were the scholars of the Dark Ages in Europe. The *Navigatio* also made a reference to this creature when Brendan was in the area of the West Indies.

There is a second instance in which Ferdinand mentions information found only in the *Navigatio*: " . . . the islands called St. Brendan, of which so many marvels are told, were probably of the same nature. One finds mention of still others that lie much farther north. In those regions there are other islands which burn perpetually" (Colon 1959:25). In the *Navigatio*, two islands are described as burning, and they do indeed lie much farther north (Chapman 1973:130).

Ferdinand is well regarded for his scholarship. His book and that of Bartolome de Las Casas are the principal sources for information on Columbus. Las Casas, also a contemporary, is known as 'the Apostle to the Indies' for his compassionate work with the natives. He joined Ferdinand in recognizing that Columbus had withheld one critical piece of information from the Spanish Monarchs (Las Casas 1971:27). That information was the route for reaching the other side and returning. The route: sail south down below the dreaded, windless Sargasso Sea to the region of the Canaries; then sail west to cross; to return, sail north, passing above the Sargasso, and turn east toward home.

Columbus himself furnished still more evidence of his awareness of Brendan's voyage, though unintentionally. As a matter of fact, he tried to cover it up. In his logbook, as they approached the West Indies, there is an entry stating his expectation of seeing "certain Islands." He had taken with him a copy of a map of the Ocean Sea, drawn by Paolo dal Pozzo Toscanelli of Florence, a physician and cosmographer. This map, like much of the other Columbus material, has long since disappeared; we know of it only through references. But when the Swedish author-researcher-painter Bjorn Landstrom went looking, he found a graticule of the map in the Toscanelli family papers. His careful reconstruction clearly shows the Isle of St. Brendan far to the west in Mare Oceanum (Landstrom 1966:19).

Christopher Columbus was well educated. He had "learned his letters at an early age" and then proceeded to learn the sciences involved in cartography, a trade at which he became proficient as shown by his success in Portugal. The contemporary Royal Historian, Gonzales Fernandez Oviedo, states: "Columbus had good Latin and great cosmographic knowledge" (Cohen 1969:28). So, reading the *Navigatio* manuscripts (one hundred and twenty copies of which are still extant in the museums and monasteries of Europe) was not a problem for him. Columbus was an avid reader of everything available on the Ocean

Sea. He had been a sea captain, sailing for twenty-three years, before he approached the Spanish monarchs with his proposed enterprise. He was certainly capable of understanding the navigational information embodied in the *Navigatio*.

The route to 'The Indies' is so critical that G. E. Nunn in a study for the American Geographical Society concluded: "There were really three discoveries made by Columbus instead of one. His discovery of the two ocean routes (outbound and return) was so overshadowed by the discovery of land that it passed unnoticed . . . over four hundred years of experience in sailing the Atlantic has not suggested any material change in the route chosen by Columbus on his first voyage" (Chapman 1973:89).

The basic problem in sailing across the Atlantic is and was wind direction. In times when wind was the means of propulsion, it was necessary to have favorable winds for at least a good part of the time. In the North Atlantic, there are the 'Prevailing Westerlies,' and the name means exactly what it says. The wind comes from the west most of the time; it is in the face of those headed west. The old square-rigger could sail only with a wind behind.

It was essential for Columbus to have knowledge of the route by which Brendan had succeeded. It is the only one which was practical in sailing days. Even the English colonists who came a hundred years later used this route (discovered by their buccaneers following the Spanish). The dedicated crew of monks had found the route by making five concerted attempts at various latitudes before succeeding. For a group of men who had prepared themselves by fasting every other day, the rigors of such voyaging could be tolerated; they were able to go on longer. While there is no limit to how far a ship can sail, there is a limit to how far a man can sail. Ordinarily, scurvy sets in at six weeks. Men become incapacitated, and, if not reinvigorated with fresh food, they die.

How did Christopher Columbus relate to Brendan and recognize the significance of the information contained in the *Navigatio*? Saint Brendan's original attempt, leaving from Ireland, had been in a northerly direction, but he was twice blown back into the Faeroes. Columbus was familiar with this area, as he had made at least one voyage to Iceland (in 1477); the Faeroes carried the same name which Brendan had given them (and still do): *Faeroe* means 'sheep island' in Norse.

As the westerlies prevail all the way down to the Azores, Brendan was turned back on his third try, making it only as far as Flores, the Azores island which has the unique feature of hot and cold running water springing forth side-by-side on its seashore. Sailing from Flores, in his fourth attempt Brendan went into the Sargasso Sea. It is an area of heavy seaweed and wind calms. This can be, and sometimes was, deadly to a sailing ship. After fifteen days they floated out, only to be blown back eastward, this time to Sao Miguel in the southeastern Azores. Here the island is identifiable by its lakes of mineral waters.

Finally, on his fifth attempt, Brendan succeeded. He did so when he elected "to let God tend the sails." Columbus, with his years of experience at sea, would read this loud and clear: they were willing to go wherever the winds would take them. The winds took Brendan down to the latitude where they start to blow from the east, off the west coast of Africa. From here the winds continue to blow from the east, and so the *Navigatio* indicated, all the way to the islands on the other side of the Ocean Sea. This route is known today as the Trade Wind Route, because it carried trade during the Colonial Period.

This brings us to another factor favoring the Abbot's venture, the discipline of a religious order. It kept the mission focused. By contrast, after five weeks at sea Columbus withstood a mutiny only by promising to turn back if land was not sighted within three more days. (In fact, it took two more.) Without Brendan we would not have had Columbus. Some say that America would have been discovered anyway by someone else. This is not necessarily so, at least not until invention of the steam engine allowed ships to 'sail' against the Prevailing Westerly winds of the North Atlantic.

What about the Norsemen—didn't they reach America? Yes, but they did so using Greenland as a stepping stone to Vinland. And then the climate changed, clogging up those sea lanes with ice. The Great Plague of the 14th century subsequently wiped out the Norsemen's merchant marine. Even the Portuguese, who were Europe's exploration leaders, failed in their attempt to resurrect the northern route. Columbus had sailed for the Portuguese for fourteen years, and they had also practiced going down along the hump of Africa and returning by a swing out to the Azores to take advantage of the westerly winds in that area.

Columbus thought the islands which had been described in detail by Brendan were the same islands described by Marco Polo, off China (the Indies). And this, coupled with the incorrect measure of the extent of the Eurasian land mass by the highly respected geographers, Claudius Ptolemy and Marinus of Tyre (Phoenicia), was responsible for Columbus' miscalculation of the distance to China. When he reached the Caribbean, Columbus named the islands there the 'West Indies,' believing them to be the westernmost of the Indies.

The Trade Wind Route is the route Columbus used to cross the dreaded 'Sea of Darkness.' Some say that he first sailed to the Canaries off Africa in order to be five hundred miles farther west. But they ignore the essential fact that this route carried him six hundred miles farther south. He did not—repeat, did not—sail west, until after the first leg of the trip. He then crossed from the Canaries to the Bahamas. In sailing the same route as Brendan, Columbus sailed into the same island chain Brendan had reached. It is easily identified by the Great Bahamas Bank. Well-described in the *Navigatio*, it is the only coral sea of that size in the Atlantic Ocean.

Brendan, with God continuing to "tend the sails," next went north with the Gulf Stream to the area of the 'burning islands,' which are submarine volcanoes along the Reykjanes Ridge off Iceland. From there the Westerlies took Brendan home. As for Columbus, he attempted neither to sail east to Spain, nor to return by the way he had come. Instead, he took Brendan's route: first sailing north, then turning east at the latitude of Spain, where the Prevailing Westerlies brought him home.

Columbus and Brendan shared the same religion: both put their faith in God. If it be true, as one historian wrote, that "only God could have shown him the way" (Cohen 1969), then perhaps He did so through His servant, Saint Brendan.

POSTSCRIPT

In 1976, Timothy Severin launched an effort to cross the Atlantic from Ireland in a skin-covered boat as Brendan had done. He was sponsored by the National Geographic Society. I was present as his guest at the meeting of the International Ship Archaeologists Society in London when he began his talk explaining that the ship was not of the ancient design. Early publicity had proclaimed it to be a replica. Instead, it had been designed by a modern naval architect, carrying two masts, as did Tim's personal yacht, and having sleek lines rather than the double-ended/single masted configuration of the ancient sailing ship. He had, however, gone to great lengths to use the same materials and construction methods as of old: cow hides stretched over a wooden frame.

In one of the ironies of history, the modern craft could not match the performance of its ancient counterpart. During a heavy storm, the winds washed waves over its stern, and the boat was rapidly being swamped. Only quick work by Severin and his small crew saved them from disaster. They built up a stern post, to split the waves, using their spare cow hides, and thus achieved at sea the same beneficial design that the ancients had incorporated all along.

Severin launched on May 17, St. Brendan's Day, and sailed to the Faeroes, as Brendan had done. But from there he went to Iceland, following the 'stepping stone'

course he had picked out from a map, instead of Brendan's course. While Tim's northern route was shorter, he argued it was also tougher than the southern route used by the Irish Abbott according to my navigational plotting from the old manuscripts. With this I had to agree, as the southern route followed the gentle trade winds.

In a review of my book on Brendan in the Hispanic American Historical Review, Professor Martin Torodash had written: " . . . the only land near enough to have been visited in an open Irish curragh is totally barren Rockall Island . . ."—two hundred and eighty miles off the Irish coast. I wrote a heated, factual response, and the editor, Michael C. Meyer, printed it intact, while giving Martin the opportunity to answer. He declined the offer. (We are now both members of the Society for the History of Discoveries and have enjoyed a friendly relationship.)

After a layover in Iceland (Brendan had laid over in the Faeroes), Severin sailed on to Newfoundland on the North American continent. In sum, even in the more difficult latitudes, and despite having to correct a design mistake while at sea, Tim proved, once and for all, that a skin-covered boat was capable of crossing the Atlantic Ocean.

REFERENCES

Chapman, P.H.
  1973 *The Man Who Led Columbus to America.* Columbus GA: Judson Press (now ISAC Press).
Cohen, John M.
  1969 *The Four Voyages of Christopher Columbus.* Hammondsworth: Penguin Books.
Colon, Ferdinand
  1959 *The Life of the Admiral Christopher Columbus*, B. Keen, trans. New Brunswick NJ: Rutgers University Press.
Landstrom, Bjorn
  1966 *Columbus.* New York: Macmillan.
Las Casas, B.
  1971 *History of the Indies,* Andre M. Collard, trans. New York: Harper & Row.
Morison, S. E.
  1971 *The European Discovery of America, The Northern Voyages.* New York: Oxford University Press.
Selmer, Carl, ed.
  1959 *Navigatio Sancti Brendani Abbatis.* University of Notre Dame Press.

JOHN L. SORENSON

CRITERIA FOR THE CRITIQUE

The papers in Section IV form a residual category that cannot be characterized neatly. Of the seven papers making up this section, two, those by Wescott and Kehoe, are concerned with the nature, significance, and history of thought concerning transoceanic diffusion. Three others survey particular bodies of evidence for pre-Columbian contact: Gordon reprises materials which point to the presence of Hebrew-speakers at several American locations; Ferryn points out topics that he thinks deserve more careful consideration than has been the case to this point; Cyr summarizes his reading of ancient maps which he believes shows distant explorations by Chinese voyagers. Finally, da Silva and Chapman offer clarifications of the role of Columbus.

Two classes of comment are pertinent about these diverse presentations. First, how persuasive are they individually as pieces of scholarship, and, second, in the aggregate what difference do they make in resolving the general controversy over pre-Columbian transoceanic contact.

The persuasiveness issue can be addressed according to two standards: how does each paper strike me personally, and how likely is each to affect the opinion of scholars who are reluctant to accept the idea of ancient crossings? My view is not that of a 'neutral' scientist or observer (if there is such a thing). I am a longtime student of the subject who has probably examined more of the material both for and against contact than anyone else (see Sorenson and Raish 1990, 1996). As a result, I have become convinced that groups crossed the oceans to the Americas at many points and times. Yet, I believe that the question of what effects those visitors had on 'Native' American cultures is still to be settled, if it can be answered at all. To me, the *quality* of scholarly endeavor exhibited by a researcher is more significant than whether his or her results agree with my current opinions. And how scholarship connects with intellectual history provides a primary standard for judging how important any piece of work is.

ANALYSIS OF THE PAPERS

Given these biases, I find the seven papers in Section IV varied in both value and quality. Wescott's piece is not meant to be an argument for diffusion at all. Rather he looks to what questions ought to be asked in this intellectual enterprise. He is dissatisfied with the value of thinking of a monolithic 'diffusionism' versus a unitary 'inventionism.' To him, diffusion is a complex phenomenon which intergrades with invention under certain conditions. I laud his attempt to broaden the thinking of diffusionists in this conference and volume but wish that a significant number of inventionists, too, could be exposed to the conceptual broadening he offers. A crucial idea that could equip conventional anthropologists and others to take a new tack toward the hoary controversy of transoceanic diffusion is encapsulated in Wescott's dictum that, "When diffused, each invention has to be, to some extent, reinvented in the minds of the receivers." Earl Lubensky has enunciated a similar notion, 'dependent invention,' which consists of modifying and building upon what has been learned from others (see L-356 in Sorenson and Raish 1990).

Kehoe provides historical and cultural context for understanding the origin of the grip of inventionism on the professional mindset of anthropologists. She traces to Daniel Wilson in Victorian England the "dogmatic insistence that the oceans were an impassable barrier to intersocietal contacts before 1492." While she has sketched for us the intellectual setting for this pronouncement, the paper fails to carry us up to the present. Why this "minor element" in Wilson's position has hung on so tenaciously among archaeologists is the important point, but we do not learn why. Without knowing what are the historical, sociological, and ideological underpinnings for this dogmatism, we cannot see how to counter it successfully.

I suspect that it has to do with political ideology in large part. Kauffman Doig has acutely pointed out one relevant dimension—nationalism—in this mode of thought about "the origin of American civilizations."[1] What he calls 'alocthonism'—crediting foreign sources for a country's native cultures—is offensive to national pride in Latin America. Scholars from those countries are affected in their professional thinking by this nationalist ideological current, probably both because of their upbringing in the country's culture and because they must court support for their scholarly careers from nationalists. But nothing in the posture of Latin Americans exceeds Sylvanus J. Morley's nationalist rhetoric regarding Maya civilization: there is "no vestige, no infinitesimal trace of Old World influence . . . to detract from the genius of our [sic] Native American mind . . . . There is no room for foreign origins here,"[2] a statement made in 1927 soon after legislation had passed to exclude new Chinese immigrants from the United States.

Early 20th century national chauvinism surely played a role in the emphasis on 'inventionism' that grew to prominence at that time. Today, the stubborn insistence by American anthropologists on the inviolability of the ocean barrier could also involve the psychology and economics of scholars' anxiety to protect their academic niches. Americanists bolster their position in academe by implicitly saying, "We are very important scientists, uniquely charged with the mission of elucidating the only completely independent 'laboratory case,' in America, of the development of civilization by humankind. Without us, the nature of human beings as cultural beings can never be known."[3]

More exploration of the history of thought in the anthropological and geographical sciences through the early 20th century is needed to elucidate this matter, going beyond Kehoe's beginning.

Gordon pictures the Jews as a stubbornly unaccommodating minority in ancient Mediterranean civilization who gave abundant reason to flee from Roman pressure to conform to imperial religious norms in the 1st and 2nd centuries. Furthermore, Jews had a little-discussed maritime capability which would have allowed them to cross to America. Evidences that they did so consist of: the 'phylactery stela' from Tepatlaxco, Veracruz, Mexico; Jewish coins found in Kentucky; the Bat Creek Stone; and the Newark and Los Lunas decalogue inscriptions, together with the Green Corn festival still continued by Yuchi Indians in Oklahoma. Finally, "material for the study of the pre-Columbian Hebrew legacy to the Americas is vast," but "the evidence is fragile" and must be studied before it disappears.

Nearly all this information has been presented before by Gordon. True, the Jewish maritime tradition is not well known, but neither is it critical to the argument as he has previously presented it. In repeating this material at the ABC Conference Gordon was "preaching to the (diffusionist) choir." I would have hoped for a new angle from him, but perhaps there will have to be dramatic new findings before a substantially different argument can be presented about "the . . . Hebrew legacy to the Americas."

Ferryn brings to us a different perspective, "a European view" of diffusionist matters. Because of the international breadth of his awareness, his summation is of interest. He says that diffusionism is not popular in Europe, in part because the arguments are little known, and also because established scholars disdain "work which runs contrary to the theories they have been defending all their lives." Ferryn is concerned "better to inform and sensitize the international academic community" on these matters. To that end, he suggests the value of more research on New England stone structures in relation to little-known monuments in France. Other topics recommended for attention include archaeoastronomy, the Kensington Stone, and de Mahieu's runic material in South America. Despite certain interesting points raised in this

paper, it cannot be considered either powerful in what it reports or novel in how it argues the issues about ancient voyaging.

The material in Cyr's paper on Chinese maps has been published previously. He is frank in labelling the treatment "a speculative game that can be played," or "an exercise in cryptography," or decipherment of old maps. The game consists of subjectively assigning geographical locations on today's world map to spots characterized by the names the Chinese put on their maps. Thus, for instance, he thinks "Hairy People Country" could refer to the land of the Ainu of northern Japan, while "Black Grandson Land could be that of the Pygmies of Africa." Indeed, one may play such a game, but it is quite clear that the results can never persuade anyone about early Chinese explorations of America or the rest of the world unless they have abiding faith in subjective guessing. Scholarship requires faith, but not this kind. I cannot see how doing this indeterminate sort of thing contributes to improving scientific or scholarly understanding of pre-Columbian voyaging across the oceans.

Da Silva's aim is to analyze "the ciphers written by the Navigator's (Columbus') own hand." When they are examined correctly, in conjunction with other documentary information, the author maintains, the great discoverer turns out to be exclusively Portuguese, not Italian at all (he did not even know the Italian language). For those with a deep concern with Columbus' career, this treatment may or may not be persuasive and cogent. It is obviously induced by ethnic pride on da Silva's part; I suppose the paper was included as a bow to the Portuguese ancestry of a part of the population of Providence, the host city for the ABC Conference, but as to the major theme of the meeting it has no value.

Chapman's discussion sketches what he sees as Columbus' debt to Brendan, the Irish monk. The major contribution is supposed to have been Brendan's knowledge of the wind patterns on the Atlantic and thus of the two routes, outbound and return, that were essential to follow if Columbus was to succeed. But he tried to conceal his dependence on his Celtic predecessor. What this short piece shows is that the large argumentative literature on the Brendan matter cannot successfully be dealt with in the brief compass of a short article. The major point is probably sound—there was a Celtic voyager (some 'Brendan' or other, whether 'St.Brendan' *per se* existed or not), and Celtic seafarers likely passed on to succeeding generations significant knowledge about sailing in the Atlantic, which at length aided the 15th century discoverers of America. It remains unclear why this matters in terms of "across before Columbus?"

How will unbelievers—scholars who have not been converted to the diffusionist faith—be likely to react to the papers in Section IV? On any careful scale of persuasion power, these seven papers are likely to fall lower than the best of the articles contained in the other parts of the book. This is because they have been keyed to presenting only specific topics, not bodies of evidence intended to persuade readers about the issue in general.

ANALYSIS OF THE VOLUME

What about the book as a whole? Its chief merit is that it combines under one cover some effective summaries of current diffusionist thought and data. In some ways it serves the purpose *Man Across the Sea* did a quarter-century ago. However, this new work is not nearly as careful a summary nor as prudent or balanced a critique as the older volume was. Diffusion enthusiasts will find it useful and comforting, but little of it is substantively new (Jett's paper on dyestuffs is a notable exception). Nothing in it sheds bright new light on, let alone challenges, views that have been published in recent years by serious students of diffusion, among whom the present authors stand out.

Well then, how will non-diffusionists respond to the volume? Few will be moved positively, I expect. This is not particularly good evangelism literature for the diffusionist cause (and it is considered a 'cause' by most of the contributors). In fact, some of it is not good science or scholarship. There are places where sound scholarly or scientific work shows up in the papers, but these are mixed with material that will not impress the fictional 'neutral observer.'

When I look at the individual papers beyond Section IV, I see two problems that stand out. First, most of them are repetitive and derivative; they present ideas and information that have been given before, often in greater detail than here. The repetition leaves the impression that 'diffusionists' nowadays tend to sit in a corner fussing around with old data, or at least with the familiar types of less-than-decisive evidence. Second, a number of the presentations are only suggestive. Rarely is a diffusionist position argued and documented in a way that demands acceptance of the interhemispheric proposition. Some authors *assert* that voyagers arrived in America and had specific influence, but they fail to powerfully argue a diffusionist view because they ignore competing explanations and contrary data.

At a grander level, the conference and volume suffer from lack of an overall plan. The papers seem to have arisen spontaneously—a proposal from this corner and another from that corner—resulting in a melange of articles containing some interesting things but without any guiding design intended to move the diffusionist case to a new level. Some may, of course, believe that "we" are not ready to come up with an integrated presentation that will make naysayers pay attention. If that is the case—if diffusionists are still at the stage of making bricks, a pile here and a pile there—but there is no architectonic plan for the structure in which the bricks are to be utilized, who can blame the doubters for not making plans to move in?

It would be presumptuous of me in this venue to undertake to sketch out the required design, but, at least in the role of commentator, I will note some of the features in the present work that should be avoided in the future if a proper diffusionist house is to be made intellectually habitable and functional for regular scholars. Other problems could be adduced, but three are enough for now.

Flawed Materials

For generations conventional scholars have been pointing out logical, epistemological, methodological, and factual flaws in diffusionist presentations. Not all their critiques have been apt, but some of the errors they have pointed out are so fundamental and egregious that to continue to include them in diffusionist literature is to invite instant discard of one's argument. Too many of the papers from this conference persist in repeating some of those flaws—doubtful documentation, special pleading, conceptually diffuse "traits," unexplained chronological gaps. At least, there ought to be developed a tradition of critique among diffusionists which points out poor work in order to enhance the larger enterprise. As things stand, there is too ready an acceptance of errors out of exaggerated courtesy to those 'on our side.' One particularly unfortunate consequence of the willingness to publish poor papers along with superior ones is that the best are then inevitably devalued, in the minds of unbelieving scholars, by appearing side-by-side with presentations which have been inadequately thought through.

Lack of Comprehensive Knowledge of Prior Work

Nearly every anti-diffusionist writer can be faulted for selective ignorance of vital data and thought on diffusionist issues. We all know that. However, that does not justify those who propose transoceanic voyages themselves to argue from ignorance. There is far too much reinventing of the wheel in current argumentation, including papers in this volume. Is the literature of diffusionism to be cumulative and progressive or not? The strengths and weaknesses of the present corpus seem to be about the same as was the case fifty or even seventy-five years ago.

Failure to Deal with Established Findings in the Human Sciences

An immense, cumulative body of information and theory has been developed by scientists about human history and behavior. Persuasive diffusionist argument must be fully informed about this corpus and has to deal with it intelligently. It simply will not do, at the end of the 20th century, to claim, say, that a boatload of folks from ancient Troy dropped into interior Argentina and continued using imported decorative motifs little changed for a couple of millennia. Or that Iberians came into New England, Chou Chinese into Mexico, or Yuchi into the Southeast. If panpipes with similar musical scales were made in both lowland South America and Melanesia, what scientifically informed proposal can be offered to connect the two cases? In cultural terms how could such a thing be? What kinds of relationships would have prevailed between intrusive foreign enclaves and the 'indigenous' populations who obviously were present? Where is the evidence for the assumed chronology and supposed continuity? This is not to say that there cannot have been a connection. It does mean that it is incumbent on diffusionists to come clean with reasonable propositions that are documented with adequate case material and elucidated by sound theory, if doubters are expected to believe these things.

The contributors have labored diligently in a time-honored manner according to the diffusionist tradition. They deserve our respect for what they have given us. I am grateful personally for what the conference and papers taught me. Yet I fear that the greatest impact that can be expected from this volume and repetitions of eclectic conferences of this type will be barely constructive enough to keep the diffusionist building permit in force, but not constructive enough to raise sound walls or put on a viable roof.

NOTES

1. See F. Kauffman Doig's 1980 "El período formativo." Pp. 253-349 in *Historia del Perú*. Vol. 1. Lima: Editorial Juan Mejia Baca. Also see K-016 in Sorenson and Raish 1990.

2. See "Maya civilization 100% American." Pp.226-236 in *The Forum* 78 (1927). Also see M-418 in Sorenson and Raish 1990; and compare Spinden's statement in R-010.

3. Compare E. James Dixon's phrasing, despite his personal open-mindedness about possible early voyages, in "The origins of the first Americans," *Archaeology* 38 (1985):22-27: "The American continents constitute two enormous fossil laboratories in which to study the last major dispersal for the human species on our planet." Or one might choose John Howland Rowe's aggressive botanical metaphor "Diffusionism and archaeology," *American Antiquity* 31 (1966):334-337. Also see Sorenson and Raish, R-193: Americanists are fighting the "hardy weed" of diffusionism, which continues to "infest" the virgin field of archaeology.

ALICE B. KEHOE

The taboo, in mainstream academic archaeology, on discussing pre-Columbian transoceanic contacts persists in part through simple inertia, the passing on from generation to generation of the standard *doxa* of the orthodox. It persists also because the social framework of a Eurocentric dominant society remains relatively little changed from the 19th century. Until the 1970s, American archaeology was a nearly pure WASP male profession, comprised of men educated to revere European philosophers and historians and to consider all non-Western nations inferior. Taught that the Titanic represented a great example of sophisticated shipbuilding, whatever her fate when attacked by a giant iceberg, these men assumed without serious analysis that alternative traditions of seafaring and boatbuilding are inferior and incapable of supporting European voyaging. The unquestioned 'evidence' of European superiority made challenges appear foolish—and 'European' meant Roman Empire and its successors, not Celts or Basques.

A second factor in the persistence of the mainstream *doxa* has been the National Science Foundation's support of archaeology since World War II. This principal source of funding favored positivist science on the model of the conventional natural and physical sciences. Projects oriented to discovering environmental factors, artifact manufacturing technology, and similar measurable data were valued. Pre-Columbian transoceanic contacts are less amenable to experimental evaluation, far less numerous than potsherds or stone blades or pollen, and therefore unsuited to statistical handling. There is a common misconception that science and statistics are synonymous.

One breakthrough has been made, however: the acceptance of L'Anse aux Meadows as 11th century Norse. It is a model of how resistance can be overcome by a site with a suite of distinctive *in-situ* features (Norse-style hall foundations, iron working), professionally excavated, and displayed *in situ* to several skeptical but fair-minded, respected, experienced archaeologists (such as Junius Bird, who had worked in Labrador). *National Geographic* acceptance and support helped, too.

I could sum up the "historical, sociological and ideological underpinnings" for the *doxa* by the phrase 'Manifest Destiny': the concept legitimated modern European invaders' genocidal conquests of the Americas, and if it were shown that transoceanic contacts have not inevitably been so destructive and overwhelming, then the post-Columbian conquests, of which Euro-Americans enjoy the fruits, cannot be held to be inevitable destiny. Admitting the possibility of earlier transoceanic contacts, American archaeologists might be compelled to respect the strength of America's First Nations and to recognize that post-Columbian holocausts have been, in part, the result of Euro-American policy decisions of questionable morality. A great number of Euro-Americans, including some archaeologists, are reluctant to discard the comfortable cloak of Manifest Destiny.

PAUL CHAPMAN

The inclusion of opposing opinions is welcomed. The lack of substance is regretted. Sorenson describes himself as "a longtime student of the subject who has probably examined more of the material both for and against contacts than anyone else." But he proceeds to criticize without recognizing a single one of the salient facts presented in my talk. These were taken from my book *The Man Who Led Columbus to America*, containing 180 pages of facts on the subject. To the best of my knowledge no one has challenged a single one of these in the twenty-six years since publication. This in spite of a cash offer of one thousand dollars made to academia for the finding of any factual error.

He correctly describes my thesis: "The main contribution is supposed to have been Brendan's knowledge of the wind patterns on the Atlantic, and thus the two routes, outbound and return, were essential to follow if Columbus was to succeed." He then concludes with: "It remains unclear why this matters in terms of 'Across Before Columbus?'." Someone should explain to Dr. Sorenson that wind propels a sailing ship and that the square-riggers required following winds; thus, the requirement for a following wind throughout the circuit. It begins with the world turning, and this results in the circular wind and sea pattern on the oceans.

As stated in the paper presented, Columbus followed the Trade Wind pattern, as found by Brendan, through trial and error; and even with favorable winds he was faced with a mutiny after five weeks en route. He landed with just two days to spare. Thus, "Without Brendan we would not have had Columbus."

To ascribe to other unnamed and unreported seafarers the knowledge gained by Brendan and recorded in 120 manuscripts still in existence in monasteries and museums in Europe is gross negligence.

Manuel da Silva

Dr. Sorenson's comment on my paper, "Columbus was 100% Portuguese!", was as brief as it was disappointing.

Unfortunately, he declined to criticize the thesis on its merit, while at the same time asserting that the purpose of my effort was simply a manifestation of ethnic pride to please the local Portuguese-American populace. This would be equivalent to an assertion that Dr. Sorenson's comments were made with the purpose of currying favor with his academic colleagues. Objective findings serve no groups. However, the reverse may be true.

Researchers with a thorough knowledge of the Portuguese language and its unique characteristics may be the only ones who are sufficiently prepared to discover the Portuguese connection to Christopher Columbus, or better, Cristóvão Colon. Quite naturally, most scholars with a knowledge of the history of the Portuguese language happen to be Portuguese.

Linda S. McElroy—Co-Editor

Dr. Sorenson's critique of the volume as a whole provides a springboard for an apologia which, as co-editor, I have felt should be presented to balance the diversity of viewpoints such a volume is bound to elicit. My issue is not so much whether the scholarshp herein supports or fails to support the diffusionist position, as whether it demonstrates the *validity* of the various approaches by which knowledge about such a subject may be acquired.

I do not disagree with Dr. Sorenson that the established orderly processes of scientific scholarship ought not be flaunted by wildly *speculative* claims in support of any new thesis. However, what mainstream archaeology/anthropology seems to need to take more seriously is the growing awareness among forward-looking scholars and knowledgeable lay people alike that there may be more than one path to 'truth,' and that having a PhD or the backing of a prestigious institution is not the only way of finding it.

Dr. Kehoe's observations concerning the very limited approaches to archaeology—not only in respect to the background and training of its practitioners but also in its reliance on only what can be measured and quantified—that have dominated this discipline up until very recent times seem to be key here. With the advent of the 'Scientific Era,' it was the initiated *scientists* (from the Latin, *scire*, 'to have knowledge about') who became the western world's new priesthood—a priesthood comprised predominantly of men who had put in their time, first as acolytes and then as novitiates, in order to become full-fledged Keepers of the Word. Gradually, scientists assumed the dominant role, both sociologically and practically, of interpreting and regulating the culture's evolving belief systems, a role formerly assumed by *religious* priests, first during the pagan era and subsequently during the Christian era. Although the locus of power shifted, it still lay securely within the largely hierarchical societal structure which, at best, patronises and, at worst, punishes the uninitiated.

As the historical dialectic process moves inexorably forward, we are now witnessing, in a whole array of scholarly disciplines, the emergence of a new synthesis which integrates the grist of recently popular paradigms with alternative approaches to the elucidation of a particular corpus of knowledge and practice. Two examples will suffice: Modern medicine, long a major power-center, is slowly realizing that its rightful business is to heal; now certain time-proven practices outside medical orthodoxy are gaining acceptance for their observed efficacy in achieving that goal, particularly when combined with current medical technologies. In a different arena, a few modern archaeologists, constrained by time and limited budgets, quietly dowse their sites to determine where to dig—a sort of pragmatic demonstration that the best archaeological practice turns up nothing until the precise location of the evidence has been determined.

Dr. Kehoe points to another key issue, namely, that the topic of diffusionism, by its inherent *nature*, does not lend itself well to the established orderly processes of scientific scholarship. What are we to do then? Wring our hands and give up for lack of an 'approved' methodology? Or thoughtfully develop alternatives, building on the processes that *have* proven successful when applied to less broad topics?

Something should be said regarding Dr. Sorenson's criticism that this volume lacks a plan. Many scholars from wide-ranging backgrounds, disciplines, and institutions were invited to present at the ABC Conference. Initial choices were determined primarily by the relevance of a researcher's known area of interest to the focus of the conference. Some scholars who could have added significant perspective to the diffusionist debate declined the opportunity; some of our Native American associates were unable to attend.[‡] But quite a few scholars, both distinguished and not so distinguished, did accept, apparently welcoming the opportunity to be *heard*. What they have in common is the dedication of a portion of their professional lifetimes, against the grain of entrenched establishment positions, to the unraveling of a variety of archaeological and anthropological enigmas, many of which have been conveniently shelved in the dusty basements of prestigious institutions.

This unwanted selective filtering of eventual participants led to a conference program which was sometimes unbalanced and sometimes displayed significant gaps in the spectrum of topics that it would have been appropriate to include. So, if the book seems to lack a coherent plan, it may be that the conference itself lacked a plan, in the sense that I think Dr. Sorenson uses that term. On the positive side, however, there are those who might argue that having too set a plan—too rigid an agenda—would have produced its own filtering process, forcing, as it would have, the content of the presentations into some predetermined polemic structure. This approach could be appropriate in a traditional discipline with well-drawn battle lines; but in one still trying to find its center of gravity, such an approach seems to this observer more backward- than forward-looking, introducing as it would, the organizers' own biases.

We pointed out in our opening remarks that NEARA has tried to provide a forum in which serious scholars could present their findings, assured of a respectful hearing and non-acrimonious debate. Some material presented here was, indeed, presented earlier. Perhaps, not having been 'heard' the first time, it merited another hearing, or at least a hearing by a different audience. Some material was, indeed, preliminary in nature and has been labeled as such, but let's not forget that it is the establishment's 'publish or perish' banner which, in an already competitive society, has encouraged the routine rushing of scholarly articles into print. Some scholarship in this volume may not measure up to establishment standards, but nevertheless, if it triggers an insight in just one thoughtful, open-minded reader/researcher because it breaks up the ingrained mindset that has been causing his mental logjam, then who can say it shouldn't have been included? Throughout history, the chemistry of different mindsets mixing in the crucible of open-minded debate has produced amazing new intellectual compounds.

Thus, some ABC contributors will be seen as earnest seekers of the truth, others as zealots already exploiting new niches of intellectual inquiry; still others may be regarded merely as 'fringe' types. However, in any period of profound transformation, zealots create the momentum that helps to launch the new cause, and 'fringe' types will provide its foils. It is from precisely this kind of intellectual soup that the new paradigm arises. As the world moves with frightening speed toward a global culture, the Bering Strait doctrine will yield to a higher synthesis just as surely as the ice yielded to a changing climate. The present priests of the archaeological/anthropological precinct may well emerge from their orderly matins one cultural morning to find that the diffusionist ship has already sailed to hazard the intellectual seas, and that they weren't on it.

‡   See the Acknowledgments for names of scholars who participated in the conference but whose papers or panel contributions are not represented in this volume.

For most of this century, it has been argued in traditional academic circles that Old World peoples did not come to the Americas across either great ocean during the several millennia before 1492 simply because they couldn't. Neither their vessels nor their maritime skills, it was alleged, were sufficiently advanced to complete ocean-spanning voyages. The only practicable route for the peopling of the Americas, therefore, had to be via the Beringia land bridge. And the only reasonable time frame that would allow for the development of the cultural diversity and level of sophistication among Native Americans observed by the 'first' Europeans had to have been much, much earlier. Evidence challenging this doctrine was routinely dismissed as fake, fanciful, or misinterpreted.

In recent decades, however, the exclusivity of the Beringia land bridge doctrine has been steadily assailed by open-minded scholars—those whose intellectual integrity was challenged by a theory clearly shown in a developing corpus of knowledge to be too limited or those driven by a clear insight, perhaps happened upon accidentally in the pursuit of some scarcely-related endeavor. Not only were they willing to undertake the necessary research, but they were undaunted by the certainty of academic opposition. The authors whose research appears in this volume are among those who have most clearly demonstrated the courage to take up the challenges, pursue their insights, and initiate the research.

In our introductory comments we expressed our belief in the need for a multi-disciplinary approach to the area of research with which this volume is concerned. We have also supported the opinion of others that a *rigid* adherence to traditional scholarly processes could not provide the breadth of approach necessary adequately to explore the diversity of evidence and contexts that this particular research requires.

Among those who took up the scholarly challenge early on are Alice Kehoe and Betty Meggers. Both scholars evaluated evidence which persuaded them that pre-Columbian ocean crossings to this hemisphere were not only possible but probable, and they persevered despite the negative criticism heaped upon them by some of their more orthodox colleagues. Kehoe's definitive paper, "Small Boats upon the North Atlantic," presented at the 1968 Santa Fe symposium and subsequently published in *Man Across the Sea,* demonstrated that ocean crossings could have been made earlier than previously thought possible. Whether such voyages actually had occurred and what effect they might have had on either the receiving or donor culture was yet to be determined. But the door for considering those questions was clearly open.

Also presented, though less noticed, in Kehoe's paper was a discussion of northeast America's earliest pottery, Vinette 1, from 1000 BC. A type without North American antecedents, it was of the same coil-formed, grit-tempered, conical-shaped, and cord-roughened tradition as some contemporary pottery made/found in northwestern Europe. Kehoe's research on an Atlantic route was reinforced in 1975 by James Tuck's excavation report on a much earlier 'Red Paint' burial cist at Labrador's L'Anse Amour site, dated to 5000 BC. This burial was so like those found in north coastal Europe from the same time-frame that they seemed to be of a common culture. Tuck coined the term 'Maritime Archaic' to describe what appeared to be a significant, ancient, seafaring culture which flourished around the north Atlantic rim from Denmark and Norway to the maritime provinces of Canada. The descendants of this culture had apparently maintained the tradition by kayak and curragh until the knarr and other planked and framed vessels became more generally available.

Interested in the other great ocean 'barrier,' the Pacific, Betty Meggers and her colleagues Clifford Evans and Emilio Estrada, beginning in the mid-sixties, published their research on the possibility of a Jomon-Valdivia (Japan-Ecuador) connection that existed 5000 years ago. Most of the archaeological world was more than a little discomfited by the presumption of this fresh challenge to the Beringia doctrine. Despite the skeptics, Meggers persisted, refining her analysis and answering her critics. The assault on Beringia continued.

In the seventies, shifting her focus to Middle America, Meggers presented a body of evidence strongly suggesting a link between China's Shang dynasty and Mexico's Olmec culture. The complex Olmec civilization had been an archaeological enigma because of its relatively sudden appearance on the Mexican scene, seemingly full-blown, without evident antecedents in the New World. Meggers' analysis of the Shang of 1750 BC (China's earliest civilization) showed numerous traits similar to the Olmec in Mexico of 1200 BC—in writing, in the use of jade and of batons as symbols of rank, in settlement patterns and architecture, in worship of mountains, and in many other traits—more similarities than could be expected from the processes of independent human invention or reaction to environment.

In her 1975 Shang-Olmec work, Meggers tackled head on the broad problem of distinguishing diffusion from independent invention and offered a list of criteria for distinguishing the two. "In theory," she wrote, "a trait or complex acquired by diffusion should have the following characteristics:

1. It should appear fully developed in the receiving area and, in the case of a complex, most of the constituent elements should be absent in the antecedent local archaeological record although incorporation of some indigenous elements can be expected.

2. Its evolution should be traceable in the archaeological record of the donor area; if a complex rather than a single trait is involved, however, the evidence may be insufficient to demonstrate that all its components are more recent in the receiving area.

3. Its extinction in the donor area should postdate its appearance in the receiving area if a direct transfer seems probable; if dissemination proceeded slowly, however, the trait or complex may have died out in its place of origin before reaching its maximum distribution.

4. It should not have evolutionary, environmental, or functional limitations that make it subject to independent origin. This qualification applies to certain aspects of social organization that are correlated with population size and concentration, and to material traits such as house type, which may be influenced by climate and local raw materials. Tools may be independently invented if their efficiency is correlated with their form."[1]

Meggers recognized that, while the criteria were easy to specify in theory, they were often difficult to apply in concrete situations. Yet, when she applied these criteria to the similarities in Shang and Olmec cultures, she found it "difficult to avoid the conclusion that transpacific communication took place."

Lending substantial, if as yet tentative, support to the Meggers theorem is the discovery cited by George Carter on page 158 wherein Chinese specialists in Shang era inscriptions, Dr. Mike Xu and Han Ping Chen, find they can 'read' the incised markings on several slender jade Olmec celts. The 1996 event attracted major media attention[2] and provoked further, sometimes scathing, scorn from many corners of the academic world. Xu stood his ground, however, asserting: "Recent discoveries of ancient relics from both Olmec land and Shang sites, plus intensive new studies on the Olmec and Shang writings and DNA testing, have proved Meggers' original ideas to be even more relevant, visionary, and correct."[3]

While it is tempting to characterize these findings as the long-sought, conclusive archaeological evidence 'proving' the Shang-Olmec connection, it is probably more accurate to describe these new findings as additional building blocks which strengthen and help to define the shape of the postulated diffusion edifice.

We have presented this series of scholarly events because it seems to us to provide a model for one kind of movement towards confirmation of cultural diffusion. It follows largely the orderly progression of disciplined research, publication, critique, rebuttal, and further research that is the hallmark of the established academic process. However, there are other routes to knowledge, other building blocks which have the potential of supporting the diffusion edifice, and there are different ways of incorporating them into the structure. Alice Kehoe's final paragraph on page 270 cogently states the problem that has arisen from the conventional 19th century position that the oceans were "an impassable barrier to intersocietal contacts before 1492." Pointing to the many documented crossings of the oceans in small craft, Kehoe writes that that "should be enough to prove the probability of pre-Columbian ocean crossings. That probability is resisted out of an obsolete belief that replication of experiments is the essence of science." Independent inventionists will be reluctant to abandon that 'isolated laboratory' concept, but, as commentator Gade observes, ". . . science is increasingly asked to defend what it has always taken for granted. Conclusive 'proof' for just about anything is a grand illusion of modernist thought."

Several of our contributors, following those alternative routes to knowledge, have opened windows which may allow more light into the diffusion edifice. By the simple method of comparison of artifacts—or inscriptions, or language and mythic elements, or biological traits—which exist on both sides of an ocean in such *quantity,* or in such circumstances, that dismissal of them as evidence for contact becomes difficult, these researchers *collectively* let a lot of light into the building. If we are intellectually honest, we are forced to ask, "Could such a diverse body of evidence, all pointing to the same conclusion, have accumulated on both sides of an ocean only in isolation?"

While Norman Totten defines his comparison of certain artifacts of North Africa with those of the Andean area of South America as rather 'soft' evidence, he adds, "My case for Magreb-to-Tiwanaku is underwhelming, but not *invalid* [italics, eds.] for this reason. It should be tested against existing evidence and new data as they come to light."

Similarly, Celia Heil's study of the possible migration of metallurgical techniques and Neil Steede's efforts to probe the mystery surrounding the features and artifacts of the Comalcalco site should be viewed cautiously for the present. But in Steede's case, it is the 'inscriptions' and drawings on thousands of fired bricks in the complex which grab our attention and may provide evidence that is difficult to dismiss. And Heil, because of her Mexican background, may be uniquely qualified to recognize particular traits in a New World culture which correlate with those of Old World peoples. These special circumstances should make us pause before concluding that the hypothesis is invalid simply because it is preliminary and untested.

The three papers on archaeoastronomy may seem at first glance relatively unrelated to the thrust of other research in this book. But, when we consider the great significance of cosmology in the everyday lives of common people in earlier eras, the importance of an understanding of this widespread cultural practice in laying the foundation for researchers involved in comparative studies may be better appreciated.

In Section II, some of the evidence presented on biology and plant geography seems particularly persuasive. Species of maize or chicken can arise naturally only once, and they do not travel or propagate elsewhere as domesticates unless by human intervention. George Carter (chickens from Asia) and Carl Johannessen (maize to Asia) continue to hone their analyses of the evidence for pre-Columbian cultural transfers. The depictions of maize in 11th to 13th century temple art in India, as illustrated and discussed by Johannessen (and confirmed by botanists), bolster the fine historical and linguistic case for its early transfer to Asia made by the South African anthropologist, M. D. W. Jeffreys, in *Man Across the Sea*. Stephen Jett makes a strong case for the transfer of dyeing techniques and dyestuffs from the Old World to the New, while Nancy Yaw Davis cuts a wide window opening in the diffusion edifice with her "fascinating hypothesis" (Dan Gade) of a late transpacific migration of the Zuni people. Obviously, it is the less ambiguous nature of biological data which draws serious scholars to this arena of diffusion studies.

In Section III, we placed papers on inscriptions along with those on linguistics, as both represent means of communication among people that involve language. However, there are profound differences in the weight that can or should be given to each as possible indicators of cultural diffusion.

An authenticated, incised inscription on an immovable stone face—a sort of "Kilroy was here" declaration—may signify only that there was person-to-rock contact, probably by the visitor. But, absent other evidence in the same context, little can be inferred or proved about whether cultural traits may or may not have been transferred as well. Still, Dave Kelley's admirable analysis of the Peterborough, Ontario, glyphs may someday provide a key to broader conclusions. In like manner, an inscription (or glyph) found on a small lithic such as Huston McCulloch's Bat Creek stone or Donal Buchanan's Michigan stone, however alluring, may be significant only if supported by other related evidence, such as the brass and wood found with the Bat Creek stone. Did the creator of the artifact actually come to the place where it was found, or did the isolated artifact merely drift ashore from a shipwreck, become a keepsake curiosity, and end up lost, forgotten, or merely in the last owner's grave? Intriguing as such items are, researchers are understandably wary of inferring too much from such enigmatic finds until corroborative evidence is discovered.

The spoken language, however, is fundamentally different in respect to its potential as evidence for diffusion. Through the arcane science of linguistics, scholars are able to determine patterns of borrowings or influences among languages and to calculate the mathematical chances of same or similar forms arising independently. Key, Wescott, and Stubbs show us the merit of careful analysis. With enough evidence, a convincing case for cultural diffusion can be made. Changes in language related to outside influences, difficult though they may be to trace, do demonstrate much more about the nature or significance of contact than does an isolated artifact. There has to have been considerable exposure to the foreign influence for borrowing of language to have occurred. . . . Not as captivating as the carving in stone, but infinitely more solid as evidence for diffusion. However, both kinds of evidence are valuable in the final determination, as it is the gradual stacking of the building blocks which finishes the edifice.

As new evidence comes to light and research is refined, there is growing acceptance of many contacts with the Americas having occurred over a long period of time. The real crux of the debate, now, involves determination of which of these contacts impacted cultures in either the donor or receiving cultures, and in what kinds of enduring ways. So much has been lost, perhaps forever, that we may never have enough 'hard' in-ground evidence to satisfy the most demanding of the archaeologists.

The dearth of objects from one hemisphere found in confirmed context in the other thus remains a problem for diffusionists. Consequently, until more such artifacts are brought to light, the array of carefully researched circumstantial evidence serves to make the diffusion case by demonstrating transfer of cultural traits in various ways: through the imitation of techniques or design elements in pottery (Meggers, Totten, Kehoe); in architectural style and brickmaking (Steede and Penhallow); via symbols, glyphs, and inscriptions (Rudolph, Davis, Kelley, Buchanan, McCulloch, Carlson, Farley, and Gordon); by means and routes of transport (Meggers, Heil, Ferryn); through language (Carter, Key, Wescott, and Stubbs); and in botany and biology (Johannessen, Davis, Jett, and Carter). But the circumstantial evidence, when added up in a volume such as this, may become so overwhelming as to leave little doubt in the mind of the well-informed reader, or even the skeptical student, that significant contacts did take place many times in the past, contacts that may account for some of the enigmatic traits or features we find in the Americas as well as for the depiction of New World maize in India's 12th-century temple statuary.

The great harm done by the earlier, narrow insistence on Beringia as the only migration or diffusion route is that it discouraged the airing of alternative explanations. Avocational or credentialled scholars who would explore this arena of world history can make the most useful contribution by examining all the evidence, including alternative explanations, without a polarizing bias. The provenience of artifacts must be recorded and researched systematically and dispassionately. Light is needed, not heat. Ultimately, as researchers examine its many small parts, the full shape of the diffusion edifice will emerge.

Donald Y. Gilmore and Linda S. McElroy
March, 1998

1. *NEARA Journal* 1997, 31(1). Reprint of Meggers' article from *American Anthropologist*, 77:1.
2. *US News and World Report*, Nov. 4, 1996.
3. *NEARA Journal* 1997, 31(1).

DAVID P. BARRON A retired clinical speech pathologist/audiologist, Barron is also an avocational archaeologist and a writer, editor, and publisher of *Stonewatch*, the quarterly newsletter of The Gungywamp Society, which he helped to found and has led since 1979. He has also authored novels, guidebooks, and magazine articles, including those related to his interest in history and pre-Columbian archaeology. His professional articles have appeared in medical and speech/hearing journals.

DONAL B. BUCHANAN Born of missionary parents in Japan, Buchanan took his BA in history at the University of Colorado and has done graduate study in archaeology, Old Norse, Old Irish, Early Welsh, and computer programming. He retired from the federal government in 1976 after serving twenty-five years in the US and overseas. He has traveled widely in Europe and Asia, has conducted linguistic and epigraphic research for over thirty years, and has published numerous articles and cartoons. Currently he is secretary/treasurer and assistant editor of the Epigraphic Society.

SUZANNE O. CARLSON An architect specializing in historic preservation, Carlson is an avocational student of language. Her interest in ancient language began when, as an architectural student in Italy, she was confronted with medieval Italian and Latin, which led to the study of Greek and the Scandinavian languages. Her pursuit of the mastery of Old Norse has led to research in Iceland and Denmark. She has been a frequent contributor to the *NEARA Journal* on a variety of topics related to her expertise in both architecture and languages, and her understanding of the challenges of translation and transliteration.

GEORGE F. CARTER Distinguished Professor Emeritus of Geography at Texas A&M, Carter is a native of San Diego, California. His early archaeological training and field experience was with the San Diego Museum of Man. He took his AB in anthropology and his PhD in geography at the University of California, and his pioneering PhD thesis has become a frequently-reprinted book: *Plant Geography and the Cultural History of the American Southwest*. The research for that study involved the first definitive collections of corn, beans, and squash. Carter's research on the very early human presence in North America led to the books: *Pleistocene Man in San Diego* and *Earlier Than You Think – a Personal View of Man in America*. He was Honorary Chair of the ABC Conference.

PAUL H. CHAPMAN Educated in history at Furman University and in navigation for ferrying World War II planes to Europe, Chapman draws on that background for research, lectures, and writing. His books include: *The Man Who Led Columbus to America, The Norse Discovery of America, Discovering Columbus,* and *Spirit Pond Runestones, A Study in Linguistics*. He also writes business articles and has founded his own media brokerage firm as well as the Atlanta-based Foundation for Improvement of Justice.

DONALD L. CYR As founder and editor of *Stonehenge Viewpoint* Publications, Donald Cyr brings to his readers a wide range of information on archaeology, astronomy, geology, meteorology, and related arts and sciences. Trained in engineering, he has been interested in megalithic subjects for some twenty years and epigraphic inscriptions for over ten years. His aim is to facilitate public access to information on these subjects.

MANUEL L. DA SILVA A Bristol, Rhode Island, physician in internal medicine, Dr. da Silva was educated in his native Portugal, New York University, and the Lahey Clinic. His activities in medical, historical, and civic matters in the US and Portugal for over forty years have earned him many high level civic and governmental honors and distinctions. He has lectured extensively and has conducted radio and television programs to educate the public on Portuguese-American history. His prolific writing includes the book, *Portuguese Pilgrims and Dighton Rock*.

NANCY YAW DAVIS Alaskan-born, with an MA from the University of Chicago and PhD from the University of Washington, Davis taught for fifteen years in Alaska and was also a visiting scholar at Stanford. She has conducted her own anthropology business, *Cultural Dynamics*, for twenty years and has published on a variety of subjects. She chaired the Asian session of the ABC Conference.

GLORIA FARLEY A native of Heavener, Oklahoma, Farley is a self-trained epigrapher and lecturer who, for fifty years, has pursued the evidence on stone of early Old World contacts with America. Her research has led to dozens of articles and to her 1995 book, *In Plain Sight: Old World Records in Ancient America*. She is a Fellow both of the Epigraphic Society and of the Explorers Club, based in New York City, and has been active in a number of other organizations researching the prehistory of North America.

PATRICK FERRYN   Director of the company, *Video Formation*, in Brussels, Belgium, which conducts training through television and video-conferencing, Ferryn is often involved in the production of promotional, training, and documentary films, in which he draws on his earlier experience as a professional photographer. He is a founding member of the non-profit association, *KADATH*, and editor of its journal, *KADATH – Chronicles of Lost Civilizations,* published since 1973. He has traveled widely for his research on many of the subjects featured in *KADATH*, further described in his paper.

DANIEL W. GADE   Professor of Geography at the University of Vermont, Gade earned his BA at Valparaiso University, his MA at the University of Illinois, and his MS and PhD degrees at the University of Wisconsin. His major research interest is cultural-historical geography and its overlap with biogeography. He has published extensively in various media, including books on Madagascar, and on Peru. He has performed editorial functions and received numerous grants and awards, especially in Latin American geography. From 1979–1980 he directed the University of Vermont's Overseas Study Program in France. Extensive research and travel have taken him to Andean Latin America, the Mediterranean lands, and Madagascar.

DONALD Y. GILMORE   A retired Foreign Service Officer with public diplomacy experience in North Africa, Europe, India, and Colombia, Gilmore has an AB from Middlebury and MA from the Fletcher School of Law and Diplomacy, Tufts University. He served as a navy flight instructor in World War II, and did aviation research in industry and at the CIA. With several years' field and lab school experience in prehistoric archaeology, he is on the board of the New Hampshire Archaeological Society and was elected President of NEARA in 1997. He was moderator of the ABC Conference and is co-editor of this volume.

CYRUS H. GORDON   After studying Semitics and Greek and Latin Classics at the University of Pennsylvania, Gordon served as a field archaeologist in Iraq and Palestine from 1931 to 1935 and as a Fellow of the American Schools of Oriental Research in Baghdad and Jerusalem. He has participated in expeditions to many parts of the world and has examined numerous antiquity sites in North, South, and Central America. Gradually, his field has expanded into the study of global diffusion. His more than 600 publications include two books on pre-Columbian America: *Before Columbus* and *Riddles in History*. Gordon is now Director of the Center for Ebla Research at New York University. He is also Professor Emeritus of Mediterranean Studies at Brandeis University and Professor Emeritus of Hebrew and other Near East Languages and Literatures at New York University. He is an Honorary Fellow of the Royal Asiatic Society for his contributions to the fields of Comparative Semitics, Ugaritic, and Minoan.

CELIA HEIL   Born in Mexico, Heil came to the US as a young woman, received a BS in cultural anthropology at Lindenwood College, did graduate work at George Washington University and the Corcoran School of Art, and has also lived in Australia and traveled widely. With ten years on the National Science Foundation staff, she was the first Mexican woman to go to the South Pole, during the 1979–1980 US Antarctic Research Expedition. Formerly the Quincentenary Program Coordinator for the Smithsonian's Center for Folklife Programs and Cultural Studies, she now operates her own business.

CURTISS HOFFMAN   Professor in the Department of Sociology and Anthropology at Bridgewater State College, Bridgewater, Massachusetts, Hoffman received his undergraduate degree in Mediterranean Studies at Brandeis in 1967, at a time when Dr. Cyrus Gordon was the Chair of that department, and his PhD in Near Eastern Languages and Literatures from Yale University in 1974. He has since specialized in the archaeology of Northeastern North America and is Past President of the Massachusetts Archaeological Society, but he maintains a strong interest in the ancient Middle East and in world mythology.

STEPHEN C. JETT   Formerly Professor and Chairperson in the Department of Geography, University of California at Davis, Jett is currently in UCD's Division of Textiles and Clothing. He received his AB in geology from Princeton and his PhD in geography from Johns Hopkins. His research interests include the Navajo Indians and possible pre-Columbian transoceanic influences. He has written two award-winning books on the Navajo and their country as well as numerous classic papers on the transoceanic controversy. Jett is editor of *Pre-Columbiana, a Journal of Long-Distance Contacts*.

CARL L. JOHANNESSEN   Professor Emeritus of Geography at the University of Oregon, Johannessen studied primarily at the University of California, Berkeley, receiving his BA in wildlife conservation and management, his MA in zoology, and his PhD in geography. He also taught summers in Central America for Oregon and in 1970 for the Organization of Tropical Studies geography program. At Oregon, he was Department Chair from 1978 until 1981. For thirty years he carried out research in Latin America. During the past decade his field research has focused on Asia, integrating these two regions, studying American crop plants in India and China and Asian chickens in the Americas.

ALICE B. KEHOE   Professor of Anthropology at Marquette University, where she has taught since 1968, Kehoe has been President of both the Central States Anthropological Society and the Milwaukee Society of the Archaeological Institute of America, and has served on the Board of Directors of the American Anthropological Associaton.   Among her publications are many articles and the books: *The Land of Prehistory: A Critical History of American Archaeology; Humans: An Introduction to Four-Field Anthropology; The Ghost Dance: Ethnohistory and Revitalization;* and the widely-used textbook, *North American Indians: A Comprehensive Account,* now in its second edition.   Her BA is from Barnard, her PhD from Harvard.

DAVID H. KELLEY   Professor Emeritus, Department of Archaeology, University of Calgary, Alberta, Kelley was born in Albany, New York, and did both undergraduate and graduate study at Harvard.   He has taught some forty different courses, including physical anthropology, linguistics, archaeoastronomy, and Mayan writing, in Peru, Texas, Uruguay, Nebraska, and, from 1968 to 1989, at the University of Calgary.   Dozens of his research articles have appeared in professional journals.   A major contributor to the decipherment of Mayan hieroglyphic writing, Kelley has also been deeply interested in problems of long range contacts between cultures and did his PhD thesis on a hypothesized movement of Uto-Aztecan speakers from Mexico to Polynesia, perhaps about AD 300 – 400.

MARY RITCHIE KEY   Professor Emeritus of Linguistics, University of California at Irvine, Key has been actively involved for over five decades in linguistic research into more than a dozen languages.   Key has published and lectured in the Americas, Europe, and Asia, and she is on the editorial board of several journals.   Among her seventeen books are: *Comparative Tacanan Phonology; The Grouping of South American Indian Languages; Polynesian and American Linguistic Connections;* and *Comparative Linguistics of South American Indian Languages.*   Her PhD is from the University of Texas.

JOSEPH B. MAHAN, JR.   At the time of his death in 1995, Mahan was executive director of the Institute for the Study of American Cultures.   He earned AB and MA degrees in anthropology at the University of Georgia, and a doctorate at the University of North Carolina.   He later taught at the University of Georgia, and was curator of several museums and a planner in historic preservation.   In India and Pakistan, he examined evidence for ancient cultural ties to the Yuchi and other American tribes, authoring the book, *The Secret: America in World History Before Columbus.*

JAMES W. MAVOR, JR   A naval architect, and designer of the deep-sea submersible, *Alvin,* Mavor also taught at M.I.T, Woods Hole Oceanographic Institution, Northeastern University, and the US Naval Academy.   He retired in 1980 to devote full time to studying past cultures.   His 1969 book, *Voyage to Atlantis,* is about the excavation of a Minoan town on the island of Thera.   From 1978 to 1993, Mavor collaborated with the late Byron Dix on anthropological research into Native American astronomy and landscape architecture, a partnership which led to dozens of articles and their 1989 book, *Manitou: The Sacred Landscape of New England's Native Civilization.*   BYRON DIX was an optical mechanical designer in the aerospace industry who studied the technical achievements of ancient Mayan and Peruvian societies as well as the archaeology and ethnohistory of the northeastern United States.

J. HUSTON MCCULLOCH   Professor of Economics at the Ohio State University in Columbus, McCulloch has written on the Bat Creek Stone in *Tennessee Anthropologist* as well as *Biblical Archaeology Review* (June 1993).   He also has an article on the Newark, Ohio, Hebrew Decalogue stone in *Epigraphic Society Occasional Papers* (1992), and another on "Ohio's Hanukkiah Mound" in *Ancient American* (July/Aug. 1996:14).   He maintains a website of these and other 'archaeological outliers' at http://www.econ.ohiostate.edu/jhm/arch/-outliers.html.

LINDA S. MCELROY   With a BS in experimental psychology from Simmons College, McElroy performed research at both M.I.T. and a Cambridge-based consulting firm and developed early software techniques for implementation of real-time psychological research projects.   As an independent consultant on databases, she more recently added publishing of databased information to her skill base.   She is an eclectic reader of pre-history, psychology, philosophy, and the evolution of consciousness in man.   As co-editor of this volume, she has shared the editing and been responsible for the technical production.

BETTY J. MEGGERS   As Research Associate, Department of Anthropology, in the Smithsonian Institution's National Museum of Natural History since 1954, Meggers has participated in numerous archaeological expeditions and investigations in South America, the Antilles, and the Pacific, leading to several books and many articles in professional journals.   She has also held a variety of professional offices and has served on numerous committees in her field.   Her MA is from Michigan and her PhD from Columbia.   Her book, *Amazonia: Man and Culture in a Counterfeit Paradise,* originally published in 1971, was recently reprinted with an epilogue by the Smithsonian Institution Press.

WILLIAM S. PENHALLOW   Professor Emeritus of Physics at the University of Rhode Island, Kingston, Rhode Island, where he taught physics and, especially, astronomy for thirty-two years, Penhallow received his ScB degree from Brown and his MS from the University of Maine, and did graduate work at Indiana University.   He taught and conducted research at both Brown and Wesleyan.   He is founder of both the Quonochontaug (RI) Observatory and the Frosty Drew Public Observatory in Ninigret Park, Charlestown, Rhode Island.

JOHN H. RUDOLPH New Jersey-born, with BA and MFA degrees in architecture from Princeton University, Rudolph moved to Bainbridge Island, Washington, in 1954 and started his own office there in 1959. His most recent focus has been on archaeoastronomy as an aid in the interpretation of petroglyphs. He is a founder and facilities director of the Edwin E. Ritchie Observatory being established on Bainbridge Island.

JOHN L. SORENSON Professor Emeritus of Anthropology at Brigham Young University, where he obtained his BA and MS degrees in archaeology, Sorenson also has an MS in meteorology from the California Institute of Technology and his PhD from UCLA in social anthropology. He is Director of Social Sciences, General Research Corporation, Santa Barbara, and President of Bonneville Research Corporation, Provo, Utah. He has published more than 165 papers, reviews, monographs, and books, notably *Pre-Columbian Contact Across the Ocean with the Americas: An Annotated Bibliography,* in two volumes, now in its second edition.

NEIL STEEDE A field archaeologist who has worked at a dozen Mexican sites, including Comalcalco, Teotihuacan, Palenque, and Tulum, Steede was under contract to the Mexican government from 1978 to 1987. He also has five years of study in anthropology and archaeology (University of the Americas) to his credit, as well as six books and more than 300 articles, most of which have appeared in Mexican government publications. Now based in the United States, Steede is currently president of the Early Sites Research Association, West.

BRIAN D. STUBBS A teacher of languages and linguistics at the College of Eastern Utah, Stubbs earned his MA in linguistics at the University of Utah and has completed postgraduate study toward his PhD in Near Eastern languages and linguistics. Involved in research on several Native American languages, principally the Uto-Aztecan and Kiowa-Tanoan language families, Stubbs has presented papers to linguistic conferences, published articles in linguistic and epigraphic journals, and has dictionaries and comparative vocabularies in preparation in Uto-Aztecan, Rio Grande Tewa, and White Mesa Ute.

NORMAN TOTTEN Professor of History at Bentley College, Waltham, Massachusetts, Totten has MA, MDiv, and PhD degrees from Boston University. He is President of The Epigraphic Society, a Trustee of the Institute for the Study of American Cultures, and a Board Member of the New England Journal of History. Totten has conducted archaeological tours to Morocco and several countries of the Middle East, as well as to Peru, Guatemala, Honduras, China, and eastern and western Europe. He has written numerous articles on history and numismatics and has books in preparation.

ROGER WILLIAMS WESCOTT Professor Emeritus of Anthropology and Linguistics at Drew University, New Jersey, Wescott founded Drew's Anthropology Department. At Drew, he directed both the Behavioral Science Program and the Linguistics Program. He had earlier founded and directed the African Language Program at Michigan State University. Of his 500 publications, forty are books. He has served as co-editor of several linguistic journals and is past president of the Linguistic Association of Canada and the United States. After receiving his PhD in linguistics from Princeton in 1948, he held a Rhodes scholarship at Oxford. Wescott is also past president of the International Society for the Comparative Study of Civilizations (ISCSC).

* OW-NW: Old World-New World